HANDBOOK OF THE POLITICS OF CHINA

HANDBOOKS OF RESEARCH ON CONTEMPORARY CHINA

Series Editor: David S.G. Goodman, *Xi'an Jiaotong-Liverpool University, China*

China has undergone a period of intense and rapid social and economic change in its path to becoming a modern industrial superpower. This timely and exciting multidisciplinary series includes *Handbooks* that offer comprehensive overviews of the very latest research on contemporary China. Prestigious, high quality works of lasting significance, the *Handbooks* explore a range of issues affecting China in the 21st Century. The emphasis of the series is on the most important concepts and research as well as expanding debate and indicating the likely research agenda for the future.

Titles in the series include:

Handbook on China and Developing Countries
Edited by Carla P. Freeman

Handbook of the Politics of China
Edited by David S.G. Goodman

Handbook of the Politics of China

Edited by

David S.G. Goodman

Xi'an Jiaotong-Liverpool University, Suzhou; Nanjing University, China; and University of Sydney, Australia

HANDBOOKS OF RESEARCH ON CONTEMPORARY CHINA

Cheltenham, UK • Northampton, MA, USA

© David S.G. Goodman 2015

All rights reserved. No part of this publication may be reproduced, stored in a retrieval system or transmitted in any form or by any means, electronic, mechanical or photocopying, recording, or otherwise without the prior permission of the publisher.

Published by
Edward Elgar Publishing Limited
The Lypiatts
15 Lansdown Road
Cheltenham
Glos GL50 2JA
UK

Edward Elgar Publishing, Inc.
William Pratt House
9 Dewey Court
Northampton
Massachusetts 01060
USA

A catalogue record for this book
is available from the British Library

Library of Congress Control Number: 2015940683

This book is available electronically in the Elgaronline
Social and Political Science subject collection
DOI 10.4337/9781782544371

ISBN 978 1 78254 436 4 (cased)
ISBN 978 1 78254 437 1 (eBook)

Typeset by Servis Filmsetting Ltd, Stockport, Cheshire

Printed and bound in Great Britain by TJ International Ltd, Padstow, Cornwall

For Elzbieta

Contents

List of contributors	x
Preface	xv
List of abbreviations	xvi

The study of contemporary Chinese politics: a reader's guide   1
David S.G. Goodman

PART I   LEADERSHIP, INSTITUTIONS AND STRUCTURES

1   The study of elite political conflict in the PRC: politics inside the 'black box'   21
Frederick C. Teiwes

2   Ideology of the Chinese Communist Party   42
Kazuko Kojima

3   The Chinese Communist Party: an institutional perspective   57
Zheng Yongnian and Chen Gang

4   The central government   76
Yan Xu and Dali L. Yang

5   Provincial politics   95
Bo Zhiyue

6   Local governance: the roles of the People's Congresses and the People's Political Consultative Conferences   104
Minglu Chen

7   Post-Deng transformation of the People's Liberation Army: changes, continuities and consequences   117
You Ji

PART II   PUBLIC POLICY

8   Managing government finance   137
Linda Chelan Li

9   Administrative territory   147
Carolyn Cartier and Hu De

10   Economic policy   165
Barry Naughton

11   Regional development policy and regional inequality   187
John A. Donaldson

12	China's nationality policy from the perspective of international minority rights *Xiaowei Zang*	205
13	Education: from egalitarian ideology to public policy *W. John Morgan and Fengliang Li*	217
14	Welfare and social security *Wang Guohui and Jane Duckett*	238

PART III   POLITICAL ECONOMY AND SOCIAL CHANGE

15	Corruption and anti-corruption *Dali L. Yang and Yan Xu*	253
16	The class politics of the Chinese Communist Party *Yingjie Guo*	271
17	From Xianglin's Wife to the Iron Girls: the politics of gender representation *Wang Zheng*	288
18	Rural development *Jean C. Oi*	310
19	Non-governmental organizations *Jennifer Y.J. Hsu*	331
20	Reports of social unrest: basic characteristics, trends and patterns, 2003–12 *Lynette H. Ong*	345

PART IV   INTERNATIONAL RELATIONS

21	China on the world stage *Shaun Breslin*	363
22	Economic statecraft *James Reilly*	381
23	East Asia *Shogo Suzuki*	397
24	Admiration, ambivalence, antipathy: the past and future for US–China relations *Bates Gill*	413
25	Southeast Asia *Alberto Camarena and Jörn Dosch*	426
26	China and the European Union *Kerry Brown*	442

Glossary of Chinese terms	453
References	454
Index	531

Contributors

Bo Zhiyue is Director of the New Zealand Contemporary China Research Centre and Professor of Political Science at Victoria University of Wellington, New Zealand. His research interests include China's elite politics, Chinese provincial leaders, central−local relations, cross-strait relations, Sino−US relations, international relations theories and global governance. He is the author of a trilogy on China's elite politics, including *Chinese Provincial Leaders: Economic Performance and Political Mobility since 1949* (2002), *China's Elite Politics: Political Transition and Power Balancing* (2007) and *China's Elite Politics: Governance and Democratization* (2010).

Shaun Breslin is Professor of Politics and International Studies at the University of Warwick, UK, where he is also Director of the Centre for the Study of Globalisation and Regionalisation. He is an Associate Fellow of the Chatham House Asia Programme, and co-editor of the *Pacific Review*. His research focuses on the international political economy and international relations of contemporary China, with a side interest in the comparative study of regional integration processes.

Kerry Brown is Director of the China Studies Centre, University of Sydney, Australia, where he is also Professor of Chinese Politics.

Alberto Camarena is currently a lecturer at the Panamerican Institute Business School (IPADE) and the Universidad Iberoamericana, both in Mexico City. His main research interests are the international relations of the Asia-Pacific, China−Southeast Asia relations and Chinese nationalism.

Carolyn Cartier is Professor of Human Geography and China Studies at the University of Technology, Sydney, Australia. She works on comparative analysis of changes to the administrative divisions in China.

Chen Gang is Research Fellow at the East Asian Institute, National University of Singapore. His research focuses on China's environmental policies, and he provides consultancy for the Singapore government on environmental and energy issues in East Asia. He is the author of *China's Climate Policy* (2012).

Minglu Chen is a lecturer in the China Studies Centre and the Department of Government and International Relations at the University of Sydney, Australia. Her research concentrates on social and political change in China, especially the interaction between entrepreneurs and the state. She is the author of *Tiger Girls: Women and Enterprises in the People's Republic of China* (2011).

John A. Donaldson is Associate Professor of Political Science at Singapore Management University. His research focuses on China's regional development issues. He serves as a Senior Research Fellow with the Lien Centre for Social Innovation, working with the Singapore Management University Change Lab to research and design innovative solutions to unmet needs in vulnerable communities in Singapore. He is the author of *Small Works: Poverty and Economic Development in Southwestern China* (2011).

Jörn Dosch holds the Chair of International Politics and Development Cooperation and is Head of the Department of Political and Administrative Sciences at the University of Rostock, Germany. He is also Adjunct Professor at Monash University, Sunway Campus, Malaysia. He has published widely on the international politics of the Asia-Pacific region, the foreign policies of Asian nations including China, and the Association of Southeast Asian Nations (ASEAN), and is co-editor of the journal *International Quarterly for Asian Studies*.

Jane Duckett is Edward Caird Chair of Politics and Director of the Scottish Centre for China Research at the University of Glasgow, UK. Her research interests are in contemporary Chinese governance and politics, particularly social and health policy. Her publications include *The Entrepreneurial State in China* (1998), *The Chinese State's Retreat from Health: Policy and the Politics of Retrenchment* (paperback 2013), and (with Beatriz Carrillo) *China's Changing Welfare Mix: Local Perspectives* (2011).

Bates Gill is Chief Executive Officer and Professor of Politics at the United States Studies Centre at the University of Sydney, Australia. He formerly led the Stockholm International Peace Research Institute as well as Asia-focused policy research programmes at the Brookings Institution and the Center for Strategic and International Studies in Washington, DC. He is the author, co-author or editor of a large number of publications, including *Rising Star: China's New Security Diplomacy* (2010).

David S.G. Goodman is Professor and Head of the Department of China Studies at Xi'an Jiaotong-Liverpool University, Suzhou, China, and Professor in the School of Social and Behavioural Sciences at Nanjing University, China. His recent research has focused on issues of class and the formation of elites in China, and he is the author of *Class in Contemporary China* (2014).

Yingjie Guo is Professor of Chinese Studies at the University of Sydney, Australia. His research interests include class discourses in the People's Republic of China and cultural nationalism in the post-Mao era. He is currently working on two volumes, *Handbook of Class and Stratification in the People's Republic of China* and *Local Elites in Post-Mao China*.

Jennifer Y.J. Hsu is Assistant Professor in the Department of Political Science at the University of Alberta, Canada. She is currently researching the internationalization of Chinese non-governmenatl organizations (NGOs) and their role in international development.

Hu De is a lecturer in the School of Urban and Regional Science at East China Normal University in Shanghai, Cnina. He writes on China's spatial economic development and is the author of *The Spatial Process of Power and Regional Economic Development* (2011).

You Ji is Professor of International Relations in the Department of Government and Public Administration at the University of Macau. He is author of three books, including *The Armed Forces of China* and *China's Enterprise Reform*.

Kazuko Kojima is an Associate Professor, Faculty of Law, Keio University, Japan. Her research focuses on Chinese politics and social organizations. Her recent publications in English include (with Masaharu Hishida, Tomoaki Ishii and Jian Qiao) *China's Trade Unions: How Autonomous Are They? A Survey of 1811 Enterprise Union Chairpersons* (2010).

Fengliang Li is an Associate Professor of the Economics of Education, the Institute of Education, Tsinghua University, China. He has published extensively in both Chinese and international journals, especially on issues concerning the graduate labour market in China.

Linda Chelan Li is Professor of Political Science at the Department of Public Policy and Associate Provost (Strategic Planning) at the City University of Hong Kong. Her research on China covers topics of central–local relations, politics of public finance, government reforms, policy implementation, law and reform, and institutional change processes. She is the editor of *Good Governance in Asia* (2015) and the author of *Rural Tax Reform in China* (2012).

W. John Morgan is United Nations Educational, Scientific and Cultural Organization (UNESCO) Chair of Political Economy and Education, School of Education; Senior Fellow, the China Policy Institute, University of Nottingham, UK; and Honorary Professor, School of Social Sciences, Cardiff University, UK. His current research is on post-school education and economic and social change in the BRICS countries (Brazil, Russia, India, China, South Africa), especially China and Russia. He is the editor (with B. Wu) of *Higher Education Reform in China: Beyond the Expansion* (2011 and 2013) and of *Chinese Higher Education Reform and Social Justice* (2015). He is a Fellow of the Royal Society of Arts, the Royal Anthropological Institute and the Learned Society of Wales.

Barry Naughton is Professor of Chinese Economy at the University of California, San Diego, USA. His work concentrates on issues relating to industry, trade, finance and China's transition to a market economy.

Jean C. Oi is the William Haas Professor in Chinese Politics in the Department of Political Science and a Senior Fellow of the Freeman Spogli Institute for International Studies at Stanford University, USA. She directs the Stanford China Program and is the founding Lee Shau Kee Director of Stanford's Center at Peking University, China. Current writing projects include the politics of corporate restructuring, as well as the challenges of governance in China's rapid urbanization. Most recently she has been doing fieldwork on the organization of rural communities and the provision of public goods, especially affordable housing. She also continues her research on rural finance and local governance in China.

Lynette H. Ong is Associate Professor in the Department of Political Science, and Asian Institute, Munk School of Global Affairs, at the University of Toronto, Canada. She is the author of *Prosper or Perish: Credit and Fiscal Systems in Rural China* (2012). Her research interests are authoritarian politics, social mobilization and the political economy of development.

James Reilly is a senior lecturer in the Department of Government and International Relations at the University of Sydney, Australia. He is the author of *Strong Society, Smart State: The Rise of Public Opinion in China's Japan Policy* (2012), and the co-editor of *Australia and China at 40* (2012). He previously served as the East Asia Representative of the American Friends Service Committee (AFSC) in China from 2001 to 2008.

Shogo Suzuki is a Senior Lecturer in the Department of Politics at the University of Manchester, UK. His work concentrates on Chinese and Japanese foreign policy, and Sino-Japanese relations.

Frederick C. Teiwes is Emeritus Professor of Chinese Politics at the University of Sydney, Australia. His publications include *Politics and Purges in China* (1979, rev. edn 1993), *Politics at Mao's Court* (1990), and various co-authored books with Warren Sun, notably *The Tragedy of Lin Biao* (1996), *China's Road to Disaster, 1955–1959* (1999), *The End of the Maoist Era* (2007) and *Paradoxes of Post-Mao Rural Reform* (forthcoming).

Wang Guohui is an Associate Professor at Yantai University, China, and a postdoctoral researcher in the Center for Comparative Politics and Economics at the Central Compilation and Translation Bureau. He is author of *Tamed Village Democracy: Elections, Governance and Clientelism in a Contemporary Chinese Village* (2014).

Wang Zheng is an Associate Professor of Women's Studies and History and Associate Research Scientist of the Institute for Research on Women and Gender at University of Michigan, USA. Wang Zheng's publications concern feminism in China, in terms of both its historical development and its contemporary activism, and changing gender discourses in China's socio-economic, political and cultural transformations of the past century. Her recent research projects deal with gender and socialist state formation in the Mao era, and contemporary feminist activism in China in a global context. An academic activist, Wang Zheng is a founding member of the diaspora organization, Chinese Society for Women's Studies. She is the founder and co-director of the UM-Fudan Joint Institute for Gender Studies at Fudan University, Shanghai, China.

Yan Xu is a doctoral student in political science at the University of Chicago, USA.

Dali L. Yang is the William Claude Reavis Professor in the Department of Political Science at the University of Chicago, USA and the founding Faculty Director of the University of Chicago Center in Beijing, China. His current research is focused on the politics of China's development, particularly risk regulation and governance, and state–society relations.

Xiaowei Zang is Chair Professor and Dean of the College of Liberal Arts and Social Sciences at City University of Hong Kong. His recent publications include: *Ethnicity in China: A Critical Introduction* (2015); Chien-wen Kou and Xiaowei Zang (eds), *Choosing China's Leaders* (2014); and Xiaowei Zang and Chien-wen Kou (eds), *Elites and Governance in China* (2013).

Zheng Yongnian is Professor and Director of East Asian Institute, National University of Singapore. He is the editor of *China: An International Journal* and *East Asian Policy*. He has studied both China's transformation and its external relations. He is author of *The Chinese Communist Party as Organizational Emperor* (2010), *Technological Empowerment: The Internet, State and Empowerment in China* (2007), *De Facto Federalism in China* (2007), *Discovering Chinese Nationalism in China* (1999) and *Globalization and State Transformation in China* (2004). He was a recipient of a Social Science Research Council–MacArthur Foundation Fellowship (1995–1997) and a John D. and Catherine T. MacArthur Foundation Fellowship (2003–2004).

Preface

It is a daunting prospect to be asked to edit a handbook of anything, let alone a *Handbook of the Politics of China*. This is a subject that has not only very broad and porous borders, but also a continually expanding literature. Even getting to the planning stage would not have been possible without considerable discussion across and support from a range of colleagues. In particular, a recognition of particular gratitude must go to my colleague at Nanjing University, Zhou Peiqin; Sujian Guo, at Fudan University; Lu Peng at CASS; as well as to many of the contributors to this volume.

The chapters of this *Handbook* were first presented to a workshop at Nanjing University in May 2014, and a recognition of particular gratitude must go to Professor Zhou Xiaohong, who hosted the event. In addition to those who have contributed to the final product a recognition of particular gratitude should also go to Bruce Dickson, Jean-Louis Rocca, Deborah Davis and Suisheng Zhao, who participated in the workshop as principal discussants and gave freely of their time and expertise in discussing large numbers of the papers and the issues. It was an exceptional intellectual event, ably organized by Kai Zhang (University of Sydney).

The editor and the contributors owe a considerable debt of gratitude to the publishing team at Edward Elgar, who have been a tower of strength in seeing this *Handbook* through production, not least because of its length.

The purpose of the *Handbook of the Politics of China* has been primarily to provide a study tool for students – undergraduates and postgraduates – interested in academic research on the various different aspects of politics as a field of study. In producing their chapters, contributors were asked to review the literature, and to both present and comment on the latest findings of research. The goal was to produce a useful work of reference with some challenges to received wisdom. Of necessity there will and should be debate about both the topics to be included, and the judgements that are presented. The production of a handbook, like the practice of politics itself, is the art of the possible as well as the discussion of interesting ideas.

David S.G. Goodman
February 2015

Abbreviations

ABC	Agricultural Bank of China
AFP	Agence France-Presse
AP	Associated Press
AQSIQ	General Administration of Quality Supervision, Inspection and Quarantine
ARF	ASEAN Regional Forum
ASA	Association of Southeast Asia
ASEAN	Association of Southeast Asian Nations
ASPAC	Asian and Pacific Council
BRICS	Brazil, Russia, India, China, South Africa
CAAC	Civil Aviation Administration of China
CAFTA	China–ASEAN Free Trade Agreement
CASS	Chinese Academy of Social Sciences
CBRC	China Banking Regulatory Commission
CC	Central Committee
CCB	China Construction Bank
CCP	Chinese Communist Party
CDB	China Development Bank
CDIC	Central Discipline Inspection Commission
CEO	chief executive officer
CIC	China Investment Corporation
CICIR	China Institute for Contemporary International Relations
CLSG	central leading small group
CMC	Central Military Commission
CMI	Chiang Mai Initiative
CMIM	Chiang Mai Initiative Multilateralization
CNMC	China Nonferrous Metals Co.
CNPC	China National Petroleum Corporation
CoC	Code of Conduct
CoE	Council of Europe
CoSTIND	Commission of Science, Technology and Industry for National Defence
CPI	Corruption Perceptions Index
CPLC	Central Political and Legal Commission
CPPCC	Chinese People's Political Consultative Conference
CSSTA	Cross Strait Services Trade Agreement
CYLC	Communist Youth League of China
DAC	Development Assistance Committee
DFA	Department of Foreign Aid
DIC	Discipline Inspection Committee

DoC	ASEAN–China Declaration on the Conduct of Parties in the South China Sea
DPP	Democratic Progressive Party
DPRK	Democratic People's Republic of Korea (North Korea)
ECFA	Economic Cooperation Framework Agreement (PRC and Taiwan)
EEZ	Exclusive Economic Zone
EHP	Early Harvest Programme
ENGO	environmental NGO
EU	European Union
Ex-Im Bank	Export-Import Bank
FDI	foreign direct investment
FELSG	Finance and Economics Leadership Small Group
FPDA	Five Power Defence Arrangements
GAC	Government Administrative Council
GATS	General Agreement on Trade in Services
GDP	gross domestic product
GFC	global financial crisis
GMD	Guomindang (Nationalist Party)
GNP	Good Neighbourliness Policy
GONGO	government-organized non-governmental organization
GPAD	General Political Affairs Department
HRC	Human Rights Council
HURD	Ningbo Government Commission of Housing and Urban–Rural Development
ICAC	Independent Commission against Corruption
ICBC	Industrial and Commercial Bank of China
IMF	International Monetary Fund
IPO	initial public offering
IT	information technology
KMT	Kuomintang (Nationalist Party)
LSG	leading small group
Maphilindo	Malaysia, the Philippines and Indonesia
MEP	Ministry of Environmental Protection
MIIT	Ministry of Industry and Information Technology
MITI	Ministry of International Trade and Industry
MOF	Ministry of Finance
MOFCOM	Ministry of Commerce
MOOTW	military operations other than war
MoE	Ministry of Education
MoR	Ministry of Railways
MOT	Ministry of Transport
MOU	memorandum of understanding
MPA	Masters of Public Administration
MPLA	Popular Movement for the Liberation of Angola
MSM	men who have sex with men
NATO	North Atlantic Treaty Organization

NBS	National Bureau of Statistics
NDRC	National Development and Reform Commission
NEA	National Energy Administration
NGO	non-governmental organization
NOC	national oil company
NPC	National People's Congress
NRCMS	new rural co-operative medical scheme
NRPS	new rural pension scheme
NSC	National Security Council
ODA	overseas development aid
OECD	Organisation for Economic Co-operation and Development
PAP	People's Armed Police
PBoC	People's Bank of China
PBSC	Politburo Standing Committee
PC	People's Congress
PKI	Partai Komunis Indonesia (Communist Party of Indonesia)
PLA	People's Liberation Army
PLC	Political and Legal Affairs Commission
PLWHA	people living with HIV/AIDS
PONGO	Party-organized NGO
PPCC	People's Political Consultative Conference
PPP	purchasing power parity
PRC	People's Republic of China
PSC	Politburo Standing Committee
R&D	research and development
REE	rare earth elements
RMB	renminbi
ROC	Republic of China
ROK	Republic of Korea (South Korea)
SAFE	State Administration of Foreign Exchange
SAIC	State Administration for Industry and Commerce
SAR	Special Administrative Region
SARS	Severe Acute Respiratory Syndrome
SASAC	State-owned Assets Supervision and Administration Commission
S–C–A	structure, consciousness and action
SCOPSR	State Commission Office for Public Sector Reform
SCPSR	State Commission for Public Sector Reform
SDPC	State Development and Planning Commission
SEATO	South East Asia Treaty Organization
SEC	State Economic Commission
SETC	State Economic and Trade Commission
SEZ	Special Economic Zone
SOE	state-owned enterprise
SPC	State Planning Commission
SUIC	Social Unrest in China (dataset)
TVEs	township and village enterprises

UN	United Nations
UNCLOS	United Nations Convention on the Law of the Sea
UNITA	National Union for the Total Independence of Angola
UNSC	United Nations Security Council
USAID	United States Agency for International Development
USSR	Union of Soviet Socialist Republics
WB	World Bank
WTO	World Trade Organization

The study of contemporary Chinese politics: a reader's guide
David S. G. Goodman

This is a primer for the study of China's politics. It makes no claim to provide the last word on everything political in the People's Republic of China (PRC) but it does aspire to provide an introduction to most of what the student of China's politics will need to address, and to point to where that student might go next, not least in terms of the References section and further reading. There is always a need for such introductions but since Mao Zedong died (in 1976) and the Chinese Communist Party (CCP) adopted a new development strategy (in 1978) that need has become more acute. The changes of the last four decades have seen not only China's rapid economic growth but also, as a result, an exponential growth in the literature on and related to China's politics. This introduction to the study of China's politics interrogates the range of perspectives, synthesizes the arguments, and sorts through the detail.

Just as the PRC has changed during the last four decades, so too has the academic world of political studies more generally. The latter have become more methodologically sophisticated and quantitative, and cover a broader range of topics.[1] These trends are also apparent in the study of China's politics, particularly in the broadening of scope, which was previously largely elite-centred. In part, of course, this change occurred because of greater access to China in general and to source material specifically, as the PRC has become dramatically more open.

Until the 1980s few graduates in China Studies had had the opportunity to live, let alone study in China. Four decades ago there was no access to archives and conducting surveys was near inconceivable. Documentary sources were largely limited to official publications, the newspapers and magazines produced by the party-state's propaganda system, and the materials provided by the Red Guards during the height of the Great Proletarian Cultural Revolution (1966–68). Interviews in China (as opposed to interviews with refugees in Hong Kong or elsewhere) were occasionally possible but almost always under the most restricted of circumstances. At the same time as China has become more open to students of politics, training programmes have improved immeasurably. Today's graduates are considerably better prepared to engage in research on China. They have good language skills, are methodologically more aware, and have usually had direct exposure to life in China.

One important result of these various trends is that the study of China's politics has moved away from a predominant concern with elite politics to embrace other activities more fully. China's international relations were always a focus for study, even before the reform era started in earnest. Governments have always had a necessary interest in China's international relations, and governments provide both funding and direction to much of what is studied and researched relating to China's politics. Nonetheless, the relative isolation of the Mao era meant that there were obvious limitations to the range of analysis applied in the study of China's international relations. The changed world order after the end of the Soviet Union, and China's growth as an economic centre, with the necessary political possibilities and consequences that follow from both, have meant that the study of China's international relations has become a significant subfield of China's politics.

A second area of growth has been the concern with policy studies. Again, the restrictions on access to China four decades ago and the reliance on documentary analysis meant that while policy was often a key focus of studies on China's politics (particularly for development issues, such as education or enterprise management) these studies were limited in their analytical reach. Before China became more open, policy studies were based overwhelmingly on official sources, with much of the research limited to official statements, only occasionally leavened by interviews with refugees undertaken in Hong Kong. There was limited ability to independently assess the socio-economic impact of policy and policy change, let alone the processes within government that have occasioned change or the attempt at change. This has clearly changed with increased openness and reform in the PRC. Policy studies can now be concerned more fully not only with the social causes and impact of governmental initiatives, but also with the internal operation of the party-state itself, a third area of growth in the study of China's politics.

As these comments on PRC policy studies indicate, the study of state–society relations has been the final and most significant development in the growth of China's politics as an area of academic endeavour. Four decades ago a totalitarian perspective dominated the study of China's politics. There was little appreciation of state–society relations, for the latter was seen as being largely subsumed by the former. While the PRC remains a party-state and maintains many of the features and characteristics of its earlier pre-reform operation, there has nonetheless been the emergence of some social space apart from the political system. Some would question whether there can be a 'civil society' under those circumstances, but there is now a wider and visible politics of society.

These observations lead directly to the structure of this *Handbook*, which is presented in four parts. The first deals with leadership, structures and the institutions of politics. The second examines the PRC's public policy. The third concentrates on topics in the PRC's political economy and social change; and the fourth and final part examines the most distinct subfield of China's politics, that of international relations. Each of the chapters reviews the secondary literature on the topic under examination, and presents the latest view of research in the area.

THE BIGGER PICTURE

Two very large questions inevitably lie behind the study of China's politics. The first is whether the PRC's political system is unique, as is often assumed. Chinese exceptionalism has always been a powerful approach to the study of China, and is a doctrine heavily embraced within the PRC in recent years. The second question is whether the PRC will change. Indeed, large as these questions are they are often the reason that students are attracted to the study of China's politics in the first place. The short answers are simple: yes and no, and that change is inevitable and current. At the same time more considered responses may be more intellectually satisfying.

Contemporary Chinese politics 3

All political systems are of course both unique and comparable. Analysing and understanding the similarities as well as the differences is part and parcel of the study of politics. In the case of the PRC there are three models that have dominated the understanding of the political system: the Communist party-state; the East Asia developmental state; and the Chinese civilization state, which is of course to some extent the model of Chinese exceptionalism. Clearly there may be elements of all three in operation in any analysis and at any one time, though it is equally as clear that there is a historical evolution. Ideas of the PRC as a Communist party-state dominated through to the 1980s, followed by discussion of the PRC as a developmental state during the 1980s and 1990s, and more recently with even greater emphasis on the PRC as a civilisation-state and the successor to Chinese imperial history.

The PRC has been and, even after the developments of the reform era, remains self-evidently a Communist party-state. The CCP is the institution around which politics revolves, and with the post-Mao institutionalization of politics this has been recognized with the appointment of the CCP General Secretary as President of the PRC, a practice which did not occur before. The system of governance centres on the CCP Politburo and its Standing Committee, with subordinate hierarchies of government and parallel CCP organization. Although there have been changes in the reform era (see especially Chapter 3, Chapter 4 and Chapter 6) essentially much of the political system is as described by Schurmann in his monumental pre-Cultural Revolution *Ideology and Organization in Communist China*, which detailed the PRC as a Communist party-state that was not totalitarian (Schurmann 1968).

There have, though, been changes, not least in the CCP's ideology (Chapter 2) and the PRC was never a Communist party-state in quite the same way as many of those that existed in Eastern Europe. One clear difference was and is scale. China is so much bigger in both land area and population than other Communist party-states that political command hierarchies and issues of domestic security are differently structured. Although the PRC had a period of overcentralization, in general the political system was always more decentralized than other Communist party-states, and decentralization has increased still further with the changes of the last four decades. Some four-fifths of government expenditure is now local government expenditure (Landry 2008). The PRC's relationship with the former Soviet Union was always different to that of the Communist party-states of Eastern Europe, even when as in the early 1950s the two were attempting a close alliance, so that subsequent developments were different. Moreover, in the PRC the peasantry were a more significant political factor, not least because of the CCP's path to power before 1949 (Feng and Goodman 2000).

Parallels with the East Asian development state also invite comparison. For most of its first 30 years the PRC pursued an import substitution development strategy. When this changed in the late 1970s it was because not only Japan, Singapore and Hong Kong, but also South Korea and Taiwan had successfully negotiated an export-oriented growth strategy. Behind this strategy lay a withdrawal of direct government involvement in economic enterprises, the corporatization of state assets, and government leadership in the direction of economic development. During the 1980s the greatest change in the PRC's political economy was government's withdrawal from the direct management of economic enterprises, as well as decentralization in the responsibilities for government functions. One immediate result was the overall transfer of resources from heavy to light industry which significantly impacted upon the PRC's export capacity (Solinger 1991). State-owned enterprises were encouraged to corporatize their activities from the mid-1990s and the number of state-owned enterprises was significantly reduced through asset sales, management buy-outs and various other devices (Garnaut et al. 2006).

There are some ways in which the PRC is not so easily equated with other East Asian developmental states. Although the government through various agencies provides considerable guidance to economic development, there is no single MITI agency in China that has the authority to lead growth and to override other agencies. Most importantly, the PRC is not a capitalist state. The period since 1978 has seen the development of a reforming socialist market economy, not the breakdown of Communist rule and the establishment of a capitalist or similar system. Indeed, to the extent that China's developmental state resembled that elsewhere in East Asia, the emphasis in its statism was at the local level, in the emergence of local state corporatism, especially during the 1980s and 1990s as the processes of change began. There is no land market, and indeed economic activities are often subject to party–state interference. There is a labour market but it is maintained in its present form by the state's household registration system which determines the creation of a migrant peasant worker reserve pool of labour. Entrepreneurs pay considerable attention and devote considerable expenditure to their political connections. The state sector of the economy remains dominant in many ways despite no longer producing the majority of GDP. The banking system works to support SOEs overwhelmingly more than other kinds of enterprises with destabilizing consequences for the entire economy.

Moreover, although the PRC has been transformed since 1978, and growth spectacular – gross domestic product (GDP) grew by a factor of 130 between 1978 and 2011 – the comparison with other East Asian states falls short economically. GDP per capita remains limited (2014) at US$12 813 (purchasing power parity, PPP). This compares to US$43 600 for Taiwan, US$37 683 for Japan, US$35 485 for South Korea and US$55 167 for Hong Kong. The PRC's 2013 GDP per capita was roughly at the same level as the Soviet Union was in 1989 – US$9211 – at the height of its economic growth (CIA 1990, 2015).

The apparent paradox of economic openness and growth while maintaining the structures and practices of a Communist party-state has not been lost on many commentators, especially those who heralded the 'end of history' with the collapse of the European Communist party-states or who otherwise had a propensity to look for alternative interpretations of social and political change. Appeals to Chinese culture have always been part of the explanation of China's political system, particularly in terms of language (Schram 1965), long-established social practices (Chow 1966; Pye 1982) and systems of political thought, especially Confucianism (Townsend 1969). In the last decade, though, there have been attempts to explain the emergence of an economically successful authoritarian political system solely in terms of a specific 'China Model' with its roots in Chinese culture (Chen and Goodman 2012).

Out of this discussion has come the notion that China is a civilization-state. Its society, decision-making, economics, social development, international relations, system of governance and culture have all been historically determined over several thousand years, leading to non-conflictual politics domestically and a dominant position in international affairs. This idea has been embraced outside the PRC by a number of commentators, most notably Martin Jacques in his *When China Rules the World* (2009). This is an exercise in not just Chinese exceptionalism but also Chinese triumphalism, and is equally matched within the PRC by the work of authors such as Pan Wei (2010) and Zhang Weiwei (2011). To quote the latter: 'China is the only nation where a millennia-old civilization fully coincides with the morphology of a modern state.' While no political system can be totally detached from the past experience of its society, there are some clear problems with taking such arguments as a total explanation of the current political system. Leaving aside the obvious over-essentialization of China's history in terms of continuity, cultural homogeneity and maintenance of land area, it is clear that the nation-state in the twentieth and twenty-first centuries has different functions to the earlier imperial system. Citizens have different expectations to subjects, and government is fundamentally no longer non-interventionist.

THE POLITICS OF CHANGE

The second big question behind the study of China's politics is whether the political system will change, or indeed is in the process of changing. The juxtaposition of economic reform without fundamental political change has challenged many commentators outside the PRC who see a certain inevitability in the relationship between the new social forces generated by economic reform and regime change. In particular, there is a general expectation that, as in Western Europe during the nineteenth century, the emergence of industrial entrepreneurs and new middle classes will lead to demands for liberal democracy (Glassman 1991). This expectation of democratization, or at least that the new social forces released by economic reform will come to the fore politically, has also been reinforced by the experience of Eastern Europe, especially the Communist party-states of Hungary and Poland during the 1980s, even before the collapse of the European Communist party-states. There is a substantial and influential (if sometimes controversial) body of research on this topic, led by Victor Nee, that focuses on the changing nature of the political elite in China, arguing that the PRC is in the throes of a 'market transition' (Nee 1989; Nee and Matthews 1996; Nee and Cao 1999, 2002).

The starting point for Nee's argument is the earlier work of Ivan Szelényi who pointed out that state socialism (as in Eastern Europe) produced a 'redistributive economy' in which state-owned resources were distributed by the political elite, leading to politically determined inequalities (Szelényi 1978). As market reforms are introduced into a redistributive economy, the key question is whether political capital retains its power as the major determinant of inequality and stratification, or whether the forces of the market replace political capital with skills, knowledge and enterprise. In Nee's view a market transition would lead to a 'transfer of power favouring direct producers over redistributors' (Nee 1989: 666). Nee followed up his initial statement with a series of studies showing, amongst other things, that rural stratification has moved to market determination (Nee 1996), that cadres have incentives to move into the private sector because of the market transition (Nee and Lian 1994) or out of state-owned enterprises (SOEs) and into private enterprise (Nee and Su 1998). The analysis of market transition is predictive: 'the spread of markets erodes commitment to the party and paves the way for regime change' (Nee and Lian 1994: 285).

Against this view of a market transition, a 'power persistence' theory has also been proposed. In this interpretation 'politically-based privilege' is regarded as 'more permanent and more deeply embedded in the economic situation' (Bian and Logan 1996: 741). Interestingly enough this too was derived from Nee's work. While he had based his ideas of market transition on analysis of rural China, he accepted that change might come more slowly in urban China, dominated as it was by the public sector: there the market creates a hybrid system with the work of the existing bureaucracy (Nee 1991, 1992). More generally, and later, Nee also developed ideas about how the path-dependent influence of political capital remains part and parcel of the market transition (Nee and Cao 1999).

There is research other than that done with or by Nee himself, especially on the local level in rural China, which seems to support his hypothesis about market transition. In some places, local politics has been subsumed one way or another by economic elites (Saich and Hu 2012). Moreover, there is also research that shows both the continued and sometimes the increased influence of local political leaders in economic decision-making (Solinger 1992; Goodman 2001; Dickson 2003; Chen and Dickson 2010). Nee himself has argued that inevitably in a system undergoing such change there will be residual state power acting alongside the market transition until a 'tipping point' is reached: 'Market transition theory is not a theory of radical change; instead it turns on the cumulative causation of decentralized market processes in promoting discontinuous change at the margins of the pre-existing stratification order' (Nee and Cao 2002: 36).

Moreover, as Nee has also pointed out, one clear consequence is that the process of change is highly localized with different impacts on the changing power of state and market, according to the economic environment and political structures. In this process he identifies differences between the maritime provinces (impacted upon by foreign investment) and the inland provinces, as well as differences in the emergence of specific hybrid local economies where industrial production is dominated by the state sector, the collective sector or the private sector, though containing elements of each (Nee 1996; Nee and Cao 1999).

Nee's argument has been met with claims that it is methodologically tautological since there was no market before 1978 (Walder 1996), and considerable scepticism that the returns to political capital are declining compared to the development of the market. A series of studies has indicated the relative importance of political capital (for example, class background, membership of the CCP and political position) while accepting that market factors (for example, education, skills, enterprise) also play a role in determining inequality (Xie and Hannum 1996; Walder 2002, 2003; Bian and Zhang 2004; Gustafsson and Sai 2010; Goodman 2014a). Against the theory of market transition the majority position favours the co-existence of redistribution and the market as principles in the determination of inequality, stratification and ultimately elite position (Walder 1995; Bian and Logan 1996; Parish and Michelson 1996; Walder et al. 2000; Zang 2001, 2004; Goodman 2014b). This dualism is also the view of Szelényi and Kostello, who bring to the interpretation of the PRC a perspective that differentiates strongly between a socialist mixed economy, such as now exists in the PRC, and the contemporary capitalist economies of post-socialist Eastern Europe. In particular they argue, from the experience of Eastern Europe, not only that the economic elites cannot replace the political elite while the party-state still exists, but also that if the regime was to change dramatically then under those circumstances it would be 'the technocratic fraction of the former *nomenklatura*' who would become the new system's political and economic elite, not the current private entrepreneurs (Szelényi and Kostello 1998: 318).

Necessarily, the behaviour of entrepreneurs and officials is at the heart of the debate and of research. Most recently Nee (with Sonja Opper) through a study of entrepreneurs in East China has argued that there has been a market transition or, as their book is titled, *Capitalism from Below*: private enterprise is represented as growing despite the political opposition of the state; the market has clearly replaced redistributive power and political capital no longer leads to economic success (Nee and Opper 2012: 255). This conclusion contrasts with that of Ivan Szelényi who denies the prospects for 'capitalism from below' and characterizes China as a form of state capitalism (Szelényi 2008); and that of Bruce Dickson who describes the development of the private sector in terms of 'crony capitalism'. This he defines as 'a system of interaction between economic and political elites that is based on patrimonial ties and in which success in business is due more to personal contacts in the official bureaucracy than to entrepreneurial skill or merit' (Dickson 2008: 22). The question of an 'inevitable' or indeed any transition away from redistributors to the market would then seem very much still to be determined, requiring somewhat more of a long-term perspective (and more longitudinal studies) than has been the case to date.

Regardless of the particular focus on market transition there is very little evidence of political change being desired by or coming from the new middle classes who have been the prime beneficiaries of economic reform. On the contrary, a large range of studies of both middle-class entrepreneurs and the professional and managerial middle classes emphasizes their close political relationship to the party-state (Li Chunling 2010; Chen Jie 2013; Chen and Goodman 2013; Li Chunling 2013). Entrepreneurs on the whole either emerge from the party-state, or are accommodated in it in a range of different ways once they are successfully established (Goodman 2014b: 74ff) A survey from 2006–07 found that 51 per cent of private entrepreneurs had previously worked in the state economic sector and 19 per cent had previously been a cadre (Chen and Dickson 2010: 37). The professional and managerial middle classes are overwhelmingly part of the party-state (Goodman 2016).

Concerns about the social basis of change apart, there are other forms of political change that may be regarded as substantial, even if they are not considered to amount to regime change. As Suisheng Zhao points out in his discussion of the China Model (Zhao 2010b), the PRC's political system has changed fundamentally with reform. It has become routinized and institutionalized in many ways, including notably the delivery of political stability in contrast to the first 30 years of the PRC; it has not become a liberal democracy. Moreover, change is ubiquitous in the more detailed chapters that follow this one. For those predicting more fundamental regime change it is worth recalling the work of Goldstone, Gurr and Moshiri examining political change. Revolutions only occur, they argue, when a state crisis (usually financial) and mass unrest coincide with a split elite. All three conditions must be met simultaneously for revolution to occur and even then the result may not be liberal democracy (Goldstone et al. 1991).

LEADERSHIP, INSTITUTIONS, STRUCTURES

Chapters 1, 2 and 3 in this volume provide much necessary historical background to both the evolution of China's politics and the study of China's politics. This is particularly true of Frederick Teiwes's analysis of both elite politics and studies of elite politics since the establishment of the PRC in 1949. In Chapter 1, Teiwes sets out the difficulties and pitfalls inherent in attempting to discover what happens inside the 'black box' of the decision-making process. An opaque art at the best of times, as Teiwes points out, analysis is often as not hindered by some of the approaches and techniques employed to find interpretation. These include the too-easy acceptance of self-evidently flawed sources, the substantial role of CCP propaganda, appeals to theories and models of politics that are not grounded in the PRC's experience, an over-reliance on unproven factional analysis, and the assumption that politics is always about 'succession struggles' when the evidence suggests otherwise. Teiwes then proceeds to provide a periodization and analysis of elite conflict in the PRC from 1949 to the present. His major arguments highlight the unchallenged and unchallengeable authority of Mao Zedong until his death, the rise of Deng Xiaoping to paramount leader status through historical prestige rather than political-ideological conflict with Hua Guofeng, and the self-consciousness since 1990 of a leadership reluctant to reveal divisions within the elite. As Teiwes concludes, a detailed examination of the post-1990 period remains difficult if not impossible, until key documents are made available for this period as for earlier times.

Kazuko Kojima (Chapter 2) similarly provides a historical approach to understanding the ideology of the CCP. Although in the post-Cold War world the role of ideology seems to have been displaced by other considerations (often economic growth) as drivers of politics, Kojima details how this really has not been the case in the PRC. She details the CCP's ideology in terms of three value-sets: Marxism–Leninism Mao Zedong Thought, the theory of developmental autocracy, and nationalism. Clearly there has been a historical dynamism to these value-sets as the CCP has sought to replace ideas of class with ideas of economic growth and national identity and unity. At the same time, as Kojima points out, this is by no means an easy or effective task for the CCP: identification with a Chinese nation may ultimately subvert identification with the CCP.

Zheng Yongnian and Chen Gang explain in Chapter 3 the development of the CCP as a political institution; indeed, as the institution around which the entire political system revolves. They trace the evolution of the CCP's organization from its foundation in 1921, through civil wars, the War of Resistance to Japan, the establishment of the PRC in 1949, the Great Leap Forward, and the Cultural Revolution to the death of Mao Zedong. The chapter then deals in greater detail with the development of the CCP in the reform era. It concentrates on explaining how the CCP selects and controls its own cadre force, and the relations between the CCP and the state. In particular, it highlights three important current institutional practices: the establishment of central leading small groups to ensure direction in specific policy areas; the importance of the *xitong* (system) into which the party-state is organized and through which the CCP controls the work of the government; and the Party groups that exist in all government agencies and departments. The CCP's theory of governance is that the CCP makes policy, and the government implements it. These are the mechanisms through which this approach is effected.

The development and institutions of central government are outlined in Chapter 4 by

Yan Xu and Dali Yang. Central government in this context is formed by the institutions of the state administration, centred on the operation of the State Council. The chapter highlights the role of the National Development and Reform Commission, which is the main institution under the State Council for macroeconomic policy formulation, with responsibility for drafting annual and five-year development plans. It also details how the policy-making process attempts to balance competing interests amongst companies, regions and state agencies. Consensus has become the norm or at least desirable in the process, and both regional governments and state agencies are often granted considerable latitude in developing policy and policy implementation. CCP control of central government in the early years of reform often led to minor conflicts over areas of responsibility, though these problems appear to have been solved in the last two decades. In a sense these could be seen as teething problems as central government moved out of direct economic involvement. In the event, the reform of central government has seen administrative rationalization as its various agencies moved towards a focus on regulatory and supervisory functions.

Bo Zhiyue (Chapter 5) takes the discussion of the PRC political system to the provincial level. This includes not only the 22 provincial jurisdictions, but also the directly subordinated metropolitan areas (Beijing, Shanghai, Tianjin and Chongqing) and the five large national minority autonomous regions (Tibet, Xinjiang, Ningxia, Inner Mongolia and Guangxi). Generally speaking provinces (and their equivalents) are country-sized units of administration. Bo Zhiyue discusses the literature on central–provincial relations, the role of provincial leaders in national politics and the political mobility of provincial leaders. He concludes that research has done a good job of identifying that the networks of provincial leaders are important political tools for their performance of their duties; but has done a poorer job of actually identifying those networks and the characteristics of interaction. This, he argues, must be the next step.

In Chapter 6, Minglu Chen takes the examination of political institutions to an even more local level (below the provincial) to consider how governance involves diverse social interests beyond simply the CCP and the state administration. She concentrates on the operation of two specific political institutions: the people's congress and the people's political consultative conference. The people's congress is the legislative and representative assembly; the people's political consultative conference is a body representing social groups and functional constituencies managed by the CCP's United Front Work Department. As might be imagined the composition of both bodies at all levels is heavily controlled and dominated by the CCP. At the same time, as Chen outlines, neither body is totally powerless. Representatives to local people's congresses increasingly see themselves as delegates of local constituents; and members of people's political consultative conferences often see themselves as the social conscience of the government system, a feeling reinforced by the requirement on them to exercise supervisory functions.

In Chapter 7, the final chapter in Part I, You Ji looks at the changing CCP–PLA (People's Liberation Army) relations during the last two decades. The PLA has moved from being the Party's Army to being a more technocratic and meritocratic institution. The most startling aspect of change in the PLA has been its transformation from a largely peasant-based military to one with relatively highly educated soldiers. Nowhere is this change more clearly exemplified than in the date of the annual recruitment to the PLA, now moved to coincide with high school and university graduation. You Ji concludes that the changes of the last two decades have meant that the PLA has gained greater control over its own operations and administration.

PUBLIC POLICY

In Chapter 8, Linda Chelan Li examines the important area of government finance. She considers the objectives, the organization and the governance of government finance. The discussion of objectives necessarily entails debate on the role of government, especially in reforming China. The discussion of government finance examines budget design and how budgets are managed across both regions and the functional and sectoral boundaries of government departments. Consideration of governance focuses on decision-making about revenue and expenditure, including examination of the decision-makers, the dissemination and evaluation of results. One of the key outcomes of the reform era has been the dramatic decentralization in government expenditure. This chapter suggests that 'guided decentralization' will continue even further, but that at the same time regional differences in resource distribution and organizational capacity will require greater inter-level and regional cooperation.

Carolyn Cartier and Hu De (Chapter 9) examine the rarely studied question of administrative territorialization below the national level. As they indicate, this ignorance is remarkable given that every dynasty and modern regime has made changes in administrative territorialization in line with political agendas and economic interests. In particular they concentrate on the provincial and county levels of administration. With reform, the most remarkable characteristic of administrative territorialization has been the formal establishment of cities. Cities exist at provincial, prefectural and county levels. In the 1970s there were not even 100 cities; by the 1990s there were more than 650. Prefectural-level cities doubled in number, but the number of county-level cities multiplied five times. Clearly these changes reflect the policies of the reform era and the emphasis on urbanization, but changes also reflect the complex interplay of economic goals and political agendas, as the two case studies of Suzhou and Pudong demonstrate.

In Chapter 10, Barry Naughton considers how the PRC's economic policy is understood and differentiated from other forms of policy, examines the policy process, and analyses the interest and opinion groups influential in the development of economic policy. He concludes that until recently economic policy was shaped in a top-down process, but with the Premier as the single most important actor. There may be consultation in the development of policy, but this process is carefully managed by the Premier, although broad participation is elicited both from the community and within the bureaucracy. Interestingly, there appears to have been a slight change in the last two years (2012–14), with Xi Jinping reducing the power of government (as opposed to the CCP) and limiting the areas of responsibility of the Premier. In the short term it seems that the role of the National Development and Reform Commission may have been reduced, although clearly the longer-term impact of the current leadership is still to be tested.

Regional development has been a key issue for the PRC ever since 1949, not least because of its size and scale, and the differences in resource allocation. In the Mao-dominated years of China's politics each region was urged to self-sufficiency, but part and parcel of the reform agenda has been the principle of competitive advantage. Regional inequality has increased in consequence and regional development policy to meet this situation is the subject of John Donaldson's Chapter 11. Donaldson considers both the efforts of local governments to develop their immediate economies, and the attempts by central government to provide regional development policies on a larger scale. He suggests that the attempts to ameliorate regional inequality have, ironically, actually exacerbated it. The best that could be said is that under Hu Jintao and Wen Jiabao (2002–12) social development policies did more to ameliorate regional inequalities than the policies apparently designed to meet the challenge of regional economic inequality.

The PRC is a multi-nationality state with a recognized 55 minority nationalities (comprising just over 8 per cent of the population in total) alongside the majority Han Chinese. In the China Studies literature, relations between the minority nationalities and the PRC are sometimes described as discriminatory, sometimes described more neutrally, or even positively. In his Chapter 12 on the topic, Xiaowei Zang examines the PRC's record against the current global norms on human rights. The chapter examines minority nationality inequality on education and labour markets; the preservation of minority cultures and languages; the representation of minority nationalities in the political system; and the degree of local autonomy for minority nationalities. Overall, Zang concludes that the party-state's policy towards minority nationalities is too homogenizing and assimilationist to meet the current international norms of human rights.

Education policy is crucial to a society for human capital and skills development as well as for socialization. In Chapter 13, W. John Morgan and Fengliang Li examine the not inconsiderable changes to the provision and content of the formal education system, as well as the changing relationships between education, the social market economy and the labour market. Overall they highlight the various ways in which education has moved from being egalitarian in outlook to being more market-focused. The result has been considerable expansion of educational provision, but a significant increase in inequality of educational opportunity. One reason for this apparent paradox has been that primary and secondary education are paid for by provincial local governments, and there are serious regional differences in resource distribution. Another has been that primary and secondary education are significantly more important to the development of educational opportunity than higher education, which has received considerable attention because of its enormous expansion since the mid-1990s. The missing link is the university entrance examination (*gaokao*) which is now in the early stages of a badly needed reform.

In Chapter 14, Wang Guohui and Jane Duckett consider the development of policy on welfare and social security as a central plank in the party-state's platform to maintain a social base of support. Their analysis starts with a review of developments before the start of the reform era, indicating the very stark differences in the levels of welfare provided by the state to urban and rural communities. Particularly for workers in heavy industry, the party-state catered to the welfare needs of urban citizens with public housing, health care, education and pensions. With the introduction of economic reform, welfare change in urban China was mediated by the pace of change and the transfer of welfare functions to various bodies. In rural China, however, welfare provision essentially collapsed completely. It was only under the leadership of Hu Jintao and Wen Jiabao that attempts were made to provide a framework for rural welfare provision. Inequalities and problems, though, still remain, and not just between rural and urban China. These include the difficulties faced by a rapidly ageing population and a pension fund deficit; the lack of social security for migrant workers; and overall poor management of the social security system.

POLITICAL ECONOMY AND SOCIAL CHANGE

Part III on state–society relations starts with a chapter on the phenomenon of corruption, which became headline news in 2013–14 with the campaign launched by General Secretary of the CCP, Xi Jinping, to hunt down and prosecute those engaged in such practices on both a large scale (the 'tigers') and a small scale (the 'flies'). In Chapter 15, Dali Yang and Yan Xu examine the prevalence of official corruption – the exchange of official power for private gain in violation of regulation – in the PRC, and the party-state's organization and implementation of anti-corruption work, and end by considering the specific anti-corruption initiatives undertaken by the current leadership since it came to power at the end of 2012. As the authors indicate, corruption is not a new phenomenon in the PRC, and while there can be no gainsaying the current (2013–15) intent to deal with the problem, there are systemic reasons for scepticism about its total eradication.

It might come as a surprise to some that the idea of class still plays a central role in China's politics. The CCP remains the 'vanguard of the proletariat', and the PRC is described in the Constitution as 'a socialist state under the people's democratic dictatorship, led by the proletariat and based on the alliance of the workers and peasants'. In Chapter 16, Yingjie Guo considers how the CCP has conceptualized and operationalized the concept since the Party's formation in 1921; not simply to explain how it has mobilized the politics of class, but to show how the apparent paradoxes can be explained. From a Marxian perspective, class consciousness leads to class action and class struggle. The CCP has, though, always been considerably more instrumentalist in its discussion of class. The departure from a commitment to class struggle in the post-Mao era simply reinforces the CCP's instrumentality, though it may also be ultimately self-defeating.

There have been dramatic changes in gender discourses and practices since the establishment of the PRC. Discussion and contestation of gender norms and gendered power relations have been a central part of the changing social, political, economic and cultural environment. Gender has been the subject of power struggles, overlapping with changing class relations and ideologies seeking dominance. Through the detailed examination of two particular symbols – Xianglin's Wife and the Dazhai Iron Girls – gender representations that have been both influential and controversial, Wang Zheng (Chapter 17) analyses the nature of the gendered power struggles, highlighting the increase in class and gender polarization in the last few decades.

In Chapter 18, Jean Oi discusses the reasons behind the substantial development of rural China in the 1980s, which lifted so many out of poverty, and the evolving policies in the ensuing decades. The foremost reason for increasing incomes was the creation of rural industry and non-agricultural wage labour soon after the reforms began. An advocate of the local state corporatism model, Oi also recognizes the variation across place and time within China with regard to the role played by private and local state actors in the development process. Regardless of whether cadres spearheaded or played a subordinate, supporting role, the key to China's development success is that cadres did not obstruct reform, but promoted it. There were effective incentives for those directly responsible for the implementation of reform to lead rural industrialization directly through support of private entrepreneurs. While highlighting the attractiveness of China's growth for other poor developing countries, Oi also points out the pitfalls and problems with this model. A theme in the chapter is that each round of rural reforms had its success, but also entailed new problems. Decollectivization increased incentives but laid the basis for the peasant taxation problems and political unrest. Eventually the central state took decisive action to eliminate the sources of peasant burdens and discontent, eliminating fees and taxes, but that has left many localities with deep fiscal inadequacies. Over time, inequalities and the persistence of pockets of poverty have necessitated a renewed emphasis on policies for poverty alleviation and welfare systems. This has also come with an increasing recentralization of power. The centre designs well-meaning programmes like the formation of new rural commnunities under the 'New Socialist Countryside', but localities have taken such policies as opportunities to engage in land grabs, as one of the few remaining sources of local revenue subject to local control.

Non-governmental organizations (NGOs) have come to play an increasingly important role in the transformation of Chinese society, especially active in those areas where the party-state either finds it undesirable to act, or is unable to. The political role of NGOs is, though, potentially equally as significant in a Communist party-state, as occurred in Eastern Europe before 1989. In Chapter 19, Jennifer Hsu considers the extent to which the emergence of NGOs represents the emergence of a civil society, both generally and through the examples of four specific areas of operation. She distinguishes the roles of NGOs involved in environmental mobilization, dealing with HIV/AIDS, migrant workers, and general social service delivery. The chapter argues that while the NGOs are clearly constrained by the party-state and have little or no direct political impact, they remain important to China's social transformation.

In Chapter 20, Lynette Ong examines the incidence of social unrest in the PRC and what this may say about the political stability and durability of the regime, concluding that, far from threatening the regime, such manifestations are a necessary safety-valve in an authoritarian political system. Her analysis is based on a dataset constructed from more than 2500 reported cases of social unrest during 2003–12. The chapter, and the dataset, differentiate distinct forms of social unrest: land grievances, labour disputes and social anger-venting incidents (usually related to feelings of unofficial injustice). Grievances related to land expropriation, demolition and relocation are the largest category, amounting to 36 per cent of all cases; labour disputes are the second-largest, accounting for 14 per cent. In general the number of cases has increased over the period surveyed, with the proportion of land grievances also increasing. Interestingly it is the social anger-venting incidents that have the tendency to include outright street violence, and to be larger in scale. These are the cases motivated largely by presumed miscarriages of justice, and police and city patrol brutality.

INTERNATIONAL RELATIONS

The final part of this volume is devoted to the PRC's international relations. It starts with Shaun Breslin's account (Chapter 21) of the PRC emerging from relative isolation to become an actor on the world stage that could influence global politics. The chapter examines how the PRC itself sees and has changed its view of the world order and its place in it. To a large extent the PRC has come to accept the established world order and adapt to it, rather than pushing for change, although there have clearly been times and issues when it has expressed dissatisfaction. This is particularly the case with the distribution of power within the major institutions of world governance, where it sees the dominant position of the Western liberal democracies exerting disproportionate influence. Breslin concludes that the PRC has played three different roles on the world stage. It started out as a global issue, became a global actor, and has now become a global power. It is not the predominant global power, but its actions and interests do have disproportionate influence across the world. Remarkably, as Breslin argues, China's rise has occurred not only because Western powers have declined in importance, but also because the West has actually contributed more positively to the rise of China.

In Chapter 22, James Reilly examines the PRC's economic statecraft: its use of economic resources to exert influence in pursuit of foreign policy objectives. As Reilly points out, this is a fairly new development in the PRC, as for much of the post-Mao era foreign policy was primarily used to pursue economic interests. It is only more recently that those roles have been reversed. Reilly outlines the emergence of economic statecraft in the PRC and explains how Chinese scholars have themselves become active in promoting its use, before going on to detail how economic statecraft actually works and who is involved. While it would be easy to descend into simple triumphalism about the scale of the economic benefits the PRC can deliver, Reilly points to some obvious constraints that need to be kept in mind. Economic, foreign policy and strategic goals may not always march in step, as the obvious case of PRC–Taiwan relations clearly bears witness. At the same time, differences within the PRC bureaucracy and the need for coordination across various systems, ministries and government agencies make a mockery of the idea that the PRC can always act simply and effectively, even in providing aid and economic statecraft.

The last four chapters deal with the PRC's international relations with specific parts of the world. In Chapter 23, Shogo Suzuki examines the PRC's international relations in East Asia, with Japan, Taiwan, the Republic of Korea (South Korea), and the Democratic People's Republic of Korea (North Korea). East Asia is the PRC's 'back yard', and it has significant economic relations with Japan, Taiwan and South Korea; while North Korea and Taiwan are more important for political reasons. On Japan, Suzuki discusses the economic closeness between the two governments, in contrast to their political separation, exacerbated still by the 'history' issues related to the interpretation of war-time behaviour and ownership of areas of the East China Sea. Taiwan is regarded as potentially the most dangerous flashpoint in the PRC's international relations, heightened by the democratization of Taiwan, but mediated to some extent by the degree of Taiwan's economic integration with east and southeast PRC. The PRC's relations with South Korea have clearly moved from confrontation to close partnership, despite South Korea's close alliance with the USA. On the other hand, the PRC's relationship with North Korea presents numerous headaches to Beijing, not only because of the former's unpredictability but also due to the latter's desire to move closer to South Korea.

Bates Gill (Chapter 24) examines the literature on relations between the USA and China, and the view each has of the other. Interestingly, he starts with the observation that from both sides there appears (according to the literature) to be a knowledge gap about the other, leading to misperceptions, misunderstandings and ignorance. While this knowledge gap may be more imagined than real, it does highlight the mutual mistrust that still exists. In the past there have been debates in the USA about containing or engaging China, which still to some extent seem to play out in contemporary debates. As Gill describes it, there is a divide between those who see USA–PRC conflict as inevitable, and those who see the PRC as more willing to accept the norms of the international community, even when, as is likely to be the case, the prospects for democratization are held to be low. Chinese commentators, in contrast, almost universally argue that a peaceful international power transition, to allow China its place in the world order, is both desirable and likely. In the end, Gill concludes, there is no choice but to adopt a position of 'engage but hedge'; not the most satisfying of policy messages, not the most stable, but probably the most realistic.

In Chapter 25, Alberto Camarena and Jörn Dosch consider relations between the PRC and Southeast Asia. Much of the literature on this topic is dominated by the USA's view of the region, and determined to some extent by relations between the USA and China. As they argue this is to forget that China has been a long-term influence in the region and that Southeast Asia is actually quite a diverse region of different national state interests and activities. While much of the discussion may devolve to a consideration of Southeast Asia as Association of Southeast Asian Nations (ASEAN), this is clearly not the whole story. The chapter examines relations between Southeast Asia in terms of three periods: 1949–76, 1976–92 and since 1992. The differences between those periods are shaped by the international environment, developments in each of the countries and in China, and the role of the USA. Clearly the most productive era has been that of the last 25 years, in which diplomatic relations have been completely restored and a free trade area (China–ASEAN Free Trade Agreement, CAFTA) discussed and then established (in 2010). On the whole, economic rationalism has led the move away from the earlier mutual hostility, although conflicts over stretches of the South China Seas still impinge.

Finally, in Chapter 26, Kerry Brown looks at relations between the European Union and the PRC. China and the countries of the European Union are economically mutually important, and interdependent, but there are clear political problems with some of the countries which play out substantially at the level of the European Union, which since 1993 and the Treaty of Maastricht has political, moral and social desiderata written into its agenda. It is the clash of values between the European Union and the PRC that is the subject of this chapter. Through an examination of policy documents, Brown concludes that this value clash is not actually very helpful in developing working relations. In the first place, neither the European Union nor the PRC do a good job of understanding the political actions of each other. Secondly, while the European Union talks extensively about its common values (especially in dealing with China), in fact those values are often contested within Europe, especially on the question of engagement with the PRC, where some countries are more pragmatic and some argue more from a priori principles.

KEY CONCEPTS

The study of China's politics, like every other field of academic enquiry, has its own private language. There are terms taken direct from Chinese and used fairly freely by

16   *Handbook of the politics of China*

writers and commentators. There are also terms in English which acquire a specific meaning when used within the study of China's politics. This section provides a guide to a few of the more high-profile terms. Others, which tend not to cross the boundaries of specific topics, are dealt with in the following individual chapters.

- *Apparat* or 'system'. An *apparat* is a hierarchical structure of the state, running from the top to the bottom, and largely self-administering. Public security would be one such *apparat*, comprising not just one but several ministries. It was once fashionable to talk of Eastern European Communist party-states as Apparat-states, because they were characterized by such systems within their governance practices. The *apparat* structure persists in the PRC where it is referred to as a 'system' (*xitong*). Most officials would spend their whole careers in a single *apparat* or system.
- 'Autonomous', as a term applied to a territorial administrative jurisdiction (region, district, county) indicates that a proportion of the population of that area are members of at least one minority nationality. One important logic of this identification is that every state-recognized minority nationality group is required to have a designated homeland, although the minority nationality may not necessarily be the majority population in that area (see Chapter 12). The title of 'autonomous' is approved by the PRC State Council in this context. Though in English 'autonomous' may mean both self-determining and self-governing, in Chinese there are two distinct terms, and in this context the meaning of self-governing (*zizhi*) is employed. An autonomous region is a provincial-level jurisdiction and there are five: Inner Mongolia, Tibet, Xinjiang, Ningxia and Guangxi. Autonomous areas are known by a combination of the territorial and minority nationality name, as for example in the Ningxia Hui Autonomous Region, or the Guangxi Zhuang Autonomous Region.
- Class composition (*chengfen*) and class background (*chushen*): in the early 1950s the CCP classified all citizens in order to direct political campaigns and organize socio-economic development. Class composition was initially the individual's class position (based largely on occupation) in the three years before 1949. Class background was an identifier based on the individual's family, and particularly their parents. The distinction was designed to create some dynamism in the classification system, but in the event simply led to confusion. Nonetheless, class labels from the early 1950s remained as drivers of political campaigns and socio-economic policies for government until 1984.
- *Danwei* is a Chinese word meaning 'unit'. It is used in the PRC to refer to social and production entities, such as government offices, schools, hospitals, factories, enterprises, and so on. In the era of state socialism (1949–84) most of urban China was organized into these kinds of *danwei*. A person and their family would not only work in, but also live in and have their welfare needs met by their *danwei*. This form of socio-economic organization on this scale is sometimes called *danwei*-society.
- The Falungong is a movement of practitioners of Chinese spiritual practices that challenged the authority of the CCP in mid-1999 and has since been outlawed from the PRC. Established in 1992 in Northeast China it has also gained adherents worldwide where it campaigns vigorously against the CCP.

- *Guanxi* is a term meaning literally in English 'relationship', but which in the context of the study of China's politics should perhaps more accurately be rendered as 'special relationship'. Even before the establishment of the PRC, the Chinese knew that if one wanted to get things done effectively one should not try the official front-on approach, but 'go through the back door, and use the special relationship' (*zou houmen, la guanxi*). This practice undoubtedly continues. One certainly needs *guanxi* to do many things, and equally as certainly, people who have such influence can achieve things that others cannot. At the same time it may be misleading to see *guanxi* as the sole factor required for action, as is the case with some studies of Chinese society and economic development.
- *Hukou* is the household registration system that applies to all citizens. Everyone has a registration based on their mother's birthplace that conveys a right to live in that area. Household registration also historically entails a right to food only in the case of those with an urban *hukou*. In the contemporary period the effect of the household registration system is to limit entitlement to citizenship rights (education, health, welfare) of migrant workers in their place of work as opposed to in their place of household registration.
- *Neibu* material: *neibu* is Chinese for 'internal', and the word applies particularly to restricted-circulation publications and papers, usually for the purposes of the party-state. There are necessarily different levels of restriction and circulation, though all are referred to as *neibu* materials. In addition to the bureaucracy's paperwork, the term also used to applied to books, magazines and newspapers that were produced for restricted circulation as opposed to open sale. Permission to purchase was granted by virtue of position in the party-state.
- *Nomenklatura* is a Russian word, imported via the former Soviet Union. It refers to the table of ranks in the party-state and is an instrument of appointment control. Each position in the party-state has a rank and grade. To be appointed to such a position the individual is also required to have been assessed at that rank and grade. Certain positions can be approved at the same level, and some at more senior levels. In China Studies the Russian word for this practice is most usually employed, although *bianzhi* is the Chinese (and lesser-utilized) word.
- *Weibo* means 'micro-blog' in Chinese. The term is more often than not applied to Sina Weibo, a particular micro-blog. Sina Weibo is similar to both Facebook and Twitter, although allowing for a larger number of characters, pictures and networking.
- Wechat is the English name for Weixing, a form of social media owned by Tencent, which is wireless-based and has replaced Sina Weibo in popularity in China. Wechat supports messages, file transfer and face-to-face calls.

NOTE

1. Details of China Studies before the start of the PRC's reform era may be found in Goodman (1984b).

PART I

LEADERSHIP, INSTITUTIONS AND STRUCTURES

1. The study of elite political conflict in the PRC: politics inside the 'black box'
Frederick C. Teiwes

This is a cautionary tale. The dominant contemporary Western scholarly assessments of Chinese Communist Party (CCP) elite politics in almost every period of the history of the People's Republic of China (PRC) have been either dramatically wrong, or a very mixed bag, or in critical respects speculation that cannot be verified on existing evidence. Moreover, in some important cases erroneous findings have remained conventional wisdom even as new information and analysis has appeared, supporting alternative interpretations. This chapter will review the shifting circumstances and conclusions of Western scholarship as they apply to the very top leadership that operates in a 'black box' that is largely opaque not only to outsiders, but even to highly positioned members of the elite itself.

The focus here is on how important national decisions have been made, the contending forces in the decision process, and the nature of and extent to which power struggles or succession struggles have been key features of PRC political history. The Politburo Standing Committee has generally stood at the centre of this institutionally, but a range of other elite actors down to the top-ranking provincial Party leaders have been involved in various instances and respects. In any political system much of what goes on regarding major developments is partially obscure, but in authoritarian Leninist systems impediments to understanding are much more systematic, making the concept of a 'black box' more than appropriate. Norms of Party discipline are strong, restrictions on the right to know and have a voice are extensive even if varying over time, and mistrust among leaders can inhibit communication and create misperceptions. Moreover, the ability of the regime to create an official narrative that distorts reality has not only misled foreign scholars, but also affected the ongoing dynamic of Party politics itself.

Yet it has been possible to penetrate the 'black box' to varying degrees in different periods as new sources have become available, although the results have often been limited. While the limitations of Western studies have been broadly due to restricted information, also significant has been the decline of scholarly attention to elite politics. As Joseph Fewsmith observed more than two decades ago, 'The study of elite politics has generally gone out of favor in recent years' (Fewsmith 2001: xi), a development going back to the opening up of China to foreign scholars in the early 1980s. This opening up of research in a wide variety of previously closed areas, including state–society relations, institutional development and village studies, drew scholars away from the more opaque area of elite politics. More generally, there has been a relative dearth of the type of detailed, deeply researched investigation necessary to present central CCP politics in all its complexity. But this does not mean that central elite politics has been ignored. One type of study, involving some impressive work (e.g., Solinger 1991; Yang 1996; Shih 2008), focuses on specific policy sectors and provides important insights into the broader political setting, but too often applies erroneous preconceptions concerning the nature of central leadership politics. Another approach adopts a thematic perspective, identifying key issues such as 'old man politics' or the relationship of informal and institutional factors; while perceptive, these studies rely on a general reading of sources rather than deeply focused research (e.g., Fewsmith 2001; Teiwes 1995; Tsou 1995).

In what follows, to both explore the evolving state of Western studies and offer concise personal assessments of different phases of CCP elite politics, I first address in broad terms problems causing misleading conclusions, and then examine five periods of PRC history, bringing in scholarly assessments of each period and how they have changed. Finally, concluding remarks will be offered on the possibilities and limits of studying elite politics going forward.

FLAWS IN WESTERN STUDIES OF CCP ELITE POLITICS

The essential problem facing analysts is the inevitable inadequacy of information for fully penetrating the 'black box'. This does not prevent painstaking research from demonstrating the wrong-headedness of various conventional wisdoms, nor from providing persuasive analyses of particular events and broader trends. But given the gaps in data, scholarship has fallen prey to flawed approaches in attempting to create coherent narratives that are not necessarily justified. Here are five of the most significant.

The Use and Abuse of Sources

Western scholarship has not been deterred from constructing, on the basis of thin albeit genuine PRC source material, analyses that cannot be sustained as more revealing sources become available. A case in point is foreign policy in the 1970s at the end of the Maoist era, whether Lin Biao's alleged opposition to US–China rapprochement, essentially based on a single after-the-fact assertion by Mao, or ongoing differences over the Soviet Union deduced from a close reading of public PRC sources.[1] In reality, Mao so dominated foreign policy that there was no room for genuine disputation; as one significant Ministry of Foreign Affairs figure put it, 'What debate? It was just a matter of doing what Mao decreed' (Teiwes and Sun 2007: 85). Beyond the problem of overreaching with the limited sources available has been the tendency to use sources that cannot be verified, and in various cases are demonstrably false. This is particularly the case with journals, books and documents published in Hong Kong and Taiwan. This is not to say that Hong Kong and Taiwan publications are inherently dubious, nor that PRC sources avoid the same uncertainties, but it is to say that there has sometimes been a cavalier acceptance of such material. Concerning documents, Taiwan publications have over many years published purported CCP documents that have on balance been credible, but flawed by fakes that have been taken up in the Western literature.[2] Arguably more significant has been the use of journals and books from Hong Kong providing 'inside information' on leadership conflict. In particular, especially in the early reform period, magazines linked to the reform perspective provided claims feeding the reform versus conservative narrative that became a key basis for influential Western analyses. While not inaccurate at one level, such studies provided an oversimplified narrative and numerous misleading details.[3]

Paying Attention to the Party Line

Overall, the foreign scholarly community has been sceptical of official and other PRC characterizations of internal elite politics, but with two glaring exceptions: the 17 years before the Cultural Revolution that was presented as a 'two-line struggle' between Mao and his alleged enemies; and the initial period following Mao's death that was treated as a struggle between a reformist faction led by Deng Xiaoping, and neo-Maoists or 'whateverists' led by Hua Guofeng. The 'two-line struggle' motif for the pre-1966 period dominated Western studies of elite politics from the time it was raised in the Cultural Revolution through the 1970s. One version adopted the fundamental tension between two camps, whether personalized as Maoists versus Liuists, or given social science respectability as, for example, revolutionary modernizers versus managerial modernizers (Ahn 1976). Alternative versions provided more complex configurations, but the central factor was that Mao was frequently opposed, and forced into periods of retreat (e.g., Chang 1975). The 'two-line struggle' interpretation was only decisively overturned when the regime treated it as a distortion, tentatively at the 1978 Third Plenum, and frontally with the 1981 Historical Resolution (see *Beijing Review* 1981).[4] Nevertheless, the literature, while no longer advancing the concept itself, still contained various analyses of a contested Mao (e.g., Huang 2000). There are similarities, but also differences, in the scholarly community's adoption of the conflict between Hua's neo-Maoists and Deng's reformers. A major difference is that analysis of alleged Hua–Deng conflict along these lines appeared in Western sources based on readings of open PRC sources before the Party adopted the overview, but the authoritative endorsement in the Historical Resolution largely put the narrative beyond doubt for the field. Hence another difference: when the CCP reversed its line on the 'two-line struggle' and provided ample evidence in support, its full version was largely abandoned in the West; when the regime's interest lay in maintaining the Hua–Deng conflict myth with minimal convincing evidence, there was little scholarly interest in pursuing the question.

Remember the Discipline

Given the gaps in the sources on elite politics, it is understandable that analysts have applied concepts from the broader political science literature in an attempt to understand the workings of leadership politics. Such efforts have been particularly notable since the 1980s when, undoubtedly not coincidentally, the trend started that weakened area studies centres and privileged disciplinary departments, particularly in the USA. Of course, testing such concepts is valid; China is not a totally unique political system where broader comparative considerations of bureaucratic interests and conflict structures are irrelevant, and theory should always be considered when assessing leadership politics. The problem has been the (mis)application of such concepts and theories to elite conflict, especially concerning the Mao period. Here I address two examples, both by first-rate scholars, both making coherent and well-regarded arguments. David Bachman's book on the origins of the Great Leap Forward, which appeared as 'new institutionalism', became a major trend in US political science, it provided an institutional interpretation of the emergence of the Great Leap as the victory of a 'planning and heavy industrial coalition' in a bureaucratic conflict, with Mao only playing a secondary role (Bachman 1991). The problem with this analysis is not only that the absolute dominance of Mao in launching the Leap Forward has become even clearer with new evidence, but also that leaders of the 'planning coalition' were equally responsible, with their purported antagonists, the 'financial coalition', in shaping the policies Mao bitterly rejected when deciding on the Leap. The second case is Avery Goldstein's attempt, drawing on systems theory, to explain differences between the 'hierarchical' elite politics of the pre-Cultural Revolution period and the 'anarchical' structure of 1966–76 politics, an effort that involved no primary research, but instead relied on existing secondary studies to illustrate his structural explanation (Goldstein 1991). While the result is interesting and in some respects closer to the mark than many previous Western efforts, nothing new is uncovered concerning events or the underlying dynamics of elite politics. The over-reliance on theory in these and other cases had the effect of downgrading the essential importance of empirical research.

Finding Factions

Conflict is the stuff of politics, and applying 'faction' to contending forces is a reasonable if slippery approach. The main problem is not simply the frequent looseness of definition, but more importantly of relating the existence (or otherwise) and roles of designated factions to actual political conflict. 'Factions' have been widely adopted in the literature, whether to refer to revolutionary 'mountaintops' binding individuals and structures in the pre-1949 period,[5] personal networks of reciprocity organized around senior leaders (e.g., Shih 2008), organizational careers or political associations,[6] or perceived policy orientations, as in the previously noted reform versus conservative analysis of the post-Mao period. One problem often left unclear in the literature is that while groupings or potential factions exist, when do they manifest as factional behaviour outlawed by Party rules? For the Maoist period the crucial factor was Mao himself in creating tensions that pushed matters over the line. The early 1950s Gao Gang purge was a case where Mao's displeasure with Liu Shaoqi, as relayed to Gao, set off a factional mobilization on Gao's part, but no counter-mobilization by Liu, and finally Mao pulled back in view of the threat to Party unity. Underlying tensions were there, but without Mao there is no reason to think they would have developed into a major crisis.[7] Another Mao creation, the 'Gang of Four', illustrates a further issue: the tendency to take as given official characterizations of 'evil' factions. The literature almost universally treats the 'gang' as a unified radical group, when in fact important tensions existed among them. In the reform era there has been a related tendency to classify leaders as reformers and conservatives without any nuance. A case in point is Xi Zhongxun, a figure deserving his place in the reform pantheon, even if overlionized now. Xi did play a leading role in some but not all reform projects. His role in establishing Special Economic Zones (SEZs) in Guangdong was significant, although his main supporter in that matter was Hua Guofeng, not 'reform faction head' Deng Xiaoping, while Xi opposed household contracting in agriculture, an area where Deng was very late in becoming engaged.

Let's Struggle for the Top Job

Given the history of purges or removals of top leaders including Liu Shaoqi, Lin Biao, Hua Guofeng, Hu Yaobang and Zhao Ziyang, it is hardly surprising that the literature is replete with claims of succession struggles. None of these cases involved struggles against pre-eminent leaders Mao and Deng, while only Hua as a genuine Number 1 leader (as opposed to Hu and Zhao who only formally held the position) was the target of actual struggles, disjointedly from the Gang of Four, and decisively from Deng in a manner hardly reflecting the ferocity notionally associated with such conflicts. If there were struggles, they were over the position of successor rather than the top job itself. During Mao's time, the only such conflict was the Gao Gang affair that, as discussed above, while a genuine attempt by Gao to unseat Liu Shaoqi, was the result of Mao's meddling. After that, until the Cultural Revolution there is no evidence of any challenge to Liu, notwithstanding Mao's occasional hints of a preference for Deng. The succession seemed set with Mao, as he affirmed in 1961, ostensibly envisioning Liu's succession, most likely followed by Deng (MacFarquhar 1997: 433, 640n14). Crucially, no possible alternative leader undertook any known efforts to undermine Liu, whether due to a feeling that this was required for regime stability, or because of uncertainty as to Mao's real intent. Strikingly, Lin Biao did not want to be the successor and tried to avoid it, and given the dubious possibility that he was intending a coup against Mao in 1971, it could only have been a desperate defensive measure (see Teiwes and Sun 1996: 57–65, 152–160). As for Hua, he also did not seek the successor post, in fact attempting to position more senior colleagues for it in 1976 (see Teiwes and Sun 2007: 439–441, 582–583), and, as we shall discuss subsequently, offered no resistance to his removal in 1980–81. Following Hua's ouster, like Hua and Lin Biao before them, neither Hu Yaobang nor Zhao Ziyang sought the position, and in fact seemingly tried to avoid it.[8] Real power lay with the Party's elders, while vulnerability accompanied the leading position on the 'first front' of managing Party and government affairs.

A PERIODIZATION, 1949–2014

The scholarly understanding of each successive period of PRC history has varied in accord with the factors discussed above and the evolving availability of sources. I address these contextual developments for each of the five periods below, and present my own summary overview of what can realistically be said about the elite politics of each period.

The Pre-Cultural Revolution Period, 1949–66[9]

During the 17 years before mid-1966 when, according to the Cultural Revolution narrative, a 'two-line struggle' existed between Mao and his alleged enemies, there was little attention to CCP elite politics in foreign scholarship. The dominant feature of this scholarship was in the Sinological tradition with historical enquiry focusing on the traditional and Republican periods, although the infusion of US government and related foundation funding in the early 1960s saw a take-off period of political and historical studies on the PRC. But little was done on elite politics, and those who did undertake such enquiries were largely limited to official public sources that naturally represented the Party line. These included the daily media, always necessary for placing politics in a hopefully precise context; major documents from key Party and state meetings or on political themes of particular salience to the leadership; and documents on some high-level purges.[10] Valuable additional sources included the Hong Kong newsletter *China News Analysis* (1953–98) that summarized and analysed PRC developments, and various compendia of meetings and personnel compiled by the US Consulate in Hong Kong. None of this, however, did much to bolster elite studies: two of the most significant books emerging from the early 1960s fundamentally avoided elite conflict (Barnett 1967; Lewis 1963),[11] while arguably the most influential (Schurmann 1966) addressed 'Mao's opponents' based on a classic Kremlinological reading of speeches by different leaders without access to any behind-the-scenes developments, and identified a struggle between Mao and Gao Gang based on the official denunciation of Gao.

As already indicated, the Cultural Revolution reversed this situation. Now there was a surfeit of 'inside' materials, as well as an official line emphasizing conflict over the 17 years. Of course, the line was not as strict and consistent as before, with Red Guard publications in uncoordinated fashion presenting a vast array of (unverifiable, but in broad terms generally credible) exposés of the views and actions of assorted Mao 'enemies'. This was bolstered by the official press along similar lines, and some extremely valuable collections of Mao's speeches and comments largely emanating from Red Guard sources.[12] This led to the most fecund period of studies on elite politics to date; a number of major books sought to explain the origins of the Cultural Revolution and the unfolding of the movement, while monographs and articles further dealt with specific aspects of leadership politics. The problem did not so much concern the accumulation of data from the new treasure trove of Cultural Revolution sources, as fitting this information into the now dominant 'two-line struggle' model. A key failure was in contrasting the opinions and actions of top leaders at one point in time to Mao's views at another as illustrating sharp conflict, ignoring that Mao almost always endorsed the offending views at the time they were raised, or at least indicated a willingness for them to be tried out, or was ambiguous, or simply made no comment.

A further reversal inevitably occurred in the post-Mao period, with the regime changing its overview and providing an enormous range of materials in support. These included an invaluable set of officially produced Mao manuscripts (*Jianguo yilai Mao Zedong wengao* 1987–98), chronologies of events, the *nianpu* or chronicles of specific high-ranking leaders,[13] an official series of biographies of deceased leaders (*Zhonggong dangshi renwu zhuan* 1980–), many memoirs of leaders including some that are exceptionally revealing (e.g., Bo Yibo 1991, 1993), major books by Party historians that while constrained by official orthodoxies nevertheless present details and analysis going beyond those limits,[14] and many articles in the same vein by serious scholars in Party history journals. Finally, an important additional source emerged with the PRC's opening: access to retired elite members and excellent Party history scholars who provide both details and perspectives that are invaluable. Thus while inevitably incomplete and leaving important questions open, this array of sources has provided the basis for deep detailed research that can correct past official misrepresentations as well as those continuing to the present. Unfortunately, some good specific studies notwithstanding, with the general turn away from elite politics since the early 1980s, erroneous claims of limits on Mao's power persist in the literature, and overall studies utilizing deep research enabling comprehensive assessments of leadership politics before 1966 are few and far between.[15]

What, then, utilizing the full range of sources available, can we conclude about elite politics before the Cultural Revolution? The central factor was the dominant, unchallengeable position of Mao. Given authority to make final decisions in 1943, such formal authority was immeasurably enhanced by the fact of the victory of the revolution in 1949; a new dynasty was established, and as the leader perceived by his colleagues as the strategic genius responsible for this unimaginable victory, Mao was the new emperor in all but name. While his status and authority were never challenged, the Chairman was sensitive to his own power, most notably by assuming virtual sole control of the military, in effect revising his dictum that 'the Party controls the gun' to 'Mao controls the gun'.[16] Mao was also highly judgemental, and had his personal favourites. These did not include his ranking colleagues Liu and Zhou who had comparable status in the early history of the Party, and these leaders would suffer in very different ways during the Cultural Revolution decade. The Chairman's favourites were more junior officials – Gao Gang, Lin Biao and Deng Xiaoping – presumably perceived as less of any possible threat, and in each case having qualities Mao admired.[17] While Gao and Lin suffered rejection and terrible fates, all three only attained positions near the very top because of Mao's actions.

While Mao exercised absolute power during the entire 17 years to 1966, this period can be divided into two distinct periods in terms of Mao's leadership style and its impact on elite politics. Up to the first signs of the Great Leap Forward in late 1957, Mao could be considered as a very strong-minded chairman of the board, one who delegated policy formulation in areas where he felt less competent; especially the economy, where Zhou Enlai and Chen Yun played the dominant role. But Mao retained direct control of the areas where he felt most comfortable, notably foreign affairs and agriculture, and forced through measures apparently opposed by most of the Politburo, notably entry into the Korean War and stepping up the pace of agricultural collectivization in 1955. Mao's policy-setting was broadly centrist, but with a predisposition to push ahead faster, as in the transition to socialism in 1953, and the 'high tide' of collectivization in 1955. Mao not only got his way, but he also imposed career setbacks on key players, although without purges.[18] Mao's colleagues apparently concluded that while they could not directly challenge the Chairman, they could try to persuade him. A telling case occurred in spring 1956 when Zhou and the bulk of the top economic leadership determined that the 'little leap forward' following the surge in collectivization was unsustainable and had to be cut back. Mao was unhappy, and at the relevant Politburo meeting instead proposed an increase in investment. Hardly anyone was supportive of this, but no one voted against it. However, several days later Zhou approached Mao to argue the case privately, and after an initial outburst of anger, the Chairman accepted the Premier's position and 'opposing rash advance' became the policy of the day (Teiwes and Sun 1999: Ch. 1). Many Western analyses treat this development as a defeat forced on Mao, and he subsequently singled it out as a major deviation. But Mao approved the policy and did not object to any specific measures at the time. He still gave leeway to Zhou and others as a matter of choice.

A new dynamic appeared with the Great Leap, a policy initiative reflecting various factors,[19] but arguably driven by Mao's coming to terms with his first significant failure since becoming CCP leader: the 1957 Hundred Flowers experiment he had pushed through which resulted in sharp criticism of the Party. Now Mao sought a new personal policy initiative, and blamed his earlier failure on others, most illogically for 'opposing rash advance'. From January 1958, Mao imposed an extreme radical economic policy on the Party, sharply criticized Zhou, forced formal self-criticisms by Standing Committee members for the first time, and created an atmosphere where Zhou felt obliged to offer his resignation. Thus the incredibly destructive Leap, which eventually cost 25 to 45 million peasant lives through starvation, was launched, with opposition within the top leadership notable by its absence, and with Liu Shaoqi and Deng Xiaoping playing key roles in pushing it forward. Of particular note is that as early signs of the disaster began to filter through, it was Mao who first called for pulling back from the extremes, with the very highest officials following cautiously. As the Lushan meeting approached in summer 1959, Mao indicated a willingness to consider further measures, but he took Peng Dehuai's critique of Great Leap excesses as a personal attack, resulting in Peng's dismissal, a new upsurge of radical policies and with it a big spike in famine deaths. But as in late 1958, it took Mao's authority in autumn 1960 to reorient policy, this time more profoundly toward ending the Leap. It also set in motion a new leadership arrangement with Mao retreating to the 'second front' to deal with overall direction and theory, leaving his colleagues on the 'first front' to run the concrete business of the party-state and clean up the Chairman's mess (see Teiwes and Sun 1999, Chs 2–4 and Epilogues 1–2).

Mao's withdrawal to the 'second front' has been treated in Western studies as another forced concession, and it is clear the Chairman's prestige within the Party had reached its nadir, as seen in his tepid self-criticism at the 7000 cadres conference in early 1962. But there is no evidence of senior leaders organizing against him; instead, Deng Xiaoping and Lin Biao made fawning speeches of support at the conference, while Liu Shaoqi tried to assume personal responsibility for what had gone wrong. Further policy adjustments occurred in the following months with Mao's tacit acceptance, until he felt matters had gone too far. He then intervened to reverse the trend in the summer, and put Chen Yun and others on the sidelines for the remainder of the Maoist era. Now Mao offered a new guideline, 'never forget class struggle', but was unable to provide a clear sense of what this meant in practice, observing that class struggle and work were two different things, and class struggle should not interfere with work. The following years up to mid-1966 saw a politics of ambiguity, with Mao on the 'second front' able to reorient policy at any time, and also capable of downgrading powerful bureaucratic institutions like the State Planning Commission in 1964. The leaders on the 'first front' sought to construct policies they believed would be acceptable to the Chairman. Differences naturally existed among these leaders, but the basic approach was cooperative rather than to compete for Mao's elusive approval. While some of the Chairman's interventions were potentially fraught, as the Cultural Revolution approached there was no sense of an impending major rupture (see Teiwes 1979 [1993]: xxxvi–xliv, Chs 10–11). Mao's motives undoubtedly included dismay at the loss of revolutionary fervour in society, fear that the revisionism he saw in the Soviet Union was China's future, an unfounded worry that he was losing control, and a particular venom concerning the perceived apostasy of some, but hardly all, of his colleagues. But none of Mao's ruminations could alert the elite to the coming onslaught.

The Cultural Revolution Decade, 1966–76

While 'the Cultural Revolution' has been variously applied to different periods in this decade, in particular two strikingly different situations existed. First, the Cultural Revolution proper from mid-1966 to mid-1968, the rebellion from below unleashed by Mao, severely attacked top leaders and the broader elite while destroying the Party organization that held the system together. Subsequently, organizational regularity was fitfully restored and, especially from 1972, elite politics itself, while much more fractious and unpredictable, was again largely a game within the (re)established official hierarchies. The basic source material for the conflicts of the Cultural Revolution proper during the period itself were the same Red Guard publications that had so influenced scholarship's inclination to accept 'two-line struggle';[20] paradoxically, analyses addressing the actual events of 1966–68 rarely posited a struggle against Mao, instead focusing on presumed moderate and radical forces in the leadership. Various documentary collections at the time, and those covering political developments over the rest of the decade, supplemented these sources; they were quite limited from the PRC itself, but generally credible versions of CCP documents were collected in Taiwan and Hong Kong.[21] Finally, copies of purported speeches by leaders over the entire decade, often handwritten, appeared in leading Western libraries. Thus source material from 1966–76 was substantial during the decade itself,[22] yet very few Western monographs in the period attempted a comprehensive analysis of ongoing elite politics.

The reticence to address these questions at the time was sensible, given the polemical sources and rapidly changing events, but with the opening of China in the 1980s, much like the case for the pre-1966 period, the situation changed dramatically. The same array of new sources were now available: PRC documentary collections of considerable detail; extensive general and subject chronologies and leaders' *nianpu*; memoirs by, biographies of and remembrance collections on important leaders; serious scholarship in Party history journals and books;[23] and interviews with participants and scholars. Something of a new twist were accounts by people associated with the 'bad guys' of the official narrative, Lin Biao and the radicals dubbed the Gang of Four.[24] But the very explosion of accounts of the period underlined the need for discrimination; some books were aimed at popular audiences in China, some pushed a decidedly anti-Cultural Revolution agenda, and others exaggerated the roles of individual leaders. As always, the task is to determine what is credible from this large array of sources. The basis now exists for serious analyses of the tumultuous elite politics of this decade, but with the field's turn to other areas, only a few studies have been attempted.[25]

Notwithstanding the tensions evident during the post-Great Leap 'politics of ambiguity', the launching of the Cultural Revolution astonished the top leaders and broader elite, with only a small group of conspirators recruited by Mao and led by his wife Jiang Qing having any inkling of what was in store. Mao's authority was never more obvious, in that none of his colleagues challenged him or the overall thesis of the movement even though it put them in perilous circumstances personally, and gutted the organization they had fought for over decades. Their resistance was defensive, in denying allegations made by radical forces, while the boldest steps, such as the 'February adverse current' of 1967 when seven vice-premiers and PLA marshals challenged Jiang Qing's Cultural Revolution Group, were based on hopeful readings of Mao's attitude; in that case, recent Mao criticisms of Jiang's extremism (see Teiwes and Sun 1996: 72–79). Moreover, while arguably more deeply on the 'second front' than previously, intervening from Olympian heights above the fray, the Chairman periodically altered the course of the movement between radical mobilization and curbs on excesses, until mid-1968 when he finally moved to end the movement by dispatching students to the countryside for education by the masses, and authorizing the rebuilding of institutions. Throughout all this, prominent leaders had their own objectives: Zhou Enlai to protect some established leaders and limit institutional destruction; and Lin Biao more narrowly to protect the professional interests of his beloved PLA, but only within the scope allowed by Mao. Lin's mantra was 'do whatever the Chairman says', while, as Deng later observed, Zhou's hailed efforts to protect senior leaders were only possible because of Mao's attitude. Indeed, where Mao was relentless, Zhou joined the chorus, notably in the case of Liu Shaoqi who the Premier declared deserved death.

One of the key effects of the disruptions of the Cultural Revolution was the undermining of historical Party status that had underwritten high office before 1966. While some senior figures survived on the new 1969 Politburo and in other offices, a new injection of radicals led by Jiang Qing, military officers who, although revolutionary veterans, would never have attained such high office without the disruption of 1966–68, and comparatively junior largely provincial officials such as (somewhat later) Hua Guofeng, ended the close link of formal office and historical prestige. The type of long-accustomed working relations of people with major merit in the victory of 1949 who had unsuccessfully tried to meet the Chairman's ambiguous demands in the early 1960s no longer existed, and crucially contributed to fractious relations involving Lin Biao, and particularly the Gang of Four. While much remains obscure about the Lin Biao case, a major contextual factor was multiple disputes between the civilian radicals around Jiang Qing and military figures under Lin, in large measure due to civilian interference in military matters. These tensions came to a head at the 1970 Lushan plenum, and even though an array of forces, including Zhou Enlai, the veteran revolutionary but prominent Cultural Revolution radical Kang Sheng, and Mao's own top bodyguard Wang Dongxing, had positioned themselves against the civilian radicals, Mao decided in favour of the Gang of Four (Teiwes and Sun 1996: 134–151). Over the following year, Lin and his top military commanders were placed under growing demands until, under still mysterious circumstances, Lin and his closest family fled China in September 1971, with his flight crashing in the Mongolian desert, killing all aboard.

The Lin Biao affair was a body blow to Mao's prestige, but it did nothing to undermine his authority in orchestrating either the immediate response, or the twists and turns in overall policy over his final years. While Zhou Enlai and Deng Xiaoping have gained much credit in both the official narrative and foreign scholarship for 'opposing ultra-leftism' in 1972 (Zhou) and the consolidation programme in 1975 (Deng), in both cases the direction was set by Mao. Particularly revealing is Deng's case in 1975 when Mao placed him with full authority at the top of the 'first front'. Rather than proceeding by building a moderate coalition against the radicals on the basis of institutional interests, as sometimes asserted, Deng spent time studying Mao's canonical works and attempted to hone measures reflecting Mao's current wishes. Deng was confident, as seen in his assured reply to Chen Yun's cautious mid-1975 query over whether he fully understood the Chairman's intent. Yet Deng had not fully understood, and was astonished when Mao began to turn against him in October. Mao was caught between the contrary desires of continuing the revolutionary impulse, and achieving a strong economy and substantially stable state. But now he became persuaded that Deng had gone too far and was not paying homage to the Cultural Revolution. In this case he was persuaded not by the largely overestimated Gang of Four, but by Mao's radical nephew, Mao Yuanxin. With Deng removed and Zhou dead by January 1976, Mao surprised everyone by choosing as his latest successor Hua Guofeng, perhaps optimistically seeing the mix of qualities he desired in the absence of compelling alternatives. But most telling of both the immediate situation and the entire course of elite politics since 1949 was that when Mao fell into a virtual coma in early June, despite deep hatreds and anxieties within the elite, no one challenged Mao's actions since late 1975, or his Cultural Revolution project. To his last breath the Chairman could not be opposed (see Teiwes and Sun 2007: Chs 5–7).

From Hua to Deng: A Soft Transition, 1976–80

Mao had seriously misjudged Hua. Within a month of the Chairman's passing, Hua organized the arrest of the Gang of Four. While PRC sources following the Historical Resolution, echoed in the West, attempted to downgrade Hua's contribution to this defining moment of PRC history, the regime formally acknowledged his 'decisive role' in the traditional career assessment following Hua's death in 2008. The central problem facing Hua and the leadership generally was how to dismantle Mao's policies of the preceding decade while maintaining fealty to the Chairman himself; this, inevitably, became intertwined with the return of Deng, ousted (although repeatedly protected) by Mao, but widely seen within the elite as the author of the hopeful policies of 1975, and as possessor of the revolutionary status (which Hua lacked) that was required for a Party leader. The regime launched extended propaganda campaigns to attack the 'gang', and thus underline ongoing issues that had to be dealt with, while seeking to bolster Hua's prestige among the populace for whom he was largely a mystery, by making claims hardly credible to seasoned members of the elite. As events evolved over the following four years, regime media and official documents remained key sources, exposing different viewpoints and tensions within the elite. A significant additional source was the direct exposure to Chinese society by growing numbers of foreign diplomats, journalists and students since the mid-1970s, allowing such individuals to be on the scene at important events like Democracy Wall in 1978–79 (see Garside 1981). Rumours about elite conflict reached their ears, but the reality remained opaque.

While, as previously noted, at the time open sources provided a basis for speculative journalistic reports and academic articles that posited political and policy conflict between forces aligned with Hua and Deng (e.g., Lieberthal 1978b), it was only following Hua's ouster in 1980–81 that this solidified along the official narrative of Hua as a leftist endorsing 'whatever' policies Mao had approved, versus Deng as leader of the reformist coalition. In Western literature, moreover, 1976–80 was sometimes treated as the tail-end of the Cultural Revolution decade, or the preamble to Deng's reform era, with little attempt to dig deeper beyond these stereotypes. Yet as with the two preceding periods, the 1980s and beyond provided a range of the same type of sources – serious Party history accounts, chronologies, memoirs, detailed documentary collections and interviews – that provided a basis for conclusions that need not echo the Party line. In this respect, arguably most noteworthy are the reminiscences of relevant officials during the period, whether in published works in the PRC or Hong Kong, or in interviews. A much more realistic picture emerges from such recollections than the denigrated neo-Maoist Hua and the glorified Deng. This was perhaps summed up nowhere better than in a 2009 interview with a leading Guangdong official crucial in the establishment of SEZs: 'The worst thing in our Party is just to speak of one person for good things, and one person for bad things. Is this Marxism? I don't think so.'

If a struggle between neo-Maoist and reformist forces did not exist, what explains the fall of Hua and Deng's assumption of the paramount leader role? Several things have to be taken into consideration. First, the need to protect Mao was not simply a priority for alleged 'whateverists' like Hua; it was a concern for seasoned senior leaders like Deng and Chen Yun as well. The instance linking Hua to 'whateverism' was the famous 'two whatevers' editorial in February 1977, a piece that was a moderate statement emphasizing the centrist Mao of the mid-1950s, and in fact much more moderate than Deng's own inner-Party assessment of Mao offered in September 1979.[26] Nevertheless, the 'two whatevers' became both a stick with which to beat Hua from late 1978, and a basically unquestioned theme of Western analyses. Second, in examining the by now quite extensive information on various policy areas, it is difficult to find any areas of significant policy differences between Hua and Deng, with the possible exception of the invasion of Vietnam where Hua, as well as many civil and military leaders, apparently initially doubted Deng's venture, but in the end provided unified support. Third, Hua had no factional base despite official and scholarly efforts to claim one, the so-called 'little gang of four' of Politburo members left over from Mao's time.[27] These four had few career ties with Hua or among themselves, soon played reduced roles after the arrest of the actual 'gang', or in the case of the one major player in 1977–78, Wang Dongxing, was actually a detriment to Hua's cause.

Of course, consensus at the top on key issues in 1977–78 did not mean consensus within the overall elite, and both before and especially after the late 1978 Third Plenum the top leadership often found itself mediating conflicting views and interests lower down in the system. The Third Plenum was significant, but has been distorted in the literature to accord with the official narrative that, succinctly, the Third Plenum equals reform, and both equal Deng Xiaoping.[28] The plenum did take important steps toward more flexible policies, especially in the ideological sphere, but 'reform and opening' did not emerge as a unifying slogan for several years, and as separate concepts they were barely mentioned in the plenum communiqué. Moreover, reform measures had begun before the Third Plenum under Hua's auspices, and Hua played a more significant role on economic reform than Deng throughout 1979. Finally, both Hua and Deng were caught by surprise when Chen Yun and others raised the issue of 'reversing verdicts' on Party leaders purged in the Cultural Revolution and earlier, a matter both had addressed in preceding months in a roughly similar manner, but had placed below the economy as the priority concern for the Party meeting. But the verdict reversal issue and the now revived question of the 'two whatevers' significantly weakened Hua. The Party Chairman was not directly attacked, but his self-criticism indicated a recalibration of leadership power. So did the return of Chen Yun to the Standing Committee, and that of a number of senior cadres to the Central Committee.

Hua's decline essentially had nothing to do with policy disputes; it had everything to do with historical status in the CCP. Within days of the arrest of the Gang of Four, children of various senior revolutionaries, despite having viewed the 'gang' as personally and politically threatening to their parents, were asking privately whether Hua, a mere youth who had only joined the Party in 1938, could be the leader. In contrast, Deng, who had not only risen to become one of Mao's close comrades-in-arms, but was also considered one of the great military figures of the revolution, had enormous prestige. A telling incident occurred at a People's Liberation Army (PLA) ceremony on the eve of

Army Day in July 1977, shortly after Deng's self-criticism and formal return to work. Against all precedent, a large photo of Deng appeared on stage, to the loud applause of the assembled generals. More than a year later, the elevation of Chen Yun to the Standing Committee furthered the clout of old revolutionaries at the Party centre. While timing and mechanisms remain unclear, sometime in 1979 Deng and Chen were working together to undermine Hua, not on any policy agenda, but on the understanding that the time had come to fully restore proper status within the Party. New younger leaders, particularly Hu Yaobang and Zhao Ziyang, were installed in top positions at the February 1980 Fifth Plenum, and Hua soon had no real role. Hua did not fight, perhaps simply realizing that he could not win, but also more than plausibly because, as he claimed, he did not want to subject the Party to the struggles of the recent past. By the middle of 1980 'old man politics' had truly arrived.

Deng Ultimately in Charge Through Tumultuous Times, 1980–92

This period, which arguably could be extended to 1994,[29] has been characterized in the literature by a broad, and correct as far as it goes, consensus on political tension between reform and conservative wings of the Party, something often personalized as Deng versus Chen Yun. Nevertheless, this has resulted in relatively few monographs focused on elite politics, the most notable being Baum (1994) and Fewsmith (1994).[30] Baum approaches the presumed seesawing struggle more broadly, while Fewsmith moves from a sophisticated analysis of economic debates to claims of 'line' and power struggles at the top. Both noted the array of other approaches to the Chinese political system since the opening of the 1980s, and declared elite politics to be the key neglected piece in understanding reform. In constructing their analyses, these scholars relied heavily on PRC public media and documents, thus providing a rich discussion of different policy proposals and advocacy, often including expressions of quite sharp conflict. Yet the problem remains how much such differences can tell us about the power equation within the leadership; and supplementary sources such as Hong Kong publications and the regime's own verdicts on key cases of political conflict provide only a partial if not misleading guide to understanding what really went on. Moreover, foreign collections including ostensible internal *neibu* (restricted circulation) material on the most important events, most famously the flawed *Tiananmen Papers* (Zhang 2001), contain documents of dubious authenticity. Other promising sources exist, but the 'black box' remains formidable.

These other sources include all those mentioned for the preceding periods – serious Party history studies, chronologies and *nianpu*, memoirs and detailed revealing biographies, internal documents obtained from various sources, and interviews. As with the 1976–80 period, the insights provided by participants in the events of the 1980s are particularly rich. Many retired officials who played significant roles have had the opportunity to reflect on the past, and feel obliged to tell the truth whether or not it fits smoothly into the official narrative. Another source is former significant figures from the reform wing of the Party who have written their own 'behind the curtain' accounts of the period abroad after leaving China in 1989, or within China after suffering from the Tiananmen fallout: for example, former leading theoretician Su Shaozhi, influential advocate of rural and economic system reform Chen Yizi, and Wu Wei who worked on measured political reform for Zhao Ziyang. Their writings, and sources from within the PRC, advance the reform perspective, as opposed to the official narrative; yet while providing important insights, such accounts carry their own biases. Relatedly, care must be taken with sources lionizing reform leaders, none more so than Hu Yaobang who has become a symbol of reform; and difficult information is often downplayed or excluded from the record.[31] It is not only the Party's account that must be approached with scepticism. More broadly, reliable information on elite politics began to decline concerning the period after 1984, and more strikingly for the years following the Tiananmen crisis to the 14th Congress in October 1992.

What can be said with some confidence concerning the period from Deng's assuming the paramount leader role in 1980 to his triumph at the 14th Congress?[32] The focus is inevitably on Deng Xiaoping. Clearly Deng was the decisive actor in the unfolding of reform, but key questions remain. What was the structure of elite power around Deng? What were his abiding goals and modus operandi? Ultimately, how much power did he have, and in what sense was he opposed? And how did all this interact with the struggles faced by his designated successors, Hu Yaobang and Zhao Ziyang? The key structural element was the emergence of 'old man politics' that marked the fall of Hua Guofeng. By spring 1980 Chen Yun was intervening on economic policy from his hospital bed, while in the summer the formal top officials of the regime flew to Wuhan seeking authoritative guidance from Deng, a visit eerily reminiscent of officials including Deng seeking out Mao in this and other provincial capitals in 1974–75. As the 1980s moved on, Deng and Chen rarely attended Standing Committee meetings, instead delegating their secretaries to participate. Zhao Ziyang would reflect after his fall that he was no more than a 'big secretary' himself to the senior leaders in terms of power, yet considerable authority was vested in the top figures on the 'first front'. Indicative was the working out of rural reform in 1981 and beyond where, according to people involved, Deng and Chen essentially endorsed whatever proposals Zhao, Hu and Wan Li, the Party leader responsible for agriculture, could agree on. More broadly, however, the role of the Party elders is murky, including who truly counted, and how these elder figures worked out their own differences.

In assessing Deng's power, the literature has frequently adopted facile assumptions about his objectives. At the most general level, the consensus that he pursued higher growth and economic reform measures to achieve it, while being much more ambivalent about and ultimately opposed to meaningful political reform, is undeniable. But on specific issues the matter is more complicated; according to an official with long experience with Deng, he was all about tactics, with CCP power and economic growth his only constant objectives. A case in point is the SEZs, usually regarded as a jewel in Deng's reformist crown. Officials directly involved in Guangdong report not only, as previously mentioned, that Deng was less of a factor than Hua in the initial formulation of the policy, but also that he made no effort to defend the zones when they came under attack from Chen Yun and others in 1982, and when setting out on his southern tour of 1984 Deng had no clear position one way or the other. In fact, local officials were deeply worried, fearing that Deng would abandon the project. Deng apparently became convinced of the promise of the SEZs on the tour, leading to a major expansion of the open policy after he returned to Beijing, making some concessions to Chen in the process. The tactical consideration was sustaining Party unity; there is little evidence suggesting the concession was forced on him. The extent of Deng's authority was further indicated by his more risky venture of price reform in 1988, something of concern to conservatives and economic officials generally. But according to Wu Wei, although opposed by Chen Yun, Premier Li Peng and other top officials, with Deng's imprimatur on the policy none of these leaders submitted objections to the Standing Committee or Politburo (Wu Wei 2013: 369–374).

That Deng's price reform was reversed under the threat of escalating inflation has been considered a policy defeat, but a more telling perspective is that Deng's pragmatism meant that, unlike Mao, he would not persist with measures that were clearly not working. Yet while Deng's position remained inviolable, there were significant policy divisions that inevitably spilled over to the personal position of other leaders, particularly Zhao. Thus the literature often posits a notionally nasty struggle involving Zhao and Li Peng culminating in the Tiananmen crisis, yet this was not necessarily the reality or the perception of the actors at the time. While the evidence suggests a decline in Zhao's authority from late summer 1988, again according to Wu Wei, in the run up to Tiananmen Zhao never anticipated that different views in the Party would become confrontational and acute, arguably a sign of Zhao's naiveté, but something suggesting the need for further research into the early months of 1989.

And what of Deng in this new situation? Much of the literature argues that the ultimate target of the conservatives in the demonstrable clash of different policy views was Deng himself, sometimes manifested in (implausibly) dismissive ways (e.g., Fewsmith 2008: Part I). The policy conflict was real and sharp, and conservative policies prevailed for most of the three-year consolidation period (1989–91) that was approved as Party policy in 1988 after the price reform fiasco. But raising this to level of a political attack on Deng is a massive leap. Clearly Deng became increasingly impatient that reform had stalled, and there is credible evidence that he contemplated removing yet another successor in Jiang Zemin; something suggesting confidence in his power. Of course, further investigation is necessary, but the view of a weakened Deng under threat sits oddly with his ability as a Party member with no official position to initiate a profound system shift against the majority position of both the Politburo and the surviving elders. The paramount leader remained paramount due to his revolutionary prestige.[33]

From the 1990s to 2014: Analysis from the Fringes of the 'Black Box'

In an ironic way, the early 1990s mark a similar transition in elite studies to the start of the Cultural Revolution, but in reverse. Starting in 1966, the previous dearth of useful information on elite politics was overwhelmed by the new plethora of 'revelations' concerning elite conflict, and an upsurge of scholarly books and articles resulted. While the amount of scholarly attention to leadership politics was already in decline as China's opening offered other avenues for academic investigation, there has been a huge regression in reliable, useful information on the inner workings of the 'black box' since Deng's 1992 success. Much has been published in Hong Kong on the new period, but it has rarely approached the quality achieved by serious PRC scholars using Hong Kong outlets for their analysis of earlier periods, with most writers little known or, even if well connected, relying heavily on often misleading inside stories, speculation and rumour. On this theme a particularly vexing development has been the explosion of internet sources presenting unverified and often sensationalist claims that reverberate in the general PRC public, among Western observers, and among members of the princeling class.[34] In this array of written sources, the voice of actual participants at the highest levels has rarely been heard.[35] Interviews with members of the broader elite also produce results that are often both speculative and contradictory.[36] Even when done to a high standard, as by John Garnaut (2012) on the purge of Bo Xilai, who skilfully utilized many undoubtedly truthful accounts by people familiar with Bo, the result is an excellent contextual picture, but it could not truly penetrate the leadership's decision on Bo's case. Fundamentally, what undoubtedly happened concerning sources for this period has been a consequence of the leadership's conclusion that the Tiananmen crisis was in large part due to divisions at the top and popular perceptions of a Party split, resulting in a determination to prevent information on conflicts within the 'black box' from leaking out – such matters are simply off limits. Speculation by those outside the 'box' inevitably sought to bridge the gap, but little of this can be treated with any confidence.

Given these problems, it is not surprising that there have been relatively few monographs on post-Deng leadership politics. Significant events like Party congresses generate analysis in articles and other forums, while the *China Leadership Monitor* (2002–) provides regular assessments of developments related to elite politics. All of this is on the fringes of the 'black box', substantially relying on open PRC media, personnel and other organizational data, and a reading of political and social trends relevant to leadership decisions and conflict. Such factors have always been an essential baseline for understanding leadership politics, but their importance has grown in the absence of convincing 'inside' sources. The question is how far they can take us. PRC media reports and documents are invaluable guides to the issues under consideration and key policy decisions, but cannot demonstrate the texture of bargaining and consensus within the leadership, or the relative power of individual leaders. Personnel data can provide overall analysis of elite composition, but attempts to use such data for factional analysis are questionable. A case in point is analyses, on the basis of career connections, claiming Jiang Zemin stacked appointments at the top, thus making his 'Shanghai gang' the most influential bloc within the leadership. But how this works in practice is not demonstrated; moreover, the fact that Shanghai leader Chen Liangyu was purged from the Politburo in 2006 and imprisoned (ostensibly) for corruption, hardly suggests the degree of clout often imputed to Jiang. And while current policies under Xi Jinping are arguably explained by perceived threats to regime legitimacy, the debate within the top leadership remains unknown. In short, while these considerations are essential for understanding CCP elite politics, they can only provide context and clues for interaction within the Standing Committee and Politburo.

The one aspect of leadership politics that we can be quite sure of is that the initial post-Tiananmen successors, Jiang Zemin and Hu Jintao, came to the top post as a result of decisions centred on Deng,[37] while current leader Xi Jinping emerged from a quite different but poorly understood process. The process of selection of not only the General Secretary but also the top leadership generally is murky. While this undoubtedly is a top-down process, who has the strongest voice? The outgoing leader and Standing Committee are clearly central, and while speculation that Hu Jintao failed in efforts to anoint his successor cannot be dismissed out of hand, neither can it be verified. Party elders, whether simply retiring top leaders or true revolutionary elders,[38] undoubtedly have input, but the degree of influence and how it is exercised remains opaque. There have also been occasional efforts to sample broader elite opinion, but these are unclear and have not been consistent. More broadly, while some form of bargaining surely went on, uncertainty surrounds what are considered the parameters of acceptable compromise, and which regime interests have to be represented. Once in office, the power of the leader within the proclaimed collective leadership is an issue currently under debate in the field concerning Xi (see Miller 2014). While many clues exist, they are often ambiguous, making speculation by those on the edge of the 'black box' just that. What is likely is that the position of leader imparts a considerable degree of power, particularly given that a ten-year period in office is the widely accepted norm, but we can only speculate concerning the dynamics of debates in contentious cases. In any case, leadership politics has been significantly affected by the emergence of rules, particularly term and age limits, and less formally by tacit guarantees against removal at the highest levels. Although under considerable stress as of mid-2014 due to anti-corruption measures involving high-ranking figures,[39] these guarantees have hitherto provided a degree of predictability and security for top leaders determined to avoid the uncertainties suffered by their predecessors under Mao and Deng. They have generally been honoured since the early 1990s, although the exceptions will be examined below, and the extent to which they will or will not be honoured in the future is uncertain.

Two broad overviews of contemporary elite politics are sustainable: one following evidence of rule-bound practices and pragmatic efforts to deal with policy issues; the other reflecting the pressures created by a system which has become a self-enrichment machine distributing vast benefits not only to vested organizational interests, but also to families and individuals connected to both the Party's history and current and recent leaders, sometimes involving spectacular corruption. Alice Miller (2011: 533–534) has provided a succinct statement of the former view: 'Increasingly, appointment to the [Politburo and Standing Committee] no longer was allocated simply on the basis of political connections . . . and factions, but also on the basis of . . . decision-making abilities. . . . factional competition continued . . ., but [now] circumscribed by still informal but increasingly binding norms and pressures for a politics of consensus'. The other overview picks up on the continuing factional competition, a process ironically involving a degree of struggle for position and benefits, but also a degree of mutual tolerance in the effort to avoid the Party split seen as central to the Tiananmen crisis. Bo Xilai's rise and fall is a case in point. Whatever Bo's administrative and political skills, it is reasonable to (speculatively) say that his rise was due to his political family background and his adoption in Chongqing of populist policies drawing on the Party's traditions. Yet it is clear that in Chongqing, Bo used brutality against enemies and ran roughshod over legal procedures, while pursuing political campaigns (most famously the singing of 'red songs') at odds with a problem-solving approach, and generally acted as a local emperor. But until late in the game Bo was seen as a rising star, and top leaders including Xi Jinping endorsed his efforts. Both types of elite politics exist. How they interact is an important but elusive question.

While not answering this large question, a necessarily speculative examination is in order for the three cases of sitting Politburo members – Chen Xitong, Chen Liangyu and Bo Xilai – where neither tolerance nor security in office persisted. While corruption was a central charge against all three leaders, it would appear that their misdeeds did not obviously set them apart from other Politburo members in this regard. Nor is the suggestion that they were threats to the position of the then leader or, in Bo's case, the designated successor, convincing. Chen Xitong's case in 1995 can be seen in the context of Jiang Zemin emerging from the shadow of the now incapacitated Deng. Chen, where we do have his own voice, apparently did not have a particularly high regard for Jiang, regarding him as an outsider in comparison to his own experience in running Beijing municipality. Moreover, Chen thought he had Deng's trust, which would have intensified independent tendencies, and he initially would not budge on many matters. But this was not a direct challenge to the 'core of the third generation', something that would have been profoundly destabilizing. A plausible explanation of Chen's purge is simply that he had become a thorn in Jiang's side, the corruption case provided an excuse to remove him, and Deng's decline eliminated any remaining inhibition. Plausible, but clearly leaving out much of what went on in the 'black box' to achieve the outcome. A similar narrative for the Chen Liangyu case in 2006 is possible. A new leader, Hu Jintao, was attempting to consolidate his leadership; Chen was charged with a major pension fund scandal in Shanghai, and reportedly Chen had repeatedly refused to slow investment in Shanghai despite directives from the centre. Again plausible, to be sure, but with even less evidence than the Chen Xitong case. And certainly it involved no direct challenge to the position of the leader.

The Bo Xilai case was different. Bo was without doubt an ambitious politician. Beyond that he had a style that set him apart from the usually grey presentation of most top leaders. In addition to his distinctive policies in Chongqing, Bo was the leader most likely to say something unscripted. But Bo's ambition and energy could not turn into a challenge for the top job because of the rules. Four years older than Xi Jinping, Bo was simply too old to serve two full terms. Thus his objective had to be a seat on the Standing Committee. How much support Bo had in the broader elite is unclear, even granting that his appeal to (selective) Maoist values had an audience. His backing among the highest officials past and present is also uncertain, notwithstanding claims of Jiang Zemin's support. While the degree of opposition to Bo assuming a Standing Committee position cannot be gauged, it would be remarkable if there were no reservations concerning such an unpredictable politician, or fears that he would be a disruptive actor in a system relying on consensus. We simply do not know, if the events that unfolded in 2011–12 had not happened, whether Bo would have received his seat on the highest body. But the time line suggests increasing concern within the leadership over Bo's brutal treatment of his enemies in Chongqing by 2011. And the bizarre murder of a British businessman by his wife in late 2012, followed by the flight of Bo's top policeman to the US Consulate in Chengdu, in effect took the matter out of the leadership's hands. If there had been an impulse to protect Bo for considerations of regime face, or even a willingness to allow him a Standing Committee position because of factional support, the affair was now public, domestically and internationally. As usual, the matter was opaque at the leadership level, but Bo's fall appears less due to any clearly defined struggle than to concern over his disruptive potential, a situation brought to a head by events no one could have anticipated.

CONCLUDING REMARKS: A HARD TASK, A NECESSARY TASK, SOMETIMES AN IMPOSSIBLE TASK

There will always be mysteries concerning what went on inside the 'black box'. Developments at the political centre of any system are crucial for understanding the overall trajectories of nations, particularly so in Leninist authoritarian systems, even if the increasing complexities of society have diluted and made more diffuse the impact of elite politics in the contemporary PRC. As indicated in the above discussion, the sources available to foreign scholars have varied significantly over time, with CCP authorities providing misdirection that the Western literature has sometimes accepted too readily. But this need not be so, at least for the leadership politics from the establishment of the regime to the start of the 1990s. A vast array of often underutilized sources exists, but this research requires much digging, critical assessment of different claims in sources that are prone to the vagaries of human memory and biases, and an acute sensitivity to political context for the construction of convincing analyses. There is much scope for further research for this period. A particular case in point is the period between the adoption of conservative economic policies in autumn 1988 and the Tiananmen crisis, a period when Zhao Ziyang reportedly did not anticipate a confrontational struggle.

From the early 1990s a totally different situation emerged, one marked by the cutting off of virtually all detailed, apparently reliable information on contemporary conflicts inside the 'black box'. Analysts have been reduced to assessing personnel and procedural patterns and open statements of policy issues from the edges of the 'box' – an honourable and necessary undertaking – and to trying to sort out sometimes wild and generally unverifiable claims, including those of purported insiders, concerning who was doing what to whom within the elite. A better understanding must await the opening of key documents, or at least allowing serious PRC scholars access to them. Meanwhile, foreign scholars, whether dealing with earlier periods where materials exist in considerable measure, or with the comparative wasteland of the contemporary period, should avoid preconceptions, aim to eliminate errors, and seek greater realism concerning the inevitable conflicts of elite politics.

ACKNOWLEDGEMENTS

Frederick Teiwes acknowledges the support of the Australian Research Council and the Chiang Ching-kuo Foundation that has facilitated this chapter. He also thanks the participants at the Nanjing workshop of May 2014 which produced this volume; and Chris Buckley, Alice Miller and especially Warren Sun for their helpful comments.

NOTES

1. On Lin Biao, see Garver (1982). On purported differences over the Soviet Union, see Lieberthal (1978a).
2. A case in point is an alleged 1978 report by Hu Yaobang on the crimes of Kang Sheng. Byron and Pack (1992) used this fake document as a key source.
3. The influential study of the initial reform period, Baum (1994), makes significant use of these sources and very much follows their narrative of fluctuating reform–conservative struggle. Baum admits (p. xvii)

40   *Handbook of the politics of China*

that many of these sources are questionable, but proceeds on the basis of his ability to assess the likely credibility of specific claims. The present author is not blameless in utilizing reform-oriented Hong Kong sources; see Teiwes (1984: Chs 2–3).
4. It was, however, possible to challenge the 'two-line struggle' interpretation on the basis of sources predating the change in the official narrative. See Teiwes (1979 [1993]).
5. Huang (2000) does a good job in highlighting this aspect, although his application of it to particular events is often questionable.
6. Notably Cheng Li (2014) in his analysis of princeling and Youth League factions in the post-Tiananmen period.
7. For overlapping but contending analyses, see Huang (2000: Ch. 4) and Teiwes (1990).
8. Hu Yaobang sought to avoid the Chairmanship in 1982, instead proposing a rotating leadership. The matter is somewhat less clear in Zhao's case, but there are credible reports that he tried to retain the Premiership rather than become General Secretary after Hu's removal in 1987. For an argument positing succession contention between Hu and Zhao in 1980–87, followed by similar conflict between Zhao and Li Peng in 1987–89, see Shirk (1993: 14).
9. For a relatively detailed overview covering developments in both this and the following section, see Teiwes (2014).
10. A formal verdict on the Gao Gang case was presented in 1955, but there was no such document dealing with Peng Dehuai, who formally remained on the Politburo following his removal as Minister of Defence in 1959.
11. Although largely discussing leadership techniques, Lewis referred to 'the militant group led by Mao [Zedong] and Liu [Shaoqi]' (Lewis 1963: 278).
12. Notably the Taiwan collection, *Mao Zedong sixiang wansui* (Mao Zedong 1967, 1969).
13. Including Zhou Enlai, Liu Shaoqi, Deng Xiaoping, Chen Yun and Ye Jianying, and in 2013 Mao.
14. For example, Volumes 1 and 2 in the China 1949–1989 series: Lin Yunhui et al. (1989) covering 1949–56, and Cong Jin (1989) covering 1956–66.
15. The outstanding examples of detailed research are MacFarquhar (1983, 1997).
16. Particularly by reorganizing the CCP's Military Commission in 1954 to exclude senior Party leaders Liu Shaoqi and Zhou Enlai; the only 'civilian' placed on the body was the more junior Deng Xiaoping.
17. For overviews of Mao's notional successors of both types, see Teiwes (1988: 56–72).
18. Notably Bo Yibo in 1953 (see Bo Yibo 1991: Ch. 11) and Deng Zihui in 1955 (see Teiwes and Sun 1993).
19. Notably doubts created for a policy utilizing intellectuals and specialists given criticisms from these quarters during the Hundred Flowers movement, a slowdown in economic growth especially in the rural sector, withdrawals from collectives and urban strikes, and a complicated competitive relationship with the Soviet Union.
20. As supplemented by official media accounts of events, and wall posters reported by foreign, especially Japanese, journalists. For serious analyses using these sources, see Robinson (1971).
21. See Kau (1975), on the Lin Biao affair. While the documents in this collection appear genuine on the whole, the editor endorsed the official narrative of a planned military coup, something very dubious at the very least.
22. A comprehensive collection only appeared more than two decades later: Song Yongyi (2002).
23. Worthy of particular praise is the third volume in the China 1949–89 series, Wang Nianyi (1988). While under the normal constraints of a Party historian, Wang's detailed discussion goes far to explode the official verdict on Lin Biao.
24. Notably Lin Biao's secretary, Zhang Yunsheng (1988), and the early Cultural Revolution radical, Wang Li (2001).
25. The most significant overall accounts are MacFarquhar and Schoenhals (2006) and Teiwes and Sun (2007).
26. See Deng's (1979) assertion that '[all] policies formulated by Chairman Mao were correct, our mistakes came from not insisting on Chairman Mao's line' (Deng Xiaoping guanyu qicao guoqing sanshi zhounian jianghua gao de tanhua jiyao).
27. Wang Dongxing, Ji Dengkui, Chen Xilian and Wu De.
28. For a brief critical discussion, see Buckley (2013).
29. The 14th Party Congress in 1992 clearly marks the 'ultimate' victory for Deng in the adoption of an expansive economic reform agenda. Deng's subsequent role is unclear, but with the ravages of advanced age, the closure of his personal office in 1994 arguably ended his period as 'boss'.
30. In addition, Vogel's (2011) biography of Deng treats elite politics in some depth but from an overly positive Deng-centred perspective.
31. Notably in a centrepiece of the Hu Yaobang industry, *Hu Yaobang sixiang nianpu* (Hu Yaobang 2007). While providing very useful texts of Hu's speeches, deliberate editing has attempted to present him as more consistent on reform issues than was actually the case.

32. Consistent with my view that deep research is required for confident statements, I must note that while I believe I have achieved such research for the preceding periods, notwithstanding considerable work on the 1980s, it has not reached the same standard. This is even more dramatically the case for the post-1992 period, where I have done little more than survey major sources and the scholarly literature.
33. Various additional factors have been cited, notably PLA support, yet surely this derived from Deng's historical status.
34. This is not to dismiss internet sources per se. Many, especially concerning earlier periods, are excerpts from publications by serious PRC scholars or former participants in elite politics. The value of others can initially be assessed by the identity of the author. The general point, however, is that a huge portion of what appears on the internet, especially as it relates to contemporary developments, is inherently unreliable.
35. A rare example published in Hong Kong is interviews with former Politburo member Chen Xitong, who had been purged and jailed for corruption (Yao Jianfu 2012).
36. While interviews with inside sources who may have some knowledge of internal elite politics can be useful, they can also result in very wrong conclusions. Particularly in the current period, there is a journalistic tendency to provide credibility for a story by citing three sources with asserted knowledge of Politburo decisions or some other claimed knowledge. The cautionary example against this tendency was a prominent May 1989 report based on three such sources that claimed moderates around Zhao Ziyang had won the debate on handling the Tiananmen demonstrations. Two days later, martial law was declared and Zhao had lost all power.
37. This does not mean they were both initially Deng's idea, although by appointing Hu to the Standing Committee at the 14th Congress Deng placed him in a position to take over from Jiang. The push for Jiang in 1989 apparently came more from Chen Yun and Li Xiannian, but surely gained the approval of Deng who dismissively rejected Li Peng, who had been implementing Chen's economic policies.
38. Particularly Bo Yibo, credited in some accounts for having smoothed the way for Jiang to remain as head of the Military Commission in 2002.
39. Especially by building a major corruption case against recently retired Standing Committee member Zhou Yongkang.

2. Ideology of the Chinese Communist Party
Kazuko Kojima

This chapter presents perspectives for discussing the ideology of the Chinese Communist Party (CCP) by reviewing the history of the People's Republic of China (PRC) and the arguments raised in previous academic works examining the CCP's ideology. As a preliminary step, the functions of ideology in politics, especially under authoritarian regimes, will be discussed.

Ideology is defined as 'a set of beliefs, especially the political beliefs on which people, parties, or countries base their actions' (Collins COBUILD 2006: 718). Governments, especially authoritarian governments that lack 'rational-legal authority' as proposed by Max Weber, tend to place importance on ideology as an inexpensive tool with which to cloak their 'coercive power' or 'utilitarian power' in a veil of 'normative power' (Etzioni 1961) and thus avail themselves of a normative justification of authority.

The CCP has also consistently established ideological work as one of the pillars of its rule and shown dedication to instilling official ideologies in its subordinates to claim normative power. The importance of ideology under the CCP's rule has been emphasized in previous studies on Chinese politics. Franz Schurmann, in the introduction to his renowned work *Ideology and Organization in Communist China*, wrote, 'China is like a vast building made of different kinds of brick and stone. However it was put together, it stands. What holds it together is ideology and organization' (Schurmann 1966: 1). David Shambaugh also focuses on these two spheres – the ideological (theoretical) sphere and the organizational sphere – in evaluating the CCP's adaptive ability (Shambaugh 2008).

As discussed below, the CCP has demonstrated its resilience in the ideological realm as well as in other governmental realms.[1] Because the CCP has attempted to remould and modernize its ideology to adapt to the changing internal and external environment, it has continued to remain in power even after experiencing adverse challenges such as the Tiananmen Incident, the collapse of the Soviet and the East European regimes between 1989 and 1992, and economic globalization in the post-Cold War era.

In this chapter, the CCP's ideology is discussed as comprising three value sets: Marxism–Leninism Mao Zedong Thought, the theory of developmental autocracy, and nationalism. The CCP, which was originally organized under the guidance of the Comintern, was a political group that was highly regulated by Marxist–Leninist ideology. However, the CCP did not hesitate to emasculate this ideology by reinterpreting it when with the changing times it lost the capacity to enhance the legitimacy of the CCP's rule. Thus, the emphasis in the CCP's official ideology shifted to developmental autocracy and nationalism instead.

Under what internal and external circumstances and for what reasons were these three ideologies adopted by the CCP? How has the emphasis shifted in the CCP's ideological work? Which points in each ideology have been debated by academic communities? In the following sections, the real politics of China and the academic arguments surrounding

Marxism–Leninism Mao Zedong Thought, developmental autocracy, and nationalism will be discussed.

MARXISM–LENINISM MAO ZEDONG THOUGHT

Marxist–Leninism Mao Zedong Thought is the CCP's most essential ideology and, to date, is stipulated in the constitution as one of the 'Four Cardinal Principles' (the socialist path, the dictatorship of the proletariat, the leadership of the CCP, Marxism–Leninism Mao Zedong Thought). This section introduces two main arguments related to Marxist–Leninist ideology in the CCP's ideological work.

Marxist–Leninist Ideology and 'Socialism with Chinese Characteristics'

From the founding of the PRC (1949) to the 1970s, the main academic and political arguments were developed concerning the question of whether Marxist–Leninist ideology advocated by the PRC should be equated with that of the Union of Soviet Socialist Republics (USSR) and other Communist countries or whether it should be regarded as an original version that reflected Chinese tradition and culture. From this question emerged another question regarding the relation between politics and ideology in China: whether an absolute and fixed ideology regulated the real politics of China or whether the ideology should be interpreted as no more than a convenient tool used for political purposes.

In the 1950s, during the early Cold War era, many scholars of China identified the PRC with the USSR as a Communist country regulated by Marxist–Leninist ideology. In other words, the PRC was recognized as a 'new' country that had departed from its feudal traditions through the introduction of Communism. For example, Richard Walker defined the situation of Mao Zedong and the CCP as 'follow[ing] the path blazed by the USSR under Stalin as closely as conditions in China permit', and further said, 'China is no longer the China of even five years ago'. 'It is important to understand that the changes brought about by the Communists reach far down into the thought patterns and speech habits of the people' (Walker 1955: ix, xi, xii). In addition, Walter W. Rostow analysed the PRC's politics, economy, society and diplomacy using the analytical framework of the totalitarian model and concluded that China sought to 'repeat on the Chinese scene the pattern of domestic transformations carried out by Stalin in the early 1930s' (Rostow 1954: 299).

Conversely, some scholars proposed different perspectives in which Communism in the PRC was of a particular version determined by Chinese history and culture. Throughout the 1950s, the focus of this argument was directed toward the question of the characterization of Mao Zedong Thought. This debate appeared in several issues of the *China Quarterly*, which was first published in 1960 (Wittfogel et al. 1960). In his reasoning, Benjamin Schwartz insisted that even though it was based on Marxism–Leninism, 'Maoism' had considerable originality that had evolved in the context of power struggles and in the course of efforts to cope with situations that were not provided for by a pre-existing doctrine (Schwartz 1951, 1960). In contrast, Karl Wittfogel contended that Mao's basic strategy, including the strategy of considering the peasantry as the main force of the revolution, could be traced back to that propagated by Karl Marx and Lenin (Wittfogel 1960).

The belief in the close relationship between the USSR and the PRC was destroyed by the Sino-Soviet split triggered by Nikita Khrushchev's speech denouncing Joseph Stalin. Mao Zedong launched mass campaigns like the Great Leap Forward and the Great Proletarian Cultural Revolution in the search for a 'Chinese road' to socialism. Reflecting such a situation, many studies on the personality of Mao Zedong, exemplified in the publications by Jerome Chen and Stuart Schram, were published in the 1960s (Chen 1965; Schram 1966).

As the varied forms of Communism became evident, the roles that ideology played in Chinese politics were analysed more carefully and objectively. The stance that emphasized the role of the Communist ideal – whether it was the 'orthodox' Marxism–Leninism or the original Chinese Maoism – as an independent variable in the CCP's revolution and politics since 1949 lost its rhetoric. Scholars now paid more attention to the aspects of real politics that regulated the role of ideology. As Schurmann said:

> Ideology is the functional equivalent of the former ethos. Just as the ethos held the social system together, so does ideology hold organization together. When the decision was made to study the ideology, it was quite early apparent that little would be gained by exegesis of the voluminous ideological literature that has appeared in China. Given the Chinese Communist stress on the unity of thought and practice, the only meaningful way to study ideology seemed to be to see how it was used. (Schurmann 1968: 9)

According to Schwartz, there were several broad definitions of Communism that rejected the 'narrow' insistence on the prevalent ideology of the time. For instance, there were those who asserted that Communism was not an ideology but a political or an economic development that would inevitably emerge at a given phase of the modernization process or that would most probably emerge unless it was prevented from doing so (Schwartz 1968: 23). The ten articles included in *Ideology and Politics in Contemporary China*, edited by Chalmers Johnson, analysed the interaction between ideology and real politics (Johnson 1973). James R. Townsend also emphasized that ideology had variability as a tool of politics. According to Townsend, ideology required that all political decisions be justified in terms of the basic tenets without providing concrete solutions to all crucial policy choices, and thus had been a source of both unity and conflict. Townsend stated, 'As a result, Chinese Communist ideology, like other aspects of the system, has been in flux' (Townsend 1974: 169).

The new position of ideology as a tool of real politics has provided a way of interpreting the Chinese revolution and politics in a more pragmatic context. As for the relativization of the roles that Communism had played in the revolution, many scholars instead regarded Communism as a dependent variable manipulated by practical aims such as nationalism and economic development. For example, Johnson, in his *Peasant Nationalism and Communist Power: The Emergence of Revolutionary China, 1937–1945*, concluded that it was the CCP's anti-Japanese stance rather than the peasants' economic grievances and the party's platform of socio-economic reform that gave the CCP a popular mandate and brought it victory in 1949 (Johnson 1962). Although Johnson's argument was criticized in the 1970s – a period in which most scholars (as represented by Mark Selden) criticized Johnson's analysis for underestimating the effects of the

CCP's revolutionary programme, including land reform[2] – interpretations of the Chinese revolution evolved in a direction that relativized its characteristics as a socialist revolution, as empirical studies based on new materials and empirical data were published in the 1980s. The Chinese revolution has revealed its multifaceted nature, which was often influenced by contingent factors in a chaotic time, as the authors of a collection edited by Kathleen Hartford and Steven M. Goldstein illustrate through interviews and the examination of local archives (Hartford and Goldstein 1989).

The relativization of the socialist revolution led scholars to focus increasingly on the continuities between the pre-Communist Chinese ideologies and the latest situation of the current regime. For example, John Israel's essay, 'Continuities and Discontinuities in the Ideology of the Great Proletarian Cultural Revolution', in *Ideology and Politics in Contemporary China*, examined the ideological continuity between the New Culture movement (1915–1923) and the Cultural Revolution (1966–1969) (Israel 1973).

Through these various studies scholars began to view Chinese politics as action on the ground, rather than as it had been earlier viewed, through the ideological veil of Marxism–Leninism.

Marxism–Leninism Mao Zedong Thought as a Façade?

Since the 1980s, Marxist–Leninist ideology has lost its substance as an ideology due to the actions of the CCP, even though it is stipulated in the Chinese Constitution as one of 'Four Cardinal Principles'. Kalpana Misra presented, in detail, the inner party debates between conservatives and reformists over 'ideology' in the first stages of 'reform and opening up' (Misra 1998). Deng Xiaoping and the reform-oriented leadership of the CCP continuously moved forward on ideological reformation to establish an ideological foundation for the ongoing reform and opening-up process. At the 12th National Party Congress held in 1982, Deng Xiaoping proposed the idea of building 'socialism with Chinese characteristics'. Deng said, 'We must integrate the universal truths of Marxism with the concrete realities of China, blaze a path of our own, and build a socialism with Chinese characteristics. That is the basic conclusion we have reached after reviewing our long history' (Deng 1993a). The phrase 'with Chinese characteristics' allowed the CCP to make diverse choices in applying Marxism–Leninism to the Chinese context. The concepts of the 'primary stage of socialism', introduced in 1987, and a 'socialist market economy', introduced in 1992, were also rhetoric that permitted a more radical marketization under the official ideology of socialism.

In the 1990s, China achieved rapid economic development under a socialist market economy. General Secretary Jiang Zemin proposed the concept of the 'Three Represents' in February 2000 to help the Party adjust to new circumstances for further marketization. Jiang (2006b) stated that the CCP should represent the 'most advanced mode of production, the most advanced culture, and the interests of the majority of the population' to hold on to power forever. Jiang's aim in proposing this new concept was to enlarge and enhance the Party's social basis by redefining the Party from a revolutionary vanguard of the proletariat to a catch-all party that could represent the economic elites (that is, 'the most advanced mode of production'), including private entrepreneurs who had been assuming increasingly vital roles in economic development. In fact, in his famous speech at the CCP's 80th anniversary celebration on 1 July 2001, Jiang implicitly proposed that the Party should recruit more members from the new private entrepreneurs class. Despite strong resistance from leftists in the Party, the 'Three Represents' concept was incorporated into the Party Constitution at the 16th National Party Congress held in 2002 and was also included in the Constitution in 2004.

No one in either the academic or the non-academic community would deny that Marxism–Leninism Mao Zedong Thought lost substance in the reform era. The reduction in the centripetal force of the ideology of Marxism–Leninism has been demonstrated with data in recent studies. Some chapters contained in the book *CCP's Survival Strategy*, edited by Masaharu Hishida (2012), provide survey data on the views of different strata of Chinese people towards socialist ideology. In a survey targeting 1864 undergraduate and graduate students at Peking University,[3] 70.9 per cent of CCP members and 82.2 per cent of Communist Youth League of China (CYLC) members agreed with the proposition, 'Socialism is a kind of unrealistic ideal', and the proportion is higher among CCP members in the younger generation (Kojima 2012; see Figure 2.1 and Figure 2.2).

However, Heike Holbig and Bruce Gilley argue that the CCP has recently implemented 'a clear shift in emphasis from an earlier economic-nationalistic approach to a more ideological-institutional approach' after dedicated efforts to 're-legitimate

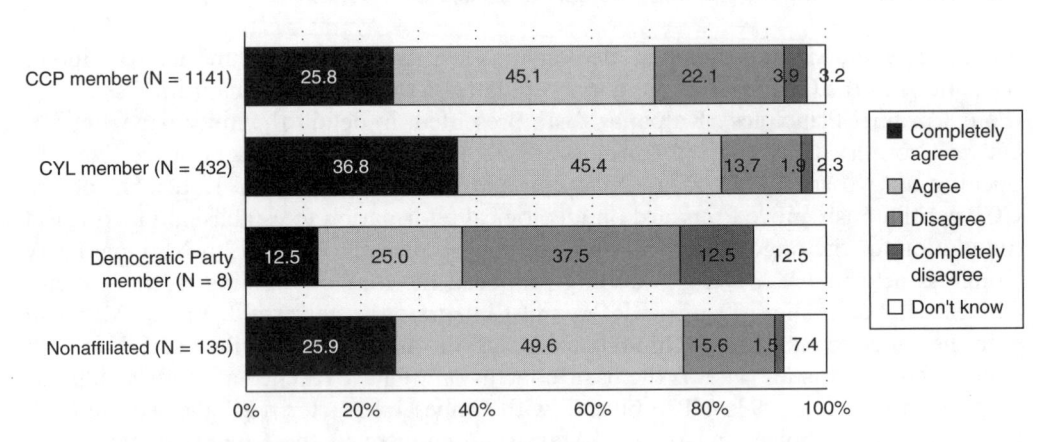

Figure 2.1 Socialism is a kind of unrealistic ideal

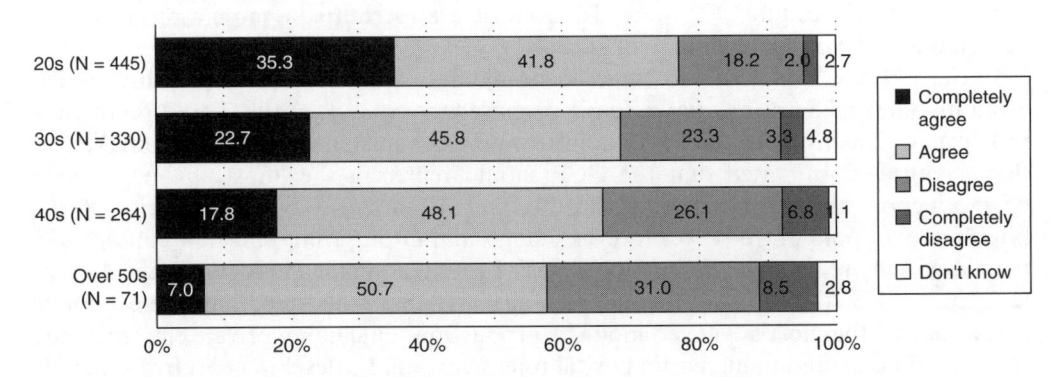

Figure 2.2 Socialism is a kind of unrealistic ideal (CCP members)

the post-revolutionary regime through economic performance, nationalism, ideology, culture, governance, and democracy' (Holbig and Gilley 2010: 83). According to Holbig, ideology 'still plays an indispensable role in the quest to legitimize authoritarian rule in contemporary China' (Holbig 2013: 62) even though 'ideology in contemporary China should be analysed not as a matter of belief but of playing by the rules of the official language game' (Holbig 2013: 63), such as making puns based on the homophonous (mis) use of official slogans or using authentic official language out of context. She admits that cynicism toward Marxism–Leninism and the socialist ideology is spreading in China but further insists that ideology can serve to legitimize the regime's hegemony in the public sphere as long as people are playing by the rules of the official language game as per the ideology (Holbig 2013: 74, 77). Further studies are needed to evaluate how the official language game is meaningful when ordinary people have no internalized belief.

DEVELOPMENTAL DICTATORSHIP

This section discusses the second stream of ideology: developmental dictatorship. The term 'developmental dictatorship' has not been used in China itself, because the concept, interpreted as part of the vocabulary of capitalism, is not compatible with the CCP's official ideology of socialism. However, the CCP's practical policies in the reform era can be characterized by this term.[4]

The Logic of Dictatorship for Power and Wealth

Starting in the mid-1970s, after ten years of chaos under the Great Proletarian Cultural Revolution, the CCP redirected the axis of its policy course from the class struggle under Marxism–Leninism Mao Zedong Thought toward economic construction through marketization. This reform signalled a radical change in the CCP's ideological work. On the one hand, before the mid-1970s, when economic propaganda was a politically sensitive matter, the 'market' was considered taboo, to be abolished as a capitalistic idea; however, the CCP has since justified it carefully and gradually, simultaneously maintaining the existing framework of socialism. On the other hand, the CCP has sustained a tough position against bottom-up pro-democratic movements that have occurred intermittently since the 1970s, as symbolized by the two Tiananmen Incidents in 1976 and 1989, both of which led to immediate suppression.

The above-mentioned policies were formulated as an official ideology of 'One Central Focus, Two Basic Points' at the 13th Party Congress in 1987. 'One Central Focus' is a reference to economic construction, and the 'Two Basic Points' denotes the 'Four Cardinal Principles' and 'reform and opening up'. By proposing this ideology, the CCP facilitated the promotion of marketization and opening up on the economic front without abandoning the concept of one-party rule.

In 1988, reformist intellectuals in China engaged in major arguments concerning the desirable relationship between economic and political reform. The liberals argued that political reforms, including democratization, would guarantee and accelerate economic reforms, whereas neoauthoritarians claimed that the role and authority of the central government should be enhanced under the CCP's absolute leadership to accelerate economic development. Wu Jiaxiang (research staff, investigation department, General Office, Central Committee of the CCP), who represented the neoauthoritarians, emphasized that centralized rule by a 'strong man' and a small cadre of elites was essential to modernize a traditional society such as China. Their envisioned model was the developmental dictatorship model of South Korea or Taiwan, which had successfully achieved rapid economic growth in the 1970s and 1980s. The debate ended in the victory of the neoauthoritarians, who gained support from Deng Xiaoping. Consequently, China has pursued the path of developmental dictatorship ever since.

Developmental dictatorship remains one of the most important ideologies of the CCP. The term that describes the policies of the Xi Jinping leadership, 'politically left, economically right', can also be positioned in the context of developmental dictatorship.

The regime in the reform and opening-up era can be categorized as a development-oriented regime, characterized by Ikuo Iwasaki as sharing the following tendencies with the 1960–1990s regimes in the Association of Southeast Asian Nations (ASEAN) countries: (1) the political society, economy and administration are unified under the regime; (2) the regime formally incorporates a parliamentary democracy, but the parliament tends to lose substantial functions because the army or a political party occupies the core of the power with the assistance of bureaucrats; (3) the regime, pursuing a state-led development strategy, is driven by a strong incentive to introduce foreign capital; and (4) sustained economic growth under the regime enhances its power and makes it stable and long lasting (Iwasaki 1994: 36). The Chinese regime can be said to reflect these features.

However, there are differing interpretations of the origin of developmental dictatorship in China. Numerous previous studies interpret this system as a consequence of the CCP's survival strategy. In this interpretation, development is not a goal but a means for the CCP to achieve its principal aim of maintaining dictatorship. For example, Shambaugh discusses the process by which the CCP leadership learned a lesson from the collapse of the Communist regimes in the Soviet Union and the East European countries, and cautiously chose a way of promoting comprehensive economic reforms, accompanied by a watering down of socialist ideology without engaging in political liberalization (Shambaugh 2008).

In contrast, some previous studies regard the combination of development and dictatorship not as the consequence of the CCP's strategic choices but as a corollary of Chinese traditional culture. Timothy Cheek and Juan Lindau discussed the lack of civil society in China through an analogy with Mexico. They stated that in both China and Mexico, powerful assumptions within the political culture (for example, a passive conception of citizenship based on strong family values, and public order as a tenuous and delicate achievement) operate as independent variables that impact upon Jürgen Habermas's equation of market and democracy (Cheek and Lindau 1998: 6).

Sustainability of Developmental Dictatorship

There are differing opinions regarding how long the ideology of 'dictatorship for power and wealth' will maintain its effectiveness. Joshua Cooper Ramo's paper 'The Beijing Consensus', which was published by the United Kingdom's Foreign Policy Centre in 2004, proposed an optimistic viewpoint on this question. According to Ramo's analysis, China's path to economic development, accompanied by a commitment to innovation and constant experimentation as well as a distribution of wealth and independent efforts to cope with globalization, will become a sustainable model as an alternative to the Washington Consensus (Ramo 2004).

However, many scholars pointed out the instability of developmental dictatorship in China. For example, Minxin Pei indicated the limits of a developmental autocracy by discussing the self-destructive dynamics of the Chinese political system (for example, low political accountability, unresponsiveness, collusion, corruption) and the ever-increasing economic problems (for example, rising inequality, underinvestment in human capital, damage to the environment) (Pei 2006).

NATIONALISM

The CCP vigorously promotes nationalism as an ideology to enhance the legitimacy of its rule along with developmental dictatorship. Nationalism means a person's fervent love for their nation and is often associated with the belief that a particular nation is better than any other nation (Collins COBUILD 2006: 949). As Holbig and Gilley summarized, based on previous studies of nationalism, present-day nationalism has two interrelated aspects: state nationalism (top-down mobilization) and popular nationalism (bottom-up mobilization) (Holbig and Gilley 2010: 13–14). This section focuses on state nationalism and reviews the discussions in previous studies.

Integration of Marxism–Leninism and Nationalism

As mentioned above, there is a consensus in previous studies that Marxism–Leninism as promoted by the CCP has retained Chinese characteristics that originated in the history, culture and real politics of China. One of the most distinctive features of the CCP's ideology was the integration of Marxism–Leninism and nationalism. Many other scholars besides Johnson indicate the importance of nationalism as one of the reasons why Chinese intellectuals and the people accepted Marxism–Leninism in the stage of the revolution. For example, Lucien Bianco, in his book *Origins of the Chinese Revolution: 1915–1949*, attributed most Chinese intellectuals' commitment to Marxism after the May Fourth Movement to the absorption of nationalism by Marxism. He wrote, 'Marxism proved itself the most effective system (the most effective "ism") not only for attacking social iniquities but also for restoring a national pride that had been sorely tried for a century' (Bianco 1971: 50). Indeed, we can recollect Marx's claim that 'any people that oppresses another people forges its own chains' (Marx 1985), and Lenin's more decisive assertion that proletarian movements should be combined with national liberation movements. Marxism–Leninism attracted the first CCP leaders, including Mao Zedong, because it specified the practical programme of realizing the unification and independence of a nation. Roland Yew expounds on this fact clearly, referring to Chinese Communism as nationalistic in the sense that it established the defence and unification of the nation as a core doctrine; indicated by the fact that the slogan 'National Salvation' spread in the resistance against aggression by the imperialist Great Powers in the 1920s. 'Existing Socialism' in China is, in truth, a variety of nationalism. The people's aspiration for liberation cannot be achieved unless it coexists with the logic of party-state, development of national power, and peoples' obedience to a revolutionary, overwhelming mobilization by the state (Lew 2004).

In contrast to the early leaders, the CCP leaders from the 1990s onward have deliberately blurred the boundaries between nationalism and socialism (Zhao 2004: 9) to demonstrate theoretical consistency in the worldwide crisis of Communist regimes. In his speech at the Capital Youth May Fourth Memorial debriefing meeting in May 1990, Jiang Zemin said, 'In China today, patriotism and socialism are unified in essence.'

Reintroduction of Nationalism in the 1990s

Nationalism was reproduced in the 1990s. Faced with a regime crisis at the end of the 1980s, the CCP implemented a nationwide Patriotic Education Campaign to ensure loyalty in the population and enhance the regime's political legitimacy through the glorification of the CCP. A document titled 'A Program for China's Education Reform and Development' issued by the State Education Commission in January 1993 presented patriotism as a guiding principle for educational reform. Subsequently, two documents, 'Guidelines for Patriotic Education' and 'Outline for Conducting Patriotic Education', were issued in 1994, which opened a nationwide patriotic education campaign from kindergarten all the way through to university. According to Zheng Wang, the campaign was 'another massive attempt by the party at ideological reeducation', and through the campaign, 'the content of history and memory has become institutionalized in political institutions and education systems, as the CCP's new ideological tool' (Wang 2008: 795).

Nationalism has been advanced further in recent years. Ian Seckington's analysis showed that a decline in the attractiveness of socialist ideology, economic recession and the emergence of a less ideological post-revolutionary ruling generation have driven China's fourth-generation leadership to 'be either more inclined, or be forced to, place a greater emphasis on nationalist rhetoric both in China's international relations and in domestic policy' (Seckington 2005: 24). The Xi Jiping leadership's famous catchphrases, 'Great Revival of the Chinese Nation' and 'China Dream', reflect Xi's intention to use nationalism as a tool of national unification. When he visited the exhibition The Road toward Renewal on 29 November 2012, Xi said:

> Nowadays, everyone is talking about the 'China Dream.' In my view, to realize the great renewal of the Chinese nation is the greatest dream for the Chinese nation in modern history. The China Dream has conglomerated the long-cherished aspiration of Chinese people of several generations, represented the overall interests of the Chinese nation and Chinese people, and has been a common expectation of every Chinese.[5]

The evolution of nationalism in China has motivated many scholars to investigate the phenomenon. Recent studies include *Discovering Chinese Nationalism in China: Modernization, Identity, and International Relations* by Yongnian Zheng (Zheng 1999), *China's New Nationalism: Pride, Politics, and Diplomacy* by Peter Hays Gries (Gries 2004), *A Nation-State by Construction: Dynamics of Modern Chinese Nationalism* by Suisheng Zhao (Zhao 2004) and *Chinese Nationalism in the Global Era* by Christopher R. Hughes (Hughes 2006). All these books examine the process of the reinstitution of nationalism in the 1990s by tracing it back to the late Qing dynasty and evaluating its impact on domestic and international politics.

According to these works, the nationalism that has been reproduced has a distinctive feature: it highlights today's glorious prosperity in contrast to its 'humiliating history'. The Chinese nation, in the official narrative of 'one hundred years of humiliation', has been described as a victim of the imperialist aggression of the Western powers in the nineteenth century and of cruel behaviour during the Sino–Japanese war.

Such nationalism that is based on a victim mentality inevitably becomes exclusionist nationalism, which is accompanied by negative attitudes toward other nations' power and value systems. It is not uncommon for the Chinese government to fiercely blame 'foreign enemy forces' as the principal offenders that have brought hardship to China. For example, in the midst of Western sanctions after the Tiananmen Incident of 1989, the Chinese government made the accusation that 'a small number of Western countries feared lest China should grow powerful, and thus imposed sanctions against her, contained her, and placed great pressure on her to pursue Westernization and disintegration' (Zhao 2004: 9). The repeated riots by the Uyghur and the Tibetan people are also explained as resulting from instigation by foreign enemy forces.

In recent years, the CCP leaders, who have gained self-confidence through China's remarkable development, have projected more clearly an anti-foreign rhetoric in rejecting universal values and advocating a China Model. The dispute over universal values arose during 2008–2009, after advocates of Tibetan independence and people protesting against China's human rights record attacked the torch relay for the Summer Olympics in Beijing. In the dispute, the reformists (supposedly in line with Hu Jintao and Wen Jiabao) argued that China would not be able to sustain development without accepting the values of freedom, democracy and human rights as universal values. In contrast, the old-guard intellectuals, led by the propaganda department of the CCP and the Chinese Academy of Social Sciences, advocated that such values were the same as the values proclaimed by the West and were by no means applicable to China. The debate ended in a victory for the latter. The CCP journal *Seeking Truth* (*Qiu Shi*) (16 March 2009) published the CCP's view that it was a challenge against Marxism to advocate Western ideas of democracy and constitutionalism as universal values that China should accept. The conservative groups' claim of rejecting Western values and pursuing China's own method of development reinforced measures and persectives provided through the discourses of the China Model and the Beijing Consensus.

In May 2013, it was reported that the General Office of the CCP had distributed a document titled 'Concerning the Situation in the Ideological Sphere' (Document No. 9) to Party provincial offices and governments.[6] The exact content of Document No. 9 was unknown, but in August 2013, the *New York Times* and the Hong Kong monthly *Mirror News* reported that the document listed seven dangerous ideological currents that were undermining the Party's authority: Western constitutional democracy; universal values; civil society; new liberalism; press freedom and other Western-inspired views of the media; the promotion of historical nihilism; and the sowing of doubt about reform and openness. The reports described how Party officials, in a call for renewed ideological discipline, were concerned about the spread of such 'erroneous' ideas and assertions in China through the internet and underground channels and that they would remain vigilant against schemes to spread the influence of Western anti-China forces and anti-government forces in the ideological sphere. The report added that officials asserted that authority over newspaper media must remain in the hands of comrade General Secretary

Xi Jinping and the Party Central Committee, and they called for reinforcing ideological education.[7]

Wu Guoguang discussed the features of the nationalism in the 1990s compared with that of the early twentieth-century May Fourth Movement. According to Wu, the Chinese nationalism of the 1990s reversed all the radical features of the early twentieth-century developmental and cosmopolitan nationalism and became a conservative and anti-foreign nationalism, because it defended the Chinese model of development, endorsed the legitimacy of the Communist regime, and sought sources of legitimacy and identity in traditional Chinese culture (Wu 2008: 467–468).

Many scholars have issued warnings about the aggressiveness of Chinese nationalism, which is backed by the country's rising economic power. We need to recognize two aspects of Chinese nationalism to estimate the direction in which it is headed. Chinese nationalism is an engine of Chinese politics as well as an instrument by which the CCP can achieve different purposes. Suisheng Zhao labelled the nationalism under the CCP regime 'pragmatic nationalism', saying:

> The most important feature of this pragmatism is the state's emphasis on the instrumentality of nationalism for rallying support in the name of building a modern Chinese nation-state. It is therefore not surprising that Chinese pragmatic nationalism is essentially contextual, without a fixed, objectified, and eternally defined content. Those in power and authority are at an advantage in creating and propagating a nationalism that would promote their own interest. (Zhao 2004: 209)

The Limitations of Enhancing Legitimacy through Nationalism

Nationalism as a source of legitimacy may have become a discourse of increasing importance, but limitations remain. There is a mismatch between official nationalism and popular nationalism. Popular nationalism in China does not necessarily coincide with state nationalism, which entails appreciating the CCP regime. Zhao analysed Chinese nationalism in terms of state propaganda, intellectual discourse, and populist sentiments (Zhao 2004: 11). Though state propaganda regulates the latter two to a significant degree, these three elements exist separately.

In fact, there are differing opinions on nationalism among intellectual and political elites. The results of the questionnaire survey mentioned earlier of 1864 undergraduate and graduate students at Peking University illustrate that intellectual elites do not identify loving the nation with appreciating the CCP, nor with valuing socialism. The proportion of respondents who answered 'completely agree' or 'agree' with the proposition 'Loving China means loving Socialist China under the leadership of the CCP' was 66.0 per cent (N = 133) among CCP members, 46.0 per cent (N = 432) among Communist Youth League of China (CYLC) members, 49.7 per cent (N = 133) among non-affiliated people, and 40.0 per cent (N = 10) among members of the democratic parties; further, the proportion is lower among CCP members in the younger generation (Kojima 2012; see Figure 2.3 and Figure 2.4). Notably, more than 30 per cent of CCP members and more than half of CYLC members did not share the same opinion. These results imply that ordinary people who have fewer chances to be involved in the CCP's interest circle may, even more remarkably, have the same orientation.

As for populist sentiments, John Fitzgerald used the words 'the nationless state' to

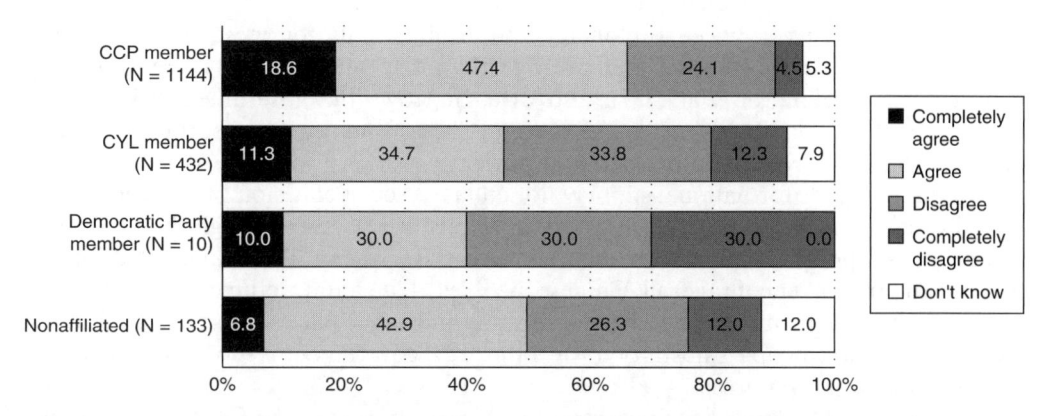

Figure 2.3 'Loving China means loving Socialist China under the leadership of the CCP'

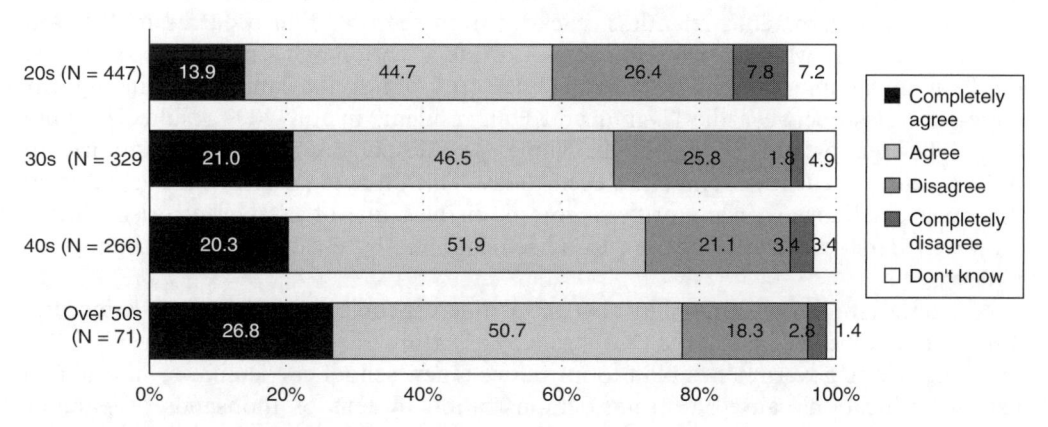

Figure 2.4 'Loving China means loving Socialist China under the leadership of the CCP' (CCP members)

underscore the problem. According to Fitzgerald, although 'the nations of citizen, race and class may well have been inventions of the state designed to overcome differences dividing the people of China', the Chinese people have sustained some alternative notions of how they belong together, and 'the relationship between state and nation is under negotiation in China today to an extent that defies all precedent' (Fitzgerald 1996: 83). In this situation, 'patriotic nationalism has taken root outside the state itself' (ibid.: 85).

The distance between popular nationalism and state nationalism means that nationalism has the potential risk of going beyond the CCP's control if used incorrectly. The slogans in the anti-Japan demonstrations in the autumn of 2010 included not only anti-Japan appeals but also people's complaints against the party-state, such as 'Attack corrupt cadres', 'Real estate is too expensive' and 'Introduce a multi-party system!' Consequently, the difference between official nationalism and popular nationalism has negatively affected the CCP's rule instead of providing it with legitimacy.

First, an exclusive popular nationalism tends to fuel people's emotional anger toward the government's weak-kneed diplomacy. It certainly calls for more decisive action in defence of China's interests and prestige than the party-state may be willing to countenance (Seckington 2005: 27), and often narrows the government's diplomatic options. Exclusive nationalism can also prevent China from acquiring soft power that is compatible with its rising status as a major power.

Second, demands for nationalism may not enhance social cohesion but rather subvert China's fragile national unity (Holbig and Gilley 2010: 14). Even though the Xi Jinping leadership proposed catchphrases such as 'Great Revival of the Chinese Nation' or 'China Dream' to encourage all Chinese peoples – including ethnic minorities and Chinese nationals living in Hong Kong, Taiwan, and other places – to rally around the CCP, part of these people's hostility toward the CCP government is too deeply rooted to be overcome by a few phrases.

In recent years, ethnic minorities' mounting frustration with the CCP's rule has surfaced in various forms such as demonstrations, stabbing sprees and self-immolations. The Chinese government's relentless crackdown on the riots that occurred in Tibetan-inhabited areas in March 2008 received worldwide attention and led to protests against the Beijing Olympic Torch relay in some cities. In Urumqi, the capital of Xinjiang, the large-scale clash between the Uyghur and Han residents in July 2009 resulted in more than 1700 injuries and 197 deaths. In Xinjiang, widespread clashes have continued to intermittently occur in several cities even today. The Chinese government has enforced thorough crackdowns on minorities' protests in the name of counterterrorism duties. However, harsh repression has led to a vicious circle by escalating the exchanges of violence.

Not only ethnic minorities but also the Chinese people living in Hong Kong and Taiwan have rebelled against the CCP's rule by asserting their own identity. In July 2012, the Hong Kong government's plan to introduce a new school curriculum of 'moral and national education' caused a strong demonstration by tens of thousands of parents, students and social activists, who claimed it amounted to brainwashing impressionable young minds with pro-mainland propaganda. Massive student protests occurred again in September 2014: an outburst of the people's strong demand for full democracy, triggered by a decision of the National People's Congress requiring that all candidates for the chief executive position be approved by at least half of a Beijing-friendly nominating committee.

Anti-mainland demonstrations have occurred in Taiwan as well. Taiwanese students who opposed the Cross Strait Services Trade Agreement (CSSTA) occupied the Taiwan legislature in March and April 2014. Faced with the stiff opposition, the Ma Yingjeou administration had to review its conciliatory policy toward the mainland. In June 2014, in response to a statement by the spokesman from the Taiwan Affairs Office of the State Council, Fan Liqing, that every matter concerning China's sovereignty and territorial security must be decided by all the Chinese people including Taiwanese compatriots, the presidential spokesman, Ma Weiguo, emphasized that the future of Taiwan would be determined by 23 million Taiwanese people under the framework of the Constitution of the Republic of China.

The failure of the CCP to deal with conflicts over identity cannot be addressed by shifting the blame to a small number of external enemies and internal separatists. The CCP has to evolve its governance to respect various identities; otherwise, nationalistic slogans will have limited effects in unifying people or, rather, will escalate the hatred and violence among the people from different cultural backgrounds.

IDEOLOGY, VALUES AND MOTIVATION

As numerous empirical studies have demonstrated, the CCP, which wishes to maintain an authoritarian, one-party regime, has used ideology as an inexpensive instrument to achieve national unity and political legitimacy. Moreover, the CCP has changed the substance of its official ideology from Marxism–Leninism to developmental dictatorship and, further, to nationalism to adapt to changing conditions over time. Unquestionably, such a pragmatic approach to its ideology has enhanced its resilience.

Because of the importance of ideology in the CCP's rule, Chinese observers of the country's conditions have focused on the CCP's decisions, leaders' comments and inner-party debates over ideology in examining various materials, including CCP newspapers and journals. They have tried to find convincing answers to the questions of how and for what purposes each ideology was formed by the CCP, and in which direction each ideology would lead the CCP and China. The CCP's ideology has been interpreted to demonstrate China's unique stance in many instances, for example its emphasis on socialism in the Cold War era, developmental dictatorship in the Third Wave of democratization, and nationalism in the era of globalization. Therefore, this seemingly anachronistic topic continues to attract Western researchers' interests.

In addition, foreign scholars have always been confronted by difficult situations when explaining the possible variance between official ideology and the value system that stems from history and culture in local and basic-level societies. The effects of each official ideology are guided by mutual interactions with indigenous value systems. What we need now are empirical studies focusing on the interactive influences between official ideologies and the reality of local communities. By what historical context, indigenous culture, and circumstances of the moment has each official ideology – Marxism–Leninism Mao Zedong Thought, developmental dictatorship, and nationalism – been determined? How and to what extent has the promotion of each official ideology and the shifts in the gravity of official ideologies exercised influence (or otherwise) on social activities in local communities with various ethnic groups and diverse cultures? We will become able to clearly evaluate the force and the effect of official ideologies, as well as the resilience of the CCP regime, only by paying attention to the interactions at multiple levels in various localities.

Combining macro and micro perspectives, each of the three official ideologies has shown its limitations in building a unified national identity. It seems to be nearly impossible to rally more than 13 000 million people under a single value system. The next pragmatic shift in the CCP's ideological work may relate to whether the Party can establish a new value system that co-opts diverse value systems and identities.

NOTES

1. Many scholars ascribe the sources of the 'strength' of the CCP and its one-party regime to its 'resilience'. For example, Andrew Nathan concluded that the Chinese authoritarian regime had become resilient and increasingly stable through institutionalization (Nathan 2003). David Shambaugh also regarded the regime as a 'reasonably strong and resilient institution'. Compared with the experiences of the former Soviet Union and the Eastern European countries, he placed the source of the CCP's longevity in its proactive stance toward making the necessary adaptations and enacting necessary reforms (Shambaugh 2008). There are also opposing views on the 'resilience' of the CCP regime. For example, Cheng Li in his article titled 'The End of the CCP's Resilient Authoritarianism?' criticized the main arguments for resilient authoritarianism, citing the CCP's underestimation of the vulnerability of the authoritarian one-party system in the face of various challenges such as factionalism within the Party, interest groups as resistance forces against reform, and socio-economic forces in the country (Li 2012).
2. Mark Selden, in his book titled *The Yenan Way in Revolutionary China*, attributed the CCP's victory to its successful realization of an egalitarian society through land reforms (Selden 1970).
3. The questionnaire survey was conducted in connection with the research project Empirical Study of the Chinese Communist Party from a Political Sociological Perspective, a grant-in-aid project of the Japanese government's Ministry of Education, Culture, Sports, Science, and Technology with the cooperation of a team at the School of Government, Peking University, from December 2008 to May 2009. This questionnaire surveyed political attitudes among graduate and undergraduate students studying at various schools, including those studying in a Masters of Public Administration (MPA) course. The valid sample numbered 1807, with a response rate of 96.9 per cent.
4. Robert Schaeffer poses an objection against using the term 'developmental dictatorship' to characterize Chinese politics in the reform era. Schaeffer persuasively states that it is incorrect to excessively emphasize the economic discontinuity between the Maoist period (1949–1978), when the Chinese Communist Party promoted 'socialism', and the reformist period (1978 to the present), when Deng and his successors promoted capitalism (Schaeffer 2012: vii). According to Schaeffer, though Mao failed to promote economic growth, he did create social structures that enabled Deng to achieve economic growth in the latter period. In this regard, Mao contributed to the development of capitalism, not socialism, in China (Schaeffer 2012: 2).
5. http://j.people.com.cn/94474/8041295.html.
6. 'Zhonggong xiafa yishi xingtai wenjian tongbao shenlong bujian shouwei' (CCP issues a briefing note on comprehensive development), BBC, in Chinese, http://www.bbc.co.uk/zhongwen/simp/china/2013/05/130513_china_politics_ideology.shtml.
7. 'Mingjing yuekan dujia quanwen kan fa zhonggong 9 hao wenjian la qingdan' (*Der Spiegel* magazine exclusive full-text document published of Document No. 9), http://www.laqingdan.net/?p=2993.

3. The Chinese Communist Party: an institutional perspective
Zheng Yongnian and Chen Gang

The Chinese Communist Party (CCP) is the largest political organization in the world today, and one of the most powerful, and has played a crucial role in initiating most of the major reforms of the past three decades in China. China's rapid rise has enabled the CCP to extend its influence throughout the globe, but the West remains uncertain whether the CCP will survive China's ongoing socio-economic transformation and whether China will become a democratic country in the Western sense. This chapter focuses on the CCP as an institution, trying to assess its durability and adaptability through looking at the CCP's institutional and ideological strengths and weaknesses. The chapter aims to depict major stages concerning CCP's institutional evolvement and to explain some key concepts in the ideological framework constructed by the CCP over time.

ORGANIZATIONAL EVOLUTION OF THE CCP

Founded in 1921 in Shanghai, the CCP has gone through dramatic transformation in the past century. From a party of merely 53 members in 1921, the CCP survived the political onslaughts of the KMT (Kuomintang) in the 1920s and 1930s and expanded drastically in subsequent decades. Under the revolutionary leadership of Mao Zedong, the CCP won the Civil War (1946–49) with the KMT and founded the People's Republic of China (PRC) in 1949. The CCP also survived Mao's 'continuous revolution' after 1949, including the Great Leap Forward and the Cultural Revolution. After Deng Xiaoping took power, the CCP embarked on an unprecedented socio-economic transformation of China.

In the past three decades, the CCP itself has experienced even more drastic changes. The CCP had only 4.5 million Party members in 1949, and by the end of 2012 the ruling Party already had 85.13 million members (Xinhua 2013f), with an annual increase of about 2 to 3 million new members in the reform era. The newly recruited members are usually younger and better educated. More than 44 per cent of these new members are frontline workers, such as industrial employees, farmers, herders and migrant staff, and of the total Party members, 20.27 million, or 23.8 per cent, were women and 5.80 million, or 6.8 per cent, were from ethnic minority groups. In terms of occupation, farmers, herders and fishermen totalling 25.35 million was the largest group, while 7.25 million Party members were industrial workers. Another 7.16 million members worked in Party and state agencies, and 20.20 million were managerial staff and professional technicians working in enterprises and non-profit organizations.

While the CCP remains a highly authoritarian structure, the composition of its membership has changed. The structure of the CCP's membership has been enhanced with younger and more higher-educated people joining. In 2012, more than a quarter of members were 35 years or younger and about 34.09 million had obtained degrees in higher education institutions. Students alone made up 2.91 million (Xinhua 2013f).

In addition to the increasing membership, the number of the Party's grassroots organizations has also been growing rapidly. In other words, Party organizations have penetrated into all forms of firms, institutions and social organizations. The CCP had 4.20 million grassroots Party organs across the country at the end of 2012, an increase of 4.3 per cent from a year earlier. These grassroots organs were set up in 7245 urban subdistricts, 33 000 towns, 87 000 urban communities and 588 000 villages. Party organs were established in nearly all government organs, state-owned and private enterprises, and social organizations. The CCP trained 1.48 million village Party branch secretaries and offered employment and skills training to 15.23 million members in 2012. The CCP also set up 11 000 Party organs and 456 000 service centres in order to improve the education and management of floating Party members in the same year.

CCP: From 1921 to 1949

In retrospect, CCP leaders in various historical stages, including those founding fathers in the early days, have all paid enormous attention to the institutional growth since the birth of CCP. In August 1920, the brilliant intellectual activist Chen Duxiu established the first branch of the CCP, comprising seven members. In September, a Shanghai unit of the Socialist Youth League was begun, as was a foreign language school that sent its first eight students to Moscow's University of the Toilers of the Far East (later renamed Sun Yat-sen University) that winter. The Peking branch of the CCP began in September with nine members, expanding to 15 by November, after allowing anarchists who had originally signed on to depart peaceably (Sheng 1971: 128). In November 1920, Mao Zedong established a very active branch at Changsha, Hunan, and other branches appeared in places like Wuhan, Tianjin, Jinan, and even Paris, France. These initial branches became very active in propaganda work, in publishing and distributing magazines and pamphlets, and in organizing and educating youth and workers (Uhalley 1988: 17). Twelve delegates, representing 59 Party members, participated in the First Congress of the CCP in July 1921. Chen Duxiu was elected as the first Party chairman despite his absence. Chen, Li Da and Zhang Guotao formed the Central Bureau, the leadership core of the CCP at that time. Li Da was in charge of propaganda affairs and Zhang Guotao took charge of organizational work. In the year between CCP's First and Second Congresses, the youthful Party became a beehive of activity. It further extended its work in propaganda and among youth, workers and peasants, gaining invaluable experience in these areas. It expanded its own organizational network to embrace regional secretaries and branches in ten provinces; by mid-1922 some 120 members were spread throughout 18 provinces (Harrison 1972: 39). At the same time, the Party was becoming more disciplined, and it weeded out those who would not submit to the severe requirements of Leninist democratic centralism (Uhalley 1988: 20). In September 1922, the magazine *Guide Weekly* replaced *New Youth* as the official Party youth organ, the later becoming a quarterly theoretical journal until it ceased publication in 1926 (Harrison 1972: 38).

The CCP showed its impressive capability in organizing workers in the early 1920s. In mid-1921, the CCP founded a Labour Secretariat in Shanghai that published the *Labour*

Weekly until it was suppressed in June 1922. Branches of the Labour Secretariat were established in Wuhan, Jinan, Guangzhou, Changsha and Beijing. In June 1922, the CCP officially accepted the concept of the united front aimed at liberalization of the Chinese people from the dual yoke of foreigners and of powerful Chinese militarists. The CCP decided to collaborate with the KMT under the united front policy since its Third Party Congress in 1923, in which Mao Zedong replaced Zhang Guotao as director of the organizational department, and Qu Qiubai was made propaganda chief. The KMT–CCP alliance won the Northern Expedition warfare against warlords quickly, but on 12 April 1927, KMT leader Jiang Jieshi suddenly disarmed the CCP-led unions in Shanghai and began a purge of the communists. During its first civil war with the KMT from 1927 to 1937, the CCP reshuffled its leadership many times and adopted organizational measures to facilitate underground activities. In 1927, a seven-man Emergency Political Bureau was formed within the Central Committee, with its own secret communications systems (Chang 1972: 95). Branch organizations were similarly organized. During the Sixth CCP Congress held in Moscow, Xiang Zhongfa, a rare genuine proletarian worker among the CCP leaders, replaced Qu Qiubai as general secretary, while Li Lisan had the real power in the new Political Bureau. The Sixth Party Congress consolidated the CCP's dependence upon the Kremlin, while Mao Zedong and other revolutionaries from the rural bases were removed from Party posts.

In April 1928 Mao Zedong was joined at Jinggangshan by Zhu De and his Fourth Army, increasing the Red Army fourfold, but his efforts to concentrate on the building of the revolutionary base area were disrupted by continued differences within the central Party leadership. The turning point came in 1931, when the CCP Central Committee in Shanghai abolished both the General Front Committee and the Provincial Action Committee; instead, it created a Central Bureau for the Soviet Areas, in which Mao and his supporters were given enhanced authority. However, Mao's authority in the Central Bureau for the Soviet Areas was continually eroded by the manoeuvring of his political opponents, the 28 Bolsheviks, who had taken control of the Politburo in 1931. In November 1931, the Chinese Soviet Republic was established in Ruichin, Jiangxi Province, with a constitutional outline, land and labour laws, resolutions on the Red Army and economic policy, and other laws approved. Despite Mao's victory over the KMT's first three encirclement campaigns, he gradually lost control of the Party apparatus and the army from 1932. The Red Army was defeated by the KMT in Jiang Jieshi's fifth encirclement campaign and during its military retreat, the Long March, Mao regained his leadership in the Zunyi Conference in January 1935, and from then onwards he controlled CCP's top-level decision-making, until his death in 1976. After the Long March to Yan'an, the CCP underwent a fundamental transformation and experienced spectacular growth in its second collaboration with the KMT when Japan invaded China from 1937 to 1945. The CCP had by this time learned to place the loosest construction on its Marxist ideology, while Mao's dictum that 'political power grows out of the gun barrel' became the maxim for the whole Party (Uhalley 1988: 55). Between 1942 and 1944, Mao launched the rectification campaign throughout the Party to consolidate his power and to set down the Party's line with regard to the arts, literature and propaganda. Mao advocated the 'mass line' in Yan'an, which required Party members to be sympathetically involved with and responsive to the rural masses, and subsequently helped the CCP to secure support from the peasantry. On the eve of the victory of the Anti-Japanese

War, Mao firmly controlled the CCP's leadership through incorporating many of his ideas into the new Party Constitution, referred to in the text of the Constitution as the 'Thought of Mao Zedong'. The Seventh Party Congress was held from April to June 1945, which established a new Central Committee, Political Bureau, and Secretariat, all of which were headed by Mao himself. After the Japanese were defeated in August 1945, both the KMT and CCP were preparing for an impending civil war, which broke out in 1946, and finally ended the KMT's rule of mainland China in 1949.

Early Stage of the Party-State: 1949-78

The CCP continued its united front tactics under the rubric of New Democracy for the preparation of the establishment of the People's Republic of China, with the Chinese People's Political Consultative Conference (CPPCC) held in Beijing in September 1945 to enact the Organic Law of the People's Central Government of the PRC and a Common Programme, which served as an interim Constitution for the new China. All the organizations established thereafter within the regime, including the State Council, People's Revolutionary Military Council, Supreme People's Court, Supreme People's Procuratorate and the National People's Congress, were under the ultimate authority of the CCP. The CCP also quickly moved its governance to various layers of localities, from provinces and special districts down to county and township level. In the meantime, the CCP was penetrating more deeply into society through expanding its grassroots organizations in various districts, government departments, enterprises and public service units. CCP cadres played important roles in local residents' committees and mass organizations like the Youth League, the Young Pioneers, the Women's Federation and the Federation of Trade Unions, which became exceedingly important mechanisms for involving all members of society in the new politics and social life of the country (Barnett 1964:29-44).

After the Fifth Plenum of the Eighth CCP Central Committee was held in May 1958, the Party became even more intrusive into the affairs of government, although the Party's assumption of a central role in policy implementation could really date from the CCP's Yan'an period in early 1940s (Martin 1981: 17). With enhanced power in the socio-economic realm, Mao launched the Great Leap Forward in 1958, with the emergence across the country of the people's commune, an organizational entity encompassing not only agriculture, but also industry, commerce, education and military affairs. The Great Leap Forward and communization ended up with a three-year famine, with Mao's authority conceded to a collective leadership under Liu Shaoqi. In 1962, however, Mao persuaded a CCP plenum to approve of a new rectification campaign, which was to include a socialist education campaign, a crackdown on intellectuals, and a new anti-corruption campaign within the Party. The plenum also strengthened the Party's Central Control Commission (Ahn 1983: 79-80).

In May 1966 Mao launched the Great Proletarian Cultural Revolution that lasted for ten years, with alleged goals of eliminating bourgeois, traditional and cultural elements in the Chinese society, and of imposing Maoist orthodoxy within the Party. The movement that spread into the military, workers, peasants and the CCP leadership itself paralyzed China politically, and significantly affected the country economically and socially. It resulted in widespread factional struggles in all walks of life. In the top leadership, it led to a mass purge of senior officials who were accused of taking a capitalist road, most notably Liu Shaoqi and Deng Xiaoping. During the same period Mao's personality cult grew to immense proportions. On 9 September 1976, Mao Zedong died, and soon the Cultural Revolution ended. One year later, Deng Xiaoping came back to power. On 18 December 1978, the pivotal Third Plenum of the Eleventh CCP Congress was held, in which Deng officially established the policy of economic reform.

The CCP in the Reform Era

The Party had been nearly destroyed and for a time actually ceased to perform its leadership function during the Cultural Revolution, so after Deng took power, one of his priority jobs was to revive the Party apparatus, the legal system, and to deal carefully with the military that had quieted the political storm at the end of the Cultural Revolution. Deng remained the Chairman of the Central Military Commission, but formal power was transferred to a new generation of pragmatic reformers, who reversed Cultural Revolution policies almost entirely. To speed up reform and opening-up that might be hampered by Marxist–Leninist orthodoxy, Deng proposed his famous pragmatism that composed of the 'black cat – white cat theory', the 'don't debate theory' and 'across the river through feeling the stones theory'.

CCP General Secretaries Hu Yaobang and Zhao Ziyang were forced to step down in 1987 and 1989, respectively, due to widespread student protests in the two years. Since the political crisis of 1989, the CCP had to make significant changes both institutionally and ideologically to adapt itself to an utterly new world order in the post-Cold War era, through drawing lessons from the collapse of the Soviet Union and other communist party-states, and through learning positive experiences from non-communist systems. In 1992 Deng Xiaoping formalized the marketization reform in his tour to Southern China. In 2001, CCP General Secretary Jiang Zemin proposed the theory of 'Three Represents', which indicated an important, even radical, shift in Party ideology, Party composition and Party orientation (Shambaugh 2008: 112). The new ideology, which reflected an opening to recruit private entrepreneurs and high-income professionals into the Party, could be regarded as an expanded and bold tactic of united front, and a break with the 80-year Marxist emphasis on recruiting workers, farmers and other proletarians into the CCP. Since Deng passed away in 1997, the CCP experienced two peaceful power transitions at the top level, namely Hu Jintao replacing Jiang Zemin as General Secretary in 2002, and Xi Jinping replacing Hu Jintao in 2012. Hu developed the 'Scientific Development Concept' while Xi proposed the fulfilment of the 'Chinese Dream'. Like other ideological campaigns launched by CCP leaders in the reform era, these two theories were actually codification of policy changes already under way.

PARTY BUILDING: INSTITUTIONS, RULES AND NORMS

Maintaining Party discipline and improving cadre management are vital issues for a Leninist party to stay in power. Due to lack of political pressures from opposition parties or institutionalized supervision from civic organization, the ruling CCP has to improve its 'ruling capacity' and meritocracy of cadres through repetitive 'party-building' processes and institutional reforms. Meanwhile rapid economic development since the reform and open-door policy has created a new socio-economic environment for the CCP. The CCP has consistently reordered its relations with the administration (the state) in order to survive in this new environment. China's successful transition to modern, effective governance is still very much dependent on these changing Party–state relations. Since the CCP–state relations together form the single most important political-institutional infrastructure in China, they are central to all political activities.

The *Nomenklatura* System

The CCP's most powerful instrument in structuring its domination over the state is a system called the 'Party management of cadres' or more commonly known in the West as the *nomenklatura* system. The *nomenklatura* system 'consists of lists of leading positions, over which Party units exercise the power to make appointments and dismissals; lists of reserves or candidates for these positions; and institutions and processes for making the appropriate personnel changes' (Burns 1989: ix). The system established was based on the Soviet model, and changes occurred from time to time, albeit not drastic ones (Burns 1994: 458–491). The *nomenklatura* system is the most important organizational pillar, which gives the CCP a dominant say over personnel decisions of all important positions. While the state administration has assumed part of this power since the reform and open-door policy, the Party still controls the most important personnel appointments. The two most important principles of China's political system are: Party control of the government, and Party management of cadres (Lieberthal 1995: Ch. 6; Huang 1996: Ch. 4; Shirk 1993). The CCP selects all government officials; almost all government officials and all top officials are themselves Party members; and in each government agency, Party members are organized under a Party committee that is subordinate to the Party committee at the higher administrative level. The hierarchy of government organs is overlaid by a parallel hierarchy of Party committees that enables Party leaders to supervise Party members in the government and lead the work of the government, not from outside.

The current practice is 'one level down', that is, each level of the Party structure is responsible for political appointments that are one level below them. For example, all positions above vice-ministerial level (such as state resident, vice-state president, premier, vice-premier, state counsellor and others) fall under the jurisdiction of the Political Bureau of the Central Committee (more specifically, the Standing Committee). In this case, the Political Bureau first selects the candidates, then passes the nominations to the National People's Congress (NPC) – China's parliament – for approval.

The 'Party management of cadres' system is also the most effective means for the CCP to control localism in the country. The Political Bureau and its Department of Organization keep a tight rein on the selection and appointment of provincial Party secretaries and governors. To prevent provincial Party secretaries and governors from becoming deeply rooted in locally vested interests, the CCP exercises the so-called 'cadre exchange system'. This system allows the CCP to curtail localism. All important provincial leaders and cadres are appointed and managed by the central government. From the mid-1950s until 1984, the *nomenklatura* system allowed the Central Committee to make appointments two levels down in the system. In 1984, the Party leadership under Hu Yaobang introduced a major reform, changing the two-level-down system to a one-level-down system, meaning that the Central Committee directly managed leaders only at the ministerial and provincial level. This change greatly reduced the number of cadres directly managed by the Central Committee. It is important to point out that by decentralizing *nomenklatura* authority, the Central Committee aimed to strengthen its power and management efficiency over provincial leaders. The huge number of cadres under the two-level-down system had too often resulted in pro forma consideration and de facto approvals of whomsoever the lower territorial unit nominated. The system was thus rather inefficient. By contrast, the one-level-down system enables 'the central authorities to exercise their nomenklatura powers in a more serious fashion' (Lieberthal 1995: 211). While the 1980s witnessed a great degree of liberalization, efforts were made to tighten this system in the aftermath of the 1989 pro-democracy movement. The system has remained intact ever since then.

In the post-Mao era, the Party ideology successfully shifted from that of class struggle to one of economic development, first under Deng Xiaoping and then under Jiang Zemin, and then to one of building a harmonious society under Hu Jintao. This would not be possible without the *nomenklatura* system. During stages of reform, resistance to changes from vested interests are inevitably strong. To counter that, the CCP leadership has to resort to the *nomenklatura* system to retire, or even forcefully remove, those who have resisted. The system also allows the CCP to select the 'right types' of cadres and government officials to implement its reformist policies. Hence, the CCP has served as an important facilitator for the state administration to carry out its reformist policies. Besides cadre management, the CCP also helps the state administration to mobilize resources required for the country's socio-economic transition.

The *nomenklatura* system presents a typified weak state and strong party phenomenon, and this is a dilemma for China. On the one hand, continuing one-party rule stifles the development of strong state mechanisms, a prerequisite for a modern state; on the other hand, without the Party and its apparatus, the state administration is incapable of moving ahead with anything at all, let alone its reformist agenda.

CCP's System of Selecting Cadres

In the reform era, the objective of the CCP's cadre selection process is to make sure that professionally competent people are recruited and promoted, and that they remain loyal to the CCP's ideologies and political views (Brødsgaard 2001: 1–2). All Party and government officials are managed by the Party according to detailed regulations relating to recruitment, appointment, transfer, reward, training and so on (CCP Central Organization Department and the Ministry of Personnel, 29 February 2008), which supplement the Civil Service Law. Concerning the management of cadres above county and division level, the most important provisions are contained in the 'Regulation on Selection and Appointment of Party and Government Leading Cadres' issued in 2002 by the Central Organization Department.

All these regulations emphasize that when selecting and appointing leading cadres in the Chinese civil service system, a number of basic principles including openness, equality, competition and the selection of the best must be adhered to. Although the selection and appointment are based on meritocratic principles, cadres should also have both political integrity and ability, and are ultimately managed by the Party (CCP Central

Organization Department 2002: Article 2). Civil servants to be promoted to leading Party and government posts at section (village) head level are required to have at least a college diploma and to have worked at a deputy's post for more than two years (CCP Central Organization Department and the Ministry of Personnel 2008: Article 19). Candidates to be promoted to posts higher than the county (division) level must have held at least two posts at lower level organs, and candidates who are promoted from deputy post to a head post generally must have worked at the deputy post for more than two years (CCP Central Organization Department 2002: Article 7). Leading cadres at bureau level or above should at least have a bachelor's degree (CCP Central Organization Department 2002: Article 7).

Candidates to be considered for selection and appointment to leading posts should be proposed through the so-called democratic recommendation (CCP Central Organization Department 2002: Articles 10–19) process conducted by the Party committee at the same level, or by a higher-level organization or personnel department. At the time of an official's change of term, various people and personnel are consulted, and they include Party committee members, leading members of government organs, leading members of the discipline inspection commissions and people's courts, and leading members of lower-level Party committees and governments. Members of democratic parties and representatives of groups without Party affiliation will also be consulted.

A candidate who has been nominated will have to undergo evaluation (CCP Central Organization Department 2002: Articles 20–28) based on elaborate procedures, which may include interviews with a number of leading officials in their own department. Evaluations are held throughout the term in office. Leading members of Party committees and government departments are also evaluated in the middle of their term. Any promotion or dismissal arising from the evaluations must undergo a process of deliberation and be reported to the Party committee at the higher level.

The regulations require a two-thirds quorum of members of a given committee when appointment and dismissal of cadres are involved. The regulations include details concerning job transfer. Any leading member of a local Party committee or government who has served in the same post for ten years must be transferred to a new post. The Party has worked out a new plan for 'deepening the cadre management system' covering the 2010–2020 period (CCP General Office 2009). The plan further details and expands the provisions of the 2002 regulations, which are applicable to the whole cadre corps and not just leading cadres. The plan, with the emphasis on 'democratic recommendation', 'public opinion polls' and 'contested election', is a reflection of China's leadership's preoccupation with selecting qualified cadres. The focus of this theme goes back to October 2004, when former Vice-President Zeng Qinghong published an important article in the *People's Daily* in which he stressed the importance of strengthening the Party's governing capacity. Zeng discussed the 'painful lesson of the loss of power' by the communist parties in the former Soviet Union and Eastern Europe (*People's Daily* 2004: 2–3). Zeng attributed the collapse of the Soviet Communist Party to the rigidity and inflexibility of its governing system which ultimately led to the Party's diminishing capacity to govern. To Zeng, establishing clear rules and regulations, and ensuring constant cadre renewal were necessary to attract new talent.

Party–State relationship

The CCP is, strictly speaking, not a 'political party' by Western standards. In a modern state, political parties are political groups that compete for public offices through candidacy in elections. Mostly, political parties are subsumed within the greater state structure; that is to say, political parties are mere institutions of the state. But in China, the CCP is in many ways equivalent to the state itself. The Party is the personification of a modern emperor. It is a highly organized emperorship that attempts to exercise domination over the society and integrate with the state (Schurmann 1968). The CCP's particular role is determined by China's unique historical experience. China has always been a continental power. Rulers throughout history had to rely heavily on ideological indoctrination and local gentries to secure their reign. For this reason, the power of the political centre is usually not fixed and institutionalized. Unlike a modern Westphalian state where the central authority is contiguous throughout its bounded territory, China's historical experience has been that of concentric rings of graded power emanating from the centre. Despite many attempts to modernize the state, China is still far from being a modern state in a Western sense. China lacks the defining characteristic of a modern state: the rule of law. The state is largely incapable of performing the regulatory function entrusted to it. In this context, the CCP becomes the most important pillar supporting a seemingly modern state. In other words, the CCP is the pillar of the Chinese state.

The unitary rule of the CCP, or the domination of the Party over the state, was a consequence of the history of the Party, since the revolutions and wars that the Party led and engaged in required the Party to be a highly centralized organization. Between its birth in 1921 and the establishment of the PRC in 1949, the CCP was an opposition party, but even during that period, the form of the party-state was taking shape in the revolutionary base areas. Although the CCP performed as the government in the areas under its de facto jurisdictions before 1949, it was basically a revolution and war machine. After it took power in 1949, the Party leadership began to explore a rational relationship between the Party and the government. Among leaders, the Party was perceived to play the role of political leadership, and the government to perform the role of governance. For example, according to Peng Zhen, then the Vice-Chairman of the National People's Congress (NPC), the leadership of the Party over the government is a political one, and there should be no organizational subordination of the government to the Party (Peng 1991: 226–227). Dong Biwu, then the Vice-Chairman of the Chinese People's Political Consultative Conference, also pointed out that:

> the Party committee of all levels should realize its leadership over the government of all levels through Party members who are working in all government bodies; if there are more than three party members in a government body, there should be a Party group in order to guarantee the leadership of the Party. (Dong 1985: 314)

However, the Party leadership under Mao Zedong continued to engage what he called 'continuous revolution', and was not able to transform the Party from a revolutionary party into a normal ruling party. In mobilizing waves of political movements and campaigns, particularly the Anti-Rightist movement, the Great Leap

Forward and the Cultural Revolution, the CCP became increasingly centralized and personalized.

In order to guarantee the leadership of the Party over the government, the Party established many (intra-Party) organizations which were parallel to those in the government. Those organizations enabled the Party to exercise its direct control over relevant government bodies. A Party-centred political hierarchy was formed: the Party made all decisions over state affairs, and the power of the Party at different levels was centralized in the hands of Party secretaries, and all ultimate power nationwide was centralized in the hands of Mao Zedong. Through this system, 'power to one party' (the CCP) was transformed into 'power to one man' (Mao Zedong). This hierarchy changed the nature of the Party itself on the one hand, and the nature of the government on the other. The Political Bureau of the Central Committee decided all major policies for the whole nation, and at the local level all major decision-making powers were centralized at the Party committee. In theory, the government (including administration and judiciary) at different levels should report to the People's Congress at the same level, but in reality, it reported to parallel Party organizations at the same level. The Party committee issued directives to the government body through the Party group within that government body, and the government reported to the Party committee through the Party group. As a matter of fact, for a long period of time during the Cultural Revolution, the government at local levels was abolished, and was replaced by the revolutionary committee, which was initially a combination of revolutionary mass organizations, the People's Liberation Army (PLA), and revolutionary leading cadres of Party and government organizations, and later restricted its activities to the affairs of the state *apparat* with the recreation of separate Party organizations (Goodman 1981: 49).

After Deng Xiaoping returned to power in the late 1970s, he learnt a lesson from Mao Zedong and began to address Party–state relations. In 1978, in a working conference of the Central Committee, he criticized the unitary leadership between the Party and the state. To enforce these reforms will enable the Party to get away from daily management and to be concentrated on policy-making and political work, and organizational and supervision work. This is not to weaken the leadership of the Party, but to improve and strengthen the leadership of the Party (Goodman 1981: 320–343). The separation of the Party from the government was central to the discourse of the reform under Deng Xiaoping and Zhao Ziyang. Needless to say, this discourse was rather conservative since the purpose of the separation was to strengthen the effectiveness of the leadership of the Party. In other words, it was not aimed at changing the domination of the Party over the state. The establishment of this reform discourse led to a short period of so-called 'political liberalization' until the crackdown on the pro-democracy movement in 1989. After the crackdown, the separation of the Party from the government disappeared from the reform discourse of Jiang Zemin (1989–2002) and Hu Jintao (2002–present). Instead, how to strengthen the domination of the Party over the government is at the centre of reform discourse.

CCP'S INSTITUTIONS IN CONTROLLING THE GOVERNMENT, MILITARY, JUDICIARY

Central Leading Small Groups

While the 'Party management of cadres' is a general principle, the CCP has established various 'technologies of power' or 'mechanisms of power' through which the Party exercises its domination over the government. Two main technologies and mechanisms are the central leading small groups at the top, and the Party groups all over the system. In China's political system, there are two types of leading small groups (LSGs), namely, central leading small groups (CLSGs) and state council leading small groups. Both types are ad hoc supraministerial coordinating and consulting bodies formed to build consensus on issues that cut across the Party, government and military system when the existing bureaucratic structure is unable to do so (Lu 2001: 45–49; Lampton 2001a: 16–19). However, the two types of groups have radically different functions. While state council leading small groups focus on coordinating policy implementation for the government, the CLSGs focus on initiating and managing policy for the Political Bureau. Through CLSGs, the CCP effectively exercises its domination over the government.

CLSGs do not formulate concrete policies; instead, they often focus on setting up guiding principles for concrete policies. Any recommendations of leading groups are likely to be reflected in the policy-making process because they represent the consensus of the leading members of the relevant Party, government and military agencies. In some cases, the policy-making body will simply adopt a CLSG's recommendation with little or even no modification. CLSGs cover a wide range of important issue areas, including Taiwan affairs, foreign affairs, financial and economic affairs, rural work, Party-building work, publicity and ideological work, overseas publicity, Party history work and other important emerging issues. Therefore, it is difficult for CLSGs to have permanent staff. They often rely on their offices to manage daily operations and for research and policy recommendations. While the effectiveness of a CLSG often depends on the effectiveness of its office, the way it operates also gives individual leaders, usually the head of a given CLSG, room to influence policy recommendations.

In the post-Deng era, CLSGs are becoming an increasingly important tool for coordinating the work of several agencies as well as ensuring Party supervision over government activities. After the passing of strongmen like Mao Zedong and Deng Xiaoping, the young generation of leaders usually does not have a strong base of legitimacy to enable individual leaders to stand above different bureaucracies and departments. Also, China is now a pluralistic society and different interests have to be taken into account when major decisions are made. In this regard, CLSGs play an important role in coordinating different interests. CLSGs are often tools for individual leaders to exercise their personal preferences over different policies. In this case, CLSGs are very informal mechanisms for the Party to exercise its domination over key political and policy agendas.

Xitong (Systems)

Another mechanism that performs similar functions as the CLSGs is the organization of the Party-state into *xitong* (systems). CLSGs exist only at the central level, but *xitong* also function at local levels such as the province and city. As CLSGs, the purpose of *xitong* is also to enable the Party to exercise its domination over the government. The *xitong* mean that society is divided into different functional spheres, and corresponding functional Party organs and cadres supervise and control these systems, which encompass the entire political and social leadership at each level. One caveat should be added here. The *xitong* are also different from the administrative counterpart departments in the Party. The Party leadership in the *xitong* is usually not part of the formal, legally organizational structure, and in general Party leaders' names are not publicized, while the Party's administrative counterpart departments are part of the formal and legal structure. Also, as their title indicates, the Party's administrative counterpart departments have a limited function, that is, to oversee a specific administrative agency. In contrast, one *xitong* often oversees several related governmental ministries, departments and agencies.

In the early years of the PRC, the CCP established a set of Party departments at the central and provincial levels, such as the Industrial and Transportation Department, Trade and Financial Department, Education and Cultural Department, Agricultural Work Department and City Planning Department. These departments performed the same functions as the government at the same level. The administrative counterpart departments in the Party completely blurred the boundary between the Party and the government. Governmental functions were taken over by Party departments. Therefore, the Party administrative counterpart departments became a major target of the political reform that Deng Xiaoping and Zhao Ziyang initiated from 1986 to 1989. Many administrative counterpart departments were abolished, and their functions were redistributed to relevant governmental agencies.

This reform had an impact on the *xitong*. With the reform abolishing the Party administrative counterparty departments, the Party leadership had to strengthen the role of the *xitong* in dominating the government. Until today, the *xitong* have played a crucial role in exercising Party domination over the government. Each main *xitong* is usually headed by a member of the Political Bureau Standing Committee at the central level. At the provincial level, this function is performed by each member of the Provincial Party Committee. The main *xitong* include:

- The military system, covering all the armed forces.
- The political and legal system, covering the ministries of State Security, Public Security, Justice and Civil Affairs; the Supreme Court and Procuratorate; the National People's Congress; and the People's Armed Police Force.
- The administrative system. Government is divided into various smaller, secondary systems such as foreign affairs; science and technology; sport and public health; and finance and economy.
- The propaganda system, covering the State Council's ministries of Education and Culture, Radio, Film and Television; State Administration of Press and Publication; the Chinese Academy of Social Sciences; and the Xinhua News Agency, the *People's Daily* and *Qiu Shi* (Seeking Truth) journal.
- The United Front system, covering the Chinese People's Political Consultative Conference (CPPCC); the eight 'democratic parties'; the All-China Federation of Industry and Commerce; various religious, minority nationalities and overseas Chinese groups; the State Nationalities Affairs Commission; the State Religious

Affairs Bureau; and the Offices for Overseas Chinese, Taiwan, Hong Kong and Macao Affairs.
- The mass organization system, covering the All-China Federation of Trade Unions, the Chinese Communist Youth League, the All-China Women's Federation, and various subordinate trade unions, youth and women's organizations.
- The organizational and personnel system, mainly Party organization departments and the government personnel ministries or departments at each level. They manage cadres within all the organizations mentioned above.

Party Groups

If CLSGs are mechanisms through which the Party exercises its domination over the government at the top, then Party groups are the means through which the Party achieves the same purpose in all government agencies and departments. Although China is a one-party system, this does not mean that there is no conflict between the Party and the government. While the Party makes key decisions, the government implements them. During this process, conflicts arise. Once the Party delegates authority to the government, the problem of oversight arises. How do community Party leaders know whether or not government bureaucrats will carry out policies that conform to the Party's preferences? Party groups come to play a key role in the process. Party groups are sometimes called Party 'factions' or Party 'core groups'. Party groups should not be confused with another important body, namely, 'Party committees' or 'unit Party affairs committees'. The CCP established both Party groups and Party committees in all government agencies. Party committees existed in all other communist states, while Party groups were established only in the CCP. Party committees belong to the Party organizational system rather than to the governmental agencies to which they are appended. Their members are at least theoretically elected by Party members working in the same government body. They focus on Party affairs, such as supervising the behaviour of the Party members within the same agency, recruiting new Party members, directing political studies and ideological work, and collecting membership fees. In principle, they do not interfere with government work. Party committees answer to the next higher Party committee.

By contrast, the Party group within a government agency is more powerful than the Party committee. Indeed, the Party committee is under the direction of the Party group in the same governmental agency. In other words, the Party group has the responsibility of actually administering the work of the whole governmental agency. Party group members are not elected by Party members in the same organization, but appointed by Party committees at the next level up. For example, at the national level, all Party groups in different ministries are appointed by the Central Organization Department and the Central Secretariat. Below that, Party groups are appointed by the relevant provincial and local Party committees. The Party group at each level answers to the Party committee one level up, to which they owe their appointments.

The Party group was a unique creation of the CCP. It came to exist in the early years of the Chinese communist revolution. The introduction of the Party group system was to ensure that the Party had control over the military. In the aftermath of the Cultural Revolution, the Party system was greatly enhanced in order to avoid the political chaos that had taken place during the previous decade. A Party group in a governmental agency is usually made up of four to five Party members who hold senior positions in that agency. The secretary of the Party group always has the final say on all the agency's important affairs and often approves and issues important documents. The main purpose of the Party group is to oversee the important activities (e.g., policy-making, policy implementation and personnel appointment) of the governmental agency to which it belongs. The Party group must make sure that the Party's preference is reflected in all such activities. Indeed, without the Party's endorsement, no important activities will take place in that governmental agency.

Key Institutions Dealing with Party–Judiciary and Party–Military Relations

All the *xitong* identified above are mechanisms through which the Party exercises its domination over the government. Among these *xitong*, two are particularly important to the Party–state relationship, namely, the judicial system and the military. A brief and separate discussion of these two *xitong* should be able to help elaborate further the domination of the Party over the government. From the perspective of the organizational emperorship, it is not so difficult to make sense of why the Party wants to exercise total control over the judicial system and the military, since these are the most effective tools to guarantee the 'property rights' of the Party over the state.

Since the reform and open-door policy, there has been an open-ended debate on which is superior, the Party or the law. Although the Chinese Constitution stipulates that 'no organization or individual may enjoy the privilege of being above the Constitution and the law', and the CCP leadership has repeatedly emphasized that like all others, the Party has also to act within the legal framework, the Party in reality has dominated the country's judiciary through various mechanisms.

The most powerful mechanism that enables the CCP to dominate all legal affairs is the Central Political and Legal Commission (CPLC). The CPLC, founded in 1980, is a specialized organ within the Party in charge of political and legal work. The CPLC is headed by a Political Bureau Standing Committee member. Since the early 1990s, this arrangement has been highly institutionalized. Powerful political figures including Peng Zhen, Chen Pixian, Qiao Shi, Luo Gan and Zhou Yongkang used to head this organization. Since the head directly answers to the Political Bureau Standing Committee, this institutional arrangement guarantees that the CPLC is to realize the leadership of the Party over political and legal work by linking the Party centre to the political and legal front line, carrying out the Party's related policy and coordinating the relationship between/among various political and legal organs. Like the other *xitong*, the CPLC performs many governmental functions. It is actively involved in judicial work and usually gives instructions to the relevant court on how to handle cases. It has the power to jointly issue legal documents together with the Court and/or the Procuratorate.

Besides the CPLC, the Central Discipline Inspection Commission (CDIC) has also frequently intervened in judicial work. The CDIC was re-established in 1978 after a ten-year disruption during the Cultural Revolution. The CDIC usually initiates and leads anti-corruption campaigns. However, by doing so, the independence of the judiciary is severely undermined. The involvement of the CDIC in anticorruption often helps some Party members, particularly high-ranking officials, evade criminal justice. This practice is therefore 'entirely arbitrary', and has shown that it is 'improbable that China will move towards a depoliticized legal system as long as the Party treats its own members without reference to any legal process' (Becker 2000: 340). It should also be noted that the CDIC and the Ministry of Supervision share a joint office: that is, two different official names, but one working team, since January 1993. Therefore, there is no real boundary between the Party and the government in the judicial system.

The Party–military relationship merits particular attention when one examines how the Party maintains its domination over the government. It is quite confusing for many as to whether the People's Liberation Army (PLA) is an integral part of the Party or the Party is an integral part of the PLA. However, one thing is certain and well defined: that is, the military does not belong to the government. In Chinese society, there have been occasional calls for the 'nationalization of the army', meaning that the military should be under the jurisdiction of the government, not the CCP. Scholars in the West would also believe that without the nationalization of the military, there can be no hope for any meaningful political reform, especially democratization, to take place in China. Nonetheless, the issue is not that simple if one takes a close look at the triangular relations between the Party, the government and the military. For many in China, the major concern is not whether the military can become a national army, but whether the civilian government (the Party and the government) will be able to continue to exercise effective control over the military, and whether the personalized control over the military can be transformed into institutional control.

The Party–military relationship has long been defined as symbiotic. The close ties between these two most powerful political institutions were concretely indicated by many defining features, such as their common ideological and revolutionary ferment; their identical and overlapping personnel structure; a nearly equal political status; and a shared mentality in government and vested interests. With the passing of the old revolutionary guards, it is increasingly important for the younger generation of Party leaders to institutionalize the civilian–military relationship. When personal control was no longer viable, institutions had to come into being. It has not been an easy task for the Party leadership to establish effective mechanisms to exercise Party control over the military. Before Jiang Zemin firmly established himself as CMC Chairman in the mid-1990s, he experienced great difficulties in coping with military intervention.

In 1997, China passed the National Defence Law, the first of its kind in the country. The major objective of the new law was to legalize the command of the Party over the military. Legalizing the relationship between the Party and the military is in fact the rational method to institutionalize the control of the Party over the gun, a relationship that in the past has depended largely on personal power rather than on the institutional power that defined civilian–military relations. The passage of the National Defence Law has undoubtedly pushed progress towards civilian control over the military. All the reforms in the post-Deng era have institutionalized the civilian–military relationship to a great degree, and thus enabled the Party leadership to exercise effective control over the military. After Hu Jintao succeeded Jiang Zemin, he quickly consolidated his power over the military. Although Hu's pro-people policy orientation has won strong popular support, all these institutional reforms in the post-Deng era have so far rendered military intervention in civilian affairs less likely.

THE CCP'S IDEOLOGICAL VARIATION

Marxism–Leninism has been consistently the official ideology of the CCP since its birth in 1921. To the CCP, Marxism–Leninism provides a vision of the contradictions in capitalist society and of the inevitability of a future socialist and communist societies (*People's Daily* 2012). In practice, however, the CCP has developed its own ideologies over the years to cope with imminent challenges in different eras. Based on China's unique national conditions the CCP has developed the 'Mao Zedong Thought', 'Deng Xiaoping Theory', 'Three Represents', the 'Concept of Scientific Development' and the 'China Dream' as its new ideologies in addition to Marxism. Such ideological evolution, which has proved crucial for CCP to seize and remain in power, is closely linked to the power succession of the CCP itself.

In the CCP's history, ideological variation has been an important factor in handling power succession for a number of reasons. First of all, there are traditional factors. To be proficient at letters was a necessary virtue for good Chinese emperors in the past. This heritage continued even after the CCP came to power in 1949, and it was believed that Mao becoming the CCP's most powerful figure was partially attributed to his ability to theorize. Mao himself emphasized that the CCP's major leaders have to be the Party's ideological and theoretical authority. Second, with the passing of the strongmen such as Mao Zedong and Deng Xiaoping, the young generation of leaders has to turn to non-personal factors, such as organization and ideology, to elicit political support from the Party and society as well. The political legitimacy of the old generation of leaders was justified by their revolutionary experience and their networking. However, even for the older generation, ideology was important. In the pre-reform era, ideology was often used to justify and to preserve the status quo, or it was utilized to transcend and transform the status quo. This role of ideology has become even more important in the post-Deng era. Third, ideology can be used to elicit Party cadres and government officials to identify with the top leadership, orient their behaviour, and prevent their deviation from the leadership's guidelines. This is also true of the pre-reform era. These functions of ideology have declined in the post-Deng era. For the top leader, ideology is to test whether Party cadres and governmental officials are loyal to the leader, since when a given ideational identity is established, the top leader has a chance to mobilize the Party machinery, not only to propagate it but also to elicit loyalty to it – an embodiment of the leader.

Owing to these unique functions, ideological evolution has always been given the highest priority by the Party leadership and by the top leader himself, especially during periods of power succession. For example, Deng Xiaoping restructured the communist ideology and transformed the Party from a revolutionary and radical one into a reform-oriented and revisionist one. By initiating the first 'liberation of thought' campaign after he came to power in the late 1970s, Deng established a non-Maoist reform ideology and provided ideological legitimacy for his own reform agenda. At the Thirteenth Party Congress in 1987, Zhao Ziyang proposed the theory of the so-called 'primary stage of socialism' in an attempt to provide a new ideological base for China's economic development. Meanwhile, Zhao also made efforts to bring in 'political reform' as an important part of his agenda. Zhao failed, however. Despite the popularity of his political reform agenda among social groups, especially intellectuals,

Zhao was not able to elicit strong political support from elders and entrenched bureaucrats. The year 1992 was a turning point in terms of changes in the functions of ideational identity. During the Fourteenth Party Congress that year, following Deng's call for a second 'liberation of thought', Jiang Zemin made the theory of a 'socialist market economy' the core of the CCP ideology. The Deng identity was thus firmly established.

From then on, Jiang began to develop his own ideology. Jiang made great efforts in initiating a campaign of talking about politics in 1996–97, and another campaign of talking about politics, virtue and political learning in 1998–99. However, to his surprise, both campaigns got a cool reception from various levels of Party organizations and governments. Jiang thus had to search for another ideational identity. In 2000, Jiang raised a new concept of the 'Three Represents'. According to this concept, the CCP represents the most advanced production mode, the most advanced culture and the interests of the majority of the people. Over the following two years, Jiang overwhelmingly focused on establishing the 'Three Represents' as his ideational identity. In terms of power succession, this identity became the most important factor in deciding who would be recruited into the new leadership. At the Sixteenth Party Congress in 2002, the 'Three Represents' theory was added into the Party Constitution. The Preamble of the Party Constitution was also changed to reflect the CCP as the vanguard not only of the working class, but also of the Chinese nation and Chinese people. This was a significant move by the Party to distance itself from any distinct social class and to move towards a political entity that would represent and coordinate the interests of various social classes.

While later Hu Jintao, on the one hand, had to be loyal to Jiang's ideational identity, on the other hand he has also had to search for his own. Hu first raised the concept of a 'harmonious society' at the Fourth Plenum of the Sixteenth Party Congress in 2004. The concept is an extension of Hu's 'pro-people' personal leadership style. At its core, it calls for a drastic reorientation from the development-first strategies implemented by Deng and Jiang, and for a return to people-centred policies aimed at addressing the mounting social problems that China faces today.

Earlier, Deng operated under the principle of 'get rich first'. The state of the poor became a secondary priority in Deng's plans, embodied by the slogan, 'To get rich is glorious'. Then Jiang pushed Deng's directives to an extreme, as the Chinese state evolved to become what the scholarly community called a 'developmental state': a state that plays a key role in pushing economic development. It was under Jiang that gross domestic product (GDP) growth became the single most important performance indicator for local government officials, when capitalists were invited into the CCP membership and when private properties were granted constitutional protection.

But after more than a decade of the ruthless, single-minded pursuit of GDP growth, the Chinese leadership is finding it necessary to step back from its previous mode of economic development. Undesirable consequences, like income disparities and environmental degradation, are today affecting not only economic growth itself, but also social stability. Hu began to turn the wheels of China's economic growth in a different direction when he first rose to power. Hu was, however, aware that the whole idea of a 'harmonious society' was grounded in China's continuing push for economic development. The emphasis was now on the sustainability of development. Here another of Hu's concepts, the so-called 'Scientific Development', came in. This concept was, in essence, to 'strike a balance' in China's various policies, and raised the importance of social justice in the pursuit of China's long-term development, in terms of more even distribution between different regions and different social groups, of economic, legal and political rights. The 'Scientific Development' became the theme of the Seventeenth Party Congress in 2007. The Congress passed a resolution on the revision of the Party Constitution and incorporated the 'scientific outlook of development' into the core guiding principles for the CCP. The resolution also referred to the construction of a 'socialist harmonious society' as an element of the Party's strategic goal in the Party Constitution. According to the revised Party Constitution, the CCP's goal is to 'turn China into a well-off, democratic, civilized and harmonious country with socialist modernization'. While these policy articulations had been discussed at length in the past, their formal inclusion in the Party Constitution enshrined them and served to elevate the theoretical stature of their author and sponsor Hu Jintao to the ranks of the Party's pantheon of greats. Meanwhile, Hu has also made even greater efforts to refine the CCP. While Jiang Zemin opened the Party to newly rising social groups, Hu has gone one step further and wants the Party to represent the interests of all people. With this Hu presented a similar line to Sun Yat-sen. Sun's political goal was, 'Everything under Heaven belongs to all', meaning that politics was for the common interest.

For many years after he took over power from Jiang in 2002, Hu placed much emphasis on 'to build the Party for all', meaning that the CCP does not have its own interests – it is for the interests of all people (*People's Daily* 2008). Hu's ideational identity was thus firmly established. Of course, like the 'Three Represents' theory, the 'Scientific Development' concept was also a political test for Party cadres and government officials to see their loyalty to Hu and his policy. At the Seventeenth Party Congress, Hu successfully gained the upper hand over his political rivals through engineering the promotion of some of his Youth League colleagues into the Political Bureau and other important positions. The line-up of the future leadership was thus arranged.

The 'China Dream' has become a buzzword in the CCP since Xi Jinping replaced Hu Jintao as General Secretary at the Eightenth Party Congress in 2012. Xi is not the first person to propose a 'China Dream'. As William Callahan has pointed out, the mainland's foreign-policy experts, economists, dissidents and artists had been engaged in an active and public debate on the different versions of the 'China Dream' for years (Callahan 2013). Among all these visions that emphasize different aspirations in the eyes of different social groups, the part that Xi wanted to emphasize has been interpreted by the Party's theoretical journal *Seeking Truth* (*Qiushi*) as national rejuvenation, state prosperity and collective pride and happiness (*Qiushi* 2013). As a continuation of China's goals of being wealthy and strong since the national humiliations of the nineteenth century, Xi's vision of 'China Dream' definitely matters much in the country's strategic planning, but in the context of economic growth slowdown, Xi's slogan looks as if it is designed chiefly to serve as a new source of legitimacy for the Communist Party through appealing to the public emotions associated with painful memories of historical suffering at the hands of colonial powers. Different from his predecessors' stodgy ideologies, like Jiang Zemin's 'Three Represents' or Hu Jintao's 'Scientific Development', Xi's 'China Dream' contains strong nationalistic aspirations for a glorious international status and strengthened global influence in world affairs, easy to trigger resonance from the masses. Xi's 'China Dream', in contrast to its American namesake, is about something more than middle-class material comfort (*The Economist* 2013b). Xi's emphasis on national rejuvenation suggests a link between his 'China Dream' doctrine and a grand strategy of being a global power.

4. The central government
Yan Xu and Dali L. Yang

Whereas China is ruled by the Chinese Communist Party (CCP), it is the central government, or the State Council, that implements most Party policies, deals with the daunting task of running the day-to-day business of the gigantic Chinese state and, on many occasions, represents the country in its relations with the outside world. The government bureaucracy is arguably the most visible part of China's political system and the cornerstone of the CCP's rule.

This chapter will first review the history and evolution of the central government since 1949, when Mao Zedong proudly pronounced the birth of the People's Republic of China. It will then delineate the central government's current structure and policy-making processes. This will be followed by discussion of the central government's complicated relationship with the Party. The chapter then focuses on China's efforts to streamline the central government's structure and rationalize its administration.

HISTORY AND EVOLUTION

Prior to defeating the Guomindang (GMD), the CCP had formed several local regimes and gained valuable experiences for establishing a national government in 1949. These regimes varied in terms of the name of the institutions and the inclusion of social classes, but they all imitated the Soviet system by having a People's Congress which nominally possessed the highest power. As Mao Zedong and his comrades prepared for the inauguration of the new government, they frequently consulted Soviet leader Joseph Stalin and were heavily influenced by his suggestions, one of which was to establish a coalition government in order to consolidate power (Li 2001). In September 1949, the CCP convened the Chinese People's Political Consultative Conference (CPPCC),[1] which included a large portion of non-CCP delegates, to discuss the establishment of a new governance system. The conference approved the Common Programme, essentially an interim constitution, and the Organic Law of the Central People's Government, based upon which the new government was established. According to the Common Programme, the highest state power would reside in the National People's Congress (NPC), which would elect the Central People's Government Committee, the highest organ that executes state power. The Common Programme also stipulated that prior to the election of an NPC, the plenary session of the CPPCC would serve in the NPC's place. However, a CPPCC plenary meeting was not convened again until 1954, which means that in practice the Central People's Government Committee, with Mao Zedong as its chairman, effectively held highest state power between 1949 and 1954.

The Central People's Government Committee was comprised of one Chairman, six Vice Chairmen and 56 committee members and encompassed four institutions: the Government Administrative Council (GAC), the People's Revolutionary Military

Commission, the Supreme People's Court and the Supreme People's Procuratorate. The GAC, the predecessor of the State Council, functioned as the highest administrative organ. It consisted of a Premier, four Vice Premiers and 15 administrative councillors and included four commissions and 30 ministries (Common Programme n.d.). Following Stalin's advice, Mao Zedong invited a large number of non-CCP figures to join the central government leadership, including three of the six Vice Chairmen, two of the four Vice Premiers, and 14 of the 34 ministers (Bo Yibo 1991). As these 'democratic parties' had fewer than 20000 members nationwide compared with the CCP's 4.48 million (Zheng, S. 1997: 41–42) the proportion of non-CCP members was quite significant. However, Mao Zedong and Zhou Enlai held the two most important positions, the Chairmanship and the Premiership, and the CCP maintained firm control of the government. The CCP also formed Party committees and Party groups in every government agency to ensure Party leadership. Finally, some government agencies were simultaneously Party institutions. For example, the CCP's Finance and Economic Commission headed by Chen Yun was set up prior to the establishment of the central government as the Party's core institution for leading economic work. In the new regime, it functioned concurrently as one of the four commissions under the Government Administrative Council, supervised the work of 16 government ministries and reported to both the central government and the Party central leadership.

Some adjustments of the government structure soon followed. One of the most important was the establishment of the State Planning Commission (SPC) in 1952. The SPC was founded with the help of Soviet advisors and charged with the responsibilities of drafting and implementing the Five-Year Plans, the first of which was introduced in 1953. Partly to limit Zhou Enlai's power, Mao Zedong put the SPC directly under the Central People's Government Committee – that is, independent of the Government Administrative Council – and appointed Gao Gang, the up-and-coming leader of the northeast region, as its first director. Eight industrial ministries directly reported to the SPC, nicknamed the 'Economic Cabinet', leaving the GAC's power substantially reduced. The SPC, whose successor today is named the National Development and Reform Commission, was later downgraded to a subordinate unit of the State Council, but it remains one of the most powerful ministerial-ranked government entities.

In September 1954, the first National People's Congress was convened in Beijing and a formal constitution was approved. The 1954 Constitution was modelled on the 1936 Soviet Constitution in terms of the state organization structure and citizen's rights and duties (Teiwes 1987) and it named the NPC as the highest organ of state power. The NPC had the authority to amend the constitution and enact laws, elect the President and Vice Presidents (previously translated as Chairman and Vice Chairmen), approve the choice of the Premier of the State Council upon nomination by the President, and of the President of the Supreme People's Court and the Chief Procurator of the Supreme People's Procuratorate. The President would be the head of state and concurrently Chairman of the National Defence Committee. The State Council, led by the Premier, would function as the highest administrative body, and become synonymous with central government. In theory, the State Council, as well as the President, the Supreme People's Court and the Supreme People's Procuratorate, were all responsible and accountable to the NPC (Constitution 1954).

The new structure diverged from the previous arrangement in the sense that it separated legislative and executive powers, which had been combined within the Central People's Government Committee, and elevated the State Council to be the highest executive organ. On paper, the new arrangement to some extent resembled the parliamentary system in Western democracies. The NPC was the equivalent of parliament, which holds legislative authorities, decides on the composition and supervises the work of the executive branch. The State Council is essentially China's cabinet, with its premier as the head of government. In practice, the State Council possessed much more real power than the NPC, especially with the inclusion of the SPC and the abolition of the six regional administrative committees, which had been the highest level of local government. The Presidency (State Chairmanship) became a more or less ceremonial position. In fact, Mao Zedong later relinquished the Presidency to Liu Shaoqi so that he could rid himself of the formalities and duties associated with that position.

Yet Mao had no intention of building a genuine coalition government. By controlling the election of NPC delegates, the CCP kept a tight grip on personnel and policy. After 1954, the CCP took control of most top posts in the new state bureaucracy, including the Presidency, the NPC Chairmanship, the Premiership and all Vice Premierships. Non-CCP members were largely sidelined, often given ceremonial positions on the NPC or the CPPCC. Their influence over policy would be further reduced by rounds of political campaigns and purges to come.

In spite of years of political turmoil, the basic state structure established in 1954 and the key political institutions, the NPC and the State Council, have been preserved until today. However, the State Council's composition and its status in the political system were often in flux, and the number of its ministries and agencies has varied over time. In 1956, the Party centre decided to decentralize some economic decision-making power to local governments and as a result the State Council cut off 21 agencies, most of which were related to economic administration (Liu Guoguang et al. 1998: 78–81). The Great Leap Forward, which started in 1958, in particular saw the rising influence of the CCP Secretariat and provincial party committees in economic work and the relative decline of the central government bureaucracy. When this ambitious programme resulted in massive famine, the central government recentralized decision-making power. A number of ministries were re-established or added and by 1965 the State Council had almost the same number of agencies as in 1956.

During the Cultural Revolution, most formal party and government institutions were paralyzed. Struggles against the leadership took place in many ministries and in one extreme case the Minister of Coal Industry was beaten to death by Red Guards (Harding 1991). With normal working procedures disrupted, Zhou Enlai, who was also under pressure from the radicals, had to form a special group to keep the State Council functioning as much as possible (Cheng Zhensheng 2002). When the political chaos finally subsided in 1969, Mao initiated another round of decentralization and transferred a large number of central-managed enterprises to local governments. More than half of State Council ministries were also trimmed. Of the remaining 32 ministries, 13 were in effect controlled by either the military or the radicals, leaving the State Council with only 19 ministries to command (Liu Guoguang et al. 1998: 106–108). Much of the paralysis persisted till Mao and Zhou died in 1976 and a new generation of leaders began to emerge.

As Deng Xiaoping re-emerged and gained influence, he and his colleagues strived to put the country back on track, first in the areas of science, technology and education, then in other sectors of social economic development (Vogel 2011). The central government apparatus quickly recovered much of the lost ground and rapidly expanded. At its peak, the State Council was comprised of 100 different types of organs in 1981. In the following year, China conducted a major overhaul of the state machinery including the enactment of a new constitution. In response to complaints of bloatedness and inefficiency, the central government was restructured and the number of organs went down to 61. Since then, Chinese leaders have made repeated efforts to streamline and rationalize the central government (Yang, Dali 2004). This will be the subject of a later section of this chapter.

COMPOSITION, FUNCTION AND POLICY-MAKING PROCESS

At present, the State Council consists of a Premier, four Vice Premiers, five State Councillors, 24 Ministers and Commissioners, an Auditor General and a Secretary General. The Premier assumes overall responsibility for the work of the State Council. The current Premier is Li Keqiang, who majored in law and economics at Peking University and had a head start in the leadership of the Communist Youth League, a cradle for top CCP leaders. He is assisted by four Vice-Premiers (Zhang Gaoli, Liu Yandong, Wang Yang and Ma Kai) and five State Councillors (Yang Jing, Chang Wanquan, Yang Jiechi, Guo Shengkun and Wang Yong), each of whom oversees a particular aspect of government work and the relevant ministries and commissions. For example, Vice Premier Zhang Gaoli is in charge of the macroeconomy and his direct reports include the National Development and Reform Commission, the Ministry of Finance and the Ministry of Land and Resources; Vice Premier Liu Yandong has culture, education, science, sports and health in her portfolio; State Councillor Yang Jiechi, a former Foreign Minister, oversees foreign relations and Hong Kong, Macau, Taiwan and overseas Chinese affairs. With the Vice Premiers and the State Councillors intermediating between the Premier and government ministries, China's cabinet is larger in size and more complicated than those of the US and the UK. Hence the Chinese counterparts to the American Secretary of State and Secretary of Treasury in the US–China Strategic and Economic Dialogue are the Vice Premier and the State Councillor overseeing trade and foreign affairs, rather than the foreign affairs and commerce ministers. Table 4.1 shows China's Premiers and Vice Premiers since 1949.

The State Council comprises a General Office and about 60 ministries, commissions, administrations and institutions. The General Office is responsible for supporting State Council leaders, preparing for meetings, drafting and promulgating official documents. It is headed by a Secretary General, with the rank of State Councillor. There are also about ten Deputy Secretary Generals who assist the Premiers and Vice Premiers. As of 2013, the State Council is composed of 25 ministries and commissions, one special organization, 16 organizations directly under the State Council, four administrative offices, and 13 institutions. Virtually all these different categories carry the ministerial rank but only the heads of the 25 ministries and commissions are members of the cabinet, whose appointments require NPC ratification. The State Council also has about 30 deliberation and coordination organs that are set up for special purposes such as poverty alleviation and food safety. Most of these organs are chaired by a leading member of the State

80 *Handbook of the politics of China*

Table 4.1 China's Premiers and Vice Premiers since 1949

Premier	Vice Premiers
Zhou Enlai (1949–76)	Dong Biwu, Chen Yun, Guo Moruo, Huang Yanpei, Deng Xiaoping, Lin Biao, Peng Dehuai, Deng Zihui, He Long, Chen Yi, Ulanhu, Li Fuchun, Li Xiannian, Nie Rongzhen, Bo Yibo, Tan Zhenlin, Lu Dingyi, Luo Ruiqing, Xi Zhongxun, Ke Qingshi, Tao Zhu, Xie Fuzhi, Zhang Chunqiao, Chen Xilian, Ji Dengkui, Hua Guofeng, Chen Yonggui, Wu Guixian, Wang Zhen, Yu Qiuli, Gu Mu, Sun Jian
Hua Guofeng (1976–80)	Chen Yun, Deng Xiaoping, Li Xiannian, Bo Yibo, Chen Xilian, Ji Dengkui, Chen Yonggui, Wu Guixian, Wang Zhen, Yu Qiuli, Gu Mu, Sun Jian, Xu Xiangqian, Geng Biao, Fang Yi, Kang Shi'en, Chen Muhua, Wang Renzhong, Yao Yilin, Ji Pengfei, Zhao Ziyang
Zhao Ziyang (1980–87)	Bo Yibo, Yu Qiuli, Gu Mu, Geng Biao, Fang Yi, Kang Shi'en, Chen Muhua, Yao Yilin, Ji Pengfei, Wan Li, Yang Jingren, Zhang Aiping, Huang Hua, Li Peng, Tian Jiyun, Qiao Shi
Li Peng (1987–98)	Yao Yilin, Tian Jiyun, Wu Xueqian, Zou Jiahua, Zhu Rongji, Qian Qichen, Li Lanqing
Zhu Rongji (1998–2003)	Li Lanqing, Qian Qichen, Wu Bangguo, Wen Jiabao
Wen Jiabao (2003–13)	Huang Ju, Wu Yi, Zeng Peiyan, Hui Liangyu, Li Keqiang, Zhang Dejiang, Wang Qishan
Li Keqiang (2013–)	Zhang Gaoli, Liu Yandong, Wang Yang, Ma Kai

Council and serve as ad hoc platforms for coordination among related ministries and institutions.[2] Table 4.2 compares the State Council ministries and commissions in 1988, 1998 and 2013.

Each ministry is comprised of various departments or bureaus, which in turn consist of divisions and offices. For central government agencies which enjoy full ministerial status, the department or bureau heads have the same rank as the Mayor of a prefecture, and the division or office heads the rank of a county chief. Each ministry also controls various kinds of organizations including research centres, academies, publishing houses and associations, such as the China Institute of International Studies (under the Ministry of Foreign Affairs) and the Academy of Macroeconomic Research (of the National Development and Reform Commission, NDRC). Figure 4.1 summarizes the organizational structure of Chinese government.

As the highest executive organ of the state, the State Council is endowed with many executive powers, which include adopting administrative measures, enacting administrative rules and regulations, and issuing decisions and orders; submitting legislative proposals to the NPC; drafting and implementing the five-year plans and the unified national budget. Its authorities cover almost anything except Party and military affairs, but its primary responsibility concerns economic and social development. It is important to note that certain ministries that appear on the State Council's organization chart, such as the Ministry of National Defence and the Ministry of Supervision, are in fact not under the control of the State Council or the Premier.

Table 4.2 State Council ministries and commissions

1988	1998	2013
Ministry of Foreign Affairs	Ministry of Foreign Affairs	Ministry of Foreign Affairs
Ministry of National Defence	Ministry of National Defence	Ministry of National Defence
State Planning Commission	State Development and Planning Commission	National Development and Reform Commission
State Commission for Restructuring the Economic Systems	State Economic and Trade Commission	Ministry of Education
State Education Commission	Ministry of Education	Ministry of Science and Technology
State Science and Technology Commission	Ministry of Science and Technology	Industry and Information Technology
Commission for Science, Technology and Industry for National Defence	Commission for Science, Technology and Industry for National Defence	State Ethic Affairs Commission
State Ethic Affairs Commission	State Ethic Affairs Commission	Ministry of Public Security
Ministry of Public Security	Ministry of Public Security	Ministry of State Security
Ministry of State Security	Ministry of State Security	Ministry of Supervision
Ministry of Supervision	Ministry of Supervision	Ministry of Civil Affairs
Ministry of Civil Affairs	Ministry of Civil Affairs	Ministry of Justice
Ministry of Justice	Ministry of Justice	Ministry of Finance
Ministry of Finance	Ministry of Finance	Ministry of Human Resources and Social Security
Ministry of Personnel	Ministry of Personnel	Ministry of Land and Resources
Ministry of Labour	Ministry of Labor and Social Security	Ministry of Environmental Protection
Ministry of Geology and Mineral Resources	Ministry of Land and Resources	Ministry of Housing and Urban-Rural Development
Ministry of Construction	Ministry of Construction	Ministry of Transport
Ministry of Energy	Ministry of Railways	Ministry of Water Resources
Ministry of Railways	Ministry of Communications	Ministry of Agriculture
Ministry of Communications	Ministry of Information Industry	Ministry of Commerce
Ministry of Machine Building and Electronics Industry	Ministry of Water Resources	Ministry of Culture
Ministry of Aerospace Industry	Ministry of Agriculture	National Health and Family Planning Commission
Ministry of Metallurgical Industry	Ministry of Foreign Trade and Economic Cooperation	People's Bank of China
Ministry of Chemical Industry	Ministry of Culture	National Audit Office
Ministry of Light Industry	Ministry of Health	
Ministry of Textile Industry	State Family Planning Commission	
Ministry of Posts and Telecommunications	People's Bank of China	

82   *Handbook of the politics of China*

Table 4.2   (continued)

1988	1998	2013
Ministry of Water Resources Ministry of Agriculture Ministry of Forestry Ministry of Commerce Ministry of Foreign Economic Relations and Trade Ministry of Material Supplies Ministry of Culture Ministry of Radio, Film and Television Ministry of Health State Physical Culture and Sports Commission State Family Planning Commission People's Bank of China National Audit Office	National Audit Office	

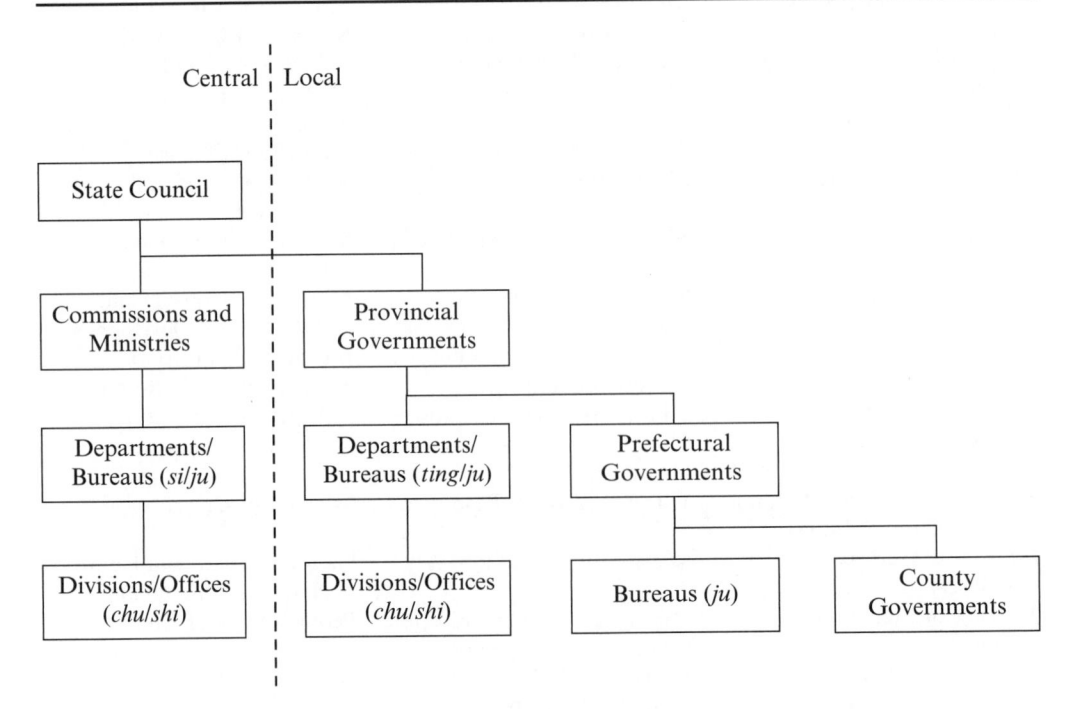

Figure 4.1   *Organizational structure of Chinese government*

The Premier convenes and chairs two types of regular meetings. The plenary meeting, attended by all members of the State Council, namely the Premiers, State Councillors, ministers and commissioners, only takes place about twice a year. It is held to discuss the Government Work Report to be presented to the annual NPC meetings in March or to ratify the appointment of the Chief Executives of the Hong Kong and Macau Special Administrative Regions. The State Council executive meetings are held much more frequently and are attended by the leading members of the State Council, namely the Premier, the Vice Premiers, the State Councillors and the Secretary General, plus heads of the relevant ministries, commissions and administrations. Premier Wen Jiabao, for example, convened 234 executive meetings between 2008 and 2013 that covered 611 topics ranging from improving school bus safety and promoting AIDS prevention to controlling housing prices and curbing air pollution. Many of the economic stimulus measures in response to the global financial crisis were also discussed and formulated in the executive meetings (Xinhua 2013b). These meetings also discuss, pass and amend regulations and rules, and national plans for specific policy areas such as forestry preservation and education reform. The plenary meetings and executive meetings are spelled out in the Organic Law of the State Council. Previously the State Council frequently held the premier's work meetings to discuss and deal with important issues, but this meeting type was abolished in 2004 as Wen Jiabao sought to make the State Council operate in accordance with the Organic Law (Guo Gaozhong 2004).

Policy-making in China usually involves discussion and coordination among multiple agencies and regions, and the need to balance competing interests. For example, China's exchange rate policy concerns not only the People's Bank of China (PBoC), the central bank, but also the Ministry of Commerce, the National Development and Reform Commission and research institutes under the State Council. Because agencies and regions represent different interests, negotiation and bargaining often take place at the State Council and other deliberation and coordination platforms such as central leading groups and work conferences. In order to reach a consensus over the Three Gorges Dam, for instance, the Ministry of Water Resources, the key proponent of the project, negotiated with other ministries and provinces and municipalities along the Yangtze River to win over support and reduce opposition (Lieberthal 2003). Such bargaining can be long and complex, especially when the parties involved possess vastly different views or the top leadership is divided over the issue, rendering the decision-making process complex and protracted (Lieberthal and Oksenberg 1988). Repeated efforts to rationalize the government have generally tended to combine agencies that differ in policy preferences so as to break policy gridlock.

In recent decades, Chinese leaders have put more emphasis on consensus in policy-making. If the ministries and local governments involved in the discussion can agree on a policy, the policy is often easily adopted; otherwise higher-level authorities need to step in and expend political capital to break the policy logjam, or the issue is tabled or dropped (Shirk 1993). To facilitate coordination in policy-making and implementation, the State Council has a variety of leading groups, inter-ministerial coordination groups and special committees.

While the State Council discusses and decides on major issues and policy directions, more specific decisions, such as whether to approve a city's subway project, license an insurance company or grant an Initial Public Offering, are made by relevant ministries or commissions. The National Development and Reform Commission, sometimes dubbed 'the little State Council', is the leading institution of macroeconomic policy formulation and is responsible for drafting annual and five-year plans. It also has the authority to allocate central fiscal construction funds and approve major infrastructure and industrial projects, foreign capital utilizing projects and overseas resource development projects, making the NDRC a favourite target for local government lobbying. When Guangdong's Zhanjiang city finally obtained approval for a major steel project in 2012 after many years of lobbying the NDRC, the city's Mayor was photographed giving a deep kiss to the approval letter and the photo captured the national imagination (*Xinkuaibao* 2012a). Indeed, the NDRC is so powerful that even a division head could enjoy enormous power over airport projects and plane procurement and cold-shoulder provincial Vice Governors, who are several levels superior in official rank (Liang Dongmei and Wang Heyan 2010). While the NDRC has joined efforts to reduce the number of government approvals, it has also gained new powers, including over anti-trust. Such powers may also provide opportunities for its officials to enrich themselves; in the anti-corruption crackdown launched by Xi Jinping and Wang Qishan, a long list of officials at the NDRC and the affiliated National Energy Administration were put under investigation or arrested (Gui Tiantian 2014). Some argue that ministries like NDRC have become vested interest groups themselves and therefore obstacles to further reform.

Since the reform and opening up, local experimentation has also become an important pathway for policy changes. Leaders in Beijing have allowed local governments to enjoy some latitude in finding locally generated solutions that can promote growth, and have adopted successful ones as national policies (Yang, Dali 1996; Heilmann 2008b). In other cases policies are deliberately tried out in restricted areas so that any possible adverse effect will be limited. One most notable example of experimentation is the flourishing of experimental zones all over the country, where local officials test various policies ranging from tax reduction to coordinated urbanization (Yang, Dali 1997). The newly established Shanghai Pilot Free Trade Zone, which will explore the transformation of government function, more openness to service and financial industries and the upgrading of trade development model, is an ambitious effort of this kind.

As the Chinese economy and society have diversified, national policies are no longer made exclusively behind closed doors, and more actors are now able to influence policy-making. Not only does the government seek advice and consultation from state-affiliated think tanks such as the Chinese Academy of Social Sciences and the State Council Development Research Centre, but non-state actors including academics, entrepreneurs and non-governmental organizations (NGOs) are also sometimes heard. Both Wen Jiabao and Li Keqiang have from time to time invited China's top economists and chief executive officers (CEOs) of large corporations, such as Alibaba's Jack Ma and Geely's Li Shufu, to Zhongnanhai to hear their opinions on the economy. The PBoC also invites renowned economics professors to sit on its monetary policy committee. In addition, firms and industry associations are increasingly capable of lobbying regulators to obtain favourable policies (Kennedy 2005). The flourishing media sector, enlivened by the internet, also enables NGOs and opinion leaders to champion their viewpoints and influence policy-making as policy entrepreneurs. There are also signs that government leaders are more sensitive, if not responsive, to public opinion, particularly in areas such as health and the environment (Wang Shaoguang 2008). The central government can no longer be viewed as a monolithic entity that dictates policy.

In theory, the State Council is responsible and accountable to the NPC, which votes on the appointment of key members of the State Council, and the annual Government Work Report and the budget. Since the elections are not competitive, and work reports and budgets are often approved with few objections, the NPC is often considered as a 'rubber stamp' parliament. In recent years, the NPC has obtained more capacity for lawmaking and has begun to command more respect from the State Council and its constituent agencies (Dowdle 1997).

RELATIONS WITH THE COMMUNIST PARTY

Ultimately the State Council still answers to the CCP leadership, which ensures the CCP's policy lines are followed by the bureaucracy. In the 1980s, as part of an evolving reform programme, some efforts were made to separate the work of Party and government, including gradual abolishment of Party groups in government bodies. The separation of Party and government was formally endorsed by the Thirteenth Party Congress in 1987, but with the ouster of General Secretary Zhao Ziyang, a leading champion of the reform, this initiative was aborted in the aftermath of the 1989 Tiananmen Crisis. Subsequent leaders have shown no sign of loosening the Party's control.

Several methods are employed to maintain the Party's leadership over the central government bureaucracy. First, the Party controls the appointments of leading positions in the State Council through the *nomenklatura* system. This makes sure that the most important positions in the government are occupied by loyal Party members (Chan 2004). As of 2014, only one member of the State Council, the Minister of Science and Technology Wan Gang, is not a CCP member. In fact the Premiers and Vice Premiers are usually themselves party leaders. It is noteworthy that while there were instances where the President, the Chairman of the NPC, the Central Military Commission (CMC) or the CPPCC was not a member of the Politburo Standing Committee (PBSC), the premiership has always been held by a PBSC member since 1949. The current Premier, Li Keqiang, ranks second on the Politburo Standing Committee while his predecessor, Wen Jiabao, officially ranked third. In addition, the Vice Premiers are usually members of the Politburo, and in recent years the first-ranking Vice Premier is also a member of the PBSC. Below the premiers, the State Councillors, the ministers and provincial leaders are all on the central *nomenklatura*, which means that their appointments need to be ratified by the Politburo (Zhao Lei 2006). In other words, the Premier, despite being the head of the State Council, is not able to choose his own cabinet. While the competency of candidates is certainly an important criterion, loyalty to the Party and patronage of top leaders are at least as important. That the Premier might not always be able to command the ministries was most obvious in much of the 1980s, when Zhao Ziyang was Premier. Zhao was not able to command the leading institution of economic work, that is, the State Planning Commission, whose ministers Yao Yilin and Song Ping were loyal to Chen Yun. Nor could he replace the SPC's leaders. Therefore he had to rely on other agencies and think tanks to promote economic reforms (Fewsmith 1996).

The second method of control is to set up parallel Party organizations in government bodies. In the central government, 'Party groups' are established in both the State Council and its subordinate organs. This practice dates back to the very beginning of the People's Republic, when many officials were not CCP members, and is analogous to the dual leadership that enshrined Party leadership in the military. While the State Council adopts an 'administrative chief executive responsibility system' according to which ministers and directors are responsible for the work of their units, major decisions are often made by the Party groups that are usually composed of the leading members of the government unit such as the Minister and Vice Ministers. The Party groups play core leadership roles especially in intra-unit party affairs, personnel management and formulating other key decisions. For example, the 2013 central government institutional reform plan was reviewed by the State Council's Party group before it was submitted to the CCP Politburo for discussion (Xinhua 2013c). The composition of a Party group is decided by the Party organization that approves its establishment. In a handful of ministries which exercise vertical leadership over all of their subordinate units or directly oversees large numbers of such units, such as the Ministries of Foreign Affairs, Public Security, State Security, and the People's Bank of China, Party committees rather than Party groups are established. The existence of Party groups and committees does not necessarily conflict with the administrative chief executive responsibility system, because in most cases the minister is concurrently secretary of the Party group or committee. As of March 2015, the only two exceptions are the Ministry of Foreign Affairs, and the Ministry of Science and Technology, whose current minister is not a CCP member. In both cases, the minister ranks above the secretary of the Party group, suggesting a more prominent role of the administrative chief executive.[3]

Thirdly, the CCP Central Committee has Party organs that often straddle Party and government, and as a result ministries usually have to answer to the State Council as well as to several party organs. For example, the powerful Central Political and Legal Affairs Commission is the paramount institution overseeing public security, armed police, state security as well as the courts, the procuratorates and the prison systems. The Ministries of Public Security, State Security and Justice are concurrently members of the Commission and are under the leadership of the Commission's secretary, who has no official position in the government. Similarly, the Party's Central Commission for Guiding Cultural and Ethical Progress guides the work of a wide range of government agencies related to propaganda, education, culture, sports and so on. Some of the central government bodies even have the same staff and office with a party organ; the so-called 'one institution with two nameplates'. For instance, the Ministry of Supervision, the State Council's Taiwan Affairs Office and Information Office share nameplates with the Party's Central Discipline Inspection Commission (CDIC), Taiwan Work Office and International Communication Office, respectively. Naturally, these units are not solely responsible to the Premier or the State Council.

The Party organ that covers the State Council's principal responsibility for economic growth and that draws the most attention is the Central Leading Group for Finance and Economic Affairs. It is comprised of the top economic policy-makers in the central government, the Premier, the Vice Premiers, the NDRC Commissioner, the Finance Minister, the Governor of the central bank, and so on, but is in fact a party organ and is responsible to the Politburo, which has the final say over economic policies. The leading group is usually chaired by the Premier, normally the second- or third-ranking member of the PBSC, but occasionally it is led by the Party's General Secretary personally (for example, Zhao Ziyang between 1987 and 1989, and Xi Jinping since 2012), enabling the Party chief to play a direct role in setting the economic agenda. The leading group also maintains a permanent office that conducts research, proposes policy options and prepares for the annual Central Economic Work Conference, an important meeting convened every December that brings together high-level central government officials and provincial leaders to analyse the economic performance of the year and sets policy guidelines for the next year.

The existence of various overarching Party organs above the government offices means that at times central government ministries are merely executors of policies, rather than independent decision-makers. It is no secret, for instance, that China's Foreign Ministry has limited autonomy because major decisions are made by the CCP's Central Leading Group for Foreign Affairs, which is usually chaired by the CCP's General Secretary. The Foreign Minister, himself a member of the leading group, can provide information and suggestions, but he needs to persuade top party leaders and other officials representing different institutions or groups, such as the military, the trade sector and the Party's International Liaison Department, in order to turn the ministry's views into actual policies. This could be quite difficult given that the Foreign Minister has had no membership on the Politburo since 2002, and is far outnumbered on the Central Committee by the military.

Finally, the Party reserves the power to determine the fate of government officials who violate discipline or do not follow Party lines closely. When an official makes mistakes, the Party's Discipline Inspection Commission (CDIC), rather than the police or the prosecutors, is the first to step in (Manion 2004). Officials of the CDIC are able to question or detain officials without warrant and transfer them to the judiciary after the investigation is complete. For instance, the former Railway Minister Liu Zhijun was held by the CDIC for about a year and a half before he was handed to the prosecutors. Since the majority of leadership positions in the central government are held by Party members, the CDIC essentially acts as the government's discipline watchdog as well. In fact, the CDIC has a discipline inspection team in every organ of the central government. Previously these teams were under the dual leadership of CDIC and the host agency. More recently there have been efforts to make these teams more independent of the host agency and more accountable to the CDIC (Yang, Dali 2004).

From time to time tensions have existed between the party's top-ranking leader (Chairman of the Central Committee before 1981, and General Secretary afterwards) and the Premier. The two positions are normally held separately by two leaders, except for two brief periods (Hua Guofeng from 1976 to 1980, and Zhao Ziyang in 1987). The fact that the formal powers of the two positions are not clearly defined implies a built-in rivalry between the two (Bachman 1992). While the Premier is legally speaking the principal of government affairs and would prefer running the State Council with more autonomy, the party's top leader, with a wider mandate, is also entitled to direct government affairs. Historically, top-ranking party leaders have often intervened when they were at odds with the Premier over economic policies, to make sure that their policy preferences would be followed. Before 1976, Mao Zedong frequently expressed his dissatisfaction with Premier Zhou Enlai, whose prudence hampered the ambitious and sometimes radical policies Mao championed. In 1958, Mao was so unhappy with Zhou Enlai and his colleagues' 'opposition to rash advance' that he substantially weakened the State Council's authority and shifted much of the decision-making to the Secretariat, then headed by Deng Xiaoping. In the early reform period, the reform-minded Hu Yaobang and Zhao Ziyang were well known for their differences. While Hu Yaobang favoured more aggressive economic policies and higher growth targets, Zhao Ziyang as Premier was worried about overheating and called for caution. At one point, Hu Yaobang would make insinuating comments about the State Council's work on inspection trips, making his disagreement with Zhao Ziyang widely known. The conflict eventually had to be settled by the personal intervention of Deng Xiaoping, who agreed with Zhao and confirmed the Premier's authority over the economy (Zhao Ziyang 2009). When Zhao Ziyang himself became General Secretary, he would find the new Premier Li Peng, with whom he had fundamental differences, difficult to work with as well.

From the 1990s onwards there seems to have been a clearer boundary of the powers between the Party General Secretary and the Premier. During his second term as General Secretary, Jiang Zemin gave Zhu Rongji much leeway in running the economy and supported Zhu's efforts to reform the state-owned enterprises (SOEs) and negotiate China's entrance into the World Trade Organization, but Zhu's influence beyond the economy was curbed over time. When Hu Jintao was General Secretary, he essentially left Premier Wen Jiabao alone. Yet the ascendence of Xi Jinping since late 2012 has seen Xi assume leadership of the Comprehensive Reform Leading Group and the Central Leading Group for Financial and Economic Affairs, and thus eclipse the role of Premier Li Keqiang in economic governance. Others believe that Xi's dominance is a necessity because only the General Secretary has the breadth of authority to lead a comprehensive reform programme (Miller 2014).

While the CCP maintains firm control of the government, it leaves much of the daily work to the bureaucrats in a sort of 'delegation relationship' (Shirk 1993). The party sets the tone, or the general direction for policies, and ministries and administrations 'play the music'. The CCP leadership has exhibited no intention of giving up Party leadership. Rather, it has been focusing on enhancing governance, including improving government efficiency and building a regulatory state.

INSTITUTIONAL STREAMLINING AND ADMINISTRATIVE RATIONALIZATION IN THE POST-MAO ERA

Mao Zedong is famous for his dissatisfaction with both market and bureaucracy that is based on legal-rational principles (Whyte 1989). In the aftermath of the Cultural Revolution, post-Mao leaders have promoted market-oriented reforms and sought institutional reform to create an efficient albeit still powerful state that is in line with a modern economy. Starting from 1982, almost every NPC has passed a government restructuring programme (1988, 1993, 1998, 2003, 2008 and 2013, respectively). Whereas in the earlier phase these initiatives focused on downsizing and improving efficiency, since 1998 the emphasis has shifted to transforming functions and rationalizing administration.

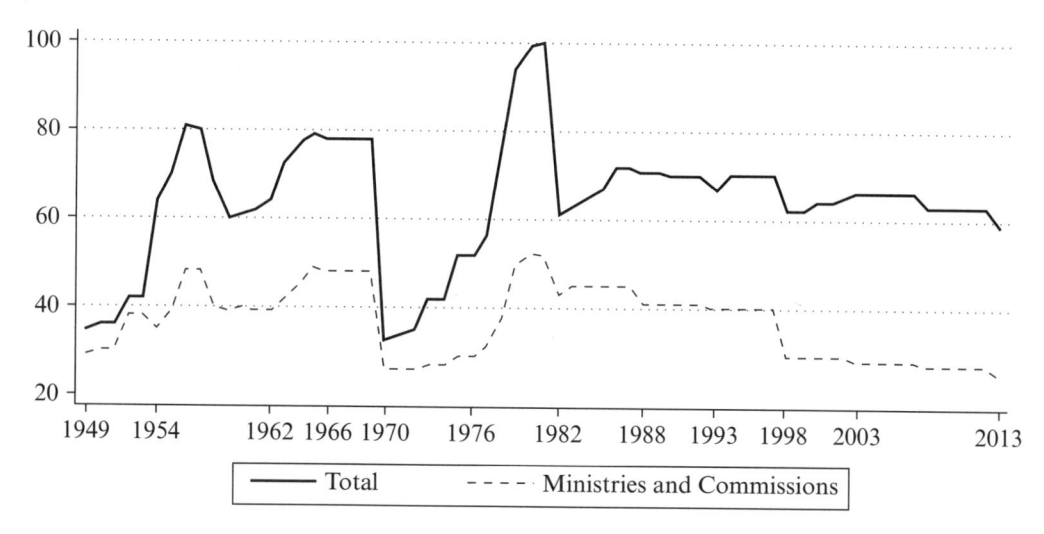

Figure 4.2 The number of State Council subordinate agencies, 1949–2013

Reform in the 1980s

In the immediate post-Mao years, the Chinese leadership took back some of the authority that had been delegated to lower levels and restored institutions that had been abolished, sidelined or merged during the chaotic Cultural Revolution. To support the opening-up policy, it also set up the Commission on Import and Export Affairs and the Commission on Foreign Investment. Between 1977 and 1981, 48 organs were restored or established and the total number of State Council organs ballooned to 100, the peak since 1949 (Luo Gan 1998; see Figure 4.2). The Chinese leadership soon realized the need to downsize. In the words of then Premier Zhao Ziyang, 'At present, the problems of overstaffing institutions, overlapping and ambiguous responsibilities and low efficiency have reached an intolerable level' (Zhao 1982). The government downsizing initiated in 1982 cut the number of State Council organs to 61 and the total number of personnel from 51 000 to about 30 000. To centralize leadership over economic policy and reform, Zhao reduced the number of Vice Premiers from almost 20 to four, strengthened the SPC and the State Economic Commission, and created a new Commission for Economic Restructuring, which Zhao Ziyang led personally.

A major effort to institutionalize in the 1982 programme was the introduction of retirement and term limits. Most officials need to retire by 60 years old, and full ministers by 65. In addition, the Premier, the Vice Premiers and the State Councillors cannot hold the same position consecutively for more than two five-year terms. This marked the end of de facto life tenure of leadership posts and helped to rejuvenate the government bureaucracy, which had been populated by old cadres.

The 1988 government reform introduced the transformation of government functions as a key objective of reform. Following the adoption of the concept of building a socialist market economy by the 14th CCP Party Congress in 1992, the central government abolished several ministries that were at the core of the planned economy. Whereas some ministries including the Ministry of Petroleum Industry were turned into central government-owned SOEs such as the China National Petroleum Corporation (CNPC), the Ministries of Light Industry and of Textile Industry were turned into industry associations.

The 1998 Reform

By 1998, a year after the death of Deng Xiaoping, China's market reform had deepened to new levels and the leadership led by Jiang Zemin had consolidated their power, setting the stage for more substantial government reforms. The Asian financial crisis and alarming budget shortfalls gave a final push (Yang, Dali 2004). The urgency was clearly stated in the reform plan: 'Institutional reform is like a revolution. It's impossible that a reform doesn't meet resistance or risk. But reform is imperative. Without reform there's no way out' (State Council 1998). Led by Premier Zhu Rongji, the 1998 government reform slashed the number of ministries and commissions from 40 to 29 and cut the number of departments or bureaus by one-quarter, or more than 200. Nine industrial ministries were subsumed into the State Economic and Trade Commission (SETC), making the SETC as formidable an institution in the State Council as the State Development and Planning Commission (formerly the SPC). Zhu Rongji, who had previously headed the SETC, then known as the Economic and Trade Office, strengthened the SETC for strategic reasons. Just as Zhao Ziyang used the State Commission for Restructuring the Economic System to work around the SPC, the conservative stronghold, and to push forward his own reform agenda, Zhu Rongji used the SETC as his organizational power base to propel his SOE reform (Zheng 2004).

The 1998 reform also sought to streamline the bloated central bureaucracy through the 'Three Fixes'. The functions, organs and the number of personnel, or *bianzhi*, of each ministry were fixed so that they could not add new organs or increase staff at will (Brødsgaard 2002). The 'Three Fixes' are implemented by the State Commission for Public Sector Reform (SCPSR), a central Party organ established in 1991. The SCPSR is usually chaired by the Premier and includes the PBSC member in charge of Party affairs, the directors of the General Office and Central Organization Department of the CCP Central Committee, and the Secretary General of the State Council. It maintains a permanent office, the State Commission Office for Public Sector Reform (SCOPSR), that reviews and monitors the 'Three Fixes' of central Party and government agencies. Although Zhu Rongji did not become chair of the SCPSR until April 1998, he oversaw the institutional reform plan and personally took part in negotiations with each minister. Zhu Rongji's aggressive push for streamlining helped to cut the headcount on the central government *bianzhi* almost by half, from 32 300 to 16 700 (Xinhua 2013d). In practice many of the redundant staff were put in state-affiliated public institutions, and various departments often borrowed personnel from affiliated units to get their work done. Meanwhile, bureaucratic responsibilities, especially approvals, have undergone consolidation and rationalization; some have been abolished and others delegated.

To improve organization efficiency, the reform also transferred into one agency similar administrative authorities that had belonged to different units. A new Ministry of Land and Resources was established that took over responsibilities previously held by four institutions. Three agencies that dealt with exit–entry management under different ministries were merged into the State Administration of Exit–Entry Inspection and Quarantine, which would later be merged with the quality and technical supervision agency to form the ministerial-ranked General Administration of Quality Supervision, Inspection and Quarantine (AQSIQ).

Reform in the Twenty-First Century

Zhu Rongji's successors have continued the government rationalization agenda. In 2003, Wen Jiabao oversaw his first institutional reform, of which a key component was the restructuring of the management system of SOEs. After a complicated process of transition, the State-owned Assets Supervision and Administration Commission (SASAC) came into being. Local governments subsequently set up their own SASACs to management SOEs owned locally. At present, the State Council's SASAC oversees 113 central SOEs, most of which are national champions such as Sinopec, China Mobile and Air China.[4]

Another important change was the creation of the Ministry of Commerce (MOFCOM) and the elimination of the SETC. Before the reform, China's domestic commerce and foreign trade were under the SETC and the Minister of Foreign Trade and Economic Cooperation respectively, an arrangement that was increasingly at odds with China's deepening integration into the global economy. The new MOFCOM, formed by combining the two agencies, was empowered to govern domestic and foreign commerce as well as other aspects of the country's economic relations with the outside world, such as foreign direct investment (FDI), foreign aid and overseas investment. Apart from the parts that went to SASAC and MOFCOM, the remnant of the SETC was grouped into the State Development and Planning Commission (SDPC), now rebranded as the National Development and Reform Commission (NDRC).

The 2003 government reform also reorganized China's financial regulation system with the formation of the China Banking Regulatory Commission (CBRC). For a long time, the PBoC, China's central bank, had been in charge of both monetary policies and financial regulation. In order to allow the PBoC to focus on its most important task and strengthen supervision of the burgeoning financial industry, the regulatory functions of the securities and the insurance industries had already been peeled off from the PBoC in 1992 and 1998 to form two separate regulatory units, the China Securities Regulatory Commission and the China Insurance Regulatory Commission. The CBRC inherited most of its functions from the PBoC and the Central Financial Work Commission, a Party organ established in 1998 to arrest the breakdown of hierarchies in the financial industry and to restore central policy decisiveness (Heilmann 2005). Now, with the CBRC as the last piece of the puzzle, China had built a Glass–Steagall-style regulatory system and the central bank could focus its attention on the formulation and execution of monetary policies.

By 2003, China's ministries and commissions were streamlined to fewer than 30, but compared to other major countries, such as US (15), the UK (18), France (16), Germany (14) and Russia (17), the number was still large. In 2008, the State Council under Wen Jiabao started to explore the so-called 'super-ministries system' by further combining organs with similar functions. The Commission of Science, Technology and

Industry for National Defence (CoSTIND) was merged with the Ministry of Information Industry to form the new Ministry of Industry and Information Technology (MIIT), a powerful institution that regulates manufacturing and communication industries. CoSTIND's nuclear power administration portfolio was given to the newly established National Energy Administration (NEA), which would receive tutelage from the NDRC. The Ministry of Personnel and the Ministry of Labour and Social Securities was combined into the new Ministry of Human Resources and Social Securities. The Civil Aviation Administration of China (CAAC) was integrated into the new Ministry of Transport (MOT), which would also administer the State Post Bureau. With the increasing salience of environmental issues, the General Administration of Environmental Protection was upgraded to become the cabinet-level Ministry of Environmental Protection.

Efforts to create super-ministries were continued in 2013, after a new leadership under Xi Jinping and Li Keqiang came into office. The Ministry of Transport absorbed the administrative functions of the Ministry of Railways (MoR), which finally fell after its last highly entrepreneurial minister Liu Zhijun was caught in a corruption scandal, and following a deadly high-speed train crash in July 2011. As China began to relax its draconian population policy, the National Population and Family Planning Commission was merged with the Ministry of Health. Moreover, the General Administration of Press and Publication and the State Administration of Radio, Film and Television were also combined, and the State Electricity Regulatory Commission was merged into the NEA. As a result, the number of full ministerial-ranked agencies of the State Council was reduced by four.

In the meantime, two changes were made in response to issues of rising importance. As food safety has become a major public concern, and also an issue in China's trade relations with other countries, the State Council set up a food safety commission to coordinate the work of related agencies in 2010 and appointed then first-ranking Vice Premier Li Keqiang as its director. But the fact that multiple agencies had supervision over the issue worked against the demand for accountability and stronger law enforcement. Therefore, the Food and Drug Administration, which was previously administered by the Ministry of Health, was upgraded to become a ministerial-ranked administration directly under the State Council. It also took over food safety related authorities that were previously held by the AQSIQ and the State Administration for Industry and Commerce (SAIC). Secondly, the State Oceanic Administration was strengthened by the addition of maritime forces formerly commanded by the Ministry of Public Security, the Ministry of Agriculture and the General Administration of Customs. The integrated force became the China Coast Guard, which has been active as China has worked hard to enforce its territorial claims in the East and South China Seas.

While the institutional restructuring has received most attention, efforts aimed at rationalizing government behaviour have also made significant progress. One aspect concerns limiting government interference with the economy and reducing administrative licensing and approval. In 2001 the State Council set up an interdepartmental leading small group to carry out the reform of administrative approvals. Six batches of approval items were subsequently abolished or delegated to lower-level or non-governmental organizations between 2002 and 2012. The new administration under Premier Li Keqiang continued to push forward on this front. Li has openly pledged that his administration would further reduce the existing 1700 approval items by at least a third (State Council 2013).

The State Council has in recent years also tried to regularize government behaviour and improve accountability by allowing more supervision both inside and outside of government. For example, a series of rules have been laid down to regulate the construction of public projects and government procurement. The National Audit Office has been granted with greater power in monitoring heads of central government ministries and commissions. According to Liu Jiayi, the Auditor General, the high-profile corruption cases of Liu Zhijun and Wang Yi, a former Deputy Governor of the State Development Bank, both resulted from work of the Audit Office (Liu Jiayi 2013). There has also been progress in enhancing government transparency, especially since the 2003 Severe Acute Respiratory Syndrome (SARS) epidemic. In 2007, the State Council promulgated Regulations of the People's Republic of China on the Disclosure of Government Information, which requires government agencies to release their structure, functions, working procedures and information that involves the interests of citizens or organizations or needs to be widely known. At present, most ministries, including the Ministry of National Defence, have their own websites which display a significant amount of government information. Premier Li Keqiang sees insistence on greater transparency, such as the release of daily information on air quality, as a key leverage that the central government has over local authorities.

CHALLENGES AHEAD

Despite the achievements, the central government is still facing many challenges. For one thing, it might find it increasingly difficult to keep up the reform momentum, as the easiest changes have been made. Major new initiatives could touch upon vital interests of certain bureaucracies, public institutions or SOEs and incur stubborn resistance. This difficulty was frankly acknowledged by Li Keqiang during his first press conference as Premier, when he quipped that to shake up vested interests may be more difficult than 'touching the soul' (Xinhua 2013d). A second challenge is widespread corruption. The Hu-Wen administration saw the downfall of two cabinet members for corruption. The anti-corruption drive under Xi Jinping has already brought down several ministerial officials within the central government as well as various powerful department-level officials, notably within the NDRC and the Energy Administration. These cases indicate the scale of corruption in the central government, and much more needs to be done to enhance transparency and accountability, especially with regard to senior officials. Moreover, the State Council and the Chinese bureaucray overall need to adapt to an era of slower growth. Yet it will take time for the bureaucracy, which has been used to stimulating growth, to adjust itself to the new task. Lack of incentives or simply inertia could lengthen the time required for this shift. Then there is also the issue of regulatory capacity. On the one hand, the growing sophistication of the Chinese economy requires strengthened regulation and oversight. On the other hand, the reduction of *bianzhi* may have limited the central government's capacity. For example, the Ministry of Environmental Protection (MEP) has only about 300 formal staff in Beijing and this raises doubts over whether it will be able to effectively enforce environmental regulations.

Counting organizations affiliated with the MEP, the number rises to about 3000, compared to about 18 000 people for the US Environmental Protection Agency. The absolute majority of China's environmental protection personnel belong to the localities.

For most of the time, China's efforts to reform its central government have been gradual and piecemeal. Since there is no successful precedent where a strong and effective central government is built in a country with a similar political system and scale, Chinese leaders have to, as they always like to say, 'cross the river by groping for the stones'. While much progress has been made and many problems tackled, new challenges are constantly rising to the surface. Pressing matters such as drug and food safety have received serious attention, but more fundamental issues, such as population ageing, may not be as easily amenable to bureaucratic solution. The Chinese government has so far done well, often by muddling through, but the current leadership centred around Xi Jinping have recognized the need for comprehensive reforms and for building a country that governs according to law. China's future hangs on the fate of Xi's reform agenda.

NOTES

1. The CPPCC is sometimes referred to as the 'new' Political Consultative Conference to distinguish it from the Political Consultative Assembly convened by the Nationalist government in 1946. See http://www.cppcc.gov.cn/2011/09/27/ARTI1317102198751744.shtml.
2. The list of these deliberation and coordination organs can be found at http://www.gov.cn/zwgk/2008-04/24/content_953488.htm
3. The State-owned Assets Supervision and Administration Commission (SASAC) was briefly another exception in which the Director and the Party Secretary were two different people. Prior to his downfall, Jiang Jiemin, the former SASAC Director, outranked the Party Secretary.
4. For a list of central SOEs, see http://www.sasac.gov.cn/n1180/n1226/n2425/.

5. Provincial politics
Bo Zhiyue

This chapter deals with the study of provincial politics in China in terms of four aspects. First, it locates provincial politics in a general framework of Chinese politics and introduces the structure of provincial politics in China. Second, it presents theoretical debates over central–provincial relations, the role of provincial leaders in national politics, and the political mobility of provincial leaders. Third, it provides a critical assessment of the state of the art in the subfield and reflects on its practical implications. Fourth, it points to promising ways forward for future study.

PROVINCIAL POLITICS IN THE FRAMEWORK OF CHINESE POLITICS

China is a country of provinces, and provincial leaders are a major group in Chinese politics. Since June 1954, provinces have been the highest level of local government in the People's Republic of China.

China's provinces are in fact composed of four different categories. First, there are 22 provinces (*sheng* in Chinese). These are governed by two chief leaders: provincial Party secretaries (*shengwei shuji* in Chinese) and provincial governors (*shengzhang* in Chinese).

Second, there are four centrally administered municipalities (Beijing, Tianjin, Shanghai and Chongqing). Their leaders are usually called municipal party secretaries (*shiwei shuji* in Chinese) and mayors (*shizhang* in Chinese). Although in theory these leaders have the same rank as provincial party secretaries and governors, they tend to outrank their counterparts in provinces in the Party hierarchy. Party secretaries of these municipalities usually are members of the Politburo (a 25-member elite group of the Chinese Communist Party at the top), while with the exception of Guangdong, none of the provincial party secretaries of provinces are Politburo members.

Moreover, Beijing's mayor also tends to rank a bit higher in the Party hierarchy than not only governors of provinces but also party secretaries of the majority of provinces. On several occasions, a candidate for the position of Beijing mayor has to have experiences as a provincial party secretary in a province previously. Jia Qinglin, for instance, had been party secretary of Fujian Province before he was transferred to Beijing as vice mayor and acting mayor in 1996. Guo Jinlong, the incumbent party secretary of Beijing and a Politburo member, had been party secretary of Tibet and Anhui before his appointment as vice mayor and acting mayor in 2007.

Third, there are five autonomous regions of ethnic minorities. They are Inner Mongolia Autonomous Region, Guangxi Zhuang Autonomous Region, Ningxia Hui Autonomous Region, Xinjiang Uighur Autonomous Region and Tibet Autonomous Region. They are governed by party secretaries (*zizhiqu dangwei shuji* in Chinese) and chairmen (*zizhiqu zhengfu zhuxi* in Chinese). Party secretaries of these regions tend to be of Han ethnicity, and chairmen are people of the dominant ethnic minority in the region. Since 2002, the party secretary of Xinjiang has been a Politburo member.

Fourth, there are two special administrative regions, Hong Kong and Macao. These are governed by chief executives, who are locally elected and are not members of the Chinese Communist Party. However, directors of the central liaison offices in these two regions are usually members of the Central Committee of the Chinese Communist Party. Peng Qinghua, former head of the Central Liaison Office in Hong Kong, for instance, was a full member of the 17th Central Committee of the CCP and is also a full member of the 18th Central Committee of the CCP. His successor, Zhang Xiaoming, the incumbent head of the Central Liaison Office in Hong Kong, is an alternate member of the 18th Central Committee. Peng is now party secretary of the Guangxi Zhuang Autonomous Region. Similarly, Bai Zhijian, former head of the Central Liaison Office in Macao, was also a full member of the 17th Central Committee. His successor, Li Gang, the incumbent head, is a member of the Central Disciplinary Inspection Commission.

China's provinces are governed by two parallel structures in addition to the provincial legislature. On the one hand, there is a provincial government structure. Headed by the provincial governor (or mayor of a centrally administered municipality or chairman of an autonomous region), the provincial people's government is the administrative arm of the provincial government apparatus. In addition to the provincial governor, there are a number of vice governors and assistant governors. Take Shanxi province, for example: Governor Li Xiaopeng works with six vice governors, a secretary general and an assistant governor.

On the other hand, there is a provincial Party structure. Headed by the provincial party secretary, the provincial Party structure is supposed to provide political leadership in the economic and social development of the province. Similarly to the national system of the Chinese Communist Party (CCP), each provincial unit holds a Provincial Party Congress once every five years. The Provincial Party Congress elects a Provincial Party Committee of full members and alternate members, which in turn elects a Standing Committee of about 13 members. Among them, there are one party secretary, two or more deputy secretaries, and a number of standing members. Take Shandong province for example: Jiang Yikang is party secretary, Guo Shuqing (Governor) and Wang Junmin are deputy secretaries, and there are ten other standing members.

There is some overlap between the provincial government structure and the provincial Party structure. In the Party hierarchy, the provincial party secretary is the Number One leader; and the provincial governor who doubles as a deputy secretary of the province is the Number Two. The executive vice governor is often a standing member of the Provincial Party Committee, while other vice governors usually do not make it to the Provincial Party Standing Committee. In addition to civilian provincial party leaders such as heads of Organization Department, Propaganda Department, United Front Department, and Committee on Politics and Law, a military leader such as the commander or the political commissar of the provincial military district also sits on the Provincial Party Standing Committee (Bo 2007b: 98).

THEORETICAL DEBATES OVER CHINESE PROVINCIAL POLITICS

Provincial leaders play at least three major roles in Chinese politics. First, they are responsible for adapting central policies according to their local conditions. Second, they provide experiments for future central policies. Third, they constitute a major source of future national leaders. Nevertheless, there are theoretical debates over critical issues on the nature of central–provincial relations, on the role of provincial leaders in national politics, and on the political mobility of provincial leaders.

Central–Provincial Relations

First, there are debates over the central–provincial relationship. In the literature, it is often taken for granted that China is a unitary state. The basic argument is that the central government is strong and that provincial governments are simply agents of the central government (Barnett 1967: 72–75). Although the degree of autonomy varies depending on functional areas and historical periods, as A. Doak Barnett argued, the vertical chain of command is all important in this highly centralized structure of power. The powers provinces exercised 'were only those delegated from the center, and the center [original quote] could centralize or decentralize authority as it saw fit' (Barnett 1967: 73). In other words, the fact that provincial leaders appear to be quite powerful during a period of decentralization does not make China a federalist state. Yet few scholars have provided a clear definition of a unitary state, followed by an explanation of why China fits this category.

As an alternative view to this popular argument that China is a unitary state, Yasheng Huang suggested that China has a de facto federalist system in which the central government specializes in political responsibilities and the local governments specialize in economic responsibilities. He argued that the Chinese de facto federalism is an optimal arrangement in three ways: political centralization alleviates excessive coordination problems; fiscal decentralization places both fiscal and monetary controls in the hands of the State Council; and fiscal decentralization is an imperfect, but the only available, constraining force on the political discretion of the central government (Huang 1996: 326–327).

Zheng Yongnian further elaborated the meaning of de facto federalism in China. In his view, in terms of formal institutions, China may appear to be a unitary state with a strong centre and weak provincial governments (Zheng 2007a: 29). But at the operational level, China resembles a federalist state. In his terms, there are two different definitions of federalism: formal institutional, and behavioural. In formal institutional terms, China is not a federalist state because 'it has neither a constitutional division of power between the different levels of government nor a separation of power within the branches of government' (Zheng 2007a: 32). In behavioural terms, China is a de facto federalist state because of the intergovernmental decentralization (Zheng 2007a: 41–46). Apparently, his view is no different from the popular argument in the basic assumption that China is indeed organized as a unitary state.

Other scholars such as Babriella Montinola, Yingyi Qian and Barry R. Weingast have simply characterized China's political system in the era of economic reform as 'federalism, Chinese style'. Instead of a political reform of Western style, these authors argue, China introduced political changes in its own style with three main characteristics. First, China's political decentralization has not only enhanced the powers of local government but has also altered central relations in several critical ways that are difficult, though not impossible, to reverse. Second, there has been a major shift in ideology from the Maoist version of Marxism–Leninism to a pragmatic and market-oriented approach. Third, China has opened its economy (Montinola et al. 1995: 52).

There are two issues on the central–provincial relationship. One is how the relationship is defined constitutionally. This is the *de jure* relationship. It may come as a surprise to many who have become accustomed to seeing China as a unitary state that China is in fact a *de jure* federalist state in constitutional terms (Bo 2010b: 108–109). According to the 1982 Constitution of the People's Republic of China and the Organic Law of the Local People's Congresses and Local Governments of the People's Republic of China, Provincial People's Congresses enjoy a wide range of legislative powers.

First, Provincial People's Congresses and their standing committees may adopt local regulations, which must not contravene the Constitution and other laws and administrative regulations, and they shall report such local regulations to the Standing Committee of the National People's Congress for record (Article 100 of the 1982 Constitution). It should be noted that Provincial People's Congresses and their standing committees have constitutional rights to make their laws and report these laws to the Standing Committee of the National People's Congress for record, not for approval.

Second, Provincial People's Congresses elect provincial government leaders such as governors and vice governors and have the power to recall them (Article 101 of the 1982 Constitution and Articles 8, 26, and 44 of the Organic Law of the Local People's Congresses and Local Governments of the People's Republic of China). In other words, Provincial People's Congresses and their Standing Committees can hire and fire provincial government leaders. And they do not even have the obligation to report these personnel changes to the Standing Committee of the National People's Congress for record.

Third, there is no leader-led relationship between the Standing Committee of the National People's Congress and Standing Committees of Provincial People's Congresses (Bo 2004: 72). Their relationship is one of communications.

The other issue on the central–provincial relationship is the relationship in reality, that is, the *de facto* relationship. China in reality operates like a unitary state. This is due to the nature of the party-state in China. For instance, provincial governors and vice governors are elected by Provincial People's Congresses by law. But they are often transferred elsewhere by the Central Organization Department of the CCP. In other words, the legislative powers of Provincial People's Congresses and their Standing Committees have been compromised because of the dominance of the CCP in personnel issues (Bo 2004: 73–98).

One specific measure for the Party to exert control over provincial governments is to make provincial party secretaries concurrent heads of Provincial People's Congress Standing Committees. In 1983, for instance, there were only two provincial party secretaries serving concurrently as chairmen of their Provincial People's Congress Standing Committees. In 2003, the number of provincial party secretaries who were concurrent heads of their respective Standing Committees of Provincial People's Congresses went up to 22 (Bo 2004: 76). Today, with the exceptions of the five autonomous regions and the four centrally administered municipalities as well as Guangdong, party secretaries of the other provinces all double as chairmen of the Standing Committees of their Provincial People's Congresses.

In sum, China is a *de jure* federalist state but a *de facto* unitary state. In constitutional terms, China is a federalist state. But in reality, China has operated as a unitary state.

Role of Provincial Leaders in National Politics

Second, there are debates about the role of provincial leaders in national politics of China. The dominant view is that provincial leaders play a very important role in national politics of China. This is because they constitute the largest bloc in the Central Committee of the Chinese Communist Party (Shirk 1993: 190–196). As a result, powerful central leaders such as Mao Zedong (Chang 1969: 100) and Deng Xiaoping (Shirk 1993: 190–196) had to gain their support for their reform measures. 'Provincial party secretaries', as Susan L. Shirk described them, 'constituted the largest bloc in the Central Committee, 43 percent of the full members of the Eleventh Central Committee (1977), 34 percent of the Twelfth Central Committee (1982), and 38 percent of the Thirteenth Central Committee (1987)' (Shirk 1993: 190–191).

Provincial party secretaries are not simply more numerous on the Central Committee of the CCP than other institutional players such as central ministerial leaders. They play a very important role in national politics because of a particular mechanism in Chinese politics: reciprocal accountability (Shirk 1993: 82–84). Instead of one-way traffic, central leaders and provincial leaders in China are reciprocally accountable. On the one hand, central leaders choose provincial leaders; on the other hand, provincial leaders also choose central leaders. 'The leaders appoint the officials, and the officials in the Central Committee choose (or at least ratify the choice of) the leaders' (Shirk 1993: 83). Following this logic, central leaders such as Mao Zedong and Deng Xiaoping initiated and sustained their policy initiatives by playing to the provinces (Shirk 1993: 162, 190–191).

David S.G. Goodman, however, is not convinced by this argument. In his view, it is true that provincial leaders, especially provincial party first secretaries, have become important in Chinese politics since the 1950s, but these political actors hardly constitute a coherent political group. Instead, they are more likely to be a categoric group than an active political group (Goodman 1984a: 71). Although provincial leaders would react to central policy initiatives, it is unlikely that they would react similarly to national politics (Goodman 1984a: 73), due to the different conditions of their provinces. More precisely, provincial leaders are important in national politics as political middlemen instead of as a political group (Goodman 1984a: 76).

Broadly speaking, provincial leaders can be classified into three categories in terms of their membership on the Central Committee of the CCP (Bo 2007a: 109–121; Bo 2010a: 92–99). First, most powerful provincial leaders are concurrent Politburo members. Generally speaking, party secretaries of four centrally administered municipalities (Beijing, Tianjin, Shanghai and Chongqing) as well as a few large provinces such as Guangdong and some important autonomous regions such as Xinjiang serve as concurrent full Politburo members. These provincial leaders are national leaders as well, and their provinces are considered elite provinces (Bo 2007a: 112–116). Second, the majority of provincial party secretaries and most of provincial governors are full members of the Central Committee. Except for the elite provinces, provinces usually have two full members on the Central Committee: one is the party secretary and the other is governor. Third, junior provincial leaders such as deputy secretaries and vice governors could also join the Central Committee as alternate members.

Yumin Sheng focused on the full Central Committee membership of provincial leaders in the era of economic reform. He argued that there was a dramatic decline of provincial shares from 1978 to 2002 in contrast to the rise of central shares in the same period (Sheng 2005: 353).

The present author tried to deal with the provincial presence in the CCP Central Committee in terms of all three categories. Based on their political weight on the Central Committee, I assigned a score to each member of the Central Committee and aggregated these scores into power indexes for all major blocs such as provinces, central institutions, the military and business corporations. In a 'power pie' of all institutions, provinces have the largest share of over 42 percent (Bo 2007a: 136; Bo 2010a: 125).

Political Mobility of Provincial Leaders

Third, there are also debates about the political mobility of provincial leaders. The conventional wisdom in the literature of Chinese politics is that political leaders in China, including provincial leaders, rise or fall because of their factional identities. In a very influential article published in the *China Quarterly* in 1973, Andrew J. Nathan proposed a factionalism model for analysing Chinese politics. Factions, in his view, are based on clientelist ties, which are non-ascriptive two-person relations founded on exchange (Nathan 1973: 37–45).

Jürgen Domes further suggested that factions are developed out of two kinds of groups: structural and functional. Structural groups act primarily on the basis of common regional origin (*tong-xiang*), common educational background (*tong-xue*) or common organizational experiences over many years (*tong-hang*) (Domes 1984: 27). Functional groups are groups 'whose attitudes in political decision-making processes are influenced by interests of functional subsystems' such as central ministries, provincial governments and military organs (Domes 1984: 28).

One school of thought specifically about the political mobility of provincial leaders is that provincial leaders who work in their home provinces tend to have a disadvantage because they could be suspects of localism, a tendency for local leaders to defend local interests at the expense of central policies (Teiwes 1967; Bo 1996). The present author, however, proposed a performance model for the political mobility of provincial leaders, especially during the era of economic reform. I believe that due to the fact that China has been both a de facto unitary state and a developmental state, provincial leaders have to perform to get promoted (Bo 2002a: 9).

Using biographical data on more than 2500 provincial leaders and provincial data on economic growth and revenue contributions from 1949 to 1998, the present author tested these models (factionalism model, localism model and performance model) (Bo 2002a). According to this study, provincial leaders with central origins tend to follow a different career path from that of provincial leaders with local origins. But this evidence does not necessarily support the factionalism model. Nevertheless, this study does show that the leaders of Shanghai are a distinct group of politicians in China and their political upward mobility has something to do with the centre (Bo 2002a: 145).

The present author contends that a native provincial leader (one who works in his or her home province) is not necessarily a localist, and my study shows that the political mobility of natives is not statistically different from that of outsiders (Bo 2002a: 145). My central conclusion is that the political mobility of provincial leaders, especially in the era of economic reform, is determined by the economic performance of their provinces. The worse the record of economic performance, the more likely it is that the provincial leader will be demoted. Moreover, the revenue contributions of a province to the centre during the provincial leader's tenure is also a determinant of the political mobility of the leader (Bo 2002a: 143–149).

In China, provinces also serve as a training ground for national leaders (Bo 2003: 66–117). In the People's Republic of China, the central authorities have often sent cadres to different localities. Hu Yaobang probably was the first person to be sent to the provinces in the early 1960s to gain additional experience for future promotions (Bo 2003: 71). One particular group of political leaders who are more likely than others to be sent to provinces for training purposes are youth league cadres, because they are relatively young with a high rank and are often well-educated.

As a result, a major common characteristic of the Politburo members has been leadership experience in the provinces. Among nine standing members of the 16th Politburo, for instance, eight had worked as provincial leaders previously. Out of the remaining 15 Politburo members, 12 were either former provincial leaders or concurrent provincial leaders (Bo 2008: 135). In the 17th Politburo, eight out of nine standing members had experience as provincial leaders, and 12 out of 15 other full members were either former provincial leaders or concurrent provincial leaders (Bo 2008: 179–180).

RESEARCH METHODS, THEORETICAL GAPS AND PRACTICAL IMPLICATIONS

Generally speaking, scholars use one of two methods in their research on Chinese provincial politics. One research method is case studies. Scholars mostly use this method to study provincial leaders in individual provinces. In a collection of essays on provincial strategies of economic reform in post-Mao China, scholars such as Zhimin Lin, Peter T.Y. Cheung, Keith Forster, Kevin P. Lane, Jae Ho Chung, Shawn Shieh, Feng Chongyi and David S.G. Goodman and Lijian Hong looked at political dynamics in various provinces such as Shanghai, Guangdong, Zhejiang, Shaanxi, Shandong, Fujian, Hainan and Sichuan (Cheung et al. 1998). The present author also carried out a case study of economic development and corruption in Beijing (Bo 2002b). Some scholars also use comparative case studies: David S.G. Goodman carried out comparative case studies of Sichuan and Guizhou in terms of central–provincial relations (Goodman 1986); and John A. Donaldson compared Guizhou and Yunnan on the issue of poverty reduction (Donaldson 2007).

Another research method is statistical analyses of provincial leaders as a group. Frederick C. Teiwes studied provincial leaders in the 1950s and the 1960s (Teiwes 1966, 1967, 1971, 1974). David S.G. Goodman offered a profile of the provincial first party secretaries from 1949 to 1978 (Goodman 1980). The present author studied four categories of provincial leaders (provincial party secretaries, provincial deputy secretaries, provincial governors, and provincial vice governors) over the period 1949 to 1998 and used statistical models to analyse the correlations between economic variables of provinces and the political mobility of provincial leaders (Bo 2002a). Yumin Sheng also used statistical models to find out the determinants of provincial presence at the CCP Central Committees (Sheng 2007).

Scholars of diverse research have generated a large body of knowledge on Chinese provincial politics since 1949, yet there are still a number of significant theoretical gaps. First, case studies are helpful to discover in-depth political dynamics of individual provinces, but their findings are not usually generalizable. This is due to the diversity of provinces in terms of population, geographic area, history, local culture, and the level of social and economic development. Based on case studies of eight provinces in terms of provincial strategies of economic reform, Peter T.Y. Cheung tried to classify provincial leaders into three types: 'pioneers', 'bandwagoners' and 'laggards' (Cheung 1998: 23–26). But more case studies are needed to confirm the existence and the balance of these types.

Second, studies of all provinces have provided overall patterns of provincial politics in general, but most of these studies tend to be descriptive. This is largely due to the availability of information on all provincial leaders. It is already an overwhelming task to keep up with the changing provincial leadership in China. But more in-depth analyses of inter-provincial and intra-provincial political dynamics will be needed.

As mentioned at the beginning of this chapter, China is a country of provinces. Many Chinese provinces are larger in population than the largest countries in Western Europe. It is impossible to fully understand China without some understanding of Chinese provinces. It is impossible to fully understand Chinese politics without some understanding of Chinese provincial politics.

Studies of provincial politics have strong practical implications. First, provincial leaders are the largest group of political leaders in China. They are not only very important in provincial politics but also very important in national politics (though not necessarily as a political group). Second, Chinese provinces are training grounds for national leaders. Many top national leaders have had provincial management experience. Third, provinces have often been used for experiments in political, social and economic policy initiatives. The success or failure of these policy initiatives is indicative of the future development of China.

FUTURE STUDIES OF CHINESE PROVINCIAL POLITICS

In the foreseeable future, studies of Chinese provincial politics will continue to benefit from the availability of data on this group of politicians and the relatively institutionalized management of provincial leaders. Future scholars will continue to be exposed to the large amount of information on this group of politicians in China and to observe similar patterns of political mobility with varying degrees of institutionalization in different provinces, but they will have to come up with a better framework to conceptualize the nature of central–provincial relations, the role of provincial leaders in national politics, and the political mobility of provincial leaders.

First, in additional to continuity, future scholars should also pay attention to political cultural shifts because of the change of the top leadership. Although Chinese top leaders have all operated in the political culture that combines the Party primacy with imperial traditions, their individual preferences are vastly different. As a result, provincial leaders work with new norms with each new top Party leader.

Second, in addition to statistics on demographic information such as age, gender, education, nationality and home province, future scholars should also look for information on the political dynamics of provincial leaders in all provinces. What is their actual political network? Do they have any patrons at the centre? Do they have any political friends in other provinces? Do they have protégés in their own provinces? How do they work with each other?

Third, future scholars should also try to uncover the actual social network of provincial leaders. Do they work closely with the business community? Who are their protégés in the local business community? Do they work with intellectuals as well? How do they promote their projects nationally and locally?

Finally, future scholars should avoid producing 'scientific outcomes' but instead aim to produce politically meaningful results. Due to the availability of information and information technology, it is easy to manipulate large quantities of data for any preconceived purpose. But it is not always meaningful to generate complicated sets of scores on any dimension of provincial leaders in one province or multiple provinces. It is more important to search for patterns of political dynamics of provincial politics, either in any single province or in multiple provinces.

6. Local governance: the roles of the People's Congresses and the People's Political Consultative Conferences
Minglu Chen

Any consideration of local governance naturally invites a clarification on the very concept of 'governance'. Despite its general popularity, '"governance" is a vague and contested term, as are many political concepts' (Bevir 2010: 1). Literally, the word 'governance' means 'rule, control', which is 'the action or manner of governing a state, organization, etc' (*Oxford Dictionaries* n.d.). The first contemporary appearance of the term occurred in the World Bank report *Sub-Saharan Africa: From Crisis to Sustainable Growth* published in 1989, which signified governance as the responsibilities of the state (World Bank 1989). In its 1992 report *Governance and Development*, the World Bank further defined governance as 'the manner in which power is exercised in the management of a country's economic and social resources for development' (World Bank 1992c: 2). Invariably, the conventional understanding on governance emphasizes the roles that formal state institutions play in governing.

Since the 1990s, a group of scholars started to argue that governance in a contemporary context involves new approaches and perspectives consequent to the 1980s neoliberal reforms of the public sector in the West featuring decentralization, marketization and privatization. Stoker argues that governance refers to the governing styles in which boundaries between and within the public and private sectors become blurred, and governing mechanisms do not rest on recourse to the authority and sanctions of government (Stoker 1998: 17). Pierre and Peters agree that governance is about the changing relationships between state and society and a decreasing reliance on coercive policy instruments, although they believe the state is still the centre of political power (Pierre and Peters 2000). And according to Bevir, governance refers to the shift in public organization and public action from hierarchic bureaucracies to markets and networks (Bevir 2010, 2013). Strong hierarchies and top-down policy-making are still recognized as remaining dominant, but are now enhanced by new strategies of broader participation (Kersting et al. 2009: 16). Noticeably, these various scholars and arguments disagree on the roles that the state and non-state sectors each play in the process of decision-making, a disagreement which is manifest in the complexity of the idea of governance itself. But these new approaches to governance invariably argue against the state monopoly in the exercise of power, and emphasize instead an emergent new relationship between the state and society.

At the same time as the understanding of governance as a more inclusive process that goes beyond formal institutions has gained popularity in liberal democracies, governance in China has been attracting more attention both within and outside the country. However, in this authoritarian system, the party-state led by the Chinese Communist Party (CCP) still enjoys absolute ruling power, exercises unchallenged control over the judiciary and media, penetrates every major social sector and has its tight grip reaching from the top of the political hierarchy to the very grassroots. Under these circumstances, does it make much sense at all to discuss the idea of governing as shared responsibilities between state and society? In fact, a number of scholars, when introducing the concept of 'new governance' to the Chinese academia, have implicitly or even explicitly questioned whether it can be readily adapted to analyse the reality in or provide any useful guidance to understanding China (Cao 2008; Xiong 2013; Ren and Qiao 2010). Indeed, the existing literature on governance in China largely focuses on formal institutions and party-state rule (Saich 2011; Yang, Dali 2004; Smith 2010).

On the other hand, China's post-1978 development has arguably featured neoliberal strategies: introduction of market forces, privatization of the public sector and decentralization of power (Harvey 2005). The reforms of the past three decades have changed formal governing institutions and processes, as well as state–society relations in unprecedented ways. In this process, the state's administrative power and public functions have been delegated to lower levels in the political-administrative hierarchy, and shared with the private sector, the market and society. For example, nowadays welfare provision is a shared task among the central and local states, the private economic sector, third-sector organizations, as well as families and individuals (Duckett and Carrillo 2011). Even when the state still plays a dominant role, the ways in which power is exercised and resources are managed are different. At the same time, inputs of various social sectors have been selectively welcomed into the process of governing. The changing relationship between state, market and society is essential to the study of governance. In the discussion of governance in China, an emergent literature has shifted its focus from fiscal and political reforms occurring in formal party-state apparatus, to how power and resources are negotiated and distributed between the state and various social groups and organizations in the context of China's marketization and globalization (Howell 2004; Kou and Zang 2013).

Beyond the party-state centre, the country's administrative hierarchy consists of five levels – province, prefecture, county, township, and at the grassroots the neighbourhood in urban areas and the village in the countryside[1] – with the political and economic powers of each level defined by the state. Except for neighbourhoods and villages, each local government is an administrative and financial entity. Since the early 1980s, a series of fiscal reforms (such as tax for fees in the early 1980s, the fiscal contracting system in the late 1980s, and the taxation reform in the mid-1990s) changed central–local dynamics in significant ways. The basic spirit of these reforms was to divide revenues and expenditures between the party-state centre and the localities, with the aim of accelerating local economic development, and increasing the local states' autonomy, responsibility and accountability. In this process, some local governments' power has grown so much with their income that they have become powerful stakeholders in the nation's policy-making. At the same time, within a single locality, policy-making involves more and more discussion and coordination among multiple sectors and agencies with the need to balance interests.

This chapter aims to add to the discussion on the dynamic process of institutional changes and the involvement of diverse social interests in governing subnational-level China. It does this by examining two formal institutions in China's political system – the People's Congress (PC) and the People's Political Consultative Conference (PPCC) – to highlight the ways in which governance beyond the central agencies of the party-state features reforms in formal institutions and the inclusion of selected key social groups in the decision-making process.

INSTITUTIONAL CONTEXT

In the contemporary Chinese political system, the CCP, the People's Government, the PC and the PPCC at both central and local levels, are commonly referred to as 'the four sets of leadership' (*si tao banzi*), which constitute China's basic political system of 'multi-party co-operation and political consultation under the leadership of the Communist Party of China' (State Council 2007). In the newly established *People's Daily* 'Local Leaders' database,[2] for instance, Party Secretary, Governor, Chairperson of the PC and Chairperson of the PPCC of all the 31 provincial-level jurisdictions (excluding Hong Kong and Macau Special Administrative Regions) have been listed as 'local executives of political power'. While the CCP is the sole ruling party[3] and the People's Government the executive body of state administration, the People's Congress is the legislature and the People's Political Consultative Conference the advisory body. Both the PC and the PPCC exist in every subnational territorial administrative area from provincial down to township levels.

The origin of the Chinese People's Political Consultative Conference dates back earlier than the PC to the period of the Republic of China, as the Kuomintang (KMT) and the CCP agreed to open multi-party united front negotiations on post-war political issues. The first PPCC was organized by the KMT in 1946 in Chongqing. When the CCP established its power in mainland China, it convened a 'new' political consultative conference in September 1949 and invited representatives from friendly parties, mass organizations and returned overseas Chinese to discuss the establishment of a democratic coalition government (Groot 2004).

The first Chinese People's Political Consultative Conference of the People's Republic of China (PRC) functioned as China's legislature (Huang 2008; Tung 1968). It elected the Central People's Government Council and decided on the national capital, the national flag, the national anthem and the calendar of the People's Republic of China. As the first Chairperson of the National Committee of the PPCC, Mao Zedong announced the establishment of the PRC on 1 October 1949. The conference adopted the Common Programme of the Chinese People's Political Consultative Conference in 1949, which served as the *de facto* constitution, until the Constitution of the People's Republic of China came into effect in 1954.

The 1949 Common Programme provided that the People's Congresses of all levels were the organs for the exercise of state power by the people, which were to be popularly elected 'when conditions permit' (Chinese People's Political Consultative Conference 1949). In 1953, after the CCP had further consolidated its rule, the National People's Congress (NPC) was finally ready to be established. One year later, the NPC held its first meeting, in which it elected state leaders, and enacted the Constitution, as well as the organic laws of the NPC, the State Council, the People's Court, the People's Procuratorate, and local People's Congresses and local people's governments at various levels. At the same time, the national PPCC transferred its function as the country's legislature to the newly founded NPC, and remained in existence as an organ of the CCP's United Front Work

Department, a department designed to unite social forces outside the CCP. Both the PC and the PPCC were interrupted by the Great Proletariat Cultural Revolution that Mao Zedong launched in 1966. The PPCC resumed its routine work in 1973, while the PC did not meet again until after Mao's death in 1976.

According to the Constitution of the People's Republic of China, People's Congresses at various levels are organs through which the people exercise state power, and People's Political Consultative Conferences play an important role in China's current political system of multi-party cooperation and political consultation by functioning as united front work organizations that provide non-CCP members, members of mass organizations, people from ethnic minority backgrounds, and those of various professions with access to politics (National People's Congress 2004). Therefore, in theory, the PC and the PPCC function as institutions through which citizens participate in decision-making and policy development process in the country. But in reality, the Party still controls nominations to both institutions and thus access to state power is only available to selected members of the society.

Constitutionally, PCs at national and various local levels 'are constituted through democratic elections' (National People's Congress 2004). For each level, quotas of deputies are allocated to different administrative districts according to the local population and populations of ethnic groups. At the same time, quotas also exist for women, workers, peasants, intellectuals, soldiers and various political parties, though they are not strictly met (O'Brien 1994). Deputies to PCs of the lowest levels (townships and counties) are directly elected by their constituents, while at higher levels they are indirectly elected by the PCs at the next lower level. Although the Organic Law of the Local People's Congresses and Local People's Governments of the People's Republic of China states that any voter or deputy, with the support of at least ten people, could nominate a candidate, in reality the Chinese Communist Party and other organizational candidates still dominate.

According to the Charter of the Chinese People's Political Consultative Conference:

> the National Committee of the Chinese People's Political Consultative Conference shall be composed of the Communist Party of China, the various democratic parties, public personages without party affiliation, people's organizations, ethnic minority groups and people of all walks of life, compatriots of the Hong Kong Special Administrative Region, the Macao Special Administrative Region and Taiwan, returned overseas Chinese and specially invited personalities, who are divided into a number of sectors. The composition of the CPPCC local committees shall be made up in light of the local actual conditions with reference to that of the CPPCC National Committee. (Chinese People's Political Consultative Conference 2012a)

Members of the PPCCs are not elected, but nominated by each of these sectors through the United Front Work Department and finally approved by the organizational department of the CCP Committee to ensure members are politically trustworthy and socially influential (Yan 2011). In China today, the expressed mission of the PPCC is to act as 'an important institution of political consultation, democratic supervision and participation in the deliberation and administration of state affairs for all democratic parties, mass organizations and representative figures from all ethnic groups and sectors of society' (Chinese People's Political Consultative Conference 2012b).

The PCs and the PPCCs meet in plenary session once a year. Both institutions have

108 *Handbook of the politics of China*

Table 6.1 Composition of the 13th People's Congress of Taiyuan City, Shanxi Province, 2014

Profession	Number
Party-state official	179
Military officer	10
Chairmen of village committee	8
Leader of mass organization	3
Professional	30
State-owned enterprise manager	27
Collective enterprise manager	5
Private enterprise owner	84
Manual worker	3
Total	349

Source: Data from Taiyuan City People's Congress official website, http://www.tyrd.gov.cn/.

a Standing Committee composed of the Chairperson, the Deputy Chairpersons and selected members, whose major responsibility is to convene the plenary sessions and manage daily affairs outside the plenary sessions. PC deputies and PPCC members both serve a fixed term of five years. The Chinese Communist Party exercises control over the PC and the PPCC not only by overseeing the nominations, but also by ensuring its own representation in both institutions. Research shows that in the PCs the percentage of the Chinese Communist Party members is maintained at around 60–80 per cent, while in the PPCCs the figure is around 40 per cent (O'Brien 1994; Yan 2011; Chen 2015). Moreover, in both institutions there is a high presentation of members of the party-state's *nomenklatura*, a system adopted from the Soviet Union, which lists the number of personnel and specifies their ranks and duties in the party-state hierarchy (Goodman 2014b).

Take Taiyuan City, the capital of Shanxi Province in northern China, for example. Table 6.1 and Table 6.2 categorize the composition of Taiyuan City People's Congress and People's Political Consultative Conference, respectively, as of the end of 2014 according to deputies' or members' profession. In the city's PC, in addition to the 179 party-state officials and ten military officers, there are eight deputies who are Chairmen of local village committees and another three who are leaders of mass organizations such as the Women's Federation, the Federation of Trade Unions and the Disabled Persons' Federation. Given that both village committees and mass organizations are subject to strong party-state control and influence (the latter with their leaders appointed by and receiving a budget from the party-state), it seems to be safe to also include these two categories as within the party-state system. Thus the party-state actually occupies 200 seats (57 per cent) in Taiyuan City PC. In the case of the city's PPCC, 156 members of the party-state *nomenklatura* and 20 mass organization leaders count for 39 per cent of the seats. These data illustrate the different designated roles that the PC and the PPCC play: while representatives to the People's Congress are often from within the party-state system, the PPCC is more of a platform where elites from outside the system participate in politics.

Table 6.2 Composition of the 12th People's Political Consultative Conference of Taiyuan City, Shanxi Province, 2014

Profession	Number
Party-state official	156
Democratic party leader	9
Leader of mass organization	20
Leader of non-governmental organization	1
Religious organization leader	8
Professional	87
State-owned enterprise manager	33
Private enterprise owner	128
Manager of private enterprise	6
Professional athlete	1
Total	449

Source: Data from Taiyuan City People's Political Consultative Conference official website, http://www.tyzx.gov.cn/.

It is such tight control by the party-state that leads to the common impression that the PC and the PPCC are 'flower vases' or rubber-stamp organizations with no real power but serving to 'window dress' forums where decisions already made by the CCP are endorsed. Indeed, there is even a popular saying in Chinese that summarizes the general impression of the PCs' and the PPCCs' lack of substantial power in the political system: 'the People's Congress raises its hand and the People's Political Consultative Conference claps its hands'.

But at the same time, the Taiyuan case also highlights the role of both the PC and the PPCC as institutions designed to create inclusion, where selected key social groups could participate in the process of governance. In 2000 Jiang Zemin, the then President of the PRC, saw the need for the CCP to expand its social basis from merely representing the proletariat to including all newly emergent social classes, and put forward the 'Three Represents' theory. It claims that the CCP now represents the development trends of advanced productive forces, the orientation of an advanced culture and the fundamental interests of the overwhelming majority of the people of China (Jiang 2000). In 2002, the CCP amended its Constitution to endorse the new ideological framework. The composition of Taiyuan City's PC and PPCC also reflects this policy direction. Apart from party-state officials and mass organization leaders, almost all the rest of the seats in the PC and PPCC are taken by private entrepreneurs, state-owned and collective-owned enterprise managers, and professionals such as lawyers, journalists, professors, doctors, accountants and so on. Obviously these are people that possess 'advanced productive forces' and 'advanced culture'[4] and thus are to be co-opted. As statistics of Taiyuan City PC and PPCC show, the most prominent group targeted is private entrepreneurs. This group occupies 84 seats (24 per cent) in the PC and 128 seats (28 per cent) in the PPCC. Indeed, the relationship between the party-state and entrepreneurs is newly emergent, yet one of the most important of state–society relationships in contemporary China, not least because the private sector is a major drive of the country's unprecedented economic growth. By the end of 2012, there were more than 10 million private enterprises registered in China, counting for over 60 per cent of the country's gross domestic product (GDP) (Pan 2013). Also, the private economic sector is contributing more than the state-owned sector in terms of exportation, taxation and employment (Ye 2011). Therefore, the state is eager to turn this group into its allies (Chen and Dickson 2010), by recruiting them to the Communist Party and minor political parties, appointing them as officials, and providing them with various awards and political titles. Clearly both the PCs and the PPCCs serve as co-optive institutions in this regard (Sun 2013; Yan 2011).

EXERCISING SUPERVISORY POWER: THE CASE OF THE PEOPLE'S CONGRESS OF ZHENGZHOU CITY, HENAN PROVINCE

The role that the People's Congress nowadays plays in China's political system has drawn much scholarly attention. O'Brien's (1994) research showed that in the post-Mao era PC deputies acted not only as regime agents, but at the same time also as people's representatives, although the former role prevailed. More than a decade later, popularly elected local Chinese congressmen and women view themselves mainly as delegates of local constituents, rather than regime agents (Manion 2014). At the same time, the role of the People's Congresses themselves have changed too. They now have more authority in the selection of local leaders (Manion 2008), lawmaking (Cho 2006), law enforcement (Cho 2003) and supervision of governments (Cho 2002). During this process, Chinese local legislatures have employed sophisticated development strategies to create a space for themselves in the political arena, including a 'network strategy' of building linkage with and gaining support from power institutions of the state system (Xia 1997, 2000) and a 'mobilization strategy to encourage social organizations and the public to participate in legislative activities' (Cho 2009). In general, all this research suggests that the Chinese People's Congresses are no longer symbolic 'rubber stamps'. Instead, they are playing an increasingly important supervisory role in China's political system. However, the current discussion has not concentrated on the aspect of the role people's congresses play in governance at local levels.

The local PCs at and above the county levels exercise various powers, including formulating and promulgating local regulations, approving governmental budgets, electing local leadership, examining work reports from local governments, courts and procuratorates, and annulling the governments' inappropriate resolutions. In 2006, the People's Congress of Zhengzhou City, Henan Province attracted much attention as its Standing Committee disapproved a governmental work report (Zhai and Zhao 2006). Similar cases of People's Congresses voting against appointments to and/or reports of local governments have been occurring repeatedly since the late 1990s, as the result of a changing relationship between PCs and governments at the subnational level (Yang, Dali 2004; Cho 2009). Current scholarship has interpreted the rejection and dismissal merely as contestation acts, rather than the dynamics of local policy-making. In fact, Manion has gone so far as to argue that 'there is little role in policy-making for local congresses' (Manion 2014: 317). However, as the Zhengzhou case indicates, policies can be shaped and developed in the process of local People's Congresses raising proposals to the governments, rejecting governments' initiatives and responses, and in the negotiation process that follows. In this way, policy-making is no long monopolized by the local state.

The rejection of the Zhengzhou Government's work report was a response to an earlier proposal initiated by Liu Muhua, a Deputy from the subordinate county-level Gongyi City to Zhengzhou People's Congress, and signed by Liu and 11 other deputies. Liu was director of the local medical insurance centre, a government-affiliated not-for-profit organization that manages local residents' public medical insurance. The proposal revealed that local urban and rural low-income groups could not afford health services and pointed out that the problem was largely the result of the government's low health care input. Therefore, the proposal discussed, hospitals had to increase charges to cover their costs. To solve the problem, it was proposed that the Zhengzhou Government's budget should include public hospitals' expenditures to guarantee salaries and benefits of medical personnel. It further suggested that the Zhengzhou Government should experiment with this strategy in selected hospitals first before promoting it broadly. At the same time, the proposal also urged the government to publish and better supervise hospitals' charging criteria.

Upon receiving the proposal, the Zhengzhou People's Congress Standing Committee organized a field trip for Deputies to visit a local hospital. The PC also arranged a discussion session on the matter and invited officials and staff members from the city's Bureau of Public Health, Price Bureau, Food and Drug Administration Bureau, Medical Insurance Centre and a public hospital. As both the field trip and the meeting confirmed the credibility of the proposal, the PC passed it on to the city government to be dealt with.

A few months later, the Zhengzhou Government made a formal report to the Standing Committee on what measures had been taken to solve the problem raised in the proposal. In the report, the government promised to pay greater attention to the issue, to strengthen the rural public health system, to develop a community-based medical network, to better regulate hospitals and to establish an efficient urban medical insurance system. After hearing the report, six members of the Standing Committee voted against it, 11 abstained and 19 voted in its favour. As the report failed to gain the majority of votes, it was rejected by the PC. An anonymous member revealed that they voted against it because the report was 'not concrete' and 'empty'. Liu Muhua explicitly commented that in its report the government only made banal remarks such as to 'pay greater attention' and to 'strengthen', without mentioning any real measures to be taken (Anyang City People's Congress 2012). Of course it would be oversimplistic to believe that the Zhengzhou People's Congress had thus obtained the upper hand over the government. After all, it is still not a common practice for PCs to contest government decisions. While exercising their political power, local PCs have been carefully targeting selected issues rather than the governments, who are treated as potential allies rather than as competitors or combatants (Xia 2000). To illustrate its stance, the Standing Committee explained that the rejection was not the rejection of the government's public health works: 'The government has already made a lot of efforts and there have been real achievements. It's only because it is much expected by the public of the government for even more improvement' (Zhai and Zhao 2006).

The PC's rejection of the government's report soon caused a series of actions from the latter. Several days after the voting, the government held a meeting with Directors of the city's Public Health Bureau, Finance Bureau, Development and Reform Commission, Bureau of Human Resources and Social Security, Disabled Persons' Federation and the local Red Cross Society, where these officials and organizational leaders carefully studied the PC proposal. Moreover, the city's Deputy Mayor visited the PC Standing Committee to seek further suggestions. After conducting research, the government came up with a much more detailed report on possible solutions to the problem raised, which included:

- To include more local residents in the public medical insurance scheme.
- To relocate two public hospitals so that the city's medical resources would be better placed geographically.
- From 2007, the city government would include community public health services in its budget and establish more community clinics.
- To promote a medicine bidding system in which multiple hospitals could purchase medicine through tendering, so as to reduce prices.
- To urge hospitals to publicize their charging criteria.
- To further promote the provincial government's decision on applying a price ceiling for the treatment of a single disease.
- To increase the number of designated hospitals where recipients of the Minimum Livelihood Guarantee – a state allowance eligible to households whose income fall below the minimum threshold determined by the local government – can go to for free or cheaper medical services.

Unfortunately, information on the Zhengzhou PC's response to the second report of the government is not available. But research reveals that almost all the earlier proposed measures have turned into governmental actions. In 2007, one year after the PC rejected the initial governmental report, the government issued the Interim Measures for Providing Basic Medical Insurance to Urban Residents of Zhengzhou City. Under the Measures, the city's basic medical insurance is available to unemployed persons, disabled persons, migrants from rural to urban areas as a result of land requisition, recipients of the Minimum Livelihood Guarantee, elderly persons with no family and orphans (Henan Sheng Renmin Zhengfu 2007). In 2008, children of migrant workers were included in the basic medical insurance scheme too (Zhengzhou Shi Renmin Zhengfu 2008). Relocation of the two public hospitals occurred in 2007 and 2010. In 2007, the city government increased its budget on community public health services by 10 yuan per every urban resident per year and established 30 community clinics (Jiu San Society Zhengzhou Committee 2007). Also in 2007, the provincial government of Henan announced that all public hospitals in in the province were to collectively purchase medicine through an online bidding system (Yang and Zhou 2007). More than 30 hospitals adopted a single disease treatment price ceiling and seven hospitals were designated to receive Minimum Livelihood Guarantee recipients (*Zhengzhou Wanbao* 2008).

PLAYING AN ADVISORY ROLE: THE CASE OF THE PEOPLE'S POLITICAL CONSULTATIVE CONFERENCE OF NINGBO CITY, ZHEJIANG PROVINCE

The People's Political Consultative Conferences have been dismissed by many as nothing more than united front 'window dressing', with no real power, a forum where what are described as democratic parties consult with the CCP and agree on whatever the CCP has already decided (Boden 2008). But recent scholarship shows that the PPCC system is playing a much more important role in Chinese politics nowadays, not least as a forum where the party-state garners feedback on governance, and elite members of society participate in the process of decision-making (Yan 2011). For example, a 2015 research report reveals that nowadays private entrepreneurs are welcomed into the PPCC, and once recruited these new rich business owners actively seek to influence local policy-making so as to protect their individual and collective interests. At the same time, the PPCCs have developed a mechanism to mobilize members to provide advice on governmental works and to receive the government's response on the proposals and opinion pieces submitted by PPCC members (Chen 2015). However, previous research fails to illustrate whether such advice does lead to government actions. After all, it is possible (and likely) that the government only pays lip service without making any real commitment. If so, the influence the PPCCs have on local governance may only be somewhat limited.

In a research report, the PPCC of Yuzhong District, Chongqing Municipality reflected on the effectiveness of its advisory work. The report commented that PPCCs brought together social elites, passed demands from the public up the state hierarchy, and provided policy consultancy to government. In this way, 'the PPCC system should well act as a think tank of the Party-state', but without a legal basis 'it is relatively hard for [PPCCs'] opinions to have real effects'. After all, it is not the legal responsibility of state organs to adopt the suggestions of PPCCs and there is also no legal redress if a PPCC's supervision and subsequent suggestions are ignored or rejected. This is the dilemma that face many PPCCs (Zhongguo Renmin Zhengzhi Xieshang Huiyi Chongqing Shi Jiangbei Qu Weiyuanhui 2013).

The case of Ningbo City PPCC illustrates how local PPCCs could seek to play a more substantial role in the process of decision-making through institutional innovation. Since 2007, Ningbo PPCC has been asking the public to put forward ideas on proposals to be submitted to the government. This has made it one of the first local PPCCs to invite input from society on its advisory work more widely; Beijing PPCC was the first to do so in 2004. Indeed, collecting suggestions from the public has become a common practice among local PPCCs nowadays. Ningbo PPCC has not been simply repeating this practice, but also made its own innovation by inviting individuals whose ideas have been adopted and developed into formal proposals to join the supervision process (Ningbo Shi Renmin Zhengfu Fazhan Yanjiu Zhongxin 2007). During its annual conference, Ningbo PPCC designates 'key proposals' based on the matters raised and the suitability (as it sees them) of the suggestions. The PPCC has set up mechanisms to supervise how these key proposals are dealt with by the relevant government departments. An important part of the supervision work is a meeting chaired by the PPCC Chairperson attended by relevant PPCC members, and Directors from the local CCP Committee and government. Citizens who put forward ideas and suggestions to the PPCC are also invited to attend these meetings.

For example, in 2007 two citizens answered the PPCC's first call for ideas and suggestions from the public by suggesting that there should be a better supply of affordable rental housing supplied for low-income households. The idea was adopted and turned into a formal proposal by the Jiu-San Society, one of the eight minor political parties, and passed on to the Ningbo Government Commission of Housing and Urban–Rural Development (HURD) to be processed. A few months later, the two citizens were invited to a meeting organized by the Chairperson of the PPCC, where the HURD reported on measures to be taken and the Deputy Mayor made further promise to revise the city's current policy on low-rent and fixed-price housing (*Renmin Zhengxie Bao* 2007).

In order for its advisory work to be taken seriously by the CCP committee and government, in 2014 Ningbo PPCC put in place a mechanism to 'democratically assess' the local state's handling of PPCC proposals. The PPCC has set up an Assessment Committee to assess the work of two state organs each year that have received the most PPCC proposals. The committee examines whether the recipients have designated specific personnel to look into the issues raised in the proposals, what measures have been or will be taken, whether and how well the problems are solved, and whether the proposers are satisfied with the response (Zhengxie Ningbo Shi Weiyuan Hui 2014a). Under this initiative, the first state organ to be assessed was the city's Civil Affairs Bureau, which had received 119 PPCC proposals over the past three years. The Assessment Committee led by the Deputy Chairperson of the PPCC visited three nursing homes, examined the Bureau's archives and had a meeting with the Bureau where the Director of the Bureau reported on how the proposals had been processed (Zhengxie Ningbo Shi Weiyuan Hui 2014b).

Another major initiative of the Ningbo PPCC to strengthen its role in decision-making was to make all-members proposals to the local state. All-members proposals were to be selected from all proposals made by individual and collective members each year, examined by the PPCC leadership and voted on by all the members. The all-members proposals were 'supreme proposals' involving 'the overall situation of the city', which were to be passed on to the city's CCP Committee and government (Zhengxie Ningbo Shi Weiyuan Hui 2014b). In 2014, a year after the mechanism was first developed, the Ningbo CCP Committee issued a document on further strengthening the role of the PPCC in political consultation, in which it required that the all-members proposals were to be processed by the Mayor of the city and the work of putting things into place to be coordinated by the Chairperson of the PPCC.

The first all-members proposal was titled 'Suggestions on Accelerating Ningbo's Urban Economic Development', originally made by the Democratic Construction Association collectively at the PPCC 2014 annual conference. The proposal suggested that Ningbo's economic development should be accelerated by restructuring the city's urban space, establishing functional areas, focusing on technology and services industries, and further dividing power and revenue between the city and its subordinate county and district governments. Upon receiving the proposal, the city Mayor invited contributions from different key departments, including the city government's Development Research Centre, the Development and Reform Commission and Economy and Informatization Commission. Several months later, the city government submitted a written document of more than 13 000 words, almost ten times longer than the initial proposal, to the PPCC. In this document, the government confirmed the significance of the issue raised and reported that it had taken action as the proposal had suggested. In detail, the governmental response listed all the policies made and measures taken on spatial restructuring, and the development of functional areas and technology and services industries, and reported that it had conducted a series of reforms in the public administrative system (Zhengxie Ningbo Shi Weiyuan Hui 2014c). In the process, the PPCC played an active role in ensuring the proposal received adequate attention from the government. The PPCC came up with a scheme on how to supervise the handling process of all-members proposals, organized an inspection trip for its leadership to inspect a district's economic development, held two bimonthly discussion sessions for its members to discuss the proposal with governmental officials, invited the Mayor to give a speech on the city's economic development, and held several meetings for relevant governmental departments to report on the progress of the proposal's handling to the PPCC.

THE DIMENSIONS OF LOCAL GOVERNANCE

Who governs in a place 'where knowledge, wealth, social position, access to officials, and other resources are unequally distributed'? This is the question raised by Dahl in his seminal work on a city political system in 1960s America (Dahl 1961). Half a century later, this is still a crucial question to ask in the examination of power distribution in any political system. By studying the People's Congresses and the People's Political Consultative Conferences, this chapter has illustrated that in the one-party system of China, at the subnational level, governance is no longer the monopoly of the Communist Party committees and governments. Instead, it is now a more dynamic process that involves inputs from outside the party-state. The People's Congresses and the People's Political Consultative Conferences have been playing an increasingly active role in local governance, by supervising works of the Party committees and governments. However, it is important not to exaggerate the extent of change and argue that the type of pluralism that Dahl has observed in New Haven can be found in such an authoritarian system too. The composition of the PCs and the PPCCs clearly show that the party-state still dominates at local levels. This point is further highlighted by the very fact that both the PCs and the PPCCs have to adopt certain tactics to overcome institutional obstacles in order to improve the effectiveness of their participation in the decision-making process.

The examination of the PCs and the PPCCs also illustrates that certain social groups are regarded as bigger stakeholders in the local political economy and thus accorded with greater legitimacy to exercise political power. In both institutions, representation of private entrepreneurs is disproportionally high, which is the result of the private sector's increasing significance in China's economic growth. In this regard, the PCs and the PPCCs have become vehicles where selected elite members of the private sector are offered access (however limited) to state power.

Of course, one should be careful when making any generalization based on a couple of case studies. Local circumstances vary greatly across China. While the PC and the PPCC in Zhengzhou and Ningbo might well have gained credible policy influence, it would be naïve to assume that every subnational PC and PPCC is playing an equally important role in local politics. Experimentalism has always featured prominently in the party-state's approach to governance, in that it is common for a successful local initiative to be adopted and promoted elsewhere until it becomes a national agenda. The possibility that this may also be the case with the development of the role of People's Congresses and People's Political Consultative Conferences in local governance, as in Zhengzhou, Ningbo and indeed elsewhere, is therefore far from negligible, particularly given the party-state's need to reinforce its legitimacy and political capacity.

NOTES

1. Villagers' Committees are not a part of the government apparatus, but rather self-government organizations of rural villagers. However, the Party structure does penetrate to the village level.
2. 'Difang lingdao ziliao ku' (Dataset of local leaders), *People's Daily*, available at http://ldzl.people.com.cn.
3. In addition to the Chinese Communist Party, there are eight registered political parties (also referred to as democratic parties) in China, which are the Revolutionary Committee of the Kuomingtang, the China Democratic League, the China National Democratic Construction Association, the China Association for Promoting Democracy, the Chinese Peasants' and Workers' Democratic Party, the China Party for Public Interest, the Jiu San Society, and the Taiwan Democratic Self-Government League. The CCP plays a leading role by controlling the minor parties' policies, major appointments and budgets.
4. According to the CCP Charter, the Chinese Communist Party represents the development trend of advanced productive forces, the orientation of advanced culture, and the fundamental interests of the overwhelming majority of the Chinese people.

7. Post-Deng transformation of the People's Liberation Army: changes, continuities and consequences
You Ji

Post-Mao reforms have driven China's military transformation, which is a key component of the country's overall social engineering. Generally the People's Liberation Army (PLA) transformation has unfolded in three major areas simultaneously. Politically its interaction with the Chinese Communist Party (CCP) has undergone substantial changes with profound impact on CCP–PLA relations. Organizationally, the PLA's personnel composition and structure has been overhauled from peasant-based to one that is increasingly cosmopolitan. In terms of force modernization the PLA is taking on a brand new look through doctrinal innovation, capability enhancement and war preparation. The PLA reform has accelerated since Xi Jinping became the Commander-in-Chief in November 2012 and ordered the PLA to concentrate all its effort on improving combat readiness in order to fight and win the next war.[1] Clearly his hands-on approach of 'commanding the gun' is very different from that of his two post-Deng predecessors, and has further reshaped CCP–PLA relations (You 2014a: 60). This chapter will concentrate on the first category of PLA transformation, namely the change in CCP–PLA relations, although the other two will also be touched upon.

THE DUAL ROLE OF THE MILITARY

CCP–PLA relations testify to the dual role of the military in authoritarian states: to protect the Party-state in domestic politics, and to safeguard national interests against external threats. The PLA's transformation has gradually affected both its internal and external functions, as the military has become more professionalized and technocratic. Conceptually, CCP–PLA interaction has gradually moved beyond symbiosis, the paradigm that has served as the academics' depiction of China's civil–military relations for most of the PLA's history (Li 2006; Shambaugh 2003b). Symbiosis had long been the political sanction for CCP leaders to involve the PLA in civilian leadership and for PLA leaders to regard involvement in domestic politics as their rightful duty. The Cultural Revolution fully exposed how a symbiotic civil–military relationship allowed an all-powerful leader to use the military to fulfil his factional purposes, and how the PLA thus became politicized once it became involved in the Party's factional conflicts (Bullard 1985; MacFarquhar and Schoenhals 2006).

There has been a qualitative change in socio-political conditions that used to serve as the foundation of CCP–PLA symbiotic relations. Survival of the CCP and the PLA post-1949 is no longer any immediate CCP–PLA concern, although organized opposition to the government continues to exist and validate the CCP–PLA symbiosis. If changing civil–military relations in other transforming societies can serve as a guide to the PRC's case – such as the examples of the Union of Soviet Socialist Republics (USSR), Taiwan, South Korea, Indonesia and more recently Egypt (Segal 1992; Bullard 1997; Graham 1991) – it is highly probable that the PLA will survive China's political changes. Furthermore, other state institutions – that is, the State Council – also exert a great influence on the Chinese government structure. In the last decade or so, PLA researchers have proposed a number of conceptual frameworks to capture the changes in CCP–PLA symbiosis, such as conditional compliance, nationalized PLA control and conflictual interest groups (Mulvenon 2001; Scobell 2006; Harding 1987; You 1999). Yet the field is still in search of a new analytical framework that can generate sophisticated and theoretically viable predictions on the long-term trend of Chinese civil–military relations (Kiselycznyk and Saunders 2010).

The PLA's transformation can be measured by its post-Mao tendency to become technocratic and meritocratic. As a highly professional entity, the PLA has followed the path of professionalization of other advanced militaries in the world that draw their occupational differentiation from social sectors. This gives rise to a pronounced PLA elitist corporate identity and value orientation. The PLA is proud of being the guardian of national security. The primary mission that Deng Xiaoping assigned to the PLA was to protect China's sovereign rights, and this has increased the PLA's influence in civil–military relations (You 2014b). For a long time to come, the PLA will continue to carry out its dual role, but the external one may become more emphasized than the internal one. The exclusionary trend is rooted in its irreplaceable responsibility in managing increasingly more sophisticated high-tech weapons, and occupational functions that endow it greater autonomy in military force administration and operations. This poses a challenge for the Party and the PLA to strike a subtle balance between effective civilian control and substantial military cohesion in running the business of war, or military occupation. The changing CCP–PLA relations reflect a shifting equilibrium in favour of PLA corporate autonomy.

Most analysts equate Chinese civil–military relations with CCP–PLA relations, which is a narrower concept than the standard Western concept which also covers the military's ties with the state and civil and political society (Muthiah 2001). Although not a focus of this chapter, changes in PLA–societal ties will deeply affect the PLA's future and CCP–PLA interactions, which will ultimately determine China's political transformation. The PLA brands itself as both the Party's army and the people's army. This creates a unique PLA–society interplay whose post-Deng evolution has contributed to PLA conscription structure and mission change. Firstly, in terms of missions it no longer serves as a CCP instrument for grassroots mobilization. The 1989 confrontation convinced the PLA top brass of the need to shield PLA combat units from direct socio-political control. Now the People's Armed Police has taken up that job (Tanner 2009). Secondly, the Maoist 'people's war' doctrine formed a traditional bond between a revolutionary military and a politicized population, which underlined the wartime symbiotic soldier–masses ties. Now that the 'people's war' is no longer relevant to the PLA's mode of future combat engagement, the effect of its call for a 'nation-at-arms' has been greatly diminished. Simultaneously the demilitarized society occasioned a visible drop in PLA prestige in terms of career assessment, in line with the general trend of military roles in Asian states as the society becomes more modernized and the middle-class population becomes more influential (Muthiah 2001). Fault lines are widening in the PLA–society integration that marked the Maoist era.

This chapter argues that PLA transformation is not only a process of military professionalization driven by new military thinking and technology, but also a process of gradual de-revolutionization as a result of deepening professionalism and a depoliticized society. The civil–military nexus no longer exclusively concerns the CCP–PLA interplay but is also subject to societal influences as the armed forces respond to an increasing state–society rift. Ultimately PLA choices will be determined by the tripartite interaction of three key dynamics: the pace of China's overall political change; the pace and impact of societal depoliticization; and the pace of PLA professionalization and its fast-changing personnel structure. This is comparable to the transformed militaries in other, formerly authoritarian regimes, which indicates that symbiosis is a temporary phenomenon in transitional societies.

PHASING OUT CCP–PLA SYMBIOSIS: A CONCEPTUAL ANALYSIS

The Party in uniform informs the origin of the symbiosis. Such a paradigm depicts a rare type of civil–military relationship built upon unique socio-political conditions. In China prior to 1949 the cruel civil war meant that the outlawed CCP and its weak military depended on each other for mutual survival. This gave rise to the lack of functional differentiation and essential organizational boundaries in CCP–PLA ties throughout their formative years (Li Nan 2010). The CCP's seizure of state power reshaped the institutional foundation for the paradigm. Post-Mao reforms have accelerated the process driven by their different organizational imperatives in China's governance. Deepening civil–military diversification of organizational interests has reshaped the pattern of Party–army interaction in a more complex way than the symbiosis paradigm can effectively explain.

Specifically, the paradigm of symbiosis is built upon four pillars of Party–PLA relations, formed in wartime: (1) common goals: political (seize state power), ideological (nationalist and communist ferment) and revolutionary (social and economic change through military force); (2) an overlapping personnel structure reflecting an integrated decision-making process at the apex of power; (3) a near equal political status; and (4) shared mentality and vested interests in governance. These provided channels for civilian penetration into the military and for PLA intervention in elite politics. As a result, PLA intrusion into Party policy-making was considered not only legitimate but also desirable.

Changes have taken place in all these four parameters. A recurrent new mode of interaction has emerged, featuring a web of CCP–PLA political and institutional interests, often shared but in conflict from time to time. First, the PLA has defined itself as a revolutionary professional army, a self-contradictory terminology. The PLA has reconciled this by way of being more professional than revolutionary, which is no longer a viable organizational objective for the PLA when the Party has transformed itself from a revolutionary party to a ruling party.[2] And the PLA is no longer an instrument to facilitate social and economic change. The word 'revolution' that the PLA still clings to simply describes its support for the Party, with an increasingly weaker ideological hold on soldiers. Now the PLA's primary objective is to build a powerful fighting force, as called for by Xi (*PLA Daily* 2013a). Professionalization, driven by the information technology (IT) hi-tech revolution, has reoriented it more toward external concerns.

Secondly, the overlapping personnel structure was completely undone. In the Maoist era when PLA officers at the 6th Grade (the rank of lieutenant general) or above were transferred to civilian posts they retained their military status. And it was common for senior CCP cadres to take commissar posts in the PLA. The practice was aborted in the 1980s. At the Politburo level the last person following this rule was General Yu Qiuli, who returned to the PLA as head of the General Political Affairs Department in 1982, from the post of vice premier in charge of China's heavy industries. Yang Shangkun was the last civilian leader to wear a PLA hat.[3] Now there is no uniformed civilian charged with PLA affairs, nor a PLA general charged with civilian affairs. PLA presentation in the Politburo is minimized and largely functional.[4] There is a deliberate disconnect in the CCP–PLA personnel structure that politically and professionally prohibits unauthorized personal contacts between civilians and soldiers, which in turn curbs mutual organizational and political interference.

Thirdly, while the PLA is crucial in Chinese politics, the imposition of codified restrictions has prevented it from pursuing unauthorized non-professional activities. For instance, generals are not 'king-makers' in terms of political succession. Its key influence is expressed by its support to the top Party leader's power consolidation, which helps him to build elite consensus on controversial policies. Moreover the PLA's status has been visibly de-privileged in the overall Party–state apparatus and in the society. Partly this was by design of the CCP leaders, learning the lesson of the Cultural Revolution, and limiting PLA representation at the apex of power and its participation in local governance. Partly this was the generals' own choice, to ease their involvement in non-professional affairs, as seen in their push to renounce the PLA's once vast business empire in exchange for guaranteed increases in the defence budget. In the eyes of the population, the PLA's lowered social status means that, while a powerful institution, it is not above others in the system, such as the State Council. A survey in Shanghai revealed that the military profession was rated behind that of taxi driver, school teacher and cook as a desired career (Li Peilin 2004). The lower PLA status and social prestige in people's minds contrasts sharply with the first decades of the PRC, when joining the army was the top preference for youth.

NEW SOCIO-POLITICAL FOUNDATIONS FOR CCP–PLA RELATIONS

The changes in the fourth category are subtler. Today the Party and the PLA stick together, reflecting the remnants of symbiosis. The PLA shares the CCP's determination to maintain the existing system, and makes itself answerable to the Party's call against organized societal opposition. Its compliance to the CCP is reciprocated with the Party's respect for the PLA, voiced on major national issues, and is reinforced by generous resources allocations. Their shared vested interests are embedded in China's quest for national rejuvenation in terms of 'rich nation, powerful military' and global status, which is the foundation of Xi's 'China Dream'.[5] PLA soldiers embrace this 'dream' and have translated it into a PLA dream to build a military superpower. This is a key component of Xi's political leadership that is marked by his willingness to use the military as his primary power base.

Common-Fate Community

These shared national goals and political agenda result in a civil–military common-fate community where the PLA has little incentive or need to disobey the Party so long as it remains a powerful institution in Chinese politics. This community serves as a regime safety belt for the PRC, from which both Party and PRC benefit. At a time short of crisis the current formula of the PLA backing the civilians' political line in exchange for its preserved privileges and civilian support of its modernization will continue to hold.

Currently CCP–PLA ties are informed by the continuation of their bond formed in their long history of mutual support. PLA subordination to the civilians is part of China's traditional military culture (Huang 1981). One should not underestimate the Party's psychological hold on soldiers, who all take an oath of obedience to the CCP on their first day in the barracks. Diversified institutional interests notwithstanding, it is the shared interests that define the existing CCP–PLA interaction. Military power is the basis for territorial nationalism that contributes to the CCP's legitimacy. Military modernization serves the CCP's efforts to raise China's global profile, which in turn enhances the Party's popularity with the soldiers and the population (Liu and Sun 2013: 12). Inevitably this entails sustained inputs of resources. CCP leaders have ensured the rise of defence expenditure in keeping with the gross domestic product (GDP) growth rate. The National Defence Law provides the legal basis for the double-digit growth in military budget in the last two decades. Few ruling parties in the world are as nice as the CCP is to its Army, and vice versa.

The core PLA interests concern its combat capability and its corporate identity. Xi's urge for the PLA to be prepared for war has reshaped the CCP's post-Mao Party line of economics in command. Now the dual emphasis on war preparation and development has tightened the civil–military common-fate community (Zhang, Yingli 2014). Eagerly following Xi's call to win the next war, the PLA has prioritized capability enhancement in its transformation. China's assertiveness in staking its territorial claims is paralleled by an unprecedented level of PLA combat drills. In 2013 more than 40 sizeable joint military exercises were conducted, many of which took place in international maritime waters. Clearly the PLA has been increasingly focused upon external threats.

Potentially Structural Dichotomy: One Servant for Two Masters

On the other hand, a common-fate community is not equivalent to symbiosis, and is basically a relationship of shared interests. The long-term and strategic challenge to this give-and-take interaction lies on the domestic front; namely, how the PLA positions itself in the tripartite relations with the Party-state and society, the latter two being increasingly in conflict. The PLA defines itself as a Party's army, a people's army and a professional army (Zhang, Weibing 2008: 70). However, the three defining features inherently clash with each other.

The number of organized protests in China is mounting due to factors such as state–society tensions and the official corruption that drove China's traditional dynastic cycles.

In 2012 about 300 000 organized events were reported. So far these protests have been social and economic in nature, posing no immediate pressure on the PLA to make a choice between loyalty to the Party or loyalty to the people. However, China's political system indicates that when these protests are resolved, they are social and economic, but when they become hard to suppress, they become highly political. The prospect remains of the PLA being ordered to do street control, as China enters a risky period of change (Tong and Lei, 2013). And the probability of the PLA being forced to make an unwanted choice between the state and the society is increasing.

The real test of how the PLA handles the off-balance tripartite ties will come in a major social crisis. In conditions of symbiosis, the PLA's support to the Party is predictable, but in a common-fate community, such a prediction is subject to an interest calculus.[6] A hypothesis thus emerges that symbiosis is a transitional phenomenon, found in transitional regimes, and reflects an evolutionary course of different stages. In these transitional societies the ties between the ruling party and the military seem to be symbiotic in the absence of state–society confrontation. Yet once they no longer see their common survival in the same boat, the military would place its own interests first. Under such circumstances the military has to calculate the cost of suppression on behalf of the Party (Kou 2000: 27–51). History proves that the symbiotic civil–military relationship is neither a given, nor unshakable. The breakdown starts when a military embraces professionalism, de-emphasizes ideology and protects its own prestige, in keeping with general social change that deconstructs an authoritarian system. The trigger for this is often irreconcilable state–society confrontation that imposes the ultimate choice upon generals. China's case is more complicated than that of other transforming societies. Yet similar catalysts for change can be identified. Organizational atrophy is inevitable in all political institutions. This is especially logical for a ruling party which is huge in size, possesses enormous resources, but is under ineffective external checks and balances. The pace of internal Party decay accelerates, as the society modernizes.

The PLA Middle-Class-ized?

The qualitative structural change in the PLA's rank-and-file membership has set the background for symbiosis to become unsustainable. The PLA has altered its recruitment criteria to recruit urban youth with high-school graduation certificate, as their computer skills are essential for the PLA's IT transformation. To this end the CMC abolished its decades-old compulsory conscription ratio of 49:51 between urbanites and peasants in 2009. Additionally, in order to lessen unemployment pressure, civilian university graduates of whom the majority are of urban origin have been targeted as a major supplement to urban high-school conscripts.[7] To facilitate the process the CMC even shifted the annual recruitment time from December to July in 2013 so that college graduates can be quickly drafted. While enhancing the technological and educational quality of PLA personnel, they are changing the PLA's time-honoured peasantry culture from the inside out.

Although it is hard to measure the precise effect of these new developments on China's civil–military relations in terms of military–societal interaction, their impact is profound in several important ways. Firstly, for the first time in PLA history, urban intakes have exceeded those from the countryside. As China gradually moves toward industrialization and urbanization, it may eventually repeat the history of Taiwan, Korea and Singapore where the bulk of the servicemen are children of the middle class. This will happen more quickly in the officer corps. Secondly, Chinese society has become highly pluralistic, especially in the urban centres. As an outcome, the conscripts are diversified in terms of class origins, including (variously) the sons of the new rich, intellectuals, white- and blue-collar workers, and farmers. This means that also for the first time in PLA history the majority of its members are not proletarian or peasants. In a way this new organizational make-up better fits the PLA's self-identification as the people's army, embracing all social stratifications of the population. However, as such, many of its institutional objectives and traditional principles in managing coercion may be rendered unsustainable. For instance, a 'catch-all' military in terms of personnel composition may mismatch the regime-stability strategy of a class-based ruling party, unless the latter becomes a catch-all party itself with shared class interests as a governing principle. Furthermore, a catch-all military would acquire the logic of an established entity, and as a result a natural impulse against the revolution it defines itself by. In fact, the PLA has been regarded as a conservative organization among Chinese institutions of power. Will this change as the change of PLA personnel composition becomes structural? This is worth close observation.

Another serious and interesting question to ask is whether the PLA is following the path of other developed Asian societies – that is, Korea and Singapore – to become 'middle-class-ized'. To a degree this is happening in China's officer corps, with technocrats (engineers, computer operators and technicians) making an ever larger percentage in services rather than the army. As the proportion of PLA officers from civilian universities rises, they change the PLA personnel structure and mentality from within. Their ties with former classmates who constitute the pillar of China's expanding middle-class bring the new popular apolitical culture to the barracks, which is often seen as heretical by the top command. And the wide use of social media in the armed forces facilitates such mutual penetration. Moreover, new conscripts join the force no longer because, as in the past, the PLA's profile attracted politically motivated youth, but because it is simply an employer whose salary level is not so bad at a time of toughened competition in job markets. And to encourage more city dwellers to the service, the demobilized urban soldiers enjoy privileges in becoming public servants and state workers. Over time the PLA's declaratory organizational objectives and those for the enlisted start to mismatch, with a profound impact on military–societal relations.

RECONSTRUCTING AN ANALYTICAL PARADIGM: CONDITIONAL SUBJECTIVE CONTROL

On the basis of gradual but visible changes in CCP–PLA relations, this chapter advances an analytical framework of conditional subjective control to conceptualize the changed CCP model of 'commanding the gun', which lies in between the two Western concepts of subjective control and objective control (Huntington 1985). Both subjective control and objective control are about civilian supremacy over the military, but with distinctively different ways and means to deliver it under the top leader. Subjective control is based on thought indoctrination and personalized domination (the strongman type). Civilian leaders encourage military participation in internal conflict as ways of supporting particular elite clusters centred on specific dominant figures. The model normally refers to civil–military ties in authoritarian states where the level of military professionalism is low, but that of social tension is high. Objective control is a model in which civilian supremacy over the military is reinforced through promoting its professionalism and institutional autonomy. The result is a natural tendency to depoliticize soldiers and dampen generals' ambitions in non-military affairs. It advocates that the military is a tool of the state, and keeps a certain distance from domestic politics, a defining feature of democratic societies. The military is encouraged to be preoccupied with high-tech toys rather than ideological ferment (Huntington 1985).

The qualifier, 'conditional', is important here as it sets the defining purview of the concept of subjective control. First of all, CCP 'control of the gun' is moving toward a level of objective control, to curtail any excessive political zeal of the top brass, but this is happening in an authoritarian system where a level of PLA politicization is necessary to service the Party's hold on power. As long as the PLA is politically committed to supporting the CCP, its interventionist impulse is inherent, although confined within certain limits. Secondly, the PLA was so deeply involved in the PRC's creation and nation-building that it still sees itself as a key and rightful player in China's governance. Thirdly, high PLA professionalism is mitigated by high domestic tension, which forces it into state–society conflicts. Fourthly, China's external security environment uplifts the PLA's role in foreign and defence policy-making, which is a prescribed area of PLA responsibility. These factors set visible limitations for the concept of objective control to be applied to CCP–PLA interaction, as subjective control is still a viable way for the Party to 'control the gun' (Lee 2006).

The PLA has been behind almost all major political events in the PRC's history, although PLA intervention was seldom on its own initiative (Joffe 1997). Mao realized this threat to CCP leadership early on, when he warned his civilian colleagues that 'the party can create an army but the army can also create a party' (Gao 2011: 200). The PLA rarely initiated any coup vis-à-vis dominant Party leaders; probably only twice in its history: 1935 in Zunyi and 1976 in Zhongnanhai. Yet it is routinely involved in internal CCP factional conflict or policy debate that changes China's political course. In 1978 it was behind Deng's launch of post-Mao reform. In 1992 it sided with Deng to force the first-line leadership to adopt marketization as the driver for reforms. More recently in 2012 its support to Hu firmed Hu's determination to purge Bo Xilai.[8]

Therefore PLA monopoly of the means of coercion is a constant source of insecurity to all civilian leaders, who have designed extraordinary measures of control over the gun: regular transfer of PLA generals to different posts; appointing the local party secretary to be first party secretary to the garrison troops; and the Politburo Standing Committee's (PSC) oversight of Central Military Commission (CMC) membership selection. The relative imbalance of power in favour of the gun tilts further with the departure of paramount civilian leaders like Deng. In the last two decades, with the traditional subjective control methods of strongman control and divide-and-rule largely renounced, and with deepening professionalization, the PLA has maintained a fair level of unity that has gradually bred a corporate identity and spirit based on structural organizational integrity as a cohesive force. This can be a double-edged sword for civilians in transforming societies. A united military contributes to the ruling party when both share strategic interests, but could be a liability if they diverge over major issues. To the CCP an exclusive PLA corporate identity can be potentially hazardous if, for instance, it is under a powerful and politically ambitious general. As a result the civilian commander-in-chief faces a conundrum in that he wants the PLA to be politically conscious in fulfilling its internal functions against his challengers in the Politburo and organized societal opposition, but he does not want the PLA to be too political, so as to intervene overzealously in the civilian decision-making process. Put another way, he would involve the PLA in the Party's factional conflicts under the condition that he was in control of its involvement. This is typically a subjective control mentality, although in a modified form.

Therefore, post-Deng CCP–PLA relations have become a complex game where the right balance is desired: the PLA needs to be less interventionist toward domestic politics and internal party affairs, allowing the civilians to govern without undue military interference, but needs to stick loyally to the CCP–PLA common-fate community. This is possible only when generals accept civilian supremacy in accordance with the PLA culture of subordination to the Party and professional values. In meeting this huge challenge, what post-Deng leaders do is similar to what most civilian leaders in the world do: ensure that soldiers obsess more about external threats, with enhanced training for fighting and war, than about elusive political ambition. Xi's push for the PLA to intensify war drills is a smart method of civilian control of the gun. Professionalism is a viable substitute for ideological ferment that induces interventionist behaviour. Meanwhile, the CCP leaders continue traditional symbiotic elements of 'absolute control' to ensure PLA compliance.

Here, a model of conditional subjective control or, to put it in reverse, conditional objective control is used to capture some visible signs of change in post-Deng CCP–PLA ties. A strong but externally focused PLA would help to alleviate the generals' interventionist impulse rooted in the legacy of symbiosis. As such, a corporate identity that distinguishes military professionals from political activists can be a plus for Party control of the gun. One attribute of the objective control model in the West is a clear division between civilian and military elites that makes elite conflict among them an inter-institutional conflict (Perlmutter and LeoGrande 1982). The end of the Maoist symbiotic personnel structure paved the way for a similar evolution, reinforced by political taboos against unauthorized civil–military personal contacts. There has been no civil–military factional construction since the Yang brothers were removed from command of the gun in 2002.

Minimum political and professional conditions exist for conditional subjective control to be practised. Firstly, functional civil–military dichotomy is highlighted in their respective policy processes. The Maoist formula that 'the Politburo runs political affairs and the CMC military affairs' sets institutional boundaries for both to abide by, and allows the PLA a good measure of administrative and operational autonomy.[9] Secondly, as with soldiers in most past dynasties, soldiers' acceptance of civilian supremacy is both reflexive and cultural. Thirdly, the PLA does not aspire to rule the country directly, especially when it benefits from CCP rule. Fourthly, it has long been a professional military, even though it was, and to some extent still is, associated with many non-professional pursuits. Professionalism creates the foundation and incentives for the PLA to seek technological modernization. Last but not least, the CCP and the PLA are bound together in countering external threats. These prerequisites for conditional subjective control are both foundational and structural.

On the other hand, the word 'conditional' is also critical, defining the CCP's continued use of subjective control measures to hedge against potential PLA disobedience. The civilian commander-in-chief commands the gun through his institutional authority as

Party leader. With an ultimate tenure of ten years, this makes it impossible for him to exercise enduring Maoist personalized control of the armed forces. Generals' days in uniform are also fixed. This prevents faction formation around a few top PLA leaders from becoming structured and long-lasting.[10]

This model of conditional subjective control reflects the fact that after Deng's departure, no Party leader can exercise effective subjective control in a Maoist 'strongman' manner, and overt subjective control may provide incentive for the officer corps to grow political ambition that forms a backlash against civilian supremacy. Thus, involving generals in play with high-tech 'toys' can be an effective tool to divert them away from unwanted political pursuits. 'Conditional' sets a subtle balance between two contradictory demands for generals: to be political enough, but not overtly, as mentioned earlier. The PLA is still depicted as an armed institution carrying out political missions (its internal function). Thence subjective control is still an indispensable mechanism for the CCP's rule of China. This is why the Party continues to indoctrinate conscripts, and maintains procedural control over PLA appointments, although mainly through CMC nominations. Recently it has stepped up its efforts to repudiate Western conspiracy to depoliticize the PLA (Liu Xinru 2012). Yet civilians' pursuit of subjective control has been balanced by their prudence in involving soldiers in non-military business and by their effort to engage them in raising fighting skills much more intensively than ever before. This subjective control is made conditional without a symbiotic foundation. It is now conducted more in terms of inducement: that is, through coalition-building (non-factional formation) and career opportunities.

ANALYSING JIANG-HU ERA COMMAND OF THE GUN

China has not registered a major civil–military event since the ouster of the Yang brothers in 1992, which testifies to sustained civilian supremacy. This is unprecedented in CCP history, especially in the post-Deng context of power balance in favour of the generals.[11] Jiang and Hu were well known for their lack of revolutionary credentials and military experience, generally two crucial prerequisites for effective control of the gun in the CCP–PLA tradition. Furthermore, their inadequate personal power was reflected in their possessing no structured factional back-up in the Party and the military at the beginning of their reign. Indeed, upon assuming office Jiang and Hu confronted a huge challenge in winning PLA loyalty.[12]

Power Institutionalization as Key to CCP Control of the Gun

At the core of this challenge to Jiang in the 1990s was the reality that civilian supremacy of the strongman type was no longer viable. Yet a new constructive model on the basis of institutionalized safeguards against mutual intervention was still rudimentary. If not handled properly, a transitional vacuum may emerge with military heavyweights or ambitious politicians inclined to manipulate civil–military fusion to their advantage. This has occurred many times in Chinese history. Most observers expressed doubt about Jiang's power consolidation (Kiselycznyk and Saunders 2010: 22). However, the transfer of power from Party–military elders to post-Deng technocrats went peacefully.

Among many attributes to this evolution institutionalization of civil–military interaction is a key one. Post-Deng civilian control of the gun relied more on formal institutional posts of Party leaders than features of informal politics, such as charisma and faction-forging. This accorded Jiang a fair chance to triumph over the PLA generals (Wilson and You 1990). The pace and smoothness with which Hu and, to a lesser extent, Jiang consolidated their commanding position vis-à-vis the PLA proved the progressive depth of institutionalization (Shirk 2002: 303). More concretely, Hu's way of commanding the gun represented a sharp contrast with all his predecessors. Risking a level of simplicity, he was the first CCP leader to consolidate power not through first controlling the gun but through first fostering a high level of popularity in the Party and society, which helped to induce military compliance. He was also the first Party leader who managed generals not through first creating a structural personnel network within the Party and the PLA, but through his institutional authority based on the one-man commander responsibility system anchored in the CMC Chair (You 2009: 55–92). Hu's command of the gun was built upon CCP–PLA institutionalization during the Jiang era. History presented him with no full military power until Jiang stepped down in 2004. Yet both of them were fully committed to the control of the gun through organizational regulations, procedures and norms. They made sure that PLA non-interventionism toward non-military affairs would be institutionalized, so that it transcended from a choice to a norm or a culture. When they left office, this was largely a reality. Even PLA elder Zhang Zhen praised Hu's leadership in an unusual manner (Zhang Zhen 2009: 49).

Institutionalization is a rule-based control mechanism, and a process by which the organization acquires value and stability (Huntington 1968: 12). Here, value may not be as important as stability for leaders who survived the Cultural Revolution. Institutionalization is especially an effective weapon for weak technocrats vis-à-vis powerful generals at a time of dynamic socio-political change. Tied to their formal posts is the official legitimacy that exerts huge constraints on anyone who intends to rock the boat, as any opposition to the leader personally could be accused as opposing the Party itself. For instance, Deng's three-in-one arrangement of institutional power for Jiang – namely, Party leader, state President and Commander-in-Chief – compensated for his lack of personal followings in interacting with his CCP–PLA colleagues. This trinity of power enabled Jiang and, later, Hu to maximize their institutional authority in running PLA affairs. Here the position of CMC Chair is of particular importance. Traditionally Mao and Deng endowed it with enormous personal power through long years of domination of Chinese politics. This legacy blurs what is the legitimate institutional purview of power and personal authority and has been inherited by their successors, although they had to build the institutional power first in order to accumulate personal power.

Jiang and Hu took advantage of this tradition, whereby the power of the CMC was somewhat derived from the power of its Chairs who represented the Party leadership. In CCP norms the authority of the CMC Chair is embedded in his paramount party position, but the reality is a lot subtler. Jiang was criticized for retaining his CMC Chair after retiring from his Party and state positions in 2002. Yet the combination of both institutional authorities was the key for weak civilian leaders to tame generals, as they could use either to deal with their civilian and PLA colleagues. It brought the strength of Party organization behind the civilian CMC Chair vis-à-vis the top brass. On the other hand this combination could also be employed as an institutional bridge for the PLA to influence the government, often in the form of the CMC Chair representing PLA interests. Jiang used this privilege to the full, while Hu was not as relentless.

One essential goal of post-Mao military reform is to channel the PLA role in domestic politics through officially designated organizational settings and state process of legal and regulation formulation, for example annual sessions of the National People's Congress and the Central Leading Groups on foreign, national security and Taiwan affairs. It was under Jiang and Hu that the body of laws and regulations to discipline PLA political pursuits and behaviour expanded greatly. Between 1990 and 2010 the Party-state and the military promulgated 104 sets of laws regarding civil–military relations. The CMC sponsored 224 pieces of laws and regulations, and PLA headquarters and military regions more than 3000 pieces.[13] For instance, enacted in 2009, the Emergency Response Law of the PRC prescribes clearly defined roles of the PLA and the PAP in times of national emergency or any circumstances or incidents that might trigger a potential crisis.[14] It contains detailed provisions on the approval process of committing armed soldiers in domestic situations. The significance of institutionalization is to avoid the worst of Mao's practice of using the gun to settle internal party disputes.

Institutionalization is embedded in abiding rules, norms and regulations including terms in office, CMC–Politburo reporting and reviewing systems on major policy initiatives, and measures of internal checks and balances. For instance, the age rule is important for institutionalized civilian–military interaction, designed to achieve two internal checks-and-balances goals. Firstly, generals' tenure in office is fixed. This prevents them from expanding their power indefinitely, a precondition for a military strongman to emerge. Secondly, it is used to tackle a thorny question of who will be in or out in forging the top brass. Age demarcation by decade defines the generation of CMC leadership. For instance, leaders born in the first half of the 1940s forged the bulk of the fourth-generation CMC with Hu as the core. Now they have all departed, paving the way for those born in the late 1940s and early 1950s to take over. This 'tyranny of age' ensures minimum fairness in personnel management: everyone is equal in the face of an age limit. The age rule also matches an objective criteria for officer selection, for example a two-term preference for the sake of personnel and policy stability (Kou 2011). Under Jiang and Hu all these measures were enhanced to curb the PLA's interventionist tendency.

The political importance of institutionalization and norm-building lies in its function as a key item in the CCP–PLA system of internal checks and balances that helps to slow down the pace of CCP–PLA organizational atrophy. This has been the driving force for the so-called Party internal reforms (Nathan 2003: 6–16). The cumulated effect of institutionalizing civil–military ties points to one fact: that it is part of an unannounced political reform. Put differently, it is the way for political reform to radiate from the periphery to the core of the political system. This was proved by Hu's 'naked exit' in the 18th Congress in November 2012; a precedent in CCP–PLA history since Mao that when the Party leader stands down he should also leave his post as Commander-in-Chief. The significance was profound. Firstly, it was the most important measure of power institutionalization that generated pressure no future leader could ignore. Secondly, it unified the first-line leadership (Party General Secretary) and the second-line leadership (CMC Chair), a long-existing phenomenon in the CCP–PLA relations that had caused repeated elite conflict since the 1950s. Thirdly, it strategically codified CCP–PLA interaction in that unifying Party and military leadership eliminated a national security hazard when the top Party and national leader was only advisor to the CMC Chair. This confused the command chain, the authority to declare war and control of the nuclear button. China was fortunate during the periods of the Deng–Jiang and Jiang–Hu transition of power that there was no major national security crisis.

Promoting PLA Professionalism and Meritocracy

No CCP leader did more than Jiang and Hu in campaigning for PLA professionalism. As engineers they both sensibly recognized the PLA's irreplaceable expertise in managing complex military technology that requires a high level of functional autonomy.[15] Professionalism is the lifeline for the PLA, as it faces realistic war scenarios with powerful, professional and better-equipped adversaries. PLA efforts to handle a sophisticated war machine create a logic to raise the level of professionalism, which is resistant to outside interference. This tendency constitutes the basis for civilians to employ conditional objective control of the gun to ensure PLA compliance.

Meritocracy: The Core Value of PLA Professionalism

Jiang and Hu changed PLA personnel management, so that it evolved around the concept of meritocracy. In a way this helped the PLA to refer back to the Chinese elitist literati tradition and culture. Meritocracy converts one type of scarcity of resources – specialized knowledge and professional skills – into another: social status and material rewards. It reflects a kind of uneven distribution of power and privileges in short supply, the stimulant for officers to venture along a progressively narrow path to the top. It rewards competence, expertise, professional judgement, efficiency and management sophistication (Larson 1997).

For meritocracy to take hold in a peasant army that traditionally enshrined egalitarianism, power has to be gradually institutionalized, its objective reasonably depoliticized, its daily focus professionally reoriented, and its internal structure suitably altered to cater for technological change. PLA meritocracy is reinforced by professionalization, driven by officer selection and promotion, hardware and software upgrades, and the daily running of combat activities. For instance, when Jiang and Hu screened PLA candidates for the 16th Central Committee, they first evaluated their tertiary qualifications, followed by a check on their age. It is said that when they found any candidate without a college degree or above a certain age, they would not bother with any further inspection of his CV but simply wrote on the front page: 'not considered'.[16]

The increasingly competitive promotion procedures have facilitated the emergence of a competitive environment, and a culture of officers improving their own ability while fostering good ties with superiors. For those candidates lucky enough to prevail in officer selection, they did so at a ratio of 1.5–2 times for officers at the tactical levels, and 2–3 times for commanders above the campaign levels (*Newspaper of the PLAAF* 2010). By the time of Hu's retirement, 20 per cent of all commanders at or below the battalion level had either PhD or MS degrees, and 25 per cent of foot soldiers had a Bachelors degree, a phenomenon previously unimaginable for an army that was so recently dominated by peasants (*PLA Daily* 2012b). The see-saw battle among conservative and open-minded officers is on between honoring history, efforts to change the present, and ambition to shape the future.

Professionalized Officer Corps

Professionalizing the PLA begins with professionalizing the officer corps. Since the Politburo took the decision to accelerate war preparations in 1999, the search for new combat capabilities (hardware and software acquisition) has highlighted the imperative to absorb new knowledge in military science and technology, the key to which is the training of new officer corps (Hao 2007: 23). These two demands have converged in bringing about a new army of technologically capable officers. The selection criteria for future PLA leaders have been formulated accordingly. In order to facilitate PLA professionalization, selection criteria have been computerized, blindly assessing candidates at divisional level or below. The difference in the pattern of cadre promotion from the past has become more obvious in that even if a candidate is strongly favoured by his mentor for a leadership role, he first has to pass the initial test of meritocratic requirements, specifically set for performance, expertise and education credentials. And he has to go through a series of internal checks-and-balances procedures. Below is a tough list of compulsory qualifications:

1. Tertiary qualifications: an essential requirement.
2. Strategic vision: reflected by a record of academic and policy-related publications, an answer to Hu's call for the PLA to become a learned military, and senior officers 'learned commanders' (Liu, Yazhou 2010: 5).
3. Experience as principal military commander: an essential criterion for an officer to climb to the very top (*PLA Daily* 2013b).
4. Chief of staff positions: the position of chief of staff and deputy chief of staff can be a short cut for promotion (Jiang 2006a: 19).
5. Crucial combat missions or missions of military operations other than war (MOOTW). The PLA's 2011 Regulation on Cadre Selection and Promotion Procedures clearly states that all candidates to enter the cadre reserve lists at senior levels must be tested in major special and routine tasks (Guo Boxiong 2010).

Professionalization of the officer corps is the foundation for overall PLA transformation. This can be measured by its changing personnel composition. By 2009, 82 per cent of PLA officers above the regimental level and 92 per cent of the officers below that level had higher education qualifications. By 2009, more than 700 officers at the brigade level or above were dispatched each year to study intensive military courses and conduct purpose-specific fieldwork trips in foreign countries. Twelve per cent of all the officers had a Masters degree. One important gauge of PLA professionalization is the proportion of technocrats in the overall officer corps. In 2008, 36 per cent of PLA officers were technological staff. In Special Services, the proportion was much larger. For instance, 70 per cent of all officers were technicians in the Strategic Missile Force (SMF) (*PLA Daily* 2012a; Xinhua 2009). Among the Navy's new recruits in 2013, one-third were graduates from civilian universities versus only 3 per cent of rural intake with middle school certificate.[17] Non-commissioned officers, who can serve in the military for up to 25 years, now make up about half of the total PLA soldier population in special services. In technical posts they account for 80 per cent of voluntary conscripts (*PLA Daily* 2012c). All this substantially contributes to the PLA's expertise and 'corporate-ness'.

Shielding the PLA from Domestic Political Missions

The PLA's transformation has made it a high-tech force, increasingly unsuitable for domestic missions of political control. Under Jiang the CMC initiated a far-reaching reform of the People's Armed Police (PAP), enabling it to shield field armies engaged in domestic duties. PLA influence on the national security policy-making process was enhanced under Jiang and Hu. It was Jiang who in 1998 put forward the idea of creating a National Security Council with the CMC playing a core role. It caused concern about excessive PLA influence in national security, although the military role in this area is seen as legitimate globally (Kohn 1994: 3). What Jiang and Hu achieved was a subtle balance: subjecting national security concerns and external PLA initiatives to serving their policy priority of domestic stability (Liu, Jixian 2008: 2).

The post-Deng leaders have realized that institutionalised civil–military relations can be achieved only when the civilians and the generals strike the right balance between effective civilian control and sufficient military autonomy. When the former is ineffective, generals may be tempted to maximize their influence at the expense of other political and social interests. When the latter is insufficient, civilian control can be intrusive, destabilizing bilateral relations and professional PLA pursuits. Jiang and Hu promoted military autonomy as a focus of professionalizing civil–military interaction, following Mao's formula of a Politburo–CMC divide, as mentioned earlier. In this politically laid boundary of responsibilities the CMC seeks strategic guidance from the top civilian leadership but enjoys substantial autonomy in its daily management. The CMC is a Party organ but is entirely composed of professional soldiers, while all but one member in the Politburo is charged with military affairs. Under the codified rules of the game mentioned earlier, this separation of organizational elite and functional responsibilities guarantees a good level of PLA autonomy and serves as the precondition for both institutions to move out of the relationship of symbiosis.

At the organizational level, thanks to unparallelled CMC power, the PLA has acquired a relatively independent status vis-à-vis the centre of Party power. In the CCP's hierarchical chain, the CMC is under the Politburo. In actuality, the CMC largely operates outside the latter's reach. This has been a long tradition since Mao's formula of Politburo–CMC division of labour. In August 1950 Mao ordered the Central Committee (CC) Central Organizational Department to formally switch PLA cadre management to the PLA General Political Affairs Department (GPAD) (Mu Song 2009). This bifurcation gave the PLA a high level of autonomy in senior appointments.

The state administration has no agency overseeing military affairs. This political division of power erects a firewall that prevents unauthorized interference from each side, but more importantly, allows the top brass to concentrate on military affairs. At the policy level, while the PSC is theoretically the ultimate forum for key military decisions, it is the PLA that takes the policy initiatives over national defence. It would be a foregone conclusion that most military policy proposals submitted to the PSC would be rubber-stamped, because these are already cleared by the CMC with the green light given by the

Party General Secretary wearing the hat of CMC Chair. While this shows civilian respect for the CMC's professionalism in terms of allowing it autonomous decision-making power, it paves the way for Party control to be abstracted. This can be seen more clearly at the administrative and operation levels where the PLA has gained most autonomy, including personnel management, budgetary allocation to the services, review of defence strategies, salary matters, troop deployment, weapons research and development (R&D) programmes and so on. The PLA's legal and disciplinary authorities are independent in handling its own criminal cases. None of these, however, can be compared with the effects of the deaths of Party and military elders who had taken it for granted to cross the civilian–military boundary. Now an unprecedented level of autonomy in managing its own affairs has resulted in the PLA's decreased need and will to get involved in civilian politics.

PARTY AND ARMY

This chapter has discussed a key component of China's military transformation, namely, the PLA's relations with the CCP. It traces various institutional and political catalysts for the country's civil–military relations to undergo great changes, with a profound impact on the overall transformation that China is experiencing now and will do in the future.

Firstly, in recognizing that the time-honoured paradigm of symbiosis has lost its explanatory power about the nature of post-Mao CCP–PLA relations this chapter has tried to construct a new analytical framework to interpret the changes in Chinese civil–military relations. Here the concepts of common-fate community and conditional subjective control are useful and pertinent to guide exploration of the PLA's new roles and functions in the altered domestic and international environment, especially in a context of CCP elite politics in transition. The chapter argues that in the foreseeable future the shared vital interests and common national goal will define CCP–PLA interaction. The military obedience to civilian supremacy can be taken for granted. However, in the long run the PLA will encounter hard choices in handling off-balanced tripartite relations between itself and the state and society, as the conflict between the latter two becomes increasingly structural. And its choice will determine the ultimate course of China's political transformation. The outcome is significant.

Secondly, the direction of China's changing civil–military relations will also be dependent on changing PLA–society relations. Chinese society is gradually becoming middle class. This is of direct relevance to the armed forces, the members of which are becoming progressively urban and worldly. The transition from a peasant-based army to a professional one composed of and commanded by urban technocrats will gradually change the PLA from the inside out. Although the immediate outcome of this structural change in personality is not clear, the long-term logic is apparent if the history of other transforming societies can be a guide. Furthermore, if we go by this guide and logic, the next thing we can assume is that the PLA would survive a colossal political event in China, as militaries in other transforming societies have done. This is an important point of this chapter, one that has been neglected by China specialists as a whole.

Thirdly, the chapter argues that there has been a general balance in CCP–PLA interaction in that the PLA reflexively yields to Party control, while the CCP respects PLA autonomy in administration and operations. However, there are institutional loopholes in such a delicate equilibrium. The Party leadership is more one of political and ideological guidance, without substantial organizational strength to underpin it. The result can be ineffective civilian oversight of PLA daily management, as seen from the Xu Caihou case. Xi Jinping's hands-on approach of commanding the gun may alleviate this fatal systemic flaw, but only sound outside and inside institutional checks and balances can address this challenge in a fundamental manner. There is a long way to go for both the Party and the PLA to work at this problem.

There is no doubt that the PLA has been a decisive force in Chinese politics and development. Its transformation is part of China's overall transformation, and is driven by it. However, PLA transformation can be an independent variable impacting on China's overall transformation in a qualitative way. As far as China's civil–military relations are concerned, the ongoing changes are visible, but their full significance cannot be adequately measured until a great event occurs that triggers a colossal socio-political change in the country. Then the PLA's role will be fully appreciated.

NOTES

1. Xi Jinping arranged a special study session for the Politburo to discuss military affairs on 29 August 2014. War preparation was the central theme, and through preparing for war in the digital era a consensus was forged at the apex of power, which contributed to both Xi's power consolidation and PLA influence in China's body politic (*PLA Daily* 2014).
2. At the 4th Plenum of the 16th Central Committee (CC) in September 2004, Jiang called on the CCP to transform itself from a revolutionary Party into a catch-all ruling Party with a wide class base (that is, admitting capitalists into the Party).
3. At lower levels the Party transfers trusted PLA officers to sensitive state agencies, for example the Ministry of State Security. A number of divisional ranking officers were allocated to the Chinese Academy of Social Sciences as its institutes' Deputy Heads after 4 June 1989 as a way to enhance Party leadership in these 'disaster zones'. Yet these were exceptional cases, rather than any pattern of mutual penetration.
4. Considering the restoration of military ranks in 1985, some Party leaders suggested that since local Party Secretaries concurrently held the position of the First Party Secretary of the regional garrison, they should be granted a military rank. Deng personally vetoed the motion (Pu Jinbao 2008).
5. 'Rich nation and powerful military' was confirmed as the national goal at the Party's 18th Congress in November 2012. Global status was added to the national goal by Xi in 2013.
6. Almost all PLA officers I have interviewed over long years of research seemed to be certain that repetition of the 1989 armed clampdown would be out of the question. Such a probability shrinks as time passes, and China's political, social and economic change deepens.
7. In 2013 there were about 7 million college graduates seeking jobs. At least 20 percent of them would have great difficulty in finding one. Military service then becomes a choice for them to transit to more stable employment later (*National News at 7pm*, CCTV-1, 25 July 2013).
8. Shortly after Bo's reported visit to the 14th GA, which was founded by his father, CCP elder Bo Yibo, in February 2012, Hu issued a brief order: 'Be sensible and sensitive to politics, sacrifice for the overall Party interests, and observe discipline'. Then Guo Boxiong and Xu Caihou made a series of tough speeches to urge PLA generals to follow Hu's line (*Daily Military Report*, CCTV-7, 25 February 2012).
9. Mao reiterated this formula at a Politburo meeting in December 1972 that decided on the circulation of eight Military Region Commanders. Interestingly, at a time of great political uncertainty, Mao added that the PLA should also involve itself in political affairs (*PLA Life*, 20 August 2009).
10. A convincing proof is that after Xu Caihou's indictment in June 2014 his influence evaporated immediately. Xu's decade-long control of PLA personnel affairs was the longest in the post-Deng era.
11. For instance, Jiang's CMC deputies – Generals Liu Huaqing and Zhang Zhen, two veterans of the Long March – enjoyed far more revolutionary prestige and military authority than Jiang.

12. Jiang used the words 'taking office at a time of acute crisis' to describe his feelings when he first arrived in Beijing (Qi Yiming 2013).
13. See www.china.com (accessed 29 December 2013).
14. Emergency Response Law of the People's Republic of China (2010), Beijing: Fazhi chubanshe.
15. Jiang and Hu issued many instructions on PLA professionalization (*PLA Daily* 2010).
16. Interview with a senior PLA researcher in Beijing, late October 2002.
17. *Naval Newspaper*, 14 October 2013.

PART II

PUBLIC POLICY

8. Managing government finance
Linda Chelan Li

Decisions on public monies are arguably the most important set of political decisions made during peacetime. They are products of protracted negotiations between diverse and often conflicting interests, but are often manifested only in government budget books as revenue and spending statistics. The neatness of numeric representation disguises the nuances of the negotiation process, which is highly opaque even in the most participative jurisdictions. The technical nature of fiscal management reduces accessibility further. A popular saying in the PRC captures the accessibility challenges: 'the outsider has no clue; the insider has no clear picture' – even fiscal workers in government complained about the murkiness of fiscal information outside their own immediate domain. A large part of the story of the public purse was at best cursorily speculated by the nosiest observer. What are the priorities informing revenue collection and spending? How are these important decisions made and what is their rationale? What are the impacts? Systematic scrutiny of these key questions in the management of government finance has been immensely difficult in all political systems (Wildavsky 1986 [1997], 1992; Goode 1984; Hillman 2009), including China.

This chapter reviews the literature on government finance in China to give a bird's eye view of the key themes of discussion. Three generic themes are identified: the objective, organization and governance of government finance. The theme of the objective of government finance refers to discussion on the ultimate purpose(s) which government activities are, and should be, directed to achieve through government finance. Permeating the discussion is the understanding of the role of the government. The literature also tends to harbour a more explicitly normative flavour than the other two themes, as starting a discussion of objectives embodies an opening to evaluate and reflect, and to seek change. The second theme, the organization of government finance, discusses how the various parts constituting the totality of public monies are managed through the design of the budget(s), and how this organization is managed both across the immense geographical spans through the multiple vertical tiers of the state, and across functional or sectoral boundaries through the departments. This subject of discussion contains both descriptive and normative dimensions, which are sometimes distinct and at other times intermingle, as the understanding of 'what is' shapes the vision of the 'desired future', and vice versa. The third theme, the governance of government finance, discusses how rules and norms of practice together define decision-making on revenue and spending, including key decision-makers, characteristics of the decision-making process, dissemination of the decisions, and evaluation. Needless to say, this is the most political theme of the three, and where opaqueness of the subject matter is the thickest. Governance is also arguably the 'short leg' of the three in terms of the distance travelled, both in scholarly discourse and in 'real world' practice. Similar to the objective, governance decisions are close to the *raison d'être* of a regime, and are thus slow to change.

A note on the literature is in order here before I start a review of the three themes.

First, the literature outside China has been visibly populated by international donor players, the World Bank in particular. A keyword search of 'China' and 'fiscal' that my colleagues and I conducted on the World Bank website on 15 May 2014 returned a total of 331 World Bank publication items.[1] Also noteworthy is the close relationship between research and policy, partly a consequence of the preponderance of World Bank works in government finance literature, which have a heavy user orientation. The World Bank teams often worked closely with the Chinese Government in their studies, while a good proportion of studies by Chinese scholars were conducted as a deliberate contribution to, at least in part, the ongoing policy discourse (Yan 2009). An examplar of research–policy collaboration is *Public Finance in China*. The 2008 volume was co-edited by Lou Ji-wei, then Deputy Secretary-General of the State Council and Finance Minister since 2013, and Shulin Wang, an economist at the World Bank. World Bank Vice-President of East Asia and Pacific Region James W. Adams complimented the book in its Foreword as representing 'the best about World Bank-sponsored analytical work . . . [as it consists of] ideas from different sources . . . [and its] contributors include some of China's most important economic reformers' (Lou and Wang 2008: xiii).

OBJECTIVE: WHAT GOVERNMENT FINANCE IS TO ACHIEVE

Getting the objective right is intuitively important for all activities, and more so for complex activities such as government finance, given the large sunk cost that would need to be invested to redirect activities at the time of goal adjustment. Ironically, precisely because of its critical importance, the question of objective is often set aside initially in the course of change, only to be picked up later when de facto changes to the original objective have made questioning it less threatening. For a full 20 years after economic reform began in China, the 'objective' of government finance remained on the sidelines of major reform policy discourse, so that the fiscal reforms embarked upon during this period mostly revolved around organizational issues, as the next section will elaborate.

Ultimately, the 'objective' of government finance refers to the role of government in society: what the government should rightfully seek to achieve through its actions in society. The conception of the government role guides the specific decisions on fiscal revenue and expenditure, as the financial side of the government should follow substantive policy decisions. Discussions on the objective of government had on the whole been conspicuous by their absence in the post-Mao reform discourse during most of the 1980s and 1990s, however. While economic reform called for radical changes in the ways the party-state managed the economy, and debates on reform directions carried a heavy ideological tone (for example, the fierce debates over the relative weight and roles of the 'plan' vis-à-vis the 'market' in the late 1980s and early 1990s), there was in fact minimal reference in the reform literature in those years to the objective, and role, of the government per se, except in passing. There was even less discussion on the linkages between changes in economic management methods and arrangements in the budget, so that budgetary reforms were executed in largely technical and organizational terms without much reference to the purposes the changes were to serve.

A closer look into the literature reveals a small stream of works on 'changing government's functions' emerging inside China in the mid-1980s, which blossomed into a steady body of work in the 1990s. The promulgation in 1984 of the landmark Decision on Economic System Reform at the Third Plenum of the Twelfth Party Congress consolidated the early successes of enterprise reform and rural agricultural reform, calling for a complete revamp of the economic system with 'enlivening the enterprises' as the core theme, and reduction of government control over micro-economic management as the key method (CCP Central Committee 1984). This triggered off a discussion over the necessity to review the theory on the role of government (e.g., Tan 1985; Chen 1986). In 1986 the first national conference on 'Role of Government' was convened in Taiyuan of Shanxi Province, and more than 60 papers were presented for discussion amongst participants from the Chinese Academy of Social Sciences, the China Public Administration Society, Shanxi officials and scholars, and other provinces (Xu 1986). Changing the role of government became a salient part of the reform agenda at the time of the Fourteenth Party Congress in 1992, after the 'Southern Tour' of paramount leader Deng Xiaopeng in January and February 1992 reinvigorated discussions on opening up and reform (Li 1992). The topic of 'changing government's role' gained a heightened sense of urgency in 1998, when Premier Zhu Rongji started drastic downsizing of State Council units (Zhu 2002). When Vice Premier Li Nanqing conceptualized the new 'public finance' approach to government finance in the national fiscal conference in December 1998, the new vision for government functions was translated and operationalized in budgetary terms (Zhu 2000; Li, J. 2001).

Since then the theme of 'changing government's functions' has become a frequent topic of scholarly and policy discourse.[2] For example, in 2004 the Chinese Academy of Social Sciences started a multiple-year research project to define a home-based theory of public finance with a comprehensive set of measurement indicators, and has published annual research reports from 2007.[3] An 815-page collection was published in 2013, consisting of 72 fiscal reform research reports written by officials from the Ministry of Finance and its regional field offices, to report the latest progress in reform experiments and ideas on possible future measures to advance the objective of 'changing the government's role' (Lou 2013). The latest developments saw further calls by the central leadership for 'comprehensively deepening reforms' to align government acts with the new vision on government roles (e.g., CCP Central Committee 2013; Li, K. 2014; State Council 2014a). Reflecting the increased popularity of the topic, the counts of journal articles on 'changing the government's role' have increased phenomenally since 2013.[4]

With a few exceptions,[5] the English-language literature outside China has not included much explicit discussion on the evolving conception of the role of government, but has dwelt more on implementation issues of the role as reflected in the execution of various sectoral segments of the budget. World Bank studies are a major source of such contributions, covering topics from rural development and public finance (World Bank 1999a, 1999b, 2007a, 2007b, 2008), uneven progress and poverty (World Bank 2004b), urban infrastructure and land (World Bank 2006a, 2006b, 2005b), to health care (World Bank 2010a). Several major sectoral reforms with significant fiscal dimensions have attracted substantial interest in the academic literature, including rural tax reform (Li, L.C. 2012; Göbel 2010; Yep 2004), transfers (Lin and Wong 2012; Liu et al. 2009), health finance (Chen et al. 2012; Zhang et al. 2013; Liu et al. 2011) and school finance (Li and Wang 2014; Li and Painter 2013; Wang et al. 2012). Through in-depth analysis of policy documents, comparative institutional data and, in some cases, data from extended ethnographic research, these works discussed in considerable detail the institutional arrangements, trends of revenue and spending as well as policy underpinning. They looked into the murky processes of implementation and decision-making of aspects of government finance to expose the intricate relationship between institutions, actors and time. The rich shades of history hence revealed added nuances to the often neat – even misleading – representation of official accounts given by government reports and fiscal statistics.

Readers are reminded that actors often harboured more complex inclinations than was assumed, which also changed substantially over time, and that upon close inspection, the actors' interactions and mutual impacts exhibited more variety and complexity than was expected. For example, in a careful re-reading of historical documents and analysis of events, Teiwes and Sun (2013) reconstructed the shifting roles of Deng Xiaoping and Chen Yun in economic policy-making in the late 1970s and early 1980s, and found that the duo had in fact held similar, not opposite, views on economic readjustment in the critical year of 1980. This is contrary to the official account and much of the literature on the subject, which had emphasized the divergence of their policy inclinations (reform versus readjustment). In Li's (2007) study of the role of central and local government officials in rural tax reform, the official account of a unilinear process stressing the natural execution of a centrally formulated master plan was rejected in favour of a more indeterminate process of strategic interactions between central and local state actors, and of multiple disjunctions between intentions and outcomes. The design and implementation of the Rural Tax Reform was a 'living' process and a result of continual mutual adaptation between actors involved, it is found. Instead of struggling with notions such as implementation deficit and agency control, the study sees policy design and implementation as dual manifestations of a dynamic and fluid process. The key research question becomes then not one of explaining the deviation of implementation from the original design in a unilinear framework, but of understanding the characteristics of the dynamic process whereby implementation and design co-evolved through actors' interactions in shifting arenas.

So far the above discussion has focused on the objective of government finance in terms of the government's role. Apart from the government's role, however, there is a second meaning to 'objective' in government finance in the literature, which refers to the synchronization of the actual revenue and spending decisions with the pronounced policy of the government. Literature of this strand asks whether the financial side of government actually follows decisions on government objectives; whether government finance is organized in a way to facilitate such compliance. It is about the alignment of the intended role of government, as approved by authorities and articulated in laws and policies, and the government's actual, executed role, as realized and expressed by how the yuan are spent and extracted in real life.

Such has been the question raised in Wong (2009): has the budget implemented the policy priorities of the government? A lead author of a number of World Bank works on China, Wong observed, by tracing the historical trajectory, that government spending had evolved over time as an outcome of concurrent processes driven by diverse actors, rather than a product of preconceived strategy of development and reform by the central government. Much of the extensively documented fiscal decentralization had not been planned but took place 'by default', and the fiscal and related institutions developed in poor coordination, resulting in misaligned incentives and implementation gaps. A notable feature of this 'broken' intergovernmental fiscal system (Wong 2009: 942) was the delinking of spending and revenue assignments to subnational governments, which precipitated problems of widening inequity in basic public goods provision at the local level, mounting government debts and risks to macroeconomic political stability. On the one hand, the government had a stated policy that it should gear toward service provision as its primary role (the shift to a service-oriented approach to government). On the other hand, the actual conduct of government finance – revenue and spending decisions – followed a different logic and could not possibly meet the intended objective without a 'comprehensive reform' of all the relevant institutions (Wong 2009: 951; World Bank 2002, 2010a). The indictment is serious: the Chinese government had mismanaged the budget, and the abundant reform measures, simply did not add up.

ORGANIZATION: HOW GOVERNMENT FINANCE IS, OR SHOULD BE, ORGANIZED

Unlike the early dormancy of the 'objective' literature, the organizational dimension of the budget has, for a long while, dominated the literature on the government budget. The pioneering works by Audrey Donnithorne (1967 [2013], 1972) on the Chinese economy and the budget of the central plan period left us with a message that still resonates well with the ongoing debates in fiscal policy today: the role and status of local governments and communities in the continental expanse of the Chinese governance system. In a famous dialogue with Nicholas Lardy in 1976 in the *China Quarterly*, Donnithorne insisted that despite the importation of the Soviet system of the plan and socialist ideology, the traditional autarchy of the Chinese local communities had survived, if clothed with new colours, and the penetration of the state and the plan was far from complete (Donnithorne 1976; Lardy 1976b). This theme of local cellularism within a totalitarian state was echoed in Vivienne Shue's 'honeycomb and web' structure in her seminal essays on state and society in China, *The Reach of the State* (Shue 1988). The continental scale of China and the immense diversity in geographical and human conditions across space and communities necessitate the salience of the intergovernmental perspective in the discussion of the polity and its finance (Goodman 1995, 1997).

Oksenberg and Tong's (1991) meticulous account of the evolution of the formal system of central–provincial fiscal arrangements over 1971–84 starts a new phase of work in understanding the management of government finance in the People's Republic of China (PRC). The 'opening up' of China and the unfolding liberalization reforms improved research access somewhat, so that more detailed works became more feasible. Still, the discussion was confined largely to the formal systems as prescribed on paper, with the gap between the formal and informal, and between prescription and the practice, up to anyone's guess. A number of influential works on policy appearing then also benefited from emerging opportunities of in-China fieldwork and collaboration (Lampton 1987; Lieberthal and Oksenberg 1988; Lieberthal and Lampton 1992). Using anecdotal evidence on defined policy issues, these studies pioneered the probe into the informal processes and the web of interacting actors in the evolution of policy design and implementation. In the same period, the World Bank literature on China's government finance also started to warm up. After a stream of pioneering studies on finance and investment (World Bank 1987), higher education finance (World Bank 1986), budget and economic growth (World Bank 1986) and tax (World Bank 1990), amongst others, several major studies on intergovernmental fiscal relations were completed in the early 1990s (World Bank 1992a, 1992b, 1993). Together with the publication of several influential academic studies on central–local fiscal relations, and central–local relations more generally, around the same time or slightly after (Wong 1991, 1992; Jia and Lin 1994; Goodman and Segal 1995; Chung 1995; Breslin 1996; Li 1998), they established firmly the salience of the intergovernmental dimension in the management of government finance.

The focus on the intergovernmental dimension in the literature mirrors the actual policy developments: adjustments in the jurisdictions between government levels – decentralization and recentralization of various sorts – have constituted a substantial share of the policy initiatives to pursue reform and development objectives in China since the landmark Third Plenum of the Eleventh Party Congress in December 1978. The central question was, and is still, 'finding the proper balance between central control and local autonomy' (Wong 1991: 691). In Mao's words, it is about the art of realizing the 'dual enthusiasms' by optimizing the interests of 'the whole' and 'the parts' (Mao 1956: 275). In the studies of government finance, this concern has led to a preponderance of a 'zero-sum' approach of assessment to identify who gets more fiscal resources at the expense of the others, as exemplified in bilateral bargaining of central–provincial fiscal contracts in the 1980s, and the scrambling for revenues in the latter part of 1993 in provinces in the lead up to the 1994 Tax Sharing Reform (Chung 1995; White 1989b; Tsang and Cheng 1994; Wang, S. 1997).

As more studies dug deeper into the interface between the formal systems and actual practices, and between the discrepancy between national prescription and local implementation, it soon became apparent that a good part of the fiscal management infrastructure had fallen short of the requirements for efficiency and efficacy. These cover not only the intergovernmental aspects but also the design and scope of the budget, its basic constituting components, and related fiscal management institutions. Soon after the 1994 Tax Sharing Reform was implemented, and especially since the late 1990s when the central government started to roll out various pilot measures, 'rationalizing reforms' entered the policy discourse in bulk. Inside China, studies on comprehensive budgeting, fiscal management reform and public finance mushroomed (Huang 1996; Wang, H. 1997; Zhongguo Caizheng Xuehui 2000; Zhang, H. 2001; Zhang et al. 2001).[6] Outside China, a steady stream of World Bank studies have assessed the baseline situations and advocated various reform strategies and initiatives, including public investment (World Bank 1995a), social spending and equity (World Bank 1996), macro management and intergovernmental relations (World Bank 1995b), subnational finance (World Bank 2002) and procurement (World Bank and OECD 2005). The academic studies have largely focused on the analysis of the baseline situation. Jun Ma gave a detailed and comprehensive statement on the major gaps in the basic infrastructure of the fiscal institutions, highlighting the implications for state capacity (Ma 2009) and the importance to get the basics right before embarking on 'more advanced' budgetary reforms (Ma and Yu 2012). The informal sector and practices are a major area of study, in particular the role and impacts of the extra-off-budget for fiscal performance and broader economic decisions (e.g. Li 1998; Wedeman 2000), and fund diversions (Liu et al. 2009; Li and Painter 2013;

Li and Yang 2014). The evolving budget rationalizing reform programmes have been the subject of an emerging literature, with a number of important pioneering studies on, for example, the rationale and problems in the reform ideas of zero-based budgeting of the Chinese reformers (Ma 2006), the institutional change processes in budget rationalization experiments and their broader contexts (Li 2005, 2003), central incentives driving central treasury management reform (Ang 2009), and the challenges and impacts in pursuing the central procurement reform (Chou 2011; Zhou 2012).

Budget rationalization remains a subject awaiting much further research, however. For instance, we still know relatively little about the important reform of departmental budgets, which has been piloted since 1999.[7] Little systematic analysis has been made in scholarly literature on the extended discussion of establishing a separate social security budget and a state assets budget to improve the management of these vital resources, which was recently reiterated in the 2014 Government Report and a 2014 State Council Document on deepening budget system reform (State Council 2014b).

GOVERNANCE: HOW GOVERNMENT FINANCE DECISIONS ARE MADE, AND MADE BETTER

A key part of fiscal governance is the budgeting process, and in particular who has a say in it. Despite general reluctance of the Chinese government in opening up budgetary decisions, there have been, since the early 1990s, localized experiments introducing a higher level of participation by local delegates and residents in local spending decisions, out of which grew a small but expanding literature on 'participatory budgeting'. This development was initially part and parcel of the governance changes unfolding in the Chinese countryside which saw relatively open popular elections, for the first time, extended all over China through the election of village committee members (He 2007). The Rural Tax Reform of the early 2000s then introduced an element of public participation in local public investment decisions through the mechanism of 'deliberation by item' (*yishi yiyi*), in order to restrain local excesses (Li, L.C. 2004). Catching substantial scholarly attention are the experiments in two townships in Wenling City, Zhejiang Province in 2005, which had scholars from Australia and United States serving as advisers and trainers to local officials (He 2011; Fewsmith 2009; Wu and Wang 2012). As in the case of village elections, the literature reflected an interest in the prospect of more fundamental, regime-level political changes. As He (2011: 123) puts it, the scholars often 'celebrated' the participatory budgeting experiments by focusing, and extending their imaginations, on their linkage with possible political reform and civic engagement developments in the future. Other important dimensions of the experiments, like the administrative logic, were often neglected in the studies. However, since the prospect of regime-level changes in reality was low, most studies turned out to converge on a similar set of limitations of the experiments: how they had not led to more drastic political changes, notwithstanding the various diverse changes in practice. The advice of Paul Cohen (1984 [2010]) in favour of 'home-based' analysis versus the application of an externally imposed frame of reference – to give due respect to history – cannot be more relevant.

In addition to participative budgeting, other new budget models and governance reforms such as performance-based budgeting and fiscal transparency have also attracted a stream of works from scholars in and out of China. In a pioneering comparative study of participative budgeting in China, Taiwan and the US, it is noted that the experimental nature of the Chinese reforms means that the focus has been mostly on capacity-building, including rallying support from more resourceful agencies, learning and information dissemination, rather than maintaining a visible performance standard and impact (Lee and Wang 2009). In some cases, even the reverse had taken place: the pioneering agencies were 'rewarded' with a larger budget than otherwise. As the learning process continued, the importance of fostering an evaluative culture and cultivating an evaluation profession with the required expertise has become more recognized (Lu 2013), which involved changes not only in the budgeting system but also in the personnel management practices and culture (Gao 2010).

Studies on fiscal transparency reform have echoed these observations on the importance of building capacity, including both institutional resources and the agency of people, in advancing the change process (Ma and Wu 2011). Also playing a significant role was the broader social context, such as the openness of the economic structure. Fiscal health hinges upon the quality of macro-level governance, apart from the technical rationality of the budget. The phenomenal growth in government debts, at the subnational levels in particular, caused considerable concern for fiscal risk and a search for a better debt governance regime (World Bank 2010b). When the second draft bill of the Budget Law was released for consultation in 2012, with escalating local debts one of the contentious issues in the background, the unprecedented volume of feedback and suggestions testified to the wide heterogeneity of views and their intensity during the protracted discussions over what sort of new budget regime was desirable.[8]

The agenda of 'deepening reform on all fronts' rolled out in the Third Plenum of the Central Committee of the Eighteenth Party Congress in November 2013 further raised the heat for fiscal reform. The pace of 'changing the functions and roles of the government' would have to be sped up, which in turn demanded a whole range of related changes and reforms in the design and management of the budget: tax structure, transfer payment, debt, intergovernmental revenue-spending sharing, transparency and public participation, and so on (CCP Central Committee 2013). Whilst the intergovernmental dimension has preoccupied fiscal reforms since the 1970s, this classical topic has now acquired added urgency and new significance. A new framework, aiming at strengthening county-level finance with improved specification of spending standards and enhanced clarity of responsibilities and resources from central and provincial levels, was enacted after the Third Plenum (State Council Secretariat 2013). More taxation authority would be decentralized to the subnational levels, reversing the revenue centralization trend since the 1994 Tax Sharing Reform, whilst spending and revenues would be better aligned (*People's Daily* 2014a). Finance Minister Lou Jiwei has stressed that fiscal governance was not just about managing spending and revenue decisions, but had instrumental significance for the governance of the country more generally (*People's Daily* 2013), and that intergovernmental jurisdiction would be a priority reform item (*People's Daily* 2014a). Candid talks about difficulties and hints of the need for better preparation suggested that there seemed to be an added will to pursue a higher degree of fiscal transparency (*People's Daily* 2014b). The enactment of the State Council Decision on Deepening Budget Management System Reform in September 2014 (State Council 2014b) gives the latest blueprint of the official reform agenda. The scope is comprehensive and broadly phrased, covering almost every topic which has been discussed recently: the alignment of budget with the new vision of government role in a market economy; governance reforms such as fiscal transparency; improving the budget system and medium-long-term planning mechanism; revenue and spending structure and management; government debt and fund management; oversight and accountability; and so on.

CONCLUSION

The critical position of government finance in politics and governance is amply demonstrated by the visibility of fiscal reform as China embarked upon the opening-up and economic reform agenda from the late 1970s. The review of scholarly and policy discourse in this chapter by three generic themes – objective, organization and governance – suggests that whilst the organization aspect dominated a large part of activities, the concerns for 'objective' and 'governance' have always underlined major policy discussions on government monies. As the scope of fiscal reform extended, there has also been a gradual convergence of the various aspects of reform, as changes in the 'objective' which government finance is to serve demand a new 'organization' of the budget and adaptations in fiscal 'governance' practices.

Where will the current wave of deepening reform lead the Chinese budget to? There is no crystal ball for the future, and social science predictions have not had much success, but the discussions of the recent trajectory allow speculation here on a few broad ideas. First, the intergovernmental dimension, which has been a major area of reform activity, will likely continue to be the venue of major changes. The changes will be in the direction of 'guided decentralization'. Whilst the central government has stepped up its role in a number of major spending areas, like education and social security, this will not reverse the subnational levels' dominance in spending but rather precipitate a more refined demarcation of spending responsibilities of the governments within a policy area. The increased interfaces and interactions will open up opportunities for collaboration, as well as challenges and new sources of tension. There will be an enhanced use of the law to reduce transaction costs. To the extent that reforms in China have been guided by large numbers of policy documents and government regulations, the impact of the law is likely to increase further, and the future development is more towards consolidation of existing laws to form a more systematic legal framework rather than adding incrementally to the current bundle of weakly coordinated pieces of regulations and policies.

The organization of the budget will require further and more extensive reform in the direction of rationalization. The centralized treasury, departmental budgets and the comprehensive budget are a few core areas requiring priority attention. Reform in these areas commenced in the late 1990s but remained still very much 'work in progress' as of 2014. The quality of reform in these areas will have important effects linked to performance in other areas, including fiscal governance reforms such as fiscal transparency, performance-based budgeting and accountability. As social tension escalates and equity has become a key issue in policy-making, the process of budget decision-making has carried as large a stake as the outcome of the decisions. The Chinese fiscal system will need to develop its instruments and tools better to address the dual needs of efficient revenue generation and equitable distribution of spending – a challenge common to the management of government finance in all governments worldwide. The immense diversity in local conditions and unevenness of fiscal reform so far across localities in the country can only further complicate all these issues and problems.

NOTES

1. Other international donor organizations have also contributed influential works, but of lesser quantity, such as the Asian Development Bank's Wong et al. (1995) and Wong (1997).
2. A keyword title search conducted in May 2014 using various phrasings of 'changing government's role/functions' found the number of articles in the China Academic Journal Database using the title keywords surged from a single-digit amount annually in the early years from 1985 to 1990, tenfold to up to 100 annually from 1991 to 2000, and then doubled to up to 200 per year during 2001–2012.
3. The most recent of these (with a national volume and a local volume) at the time of writing this chapter in 2014 were published in 2013 (Gao et al. 2013). The first volume published on this project outlines the theoretical framework (Gao 2007).
4. A keyword-title search of the China Journal Database conducted on 6 November 2014 gave 369 counts since 2013, against 218 counts for 2011–12. In addition, there were an additional 225 counts of articles with 'state governance' in the keyword-title search and 'government's functions' in the keyword-text search, reflecting the new context in which the subject of the government's role was discussed.
5. But see World Bank (2004a, 2005a).
6. A keyword-title search using 'public finance' of the China Academic Journal Database conducted in May 2014 found a count of over 4000 articles since the first articles appeared in 1984, with the lion's share published after 1998.
7. But see Ma (2009: 15), Ma and Niu (2006) and Ma and Ni (2008).
8. The recent round of revision of the Budget Law, enacted in 1995, lasted for a full decade from 2005 to 2014, when the fourth draft bill was presented and approved by the Standing Committee of the Twelfth People's Congress in August 2014. When the second bill was released in June 2012, an unprecedented 330 000 items of opinions from 19 000 members of the public were received during the online consultation period, leading to the withdrawal of the bill and a substantial revision which took almost two years to complete (http://m.hexun.com/content.php?id=163922912, accessed 11 May 2014). Over the decade 2005 to 2014 the foci of discussion have shifted somewhat but the broad themes remained the following: (a) scope and design of the budget; (b) governance issues, in particular transparency; (c) local debts; (d) management of the central treasury; and (e) role of the budget in state governance.

9. Administrative territory
Carolyn Cartier and Hu De

Administrative territory in China is the national system of administrative divisions or governing areas below the central government. The fundamental local level of government, the county, was established in the early dynastic era. The province, which defines common political maps of China, emerged in its modern form more than 700 years ago. The deep history and continuity of China's administrative territories belie the reality that every dynasty and modern regime has made adjustments to the subnational territories, including periodic major changes, in relation to political interests and economic goals. Among the contemporary levels of territorial administration in China, province, prefecture, county and town or township, and village, the province is the main meso-level of administrative territory, whereas the county has served as the main unit of local government, social life and cultural identification over the *longue durée*. For these reasons, this chapter introduces the territorial administrative system especially in relation to the province and the county, and major changes to the county in relation to widespread urbanization since the 1980s.

The significance of administrative territory and its history in China is based on co-constitution of geographical areas of state authority and hierarchical levels of government and administration. In other words, Party and government officials are necessarily appointed to govern administrative territory. Consequently, administrative territories are pivotally important for understanding 'central–local relations' in China. Relations between the centre (*zhongyang*) and local (*difang*) reflect the hierarchical administrative structure, between the capital, whether imperial or modern, and subnational administrative territory. The dyad of centre and local also characterizes how the PRC narrates its functional relationships below the central government. Because it accurately reflects how the PRC understands and represents its domestic governing relations, 'centre and local' also constitutes a 'China-centered view' (Cohen 2010) of Chinese politics, history and geography. Research about or in the framework of centre–local relations features prominently in the scholarship of China Studies. When it is not explicitly named it is often assumed, since central–local relations reflect the institutional conditions of the PRC as a single-party state.

Yet the meaning of 'local' is not simple. In the binary of centre and local, local is at once fundamentally relational and an overdetermined subject. 'Local' is overdetermined because it represents subnational territory and government in general, and stands in for all 'locals' or all levels of territorial administration and their interrelations. 'Local' could be 'anywhere'. It is relational because no place is local on its own: a place is local in relation to somewhere else, whether to the province or to the 'centre', the central government. In the general social sciences literature, local typically features in relation to the national or the global, as in 'the local and the global'. Thus the local in China, as if containing all levels of government below the central, especially asks to be unpacked, both empirically and conceptually, because different kinds or categories of administrative territory and multiple levels of government constitute the local in China. What is local in China is actually a complex, dynamic system of administrative divisions.

The administrative divisions are mapped territories as well as the spaces and place of Chinese politics; they constitute the places to which Chinese officials or cadres are appointed and the state spaces that they administer. However, this chapter, unlike other chapters in this *Handbook*, cannot draw on a rich tradition of scholarship on the Chinese administrative divisions in English-language scholarship. Changes to the administrative divisions do not feature regularly in research on Chinese politics or in studies of urban and economic development. Considering that they function as the matrix of state administration, this condition would seem rather odd. Gaining insight into why this is the case requires some comparative assessment of scholarship in the different academies; for example, comparing international scholarship with scholarship produced in China. It also begs questions about other approaches to subnational territory in China, which implicates the 'macroregion', a popular approach used especially in China Studies in the US in the late twentieth century. The macroregion uses natural physical regions to map settlement and economic development. However, macroregions are not commensurate with political boundaries in China, which suggests the state–market problematic or the problem of political versus economic causality in research design.

Next, the chapter shifts to place these topics in relation to the existing literature and current research, ultimately with particular focus on the county. The section on 'The administrative divisions and territorial governance' defines the territorial administrative system in historical perspective, its general conditions, and the main changes to the system since the start of the reform period after 1978. The next section, 'Documentation, scholarship and debate', compares background literature on local government and the administrative hierarchy from the perspective of the state–market problematic in relation to the macroregion approach. Limitations of existing approaches invite comparison of the Chinese scholarship for its definitive treatment of the history of the administrative divisions. The section on 'Reterritorialization of the county' provides a countrywide summary of changes to the administrative divisions at the county level, which shows the frequency, type and number of changes to counties, especially reterritorialization of counties into cities and urban districts. This transformation is the subject of the sections in which we discuss reterritorialization at the county level through two case studies: Suzhou, a prefecture-level city in Jiangsu province; and the Shanghai Pudong New Area.

THE ADMINISTRATIVE DIVISIONS AND TERRITORIAL GOVERNANCE

The system of administrative divisions emerged in the early imperial era before China expanded to the size and extent of its modern geographical area or 'geobody' (cf. Winichakul 1994; Callahan 2009). It is well known that the county (*xian*) originated in the Qin dynasty (221–206 BCE) and that its first Emperor, Qin Shihuang, unified the land's semi-disparate kingdoms into a coherent empire for the first time. What does not appear in the common narrative, yet which is of utmost salience for the present concern, is the question of how Qin Shihuang unified territory. A historio-biographical and political relations approach would answer the question through the formation of political alliances among elites who ruled local kingdoms (e.g. Huang 1997; Sanft 2014).

A different and complementary response takes a territorial perspective. Territory is the 'organization and exercise of power . . . over blocs of space', and territoriality is the 'the strategic use of territory to attain organizational goals' (Agnew 2009: 744, 746). From a territorial perspective, the institution of the county was the first major territorial strategy through which the imperial state organized and amalgamated extensive land areas into a coherent whole. The exercise of power over the organization of territory constituted the process of unification of state space; the emergence of an empire that became China. Over time and successive dynasties, the territorialization of land as a governing strategy led to the formation of a complex system of administrative divisions.

The Chinese system of administrative divisions evolved incrementally although not along a uniform trajectory of development. Different dynasties and regimes made different kinds of changes to the system (Chung and Lam 2010). What is clear is that each regime changed the system to suit prevailing and anticipated interests. Variation in the hierarchical levels of government demonstrates this principle. The contemporary system consists of four main levels below the capital: province, prefecture, county and township or town. Yet from a historical perspective, the prefecture and township and town levels of government, for example, existed in different forms over time (cf. Chien 2010; Zhong 2003, 2010). In the current system, the prefecture is distinctively unusual because it is not a legal level of government. It is an important de facto level that has become instantiated with the growth of prefecture-level cities since the 1980s and 1990s. The modern prefecture, or *diqu*, has a particularly complex history of varying conditions under several different names and, historically, as an administrative office known as 'field agencies' of the provincial government for rural lands between the province level of government and the county.

Comparison of the historical record confirms variation in territorial administration. The early dynasties, Qin, Han, Sui and Tang, had dual-level administrative hierarchies below the imperial capitals. The later Tang, Song, Liao, Jin, Ming and Qing dynasties maintained three-level systems, while the Yuan dynasty had a four-level system. The current People's Republic of China (PRC) actually has a mixed system in which a de facto four-level system expands to five and even six levels in some ethnic autonomous regions (Chung 2010; Zhou 2005).

A key precept of administrative territory in China is the relationship between levels of government and territory. Administrative divisions correspond to land areas and levels of government, in rank order, under the central government. Each administrative division occupies a rank which is a structural condition of the subnational territorial administrative system and correlate of administrative rank, that is, ranks of officials and cadre appointments. However, some 'extra' or additional levels of government, past and present, add another layer to the administrative hierarchy: that is, their level of governing power is higher than their territorial status. A contemporary example of this condition is the sub-province-level city, a small number of major cities whose developmental goals are nationally significant and thus maintain economic plans negotiated directly with the central government, bypassing the province (Landry 2008). No matter the level of government, hierarchy embedded in the system represents authoritarian power of the single-party state and the spatial relations of 'Party line'.

In addition, the levels of government, in rank order, are the general contexts of institutional organization under which exist different types of territory. For example, the administrative level of the county encompasses counties, autonomous counties, county-level cities and urban districts. Similarly, the province level encompasses provinces, province-level or 'directly administered' cities (Beijing, Chongqing, Shanghai and Tianjin), autonomous provinces (Guangxi, Inner Mondolia, Ningxia, Tibet and Xinjiang) and special administrative regions (Hong Kong and Macao). The level of government or rank structures the organization of the political system, interrelates these jurisdictions with higher and lower levels, and serves as the context of Party and government bureaucracies and officials appointed to them (Lieberthal 2003; Joseph 2010). The hierarchical condition of the system structures power relations at and between levels of administration, in which increased powers and rights are commensurate with higher levels of government. For example, a city at a higher level of government has more administrative and economic rights.

By comparison with counties, the provincial territories emerged much later. The provinces first took shape in the Yuan dynasty (1271–1368 CE) and gained their modern size and extent by the time of the Ming dynasty (1368–1644). Since their origins, both the provinces and the counties have been relatively stable to the degree that scholars identify the system of territorial administration as the 'most stable element in the historical annals of the Chinese state' (Fitzgerald 2002: 11). Over two millennia – across the dynastic era, through the twentieth-century reorganization of the political-economic system under socialism, and the subsequent decentralization under reform since 1978 – the territorial administrative hierarchy has existed as the administrative framework and political-geographical structure of subnational state organization. Yet its stability is not spatial fixity, as if boundaries never change or as if the same administrative divisions have continued to exist 'since the beginning of time'. Changes to the administrative divisions are periodically frequent and significant. They characterize regime change and, in the contemporary era, accompany and impel economic development, especially urban and regional growth across administrative area divisions. Thus stability does not mean immutability but functional coherence in which changes to the administrative divisions characterize and continue the resiliency of the system – in step with and structuring China's changing political economy.

Changes to the Administrative Divisions since the 1980s

From provinces to prefectures and counties, nearly 1000 individual changes to the administrative divisions have taken place over the past three decades (CADC 2014). Within the Chinese government, the Ministry of Civil Affairs adjudicates and finalizes adjustments to the administrative divisions. For changes at the county level and above, the State Council formalizes and announces the decisions, which marks the official date of change in the historical record. Major changes take place under the direct planning authority of central government offices, especially the National Development and Reform Commission. Unique, large-scale changes take place in direct relation to central government plans and projects. For example, the establishment of Chongqing as a province-level city proceeded in relation to administration of areas affected by the Three Gorges Dam reservoir (Hong 2002). Changes also take place as a consequence of policies targeting specific administrative or economic reforms, which may allow local jurisdictions to apply for adjustments.

General changes, such as reterritorializing the old prefectures as prefecture-level cities, beginning in 1983, are also administrative area reforms. General reforms to the administrative divisions typically become implemented in relation to economic reforms. Policies to allow prefectures to become cities (*di gai shi*) and counties to become cities (*xian gai shi*), which prevailed from 1983 to 1996, are key examples of changes that have taken place widely at the county and prefecture levels. These changes, referred to as adjustments to the administrative divisions (*tiaozheng xingzheng quhua*), are typically rendered in relation to one or more development goals and administrative plans at one or more local levels. The final sections of the chapter examine examples of these changes through Suzhou, a prefecture-level city in Jiangsu province, and Shanghai, a province-level city.

In general, changes to the administrative divisions are forms of state reterritorialization, including rescaling or changing the rank or level of a subnational territory in the administrative hierarchy; changing the size and boundary of the territory, typically through recombination or mergers; and changing the 'mosaic' of territories within an administrative division. A basic definition of reterritorialization is the use of state powers and practices to change an administrative territory. The PRC Constitution articulates these powers. Article 30 of the Constitution defines the administrative divisions in rank order under the authority of the central government; Article 31 allows establishment of 'special administrative regions', for example the status of Hong Kong. Item 15 of Article 89 establishes that the State Council functions and exercises power to establish and approve changes to administrative-territorial divisions. Thus administrative divisions are established by the state, at different levels, and subject to change. China does not have a federal system that guarantees constitutional integrity of subnational territory.

The most remarkable general change to the administrative divisions since the start of the reform era is the formal establishment of cities. From under 100 cities (*shi*) in the 1970s, the number of cities increased to over 650 by the 1990s (Table 9.1). In Chinese urban history, the city emerged as the standard intermediate echelon of territorial governance only in the late twentieth century. Since cities feature prominently in Chinese history, including many large cities, what does it mean to establish new cities? The answer to this question recalls the direct relationship between administrative territory and levels of government (Chan 2010; Landry 2008; Zhang and Zhao 1998). The widespread formal establishment of new cities since the 1980s demonstrates changes to the administrative divisions for industrial development and urban modernization; changing counties to cities is a major step toward aligning government administration and state power with urban space. Through urbanization based on administrative territory, the county level continues to exist while categories at the county level have changed: nearly 300 have become reclassified as county-level cities since 1978. Table 9.1 provides details of changes in city classification since 1978.

Consistent with the priority of rank, the PRC defines cities in the first instance by their position in the hierarchical system of administrative divisions: province-level city (*zhixia shi*), prefecture-level city (*diji shi*) and county-level city (*xianji shi*). These official names define cities as levels of government and establish hierarchy and rank among them as administrative territories. In addition, the term for province-level city, *zhixia shi*, is only analogous with 'province' because *zhixia* means 'directly governed', that is, under

Table 9.1 Changes in the number of cities by level of government

Year	Province	Prefecture	County	Total cities
1978	3	98	92	193
1980	3	107	113	223
1985	3	162	159	324
1990	3	185	279	467
1995	3	210	427	640
2000	4	259	400	663
2005	4	283	374	661
2010	4	283	370	657
2013	4	285	368	657

Source: Ministry of Civil Affairs (various editions).

the direct authority of the central government. The directly governed cities – Beijing, Shanghai, Tianjin and Chongqing – accept the unified leadership of the Party central committees and central government, which maintain power to guide, change or void decisions undertaken by the city. These realities of changing administrative divisions to establish cities should raise questions because, in comparative context, cities emerge as a result of concentrated economic activity and population growth, generally not as a result of changing the status of a territory. Transforming Chinese cities into administrative territories, and administrative divisions into new cities, demonstrates conditions that differ from the history of capitalist urbanization.

The next section discusses scholarship on administrative territory and related literature on local government and administration, with a focus on the county. The analysis revisits assumptions about long-term stability of the administrative hierarchy, which arguably perpetuates notions that the administrative divisions are fixed in space as if they do not appreciably change. For example, if administrative divisions are different levels of government, then why do scholars continue to research local government in China without taking into account changes to the administrative territory? We cannot answer this question definitively. One response revolves around the priority of other approaches adopted for the study of local conditions, in which the 'macroregion' has figured prominently. Its limitations and differences from the administrative divisions suggest dilemmas of the state–market problematic. This overview concludes by introducing the Chinese-language scholarship on the administrative divisions, which does not commonly appear in the (non-Chinese language) Chinese politics literature, to provide a basis for understanding the complexity and mutability of the system of administrative territory.

DOCUMENTATION, SCHOLARSHIP AND DEBATE

China's textual tradition, from the dynastic era to the present, including local histories (*difang zhi*) and contemporary documents of the Ministry of Civil Affairs, records changes to the administrative divisions. By the late Ming dynasty, when most of the eastern provinces had become established, from Shandong and Henan to the north,

Guangdong and Guangxi to the south, and Sichuan and Yunnan to the west, there were 13 provinces. But between 1368 and 1428, when the new (Ming) regime was becoming established, the number of provinces varied. In the 'Ming Government' chapter of *The Cambridge History of China*, Charles Hucker (1998: 13) writes: 'in the early decades of the Ming the number of provinces fluctuated: from three to nine in 1368, to eleven in 1369, to twelve in 1371, to thirteen in 1382, back to twelve in 1403, to thirteen again in 1407, to fourteen in 1413, and finally to thirteen again in 1428'. By the end of the dynasty there were 159 prefectures (*fu*), 240 sub-prefectures (*zhou*) and 1144 counties, whose 'numbers fluctuated throughout the dynasty as areas were upgraded or downgraded in status and as units of local administration were created or abolished' (Hucker 1998: 15). The province that was 'lost' in 1428 was the area of the Red River basin in North Vietnam, what the PRC calls Jiaozhi, one of China's historic frontiers. Thus in the transition from the Yuan period (1271–1368), the Ming dynasty became established in part through territorial reorganization: changes to the administrative divisions. The most well-known territorial change of the Ming dynasty is the relocation of the imperial centre from Nanjing to Beijing, by 1421, but moving the capital was only one of numerous changes to the administration of territory. For the Qing dynasty, however, we cannot turn to *The Cambridge History of China* for a 'Qing Government' chapter, because 'Part 2' of the 'Ch'ing [Qing] Empire to 1800' remains unpublished. Besides, exploring the historical geography of the Qing dynasty takes us in different directions.

The Manchu conquest of China that formed the Qing dynasty (1644–1911) was an expansionary empire. Its territorial interests sought consolidation of frontiers; its geobody differed substantially from the historic core of China that was the Ming dynasty. The Qing made major changes to the provinces by dividing existing ones and also by establishing new ones. Western Shaanxi was cleaved off to form Gansu. Similarly, South Zhili, the 'directly ruled' (*zhili*) area associated with the southern capital, became two provinces, Jiangsu and Anhui; each after a long, complex history of territorial-administrative change (Guy 2010; Jacobs 1999; Purdue 2005). Subsequently North Zhili, the directly governed area around the northern capital, became simply Zhili under the Qing, from which Hebei province emerged only when the Nationalist Republic moved the capital to Nanjing in 1927–28. The Qing regime brought Manchuria into the empire, which became divided into the provinces of Liaoning (formerly Fengtian), Jilin and Heilongjiang. The Qing also introduced new categories of administrative territory, namely leagues and banners of the Manchu government (Elliott 2001), which became prefecture and county-level administrative territories, respectively, in Inner Mongolia.

The numbers of provinces and counties changed again during the Republican era (1912–49) when warlord governments contended to control the regions. Sites of contention, provincial territories were established and challenged in relation to local and national politics. Provinces, especially, increased in number during the Republican era. In 1928 the Republican government elevated three governing territories to provincial status – Rehe, Suiyuan, Chahar – and reterritorialized Gansu to establish Ningxia and Qinghai. Xikang was established as a province in 1938. Only Qinghai and Ningxia have maintained their territorial integrity. Rehe, Suiyuan and Chahar were folded into the new Inner Mongolia Autonomous Region in 1947. Suiyuan was incorporated into Inner Mongolia during 1952–54. Xikang, the traditional Kham region of Tibet, became incorporated into Sichuan province after 1955. After 1945, overall, the Republic of China briefly had 20 additional provinces and the PRC had 52 provinces in the early 1950s (Donaldson, 2010: 19, 23). Table 9.2 summarizes the numbers of changes to the provinces over the *long durée*.

Table 9.3 and Table 9.4 summarize the numbers of changes to counties. Comparison of Table 9.3 with Table 9.4 shows, by sheer numbers, the presence and significance of the county over time. It also suggests that the idea of the county as the most stable unit of state and society is not entirely correct, if the assumption of stability is the absence of change. The numbers also show considerable change: the number of counties has fluctuated over time. In Table 9.3, the relatively high number of counties in the Qing dynasty reflects the expansion of territory under the Qing. But the expansion of counties in

Table 9.2 Number of province-level administrative divisions

Yuan	Ming	Qing	Republic	PRC
11	15	23	28 (48)	34 (52)

Source: Donaldson (2010).

Table 9.3 Number of counties in the dynastic era up to 1949

Han	~ 1000
Western Han	1587
Eastern Han	1180
Three Kingdoms	1190
Tang	1573
Song	1234
Ming	1138
Qing	1456
Republican – 1913	1791
Republican – 1947	2016

Source: Liu et al. (1999).

Table 9.4 Number of counties from 1949 with county-level cities

1949	2067	66
1957	1972	81
1959	1560	102
1961	1853	126
1965	2004	90
1977	2009	90
1983	1942	142
1997	1520	442
2007	1463	369
2013	1464	364

Sources: Lam (2010) and CADC (2014).

the Republican period reflects not expanded territory, but changes to government and territory, and territorial practices of the state.

Despite knowledge of numerous changes to the provinces and counties, and their pivotal significance in regional politics and regime change, no single major source exists in English on the history of these administrative divisions in China. We can point to only two summaries, and one extended historical treatment. John Fitzgerald's (2002) succinct history, Chapter 2 in *Rethinking China's Provinces*, examines changes to the province from the dynastic era to the contemporary PRC, ultimately identifying the state–market problematic in the development of marketizing economies within administrative divisions: 'Today the boundaries of many of China's new cities conform more closely with these old socialist administrative units than with ideal market networks; or, to put the problem more concretely, new urban marketing networks have developed around old patterns of territorial administration' (Fitzgerald 2002: 30). Contemporary administrative territories not only structure the subnational administrative landscape and the political system, but also work as a cellular grid of quasi-discrete areas of economic development.

In *China's Local Administration: Traditions and Changes in the Sub-national Hierarchy* (Chung and Lam 2009), John Donaldson (2009: 14) pursues the analytical question of the province as 'both indispensable and threatening to central rulers' of imperial as well as modern Chinese governments. Donaldson finds contemporary provinces losing administrative and economic power to expanding prefecture-level cities, which have taken over many meso-scale functions with county-level administrative territories. In a treatment of Qing provincial administration, *Qing Governors and Their Provinces: The Evolution of Territorial Administration in China, 1644–1796*, R.K. Guy (2010) illuminates how the dynasty governed the provinces, including through formalization of an additional level of officials appointed as governors-general between the provinces and the imperial capital. Yet this analysis does not focus on territorial conditions of the provinces.

Outside China, the China's Provinces in Reform project, in the Australian academy, has been the outstanding collective programme to develop research on local perspectives from the province and the county. Drawing on his foundational work, emblematic in Sichuan and Guizhou (Goodman 1986), and through a series of collaborations, David Goodman has developed comparative research on local China and established the 'provincial China' paradigm, beginning with *China's Provinces in Reform: Class, Community and Political Culture* (Goodman 1997), which was followed by *The Political Economy of China's Provinces* (Hendrischke and Feng 1999), *Rethinking China's Provinces* (Fitzgerald 2002) and *China's Campaign to Open Up the West* (Goodman 2004b). The scholarly legacy of the research programme continues in diverse projects of its historic members.

Given the limitations in the international scholarship, we need to assess how the field of China Studies itself has contributed to the lack of research on administrative territory and interdisciplinary approaches informed by spatial thought in contemporary geography. One factor, particularly salient in US-based China Studies, is the use of the macroregion, which appeared in the 1970s, for research on local conditions (see Cartier 2002). The macroregion approach consists of nine mapped regions, fixed in space over time, which contributes to the lack of a dynamic spatial perspective in contemporary research on local governance in China. The second set of factors limiting international scholarship on the administrative divisions concerns the primary Chinese source material (see also Cartier 2015a). First, let us consider a brief history of the macroregion in the context of research design practices.

In contrast to subnational territories defined by political boundaries, William Skinner (1977) developed the idea of the macroregion based on natural regions or watersheds, that is, drainage basins or river valleys with agricultural settlement in pre-industrial societies. From rural industry in macroregion cores, posited Skinner, market towns developed and became networked into nested hierarchies of economic places. This market-centric approach bracketed the state and vigorously declaimed contextual significance of administrative territories, especially the province. Skinner indeed promoted the macroregion and argued against the province: 'it is "methodologically indefensible and generally misleading" to employ the province as a unit of comparison for urban studies and, by extension, for studies of socio-economic space more generally' (quoted in Fitzgerald 2002: 14). Yet in the context of contemporary standards in research design, characterized by mixed-methods, contextual theory and original interpretations of theory, the notion of any single approach falls short of commensurability with research standards in the humanities and social sciences.

Developed before the late twentieth century spatial turn in social thought, the macroregion reflects instead mid-twentieth century research design which drew on systems theory to frame social and economic dynamics. The world-view of systems theory, characterized by network logics, did not encompass the reach of spatial dynamics at multiple scales that would come to characterize epistemologies of knowledge in an era of globalization. For example, contemporary approaches in spatial theory recognize how spatial contexts change as a consequence of social, political and economic change: the administrative divisions in China change over time. In contrast, the macroregion is characterized by fixed space: macroregions are fixed in space, mapped in approximation to watersheds (Cartier 2002). Nevertheless, Skinner continued to promote the suitability of the macroregion for research on urban China up to the 2000s (Womack 2009), even as the administrative divisions have been subject to particularly rapid change under reform since the 1980s. With its assumptions of market causality that bracket state space, the macroregion approach especially exemplifies the state–market problematic in epistemologies of knowledge about China.

When China opened to the world economy after 1978, widespread interest predicted its economic transition from the socialist planned economy to a market economy. Anticipation of the market in China arguably energized continuing interest in the macroregion model for its prioritization of market networks. Yet over three decades later, the PRC continues discussion of market reforms, and the role of the state in the Chinese economy remains significant. Typically, the idea of the role of the state in the economy equates with state regulation, state subsidies and state-owned enterprises. In China, we need to understand that the role of the state continues to structure urban and regional economies through the administrative divisions. The reality of local economies governed within administrative divisions is another way in which economic development in China is evolving in relation to state institutions, producing hybrid state–market conditions. More research is needed to understand these complexities.

The second set of factors limiting international scholarship on administrative territory concerns the primary Chinese sources on the administrative divisions. These limitations include interpretation of Chinese characters and terms, conditions of the primary data and development of comparative information. Let us consider first another example of the state–market problematic through language.

Most of the international analysis on the Chinese economy minimizes analysis of linguistic matters. Yet in the case of the administrative divisions, some attention to the Chinese terminology brings the administrative divisions more clearly into view. The state–market problematic is especially evident in the case of 'special economic zones'. China opened to the world economy via Shenzhen and other 'special zones' in the 1980s. Narrating their development has been a preoccupation of the international literature, often in relation to conditions of Asian developmental states. Such discourses continue. For example, reforms introduced in Shanghai in 2013 widely regenerated international interest in Pudong as a free trade zone. Yet the idea of zones as places in synchronization with global markets belies the reality of zones as administrative divisions, governed by the usual dual structure of Party and government bureaucracies. Confusion likely arises as a consequence of the word *qu*: it appears in *jingji tequ*, translated as 'special economic zone'. Yet *qu* is the general word for administrative divisions in *xingzheng quhua*. Understanding that *qu* is an area or district of the system of administrative divisions offers a corrective to notions about economic zones as if somehow separate from the political system of China.

The primary Chinese data on changes to the administrative divisions also present limitations. The Ministry of Civil Affairs has documented changes to the administrative divisions since 1978 through lists of place names and dates of change, but these year-by-year, province-by-province lists lack summaries or organization by type of change. These lists of changes appear in the Ministry of Civil Affairs annual *Handbook of the Administrative Divisions of the People's Republic of China*, and online, but they are unaccompanied by historical context or political-economic rationale. The Ministry's documentary record is otherwise closed. Historical compilations of changes to the administrative divisions also similarly list administrative changes by place and date, without historical context or aggregate data (e.g. Chen, C. 2007; Tian et al. 2006). Information exists on thousands of adjustments to the administrative divisions but making use of the primary source material requires translation, organization and contextual analysis. A major step toward historical synthesis is the 12-volume *History of the Administrative Divisions of China* (Zhou 2007–12), which provides a narrative compilation of records from the Qin dynasty to the Republican period.

Where the recent Chinese-language literature includes historical surveys of the administrative divisions, the international literature tends to feature disciplinary approaches. Yet the international literature, curiously, does not focus squarely on the administrative divisions. Where the international literature coalesces in a unified approach, the scholarship treats administrative divisions through the 'spatial administrative hierarchy' (Chan 2010; Cartier 2005; Fitzgerald 2002; Ma 2005; Chung and Lam 2009). The spatial administrative hierarchy approach examines levels of government and cities as governing areas at different levels. The only partially systematic treatment of the spatial administrative hierarchy in English, the collection by Jae Ho Chung and Tao-Chiu Lam (2009), examines levels of government in relation to the level above and below, based on the Chinese literature. In general, the spatial administrative hierarchy approach recognizes levels of government in relation to subnational territories and their differential powers, but gives only preliminary attention to how the party-state strategically reterritorializes through changes to the administrative divisions. In effect, the administrative hierarchy approach does not address the state–market problematic.

Widespread, extensive change to the administrative divisions over the past three decades is leading to increased research on administrative territory in China, including analytical work on strategic changes to the administrative divisions. The scholarship of Liu Junde especially examines changes to the administrative divisions in relation to economic development since the 1980s (Liu 1996, 2002; Liu et al. 1999; Liu et al. 2011; Liu and Wang 2000; Ma and Liu 2009). This body of work recognizes how the state adjusts the administrative divisions to attain economic goals and address particular developmental problems. Liu's (1996) approach, the 'administrative area economy' or 'administrative district economy' (*xingzhengqu jingji*) conceptualizes the role of the state in guiding economic dynamics through adjustments and interrelations between adjacent jurisdictions. The approach takes into account the relationship between state administration of territory and the interrelated conditions of an administrative division: boundary, government, land territory, economy and population. Related to a territoriality approach in political geography (Agnew 2009), it assumes that conflicts may exist between adjacent territories, in part because officials advance the interests of their own jurisdictions, by which the Party evaluates them. As an applied approach, the administrative district economy estimates and weighs overall conditions of administrative divisions and their potential for change. Problematizing domestic economic dynamics through changes to the administrative divisions contributes to general understanding of the Chinese political economy.

Next we turn to introduce our recent development of a database that organizes and summarizes all changes to the administrative divisions at the province, prefecture and county levels since 1978 (CADC 2014). Here we present an abbreviated approach to the adjustments to the administrative divisions at the county level.

RETERRITORIALIZATION OF THE COUNTY

The establishment of hundreds of new cities in China under reform has had the greatest impact on changing the administrative divisions of historical counties and prefectures. Because of its significance in defining 'local China', in this section we focus on changes to the county. Changing counties into county-level cities has been one of the most common adjustments to the county. Nearly 600 changes to counties have taken place since 1978 through 'repealing' in order to change the county into another type of administrative division.

The main change is repealing the county to establish the county-level city, which started in the early 1980s (Ma 2005; Zhang and Zhao 1998). This change was popular with county officials because only urban territories could formally lease land for real estate development, and by the 1990s real estate development started to outpace manufacturing to become the most profitable sector of the economy (Cartier 2001). But the central government ultimately stopped the policy in 1996, since rampant land development had become a widely recognized problem. By the late 1990s, policy on urban change shifted to favour more uniform administration over larger areas: the creation of larger cities or urban mosaics of historic counties. The government has reterritorialized many former counties and county-level cities as districts of cities, which has significantly expanded the area, population and land resources of cities nationwide.

Historically, the county is the fundamental spatial unit of administrative territory in China. Although it became formally established in the Qin dynasty, the county likely first emerged in the Western Zhou before 690 BCE. As the main context of identity and government, the county has endured a long history over many dynasties while remaining the most stable administrative division in the hierarchy of the territorial system. Many counties in modern China have existed in approximately the same territory for more than 1000 years and have kept the same name. A popular proverb, 'the emperor's power stops at the county' (*huangquan buxia xian*), demonstrates the role of the county as the fundamental governing unit in dynastic China, and its significance for defining 'local China'.

But in the past three decades, in the process of urbanization, hundreds of counties have been repealed and reterritorialized as county-level cities. This transformation, from the county to the city, is the single greatest structural change to the system of administrative divisions in the reform era. Yet changing counties into county-level cities is only the most common adjustment to the level of the county, and so next we examine definitions and descriptions of different types of changes, analysis of the changes in time and space, and significant impacts of the changes.

In the records of the Ministry of Civil Affairs, there are different categories of adjustments to counties that take place by repealing the county. Here we analyze the main category, repealing a county in order to change the county administrative division. The first subcategory of change is repealing a county in order to reallocate its territory to other administrative unit(s). The county effectively disappears since it no longer exists as a united administrative district. This reterritorialization can take different forms. The subordinate towns and townships of the former county may be merged into the neighbouring counties and cities. The whole territory of a county may be merged into another county or city, or the county divided into several parts to be merged into neighbouring counties and cities. In Shanghai, the Pudong New Area is a product of repealing administrative divisions and dividing their territory to establish new ones.

The second subcategory is repealing a county to establish a city. The repealed county is redesignated as a county-level city or a prefecture-level city. The significance of this type of change is redesignation of the 'rural' status of the county to 'urban' status. When the county is redesignated as a prefecture-level city, the change also refers to scaling-up the territory to a higher level of administrative hierarchy. Yet the change can be complicated because the change in status from rural to urban does not necessarily apply uniformly. For example, land use change is a significant factor in development of the local economy, because urban land can be legally leased for development. Yet the change from the county to the county-level city does not necessarily reclassify all land in the county-level city as urban land. Similarly, the population of a county-level city does not uniformly hold urban citizenship; a large proportion of residents in a county-level city may continue to hold rural *hukou* (registered permanent residence).

Repealing a county and establishing an urban district is the third subcategory of change. In contrast to turning a county into a city, redesignation as an urban district results in merging a historic county (without first changing it into a county-level city) directly into a prefecture-level city. This also changes the status from rural to urban, in which the prefecture-level city directly governs the district. The fourth subcategory of

Table 9.5 Administrative changes to the county, 1978–2013

Category	Subcategory	1978–89	1990–99	2000–13	Total
Repeal of a county/ autonomous county to	allocate its territory to another area	36	6	1	43
	establish a district	6	20	44	70
	establish a county-level city (or a prefectural city*)	196 (incl. 10*)	220 (incl. 3*)	5 (incl. 1*)	421 (incl. 14*)
	establish an autonomous county (or vice versa*)	52 (incl. 5*)	2	1	55 (incl. 5*)
	resume its original administrative level	7	0	0	7
	all subcategories	297	248	51	596

Source: CADC (2014).

change is repealing a county to establish an autonomous county or vice versa, that is, repealing an autonomous county to establish a county. The fifth subcategory of change is repealing a county and assigning it to resume its original administrative status. This is an unusual type of adjustment, which suggests policy change at the local level. For example, Hanzhong county in Shanxi province existed from 1964 to 1979 but from 1951 to 1963 it was a county-level city; from 1963 to 1964 it was a prefecture-level city. In 1980 Hanzhong county was repealed and resumed its former county-level city status. Hanzhong illustrates the complexity and potential frequency of change to the administrative divisions.

Table 9.5 shows the different types of changes to counties in different time periods. From 1978 to 2013, the county experienced a total of 596 changes. Among these, the most frequent type of change was to redesignate its territory as a city, constituting more than 70 per cent of all changes during the past 35 years: 421 counties were repealed and redesignated as cities and, among these, 407 were county-level cities and 14 were prefecture-level cities.

The second most frequent change has established urban districts: 70 counties were repealed and redesignated as districts. Next, 47 counties were made autonomous counties and five autonomous counties were turned into counties. Repealing a county and reallocating its territory to other administrative units, which appears first in the Ministry of Civil Affairs list of types of changes, is the fourth most frequent type of change. In total, 43 counties were divided or merged in this way. Repealing a county to resume its original administrative institution took place only seven times (Table 9.5).

Comparing different changes to the county by periods shows some interesting patterns. In the 1990s, the central government accelerated designation of counties as cities, but after 2000 it practically stopped this type of change. From 1978 to 1989, 196 counties were repealed and redesignated as 186 county-level cities and ten prefecture-level cities (about 16 or 17 new cities were established every year). In the 1990s, 220 counties were redesignated into 217 county-level cities and three prefecture-level cities (the number increased by about 22 newly designated cities each year), but after 2000 only five counties were redesignated as cities. The central government instead increasingly changed counties

Table 9.6 Administrative changes to the county in different regions from 1978 to 2013

Category	Subcategory	East China	Central China	West China	Total
Repeal of a county/ autonomous county to	allocate its territory to another area	12	16	15	43
	establish a district	41	11	18	70
	establish a county-level city (or a prefectural city*)	193 (incl. 5*)	152 (incl. 6)	76 (incl. 3*)	421 (incl. 14*)
	establish an autonomous county (or vice versa*)	11	9	35 (incl. 5*)	55 (incl. 5*)
	resume its original administrative level	5	1	1	7
	all subcategories	262	189	145	596

Source: CADC (2014).

into districts and merged them into cities, especially prefecture-level cities. Whereas from 1978 to 1989 only six counties were redesignated as urban districts, the number of new districts increased more than threefold to 20 in the 1990s. From 2000 to 2013 the number of counties changed to districts more than doubled over the 1990s to 44 new districts.

Changes in the other three subcategories largely took place in the 1980s. From 1978 to 1989, the administrative territories of 36 counties were divided and merged into neighbouring administrative units, but in 1990s the number was just six. After 2000 the number was just one. Similarly, in the 1990s and certainly after 2000, the central government's redesignation of counties as autonomous counties slowed dramatically. Two changes of this type took place in the 1990s, and after that only one. This contrasts with earlier patterns: in the decade from 1978, it redesignated 47 counties as autonomous counties and five autonomous counties as counties. As for the number of counties being made to resume their original administrative institution, already a rare occurrence, this strategy was no longer employed after 1990. These three subtypes of changes to counties have not been common in recent years.

The administrative changes to counties also show some regional differences. Table 9.6 shows the changes to counties by region. Since adjustments take place in relation to political-economic change, most have taken place in East China, followed by Central China and West China. Comparing the changes by region, 193 counties were redesignated as cities in East China, including five prefecture-level cities. Central China had 152 counties redesignated as cities, including six prefecture-level cities; whereas only 76 counties became cities in West China, including three prefecture-level cities. These numbers are consistent with the general level of economic development in the regions. Level of economic development is the most important factor of evaluation in the process of government assessment for redesignating a county as a city.

On the merger of counties into cities as urban districts, 41 counties were redesignated as urban districts of prefecture-level cities in East China, and 18 in West China, but only 11 in Central China. In actual practice, a county or a county-level city has more rights to administer urban and economic planning, land use and finance. Thus when a county is turned into an urban district, the county is merged into and becomes a part of a city through which the city government obtains more land and fiscal resources. Through districts, the city expands its territory and developmental space, and increases population and industry, reproducing the urban process. In the last three decades, 41 counties were merged into cities in East China, yet the sum of the total number in West China (18) and Central China (11) was just 29.

Understanding changes to the administrative divisions reveals how the party-state strategically governs state space. The relationship between party-state governing authority and the administrative territorial system means that any study of cities or local political economic development must assess relevance of changes to the administrative divisions. The frequency of change to the administrative divisions also demonstrates how any fixed spatial approach to local and regional change – especially the macroregion – is, if we are interested in the role of the state, both theoretically and empirically problematic. The macroregion is theoretically problematic because it is based on physical or natural regions instead of political or administrative divisions, and empirically problematic because its regions are fixed in space but the wrong kinds of space for understanding the role of the state.

Let us turn to case studies of two cities where changes to the administrative divisions illustrate processes of economic transformation through territorial change. First we examine Suzhou, a leading prefectural city by economic rank in China, to illustrate the context of repealing a county to change the territory into an urban district of the prefectural city. The second case examines the establishment of Pudong in Shanghai to illustrate the process of establishing a new territory from historic administrative divisions and district-to-district merger.

CASE STUDY: SUZHOU

Suzhou in Jiangsu province is a renowned cultural city and an economic powerhouse, ranking behind only Guangzhou and Shenzhen among prefecture-level cities in annual economic productivity. Across the twentieth century Suzhou has served as both county-level and prefecture-level administrations, in which the larger, mostly rural prefectural territory surrounded the city. Then in 1983, leading one of two waves of establishing cities at the prefecture level, Jiangsu province reterritorialized the prefecture surrounding Suzhou as a prefecture-level city. Since then, like most prefecture-level cities in the urban coastal regions, administrative divisions in Suzhou have been subject to multiple adjustments. (For a longer treatment of this case in relation to official appointments, see Cartier 2015b.)

The main changes to the administrative divisions in Suzhou have transformed counties into county-level cities, and county-level cities near the urban core into urban districts. In 2000, Suzhou gained two districts, Wuzhong and Xiangcheng, which were established by repealing Wuxian city. Wuxian city was historically Wu county, the large county from which Suzhou was territorialized in 1949, the heart of the ancient region of Wu and its fabled kingdom (Xu 2000). In 2012 Suzhou experienced two administrative-territorial adjustments. On 4 September, the State Council announced the merger of the districts at its centre, Canglang, Jinchang and Pingjiang, into a single district named Gusu. This merger responded to the problem of diminished political-economic vitality in the historic core. Now the Suzhou city centre is a larger, single district with a uniform government. Then on 29 October, the State Council repealed Wujiang county-level city and established Wujiang district as part of the Suzhou urban core. Before 2012, Wujiang was one of five county-level cities in the administrative city of Suzhou. Compared with the other four – Changshu, Kunshan, Taicang and Zhangjiagang – Wujiang is larger, equivalent only to Changshu in land area. Reterritoralizing Wujiang significantly expanded the main city of Suzhou. Wujiang also shares a section of border with Shanghai, establishing a direct border between Suzhou and Shanghai.

Do the changes to Gusu and Wujiang interrelate? New research on the administrative divisions seeks to understand their context and rationale. Here we utilize the CADC (2014) database to compare relevant changes. The merger of the Suzhou core districts in 2012, forming Gusu, was the only district merger in Jiangsu province in 2012, a year of five district mergers countrywide. Redesignating Wujiang from a county-level city to a district was one of only two changes of this type in a prefecture-level city countrywide in 2012. Thus we propose that these changes interrelate: the expansion of Suzhou's economic base through Wujiang requires a stronger urban core to govern the larger city. The rationale for Wujiang district also relates to a policy change in Kunshan, the 'strongest' county-level city in Suzhou prefectural city. Kunshan gained direct administrative relations with the provincial government from 1 October 2012, when it became one of three county-level cities in southern Jiangsu to pilot 'direct control', which removes Suzhou from authority over political and economic approval processes in Kunshan, including appointment of Kunshan officials. In negotiations over changes to the administrative divisions, Suzhou 'gets' (*dedao*) Wujiang as a consequence of 'losing' (*shiqu*) Kunshan. Strong county-level cities seek to be removed from prefecture-level administration and control, while prefectural cities seek incorporation of adjacent county-level cities as urban districts to increase economic resources. The resulting prefectural city is a mosaic of historic territories.

CASE STUDY: SHANGHAI PUDONG

Pudong is an urban district on the eastern bank of the Huangpu River opposite Shanghai's historic Bund. To see Pudong now, its financial district at Lujiazui spiked with super-tall buildings, is to see the result of at least two decades of planning, at the heart of which have been changes to administrative divisions. (For an analysis of Shanghai Pudong as a process of territorial urbanization see Cartier 2015a.)

In 1990 when Deng Xiaoping announced that the Pudong New Area would open Shanghai to the world economy, the district of Pudong did not yet exist. The Shanghai Planning Bureau created the territorial space of Pudong by repealing and combining three districts, Huangpu, Nanshi and Yangpu; one county, Chuansha; and a township, Sanlin. Through strategic territorialization, Pudong appeared on the map. In 1992 at the 14th Party Congress, then President Jiang Zemin, a former Shanghai Party Secretary, announced that Shanghai Pudong would serve as a centre of international finance and trade. In 1993 the Shanghai government established Pudong as a district of the city, and the Shanghai international financial centre in Pudong at Lujiazui. Urban construction proceeded throughout the 1990s and the State Council approved the Master Plan of Shanghai (1999–2020) based on the 'two centres' concept. In 2000, at the symbolic turn of the century and millennium, Shanghai established the Pudong government uniquely at the sub-province level, a half-level higher than other Shanghai districts, to emphasize its power and significance.

The next stage of administrative territorialization took place in 2009 when the State Council, in a likely stimulus measure, intensified construction of the 'two centres'. But expanding Shanghai's international trade capacity presents a problem: the closest deepwater port facilities are in Hangzhou Bay, offshore from Nanhui district on the southern boundary of Pudong. Pudong could not become an international shipping centre without access to Yangshan from Nanhui district. Then in April 2009 the State Council announced the merger of Nanhui district into Pudong. The merger repealed Nanhui and added the territory of Nanhui to Pudong, more than doubling the size of Pudong from 533 km^2 to 1210 km^2. Pudong now governs places and populations in Nanhui, and the name 'Nanhui' has disappeared off the contemporary map. In the process, Shanghai gained access to the port of Yangshan, a deepwater facility in the Zhoushan archipelago, via the 32.5 km Donghai Bridge.

The State Council announces mergers often within days of related policy, but not simultaneously. Understanding changes to the administrative divisions requires research on related policy change. The State Council announced the 'two centres' policy on 14 April 2009 and the merger of Nanhui into Pudong on 24 April 2009. Territorial urbanization of Pudong also anticipated the announcement of the Shanghai Disneyland project. In November 2009, after years of negotiation, the National Development and Reform Commission approved the project. The project site, along the expressway from the Shanghai Pudong International Airport, straddles the former Pudong–Nanhui boundary.

The repeal of Nanhui district (a county-level administrative division) and the expansion of Pudong is one among several urban district mergers in major cities at the province and prefecture levels. The Pudong–Nanhui merger is an example of the type between adjacent districts with uneven levels of economic development. The government repeals the less-developed district and adds its territory to the more-developed area, which contributes directly to the growth of the more-developed district. Such mergers contribute to meeting urban-economic targets while extending developmental and governing capacity into surrounding areas. This territorial urbanization – the establishment and expansion of cities through changes to the administrative divisions – characterizes the urban process in China.

10. Economic policy
Barry Naughton

The economy has been central to much of Chinese policy-making since 1978, yet the economic policy process itself has not been thoroughly studied. Like elite politics in general (Teiwes, Chapter 1 in this volume), much of economic policy-making is a black box. How is economic policy made? Do we understand the economic policy process? Which interest and opinion groups are most influential? This chapter attempts a partial answer to these questions, acknowledging that there is much that we do not know. I begin by placing economic policy in context, and argue that economic policy has a number of distinctive characteristics in the Chinese context. The next section defines economic policy and delineates the boundaries that separate economic policy from other political economy issues. The chapter goes on to describe the policy process, emphasizing the dominant role of the Premier. Five different policy regimes are sketched out, as five Premiers grapple with rapidly changing economic and political conditions. The next section divides economic policy into two types: structural policies and stabilization policies, both defined very broadly. It argues that, perhaps counter-intuitively, the Chinese system is better suited to a kind of change-oriented structural policy than it is to ordinary stabilization policies. The chapter then considers what kind of interest and opinion groups might appear to be influential in economic policy.

WHAT MAKES ECONOMIC POLICY DISTINCTIVE?

Two aspects of the relationship between economics and politics in China are worth singling out, since a number of distinctive characteristics of economic policy follow from them. First, economic development has very high priority and a broad consensus in support of its realization. The contemporary period of Chinese politics began when the December 1978 'Third Plenum' declared that the centre of Chinese Communist Party (CCP) work would shift from class struggle to economic construction.[1] Since then, there has never been serious dissent about this objective. Gross domestic product (GDP) growth is written into the success indicators of political leaders at every level, and systemic innovations have repeatedly been justified in terms of their efficacy in accelerating GDP growth. Second, the entire post-1978 period has been one of sustained systemic transformation and change, in the general direction of market-oriented reform and international opening. Every Chinese administration since 1978 has embraced economic reform, at least nominally, and the outcomes have been varied but at times extremely impressive. In other words, there has been no permanent orthodoxy in the field of economics, and the need for economic institutional change has been ingrained into the Communist Party's world-view.

These fundamental features of economics and politics lead to several distinctive characteristics of economic policy. First, the overriding priority given to economic development means that this goal can, on occasion, override other objectives. Since the late 1970s, economics has been implicitly defined as an issue of national survival. Without successful economic development, China's leaders were convinced, China would be bullied internationally and Communist Party power would eventually collapse. As a result, economic policy gets a great deal of direct, hands-on attention at the highest level. Economic development infuses the action of government officials at all levels, and in all positions. It follows from this that effective economic policy can, under certain circumstances, override specific interest groups and even the partial interests of the Communist Party system itself.

Following on from this point, there is generally no 'wrong' side in economic policy debates, as long as one argues from a non-political, technocratic standpoint. The broad rhetorical commitment to 'reform' implies a continuous search for alternative approaches; the high priority given to economics implies that failure to locate an effective alternative would be very costly. There is no 'blueprint' for economic reform. As a result, there is (almost) free speech, and a spectrum of opinion from radical free marketers to extreme statists is tolerated. In a highly politicized system, economic policy is relatively depoliticized and can be discussed more freely. Thus, if we find rational policy-making in the Chinese system, it is more likely to be in economic policy than other arenas; and indeed many analysts have claimed to find this.

Reinforcing the previous, there is an objective standard for economic performance. Obvious mismanagement of the economy is not tolerated, and the consequences of failure are severe. This leads to an overemphasis on short-term performance at the expense of long-run economic health, but it also reinforces the technocratic orientation described earlier. In this, economic policy is very different from propaganda policy, or even defence and foreign policy, where policy failures might not emerge for decades.

These three features of economic policy mean that it is more transparent and somewhat easier to understand than other policy arenas. The criteria of success and failure are relatively clear. Finally, Chinese are proud of their economic record, so they are more likely to discuss and critique economic policy. To a certain extent, China's economic policy record fits into a lineage as an East Asian 'developmental state'. China since 1978 has resembled Japan or Korea in earlier decades, in the sense that economic development infuses the action of government officials at all levels, and in all positions. Deng's call in 1982 to quadruple GDP by 2000 carried clear echoes of Ikeda's 1960 call to double Japan's national income in ten years. China absorbed many specific ideas and policies from Japan and South Korea over the past few decades. But in another sense, China is quite different from these earlier developmental states, because so much of China's push for development has occurred through the process of marketization and opening up. The classic developmental states were concerned with shifting priorities and mobilizing resources in the context of an already existing market economy, but China pre-reform suffered from an unsuccessful strategy with an excessive mobilization of resources. Thus, much of development strategy in the current period has been engaged in relaxation, deprioritization and opening. A major task of economic policy has been to identify practical institutional strategies to achieve the broad goal of reform and opening. This makes China quite different from the classic developmental state.

WHAT IS ECONOMIC POLICY?

I define 'economic policy' as the actions taken by a government in order to influence its economy. Although almost every public policy has economic consequences, the definition of economic policy includes only those policies whose primary intention is to shape economic outcomes. Economic policy, obviously, is formulated and implemented within the context of a given economic system, and indeed, modifying the existing economic system is one of the primary objectives of economic policy, especially in a transitional economy like China. However, broader analysis of the economic system in itself is a huge task beyond the scope of this chapter. Still, certain fundamental aspects of China's economic system need to be taken account of, particularly the division between central and local government. Local governments can certainly carry out economic policies, but the emphasis of this chapter is on the central government. What is the relationship between the two?

There is a large body of existing work on the relationship between the centre and the local in Chinese economic change, much of which focuses on the development of economic initiative at the local level. This is understandable, since this work is essential to understanding China dynamically and in comparative terms. One of the most important features of China's development after 1978 was the way in which decentralized initiatives were adopted nationwide and culminated in a profound economic transformation beyond what most anticipated. One of the most distinctive features of China's economy today is the extremely hands-on and interventionist role that local governments play. In other words, local governments in China are entrepreneurial; that is, that they have strong incentives to create new revenue streams and thus to act as economic development agents. In the 1970s and 1980s, the catalytic role played by township and village enterprises (TVEs) in China's market transition attracted a great deal of attention. A body of work emerged that elucidated the political and institutional relations at the local level that empowered TVEs. These included analyses of institutions at the local level, including 'local government corporatism' (Oi 1992, 1999; Whiting 1999, 2000), and studies of the nature of ownership and incentives in the local-government owned firm (Rozelle and Boisvert 1994; Weitzman and Xu 1994). Based on these insights, a further body of work has examined the broader conditions under which entrepreneurial local governments could be expected to interact in ways that contribute to economic development (Montinola et al. 1995; Xu 2011). The key insight in these works is that competition among jurisdictions is essential to discipline local governments and ensure that entrepreneurial energies are not channelled into rent-seeking and corruption.

These works are fundamental to understanding the Chinese economic and political system, but they are not primarily about economic policy. Chinese leaders make economic policy in the context of a system that has extremely entrepreneurial local governments, to be sure, and there were certain crucial junctures at which economic policy intentionally reinforced the entrepreneurial instincts of local government. The initial development of TVEs was enabled only passively by national policy, when it relaxed earlier restrictions in the earlier rural industrialization policy and allowed local governments to seek markets and profits. However, after the success of TVEs, national policy was adapted to try to give urban and provincial governments the same kind of high-powered incentives, building GDP growth into success indicators and providing budgetary systems with high marginal retained revenues. Thus, policy sought to strengthen and spread a feature that was seen to be already intrinsic to the Chinese system. In general, though, the many things that local governments do to generate revenues and economic development are not taken as 'economic policy' in this chapter. These actions do of course 'influence' the local economy, but their objective is to create new revenue streams rather than to influence the functioning of the local economy. They are more like government-owned businesses than economic policy-makers, and are not further considered in this chapter.[2]

To be sure, Chinese local governments do carry out clear economic policies on occasion. Guangdong province famously pioneered several important policies related to economic opening in the early days, and has followed an ambitious programme to restructure and upgrade its economy since about 2005. Shanghai has pioneered a number of social security and welfare policies, including minimum living stipends to its poor. Most strikingly, Chongqing under Party Secretary Bo Xilai and Mayor Huang Qifan tried to create a local economic model and pioneered an expansion of social welfare policies. These cases are not covered in this chapter, for two reasons. First, it would simply take me too far afield, and I have chosen instead to focus the discussion on national economic policy. Second, local economic policies, as important as they are in some cases, are typically carried out 'in the shadow of hierarchy' (Heilmann 2009: 457). That is to say, local economic policies are generally adopted in response to signals from the central government that alternative approaches are being considered. Local leaders respond as political entrepreneurs, because they realize that pioneering successful policies will raise their visibility and make promotion much more likely. Understanding this, national policy-makers rely on local officials 'to try out new ways of problem-solving and then feed the local experiences back into national policy formation' (Heilmann 2008b: 1). This means that understanding the national policy context is the most important task, and it is to this that I now turn.

WHO DETERMINES ECONOMIC POLICY? THE PREMIER

In economic policy, a tremendous amount of authority is delegated to the government, and specifically to the Premier. The leadership of the Communist Party retains ultimate authority over economic affairs (as all areas), but it delegates primary control over the economy to the Premier. This relationship explains both the extraordinary concentration of power in the hands of the Premier, and the limits on that power. The delegation of economic authority to the Premier has been a fairly stable and consistent pattern since the 1980s.[3] When the reform era began, the Elders, led by Deng Xiaoping and Chen Yun, were intent on preventing the recurrence of the disasters that had occurred due to the concentration of absolute power in the hands of Mao Zedong. A new division of responsibility was intentionally devised by Deng Xiaoping, who sought to separate Party and government, and divide responsibility among different individuals within a collective leadership. The area in which this vision was most effectively realized was economic policy. Deng brought Zhao Ziyang from Sichuan and made him Premier in order to take charge of economic policy. Chen Yun had been in charge of economic policy temporarily after the Third Plenum, but he quickly turned over the direct economic leadership to Zhao. In February 1980, Zhao became head of the Party's revived Finance and

Economics Leadership Small Group to reinforce his Premier's role, and from this time until 4 June 1989, Zhao Ziyang was the most important single architect of economic policy.

Although Premier Zhao Ziyang and General Secretary Hu Yaobang were generally allies in supporting the reform process, there were persistent differences between them in the early 1980s with respect to the pace of economic growth. It took a direct personal intervention from Deng Xiaoping to establish in practice the principle that the Premier was responsible for economic policy. On 15 March 1982, he called Hu and Zhao to his home for a talk, and then two days later convened a joint meeting of the Politburo Standing Committee and the Party Secretariat. At this meeting he rebuked Hu on both content and process. Deng first repudiated 'feverish' economic policies and then declared that economic policy statements should be made through a single channel, which should be the Finance and Economics Leadership Small Group (FELSG), which was chaired by Zhao (Deng 2004: 895–896; Deng Liqun 2005: 203–205; Zhao 2009: 114–118). In Zhao's words, 'a rule was set in this conversation: the State Council and the FELSG were in charge of economic affairs'. Hu's behaviour changed markedly, and thereafter he was careful to acknowledge Zhao's precedence in economic matters (Xie 2014: 284). The principle that the Premier ran economic policy was effectively established.

Delegation to the Premier was never absolute, and it could always be revoked, since the Party remains the ultimate authority. Moreover, the highly personalized nature of elite Chinese politics and the impact of economic turbulence meant occasional interludes in which the nominal assignment of roles did not fit the actual responsibilities. First, after the fall of Hu Yaobang, Zhao assumed the General Secretary position, and Li Peng became Premier. However, Zhao remained head of the Finance and Economics Leadership Small Group, and maintained a strong influence (though not necessarily predominance) in the economic field.[4] It was not until 4 June 1989, when Zhao lost all influence, that Li Peng assumed control over economic policy. In any case, Li Peng was never able to establish an effective policy regime. Economic challenges were severe, with the impact of contractionary policies reinforced by political and international disruption. Moreover, the regime was deeply split over the fundamental direction of economic reform, and Li had to pay attention to the interventions of reformers (Deng Xiaoping) and conservatives (Yao Yilin). By the evidence of his 'Economics Diary', Li spent most of his time brokering deals to bridge over short-term economic difficulties and engaging in fruitless planning exercises, including the drafting of a Ten Year Plan that never saw the light of day and has been conveniently erased from history. When the re-emergence of reform in 1991–92 was accompanied by a surge of inflation, Li Peng's time as top policy-maker was over.

Zhu Rongji had been appointed Vice-Premier in April 1991. Zhu Rongji was brought from Shanghai by Deng Xiaoping specifically to take charge of economic policy, but Li Peng remained Premier. At first there was some uncertainty about relative power, but by June 1993, at the latest, when Zhu concurrently became head of the People's Bank of China, Zhu was unambiguously in charge of economic policy.[5] Zhu retained this dominance of economic policy for a decade, and formally assumed the Premier's job in the spring of 1998. Some of the most dramatic episodes of economic policy-making in China occurred in 1993–94, as Zhu seized full control over the economics agenda, and pushed through crucial fiscal and trade reforms based on the reform programme passed by the Third Plenum in October 1993. Overall, Zhu's tenure was marked by remarkable achievements in economic reform policy.

When Wen Jiabao succeeded Zhu Rongji as Premier in early 2003, most expectations were for policy continuity. In retrospect, however, it is clear that Wen Jiabao introduced a dramatically different set of policy priorities from the very beginning of his administration. The emphasis on economic reform dropped dramatically, and a new set of spending priorities increased in importance. Since overall economic and budgetary conditions were quite positive during this period, Wen's priorities met with general acceptance. However, after the new Xi Jinping–Li Keqiang administration came to power in 2012–13, the policy orientation again changed dramatically. Both Xi and Li stepped up the economic reform rhetoric, and rolled out an ambitious and broad reform programme at the November 2013 Third Plenum. While it is too early to assess the Li Keqiang policy regime, it is already clear that it will be quite different from that of Wen Jiabao.

This quick historical sketch reveals that each individual Premier faced distinctive conditions and shaped a distinctive approach to economic policy, and that successive Chinese Communist Party heads have delegated primary responsibility for economic policy-making to the Premier. There are important differences in the specifics of delegation in each case, and Li Peng's tenure contained two anomalous episodes (particularly around Li Peng's tenure), but the general principle of delegation is quite robust. This means that the entire 35-year period (1980–2015) has been strongly marked by five different Premierships. Of these, the three Premierships of Zhao, Zhu and Wen can be clearly characterized by their policy accomplishments. The (economic) Premiership of Li Peng was overwhelmed by economic and political difficulties; and it is too early to evaluate the Premiership of Li Keqiang.

THE POLICY ENVIRONMENT OF INDIVIDUAL PREMIERS

Chinese Premiers face an extraordinarily complex and challenging decision-making environment. Since the Premier in China has never been the top leader, the Premier must always pay primary attention to the configuration of power above, especially in the person of the General Secretary of the Communist Party. At the same time, the Premier must pay attention to his various constituencies, first of all the officials and managers of the state and Party system. The Premier must be skilled at managing up, as well as managing down. At the same time, the economic environment is constantly changing, and serious economic challenges are repeatedly presented. A Premier who failed to master the basic economic challenges would face the real danger of being swept aside, even if his support coalition otherwise seemed to be intact. Among all the important economic outcomes, it is particularly vital that the Premier be able to ensure an adequate supply of resources to the central government. In this section, I characterize the economic policy regimes of successive Premiers in terms of these changing political and economic conditions.

The configuration of power above the Premier shapes the kind of authority he is able to exercise. That configuration has changed dramatically: in the 1980s, ultimate power was dispersed among the 'Revolutionary Elders', most importantly Deng Xiaoping and Chen Yun. While Deng's paramount position was acknowledged, many of the Elders had a voice or veto power over a specific policy area, and Chen Yun's influence over economic policy was formidable. This created a complex environment of multiple centres and multiple veto-points around which Premiers Zhao Ziyang and Li Peng had to manoeuvre. Around 1993–94, this situation changed dramatically. Some of the most important elders passed away, and Jiang Zemin was able to centralize power in his own hands (Naughton 2008a). Jiang exercised power, in part, by supporting Zhu Rongji, but also occasionally balancing Zhu's more extreme positions against those of the more conservative Li Peng. Jiang consolidated the pattern of delegation of economic policy to the Premier by maintaining stable relations with Zhu Rongji, despite occasional frictions. After Jiang, successive General Secretaries have maintained their top position, but with different practices of delegation. Hu Jintao was an especially hands-off leader who seems to have rarely intervened in economic policy. By contrast, Xi Jinping has already established a much more dynamic, hands-on approach to the exercise of power. Although Premier Li Keqiang still manages the economics portfolio on a day-to-day basis, Xi Jinping chairs two important Leadership Small Groups that oversee economic policy and place much more immediate constraints on the Premier's decision-making than was the case in previous administrations. These procedural changes implemented by Xi Jinping are quite radical in the context of China's decades-long practice of delegation.

The changes in economic conditions over the past 35 years have been dramatic and multidimensional: rapid economic growth, marketization and changes in the effectiveness of economic institutions have continuously reshaped the economic environment. From the standpoint of national policy-makers, these complex changes can be drastically simplified by looking at the change in availability of government resources. As Figure 10.1 shows, government budgetary revenues as a share of GDP show a very clear and distinctive pattern: revenues declined steadily from 1978 to 1995, and then increased steadily from 1995 to 2013. These changes are themselves the outcome of a series of economic reform policies, increased competition for state-owned enterprises (SOEs) and tax reforms in particular. Here I focus on the effect of the revenue changes on the options and challenges specific Chinese administrations faced. Clearly, Premiers who preside over periods of declining revenue availability face a more challenging environment than Premiers who preside over increasing revenues. Facing declining revenues, Premiers must make difficult decisions about resource allocation that inevitably disenfranchise some stakeholders. Facing increasing revenues, Premiers can make decisions about expanding benefits and initiating new programmes. Premiers Zhao Ziyang, Li Peng and Zhu Rongji all faced prolonged declines in resource availability that changed the nature of economic policy in China by the late 1990s. Since then, Wen Jiabao and Li Keqiang have possessed many more options and made decisions about the disposition of a larger volume of resources.

It is possible to combine these basic political and economic factors to create a simplified schematic version of the policy programmes that different Premiers carried through. This is shown in Table 10.1. Each Premier faced political and economic conditions that, while complex, can be usefully reduced to two basic conditions in each of the political and economic dimensions. Politically, Premiers either worked for complex configurations of elders, with multiple veto-points, or they worked for a single top leader with a relatively unified leadership position. Economically, Premiers either faced declining resource availability, stabilization, or increasing resource availability. Given these conditions, each Premier solicited policy advice, devised strategies, assembled support coalitions and

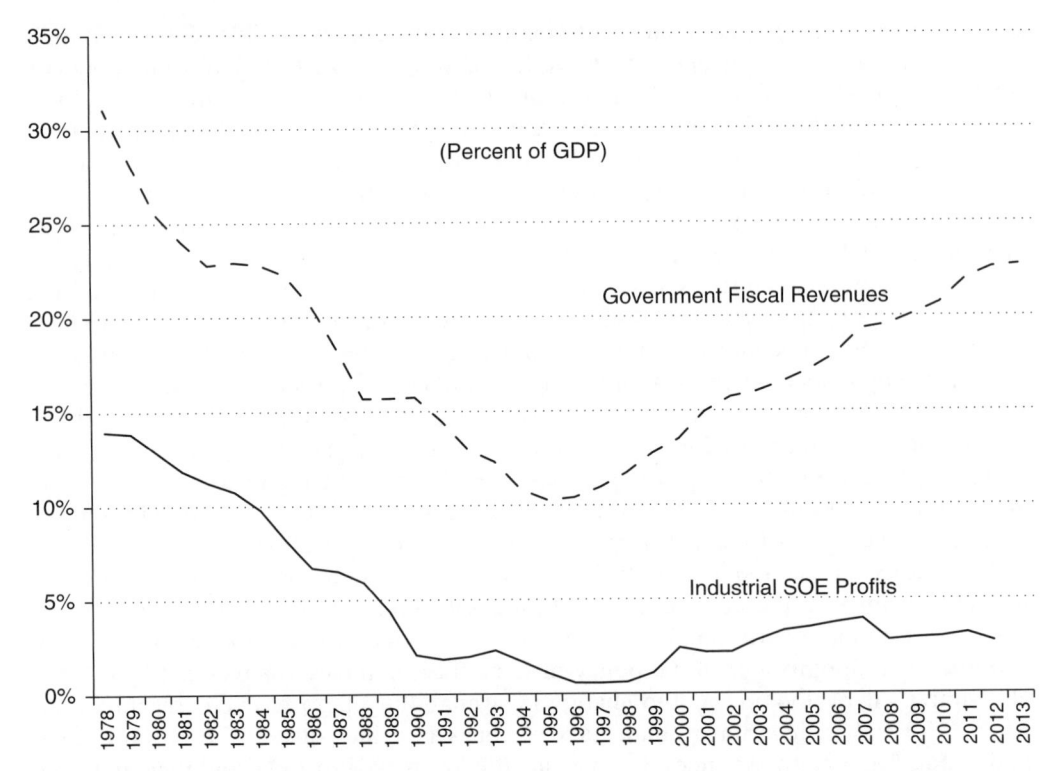

Figure 10.1 Government resources: budgetary revenues and industrial SOE profits (% of GDP)

Table 10.1 Policy-making framework

Premier	Resource availability	Apex power configuration	Policy outcome
Zhao Ziyang 1980–89	Declining	Elders; fragmented; multiple veto-points	Dual track reforms
Li Peng 1989–93	Declining	Elders; fragmented; multiple veto-points	Failure
Zhu Rongji 1993–2003	Declining; stabilizing	Unified; Jiang Zemin, balancer	Comprehensive reforms
Wen Jiabao 2003–13	Increasing	Hu Jintao; weak oversight	Redistributive politics
Li Keqiang 2013–present	Increasing	Xi Jinping: strong oversight	

carried out important economic policies. Not surprisingly, the overall outcomes were very different in each case.

This schematic matrix of external conditions tells us a great deal about each Premier's economic policies, but of course does not determine any particular outcome. Premiers differ in their vision, ideology, personality and skill. Premiers have to assemble workable coalitions, so that the bureaucracy is willing to carry out their programmes. They bring different backgrounds to the task. Making economic policy, for the Premier, is an art, not a science. The result has been very different outcomes associated with different Premiers, which are shown schematically in the right-hand column of Table 10.1. There have been two strikingly successful Premierships with regard to economic reform, but even these have been quite different in character. Zhao Ziyang presided over a remarkable stage of reform policy-making in the 1980s based on 'dual track' reforms that gave almost all major stakeholders a secure income, while providing them with an opportunity to gain higher incomes from more efficient, market-oriented activity. Zhu Rongji pushed an equally productive reform period based on dramatically different principles, pushing for comprehensive reforms to treat all market participants equally. Until today, these two Premierships stand out as breakthrough periods in economic transformation.

Zhao Ziyang (1980–89) confronted an essentially intact planned economy system, in which control of virtually all economic resources was monopolized inside the hierarchical political system. However, due to the failures of the planned economic system during the Cultural Revolution, the system had little in the way of available resources. Incomplete investment projects, misguided technological development projects and long-deferred investments in public welfare and housing all implied that leaders were engaged in cutting back outlays, cancelling projects and delaying payments. This was a 'low-power' regime, in the sense that the level of discretionary resources available to leaders was quite limited. In this regime, a pervasive politics of bargaining among insiders was in evidence. Zhao had to shape this bureaucratic bargaining environment to start the movement toward a market economy, and push the economy toward objectively determined scarcities and opportunities. In this endeavour, Zhao was helped enormously by the broad consensus in favour of change, which made many insiders receptive to opportunities to trade their privileged insider positions for the freedom to operate outside the system in the brave new world of the market economy. Insider interest groups were relatively low-powered, at least insofar as their opposition to reform was concerned. Still, Zhao faced an extraordinarily difficult political environment because of the presence of many elders whose support could not be sustained. Zhao succeeded brilliantly in shaping this environment into a successful programme through the means of a 'dual track' reform strategy (Naughton 2007a, 2008a). Despite the success in the reform direction, Zhao lost the backing of the Elders in 1989, when macroeconomic problems coincided with political events to create the unrest at Tiananmen Square.

Li Peng (1989–93), taking over from Zhao, faced the same difficult political environment, with Elders with competing views still holding dominant political positions, while a new top Party leader, Jiang Zemin, was gradually consolidating power. Economic conditions, in the immediate wake of Tiananmen, were even more challenging than those that had faced Zhao. Perhaps most important, Li was utterly lacking in any kind of vision for the future direction of the economy. A fundamentally transactional Premier, it was inevitable that Li would lose out when the economy began to recover, and Deng Xiaoping reasserted his economic reform vision. However, this very absence of vision probably made it possible for Li Peng to survive into another term of Premier. While he ceded top economic responsibilities to Zhu Rongji, Li Peng continued to preside over the bureaucracy, broker deals and coordinate investment projects, and generally keep the machinery of government running.

Zhu Rongji (1993–2003) faced new challenges and produced economic outcomes that were fundamentally different from those of Zhao Ziyang. By the time Zhu came to Beijing, China faced a fundamental crisis of state capacity. Government revenues as a share of GDP had declined to near crisis levels, and government leaders faced major challenges in prioritizing a limited number of feasible government objectives. The decline in budgetary resources posed huge challenges to macroeconomic stability. At the same time, the threat of crisis provided an enormous impetus to more fundamental reforms, since it allowed reformers to argue that survival was impossible without fundamental changes. Zhu Rongji's blunt and assertive personality fitted the situation well, and he was able to impose sometimes painful reforms in the name of the common good. Zhu's policies harnessed these economic pressures to drastically reformulate China's tax and foreign exchange systems, create a modern banking system, drastically restructure the state sector, and bring China into the World Trade Organization (WTO). Zhu's actions constituted a reform strategy quite different from that of Zhao Ziyang. Focusing on institutional development that moved toward common competitive conditions for all, Zhu carried through reforms that created obvious costs – particularly in the form of urban unemployment – in return for long-run economic benefits. Indeed, Zhu's actions laid the foundations for China's continuing growth miracle and stabilized government resources. Zhu Rongji succeeded in crafting a reform strategy that overcame the crisis of state capacity he had inherited.

At the same time, under Zhu Rongji it appeared that the nature of influence over economic policy had begun to change. As power inside the system declined, economic power outside the system grew. Multinational corporations, with enormous economic and technological resources, began to invest in China, and the Chinese leadership began to court them and bargain with them. As the Chinese economy grew, domestic business groups became significant. With the rise of economic interests outside the government, we began to see something that looks like lobbying. Zhu Rongji was a transformational leader with respect to the economy, and the reforms he helped to push through changed the basic economic environment. By the end of Zhu's tenure, it was clear that reforms had succeeded and that government resources had recovered and were entering a new period of sustained increase.

Wen Jiabao (2003–13) thus inherited a drastically different set of economic conditions from those of his predecessors. As budgetary resources increased, interests within the system, now restructured on a sustainable basis, began to reassert themselves. At the same time, a backlash against reforms grew, and some argued that reforms had gone too far, or had neglected crucial elements of the social safety net. Moreover, successful economic reforms meant that the immediate urgency of further reforms seemed low. Wen Jiabao crafted a complex response to these economic and political currents. A master of the central bureaucratic apparatus, in which he had spent his entire career, Wen built a whole panoply of new social programmes and technological initiatives. While continuing to give lip service to economic reform, Wen never in fact pushed through any significant market-oriented reform. Instead, he built a redistributive bureaucratic system that brought in, or bought off, many of the main insider interest groups. In his own terms, Wen was quite successful: he began the reconstruction of social security programmes, made government policy more redistributive, and presided over an array of technological and defence programmes that enhanced China's stature and prestige. However, he also presided over a surprising revival of some elements of the old system, and significant backsliding on economic reform.

Li Keqiang thus became Premier in 2013 in an environment that was once again markedly different from that of his predecessors. Li will continue the redistributive policies initiated by Wen Jiabao, but it may be difficult for him to do so. Although the Chinese state is far richer than ever before, a much greater share of state resources is now tied up in various projects and initiatives than was the case ten years ago. Thus, while Wen Jiabao had freedom to initiate new programmes, Li must juggle among existing commitments that demand continued and expanded funding (health insurance, pensions, military modernization and so on). Moreover, China's economy is slowing. To be sure, growth slowing from 10 per cent to 6 per cent will not reverse the scenario of an increasingly rich state with steadily expanding capabilities, but if the transition to slower growth is rocky or turbulent, a comfortable redistributive approach may not be feasible. Even more important, both Li Keqiang and Xi Jinping have strongly asserted the need to revive the economic reform process. The Third Plenum of the 18th Party Congress (November 2013) rolled out a broad and ambitious reform programme, marking a clear break with – and implicit repudiation of – the policy stance under the previous administration. Indeed, both Xi and Li display clear signs of dissatisfaction with the surface stability of the Hu–Wen period, and the failure to tackle deeper problems that may have accumulated. This creates a fundamentally new economic and policy environment for Li Keqiang.

Yet the most important change of all is that Xi Jinping has taken steps to end the almost complete delegation of economic decision-making authority to the Premier that characterized previous administrations. Xi asserted his own personal control over the Third Plenum policy process; he assumed the chairmanship of two separate Leadership Small Groups that pass on fundamental economic decisions, and he has given both unprecedented visibility. A new body, the Comprehensive Reform Leadership Small Group, is in charge of overseeing the translation of the Third Plenum reform programme into practical measures, and of overseeing their implementation. Meanwhile, the existing Finance and Economics Leadership Small Group has been revitalized and undertaken a regular calendar of meetings. These steps indicate a desire by Xi to take control of economic policy in a way not seen since Mao. This is a fairly radical shake-up of one part of the (unwritten) Dengist 'constitution'; it could be highly disruptive, and it might not succeed.

Each successive reform-era administration has dramatically reoriented economic policy-making. It is an illusion to think of a constant 'incremental reform' approach to economic policy in China over the past 30 years. To some extent, this is a reflection of the tremendous change in economic conditions that has framed policy over this period, and to some extent it is a reflection of the continued importance of individual leaders in China's authoritarian system. This makes the current policy-making environment especially volatile: new leaders are asserting new ideas and making institutional and procedural innovations. It is too early to judge the impact of these changes.

HOW DOES POLICY GET MADE?

Having established that the economic policy outcomes have been extremely personalized, it is now possible to identify certain persistent patterns in the policy process. To describe the policy process, it is necessary to divide policies into two types, which I will label 'structural' and 'stabilization'. 'Structural policies' are those that require the articulation of an objective beforehand. They include most types of economic reform (financial reform, fiscal reform) as well as policies designed to foster the development of specific sectors. They require that objectives be formulated in advance and they may require substantial coordination and design and then mobilization of supporters and perhaps neutralization of opponents. 'Stabilization policies' are those that come in response to the steady flux of economic events. They include a constant stream of short-term and policy measures, which cumulatively exert enormous influence on an economy's performance. These measures may be modest incremental adaptations to changes in the economic environment; or there may be massive responses to economic crises that have not been foreseen but require a rapid response. It makes sense to consider these two types of policy-making separately.

Structural Policies

There is an extensive literature on policy process that occurs with structural policies. This literature generally emphasizes that the Chinese policy process adapted to absorb expert and technocratic opinion and build policy consensus (Chen et al. 2010; Chen, Ling 2011; Ma and Lin 2012; Wang and Peng 2013). The literature agrees that Chinese policy-makers have developed impressive capabilities to canvass views among a broad policy community, to reach outside of official government circles for 'outside' opinions, and to synthesize these views into a 'consensus' policy. In the case of economic policy, these processes are typically structured by the Premier. He may assemble a government Leadership Small Group to control the decision process (these decision-oriented government Leadership Small Groups are different in kind from the Party's standing Leadership Small Groups). This process typically culminates in a programmatic document issued by the top political authority, that then becomes the basis for widespread implementation. Such a document is typically ratified by the Communist Party, which affirms the basic principle. Then implementation is referred back to government bodies, often the same bodies that participated in drafting the measure. A selection of important structural policies is presented in Box 10.1.

BOX 10.1   SELECTED 'STRUCTURAL POLICY' MILESTONES

1993: Third Plenum '50 Articles': outlines Zhu Rongji economic reform programme, including fiscal and bank reforms.
1994: Fiscal reform.
1995: Bank reform.
2006: Medium and long-term plan for science and technology.
2008–09: Health care reform.

Even a cursory glance at the structural economic policies of the past 35 years reveals that the Chinese system displays the ability to adopt policies that break with past practice and substantially reorient the policy framework. Perhaps the most dramatic single example is the sequence of events in the 1990s. The 1993 Third Plenum (of the 14th Party Congress) laid out an ambitious economic reform programme. Subsequently, the Premier achieved the successive passage and implementation (separately) of many of the sub-parts of this overall reform programme, starting with major fiscal and foreign trade reforms that took effect on 1 January 1994. The ability to enact fundamental changes is something the Chinese system has displayed frequently, and done relatively well, in the area of economic policy. In other words, the policy process is characterized by a fairly high degree of top-down decisiveness. A determined leadership group can achieve dramatic changes, and the Premier is the 'point man' with respect to changes in economic policy.

We can trace this ability to formulate structural policies back to the Zhao Ziyang era. Zhao Ziyang searched widely for ideas to carry out economic reform. He famously drew from uncredentialled radical young economists grouped in the Economic Reform Institute and Rural Development Research Centre to formulate 'enterprise contracting' programmes. He absorbed from the World Bank ideas about joint stock corporations and macroeconomic management. He tapped junior and middle-aged economists in more 'establishment' think tanks to craft a comprehensive reform strategy in 1987 (Fewsmith 1994; Wu, J. 2013). It makes sense to give Zhao credit overall as the prototype of a consultative Premier – canvassing opinion widely in a search for solutions – and identify economics as the arena where this policy style was first established. Yet this process was not institutionalized during Zhao's administration. In fact, Zhao's policies were implemented unevenly, but this reflected the treacherous configuration of power at the top. With several elders exercising vetoes over Zhao's decisions, and other elders jockeying to place their clients in positions of power, Zhao's room for manoeuvre was severely constricted. The resulting outcome was famously characterized by Lieberthal and Oksenberg as 'fragmented authoritarianism'.

However, subsequent Premiers gradually institutionalized this type of policy process. Typically, the Premier begins by structuring some kind of consultation process. The consensus-building process can be lengthy. Sometimes, the prolonged policy formulation process causes outside observers to despair, seeming to be evidence of policy gridlock. However, it has repeatedly occurred that, after long delays, a gradually constructed consensus has finally fallen into place, and that subsequent change has occurred surprisingly quickly, and often more deeply than anticipated. For example, many observers despaired in the 1990s over China's ability to tackle the problem of state-owned enterprise reform; or in the 2000s over China's ability to rebuild a viable health insurance scheme. In both cases, after long delays the problems were ultimately tackled head on, and with a fairly high degree of success. The successive waves of economic and institutional change that have swept over China since 1978 have given Chinese policy-makers an especially rich experience in policy design and policy change.

One of the key levers of power that the Premier possesses is his ability to structure this consultation process. In any policy formulation process, the architect of the process imposes structure on the process: certain approaches are ruled out, others are preferred, and the architect determines which opinions will be solicited by preference (Chen and

Naughton 2014). The Premier signals the type of outcome he wants to see, and in an intensely hierarchical system, advisers inside and outside the system scramble to give the leaders what they want, while also building their own interests into the advice they give. Thus, we misunderstand the process if we see it as a straightforward consensus-building exercise: it is in fact a kind of coerced consensus, in which a patient leader is able to bring various constituencies into line, getting positive outcomes while making modest adjustments and concessions to overcome objections.[6] This is one of the important roles of local policy experiments as well, giving policy leaders a chance to reduce risk by testing out important articles of their political programmes. Thus, these now-familiar policy formulation processes have shown their effectiveness in overcoming 'fragmented authoritarianism' and permitting Chinese leaders to produce qualitative changes. At the same time, the expectations about policy formulation slow down powerful leaders, and impose some partial checks and balances on them. Thus, policy-making, while far from perfect, seems to display a necessary minimum of responsiveness to diverse opinion, while still allowing for top-down initiative.

Stabilization Policy

The prominence of the Premier in coordinating all government actions gives the Premier an even greater dominance of stabilization policy than he possesses with respect to structural policies. Many day-to-day decisions simply fly under the radar screen of apex bodies like the Politburo Standing Committee, and an astute Premier can use this situation to achieve substantial parts of whatever agenda he wants to push. Zhu Rongji certainly advanced his pro-market agenda by making scores, perhaps hundreds, of small decisions that removed decisions from the realm of bureaucratic discretion, and pushing them to the market. More generally, stabilization policy requires that policy-makers respond rapidly. The Premier's importance in this area is increased by the fact that China's central bank (the People's Bank of China) does not have independence, and so monetary policy is ultimately set by the Premier.[7]

Virtually all developed market economies have independent central banks. It has been shown that independent central banks tend to create more stable macroeconomic outcomes (although they obviously do not eliminate financial crisis). When central banks are subject to direct political influence, they tend to create excessive monetary and credit growth, as policy-makers try to use the bank to satisfy multiple policy goals, including employment creation or earmarking of credit to preferred sectors or clients. Independent central banks typically concentrate on more narrow objectives of price stability and financial regulation. The Premier's control of the daily agenda combined with his control of monetary policy arguably gives him excessive discretionary power over the economy. As the literature on central banks suggests, Premiers are tempted to try to achieve many different kinds of objectives with this type of control over the financial system. Chinese Premiers have astonishingly broad spans of authority, extremely complex political and interest environments to navigate, and limited attention spans. Like policy-makers everywhere, they are in search of quick, short-cut solutions to scores of pressing problems.

In the Wen Jiabao administration, many crucial decisions with long-run consequences for the Chinese economy were made in a reactive, stabilization-policy mode. Box 10.2

> **BOX 10.2 SELECTED 'STABILIZATION POLICY' MEASURES OF THE WEN JIABAO ADMINISTRATION**
>
> 2004: Managing economic 'overheating' without adopting clear contractionary policies, raising interest rates, or allowing the RMB to appreciate.
> 2006: Adjusting attitudes toward SOEs, including sectoral distribution.
> 2008: Massive stimulus programme, 5 November.
> 2009–10: Sustained high monetary growth rate after economic recovery is achieved (absence of prompt, major reduction in stimulus).

shows a selected list of four examples. Of the four, only one is well known, the November 2008 stimulus programme. This was a decisive and large-scale policy adopted promptly in the face of the immediate global financial crisis (GFC). A policy of this magnitude could not be adopted by the Premier alone, and the 2008 stimulus programme was in fact formalized in a top-level document issued at a joint State Council–Politburo meeting. This document – Zhongfa [2008] 18 – is secret, and no copy is known to have leaked to the outside. However, we know that the document authorized the 'Four Trillion RMB Stimulus Programme' issued by the National Development and Reform Commission (NDRC), and also instructed local governments to initiate investment projects quickly. It established financial schemes to carry out these investments, and instructed banks to fund the schemes (Naughton 2009). The subsequent evaluation of the Chinese stimulus response has been mixed. On the one hand, the short-run impact was overwhelmingly positive. The massive and prompt programme undoubtedly helped China and the global economy withstand the GFC of that year (Lardy 2012). On the other hand, the programme unleashed a torrent of bank credit to poorly capitalized local government investment corporations. Moreover, it was prolonged for far too long, allowing the substantial build-up of bad loans in the banking system and flimsy financial structures at the local government level. As of 2015, the Chinese system was just beginning its efforts to deal with this legacy of accumulated problems.

The other three policies were less dramatic, and were not associated with any top-level document, but each had a major impact on economic policy. In all three cases, the result was a significant deterioration in the quality of economic policy-making. The 2004 decision on macroeconomic policy involved a substantial shift away from conventional macroeconomic policy instruments that had been successfully employed in macroeconomic stabilization in the mid to late 1990s. This shift led to a dramatic tilt toward 'financial repression', the condition of negative real interest rates for depositors and directed credit for favoured borrowers that has tended to characterize the Chinese economy since 2004 (Lardy 2012). Moreover, the same reluctance to utilize standard macroeconomic instruments let to the persistence of an undervalued RMB exchange rate that led to huge current account surpluses in 2006–08. Poor quality macroeconomic policy-making was also evident from 2010. At a time when most central banks were moving to liquidate the most extreme measures adopted during the GFC, China's total credit growth remained very rapid through late 2011, and an attempt by the People's Bank of China to rein in credit in 2012 was abandoned halfway through. In other words, China maintained overly rapid credit growth for more than two years after the success of the stimulus programme became evident. The result is a very substantial financial overhang that plagues policy-makers today, creating financial fragility and financial risks in the Chinese economy, and greatly complicating the task of economic reform policy-making.

In the Chinese case, many short-run decisions are made about the economy that do not fit into the standard macroeconomic policies of monetary and fiscal policy. These policies are sometimes called 'macroeconomic adjustment' (*hongguan tiaokong*) in China, but involve adjusting sectoral priorities. One example is government policy with respect to the sectors in which state-owned enterprises (SOEs) are allowed to operate. The state sector has changed dramatically since the Zhu Rongji years: it is much smaller (overall), much more dominated by the central government, and much more profitable than before. In the wake of Zhu reform era policies, a restructured, shrunken and protected state sector was stabilized and returned to profitability. A critical concrete policy related to SOEs is the question of which sectors SOEs will operate in. The establishment of the State-owned Assets Supervision and Administration Commission (SASAC) in 2003 left this question unanswered, but it was thus a surprise when in late 2006, SASAC head Li Rongrong specified that state firms should have 'full control' in seven sectors: military industry, electricity, oil, telecommunications, coal, civil aviation and transport. In these sectors, government capital should increase and be optimized, while in nine other sectors – including steel, electronics, machine-building and autos – the centre should maintain control over a number of technologically advanced keypoint enterprises. Li's statement was clearly meant to signal an official change in policy, but oddly the only official document published was a brief document at the end of 2006 on accelerated restructuring without any concrete details. Was this a top-level decision, made by Premier Wen Jiabao or the Politburo Standing Committee? Was there a top-level policy document? In both cases, we simply do not know. Again, the Premier's day-to-day control of policy permits large changes to sometimes be instituted by stealth, indirection, or non-intervention in lower-level administrative or regulatory actions.

Evaluation

The economic policy process in China is bifurcated. Structural policy measures can be instituted when the leadership is able to identify important long-run problems and identify solutions, even though subsequent implementation may be gradual and incremental. The process is time-consuming but thorough, and is often successful. Chinese economic policy-makers since Zhao Ziyang have been good at this, and these skills have been honed and improved in the 25 years since. Stabilization policy, on the other hand, falls into the broad range of discretion that the Premier exercises over economic policy, so that for items on the day-to-day agenda, or when issues either come up unexpectedly, the Premier exercises enormous power. In these cases, the system retains the ability to act decisively – as demonstrated by the stimulus response to the GFC – but without clear consultative arrangements, there are few checks on the Premier's authority. With a strong focus on economics, the system does not get paralyzed when confronted with difficult economic issues, and the Premier can drive a rapid response. This prompt, decisive decision-making certainly has benefits, but overall the reactive policy process suffers from the concentration of too much discretionary power in the hands of the Premier. During the Zhu Rongji era, the dearth of government resources and the need to control overt inflation pushed the Premier in a positive direction, and Zhu was a good enough economist to respond effectively as well. However, in general, the quality of the stabilization policies that emerged from the Wen Jiabao years was poor, and had implications for financial sector stability, state enterprise policy and overall development policy. Moreover, we know very little about how policy was made during these episodes. In some cases, we are not even sure that an explicit decision was made, since it is possible in some cases that policy simply drifted by default or inattention under new circumstances. The Chinese system is to have a track record of success with respect to formulated structural policies, but displays repeated failings in its reactive stabilization policies. The underlying reason for both seems to be the extreme degree of authority vested in the Premier.

WHO INFLUENCES ECONOMIC POLICY?

Policy can be influenced by insiders and outsiders, but policy is made solely by insiders.

The Insider Pyramid

Despite myriad changes over the years, it is possible to identify a roughly continuous set of influential insider groups. Bureaucratic reorganizations are undertaken periodically, and these have side effects in influencing the channels of interest aggregation. However, the constituent agencies (often 'bureaus') are rarely eliminated, and the underlying interests change relatively little.

Three comprehensive economic agencies are seen as having a legitimate voice in virtually any economic decision: planners, financial system representatives and enterprise representatives. Each of these broad interests has had some kind of organizational representation since the beginning of the reform era, and each has undergone substantial changes over the decades, including name changes. I simplify as follows:

1. The State Planning Commission (SPC) became the National Development and Reform Commission (NDRC) from 2003.
2. People's Bank of China (PBoC): peak of the financial bureaucracy in the 1980s; a true central bank after 1995.
3. State Economic Commission (SEC) became the State-owned Assets Supervision and Administration Commission (SASAC) from 2003.

Since it became the central bank, there have been only two PBoC governors, Dai Xianglong (until 2002) and Zhou Xiaochuan (through to the present). The SEC initially served a 'dispatcher' function in the economy, resolving short-term problems that SOEs had (often involving scarce materials) but generally reflecting SOE concerns. During the 1980s, the SEC consistently advocated for the interests of 'its' enterprises. Its functions were absorbed into a series of successor agencies, until it was finally split again in 2003, with its main enterprise functions transformed into an ownership role in SASAC. Of course, many sectoral ministries, provincial governments, and important enterprises may also exercise influence, either directly or through one of the comprehensive agencies.

An individual Premier in the final instance determines how much voice an organization will have, and how strongly its views and interests will weigh, just as Premiers can be architects of a specific policy formulation process. From this perspective, it is easy to characterize the reformist regimes of both Zhao Ziyang and Zhu Rongji, the two main economic reform Premiers. Both Zhao and Zhu intentionally avoided and sidelined the 'planning' agencies, and relied heavily on enterprise interests and outside intellectuals as a substitute. Such a procedure was far more difficult for Zhao, who had to deal with entrenched interests at the Planning Commission, headed for most of the 1980s by Yao Yilin, an unabashed hardliner with strong connections to elder Chen Yun. Zhao understood that enterprise interests could be enlisted on the side of economic reform, because reform could promise enterprises greater resources and decision-making authority than under the planned economy. As a result, the State Economic Commission became a reliable advocate for market-oriented reform. Furthermore, Zhao set up an Economic System Reform Commission in 1982, headed it himself, and used it to develop long-run reform proposals. In this way, Zhao was able to circumvent the power and interests of the State Planning Commission.

Zhu Rongji himself came from the State Economic Commission, and used its successors the State Council Production Office and the State Economic and Trade Commission, as an important instrument and aggregator of interests. Zhu, famously, never once set foot inside the SPC during the entire time that he ran economic policy, even though (or perhaps because) his own career had started there in the 1950s. It was easier for Zhu to ignore the SPC than it had been for Zhao, since the SPC looked ridiculous after its post-Tiananmen 'readjustment' of the economy, which had accomplished nothing. Even people at the NDRC recognized that their traditional approach to planning no longer made sense, and they began to study 'indicative planning' and 'industrial policy' in the search for a renewed sense of mission (Heilmann and Melton 2013). By 1998, when Zhu Rongji became Premier, a governmental reorganization was carried out that abolished most of the industrial ministries and restructured the SPC. At the same time, the new head of the SPC, Zeng Peiyan, was a reformist, close to Jiang Zemin, and committed to a dramatic restructuring of SPC functions. By the end of the Zhu Rongji administration, it could be reasonably anticipated that the old interest structure of government had been fundamentally altered, and a new system of divided responsibility created.

However, under the Premiership of Wen Jiabao, the old influence structure was resurrected. First and foremost, Wen Jiabao turned to the NDRC as an important source of policy-making advice and guidance. Wen Jiabao was a classic 'organization man' who understood the bureaucracy, respected bureaucrats and preferred to use official channels if they existed. Moreover, the NDRC had become more professional and well suited to its function. It was headed by Ma Kai, a competent technocratic leader close to Wen. Last but not least, Wen Jiabao simply believed in long-run planning, and he supported linking project approval to the long-run plan. In a widely quoted remark, Wen said, 'Without a long-run plan, we should not approve any project; the plan first, then the projects'. The result was that the NDRC was reinstated as a major source of macroeconomic advice. When macroeconomic imbalances emerged in 2004, Wen presided over vigorous debate between two camps of macroeconomic advice. The first camp, led by the People's Bank of China and its head, Zhou Xiaochuan, argued for standard monetary policy tools (high interest rates and slower monetary growth) to slow and rebalance the overall economy. They had grown accustomed to having their advice accepted by Zhu Rongji, and viewed the control of inflation and 'soft landing' of 1998 as evidence of their expertise. The other camp, led by the NDRC, argued for selective sectoral policies to cool only specific sectors judged to be overheated. Ultimately, the NDRC won the support of Premier Wen Jiabao and became the dominant voice in macroeconomic policy.

Even though the personnel and mission of the NDRC had changed, the fundamental interests of the NDRC continued to favour direct government intervention in the economy. Emphasizing government steerage of specific sectors inevitably strengthened the NDRC. More generally, under the guise of rectifying a 'partially overheated' economy, the system of approval of investment projects by the NDRC was revived; ironically, its abolition had just been announced in a State Council document of December 2003. These measures set up a situation in which project approval, land acquisition, credit approval and environmental evaluation were tied up together (Mu 2013; Naughton 2005). Among the many elements of the pre-existing system that is being disrupted by the Xi Jingping–Li Keqiang administration, the prominent position attained by the NDRC under Wen Jiabao seems to be slipping. NDRC was hit hard by the earliest phases of Xi Jinping's anti-corruption campaign, and NDRC's project approval powers were sharply reduced in the first wave of Li Keqiang's campaign to cut red tape and reduce required government approvals.

Outsiders: Interest Group Lobbying

How important is the influence of 'outsiders'? Private sector lobbyists are clearly active and seek to shape policies to their own interest. Kennedy (2009) describes in detail the processes of lobbying with respect to specific regulatory outcomes. Others have pointed out the interaction between business interests (mostly private) and government ministries. In the intense lobbying over China's RMB value, export interests clearly allied with the Ministry of Commerce and used the Ministry of Commerce to amplify their voices and provide channels to the top leadership (Steinberg and Shih 2012; Yuan 2012). The lines are further blurred because the downsizing of the government and state sector after 1998 was accompanied by the transformation of a number of the former bureaucracies into Industry Associations. These bureaucracy-descended Industry Associations, often headed by former bureaucrats, have systematically different lobbying objectives from the more independent private associations (Deng and Kennedy 2010). Solid research clearly indicates the presence of lobbying as interest groups try to shape policy formulation and implementation.

However, existing research has not been able to demonstrate that lobbying is the decisive factor in any important economic policy decision. Is lobbying part of the structured consultation process over which Premiers have so much influence? Or do some business groups gain control of the policy agenda for specific issues? The issue of RMB appreciation is a suggestive case. While exporters clearly lobbied against appreciation, it is striking that Wen Jiabao had already dug in his heels against RMB appreciation as early as 2004, and was partly responsible for converting the issue from one of economic policy to one of national sovereignty in which government media outlets were mobilized to insist that the US could not tell China how to manage its currency. The forces that led to rapid RMB appreciation after November 2007 were not shifts in lobbying influence, but rather accelerating inflation and intensifying imbalances that in the end alarmed even Wen Jiabao.

Exporters lobbied hard against appreciation when Wen gave them the opportunity to do so, but retreated when appreciation became inevitable. Steinberg and Shih (2012) discuss the 2008 change in the lobbying activities of exporters and attribute it to the payment of compensation. But given that exporters had no other real recourse once they lost top-level patronage, did they really have any choice?

Another lobbying group that has attracted significant attention is the real estate lobby. This is an interest group composed of highly visible, relatively independent and fairly colourful personalities who have not hesitated to use public media. It is often seen to have reached maturity in the public relations campaign it waged in 2003, after the PBoC first attempted to restrict credit to real estate development, after which policy-makers were forced to reverse direction and grant increased legitimacy to real estate development (Clarke 2014; Hsing 2006; Mei 2010; Naughton 2007b). Yet, in the long run, this lobbying campaign was unable to prevent wave after wave of central government policies designed to cap real estate prices and reduce demand for real estate. The key problem with assessing the role of lobbying in China is that the overall policy agenda is set by the political leadership. At what point does lobbying really compel the leaders to alter the parameters of the possible? We still have a way to go before we can answer that question.

Puzzles: Whose Interests does Economic Policy Serve?

Although it is easy to see the contending economic interests that have grown up during the reform era, it is far more difficult to detect how, and through what channels, they influence economic policy. This is because the Communist Party retains such a formidable control over most channels of public influence, and there is a kind of implicit 'permission to influence' going on in most cases when lobbying is observed. The enormous discretion exercised by the Premier as the agent of the Party is quite formidable. Interest groups cannot overtly challenge the process through which the Party and government aggregate interests: to do so would risk being shut out of influence altogether, even in the relatively 'depoliticized' realm of economic policy-making. If lobbyists seek to influence decisions, then, they must do so discreetly and without rocking the boat.

In the final analysis, the concept of the 'interest group' is elusive in China: everybody believes that interest groups have formidable influence on policy, but nobody can clearly identify the most important interest groups. Of course, many partial interests may have a formidable influence on policy through quiet lobbying, or through corruption, or through subtle forms of influence trading. These poorly documented activities are beyond the scope of this chapter. However, it is difficult to completely resist speculation. As the Communist Party has remade itself, it has come increasingly to draw its membership from urban white-collar professionals. While the Party's 80 million members (2010) still include 40 million farmers and retirees, it is obvious that the active participants in Party activities are increasingly drawn from the urban administrative and managerial classes. This group is mainly employed by the government. Of 32.2 million urban Party members who are currently employed, 20.6 million (64 per cent) work for the government or SOEs. Looked at from a different angle, of the total of 5.3 million managerial and administrative personnel in public enterprises, just under 3 million (56 per cent) are Party members, as are 83 per cent of the 7 million civil servants (Organization Department 2012). To some extent, the change in Party representation reflects changes in the occupational structure of urban residents who hold residence permits. Most urban *hukou* holders have made the transition to white-collar jobs in clerical, service or professional positions. Most production jobs are now held by rural immigrants: the proportion of urban *hukou* holders working in production jobs had by 2009 already declined to 27 per cent, according to a large household survey reported in Meng et al. (2013). This urban white-collar group is the most important component of Party membership. They seek to influence economic policy on occasion, but more consistently seek economic growth and opportunity for themselves and their families. This constituency demands that the Premier continues to deliver robust economic performance.

DIMENSIONS OF ECONOMIC POLICY

Economic policy is the part of the Chinese policy process that is probably the most open, yet even so, there is much about the policy process that we do not understand. While far from being a 'black box', economic policy-making is far from being well understood. The discussion of this chapter leads to the following tentative hypotheses:

- The economic policy process continues to be primarily top-down. The Communist Party retains its traditional dominance over the policy process, and delegates operational control over policy to the Premier. The Premier is subject to complex pressures and multiple demands, but also has remarkable discretionary power to address issues.
- In structural policies, which begin with the articulation of a goal that can claim wide support, the Premier will generally establish a broad consultative process to formulate policy. These procedures are fairly effective in eliciting broad participation among the policy community, while maintaining the initiative and decisiveness of producing broadly acceptable policy innovations.
- The Premier's day-to-day control of stabilization policy and other 'reactive' policy measures gives him far broader discretion, reinforced by the need to respond quickly. There are fewer checks and balances on this process, and so the policy process creates poorer-quality outcomes than does the structural policy process. The demands on the Premier are too great and scope for discretion too large.
- There is a persistent structure of interests within the government bureaucracy, but Premiers can structure their consultation processes to tilt towards the elements of the bureaucracy they prefer. Leaders are not captives of the bureaucracy.
- The policy process has expanded to allow input from many outside groups, including lobbying activity and input from experts and technocrats. However, political leaders still determine how this input is structured, the limits of consultation, and the implicit weights given to various kinds of testimony.

These observations apply rather generally to economic policy over the past 35 years, despite dramatic changes in economic conditions. Surprisingly, the Xi Jinping–Li Keqiang administration that came to power in 2012–13 has taken steps that may dramatically upset this way of doing things. In particular, Xi Jinping has taken steps that reduce the power of the government, both by taking back some of the policy authority that had been delegated to the Premier, and by reducing the strength of some of the government bureaucracies, especially the NDRC. It remains to be seen whether these changes will overturn the fundamental patterns of economic policy-making under previous administrations.

NOTES

1. In 1978, the repudiation of Maoism was a bold turn. Over the long term, however, the pursuit of economic development has been the predominant strand in modern Chinese politics, and Mao Zedong's late-life lurch away from this mainstream looks increasingly like the anomaly. Since China's traumatic defeat by Japan in the Jiawu War (1894–95), Yan Fu's call for 'rich country, strong army' has been part of the mainstream of Chinese politics (Schell and Delury 2013; Schwartz 1964). Mao Zedong, late in his life, veered away from this consensus, but only after adhering to the developmental consensus for the first decade of the People's Republic. When China's leaders again visited other East Asian countries after the Cultural Revolution, in 1977–78, they felt a profound sense of shock and backwardness. Under Xi Jinping, of course, the realization of 'rich country, strong army' has again been given the highest priority as a national goal.
2. We can contrast the Chinese system with the US one: an American state like California has economic policies, but it is rarely, if ever, entrepreneurial. Chinese townships are the opposite: they are entrepreneurial, but rarely have economic policy. This chapter is concerned with policy, not entrepreneurship.
3. This pattern does not extend prior to 1978. Zhou Enlai, Premier from 1949 until his death in 1976, was never the primary architect of economic policy. Instead, control in 'normal' years was exercised by a group of veteran economic specialists headed by Chen Yun. Unfortunately, there were only a few normal years, perhaps 11 years out of the 28 from 1950 to 1977. In other years, Mao Zedong decreed policies that profoundly shaped and distorted the basic economic environment. This was not limited to the disastrous large-scale events of the Great Leap Forward and Cultural Revolution, which are well known. For example, in 1964, Mao personally and repeatedly overruled his economic specialists in order to shift priority to the construction of the inland 'Third Front' and away from the restoration of consumption damaged by the Great Leap Forward (Chen Donglin 2003: 43–57).
4. Zhao moved the office of the FELSG out of the State Council compound and over to the Party compound at the other end of Zhongnanhai, in an effort to maintain the upper hand in economic policy-making.
5. Zhu joined the Standing Committee Politburo at the 14th Party Congress (October 1992); the Finance and Economics Leading Small Group was re-established in January 1993, with Jiang Zemin as the head, but Zhu as the acknowledged economics expert. Then at the 8th National People's Congress, 29 March 1993, Zhu was named Executive (top-ranked) Vice-Premier. Probably these designations lagged Zhu's actual assumption of responsibility over economic policy. Making the transference of responsibility unambiguous was Li's illness and absence from policy-making during four months in 1993, when some of the most crucial economic decisions in PRC history were made. From the evidence of his 'Economic Diary', Li was peripheral in economic policy-making in 1993–94, but made an effort to become more relevant in certain specific areas during 1995–96.
6. However, there is severe selection bias in that only cases in which the policy process achieved a dramatic outcome have been studied in depth. We only see this process in action when the outcome is positive; there are no detailed studies of consensus-building processes that failed. The field would benefit greatly from a study looking at cases where the process broke down, and suggesting reasons for the breakdown.
7. The Standing Committee of the Politburo undoubtedly ratifies the Premier's views on monetary policy, and could instruct him to change them. We do not know whether or not this has ever happened.

11. Regional development policy and regional inequality
John A. Donaldson

> There can be no Communism with pauperism, or Socialism with pauperism. So to get rich is no sin. However, what we mean by getting rich is different from what you mean. Wealth in a socialist society belongs to the people. To get rich in a socialist society means prosperity for the entire people. The principles of socialism are: first, development of production and second, common prosperity. We permit some people and some regions to become prosperous first, for the purposes of achieving common prosperity faster. That is why our policy will not lead to polarization, to a situation where the rich get richer while the poor get poorer.
> (Deng Xiaoping in a 1986 US television interview, cited in Fenby 2013)

What has caused China's varying patterns of regional development since the establishment of the People's Republic of China in 1949? To what extent can central and subnational regional development policies explain the varied patterns of regional development? This chapter reviews the scholarly debate that is key to understanding the prospects for China's continued development and stability. Although most scholars agree that some variation in the pace of regional development is inevitable and to a certain extent beneficial, the inequality experienced during most of the reform period has been disconcertingly high. This has resulted in dissatisfaction and even protests among those left out of China's development.

To understand regional development in China, we must first ask: what is a region? This is a contested issue. Much of the early analysis of China's regional development was based on theories derived from the European experience, the applicability of which to China's experience is dubious (Cartier 2002). There have been a number of attempts to divide China into several macro-regions. One standard account during the early reform era – by a group of Chinese geographers lead by Ren Mei'e – divides China into eight regions based on natural features (Ren et al. 1979, cited in Cartier 2002). Another approach based on China's biomes resulted in a three-tiered division: three large natural regions, seven meso-regions and 30 three smaller ones (Zhao 1986, cited in Cartier 2002). The earliest and most dominant Western approach – that of geographer G. William Skinner – is based on a regional marketing systems approach. Skinner's argument focuses on nine macro-regions characterized by the physical features of drainage basins or watersheds, and emphasizes the importance of marketing towns, which served to organize peasant life and over time reflected the increasing local diversification of the agricultural economy (Skinner 1964, cited in Cartier 2002). Skinner's arguments usefully drew scholars' attention away from capital cities to more regional concerns, and also blurred the false divide between urban and rural areas (e.g., Agnew 1990). Yet scholars have criticized these and other location-model-based accounts of China's regions by arguing that they are ahistorical, mask differences within regions, and conceal unequal development (Smith 1984, cited in Cartier 2002). The attempt to conceptualize regions along these lines has led to charges of reification of the regions in ways that promote false differences and ignore true ones (Cartier 2002).

Historically, experts focused less on differences between coastal and inland regions and more on divisions between the rice-growing south and the wheat-growing north, with the Huai River serving as a rough dividing line. Economic differences emerged: northern farm sizes were roughly double those of the south (though farms in both regions were small), and tenancy was also lower. The south enjoyed higher irrigation rates, and interlacing rivers and canals facilitated transportation of commodities. Southern farmers could harvest two or sometimes three rice crops each year, whereas in the north, spring wheat harvests would give way to the planting of maize, cotton, soybeans or other crops (Eastman 1988). Cultural divisions also emerged from these distinctions. Rice growing requires much more labour and requires irrigation across fields. This in turn demands that farmers cooperate in order to reap successful harvests. A culture of teamwork and interdependence was thus formed across the south since it was critical to survival, while there were no such pressures in the north (Talhelm et al. 2014).

However, during the more contemporary period, most scholarship divides China into coastal, central and western regions.[1] These divisions, like past attempts to regionalize China, do not reflect any absolute fact, and in truth there are some obvious inconsistencies. The provincial-level unit of Beijing is labelled coastal, though it does not border the ocean. Guangxi is often labelled western, but has a coastline. The north-eastern provinces of Heilongjiang and Jilin – neighbours of Russia – do not seem 'central' in the same way that Henan and Hunan are central. In fact, China's geographic centre is located in the western province of Gansu (*People's Daily* 2000). However, the fact that these divisions are not natural, having been constructed by human agents, makes them no less real; these divisions have had powerful political and economic effects.

However 'region' is defined, the impact of unequal development is substantial. First, if all of China's regions were reasonably well developed, consumption in China would be much higher, strengthening China's economy and enhancing the livelihoods of more people. Lack of development in areas represents a waste of potential human resources and energy for the economy. Second, while China's central and local governments spend significant resources in alleviating poverty, the costs of unequal development are only partially reflected in budgetary terms. Instability, crime, overly rapid migration – each of these has been linked to regional inequality (e.g., Lai 2002; Tian 2004; Fan and Sun 2008). Third, and perhaps most importantly, severely unequal regional development also becomes an ethical question, particularly for a regime that at one time based its legitimacy on liberating hundreds of millions from economic oppression and, in later years, promised that inequality would be temporary (Golley 2010). Deng Xiaoping's commitment to a common prosperity, reflected in the quote that opens this chapter, underscores how vital this is for China's legitimacy.

In addition to debating the effects of China's unequal regional development, scholarly discussion focuses on how to address this gap. Optimists argue that, just as market forces sparked this gap, so too will market forces begin to close it, echoing Kuznets's classical theory that inequality will increase initially before abating as wealth spreads to those previously left behind. Another group of theorists argue that policy interventions – including preferential investment policies and infrastructure financing – are crucial to closing the gap. A third group, by contrast, is more sceptical that market forces or even interventionist policies will be effective. They point to systemic or structural factors – such as the scissors gap described below – that block the equalization of incomes, and thus they expect this gap to continue indefinitely.

This chapter attempts to analyse this debate by reviewing regional development policy from the Mao era until today. First, the chapter traces Mao's largely unsuccessful efforts to promote egalitarian and security goals by developing China's inland regions. Second, it explores the part of the reform era (1978–2000) under Deng Xiaoping until the end of the Jiang Zemin era when policies designed to privilege coastal regions exacerbated regional inequality. Third, the chapter turns its focus to local governments' efforts to develop their economies and thus effect regional development. Fourth, it analyses the efforts to close the gap, starting at the tail end of the Jiang administration and continuing through much of the period of Hu Jintao's administration. Overall, the chapter argues that China's regional development policies during most of the reform period exacerbated regional inequalities. Moreover, regional development policies implemented after the turn of this new century have been largely disappointing in reversing these inequalities. Ironically, it was social rather than regional development policies, implemented under Hu Jintao and Wen Jiabao's administration, that have likely helped to ameliorate these regional divisions. Whether the reduction in regional inequalities continues depends in large part on the continuation and deepening of these social policies and on the development priorities of Xi Jinping and Li Keqiang, China's current leaders.

MAO'S ERA: EGALITARIANISM, SECURITY AND MISPLACED INTENTIONS

The regional development approach of Mao Zedong's administration (1949–76) contrasted markedly with that which came before or has come since. The country Mao inherited was poor and unequal. The vast gaps between rich and poor, and between wealthier and poorer regions, were not only a product of climate and geography (although both of these were vital factors): wealth was concentrated in the hands of the powerful few. During the pre-war Republican era (1911–49), China was only nominally unified under a central government, with different regions under the control of often predatory regional warlords, who routinely ignored central policies. What development there was, was centred in a handful of coastal cities, controlled by foreigners colluding with corrupt and rapacious local officials and financiers (e.g., Hsu 2000). Virtually all modern industry, and much of the mineral industry, was located in the five provinces of Guangdong, Jiangsu, Shandong, Hebei and Liaoning. Of all the factories in China that met the conditions established under China's Factory Law, nearly half were located in a single city: Shanghai. Modern infrastructure was similarly distributed, and mainly facilitated the movement of raw materials and finished goods out of China; such infrastructure had little ability to spread the benefit of whatever growth and industrialization could be generated under those conditions (e.g., Paine 1981). Japanese imperialism, China's long experience with a vicious world war, and its bitterly fought civil war only worsened this situation. By the late 1940s, four cities outside of the Japanese-held Manchuria – Shanghai, Qingdao, Wuhan and Nanjing – held approximately two-thirds of China's modern manufacturing industry. For its part, the Manchurian region – north-eastern China – that had during the early 1940s been a base for Japan's war effort, contained significant resources in manufacturing, construction and mining. While post-war Soviet occupation dismantled many of these capabilities, the remaining productive forces and, importantly, labour and management experience, persisted. Thus, China on the eve of liberation was war-torn, exhausted, poor and grossly unequal. Outside of a few cities on China's coast and its north-eastern areas remained the vast majority of the economic landscape: poor, agrarian and underdeveloped (Paine 1981).

After a few years of stabilizing the economy, the newly established leaders of the People's Republic of China turned to the challenge of developing this war-torn and grossly underdeveloped economy (Fan 1995).[2] Regional development was a part of the agenda, and was seen as a way of not only industrializing equitably, but also of enhancing security (Fan 1995). China's interior region received much of the investment and specific industrial projects. In addition to equity concerns, China's leaders perceived that industrial production on the coast was located too far away from the natural resources inland. Transporting these materials to production bases was costly and overtaxed China's underdeveloped infrastructure (Yang 1997). Investing in the interior was thus considered an effective way to increase industrial production overall (Fan and Sun 2008). Moreover, the lesson of the Republic of China's tragic experience during World War II made clear that concentrating industrial production on the coast left it vulnerable to military threat (Yang 1997). When Japan invaded coastal China in 1937, it quickly destroyed or captured much of the nation's industrial and war-making capabilities, while the remainder was expensively and painstakingly relocated to more secure locations inland (Paine 1981). Thus China's economic instincts and these security concerns combined to point leaders in the same direction: investing in the rapid industrialization of inland China.

As China's security situation worsened in subsequent years, these military concerns outweighed economic considerations. During the 1960s, Sino-Soviet relations deteriorated, breaking out into border skirmishes. In addition, the US-led war in Vietnam brought foreign troops close to the Chinese border, making a US-led invasion of China seem increasingly likely. Thus, in the mid-1960s, China redoubled its efforts to invest in the inland and even more remote areas of western China. Given China's technological inferiority compared to the advanced forces it faced, China's leaders doubted that an attack could be repelled at the borders. Bringing war-making capabilities inland would support China's superior numbers as they fought amidst more difficult terrain. By the late 1970s, this effort to bolster China's 'Third Front' brought nearly 30000 projects, including 2000 production centres – one-third of the nation's total – to the mountainous areas of the west, particularly Sichuan, Guizhou, Gansu and Shaanxi provinces (Paine 1981; Naughton 1988; Yang 1990).

These efforts were reflected in the state's investment in fixed assets. During China's First Five-year Plan (1953–57), interior provinces received RMB 27.6 billion in state fixed investment, nearly 56 per cent of all fixed investment throughout the country (Yang 1990). This figure ballooned to RMB 63 billion, or 71 per cent of total central investment. By the dawn of the Deng era in 1978, inland provinces still received some 56 per cent of central investment, RMB 5.5 billion more than coastal provinces. By 1983, the value of fixed assets in the interior increased from RMB 4 billion in 1952 to RMB 270 billion in 1983, about 57 per cent of China's total of such assets (Yang 1990).

Moreover, the budgetary process allowed the centre to extract revenues from the wealthier provinces, leaving just enough resources to finance expenditures, which were also determined centrally. China's less-developed provinces enjoyed low remission rates or net subsidies, while more developed provinces spent only a fraction of generated revenues. For example, while Shanghai remitted more than 80 per cent of its revenues in 1959, and the coastal provinces of Guangzhou, Shandong and Jiangsu remitted more than 40 per cent, the western provinces of Guizhou, Yunnan and Xinjiang received subsidies ranging from 18 to 26 per cent of their total expenditures. By 1972, Shanghai and Jiangsu provinces continued to remit the vast majority of their revenues and even increased their rates to 90 per cent and 70 per cent, respectively (Lardy 1976a). By compelling wealthier provinces to share revenues and by large-scale investment projects, the centre redistributed assets from coast to inland areas (Lardy 1976a; Yang 1990).

Yet, these efforts to rapidly redistribute wealth and promote the industrialization of western China took a toll on the national economy. The remote and inaccessible locations of these self-contained and self-sufficient production bases rendered them grossly inefficient (Fan 1995). By one estimate, the leadership's Third Front efforts set back China's industrial output by 10 to 15 per cent (Naughton 1988). Moreover, these efforts did little to help redistribute production. As Mao's era came to a close, coastal provinces, despite being starved for resources and investment, continued to produce the majority of China's output. For instance, in 1979 the two leading provincial-level units were coastal: Shanghai produced RMB 1106 per capita while Beijing produced RMB 513 per capita. By comparison, only two of China's non-coastal provinces (the north-eastern industrial bases during much of the Mao era of Heilongjiang and Jilin) produced more than RMB 100 per person (Yang 1990). The coastal provinces' superior location, human resources endowment, managerial experience and infrastructure trumped China's inefficient investment decisions, helping those provinces to maintain their production positions.

Thus the heavy central investment in inland areas failed to shift the balance in production, nor did it close the gap in livelihoods (Paine 1981). What is worse, these efforts meant that the economic situation that was inherited by Mao's successors was plagued by production problems and ineffective management. The twin goals of egalitarian production and enhanced security, combined with poor planning and execution, caused China's overall development to fall further behind the world average. In 1952, China's gross domestic product (GDP) per capita was around a quarter of the world's average; by 1978, that figure had fallen further to 22 per cent (Grewal and Sun 2002). Moreover, despite massive investment, regional development remained uneven, as the coastal areas remained far ahead of China's interior regions.

REFORM, COASTAL DEVELOPMENT AND SPECIAL ECONOMIC ZONES

For many of China's post-1978 leaders, the lessons of the Mao era were painfully clear. If China's new leadership was to develop the nation, the goal of equitable development had to be put to one side, at least for a time. The egalitarianism and security concerns that animated the Mao era approach to the economy in general and regional development in particular were replaced by a focus on efficiency and opening (Fan 1995). Under Deng Xiaoping, development became the 'hard truth' and the highest priority. Virtually all aspects of economic management were guided by the goal of maximizing economic growth and promoting the 'four modernizations' in industry, agriculture, national defence, and science and technology (Andersson et al. 2013). Although Deng Xiaoping hoped that all of China's regions would eventually share in the prosperity, some areas would get rich first.

Yet, as Deng Xiaoping's quote that opens this chapter also suggests, the central government in designing the policy to promote the unequal treatment of China intended that the imbalances would eventually be redressed. In theory, once the coastal provinces got wealthier, they would drive China's growth, promoting development westward to other areas (Fan 1995). In addition to relying on the market forces that would help spread the coast's largess to underdeveloped inland regions, the government also pledged that it would use the coast's resources to finance inland growth – but only after it had reached a sufficient stage of development. For instance, in 1992, Deng Xiaoping predicted that by the end of the century, people throughout the country would be 'comparatively well-off', and the state would have the resources and latitude to address the unequal regional development (Lai 2002). For the time being, however, market reform and opening to the outside world became a fundamental tenet of development, even if that implied China's regions benefited unequally.

Consistent with this, the reformist leaders abandoned Mao's effort for regional self-sufficiency in favour of assigning specific specializations to each of three macro-regions. During the 1980s, China's leaders established a policy of 'three economic belts' that divided the regions, based on the theory of comparative advantage that is accepted in Western economic thinking. The coastal area would use its location, management experience and superior infrastructure to specialize in foreign trade, manufacturing and export-oriented industry. Inland provinces were assigned to focus on agriculture and industry. The western region, which is endowed with most of China's natural resources, was to focus on mineral exploitation and animal husbandry (Fan 1997).

Another of Deng's early economic reforms was to experiment with economic reforms and preferential policies in coastal China. In contrast with the 'shock therapy' policy of the Union of Soviet Socialist Republics (USSR), China's leaders focused on gradual industrialization, through the use of regionally targeted experiments in economic reform and opening. In July 1979, China's State Council and the Central Committee of the Chinese Communist Party jointly issued a directive allowing two coastal provinces in south-eastern China the flexibility to promote foreign trade and investment. The centrepiece of these policies was the establishment of four Special Economic Zones (SEZs): three in Guangdong province, and one in Fujian. These four were the former fishing town of Shenzhen, with its strategic location across from Hong Kong, and the cities of Zhuhai, Shantou and Xiamen, this last a large city in Fujian province located across the strait from Taiwan. Subsequently, in 1988, the entire island of Hainan was carved out of Guangdong to become a separate province and China's fifth SEZ (Zeng 2011).

The SEZs were designed to attract foreign investment and technology mainly through establishing joint ventures between Chinese state-owned firms and foreign businesses. Initially, state-owned firms were shielded from competition from these joint ventures, which were required to export most of their production. Even as China's state-owned enterprises (SOEs) were reformed in a number of ways and given incentives to raise revenues, Chinese leaders realized that most of these inefficient firms could not survive competitive pressures from foreign-invested firms. Moreover, these state-owned firms were important not only to retain some element of domestic production, but also to provide jobs and social goods to millions of urban workers. Thus, wholesale reform of the state-owned sector could be put off until China's economy was more stable and developed, whereupon more painful and costly reforms could be attempted (Naughton 1996). To the joint ventures, China's reformers offered special concessions that were not offered to SOEs, including the import of capital equipment tax-free and the ability to hire and fire workers more freely. In addition, these zones featured strong infrastructure, supportive local governments, and an inexpensive and seemingly endless supply of well-educated and disciplined workers (e.g., Zeng 2011).

These zones promoted several economic objectives. First, the zones fostered more advanced and efficient firms that would drive employment growth and provide training for Chinese workers and managers in the use of advanced technology and management techniques. Second, both the foreign investment and revenues from exports brought badly needed foreign capital to China. Third, these zones served as a geographically limited experiment for China in how to undertake reforms; the most successful reforms would subsequently be expanded outside the SEZs. Finally, as China had for decades been essentially closed to much of the West, these zones served as 'windows to the outside world' that allowed both China and the outside world to learn more about each other (Heilmann 2008a). Moreover, the zones' purposeful proximity to Hong Kong, Macau and Taiwan promoted the integration of China's economy with the economies of these regions (Fenwick 1984). The zones' success in each of these objectives was remarkable. For instance, by 1981, the four zones accounted for nearly 60 per cent of the total foreign direct investment (FDI) in China, with Shenzhen alone accounting for some 50.6 per cent. By the mid-1980s, FDI in the zones were primary to driving FDI, which totalled US$1.17 billion in 1985, or some 20 per cent of China's total. Utilized FDI in the zones increased exponentially each decade after they were established: from approximately US$7 million in 1980 to US$730 million in 1990 and US$4.4 billion by 2000. Similarly, exports increased from about US$350 million in 1980 to US$10.7 billion in 1990 and US$47.5 billion in 2000 (Zeng 2011).

Reformist Chinese leaders responded to the success of these zones by extending preferential policies to others areas of China's coastal region. By 1984, Chinese leaders had opened 14 coastal cities to foreign investment. By 1985, three large coastal regions, marked by river deltas, were also similarly opened: the Pearl River Delta in Guangdong province, the Min River Delta (including the Xiamen–Zhangzhou–Quanzhou Triangle in Fujian province), and the Yangtze River Delta in eastern China. In effect, China's entire coastal area was opened to foreign investment, constituting what became known as the 'golden coastline' (Fan 1995). In 1987, additional preferential policies complemented the coastal development strategy. General Secretary Zhao Ziyang, in his October 1987 report to the Thirteenth National Congress of the Communist Party of China, ushered in an 'Advance Along the Road of Socialism with Chinese Characteristics' (Zhao 1987). In the report, Zhao declared that China should take bolder measures to engage in the global economy, and aimed to develop its export-oriented economy (Meisner 1996).

Thus, by the end of the 1980s, China's central development policy benefited primarily one region, as coastal provinces were endowed with a number of preferential policies not enjoyed by other areas. The state committed to investing in joint and local projects through loans, subsidies and direct appropriations. SEZs and other open zones were allowed to retain earned foreign exchange at a higher rate than other areas, and some open provinces were allowed to retain more revenue for their own use. Industrial inputs, including coal and other natural resources, as well as agriculture, were subsidized by the state, reducing the costs of manufacturing and allowing these areas to literally feed the workforce. Finally, coastal provinces and enterprises enjoyed greater autonomy (Fan 1995). Consistent with General Secretary Zhao's goal, the FDI and technology that had been predominantly invested in China's SEZs spread throughout the coastal region (Demurger et al. 2001).

In addition to these preferential policies, central leaders encouraged industrialization in China's coastal regions by providing subsidized inputs. The Seventh Five-Year Plan (1986–90) formalized what was already a widespread practice in coastal areas: obtaining subsidized raw materials, energy and agricultural products in exchange for more expensive finished products. Under this plan, raw materials were bought at below-market rates (Yang 1997; Lardy 1992) by the coast to manufacture added-value or high-tech goods, a portion of which were then sent back to the inland areas and sold at a higher price (Solinger 1996; Fan 1997; Yang 1997).

Inland provinces were left wanting. Over 90 per cent of China's raw materials (Zou 1998), including energy resources such as coal, oil and natural gas, are found in the naturally well-endowed inland areas (Sun 1988). Yet, the sharply increased demand for such raw materials paradoxically hampered the interior region's development. Requiring raw materials and energy to fuel the growth of coastal areas, the central government purchased raw materials for the coast at below-market prices.[3] Thus the development of coastal industries caused inland and western SOEs to absorb heavy loses (Yang 1997; Tisdell 1993). By policy, the central government constrained the latitude of firms that produced natural resources to set their own prices (Lardy 1992; Yang 1997). Paradoxically, the increased demand for raw materials suppressed the development of the better-endowed provinces.

REGIONAL GOVERNMENTS AND REGIONAL DEVELOPMENT

To be sure, the central government is not the only driver of regional development: provincial and local governments at all levels have planned and implemented policies of their own. China is far from a federal system. Regions are constrained by the central government through continued control over personnel and a targeted responsibility system that monitors the performance of regional leaders on a range of economic, social and policy indicators. Yet, from the dawn of the reform period in the late 1970s, sub-central governments have experienced increasing latitude in setting development priorities and economic policy. An early series of studies focused on the development approaches of nearly every provincial-level government (Goodman 1997; Hendrischke 1999; Fitzgerald 2002; Cheung et al. 1998). Other research compared dyads or triads of policies from different provinces. For instance, Elizabeth Remick (2004) compared the differences in tax collection in Tianjin and Guangdong, both during China's Republican period and in the early days of reform. While Guangdong focused on establishing a more institutionalized and formal system of tax collection, Tianjin's approach centred on shaming shirkers. These differing approaches had an impact on the subsequent development strategy of these provinces. Linda Li (1998) studied investment policy in Shanghai and Guangdong to argue that the provinces' use of several tools, including bargaining with the centre and leeway over implementation of central policy, gave them significant room to develop in their own way. While the relationships between these provincial-level governments and the centre varied greatly, as did their development strategies, both became important engines of growth and development for coastal China.

Some regions had policies that were sufficiently consistent and successful to be labelled models. For example, the Pearl River Delta area of Guangdong province, which includes the city of Guangzhou, along with the dynamic SEZ of Shenzhen and surrounding areas, in the early days of reform implemented a development strategy based on attracting foreign investment in basic, low-tech manufacturing. Under this model, the economy boomed. By contrast, the southern portion of the coastal province of Jiangsu developed through the promotion of township and village enterprises (TVEs). The Yangtze River Delta development model leveraged the advantages that local officials-turned-entrepreneurs had in rallying resources and labour (e.g., Frolic 1994; Oi 1995). These TVEs remained competitive through much of the 1990s, but soon lost much of their comparative advantage, after which the model declined. But for a time, this model contributed to driving the rapidly growing region of southern Jiangsu and elsewhere (Oi 1995). Prefecture-level municipalities drove some of the local initiatives, with their control over vast territories that included both cities and countryside. For instance, the coastal prefecture-level city of Wenzhou implemented a set of policies coherent and successful enough to be dubbed the 'Wenzhou model', which focuses on small-scale family-owned firms (Liu 1992; Parris 1993). While private actors were key to the model, local officials supported the development of such firms by protecting private property rights in order to tap into private ownership of capital. The restructuring of private enterprise into shareholding collectives facilitated central government receptiveness and assuaged local entrepreneurs' concerns over property rights protection. Moreover, the collectivization of enterprises also saw tax benefits and increased access to factor, product, land and credit markets, greatly facilitating their growth (Whiting 1999). Thus, Wenzhou – a prefecture-level city – became a key driver of economic growth, but in a form that differs markedly from that of the varied approaches of Pearl River Delta, the Yangtze River Delta or Shanghai.

More recently, a number of scholars – Meg Rithmire (2014) dubs them the 'new regionalists' – have compared several subnational governments to explain variation in regional development. For instance, Breznitz and Murphree (2011) examine variation in regional innovation within the information technology industry in the Pearl River Delta and Shanghai. They argue that under 'structured uncertainty' these regional governments showed different patterns of investment and promotion in the industry. William Hurst (2009) uses a historical-social approach to understand the differences in policies towards laid-off workers in four macro-regions. Donaldson (2011) compares the development approach of the neighbouring provinces of Guizhou and Yunnan. He argues that the micro-oriented state approach started by Guizhou leaders as early as the late 1980s has helped to reduce rural poverty, despite the lack of economic development. These and other studies emphasize that regional development is not just centrally driven, but driven by subnational governments themselves.

REBALANCING DEVELOPMENT? OPENING THE WEST

What were the effects of these local and central regional development policies in China during the first decades of the reform period? A variety of quantitative research on regional inequality during this period appears to point in the same direction: from 1978 to at least 2000, interregional inequality increased sharply and steadily. A number of recent analyses adopt different methods to measure this inequality. For instance, Fan (1995, 1997; Fan and Sun 2008) argues that, starting in 1978, China's growth core shifted from China's old industrial regions of Shanghai, Beijing, Tianjin, Liaoning and Heilongjiang to a new growth core, primarily the coastal provinces of Shandong, Jiangsu, Zhejiang, Fujian and Guangdong. By 1990, this core continued to grow quickly, and was joined by the previously rapidly growing provincial-level municipalities of Shanghai, Beijing and Tianjin (Fan and Sun 2008). The analysis of Andersson et al. (2013), which eliminated short-term fluctuations in order to observe long-term trends, finds similar patterns. They trace a growing east–west divide, one that peaks around 1994; although it is not until 2003 that these scholars see the inland region showing significant signs of catching up. Li and Gibson (2013) criticize most other research by noting three errors related to China's massive internal migration that skew analyses of regional development. Still, while these scholars argue that regional inequality has been exaggerated, the overall trends based on recalculated data are nevertheless consistent with these other studies. Between 1990 and 2005, they observe a rising gap (although at a much slower rate than other studies) between coastal and inland provinces, with the rate of increase slowing between 2000 and 2005. Thus, despite very different approaches to analysing patterns of regional development, these scholars come to a broadly similar conclusion. Coastal provinces grew rapidly and at a much faster pace than western provinces. The gap between the two increased rapidly for at least the last two decades of the twentieth century.

In reaction to these growing inequalities, China's then president Jiang Zemin announced the Western Regional Development Programme during the second half of 1999. Some 20 years after the establishment of the SEZ strategy that contributed to the development of the coast, central leaders sought to start to close the gap between the coastal and western regions – this being nearly the time that Deng had predicted in 1992 (Lai 2002). To be sure, the central leadership did not wait until this major policy shift to implement more modest policies aimed at improving the living standards in western China. For instance, the central anti-poverty plan promulgated in 1986 was in large part aimed at reducing rural poverty, much of which was located in the interior. In addition, as early as 1990, China's Eighth Five-Year Plan paired a number of coastal provinces and cities with specific underdeveloped areas. The wealthier areas were supposed to advise and support their less-developed counterparts. What is more, twice during the mid-1990s, China's then Premier Zhu Rongji pledged additional investment for inland and western China. Finally, the south-western city of Chongqing in 1997 was split off from the larger province of Sichuan, in large part to help manage the massive Three Gorges Dam project and to allow Chongqing to serve as a growth pole to promote western development (Lai 2002). Many of the local governments in the western region used the more open policy environment to implement their own policies. For instance, Chongqing and Chengdu, in an effort to spur agricultural production, have both experimented with different forms of land policies.

Despite these efforts, however, the gap between coastal and inland areas continued to widen, as noted above. Between 1976 and 1980, the coast's share of state investment in the provinces increased from 42 per cent in the late 1970s to nearly 54 per cent by the mid-1990s, while the inland areas' share of investment declined from nearly 50 per cent to less than 39 per cent. Similarly, pledges from the centre for more investment in inland China did not come to pass – state investment in basic construction in the region remained stable at just under 40 per cent of the country's total throughout much of the 1990s (Lai 2002). By 1997, inland and western China attracted only 10.7 per cent and 3.5 per cent, respectively, of all foreign direct investment. Whereas poverty in all of China declined in the early 1980s, most of this was experienced on China's coast. By 1996, poverty rates in seven coastal provinces declined to 1.2 per cent of the provincial population, while they remained high in north-western (18.6 per cent) and south-western (10.5 per cent) provinces – which held nearly 70 per cent of all of China's poor (World Bank 2001). Not surprisingly, more than 80 per cent of China's designated poor counties were found in China's inland and western regions (Lai 2002).

These GDP and poverty figures spurred the central government to promulgate in 1999 a more ambitious plan to develop China's western regions, the Western Regional Development Programme. As Golley (2010: 135) quoted Jiang as arguing at the time, the programme 'is an important move to carry out Comrade Deng Xiaoping's strategic thinking of "two great situations," eliminate regional disparities gradually, consolidate the unity of ethnic groups, ensure border stability and social stability, and promote social progress.' The policy was explicitly designed to develop China's western provinces that had been neglected since the beginning of the reform era in 1978 (e.g., Tian 2004). The way that the 'west' was defined underscored the point that regions are not primordial, but are instead constructed. The policy, implemented in 2000, designated as 'western' nine provincial-level jurisdictions that had already been designated as such in the start of the reform era, plus the newly established Chongqing municipality. In addition, in late 2000, two provinces that were previously classified as inland and coastal provinces – Inner Mongolia and Guangxi, respectively – were reclassified as western. The western region was expanded again one year later, by adding not more provinces, but three prefectures, one each from Hunan, Hubei and Jilin provinces (Goodman 2004a; Holbig 2004).

The Western Regional Development Programme's ambitious list of objectives seemed promising. By March 2000, Premier Zhu Rongji used the Government's Work Report announcement to the Third Plenum of the Ninth People's Congress to describe the key goals of the policy for developing western China. In the wake of the Asian financial crisis of 1998, the western development project was intended to spur exports and stimulate domestic consumption throughout China (Fan et al. 2011). Since the mid-1990s, China also faced a glut of manufactured goods; stimulating the below-average consumption levels of the west was designed to partially alleviate this problem (Lai 2002). The overall approach would channel market forces, with the government providing overall macro-economic management (Grewal and Ahmed 2011).

In addition to the social and economic development of western regions and industrial restructuring, the policy sought to enhance the western areas in numerous other respects. The comprehensive list includes consolidating agriculture, promoting education in science and technology, protecting the environment, stimulating tourism and bolstering the public health system. The plan also aimed to improve infrastructure in the west, including highways, railways and hydropower projects. The interior areas were still highly dependent on SOEs, which by the mid-1990s produced 47 per cent of industrial output in inland provinces and 69 per cent of that in western provinces. The Western Regional Development Programme was designed to improve the performance of SOEs while promoting the development of the non-state economy in the west (Lai 2002). The plan also included measures to check desertification, as well as to promote and protect the west's forested land. Through promoting the west, policy-makers also sought to boost China's economy overall by freeing up additional natural resources from the west, and expanding domestic demand by spurring the consumption from a more prosperous west (Grewal and Ahmed 2011; Onishi 2001; Lai 2002). The policy was to achieve these aims by encouraging foreign and domestic investment through tax incentives and other preferential policies. In designing the policy, the government promised to allocate funds raised domestically and overseas through its 'three 70 per cent policy': the allocation to the west of 70 per cent of state fiscal assistance, funds raised through government bond issues, and loans from foreign governments and international organizations (Onishi 2001).

Through this programme, the centre has developed a number of large-scale projects in western China. Between 2000 and 2005, the centre planned 70 major construction projects. During this period, new roads built in the west reached some 220 000 kilometres, including 6853 kilometres of highways. By the middle of the decade, the centre had invested some RMB 460 billion in construction projects; fiscal transfers and subsidies added an additional RMB 500 billion, to bring total investment to RMB 1 trillion (Yao 2009; Chen and Lu 2009).

Despite these ambitions, the impact of the Western Regional Development Programme remains contentious. Proponents argue the policy has spurred growth. For instance, from 2001 to 2010, the average annual growth rate of state investments in fixed assets in western China was nearly 31 per cent, more than that in China's eastern (22 per cent) and inland (26.6 per cent) regions. Between 1999 and 2010, fiscal transfers allocated to western China increased from 29 per cent to nearly 40 per cent of total fiscal transfers (Zheng and Deng 2011). Inward FDI grew rapidly in the region from less than US$2 billion in 1999 (less than 5 per cent of the nation's total) to US$20.8 billion in 2010 (just under 20 per cent of the country's total). In terms of impact, scholars note that the west has grown somewhat faster than the rest of China. Between 2000 and 2010, for instance, the GDP of China's western regions grew on average 13.5 per cent each year, exceeding the growth of inland and north-eastern China. While the share of GDP generated by the west has increased only slowly (from 17.1 per cent in 2000, to 18.7 per cent in 2010), the policy's defenders argue that at least the policy has helped to arrest the expanding gap between western and eastern China, and has brought more of China's largess to a previously underdeveloped region.

Sceptics counter that the policy has yet to achieve its aim of developing the Western region. In its initial years, investment in fixed assets that was promised as part of the programme did not materialize; the west's share even by the mid-2000s remained at less than 20 per cent of China's total, while the share of the centre declined. Moreover, even as western provinces' share of total fiscal transfers rose from 28 per cent in 1999 to 34.4 per cent in 2004, this was offset by the loss of the share of collected revenues retained by these provinces (Yu, H. 2010; Grewal and Ahmed 2011).

Moreover, despite the rapid increase in investments, the economic benefits from the plan were not apparent for several years. According to one scholar, the west's share of GDP actually declined between 1999 and 2007 (Yu 2010a). Even to policy supporters, the region's economic growth did not surpass that of eastern China to become the fastest-growing region in China until 2006 (Lu and Deng 2011). As noted above, this is consistent with other recent analyses: Fan and Sun (2008), Andersson et al. (2013) and Li and Gibson (2013) all see regional inequalities declining, but not until the middle of the 2000s, several years after the policy to develop the west was first implemented. As a regional development policy, the results were much more modest than expected; subsequent policy may have had more of an impact on regional development.

Further, detractors note that the types of economic growth and regional development that were generated may not have made a major impact on the lives of ordinary people. Much of the economic growth generated in inland and western China has not been in industries that generate employment and sustain consistent growth, but is instead concentrated in mining, food processing and manufacturing, petroleum processing and coking, leather and furs, and special-purpose equipment (Golley 2010). Many of these industries – which are not especially labour-intensive, according to Golley's (2010) calculations – primarily support the strategy of using natural resources in western China to fuel coastal development. Others question the sustainability of the growth, noting that much of the growth appears to be generated from increasing inputs, not efficiency (Andersson et al. 2013; Lu and Deng 2011). For those looking for an aggressive policy of concentrated regional development led by the central government and supported by coastal China, the policy was disappointing.

Finally, some sceptics charge that the Western Regional Development Programme's key objectives are not to help the west economically, but to further integrate these minority areas into China and consolidate them into China proper.[4] China had long been concerned about the separatist movements that were located in the western provinces of Tibet and Xinjiang, and to a lesser extent Inner Mongolia (Lai 2002). The promotion of the west's economy was also intended to more closely integrate minorities into the Chinese economy (Lai 2002), to spur additional Han majority migration into minority areas (Schrei 2002), and otherwise to neutralize ethnic conflict and ensure China's regional integration (Goodman 2002). As one critic argued, 'At its heart, the plan is not a humanitarian enterprise. It is instead an effort by the Chinese government to further consolidate control over troublesome regions' (Schrei 2002). If so, then the policy has failed to benefit the native population, economically or otherwise.

REGIONAL DEVELOPMENT UNDER THE HU–WEN ADMINISTRATION

If the Western Regional Development Programme was largely disappointing, what explains the regional development seen in the interior during the mid-2000s? Perhaps it was the policies and approaches of Jiang Zemin and Zhu Rongji's successors? Ironically, the subsequent administration led by President and Chinese Communist Party (CCP) General Secretary Hu Jintao and Premier Wen Jiabao has been derided for being largely ineffective in addressing a number of China's problems and priorities. The Hu and Wen administration (2002–12) has taken criticism for not prioritizing extending economic reforms, for failing to tackle corruption in any serious way, for tightening political controls on dissent, for recentralizing China's political system, and for overseeing rising income inequality. These collective failings have led some to label the regime as a 'Lost Decade' for China's reform (Naughton 2014). Yet, many of the policies implemented during the Hu and Wen administration benefited western China. Though less prominent than the launch of the Western Regional Development Programme, the Hu–Wen social policies may have contributed to slowing and even reversing the growing chasm between coastal and inland China.

Hu's policy to develop a 'harmonious society' (*hexie shehui*) moderated what had been a singular dedication to economic growth in favour of addressing other social problems, including poverty, inequality and illiteracy (Saich 2006; Heilmann and Melton 2013). In particular, Hu Jintao consistently focused on mitigating inland–coastal provincial inequality, as well as rural–urban inequality, through strategies such as agriculture reform and better public goods provision, especially grassroots health care and basic, rural education (Saich 2006, 2007). Hu's 'scientific development view' (*kexue fazhan guan*) de-emphasized his predecessors' focus on economic growth at the expense of other priorities (Wei 2005). Although powerful Chinese political figures opposed the idea (Zheng 2007b), this approach was institutionalized in 2006 as 'the policy orientation of the Party' (Zheng et al. 2006: 2).

The policy catalysed regional development by focusing not on the region but on social policy for poor rural residents. First, the Hu–Wen administration's policies aimed to establish new safety nets for poor rural farmers and to boost rural incomes. These included a number of policies such as schemes for rural education and health care, establishing a minimum living standard, and setting up a pension scheme. These were not regional development policies per se. Yet, because most of the beneficiaries of these policies were from these regions, the gap between the regions narrowed. Several specific policies contributed to this comparative rise in western fortunes. First, the distribution of some RMB 76.3 billion (US$12.5 billion) between 2002 and 2012 in agricultural subsidies helped grain production to increase and added to the coffers of China's farmers (China Data Center n.d.; Zhao 2005). Second, the launch in 2003 of the new Rural Cooperative Medical Scheme reduced the risk of those catastrophic health problems that impoverish millions of households and hamper consumption (National Health and Family Planning Commission 2012). Third, in 2006, the central government began publicly financing the rural compulsory education system, and brought additional financing for rural education from a number of levels of government. Fourth, the Rural Minimum Living Standard Security Scheme provided a basic allowance to tens of millions of rural residents – far more than under the old Five Guarantees (*wubao*) System – whose incomes are lower than minimum standards (Ministry of Civil Affairs 2013). Finally, the 2009 New Rural Pension Scheme covered millions of retired farmers with minimal support, supplementing other sources. The programmes helped rural residents throughout China, and especially those in poorer inland areas (Fan et al. 2011). Thus, the regional development that has been spurred may not have emerged primarily from regional development policy. More likely, it was an effect of anti-poverty policies that have had a disproportionate effect on regions where subsistence agriculture remained and rural poverty was more severe.

In addition, the Hu–Wen administration also established a number of initiatives that were meant to elevate regions that had benefited neither from the coastal development policies, nor from the opening of the west. These include the Revive the North-East Programme (2003), the Rise of Central China Programme (2004), and also the Pearl River Delta Programme (2008) and the Yangzi River Delta Programme (2010) (see Heilmann and Melton 2013).

Revive the North-East

As noted earlier, the three north-eastern provinces of China, along with Shanghai, Beijing and Tianjin, were part of the older industrial areas of China (Hu and Lin 2010). Since the establishment of the coastal development programme, which saw the construction and entry of more competitive foreign invested enterprises, the large-scale industrial bases in the north-east declined rapidly. North-east China's gross value of industrial output as a share of national output declined steadily, from 16.5 per cent in 1978 to 9.3 per cent in 2003 (Chung et al. 2007). Saddled with inefficient management, obsolete technology, as well as large pensions and other social burdens, the governments in this 'rust belt' were challenged by reforming these enterprises.

Just after President Hu Jintao succeeded President Jiang Zemin, his administration began touting the revitalization of the north-east as a 'fourth engine' of Chinese economic growth (Chung et al. 2007). The policy, established in 2003 and formally launched in 2004, aimed to increase wealth and promote rapid industrialization in north-east China, and to turn the region into a national and even international base for manufacturing of equipment and supply of raw materials (Dong 2005). The policy included a number of pro-market initiatives, including acceleration of ownership reform, as well as other structural and institutional reforms. In addition, the state upgraded transport and electricity networks and added modern ports and airport facilities (Dong 2005; Chung et al. 2009). The policy also intended for different provinces to focus on a handful of pillar industries. For instance, Liaoning province would focus on petroleum, iron and steel, and equipment manufacturing; Jilin would focus on modern agriculture and pharmaceuticals; and Heilongjiang would focus on equipment manufacturing, energy, pharmaceuticals and environmentally friendly food production (Zhang and Wan 2005).

Like the Western Regional Development Programme, this project was intended not only to return economic vitality to the north-east, but also to ensure the region's stability. The economic challenges of the north-east have sparked numerous protests, reason enough to revitalize the economy. Moreover, the government was concerned about the integration of Korean minorities into Mainland China. A stronger north-east would help to bring a stronger economic and political presence near the Korean peninsula (Yoon 2004), capitalize on the opportunities found in both North and South Korea, and provide additional stability and vitality to a border region.

From the little research that has been done, it appears that the results so far have been mixed. Proponents note that the three north-eastern provinces have seen faster growth compared to previous years (Zhang 2008; Chung et al. 2009). The policy brought increased investment in fixed assets, and the key enterprises within the designated pillar industries also grew faster than average (Zhang 2008). Whether these gains are sustainable remains an open question. The policy has not yet overcome the difficult barriers represented by years of state ownership of key industries, the planned economy, and the conservative governments that have managed these provinces for years. Today, the role of large centralized SOEs in the economy remains significant, and the region lacks funds for social, economic and environmental development (Chung et al. 2009).

Rise of Central China

Premier Wen Jiabao announced in 2004 the 'Rise of Central China' policy to speed the growth of six inland provinces (Shanxi, Henan, Anhui, Jiangxi, Hubei and Hunan), and to address income inequality, rural poverty and rural unrest in these regions. Due to development policies in other regions, inland China has fallen behind not only the high levels of development of the more advanced coastal area, but also the quickening pace of the west. This region has been a key grain-producing region, but incomes from both agriculture and off-farm employment have stagnated in recent years. In addition, the region suffered from the closing down of uncompetitive SOEs, increasing both unemployment and social discontent (Lai 2006).

In response, the Rise of Central China policy intended to promote the region as a major grain production base and a production base for raw materials and energy, as well a high-tech industrial base, a manufacturing base for modern equipment, and a transportation hub (Xinhua 2006a). The first two items on this list were already designated as part of the centre's responsibility under the divisions of labour policy announced by reformist leaders in the mid-1980s. Whether this scattered policy helps to develop the central regions remains to be seen.

Other Aspects of Hu–Wen Policy

Other aspects of China that have affected regional development during the Hu and Wen administration include first, a massive influx of infrastructural investment and second, the recentralization of policy. First, in the wake of the 2008–09 global financial crisis, China announced a series of stimulus packages designed to temper the effects of the crisis on China's economic growth (Overholt 2009–10). More than a third of the RMB 4 trillion stimulus included infrastructure investment for western China, including railway, rural roadway, irrigation and airport construction. These included a number of highway construction projects in western China (Ma and Summers 2009). Designed to help facilitate the spread of coastal wealth to inland China, the projects have been criticized as being wasteful and a source of official corruption. Moreover, according to one calculation, expenditure on infrastructure in western China has had an expected negative effect on economic growth (Grewal and Ahmed 2011).

Second, the recentralization policies of Hu–Wen may have helped to even out regional development. Many scholars argue that decentralization of fiscal resources and development policy has contributed to the growth of coastal China, even as it has disadvantaged inland China. The Hu–Wen administration was marked by attempts at recentralization, even during attempts to spark regional development (Heilmann and Melton 2013). For instance, Heilmann and Melton (2013) argue, 'It is a remarkable feature in the making of both the Chongqing and Pearl River development programs that the central government . . . monopolized the plan drafting process.' While regional governments could submit proposals and were consulted, these cross-provincial and cross-border development plans were 'ultimately treated as a central-government affair that transcended regional competencies' (Heilmann and Melton 2013: 593). This recentralization likewise allowed the central government to drive the process of development in favour of redressing imbalances and spreading the largess of China's growth to areas that had suffered severe gaps. In this way, the policies echoed the Mao era goal of bringing development to interior regions that remained far behind the coastal areas.

UNEVEN DEVELOPMENT AND INEQUALITY

Uneven development has characterized most of China's modern history. In the decades following the successful revolution and establishment of the People's Republic of China, CCP Chairman Mao Zedong and his colleagues tried to close development gaps through massive investment in inland and western China. Despite these efforts, though, coastal China still remained dominant in China's economy. Reacting to the failures of the Mao period and hoping to develop China's economy rapidly, Deng Xiaoping ushered in an era of unequal development. Policies to establish SEZs and other efforts to promote coastal development, combined with the coast's geographic and other advantages, worsened inequities in regional development, as did most local government-led efforts at promoting regional development. The Western Regional Development Programme and other efforts to spread development from coastal to inland areas largely failed to close the gap.

Through continued efforts in inland development, the establishment and strengthening of a social safety net in poorer areas of China, and political recentralization, the Hu and Wen administration seems to have begun the process of rebalancing regional development. The positive impact of some of these initiatives – such as the agricultural subsidies – on regional development has been indirect, but has made a distinct difference. The contribution of other policies – such as massive infrastructure investment – has been more dubious. Nevertheless, many scholars see a crossroads in regional development. The gap between coastal and inland regions has begun to reverse itself and slowly close (Fan et al. 2011; Li and Gibson 2013; Andersson et al. 2013). While most doubt that the west will ever fully catch up with the coast (Golley 2010) – complete parity is both unrealistic and probably unnecessary – the reduction of inequality could contribute to China's continued development, as well as to its social stability.

To the extent that the policies of Hu and Wen have helped to reverse regional inequality, will this alleviation continue? Some scholars point to market effects, which they argue have already facilitated the spread of wealth from east to west. These scholars are optimistic that inequality will continue to ebb, regardless of government policy. Other scholars point to policy reversals of the Xi and Li administration, and worry that they are undermining many of the positive effects of the Hu and Wen administration. Still others note that the basic structural factors driving unequal development have yet to be addressed. The debate on the future patterns of regional development thus continues.

ACKNOWLEDGEMENTS

The author wishes to thank a number of people for their help with the research. These include Jennifer Milewski, Siddharth Poddar, Yane Lee, Wilson Ho Wee Seng, Daniel

Selvakumar and Gong Weigang. The feedback from Deborah Davis, Bruce Dickson, Yang Dali and other participants at the May 2014 workshop at Nanjing University, held to discuss contributions to this volume, were invaluable. This research was supported with funding support by Singapore's Ministry of Education Academic Research Tier 2 (MOE2012-T2-2-115).

NOTES

1. At one time, the coastal provinces included Hebei, Liaoning, Jiangsu, Zhejiang, Fujian, Shandong, Guangdong, Hainan and Guangxi. The inland provinces included Shanxi, Jilin, Heilongjiang, Anhui, Jiangxi, Henan, Hubei, Hunan, Inner Mongolia and Shaanxi. The western provinces included Sichuan, Chongqing, Guizhou, Yunnan, Gansu, Qinghai, Ningxia, Xinjiang and Tibet. As mentioned below, these provinces – and even parts of provinces – have been classified differently for different purposes. The term 'central province' is confusing in a chapter that also refers to a 'central government'. For this reason, these provinces will hereafter be referred to as 'inland provinces'.
2. The overall approach adopted by Mao and his leadership to develop China is multifaceted. This chapter focuses on the regional aspects of his overall policy.
3. Although a similar relationship existed during Mao's era, inland areas at that time were partially compensated via interprovincial transfers (Fan 1997).
4. Some two-thirds of China's international boundaries are located in central and western provinces, and 20 of China's 55 minorities in these provinces live directly on these borders. Although less than one-quarter of China's population lived in western provinces in the late 1990s, 56 per cent of the nation's minorities called western China home.

12. China's nationality policy from the perspective of international minority rights[1]
Xiaowei Zang

There are 56 state-recognized nationality groups (*minzu*) in the People's Republic of China (PRC). The majority nationality group is Han Chinese, representing 91.6 per cent of the total population. The other 55 groups are classified by the government as minority nationality groups. How well has the PRC state treated ethnic minorities in China? Some people hold either positive or neutral views about various aspects of China's nationality policy (Mackerras 2011: 116–117, 124; Sautman 1999: 283, 300–302; Sautman 2012). Others however are critical of the PRC's policy toward its ethnic minorities, considering it discriminative in terms of labour market outcomes and detrimental to minority cultures including languages and religions (Barabantseva 2008: 569–570; Howland 2011: 4; also Hyer 2009; Smith Finley 2007; Schluessel 2007).

Which of the above conflicting claims is close to reality? This chapter addresses this question by measuring what the PRC has done for its ethnic minorities against the current global norms on minority rights. Its benchmark is the global norms on minority rights, rather than China's standards, since they underscore international criticisms of China's nationality policy. The 'global' norms are mainly the outcomes of the efforts by the European Union (EU) in championing minority rights as a key norm in global governance (Pentassuglia 2005: 24; Preece 1997: 358; Rupnik 2000: 123–124; Vermeersch 2004: 3). The European norms are used because 'minority standards beyond Europe are still virtually lacking' (Pentassuglia 2005: 19; also Castellino and Redondo 2006: 10). In the US, the emphasis is on equal opportunity programmes to protect individual rights, whereas the EU approach promotes both individual rights and minority group guarantees (to be discussed below). The EU approach seems to be a more appropriate benchmark than the US one for an assessment of the PRC's minority rights regime, because international attention to ethnic minorities in China focuses on both individual rights and group guarantees.

Thus, this chapter studies whether the provisions of individual rights and group guarantees are adequately provided for the ethnic minorities in China. This approach offers a solution to operationalization since it specifies the extension of the PRC's minority rights regime (which is a broad concept), making it measurable; and there are measurement units for both individual rights and group guarantees available in the existing literature on minority rights. Specifically, this chapter examines two important measures of individual rights: (1) the reduction of ethnic inequality in schooling and labour market outcomes; and (2) the preservation of minority cultures and languages. This chapter also examines two important measures of group guarantees: (1) the representation of minorities in government institutions; and (2) the degrees of regional autonomy for ethnic minorities. This chapter does not investigate other dimensions of minority rights (such as minority claims on local resources and revenues, majority perceptions and stereotypes against minorities, and so on) due to space limitation. For convenience, Beijing, China, the Chinese Communist Party (CCP) and the PRC are used interchangeably.

INDIVIDUAL RIGHTS AND GROUP GUARANTEES

In a broad sense, human rights mean equal enjoyment of basic rights for everybody, whereas minority rights are for the exclusive benefits of minority groups in order to compensate and mitigate discrimination they have suffered, with the ultimate goal to establish universal human rights in society (Human Rights in China 2007: 11; Kymlicka 1995: 6; Sautman 1999: 286). The minority groups refer to gays and lesbians, ethnic minorities and other minority groups. The rights for ethnic minorities include both individual rights and group guarantees. Individual rights include efforts to reduce ethnic inequality; freedom of religion; the right to bilingual education and use of the mother tongue; the right to establish religious, social and educational institutions; and the right to preserve the distinctive characteristics of the ethnic minority including its customs (Henrard 2001: 53–54; Preece 1997: 348; Sautman 1999: 287; the United Nations 1992). These rights are regarded as 'the global minimum standard of state conduct towards minorities' (Preece 1997: 347, 355–357). Group guarantees protect diversity, multiculturalism and self-determination, and range from 'the funding of activities and organisations of national minorities' to 'guaranteed representation, or consultation of minorities in government institutions' to 'the introduction of minority self-governments, the granting of territorial or cultural autonomy to minority groups', and secession if there are serious violations of minority rights or attempts for forced assimilation into majority society (Kymlicka 1995: 10; Vermeersch 2003: 1).

Minority Rights: A Historical Perspective

The contemporary standards of minority rights on ethnic minorities have been the outcome of a long historical process. According to Koszorus (1982), the first direct attempts at minority protection appeared in the thirteenth century and grew in importance as a result of the Reformation. Examples included the Peace of Augsburg signed in 1555, the Pact of Warsaw signed in 1573, and the Edict of Nantes signed in 1598. The Peace of Westphalia, signed in Osnabrück and Münster in 1648, raised the importance of protection of religious minorities as a matter of major international concern (Castellino and Redondo 2006: 5; Grossman 1984: 5; Preece 1998: 55–66). The 1919 League of Nations System of Minority Guarantees extended the protection to members of 'racial, linguistic and religious' minorities in East and Central Europe (Koszorus 1982). Yet the treaties and rhetoric were not taken seriously then (Anagnostou 2001: 38; Castellino and Redondo 2006: 11), and there was no immediate improvement in minority rights after World War II. In 1948, the UN General Assembly proclaimed the Universal Declaration of Human Rights. Although it is a milestone in global human rights movements, it did not explicitly deal with ethnic minority rights. This situation was partially addressed when the International Convention on the Elimination of Forms of Racial Discrimination (United Nations 1965) was promulgated. The United Nations adopted the International Covenant on Civil and Political Rights in 1966, setting the global minimum standard on state conduct directed at national minorities (Pentassuglia 2005: 10, 13–14; Preece 1997: 347).

Immediately after the end of the Cold War, the EU faced challenges from the post-1989 migrations by ethnic minority groups between European countries, the violent ethnic conflicts in former Yugoslavia, and possible further ethnic unrests in other Eastern European countries (Preece 1997: 349; Preece 1998: 30–54). The Council of Europe (CoE), the European Court of Human Rights and the EU have together played a major role in developing a minority rights regime within the framework of human rights (Fleming 2002: 533–534; Hale 2003: 208; Pentassuglia 2005: 17–18). Partly because of their work, the UN proclaimed the Declaration on the Rights of Persons Belonging to National or Ethnic, Religious and Linguistic Minorities in 1992. The International Commission on Intervention and State Sovereignty published a landmark report titled 'The Responsibility to Protect' (R2P) in 2001. In 2007, the UN General Assembly adopted a strongly worded Declaration on the Rights of Indigenous Peoples that supported self-determination, minority access to resources, and so on (United Nations 2007).

With the global diffusion of human rights including minority rights, more and more scholars and politicians in the world have advocated both self-determination, justified by the principle of free association, and the rights to minority identity and existence (Farer 2003: 405; Preece 1997: 351–355, 357–358). The recognition of state sovereignty has been increasingly made conditional upon a state's ability to protect human rights, including minority rights (Castellino and Redondo 2006: 13; Koenig 2008: 99, 107–108; Peters 2009: 513), and recommendations have emerged in favour of the prohibition against forced assimilation, minority autonomy, self-government and self-determination. These group guarantees, together with individual rights such as the promotion of ethnic cultures and languages and the reduction of intergroup inequality, have defined the current international standards on minority rights.

'Ronghe' and the CCP's Nationality Policy

The CCP's nationality policy, based on Confucian *ronghe* ideology, does not seem to be consistent with the current international standards on minority rights that promote diversity, multiculturalism and self-determination. He (2004: 112) regards *ronghe* as the fusion or amalgamation of the Han majority and non-Han groups in a historical process of Confucian cultural diffusion (also Sautman 1999: 300). A major advocate of Confucian *ronghe* ideology in modern China was Dr Sun Yat-sen, who called for 'unifying the territories of the Han, Manchu, Mongol, Hui (Xinjiang) and Tibetans as a state' and insisted that the non-Han groups were the sub-branches of the Chinese nation, which would be assimilated into a 'single cultural and political whole' dominated by Han Chinese (Barabantseva 2008: 570–572; Gladney 1996: 79–85; Hyer 2009: 259; Mackerras 2011: 114). Dr Sun supported both *ronghe* and *tonghua* to achieve national unity via assimilation. *Ronghe* assumes relatively equal status between Han people and non-Han peoples, while *tonghua* assumes a superior position of the former over the latter (Barabantseva 2008: 571–572; Dreyer 1976: 16; He 2003: 226; Leibold 2008: 113–175; Wang and Phillion 2009: 2).

The leaders of the CCP inherited Dr Sun's assimilative stance to govern nationality issues after they came to power in 1949. The PRC's Premier Zhou Enlai remarked in

1957 that 'assimilation would not be welcome if it were achieved by force. Assimilation should be promoted if it were the outcome of mutual efforts of the majority and minority peoples. Successful examples of assimilation include the Hui people and the Manchu people' (He 2003: 226; Leibold 2008: 113–175; Zhu 2012). Why was the CCP interested in *ronghe* ideology? Firstly, the Chinese community revolution was a home-grown social movement, the CCP leaders were more (Han) nationalists than Marxists, and *ronghe* has always been part of Chinese nationalism. Thus, when the CCP leaders managed nationality issues in post-1949 China, Dr Sun's Han nationalist approach offered a ready-made solution for them to promote acculturation and assimilation in the post-1949 era. In addition, the Soviet approach (other than regional autonomy) was not taken seriously because it was not judged to fit the context in China (Zang 2015). Furthermore, the PRC shut itself off from the West due to the Cold War. In fact, there were no other viable options in the West then because major breakthroughs in minority rights occurred after the end of the Cold War, as mentioned above. These historical contexts may partly explain the CCP's interest in *ronghe* ideology.

Equally importantly, during the 1950s and the early 1970s, the CCP's top priority was to build a Stalinist China, and the *ronghe* approach was an ideal instrument for the CCP to transform minority nationality groups and minority areas. The CCP insisted that the Han Chinese had formed a coherent nationality long before 1949, whereas non-Han peoples had remained at feudal or pre-feudal levels of development, had been kept from becoming modern nations, and were 'weak and small nationality' and 'backward nationality'. This storyline was used to justify the leadership of Han Chinese in the Chinese nation (Barabantseva 2008: 585; Hyer 2006: 76–77) and the official rhetoric that non-Han peoples wanted to follow the CCP because they were members of the Chinese nation and were economically and culturally drawn to Han society (Hyer 2006: 78). The CCP claimed that it wanted to help non-Han peoples catch up with Han Chinese socio-economically and then move them with Han Chinese toward a communist society where assimilation became a reality.

The pre-1966 nationality policy was replaced by political extremism that favoured outright, forced acculturation and assimilation during the Cultural Revolution of 1966–76. It was officially declared that China was not a multinational country and that the nationality issue was settled. Forceful measures were taken in an attempt to suppress the expression of minority cultures and identities (Clothey 2001: 9; Heberer 1989: 26; Leibold 2010: 17; Mackerras 1995: 152; Sautman 1999: 288, 300; Zhu 2012). The period of the Cultural Revolution seemed to be different from the pre-1966 era in the treatment of nationality issues in China, but the radical and extreme changes were in fact the continuation of the CCP's *ronghe* policy. The measures taken between 1966 and 1976 and those taken in the pre-1966 era were all designed to assimilate ethnic minority groups into Han society. The differences between them were the targeted speeds of assimilation and the methods to promote assimilation. It is important to point out that political extremism of the Cultural Revolution was not initially invented to promote assimilation; rather, it was designed and used by Mao Zedong in his power struggle against his rivals inside the CCP, but in the later stage of the Cultural Revolution was extended to many other areas including nationality governance.

The CCP abandoned the radical policy of the Cultural Revolution after 1978 mainly because of the collapsing economy and broken revolutionary ideology in China. The

CCP leaders undertook some painful soul-searching exercises and reflected on the negative consequences of political extremism (Goodman 1994). As part of this overhaul of policy-making and implementation in every aspect of governance in China, a review of radical nationality policy was undertaken and a consensus was reached that instead of promoting assimilation in the PRC, political extremism had significantly increased intergroup tensions during the Cultural Revolution. The CCP decided that it was time to move away from political extremism in nationality governance, and there was an immediate need to repair Han–minority relations through liberalization (Zang 2015).

Nevertheless, the post-1978 era change does not represent the fundamental departure from *ronghe* ideology, and the difference between post-1978 nationality policy and political extremism of the Cultural Revolution is in degree but not in kind. The CCP has continued to promote acculturation and assimilation, although its approach toward nationality governance has become increasingly sophisticated and often sugar-coated with politically correct phrases. It now uses the term 'Chinese person' (*zhongguoren*), as opposed to Han Chinese, to include all nationality groups within the 'Chinese nation' (*zhonghua minzu*). It has claimed that China is a united nation of many nationalities due to 'the historical development of the past several thousand years', that China is a 'big fraternal and co-operative family composed of all nationalities', and that ethnic minorities 'formed with Han Chinese a single, unbreakable unit' due to historical, cultural, and economic reasons (Hyer 2006: 76–77; Mackerras 2011: 114). Top PRC officials assert that *ronghe* has been a frequent and common phenomenon in Chinese history. Zhu Weiqun, then executive deputy minister of the State Ethnic Commission, wrote in 2012 that: 'the government has to guide, promote, and lead the assimilative trend. One immediate measure the government shall adopt to promote assimilation is to abolish the ethnic identity in personal ID, stop setting up more ethnic autonomous areas, and promote the mixing of students of different ethnic groups' (see also He 2003: 226; Leibold 2008: 113–175).

There is popular support for *ronghe* ideology and assimilation among Han scholars in China. Some of them claim that '*Minzu* extinction is an inevitable result of *minzu* self-development and self-improvement . . . It is the final result of *minzu* development at its highest stage . . . in this big *minzu* family every *minzu* group has a higher level of identification – *Zhonghua Minzu*' (Minzu Tuanjie Jiaoyu Caibian Yuzu 2009: 17, 37, 79). Other scholars assert that there were numerous examples of *ronghe* in Chinese history, for example many ancient nomadic people no longer exist because they had been 'sinicized' into Han people, and there shall be an eventual *ronghe* leading to the total disappearance of minority nationalities in China in the future (Minzu Tuanjie Jiaoyu Caibian Yuzu 2009: 17, 37, 79). Still others demand that public policy focus on promoting Han culture and identity through acculturation rather than the protection of minority rights. In their opinion, 'Minorities should agree to assimilate, align their identities with Han' (Leibold 2010: 19; Sautman 2012: 9–10).

THE MINORITY RIGHTS REGIME IN CHINA

Given the above discussion, one cannot help but ask what the minority rights regime in China looks like. In the West, minority rights are guaranteed by a state's constitution, by a particular law on minority protection, or by individual legislations on specific areas; for example, laws on minority language and laws on minority education. In the PRC, the 1982 Constitution elaborates a range of minority rights to be realized through national and local laws, and many new laws and policies on minority rights have been promulgated after 1982. Even the US Congressional-Executive Commission on China (2005: 15) acknowledges that there are not many flaws in the legal framework designed to protect minority rights in the PRC (see also Human Rights in China 2007: 2, 12). However, the rights enumerated in the PRC laws are generally 'non-actionable', and they do not specify legal consequences if a right is abridged (Congressional-Executive Commission on China 2005: 12, 16; Lundberg and Zhou 2009: 275–276; Mackerras 1994: 153–166, 264–265; Smith 2004: 14–15). Hence, it is necessary to examine what the CCP has done in order to grasp the perimeters of the minority rights regime in China.

Reduction of Ethnic Inequality

There is a broad consensus among China experts that with certain exceptions, ethnic minority groups trail Han Chinese in status attainment by a large margin, and minority areas are less developed than Han areas (Gustafsson and Li 2003; Hannum 2002). The CCP has pursued a twofold strategy for the reduction of ethnic inequality in China. Firstly, it has implemented affirmative action programmes to improve the life chances of individual members of minority nationalities in both Han regions and minority regions. Secondly, it has attempted to reduce Han–minority inequality by reducing socio-economic gaps between Han regions and minority regions.

With regard to affirmative action, the CCP has called for preferred hiring of minorities in the state sector in the PRC. There are leadership positions designated for candidates from minority groups in the political hierarchy, and some minority groups are exempted from China's one-child policy. Universities are required to give minority students 'priority over others with equal qualifications' and set up preparatory courses for them (Sautman 1999: 294–295; also Mackerras 2011: 113–114). However, the growth of the private sector, which is not required to implement affirmative action programmes, has been accompanied by ethnic discrimination in hiring (Human Rights in China 2007: 2, 20–21; Zang 2010), and there is solid evidence on ethnic inequalities in labour market outcomes. Johnson and Chow (1997) show that ethnic minorities earned approximately 19 per cent less than Han Chinese in rural areas and approximately 4.5 per cent less than Han Chinese in urban areas. Zang (2008) shows that Hui workers in Lanzhou face barriers in finding a job in both state firms and government agencies: 54.3 per cent of the Han respondents work in state firms, as compared with 45.2 per cent of the Hui respondents; 25.5 per cent of Han Chinese are employed in government agencies, whereas only 11 per cent of Hui Muslims report the same institutional affiliation. Zang (2010) shows that in Ürümchi, 52.3 per cent of the Han respondents work in state firms, as compared with 28.5 per cent of the Uyghur respondents. Uyghur workers earn 52 per cent less than Han workers in non-state sectors in Ürümchi (Zang 2011). Other scholars point out that post-1978 growth 'masks a large and increasing income disparity' between minorities and Han Chinese (US Congressional-Executive Commission on China 2005: 16–17; Barabantseva 2008: 244; Dreyer 2005: 82; Hansen 2005: 117; Sautman 1999: 285). Enlarged ethnic inequalities in labour market outcomes have occurred partly because of Han–minority differences in educational attainment, access to political power (because most government officials are Han Chinese), discrimination, and so on.

The CCP has not been successful in reducing the disparities between Han regions and minority regions either: 'The gap in GDP per capita between ethnic regions and the nation steadily increased from 1773 *yuan* in 1995 to 5488 *yuan* in 2006' (Lai 2009a: 10; Tapp 2010: 104; Yang and Wall 2009: 77). Over 45 per cent of the poor counties listed by the central government in 2001 were located in minority regions, and more than 80 per cent of the people who suffered from basic needs for food and clothing lived in the minority regions (Clothey 2001: 3; Guo and Wang 2010: 201; Wei Zheng 2009: 41–42). Both Han regions and minority regions have developed in the post-1978 era, but Han regions have developed at a faster rate than minority regions because of their differences in infrastructure, human capital, access to foreign capital and technologies, and so on. Many minority regions are in remote areas in inland provinces, and people in minority regions are less educated than those in Han regions.

It is not appropriate to think that the CCP is not keen on the reduction of intergroup inequality in China. In fact, the issues of poverty, education and economic development have been at the core of the CCP's nationality policy since 1978 (Ghai and Woodman 2009: 44–45). The CCP has consistently regarded the common prosperity of all nationality groups as 'the fundamental stance of China's ethnic policy' (Information Office of the State Council 2010; Gladney 1996: 91–92) because it believes that economic growth can solve 'all minority problems' (US Congressional-Executive Commission on China 2005: 14; Elmer 2011: 8; see also Zhu 2012). The CCP's belief is not correct, because ethnic relations are not exclusively economic, as they involve many other dimensions such as cultural and political issues. The CCP apparently has a strong motivation to narrow the ethnic gap in labour market outcomes, as it believes that the the reduction of ethnic inequality is vital for stability, effective governance, and eventual assimilation. In other words, the reduction of ethnic inequality serves *ronghe* ideology.

It is however appropriate to criticize the CCP for not doing its best to reduce the gap in socio-economic attainment between Han Chinese and ethnic minority groups in China. It could invest more in minority regions, enact laws against discrimination in both public and private firms, and broaden equal opportunity programmes, but it has completed none of these tasks. In the early stage of market reforms in the late twentieth century, the government was poor and relied on the principles of laissez-faire capitalism to promote competition and efficiency. Ethnic minorities, together with other disadvantaged groups, were victimized due to the pursuit of 'survival of the fittest' by the CCP. However, today China is the second-largest economy and has the largest foreign reserves in the world. It is difficult to understand why the CCP has not developed new strategies and invested more resources in its fight against intergroup disparities in China. As mentioned, the reduction of ethnic inequality is vital for its assimilation strategy. One possible explanation is the CCP's determination not to create a welfare regime in China, so much so that its obsession with China's market competitiveness in the world outweighs its conceived obligation to equality and social justice. Another possible explanation is that the masterminds behind China's nationality policy in the twentieth century, who were raised with limited access to global norms on minority rights, have remained in office, and they do not have the capacity to conceive of new strategies to reduce the ethnic gap in socio-economic status.

Minority Cultures and Languages

The CCP has declared that minority languages are valued and respected, and that minority groups have the right to use their languages (Mackerras 1994; Wang and Phillion 2009: 2; Zuo 2007). Nevertheless, the nationwide promotion of Mandarin Chinese since 1956 and the popularity of Mandarin Chinese in the post-1978 era because of China's booming economy have created unfavourable conditions for some minority languages in China. Other factors that have had a detrimental effect on minority languages include the use of Mandarin as the teaching medium at universities, and the policy that Mandarin is the official working language in the governments of minority areas (US Congressional-Executive Commission on China 2005: 19–20; Human Rights in China 2007: 2, 26–29; Mackerras 2011: 117–118; Wang and Phillion 2009: 1).

The CCP has promoted some minority performing arts, using them to showcase its multiculturalism and enhance its political mandate to govern China. This explains why these minority performing arts have become more and more integrated with and similar to Han performing arts (Mackerras 1992: 30); the increasing similarity is unavoidable since both are required to fulfil similar political functions. In this way the CCP has in fact weakened minority cultures. In addition, the CCP has had no interest in supporting grassroots non-Han performing arts and has done little to preserve these minority cultural heritages. It is possible that the CCP does not see the use value of them for its political purposes because they are grassroots and parochial and thus insignificant. As a result, some of them have become endangered because there are no successors (Feng 2007; Ingram 2011; Mackerras 1992).

In theory, the CCP respects the freedom of religion. Mackerras (2011: 118) claims that 'on the whole religions and faiths of various kinds flourish openly among the ethnic minorities'. However, the US Congressional-Executive Commission on China (2005: 4–5) asserts that the CCP requires places of religious activity to be registered with and supervised by the religious bureau of a local government. Any attempt to edit, publish or distribute religious materials, including video and audio recording, is not allowed without prior government approval. The activities of self-proclaimed preachers are strictly prohibited. No foreign donations for proselytizing activities may be accepted by any party (US Congressional-Executive Commission on China 2005: 19; Human Rights in China 2007: 2, 29–30; Mackerras 2011: 118–119; Sautman 2012: 7).

Finally, although the CCP has publicized its commitment to preserving minority cultures and languages in China, it has educated non-Han peoples to be aware that their 'outmoded institutions and customs can harm their physical and mental well-being'. Non-Han peoples have been officially 'encouraged to adopt new, scientific, civilized and healthy customs in daily life, as well as in marriages and funerals' (Liu and Alatan 1988: 154; see also Information Office of the State Council 2005). By 'new, scientific, civilized and healthy customs' the CCP unequivocally means Han customs.

Overall, the CCP is apparently less enthusiastic to promote minority cultures and religions than the reduction of ethnic inequality in the PRC. The relative lack of enthusiasm can be seen in three aspects. Firstly, the CCP has not taken steps to reverse the decline of endangered minority languages. Secondly, the CCP has selectively preserved certain minority performing arts if it sees their use value, and has let other minority performing arts fall into oblivion if it does not see their use value. Thirdly, the CCP has restricted religious activities among certain minority groups. In comparison, the CCP has devised various measures and policies to promote intergroup parity in income and employment, although it has not done enough work. At least it has not actively restricted economic activities that facilitate the reduction of ethnic inequality. Unlike the promotion of ethnic parity, the preservation of minority cultures and religions does not serve *ronghe* ideology. On the contrary, they are perceived by the CCP as a major barrier to minority acculturation and assimilation into Han society, and some of them such as Tibetan Buddhism and Islam are perceived by the CCP to be a catalyst for rising ethnic consciousness and demands for self-determination by certain minority nationality groups such as Tibetans and Uyghurs. This may explain the relative lack of enthusiasm for the protection of minority cultures by the CCP.

Regional Autonomy

In theory, the CCP has practised regional autonomy in minority areas since 1949. The exception is the period of the Cultural Revolution, as the 1975 Chinese Constitution abolished the right of regional autonomy for minority nationality groups (Mackerras 1995: 152; Sautman 1999: 288; Zhu 2012). By 2005, 30 autonomous prefectures, 117 autonomous counties, and three autonomous regions had been set up. Among the 55 ethnic minorities, 44 have autonomous areas covering 75 per cent of the total ethnic minority population and account for 64 per cent of China's total land area (Information Office of the State Council 2005; see also Chang 2003: 21; Lai 2010: 67–69; Leibold 2010: 6; Lundberg and Zhou 2009: 295, 299–300; Sautman 1999: 296).

However, some scholars in the West regard the autonomous system as deficient or as a symbolic representation rather than real autonomy rules and mechanisms (Lundberg and Zhou 2009: 319; Moneyhon 2002: 120–121; Sautman 2000: 73), dismissing the system as 'a sham' or 'paper autonomy' (Becquelin 1997: 19; Lundberg and Zhou 2009: 275; Sautman 1999: 293; Shan and Chen 2009: 17). There are other issues associated with regional autonomy. The PRC Constitution proclaims that regional autonomy is practised by minority nationalities living in compact communities, who are free to 'preserve or reform their own ways and customs'. In other words, ethnic regional autonomy is officially defined to be mainly cultural. But it shall be mainly about power to the minority nationalities (Ghai and Woodman 2009: 29, 32–33; Mackerras 1994: 153–166, 264–265; Mackerras 2003: 26; Sautman 2000: 73). Finally, the CCP makes it clear that regional autonomy has nothing to do with self-determination and secession, the PRC is a 'unitary multiethnic state', separation of any territorial units from China is strictly prohibited, and separatist activities must be severely punished (Lai 2009a: 9; also Chang 2003: 13; Hansen 2005: 169; Smith 2004: 9).

Given the above discussion, it is curious why the CCP set up autonomous regions in the first place. One possible account is that it made a promise to ethnic minority groups in an effort to solicit their support in its struggle for power before 1949, and had to deliver upon its promise when it was able to (Gladney 1996). But there is no empirical evidence to support this. Another possible account is that the CCP copied the practice of the Soviet Union after 1949. But this cannot explain why the PRC did not abolish this system after it fell out with the Soviet Union in the 1960s.

Overall, it seems that regional autonomy 'does little to protect minority rights' in China (US Congressional-Executive Commission on China 2005: 13; Lundberg and Zhou 2009: 275–276). Regional autonomy does not serve *ronghe* ideology and assimilation and thus cannot attract support from the CCP. Moreover, regional autonomy is not a preferred instrument for minority governance in China because the CCP perceives the possibility that some ethnic minority groups use it as the framework for inspiration for self-determination or even secession. This partly explains why the five autonomous regions in China 'enjoy less legislative autonomy than ordinary provinces' (Ghai and Woodman 2009: 44). 'Strict Control' has characterized the CCP's approach toward autonomous regions in China (Zang 2015).

Representation of Minorities in Government

There are two main types of the ethnic representation in the Chinese political system: (1) minority deputies in the legislature (that is, the People's Congresses); and (2) minority cadres in the executive branch of government. With regard to the minority presence in the legislature, all 55 ethnic minority groups have their deputies to the National People's Congress (NPC) and members of the People's Political Consultative Conference (PPCC). However, both the NPC and the PPCC are not real law-making machines in the PRC, they are two rubber-stamp legislative bodies. The presence of minority deputies mainly serves the CCP's need to demonstrate its political legitimacy and portray the PRC as a champion of multiculturalism.

With regard to the minority presence in the executive branch of government, the CCP has recruited cadres from minority nationality groups to govern minority areas and employed nearly 3 million non-Han party members in 2007, up from merely 10 000 in 1950. The share of ethnic minorities in the PRC cadre corps was 73.9 per cent in Tibet, 47 per cent in Xinjiang, 34 per cent in Guangxi, 23.4 per cent in Inner Mongolia, and 17.5 per cent in Ningxia (Lai 2009a: 7). While these figures are impressive, a major issue is the Leninist centralization of cadre recruitment in China: when these minority cadres are appointed by higher authorities, local minority communities are not consulted and do not have a say in their appointments. As a result, these minority officials do not always promote policies to benefit their communities (US Congressional-Executive Commission on China 2005: 12; Kaup 2002: 883; Lai 2009a: 9).

Another major issue is how much power minority cadres can actually have after they are appointed. For example, although top administrative posts in an autonomous area must be open to candidates from the local minority group(s), the secretary of the CCP committee of the autonomous area, which is where the real authority lies, is always a Han Chinese (Hess 2009: 77; Ghai and Woodman 2009: 30, 45; Lai 2009b: 9; Smith 2004: 15; Lundberg and Zhou 2009: 306–307; Shan and Chen 2009: 17). The Han secretary holds real power, whereas minority officials are often figureheads. Overall, it seems that the CCP does not trust minority cadres; 'manipulation' is a term that can be used to characterize the way the CCP appoints and manages minority cadres, and there is no sign that the CCP will change its approach toward the representation of minorities in the political system in the near future.

MINORITIES AND RIGHTS

This chapter asks whether China has a good minority rights regime. To answer this question, it discusses the underlying principle of the CCP's nationality policy and argues that *ronghe* ideology has affected how the CCP has developed its nationality policy. This effect explains why the reduction of intergroup disparity has been at the core of the CCP's nationality policy: the common prosperity of all nationality groups has been regarded by the CCP as an essential step toward ethnic unity, minority acculturation and eventual assimilation into Han society. Nevertheless, there is still major ethnic inequality in the PRC, and there are not adequate provisions in the CCP's nationality policy to address intergroup disparity.

The CCP's effort to promote minority languages and cultures has been less impressive and unequivocal. The CCP has supported some minority cultural activities since they serve its political purposes, has let other minority cultural practices fade away, and has controlled or even suppressed some minority cultural activities if they are perceived to be used to raise ethnic consciousness. Clearly, whether the CCP supports a minority cultural practice depends very much on whether it can serve *ronghe* ideology.

Furthermore, it is clear that the matters related to regional autonomy and minority representation in the political system are manipulated and marginalized in the CCP's policy-making on nationality issues. This manipulation and marginalization can be explained because group guarantees do not facilitate *ronghe*. In short, the CCP's nationality policy is built to promote minority acculturation and assimilation rather than to protect minority group guarantees which call for diversity, multiculturalism, self-determination, and so on.

From the perspective of the current global norms on minority rights, it is clear that what the CCP has done for its minority nationality groups is designed to meet the minimum standards for the state conduct toward minority rights, and the outcomes are not encouraging. Moreover, the CCP does not seem to embrace many thoughts about or carry out many actions related to group guarantees. The CCP's nationality policy is not consistent with current global norms on minority rights: it has supported acculturation and assimilation, whereas the global norms have promoted self-determination and multiculturalism; the global norms on minority rights are based on individual dignity and group equality, whereas the *ronghe* policy is hierarchal and paternal in nature, placing Han Chinese above ethnic minorities. Thus, it can be argued that the CCP has yet established a good minority rights regime in China, and the dictionary of China's nationality policy should be enlarged and edited to include individual freedom, diversity, pluralism, state responsibility, self-determination and democracy.

The PRC cannot become respected as a responsible global power if its policy toward its minority nationalities does not meet international standards on minority rights. Moreover, China's domestic policy toward ethnic minorities has international implications. For example, China has one of the world's largest Muslim populations: more than 20 million, which is more than the United Arab Emirates, Iraq, Libya or Syria. China has provided the Middle East and Central Asia with cheap labour, consumer goods, weaponry, and increasing numbers of pilgrims to Mecca. These relations could be jeopardized if there is discontent among Muslims in China over such issues as limitations on Islamic activities, uncontrolled mineral and energy development, and uncontrolled Han migration into Muslim areas.

An overhaul of the CCP's nationality policy is urgently needed. *Ronghe* owes its origin to Confucianism, is an outmoded ideology if measured by current global norms on minority rights, and will eventually be outdated. Indeed, the CCP has in recent decades shown a trend moving toward global norms on minority rights (Chin and Thakur 2010: 119–121, 129; Human Rights in China 2007: 11; Kent 2002: 344–345, 358; Mushkat 2011: 68). The PRC endorsed the key properties of R2P, first at the 2005 World Summit, and subsequently in United Nations (UN) Security Council Resolution 1674 (2006), as well as in the 2009 UN General Assembly Informal Debate and the subsequent UN resolution on the implementation of R2P (Chin and Thakur 2010: 129; Prantl and Nakano 2011: 212–214). In 2005 the then PRC President Hu Jintao called for more freedom of religion, a higher degree of ethnic regional autonomy, Han cadres learning minority languages, greater quotas for hiring minority cadres, and more recognition of their contributions (Sautman 2012: 6). The current Chinese leadership has observed this line of thinking, although it has called for more aggressive attacks on ethnic separatism in China.

The changes discussed above are an inevitable product of liberalization at home and engagement with the international community in the post-1978 era (Mushkat 2011: 43). The increasing exchange between China and the West has promoted the awareness of the international minority rights regime among Chinese scholars, which has formed a new framework with which Chinese scholars have examined government nationality policy. 'It thus seems that Chinese scholars have "rightized" every official policy towards the minority, grouping them under the "minority right" umbrella' (He 2003: 232; He 2004: 117; Leibold 2010: 20; Prantl and Nakano 2011: 213; Sautman 2012: 11).

Another reason for the changes in China's nationality policy is the pressure from Western countries to promote human rights in the PRC. Many foreign dignitaries have raised issues related to ethnic minorities in meetings with Chinese officials, and there are also institutional arrangements as a major platform for the discourse on minority rights in China. For example, China and the EU have exchanged views regularly during the EU–China Dialogues on Human Rights, including minority rights (Bi 2011; Delegation of the European Union to China 2011).

Finally, the Chinese state's paradoxical enlistment of international development actors in the task of modernizing its minority areas such as Tibet (Mackerras 2005: 28–30) has allowed these non-governmental organizations (NGOs) to adopt international norms and practices on minority rights in devising development projects (Williams 2008). These norms and practices are essential elements for the future development of a Chinese minority rights regime in line with the global trends. It is possible that China will develop a nationality policy to promote diversity, multiculturalism and autonomy as the PRC is further integrated into the international community, and the ideas of human rights and democracy become everyday concepts in China.

NOTE

1. This chapter draws on my *Ethnicity in China: A Critical Approach*, Cambridge: Polity Press, 2015.

13. Education: from egalitarian ideology to public policy
W. John Morgan and Fengliang Li

The shaping and implementation of public policy is a fundamental process in any state whether developed or developing. It is an instrument that confirms the legitimacy of the state itself, in that it is an expression in practice of its monopoly of power. It is also essential to the welfare of citizens, demonstrating the state's responsibility for this: a further example of its political legitimacy. In parliamentary democracies, such as in Europe or in the Americas for instance, the process and content of such public policy is connected intimately with public opinion. This provides evidence about what citizens believe they need if they are to prosper, and for the state itself to continue to enjoy their support. This is shown through democratic elections in which citizens choose, albeit broadly, between public policy options and the individuals or groups of individuals who will deliver these in practice. Such a process is the working out of ideologies in practice. It is also a process which builds, in Gramscian terms, an ideological hegemony that goes beyond the maintenance of power through a monopoly of force (Borg et al. 2002). In short, the population is persuaded that the ideology of the ruling state power is a commonsense expression of what is needed to provide for its welfare now and in the future. This makes public policy concerning the education of the population a matter of key importance, essential as it is to human capital and skills development, to social capital, social cohesion and a harmonious society, and to the cultural development of the population generally. As we have said, in parliamentary democracies this is put to the test through periodic elections. In the People's Republic of China the shaping and implementation of public policy has each of these characteristics, except the final one.

The chapter focuses on the evolution of education as public policy in contemporary China, that is the period since Deng Xiaoping's Opening-Up and Market Reform of the economy. This has seen extensive changes to the provision and content of China's formal education system generally, and especially higher education; and in the relationship between education, the social market economy and the labour market in China. It should be noted that the chapter does not consider education policy in Maoist China, interesting though it is as a dramatic example of social and cultural ideology in practice (Morgan 2003). The reader interested in this, from the perspective of education policy as egalitarian ideology in China, should read the comprehensive accounts of Suzanne Pepper (1996), Vilma Seeberg (2000) and, for higher education, Ruth Hayhoe (1989). The literature specifically on the Cultural Revolution (1966–76) is immense, although Jack Chen's account may be recommended for its immediacy and its graphic insights (Chen 1976), together with the scholarly assessment of MacFarquhar and Schoenhals (2006).

There is also a considerable and growing literature on current educational developments in China, both in Chinese and in English. This deals with specific policy topics such as, for example, the impact of the One-Child Policy, teacher training, teaching and learning in schools, and the changing labour market for graduates. The chapter does not consider such literature or such issues in detail, not least for reasons of space. It considers instead the policy statements made by the Chinese Communist Party and state, as the Chinese system of formal education was rebuilt on the ruins of the Cultural Revolution. The chapter focuses on mainland China and does not consider education policies in the Special Administrative Regions (SARs) of Hong Kong and of Macau. The reader interested in these should begin with the series edited by Mark Bray and Ramsey Koo (2004).

FROM EGALITARIAN IDEOLOGY TO PUBLIC POLICY

The key questions when assessing public policy are: What is its purpose? Who should it serve? Does it have a legal basis? How is it financed and delivered in practice? And, crucially, who makes policy choices and assesses their effectiveness? In Maoist China education and cultural policy generally were driven ideologically to the climax of the Great Proletarian Cultural Revolution initiated by Mao in 1966. The direction was to be determined from below by the overwhelming majority and in their interests. The result was political and social chaos and the reduction of the system of formal education to rubble. After Mao's death and the arrest, trial and conviction of the Gang of Four (Jiang Qing, Zhang Chunqiao, Yao Wenyuan and Wang Hongwen) in 1976, the Chinese Communist Party led by Deng Xiaoping brought an end to the ideological changes associated with the Cultural Revolution. In June 1981, the Central Committee stated that: 'The "cultural revolution", May 1966 to October 1976, was responsible for the most severe setback and the heaviest losses suffered by the Party, the State, and the People since the founding of the People's Republic' (CCP Central Committee 1981).

Since then, despite formal consultations of public opinion, policy decisions in China have been made in practice by the technocrats of the Chinese Communist Party and state. The initial aim was to reconstruct an effective system of formal education, to provide it with an administrative-legal basis, with financial support and to ensure its delivery in practice. The policies devised relied increasingly on the use of statistical data and other quantitative analyses. This, it has been pointed out, marked a fundamental epistemological shift from Maoism to a new pattern of public knowledge and governance (Liu, X. 2012). The justification has been that Chinese policy-makers now 'place practice-based truths above value-based truths and initiate many pilot projects' (Zhang 2012: 91, cited in Morgan 2013: 134). Although the problem of choosing among policy options remains, this is still a Chinese Communist Party prerogative. Such policy-making and implementation was carried out initially on the basis of central planning, but the technocratic policy-makers of the Chinese Communist Party have attempted increasingly to reconcile society, state and market, as do governments elsewhere (Morgan and White 2013). They did not and do not, however, subject policy decisions and their outcomes to the formal electoral test of public approval. In the following sections we shall consider some key steps in the process of transition from egalitarian ideology to public policy which, as will be seen, was achieved in a series of slow but regular steps.

LAW AND FINANCE

In order to improve the backward condition of basic education fundamentally, the State formulated the Compulsory Education Law of the People's Republic of China, approved at the fourth National People's Congress on 12 April 1986.[1] The principle that local government take responsibility for the management of compulsory education was thus formulated as law. This was accompanied by departments at all levels beginning to shoulder the responsibility for their own finances on a contractual basis. In 1988, the State Education Commission and the Ministry of Finance promulgated the 'Provisions on Strengthening the Management of the General Educational Funds'.[2] This required that, when compiling education budgets, the finance and education departments at all levels should ensure the needs of basic education development by using both quota and special funds. The administrative departments should prepare school budgets economically; take responsibility for their own financial management and for any surplus or shortages. This process was followed in 1992 by the publication by the state of 'Implementation Rules for the Compulsory Education Law of the People's Republic of China'.[3] These defined further management systems of compulsory education, implementation steps and safeguarding and inspection measures. They laid a solid foundation for the development of compulsory education in China.

On 13 February 1993, the Central Committee of the Chinese Communist Party and the State Council issued the 'Chinese Basic Education Reform and Development Compendium'.[4] This argued that increasing investment in basic education was essential if China's strategic educational objectives were to be met. The government at all levels, society in general and also individuals, should contribute to such investment in basic education. China should establish gradually a funding system by which the state would provide the core funds which would be supplemented by fees for basic education, school-run industry income, social donors, basic education funds, and by funds raised through other channels. The Compendium also pointed out that government revenues must be used for basic education, especially to ensure nine-year compulsory education. The local governments could collect other charges for basic education based on the actual needs of local development, economic conditions and the public's income capacity.

On 18 March 1995 the Education Law of the People's Republic of China established the new education funds investment system formally and legally.[5] The aim remained to gradually increase investment in basic education, to ensure a stable source of education funds supplied to public schools. In order to develop compulsory education in economically backward areas, such as West China, the State Education Commission and the Ministry of Finance organized the National Compulsory Education Programme for the Poor Regions, using the compulsory education funds appropriated by the central government and funds raised by local government at all levels. The state, through this programme, mobilized different social forces to support educational development in poor areas, and to strengthen the responsibility and obligation of local government in promoting compulsory education in the local areas.

However, in 1994 China also initiated a tax-sharing system between the central and the local governments and the fiscal revenue available to local governments fell significantly. As a result, the policy which allocated to local government the main responsibilities for investment in and management of education encountered great difficulties in practice.

For example, local primary schools financed by villages experienced a financial crisis, while government at the county level had similarly limited financial resources to invest in the junior middle schools. There was increased reliance on income from the school-run industries, the township collective enterprises, state-owned enterprises, donations from society, miscellaneous fees charged to educational consumers, and other channels; yet the township collective enterprises and the state-owned enterprises were progressively less able to provide investment funds for basic education.

In 2001 the State Council's Decision on the Reform and Development of the Basic Education was a significant policy adjustment. It confirmed that compulsory education should be carried out: 'under the leadership of the State Council with local government taking management responsibility for provision while giving priority to the county'.[6] Thus, the main responsibility for investment in compulsory education was adjusted from the local grassroots upward to the county. The expectation was that over the next several years, based on considerations of social fairness, the basic direction of China's compulsory education would also be to shift management responsibility upwards; that is to say, that the provincial government would be responsible for the finance of compulsory education. We shall next consider the development of policy and provision in each of the key sectors of China's system of education.

PRE-SCHOOL EDUCATION

China's pre-school education was destroyed during the Cultural Revolution. In July 1979, in order to restore pre-school education and to develop it actively, the state put forward a so-called 'walking on two legs' policy at a National Nursery Work Conference.[7] This said that to solve the problems of financing kindergartens, multiple channels of support should be used such as the state, the collective, the society and individuals, while facilities at enterprises and similar institutions should be provided by the organizers themselves. Later, according to a statement of 'State Budgetary Revenues and Expenditures' issued by the Ministry of Finance in 1980 (Ministry of Finance 1980), special funds for pre-school education were listed under the provisions of the local funds for education, with special allocations made for rural pre-school education. However, in practice rural pre-school education did not receive appropriate attention in many regions, especially in West China and, as a result, kindergartens there lacked adequate funds and many remained in poor conditions.

In order to address these problems, the state published its 'Opinions on Developing the Rural Pre-School Education' in 1983. This specified that multiple channels should also be used to raise funds for rural pre-school education. In addition, parents, whether in rural or in urban areas, should pay a small fee towards the educational costs. It also pointed out that rural education should be developed in a coherent way. For example, in rural areas, the kindergarten should be run mainly by the collective while fully mobilizing the initiatives of the township and the team (village). The county and the town should also encourage and support organizations, factories, mines and local communities, as well as individuals, to run kindergartens. The publication of the Opinion ensured that the pre-school educational funds would have a place in fiscal expenditure and promoted the development of the rural preschool education.

In 1985 the State Council's General Office required local governments at all levels to allocate pre-school education funds in accordance with the 'Decision by the Central Committee of the Communist Party of China on the Reform of the Education System'.[8] It made clear that government at all levels had to take responsibility for mobilizing educational funds for this purpose. The Decision also pointed out that the bringing up of children is the legal and social responsibility of parents. Early childhood education is not part of compulsory education, thus parents who send their children to kindergarten should bear related costs of their children's care and education. The local government should set a standard charge for kindergartens based on an evaluation of costs of provision. Such a standard charge should be based on the principle of: 'what is taken from the people is used in the interests of the people'. It should take parents' actual needs and economic situation into consideration and then be checked and approved by the appropriate price control department.

This regulation indicated that, under the impact of the market economy, the costs of sending children to a kindergarten were not set by the state, but determined by the market, and that the public welfare characteristics of the planned economy were under question. In 1987 the State Education Commission, with the backing of the State Council, held the first national pre-school education conference since 1949. This recommended the development of pre-school education by mobilizing various financial resources, in a planned way, step by step with multiple channels and multiple forms of support. It advocated also that the state, the collective, and the individual should all invest in the development of kindergarten provision. As a result, China's pre-school education developed rapidly, with rural pre-school education also developing significantly.

As we have noted above, the reform of the economic system also required the adjustment of the national education strategy. In this case, it put forward policies which encouraged society to contribute to the development and operation of kindergartens. The state also provided the policy basis for the development of private pre-school education, a significant political initiative. In September 1995, the State Education Commission, the Planning Commission, the Ministry of Civil Affairs and other relevant departments jointly published the 'Opinions on the Enterprises to Open Kindergartens'. These stated that:

> We should reform the current fee system for the kindergarten, encourage enterprise kindergartens to open to the society generally, gradually change the kindergarten funding practice which, formerly, was met completely by the enterprises, improve the efficiency of opening kindergartens, deepen the reform, and actively and steadily promote pre-school education. Those enterprises which do not have appropriate conditions to provide kindergartens based on the principle of smooth transition and under the guidance of the government, should transfer responsibility to the local administrative department of education. We should continue to run the kindergarten with a variety of forms, or allow it to be run jointly by the community, or by qualified groups and individuals.[9]

On 17 July 1997, the State Education Commission published its 'Opinions on the Implementation of the Goals of the National Ninth Five-year Plan Concerning Early Childhood Education'. The document pointed out that: 'the pre-school education, constituting the first stage of China's educational system, is an organic part of primary education'.[10] It also stated that China should continue the reform of the kindergarten system. The pre-school education was not only said to be part of the education system, but also retained some of the characteristics of public welfare; which was an indication of a policy tension in the social market economy. China should, with the reform of the economic system, steadily and actively modernize the kindergarten system, clarify the responsibility of the government at all levels, and review the internal management system of kindergartens. The document concluded that the country still had a long way to go before realising the socialization of pre-school education.[11] The decline of state-owned enterprises had its effect, as pre-school education, originally provided by the state in this way, was gradually removed from the enterprises and transferred to society in its various forms; the main sponsors of the kindergarten changed significantly. A consequence was that some kindergartens were themselves forced to raise operational funds. The 'socialization' of pre-school education as a concept has spread widely, and reform and expansion has taken place across the whole country.

The Education Law of the People's Republic of China, passed in 1995,[12] guaranteed financial investment in and the conditions for education: the state-run schools have a fiscal appropriation as the main funding source, complemented from a variety of other sources. The enterprises and institutions, social organizations and individuals are responsible for raising money for running the kindergarten, while governments at all levels should give appropriate supplementary support. However, no organization or individual could open educational institutions for the purpose of profit-making. In 1996 the 'Kindergarten Work Procedure' was published which stated that: 'the funds for kindergarten should be raised by the organizers themselves'.[13] In 2003 the 'Guidance on the Reform and Development of Pre-school Education' was published. This pointed out that:

> the local government at all levels should strengthen the construction of the public kindergarten, ensure investment in pre-school education, and comprehensively improve the quality of services. The government at all levels should help to establish the public-run kindergarten and increase investment to pre-school education year by year. The government at or above the county level should arrange financial funds for pre-school education to ensure its normal operation, and support the development of the rural pre-school education. The pre-school educational funds should be used with care, with no department to intercept or embezzle funds.[14]

This policy stipulated that:

> the Education Department of the State Council, together with the Ministry of Finance and the Department of Prices, according to the non-profit seeking principle, formulate the charges for the pre-school kindergarten. The education departments of the provincial government, the autonomous regions and the municipalities should set the maximum and minimum charge according to the local economic development level and the economic capacity of the residents, upon the examination and approval by the financial department and the competent department of prices, and should not be implemented unless approved by the provincial government. The private kindergarten, by the provisions of the state, sets the charge standard according to the costs of opening the kindergarten, subjected to the approval of relevant departments.[15]

This rule more explicitly stipulated the fee standards of the kindergarten since the related rules issued in 1988 and 1966.

In November 2010, the State Council published its 'Opinions on the Current Development of Pre-school Education', which again stated the goals for pre-school education: 'namely, to finance pre-school education with government-led cost-sharing, and to rely mainly on the county for provision'. The essence of this was to: 'develop the public kindergarten energetically'. The policy document stated that: 'the development of pre-school education should be based on the principle of public welfare and universality. We should strive to build pre-school education as a public service system on the basis of reasonable costs and covering both urban and rural areas'. It continued: 'The government at all levels must ... vigorously include the construction of pre-school education as part of the people's livelihood projects for the construction of a socially harmonious society and as part of the agenda of the government's programme.'[16] This was the first time that pre-school education had been seen as part of the people's livelihood projects of the state, with clear characteristics of welfare and universality. This provided the basis at the government level for the implementation of policy on pre-school education. It is expected that, over the next several years, the basic direction of China's pre-school education policy will be to improve the system of management and responsibility, lessening state and government functions, as well as the quality of early childhood education; and to enlarge the scale of provision to meet the increasing demands of the population. It is an issue which, of course, is closely connected with the introduction and current changes of China's One-Child Policy.

COMPULSORY EDUCATION

Compulsory education is the national education that children and teenagers of school-age must receive and the state, society and each family must guarantee. Its substance is the compulsory educational system that the state provides for school-age children as required by the Law of Compulsory Education.[17] This stipulates that compulsory education lasts for nine years including elementary education and secondary education. In 2013 some 266 300 schools provided compulsory education with enrolments standing at 31 914 400.[18]

In 1980, the Central Committee of the Chinese Communist Party and the State Council published the 'Decision on Some Issues of Popularizing the Primary Education'.[19] This set out the principles of adjustment, reform, reorganization and improvement of the sector; these aimed to adjust the ratio between the input of basic education and the economy. Basic education was also considered as fundamental to China's development, and the proportion of investment in basic education was to be increased to meet the lack of educational funds. The Decision also specified specific goals and related corresponding policies and measures and, subsequently, China's basic education policy focused on planning, investment and efficiency. This was necessary as, in the mid-1980s, a considerable number of rural schools still had poor infrastructure, lacked teaching equipment and tools and were short of funds. As a result the salaries of teachers remained at a low level. On 13 December 1984, to address this, the State Council issued its: 'Notice on Raising Funds for Rural Schools'.[20] It required government at all levels to take effective measures to increase investment in basic educational construction and to encourage rural collectives and other social associations to take part in the development of rural education. The Notice sanctioned additional charges by government in rural areas to raise funds for rural education. Since then, government in the rural areas has acquired more and more responsibilities and has taken the leading role in the development of rural basic education. In addition to the rural collective economic organizations, the rural population itself became an important source of educational support funds.

In 1985 the 'Decision on the Reform of the Basic Education by the Chinese Communist Party' put forward strategic goals for the comprehensive reform of China's basic educational system. It made it clear that local government should be responsible for the development of basic education and for the implementation of a nine-year compulsory education in a coherent and step-by-step way.[21] The local government was to be responsible for the investment and management of basic education in its territory, but strategic policy directions and macro-planning, as well as the declaration of the implementation of specific policies, was to be decided by the central government. As part of this pyramid system, it was made clear that the management responsibilities of the governments at the provincial, city, county and township levels should be set out by the provincial government. However, restricted by the poor rural economy, China's rural basic education continued to be relatively weak. Quite a number of rural areas failed to achieve universal primary education and many school-age children, especially girls, could not be guaranteed a fixed number of years of primary school education. As a result, many young adults remained semi-literate or illiterate. A further aggravating factor has been that many primary and secondary schools remain in poor condition, with a serious lack of teaching equipment and facilities.

SECONDARY VOCATIONAL AND TECHNICAL EDUCATION

Secondary vocational and technical education is an important element of school education in China. It undertakes the essential task of cultivating hundreds of millions of qualified and skilled workers. There are 12 300 secondary vocational and technical schools which recruited 6 747 600 students in 2013.[22] At the National Education for Work conference in 1979, Deng Xiaoping summarized the Chinese Communist Party's policy objectives thus: the number of agricultural secondary schools and secondary vocational schools would be increased; and in education planning importance would be given to the restructuring of secondary education.

Thus adjusting the structure of secondary education and developing vocational education and training became part of the policy agenda. Until 1980 there were only 3314 vocational middle schools with 454 000 students at school in the whole country. These included 2924 rural vocational middle schools, accounting for 74 per cent of the total number of schools. The number of students in these schools was 320 000, or 70 per cent of the total number (Hao and Ren 1999). Consequently, in 1980, the Ministry of Education published the 'Report on the Reform of the Structure of Secondary Education',[23] which stressed that both the collective and the individual could open professional or technical schools. This was significant in that it broke with the original system by which only the state was allowed to provide such schools, which had a profound influence on the development of vocational education and training in China. The Report also put forward a series of preferential policies to promote the development of secondary vocational education, which greatly increased the number of providing institutions.

The Report was followed in 1983 by a document on 'Opinions on Reforming the Secondary Education Structure and Developing the Vocational and Technical Education', issued jointly by the Ministry of Education and other relevant ministries and committees. This made clear the policy for reforming the secondary vocational education. Two years later the state published 'The Central Committee of the Chinese Communist Party's Decision on Reforming the Education System'. This developed further the policy direction for vocational education and training. It pointed out that the structure of secondary education should be adjusted to focus on vocational education and training, and that enterprises should give priority to vocational college graduates in recruitment.

As a result, between 1978 and 1990, the number of secondary vocational schools grew from 4773 to 20 763, while the number of enrolments increased from 704 000 to 2 861 000. The secondary vocational education system as a whole achieved unprecedented development, while higher vocational education also began to receive attention. In 1980, a number of technical secondary schools and junior schools were upgraded to colleges. The structure and the level of such higher education were adjusted, as we shall consider further below. This encouraged big cities, medium-sized cities with rapid economic development, as well as large enterprises to open high schools and vocational colleges. These included independent higher vocational colleges, and by 1985, the number of enrolments in such colleges reached 30 100. In 1991, to consolidate the reform of the vocational education and training system the State Council published the 'Decision on Vigorously Developing Vocational and Technical Education'.[24] This put forward specific policies to promote vocational education and training such as opening dedicated vocational universities and giving priority to their graduates in recruitment.

The development of education policy continued in 1993 when the Central Committee of the Chinese Communist Party and the State Council published the 'Outline on the Reform and Development of Chinese Education'.[25] This followed a now familiar line, saying that reliance on government investment should give way to finance from other 'social forces' which would be complemented by the government. This would ensure various stakeholders in the development of vocational education and training which would be of benefit to the whole society. The policy enabled the system of vocational education and training to be distinguished from the general education system. The rapid development of a social market economy in China meant that there was a growing need for technical knowledge and skills. In 1994, in order to develop higher vocational education, the National Education for Work conference suggested management reforms at the school level, attaching vocational units to existing high schools, and encouraging independent adult colleges to supplement and develop higher vocational education (Li Peng 1994). At the same time, a few qualified key secondary vocational schools were also restructured and enhanced to supplement the development of higher vocational education. The implementation of this policy satisfied to a certain extent the need of the emerging social market economy for the development of vocational education and training, noted above.

In 1996 the Vocational Education Law of the People's Republic of China was issued. This was the first to deal specifically with this sector of education. It classified vocational schools at three levels: namely, elementary, secondary and higher vocational schools.[26] It was followed by the Higher Education Law of the People's Republic of China, issued in 1998.[27] This stipulated clearly that higher vocational education was part of higher education which established its legal-administrative status. The formulation and implementation of these policies significantly promoted the development of higher vocational education in China. It should also be noted that, by the end of 1998, there were 101 independently established higher vocational colleges in China, recruiting 62 800 students.

In 1999, the State Education Commission issued the 'Opinions on Trial Implementation of the New Management Mode and Operation Mechanism of Higher Vocational and Technical Education'.[28] This put forward 'three-no' rules: namely, no diploma, no employment registration card and no work arrangements for graduates from vocational higher institutions. It also required students studying in higher vocational colleges to pay tuition fees themselves (high tuition fees, in practice). This was known together as the so-called 'three noes and one high' policy. Unfortunately this policy restricted the further development of higher vocational education. Although the development of a social market economy continued rapidly, the original policy for vocational education and training gradually lost its rationale, and the secondary vocational schools lost their appeal for junior high school graduates, aggravated by the enrolment expansion of colleges and universities. Consequently, the secondary vocational education system fell into something of a crisis.

However, since 2000 vocational education and training has again been on the national policy agenda. Between 2002 and 2005 the State Council held three annual national work conferences on vocational education. These were accompanied by a number of important policy statements, the most significant being the 'Decision on Vigorously Promoting the Reform and the Development of Vocational Education' issued by the State Council in 2002.This stated that during the Tenth Five-Year Plan (2001–05), a modern vocational education and training system adapted to the socialist market economy and the needs of the labour market should be established. This should be characterized by flexibility and the capacity for independent development. This was followed by the document on 'Several Opinions on Further Strengthening the Vocational Education Work', issued by the State Council in 2004, and by the updated 'Decision on Vigorously Developing Vocational Education'[29] by the State Council in 2005. This last said that by 2010, recruitment to China's secondary vocational education and higher vocational education should parallel that of general education. The number of enrolments in secondary vocational education should reach more than 8 million, while enrolment in higher vocational education should be more than 50 per cent of higher education enrolment in total.

Since 2004, under the guidance of national policy, the quantity and quality of vocational education and training in China has improved steadily. The enrolment proportions of general education and vocational education are now close to being parallel. In summary, since China's Opening-up and Reform, the country's vocational education has made significant progress after more than 30 years of development. Firstly, the system which gave priority to school education with vocational training as an auxiliary was established. Secondly, the legal system of vocational education was created. Thirdly, the scale of the vocational education and training expanded steadily. For example, take secondary vocational education: in 1978, there were 4774 secondary vocational middle schools with 714 900 students; in 2007 the number of secondary vocational middle schools reached 4832, with 8 120 000 students, which accounted for half of the total numbers in secondary education. It is expected that this trend will continue with support from the Chinese Communist Party and the state.

ADULT AND LIFELONG EDUCATION

On 22 April 1978, Deng Xiaoping delivered a speech at the opening ceremony of the National Work Conference on Education. In addition to commenting on the schooling of children, he also emphasized the need to develop part-time adult education as a contribution to China's economic and social development (Deng Xiaoping 1985). The continuing education and training of workers was identified as a key element in such education. This lead was followed later in the year when, on 11 October 1978, the Chinese trade unions at their Ninth National Congress confirmed the 'Articles of Association of Chinese Trade Unions'. This included a call for the development of all types of part-time education, especially continuing vocational education and training. On 21 June 1979, the then Vice-Premier, Yu Qiu Li, in the fifth session of the National People's Congress presented the 'Report on the Draft Plan for National Economic of 1979'.[30] This included the continuing education of workers, in the spirit of Deng Xiaoping's speech, which had required that educational policy should be coordinated with the State Plan for the utilization of labour.

Further policy documents followed, with the following of significant importance: on 5 September 1980, the State Council approved the 'Opinions on Vigorously Developing the Higher Correspondence Education and Evening University', prepared by the Ministry of Education;[31] on 20 November 1980, the Ministry of Education issued the 'Interim Management Regulations on School Register Management of Radio and Television University Students';[32] and on 20 February 1981, the State Council issued its 'Decisions on Strengthening Staff Education'.[33] The Decisions proposed the principles, mission, objectives and major measures for the development of staff or workers' education. This policy document marked a new stage in which a system of education and training plans for employees was established. The Decisions declared that staff should be trained in a planned way, with political education and literacy classes for young adults who had entered employment after the Cultural Revolution. In order to promote such adult education, under the guidance of the Ministry of Education, on 3 April 1981 the Chinese Adult Education Association was established in Beijing, China. This was China's first national adult education association, the establishment of which marked a new chapter of adult education, stimulating academic research as well as domestic and international exchanges and cooperation.

In order to promote the continuing education of employees, the Chinese Communist Party and the state issued a number of guidance documents. The most important of these are given here: on 20 May 1981, the State Planning Commission, the Ministry of Education and the National Workers' Education Management Commission jointly issued the 'Opinions on Workers' Education'; on 29 June, the National Workers' Education Management Committee, the State Council and the Ministry of Finance jointly issued the 'Notice on Strengthening the Workers' Educational Organizations'; on 13 July, the Chinese Communist Party's Central Committee and the State Council published the 'Regulations for the National Industrial Enterprises workers Congress' formulated jointly by the Federation of Trade Unions, the National Economic Council and the Central Committee of the Chinese Communist Party; on 21 July, the National Labour Bureau issued the 'Opinions on Strengthening and Improving the Apprentice Training'; on 18 November, the Ministry of Education issued the 'Notice about Some

Issues of Junior Middle School Workers' and Missed Cultural Lessons'; on 29 December, the Ministry of Education issued the 'Opinions on Some Issues about Approval of the Establishment of the Workers' University and Graduate Degrees'.[34] This series of policy documents listed the specific requirements for the development of workers' and employees' continuing education and training. As a result, such provision experienced vigorous development and positive results, with the cultural and technical quality of the labour force significantly improved.

However, yet again, provision in rural China lagged behind, even though it had the greatest number of illiterate people. A set of policies was developed to address this problem. In June 1982 the Ministry of Education issued the 'Interim Measures for County Farmers' Technical Schools'.[35] This stated that the farmers' technical school must be part of the agricultural (including forestry, animal husbandry and fishery industries) secondary specialized school. This aimed at helping the rural people's commune and production brigades to cultivate skills equivalent to the secondary specialized scientific and technological level. On 2 December 1982, the State Council endorsed the 'Report on Rapidly Strengthening Agricultural Technology Training Work'[36] issued by the Department of Farming and Fisheries; and in May 1986, the Animal Husbandry and Fisheries Department issued the 'Notice on Reforming and Strengthening Farmers' Vocational and Technical Education and Training Work'. In October the same year, the China Association for Science and Technology, the State Education Commission, the Department for Animal Husbandry and Fisheries, the Central Committee of the Communist Youth League and the China's Women's Federation issued jointly the 'Notice on Strengthening the Practical Technical Training for the Rural Youth During the Seven-Five Period'. Both of these notices played an important role in the development of farmers' vocational and technical education (Li, N. 2013).

Part-time adult education in China had entered a new stage with vocational and technical education as the focus, together with the comprehensive development of political, cultural and scientific knowledge. On 23 June 1987 the State Council published the 'Decision on Reforming and Developing the Adult Education by the National Education Committee',[37] which was discussed at the National Conference on Adult Education. As a result, the adult education management system, educational concepts, principles, goals, tasks and priorities underwent significant adjustment and change, necessary to adapt to the needs of economic development and social progress. The Decision confirmed that 'adult education is an important part of education in our country, and is as important as basic education, vocational and technical education, and higher education'.[38] This declaration was a milestone in the history of adult education in China.

Its position was consolidated when, in January 1993, the State Educational Commission published the 'Opinions on Further Reform and Development of Adult Higher Education'. This policy document set out a set of strategic goals. Firstly, all social forces should be mobilized to establish a variety of forms, specifications and levels of adult higher education. Secondly, a high level of job training and of university continuing education should be a policy objective. Thirdly, there should be investment in the system to enable it to adapt to changing economic and social needs. Fourthly, a management and quality monitoring system should be established. Thus, the examination and approval of correspondence and evening university education qualifications was steadily moved from the macro control of the state (Wang and Morgan 2009).

However, the concept of basic adult education gradually became less important with the development of school provision, employee training, education for literacy and lifelong education. In 1998, during the reform of the state educational institutions, responsibilities for adult education and for vocational education were brought together under vocational and adult education institutes with functions allocated to four departments: development planning, basic education, higher education and higher education students. Therefore, the distinctive adult education institutions in each province were effectively closed. It is expected that adult education in China will, in accordance with contemporary international trends, be replaced by lifelong education, which we consider next.

This concept was first written into educational policy in the 'Outline for China's Educational Reform and Development' issued by the State Council in February 1993. It said that: 'adult education is a new type of education in the transition process from the traditional school education to lifelong education, which plays an important role in constantly improving the quality of the whole nation and promoting the economic and social development'.[39] It marked the shift of lifelong education from a concept to a policy. This was consolidated in 1995 when the National People's Congress endorsed the Educational Law of the People's Republic of China, Article 11 of which said specifically that: 'in order to adapt to the needs of socialist market economic development and social progress, promote the educational reform, and promote coordinated development of various types of education at all levels, the lifelong education system should be established and perfected'. This would 'allow citizens to receive appropriate political, economic, cultural, scientific, technological lifelong education ... creating conditions for citizens to receive lifelong learning'.[40] As lifelong education became part of educational policy and law, its fundamental position was established.

Strategic policy continued to be developed when, in December 1998, the Ministry of Education published its 'Education Revitalization Action Plan for the 21st Century'. This pointed out that 'lifelong education is a common requirement for education development and social progress' and argued the necessity 'to practice experimental work for community education, to gradually establish and perfect lifelong education system, and to improve the whole nation's quality'. It also pointed out that 'by 2010 the lifelong learning system should be established to sufficiently provide personnel support and knowledge contribution for the national knowledge innovation system as well as its modernization construction'.[41]

It should be noted that in this transition-century action plan, the concept of 'lifelong learning' was mentioned three times. The policy interest continued when, in June 1999, the State Council published its 'Decision about Deepening the Educational Reform and Comprehensively Promote Quality Education'. It said that China should 'gradually improve the lifelong learning system', and 'make full use of the modern distance education network to provide life-long learning opportunity for the social members'. This was also the first time that improving 'teachers' consciousness of lifelong learning' was mentioned.[42] In summary, since 1995, lifelong education has developed from an idea to a national policy, which was reflected in a series of important educational policies issued by the Ministry of Education and endorsed by the State Council. The concept of lifelong education, a popular international concept, has now become an important educational policy for China.

Its consolidation is confirmed in the way in which it appeared with greater frequency in the Chinese Communist Party's Congress reports and resolution files, which reflected official determination to promote lifelong learning. For example, in November 2002, President Jiang Zeming at the 16th Chinese Communist Party's Congress presented a 'Report on the Construction of a Prosperous Society in an Inclusive Way; and Creating a New Situation of Socialism with Chinese Characteristics'. This said that China 'should strengthen vocational education and training, develop continuing education and construct a lifelong education system', to form 'a learning society in which everyone will learn to achieve their all-round development'.[43] Again, in October 2003, the policy document 'Some Issues of the Further Requirement by the Central Committee of the Chinese Communist Party for Perfecting the Socialist Market Economy' was published. This called for 'the further reform of the education system generally, with the aim of constructing a learning society, promoting quality education, and strengthening people's capacity for innovation and employment; transforming population pressure into a human resource advantage'.[44]

The same policy trend and its political implications may be seen in the Central Committee of the Chinese Communist Party's 'Decision on Strengthening the Construction of the Party's Governance Capability', issued in September 2004. This declared the need to 'create an atmosphere in which people will follow a process of life-long education and promote the establishment of a learning society'.[45] This was followed, in October 2006, by another Chinese Communist Party Central Committee document, the 'Decision on Building Socialism and a Harmonious Society'. This again stated that China should 'deepen the education reform, improve the quality of education, and construct a modern national education system and lifelong education system'. The policy concept received the highest endorsement in October 2007 when General Secretary Hu Jintao, in his report to the 17th Chinese Communist Party's Congress, emphasized China's need to develop distance education and continuing education and to build a learning society.[46]

The concept was included finally as policy in the 'National Plan for Medium and Long-term Education Reform and Development (2010–2020)',[47] published by the State Education Commission in 2010. In summary, lifelong education was emphasized not only in the files and work reports of the Chinese Communist Party's Central Committee, but also in state educational policy discussions, which together provide the motive power for China's public policy reform and practice. Thus, the concept of lifelong education is now accepted by more and more people in China as a key instrument in the sustainable development of the economy and the society.

It is appropriate to say something further here about the 'National Plan for Medium and Long-term Education Reform and Development (2010–2020)' mentioned above. It contains a series of important policy measures that, it is claimed, respond to public needs and requirements, and is based on the understanding that a strong China depends on first-class education and first-class human resources. It claims that the Scientific Development Concept is the overarching principle in the Plan, which is a justification of the technocratic approach to public policy-making. It promises to raise the proportion of national fiscal expenditure on education to 4 per cent of gross domestic product (GDP) by 2012, and to ensure the steady growth of this proportion in the future. It has social aims in that it favours a learner-centred approach, an entrepreneurial spirit and problem-solving skills, together developing a sense of social responsibility among students. It claims also to address issues of public concern and reasserts the public good characteristics of educational provision. This recognizes that equal access is the key to equality in education and that each individual citizen has a legal right to education, which has implications for the equitable allocation of educational resources. The Plan also addresses specific issues, not least those associated with the reform of the One-Child Policy, with educational quality, and claims that it was developed following a lengthy and widespread public consultation (*People's Daily* 2010). This is encouraging, and recognizes the key issue of social choice in public policy-making. However, it does not take this recognition to its logical conclusion, but retains final responsibility for national education policy in the hands of the technocrats of the Chinese Communist Party and state. This is formulated through the Plan's emphasis on the Scientific Development Concept, which is an administrative and managerial one in essence.

HIGHER EDUCATION

In this section we discuss policy development in the key sector of higher education. China's higher education management system reform began gradually after 1978, while in 1980 the system of state financial support was also reformed. The management system of the national budget was transformed from the 'unified collection and allocation of funds by the state' to a 'division of revenue and expenditure between the central and the local governments' (Ding et al. 2008). The reform adapted to the new policy which required separate management of the fiscal revenue by both the central and the local governments. Later, apart from the central institutions, the provincial financial departments became responsible for the expenditure of local colleges and universities throughout China, with no unified appropriation of funds from the central government. As a consequence of the increase in institutional decision-making, some colleges and universities began to lower entrance requirements in order to admit some self-financed students. This policy and the accompanying contractual programmes with the state-owned enterprises were carried out step by step. A new era for Chinese higher education was beginning.

In 1985 the State Council published the 'Decision by the Central Committee of the Chinese Communist Party on the Reform of the Education System'[48] which said that:

> the key to the current reform of higher education is to change the management system, as the government has too much control over the institutions of higher education ... The state and its education administrative departments should strengthen the macro management and guidance of higher education. Under the guidance of national united educational policy and planning, we should increase the autonomy of higher institutions, and strengthen their social contact with the production departments, scientific research departments and other various aspects of the society, to provide the institutions of higher learning with the enthusiasm and ability to adapt to the needs of the economic and social development.

This was an important decision for China's higher education system reform. It was followed in 1989 by the State Education Commission's 'Regulation on Charging Tuition and Accommodation Fees at Public Colleges and Universities'.[49] This put forward the principle of a cost sharing and recovery system for non-compulsory education, changing the original system of financial aid through scholarships, grants and loans in order to widen sources of funds for colleges and universities. The new policy transferred the management of the local colleges and universities to the local government, arguing that local governments could best cultivate the knowledge and skills needed for local economic development. Again, in 1992, the State Education Commission published its 'Opinions on Accelerating the Reform and Development of Higher Education'.[50] It pointed out that China should establish a new system of higher education governance, with the state responsible for strategic planning and macro-management, and the institutions given management autonomy, making clear the rights and obligations of colleges and universities. In the same year, in order to adapt to the socialist market economy, more and more higher education institutions in China began to charge student fees directly. This was endorsed the following year when the Chinese Communist Party's Central Committee and the State Council promulgated the 'Chinese Education Reform and Development Compendium'.[51]

This permitted a pilot fee-charging system at the Shanghai Foreign Language Studies University and at the South-East University. Subsequently, this practice became more widespread year by year; which increased the amount of cost-sharing in the financing of China's higher education. In July 1995 the State Education Commission published 'Several Opinions about Deepening the Reform of the Higher Education System'. This policy document stated that: 'the aim of the higher management system reform is to build up a new management system which adapts to the reform economic, political, scientific and cultural systems; and to promote the reform and development of higher education generally'. In 1997, the cost-sharing principle was implemented fully in higher education institutions. The Compendium also pointed out that:

> the aim of the higher education system reform is to make clear the relationship between the government and colleges and universities, between the central state and local government, as well as between the State Education Commission and the various central departments; and to build up the independent school-management system under the government's macro management.[52]

Following the 15th session of the National People's Congress in 1997, China's higher education system entered a new stage of development. Its resources are now allocated rationally and the quality of institutional management has been improved. In 1999, the Chinese Communist Party's Central Committee put forward further principles for the reform of higher education, namely: 'co-construction, adjustment, cooperation and integration'.[53] This enabled central and local governments to build higher education institutions in partnership, while the management of the higher educational institutions was transferred from central government to local government, and to the institutions themselves. A massive expansion of Chinese higher education institutions followed, including the emergence of private provision (Li and Morgan 2013). As a result, higher education in China moved from elite higher education to mass higher education, although retaining a commitment to develop selected universities as world-class institutions. In China today some 34.6 million students receive higher education of all types and the gross enrolment rate has reached 34.5 per cent.[54] China's higher education, in ruins following the Cultural Revolution, has entered a new and vigorous era. The policy aim is to move beyond expansion to the development of world-class universities and for higher education to be available for the identification and training of talent throughout China, with different types of higher education fulfilling different functions (Morgan and Wu 2013 [2011]).

THE REFORM OF THE *GAOKAO*[55]

We conclude this policy survey by considering a very important recent policy initiative: the reform of the *Gaokao* or National College Entrance Examination announced by China's Ministry of Education (MoE).[56] In future, the entry of new students to higher education will no longer be based on performance in a few major subjects, such as mathematics, Chinese and English. Instead, it will also take into account other subjects, as well as their personal and social character, not considered formerly. This change should have a potentially important impact on both individual Chinese students and the education system.

The current Gaokao system, which may be compared with the A-level examination in the United Kingdom, was established in 1977 and has been criticized widely. Chinese universities and colleges focus solely on scores from the test, taken each June, when considering applicants, with obvious consequences for students' future life-chances. In order to secure a good grade in the *Gaokao*, students concentrate on its core subjects from the beginning of secondary school, which is extremely narrow educationally. Again, parents, concerned for their only child, also try to ensure that their children go to schools which have a good record of success in the *Gaokao*. Such intensive competition has had a very negative impact on students, on schools and on social equality. The *Gaokao* has, for instance, aggravated the unequal weighting of educational resources at secondary level in favour of urban and professional families.

It is anticipated that the planned reform will influence many stakeholders. For tens of millions of Chinese students, besides studying three core subjects (mathematics, Chinese and English) examined at national level, there will be the opportunity to select three other subjects and to sit the examinations at the provincial level. In addition, results will be graded in A to E bands according to the relative performance of students within each province. Furthermore, an evaluation of the personal and social quality of students will be undertaken. This will require secondary school students to present a record of information relating to moral standards, physical health, general culture, such as hobbies, and social or community engagement and contribution, such as volunteering. The planned reform sends a clear message to secondary school students and their teachers that a narrow focus on the classroom rote learning, together with a lack of engagement with the wider community, may not be enough to ensure entry to higher education, which is so important for future life chances.

The reform should therefore have a major impact on the organization and management of secondary education in China which, for almost 40 years, has been dominated by the *Gaokao*. One effect is likely to be an end to the strict divide between the natural sciences and technology, and the humanities and social sciences. Students will be given the opportunity to select and combine those subjects in which they are interested. This will require a reorganization of school resources and impact also upon teacher education and training. Schools will also be required to provide additional resources and support for student participation in and contribution to the wider community. This will present challenges for school principals and other staff. This will require a reorganization of school resources and impact also on teacher education and training.

The likely impact will not be confined to the secondary education system. We have mentioned teacher education and training, while the planned reform could create more space for higher education institutions to evaluate and select students not only through performance in their core and selected subjects (3 + 3), but also through an assessment of their personal and social characteristics. In the longer term, there should also be an impact on the employability of graduates, which means that employers are also potential stakeholders in the reform.

The planned reform is being piloted in the Shanghai municipality and in Zhejiang province. It should be appraised not only from the perspective of student academic choice and broader educational development, but also in how it improves on the current *Gaokao* system which is very important in terms of feasibility. It would be optimistic to assume that the reform could be adopted nationwide by 2017 without opposition. The need to overcome resource shortages in many schools and to reform teacher attitudes through training is one obstacle. Parents will also need to be persuaded of the merits of chance. Given the conflict of values within Chinese society, it will not be easy to secure consensus about how university entrants should be evaluated. This is related to another fundamental issue in contemporary China, which is the relationship between equal opportunity in education and a broader social justice. This has yet to be considered in current debates or by government policy documents, and yet the proposed *Gaokao* reform will have both educational and social effects.

KNOWLEDGE, SKILLS, PUBLIC COHESION

It is clear that, given the economic and social development strategy laid down by the Chinese Communist Party, education will continue to be a key element of public policy, but in the Chinese sense. There are two fundamental reasons for this. Firstly, a comprehensive and effective education system is essential to the development of China's human capital stock. This is seen as key to China's aspiration to be the world's leading economy. This was demonstrated in an important and relatively recent collection of studies, based on empirical evidence derived from research and using a sound analytical framework (Liu et al. 2010). The substantial evidence that the collection offers about the importance of investing in human capital for economic development in China gives ground for optimism. However, it identifies also several potential problems, notably the apparently ever-widening socio-economic inequalities which will need to be addressed if the state objectives of economic growth and a 'Harmonious Society' are to be achieved (Postiglione 2006; Wang and Morgan 2012).

The concept of citizenship and citizenship education, and what it means in practice, is relevant to this aspect of education as public policy. It includes promoting the rule of law in Chinese society, the emergence of civil society and of cyberspace as sites of public discourse, and addressing the socio-political tensions that have been stimulated by a patriotic-socialist citizenship curriculum. The question is, of course, whether China, because of its size, growing economic power and relative cultural homogeneity, will prove to be exceptional (Law 2011). This raises the question of Han Chinese nationalism and of the cultural and political status of minorities, ethnic and religious, as the currently volatile situation in Xinjiang province indicates. It has been argued that the social and cultural experience of rights and responsibilities in practice has had a greater impact on ordinary Chinese people, and especially those at the margins, than formal civil and political citizenship education (Fong and Murphy 2006). There is also the possible danger of a neo-imperialist outlook developing unless China is prepared to act as a world citizen (King 2013).

Secondly, and in a similar way, education policy is also an integral part of social policy. As we have noted above, China's rapid growth during the past 30 years has been accompanied by serious social and environmental problems, inequalities of income, health care, housing and employment – and of access to education, which is key to a comprehensive and effective education system. Any assessment of contemporary public policy in China must consider the impact of market-oriented economic development on social policy and question whether the path that continues to be followed by the Chinese Communist Party can result in a sustainable and cohesive society (Zhao and Lim 2010). This is the second fundamental reason for the continuing importance of education as public policy in China.

The Chinese Communist Party recognizes that it is the development of an economically rewarded, contented and cohesive Chinese population, despite the social inequalities, that will maintain its political hegemony. The control of the provision, access to and content of public education is a key to this; although such a balance is likely to be increasingly difficult to sustain. The provision of education has usually been seen internationally as a public good or service which the state guarantees. However, neoliberalism and the competitive nature of the market economy have now challenged this. As Tilak points out, the General Agreement on Trade in Services (GATS), to which China is a signatory, regards 'the supply of education as a commercial trade' (Tilak 2011: 124; cited in Morgan 2013: 132). In the Chinese public policy context there are likely economic and individual benefits, but the potential for tension is very great as the tendency increases for social and economic inequalities to worsen. The lesson for Chinese policy-makers in education, as in other aspects of public policy, is that a balance that takes public preferences more readily into account should be attempted in the interests of social harmony and cohesion.

ACKNOWLEDGEMENT

The authors thank Miss Dan Liu for her kind assistance.

NOTES

1. The full text of this law can be found on the page of the official website of Ministry of Education of People's Republic of China, available at http://www.moe.edu.cn/publicfiles/business/htmlfiles/moe/moe_619/200606/15687.html.
2. http://www.law-lib.com/lawhtm/1988/4899.htm.
3. The original texts see *People's Education*, No. 5, 1992, available at http://www.cnki.com.cn/Article/CJFDTotal-RMJY199205000.htm.
4. The original texts see *China Higher Education*, No. 4, 1993, available at http://www.cnki.com.cn/Article/CJFDTotal-ZGDJ199304002.htm.
5. *Gazette of the State Council of the People's Republic of China*, Oct. 1995, available at http://www.cnki.com.cn/Article/CJFDTOTAL-GWYB199510000.htm.
6. *Gazette of the State Council of the People's Republic of China*, No. 23, 2001, available at http://www.cnki.com.cn/Article/CJFDTotal-GWYB200123003.htm.
7. *The Notification of Forwarding The summary of National Nursery Work Conference*, by the Central

Committee of the Communist Party of China and the State Council, according to the Chinese Women's Research Network, available at http://www.wsic.ac.cn/internalwomenmovementliterature/12721.htm.
8. *Gazette of the State Council of the People's Republic of China*, No. 15, 1985, available at http://www.cnki.com.cn/Article/CJFDTotal-GWYB198515000.htm.
9. http://www.gzedu.gov.cn/gov/GZ04/200812/t20081217_3291.html.
10. Full text is available at http://www.moe.gov.cn/publicfiles/business/htmlfiles/moe/s3327/201001/xxgk_81983.html.
11. Full text is available at http://www.moe.gov.cn/publicfiles/business/htmlfiles/moe/s3327/201001/xxgk_81983.html.
12. The full text of this law can be found on the official website of Ministry of Education of People's Republic of China, http://www.moe.edu.cn/publicfiles/business/htmlfiles/moe/moe_619/200407/1316.html.
13. Kindergarten Work Procedure, *Studies in Preschool Education*, No. 4, 1996, available at http://www.cnki.com.cn/Article/CJFDTOTAL-XQJY604.024.htm.
14. *Early Childhood Education*, Vol. 6, No. 4, available at http://www.cnki.com.cn/Article/CJFDTotal-YEJY200304001.htm.
15. The full text of this law can be found on the website of Ministry of Education of People's Republic of China, http://www.moe.edu.cn/publicfiles/business/htmlfiles/moe/moe_619/200407/1316.html.
16. http://www.gov.cn/zwgk/2010-11/24/content_1752377.htm.
17. http://www.law-lib.com/law/law_view.asp?id=163284.
18. http://www.moe.edu.cn/publicfiles/business/htmlfiles/moe/moe_633/201407/171144.html.
19. http://www.people.com.cn/item/flfgk/gwyfg/1980/112701198006.html.
20. http://www.people.com.cn/item/flfgk/gwyfg/1984/112701198401.html.
21. http://www.people.com.cn/GB/historic/0527/1738.html.
22. http://www.moe.edu.cn/publicfiles/business/htmlfiles/moe/moe_633/201407/171144.html.
23. http://www.china.com.cn/law/flfg/txt/2006-08/08/content_7058712.htm.
24. http://www.people.com.cn/item/flfgk/gwyfg/1991/112701199142.html.
25. http://www.edu.cn/zong_he_870/20100719/t20100719_497964.shtml.
26. The full text of this law can be found on the official website of Ministry of Education of People's Republic of China, http://www.moe.edu.cn/publicfiles/business/htmlfiles/moe/moe_619/200407/1312.html.
27. http://www.gov.cn/banshi/2005-05/25/content_927.htm.
28. http://www.people.com.cn/item/flfgk/gwyfg/1999/206003199902.html.
29. http://www.gov.cn/gongbao/content/2002/content_61755.htm.
30. http://news.xinhuanet.com/ziliao/2002-02/20/content_283404_1.htm.
31. http://www.people.com.cn/item/flfgk/gwyfg/1980/112701198001.html.
32. http://www.people.com.cn/item/flfgk/gwyfg/1980/206005198002.html.
33. http://www.people.com.cn/item/flfgk/gwyfg/1981/225702198101.html.
34. http://www.jse.gov.cn/art/2011/6/24/art_3904_14931.html.
35. *Gazette of the State Council of the People's Republic of China*, No. 2, 1982, available at http://www.cnki.com.cn/Article/CJFDTotal-GWYB198802007.htm.
36. *Gazette of the State Council of the People's Republic of China*, No. 1, 1983, available at http://www.cnki.com.cn/Article/CJFDTotal-GWYB198301009.htm.
37. http://www.people.com.cn/item/flfgk/gwyfg/1987/L35701198709.html.
38. http://www.people.com.cn/item/flfgk/gwyfg/1993/112701199345.html.
39. 'Outline for China's Educational Reform and Development', available at http://www.jyb.cn/info/jyzck/200602/t20060219_10718.html.
40. 'Educational Law of the People's Republic of China', available at http://www.gov.cn/ziliao/flfg/2006-06/30/content_323302.htm.
41. *Guangming Daily*, 25 Feb. 1999, available at http://www.gmw.cn/01gmrb/1999-02/25/GB/17978%5EGM3-2505.HTM.
42. 'Decision about Deepening the Educational Reform and Comprehensively Promote Quality Education', *People's Education*, No. 7, 1999, available at http://www.cnki.com.cn/Article/CJFDTotal-RMJY199907001.htm.
43. http://www.people.com.cn/GB/paper39/7683/733922.html.
44. http://news.xinhuanet.com/newscenter/2003-10/21/content_1135402.htm.
45. http://www.people.com.cn/GB/40531/40746/2994977.html.
46. http://cpc.people.com.cn/GB/104019/104099/6429414.html.
47. http://www.moe.edu.cn/publicfiles/business/htmlfiles/moe/moe_838/201008/93704.html.
48. *Gazette of the State Council of the People's Republic of China*, No. 15, 1985, available at http://www.cnki.com.cn/Article/CJFDTotal-GWYB198515000.htm.
49. http://www.chinesetax.com.cn/fagui/bumenguizhang/wujiaguiding/200507/137970.html.
50. http://www.law-lib.com/lawhtm/1993/55625.htm.

51. http://www.law-lib.com/law/law_view.asp?id=58490.
52. http://www.law-lib.com/law/law_view.asp?id=58490.
53. http://www.shedu.net/news/data/20021017207531/20021017207531_1.htm.
54. http://www.moe.edu.cn/publicfiles/business/htmlfiles/moe/moe_633/201407/171144.html.
55. A version of this section was published first by W. John Morgan and Bin Wu as 'Why Reforms to China's College Entrance Exam are so Revolutionary', available at http://theconversation.com/why-reforms-to-chinas-college-entrance-exam-are-so-revolutionary-36048.
56. http://news.xinhuanet.com/english/china/2014-12/21/c_133869221.htm.

14. Welfare and social security[1]
Wang Guohui and Jane Duckett

Research on Chinese politics has only recently begun to include welfare and social security. Studies of the Mao and early post-Mao periods concentrated on political leaders, institutions and state–society relations without taking account of social policies to provide for the poor, elderly and unemployed or to deliver health services and education. Social policy research, meanwhile, tended to describe policies and provisions rather than explain them, or to portray them as rational responses to emergent social problems (Dixon 1981; Wong 1998; Leung 2005; Yang 2003).[2] Only from the late 1990s did political scientists begin to explore the politics that shape welfare and social security policies and, conversely, the role that these policies played in Chinese politics (White 1998; Frazier 2010; Saich 2011; Duckett 2001, 2004, 2011).

Despite their neglect, welfare and social security policies have since the early 1950s been an important part of the Chinese Communist Party's (CCP's) political project of 'modernizing' China. That political project led the CCP to adopt development strategies influenced by the dominant ideologies and economic development paradigms of the major world powers, particularly the Soviet Union from the 1950s, and then the United States from the late 1980s. Although its development strategies have been very different, with one based on state planning and the other on market-led growth, the CCP's twentieth-century welfare and social security policies and provisions helped to build political support for them both as well as for the Party itself. Into the twenty-first century, as the CCP has struggled to maintain support, welfare and social security have become important, high-profile policy spheres for the party-state.

SOCIAL SECURITY AND THE POLITICS OF HEAVY INDUSTRIALIZATION, 1950s–1980s

The CCP's ideology meant that after it seized power in 1949 its land reforms and nationalization of industry did much to redistribute the resources of landowners and urban industrialists. But its social security policies from the 1950s to late 1980s were shaped more by the Soviet development model adopted in the first decade, and by the CCP's need to build political support for it in the cities. Soviet state planning enabled the party-state to extract resources from agriculture and channel them into industrialization. At the same time, and as part of the model, welfare and social security helped the new party-state to build political support among urban workers in newly nationalized industries as well as among government employees (some of whom had worked for the previous Nationalist government) by providing job security, old-age pensions and low-cost health care. It then gradually extended these provisions to privilege many state enterprises and other public sector workers.

In rural areas, meanwhile, the party-state collectivized agriculture, and from the late 1950s – as the split with the Soviet Union emerged – created rural communes that provided a modicum of security and health care for rural dwellers. Despite pro-rural Maoist initiatives and rhetoric, however, rural residents did not enjoy the same range of provisions as their urban counterparts.

Underpinning the rural–urban divide in provisions was the national registration system created in the 1950s, which segregated the population into 'agricultural' and 'non-agricultural' households, tied rural dwellers to the location of their birth and restricted rural–urban migration. In addition, the state procured grain and other agricultural produce at fixed prices under state planning, enabling it to keep food prices low in the cities and to channel resources into building heavy industry. In this way rural inhabitants effectively subsidized the cities.

Urban Social Security for the Development of Heavy Industry

From the 1950s, the new party-state gradually eliminated labour markets and tried in principle to ensure full employment. Under the 'iron rice bowl' it gave urban workers jobs for life and through their work places – known as 'work units' (*danwei*) – delivered 'welfare' (*fuli*) that included pensions, cheap housing, assistance with health care costs and education (some units even had their own hospitals, clinics, schools and nurseries) (Leung 1994). Work units also provided subsidies for everyday costs, and coupons to enable people to purchase grain. These public sector work units gradually expanded to include almost all the urban labour force. Although they did not pay high wages, they provided social security and in-kind benefits that were generous for a low-income country.

In 1951, the new national government issued the Labour Insurance Regulations (*Zhonghua renmin gongheguo laodong baoxian tiaoli*), which stipulated that enterprises should provide for employees in case of sickness, pregnancy, work injury, disability, old age and on their death. Thus work units paid for the health treatment of their current employees, as well as maternity benefits – up to 56 days of paid leave by the early 1980s – and health costs relating to pregnancy or work injury. They also paid for their workers' retirement pensions (which were non-contributory: that is, workers did not make contributions) calculated at between 75 and 100 per cent of their final wage. Finally, they permitted retirees to remain in their work unit housing (for which rent was negligible) and to continue to be reimbursed for their health care. From the mid-1960s onwards, all these expenses fell to individual enterprises after union-organized enterprise risk-pooling of welfare funds was abolished.

The state gradually extended urban enterprise worker provisions, and granted similar benefits to government and other public sector (*shiye danwei*) employees – including those working in public hospitals, schools and universities. There were, however, significant differences in the level of provision, with large state enterprises – often those in the heavy industrial sector or other key industries such as textiles – providing more generously than local government-run collectives. Provision also varied by locality, and overall women, blue-collar and unskilled workers received less generous benefits than men, white-collar or skilled workers.

The state also provided for those who fell outside the state sector in the cities. It organized employment for many with disabilities in so-called 'welfare enterprises', and it provided very basic social assistance (*shehui jiuji*) for those with no family, no work and no means of support; the so-called 'three nos' (*san wu*). Finally, the state also delivered special assistance for army veterans, retired soldiers and the families of 'revolutionary martyrs' (Dixon 1981; Wong 1998).

Local Rural Social Security in a Dualized System

The CCP had begun land reforms in areas it controlled before 1949, and extended those reforms as it seized power across China in the late 1940s and early 1950s. But its division of land among farming households was soon followed by policies that collectivized farming, and by the end of the 1950s led to the creation of the first rural communes. Through these communes the party-state decommodified rural labour, and organized rural dwellers into production brigades and teams (around 20–30 households and 100 people). It stipulated that production teams, as the basic accounting unit for production and distribution, calculate rural dwellers' work points and then convert them into grain and food provisions as well as some very limited cash.

The grain distribution system played a key role in providing collective security (*jiti baozhang*), guaranteeing minimum subsistence for every member. The communes, through its teams, allocated a basic grain ration (*jiben kouliang*) to each person, including children. Then on top of this it allocated 'work point grain' (*gongfen liang*) based on individual members' earned work points. Large families unable to earn sufficient grain could borrow from the collective (Mei 2005). The wider brigade and commune then played a redistributive role when planning and organizing public services such as co-operative medical schemes, special care for the families of revolutionary 'martyrs' and servicemen, and 'Five Guarantee Household' (*wubaohu*) support for the poorest families (Kang 2009).

During the commune era, the collective provided social relief through social mutual aid, sometimes with government support. Sometimes it subsidized commune members who fell into poverty – that is, those households whose annual income was insufficient for basic subsistence – through extra work points or grain, based on the annual income of the production team and brigade. Alternatively, it provided money from the collective's welfare funds: a sum not exceeding 2 or 3 per cent of total distributable income each year that the production team held back (Song 2003). The (county) government would provide relief for poor households in localities where the collective economy struggled to help. In addition, the Five Guarantee Household system established in the late 1950s targeted help – such as light work in exchange for work points or free grain – at the elderly, weak, widowed and disabled who had no other source of support, guaranteed food, clothing, firewood and education for their children and a proper burial when they died. It also directly provided necessities or arranged daily care and assistance (Li and Jiang 1996).

For households whose members included servicemen or 'martyrs', the Chinese party-state implemented a special nationwide care scheme. From 1956 until the collapse of the commune system in the early 1980s, it ran a Special Treatment Work Day Programme (*youdai laodongri zhidu*). Under this programme, households with revolutionary 'martyrs', servicemen or disabled/sick veterans enjoyed the benefit of extra work days, without actually having to work them, if their income did not reach the general standard of the commune (Xin 2001). During the commune period, households were granted over 400 million extra work days each year (Song 2003: 30), helping many on low incomes who had provided servicemen for the country.

From the late 1950s and especially during the 1966–76 Cultural Revolution, the party-state also adopted rural co-operative medical schemes, through which barefoot doctors (usually paramedics who also worked in the fields but were trained in basic sanitation and health) based in villages provided low-cost basic health care, including immunizations. Co-operative medical schemes and barefoot doctors extended health care into rural areas, and the government also extended the system of county hospitals and commune health centres across China, but rural dwellers did not enjoy the same level of free medical treatment and curative care as their urban counterparts.

In sum, rural welfare and social security during the commune era should be understood in the context of the state's heavy extraction from rural society and agriculture to fund industry. In this context, where the rural collective economy was weak and rural dwellers' incomes were squeezed to a very low level, an egalitarian method of consumption and goods distribution was used to ensure the subsistence of all commune members. It therefore furnished only very basic social security. People living in the countryside did not enjoy public housing, but built their own dwellings. Neither did they receive a pension when reaching old age. Instead, the collective arranged work for them until they completely lost the capacity for work, after which they were cared for by family members. Finally, rural co-operative medical schemes were underfunded in comparison with the urban system, which provided at low cost a much higher level of curative care. As a result, when rural dwellers contracted serious illnesses, they relied primarily on their families, many of whom would be unable to afford treatment.

WELFARE AND SOCIAL SECURITY IN SUPPORT OF MARKETIZATION, 1980s–1990s

The institutions created in the 1950s endured through much of the 1980s, when the CCP's development strategy shifted toward liberalizing and marketizing the economy. Under Deng Xiaoping, China's development strategy began to change from the late 1970s as the CCP allowed the economy gradually to 'grow out of the plan' (Naughton 1996). In the 1980s, the party-state – not without some significant disagreements and negotiation among its leaders – began to permit labour markets to return, to allow the private sector to grow, and then to reform its state enterprises. Through all these economic policy changes, the party-state used welfare and social security to reduce political opposition and build support for its strategy, focusing more on the cities than on the countryside and retaining the urban–rural divide in systems of provision.

Urban Welfare and Social Security in Support of State Enterprise Reform

Before the 1980s, the party-state had been committed to full employment, and unemployment (*shiye*) had been portrayed as a capitalist evil. Those without work tended to be young secondary or tertiary graduates who were waiting to be allocated work by the state (*daiye*). Very few people lost their jobs and became unemployed, although from the 1960s there were periods when significant numbers of young people were without work, for example between 1978 and 1980 when they returned from working in the countryside (Jefferson and Rawski 1992).

From the late 1980s, the party-state began to experiment with allowing state enterprise managers to dismiss workers and introducing contracts for workers that signalled the end of job tenure (Leung 1995). As a consequence, unemployment – measured only for the urban population – began to grow, rising even on conservative official figures from 2.5 per cent in 1990 to 4.2 per cent in 2004 as state enterprise reforms culminated in mass lay-offs (Duckett and Hussain 2008). And to compensate one of its core constituencies for this loss of security, from 1986 the party-state introduced unemployment insurance for state enterprise employees (Pi 1995).

Major change – to not only unemployment insurance but also other urban welfare and social security provisions – really began when CCP leaders bit the bullet of major state enterprise reform in the mid-1990s. Now that they needed to lay off large numbers of urban workers, who were the main beneficiaries of the previous system and its generous social security provisions, Jiang Zemin and Zhu Rongji oversaw reforms first in retirement pensions (with many unemployed being given early retirement), the creation of 're-employment service centres' to provide laid-off worker allowances, retraining and other support, and the extension nationwide of social assistance, the 'minimum living security guarantee' (*zuidi shenghuo baozhang*, often referred to as *dibao*), to provide a further safety net for the unemployed (Duckett and Hussain 2008).

During the 1990s, the urban work unit-based social security system declined in relevance for the many workers who moved to work in the private sector or into informal employment. At the same time, long-established state enterprises with an older workforce and many retirees were disadvantaged vis-à-vis newer state and private sector businesses. To help reduce the burden, new policies shifted responsibility for social security from individual work units to local governments. Local government social insurance or social security departments organized and managed new old-age and health insurance schemes into which enterprise employees and employers contributed. Although this meant security and continuity of provision for many, as schemes were expanded to include a majority of urban dwellers in formal employment, they left informal workers and dependants without protection in cases of illness and in old age (Béland and Yu 2004; Duckett 2004).

While reform of social security (including old-age, health and unemployment insurance) for urban enterprise employees in the 1990s proceeded rapidly, the social security system for public servants and those working in other public sector units remained largely unchanged. Particularly in terms of pensions and health care, the generous benefits to people working in the public sector were still paid for from government budgets, while individuals did not make contributions. This created a dualized urban social security system that was criticized for its unfairness. While in the twenty-first century the central government has attempted to merge the pension scheme for civil servants and other public sector workers with that of enterprise workers, this reform has been strongly resisted. Public sector employees are fearful that it would reduce their benefits (Lu 2011), and since they are a key support-base of the CCP, they have been able to stall change.

The Collapse of Rural Collective Welfare and Social Security

Rural administrative and economic policies in the late 1970s and early 1980s contributed to dramatic changes in rural welfare and social security. When the party-state abandoned the commune system and replaced it with household farming, the Five Guarantee Household programme and co-operative medical schemes, which were funded by collective economy, collapsed (for other contributing factors, see Duckett 2011). They had been organized on a pay-as-you-go basis, and so had not accumulated funds. And neither central nor local governments found alternative sources of finance. One survey showed that the share of administrative villages with co-operative medical schemes dropped suddenly from over 90 per cent in the mid-1970s to under 6 per cent in 1986 (Wei 1994: 140). By 1989 fewer than 5 per cent of villages retained them (Song 2006). Where they did survive, programmes for the Five Guarantee Households and rural compulsory education were now mainly funded through village-level public welfare deductions (*cun tiliu*) and township planning charges (*xiang tongchou*) (Song 2006: 70–72; Chen and Li 2009). Old-age assistance collapsed, however, and the family, as the basic unit of production after the commune system, now took sole responsibility for its members' security.

During much of the 1980s, the party-state did not consider rural social security to be a serious problem, and the impact of its collapse was softened by the rapid growth in average incomes. But from the late 1980s and into the 1990s, when income growth slowed and the 'peasant burden' grew heavier, rural social security issues such as health care and old-age support became a pressing political issue that the central government felt increasingly compelled to tackle. Particularly after the 1994 tax reforms, many township governments were very short of revenue and had to rely on various charges and fees directly collected from peasants to maintain their operations and public services, creating widespread dissatisfaction.

The central government had begun in the 1990s to pay some attention to rural health and old-age care, with initiatives aimed at re-establishing co-operative medical schemes and setting up a rural pension system. For example, the CCP Central Committee's 1993 'Decision Concerning Some Problems in the Construction of the Socialist Market Economy' specifically made it a requirement 'to develop and improve rural cooperative medical schemes' (Article 27) (CCP Central Committee 1993). And in 1997, the CCP Central Committee and the State Council 'Decision Concerning Health Reform and Development' stressed that it was important 'to actively and steadily develop and improve rural co-operative medical schemes' (Article 11) (CCP Central Committee and State Council 1997). Despite these Decisions, however, progress was limited to localized experiments that failed to involve a significant proportion of the rural population. Toward the very end of his tenure, in 2002, Jiang Zemin did nevertheless back a high-level Decision to tackle rural health problems, including health insurance for farmers, and this formed the basis of a concerted political push to establish New Rural Co-operative Medical Schemes (NRCMSs) under Hu and Wen during their first term in power.

As far as rural old-age care was concerned, the central government began to foresee a crisis in the family provision of care for elderly farmers following the demise of the commune system, the growth in rural–urban migration, the implementation of the one-child family planning policy and a rapidly ageing society. From 1986, the Ministry of Civil Affairs began to carry out policy research and experimented with small-scale local pilot schemes. After six years of experimentation, in 1992, it issued its 'Provisional Basic Programme for County Level Rural Social Old-Age Insurance', the first government regulation on rural pensions (Ministry of Civil Affairs 1992). According to this programme, the main form of funding for the scheme was rural dwellers' personal payments, though alongside these the collective was to subsidize and the government was to provide 'policy support'. The funds were managed at county level and took the county as an accounting unit. This programme was considered a milestone in moving rural social security from the traditional family-based model to a more 'modern', state-backed one (Song 2006: 74). It was implemented nationwide, and by 1998 some 2123 counties (including county-level cities and districts) and 65 per cent of towns or townships were organizing rural pension schemes with a total of 80 million rural dwellers participating and a total fund accumulation of 17 billion yuan (Ministry of Labour and Social Security and National Bureau of Statistics 1998).

Despite these early efforts at establishing rural social security, however, the central government's focus during the 1990s was largely on urban reform – especially state enterprise reform – and the reform of urban workers' social security programmes. Thus, for example, in 1990, total governmental spending on social security was 110 billion yuan, of which 89 per cent, or 98 billion yuan, was used for urban dwellers, who constituted only 20 per cent of the total population. Only 11 per cent, or 13 billion yuan, was used for the 80 per cent living in the countryside (Zhang 2003). With such limited government spending, rural social security in this period was established at only a low level and was characterized by limited population coverage and selective or experimental implementation. Neither co-operative medical schemes nor pensions were able to provide meaningful security for rural dwellers primarily because the government did not take responsibility and put in substantial resources, and largely left rural dwellers to pay contributions themselves. Nevertheless, in terms of reform and creating a social security framework appropriate to a market economy, this period from the mid-1980s to the late 1990s was an important time of exploration and experiment. Although the reach and impact of social security reforms were limited, experiments and small-scale pilot schemes accumulated experience and lessons that laid the foundations for developing social security into the twenty-first century.

FOCUS ON RURAL WELFARE AND SOCIAL SECURITY FOR A 'HARMONIOUS' TWENTY-FIRST CENTURY SOCIETY

Several factors combined to encourage China's central party-state to focus on improving welfare and social security provisions, particularly in rural areas, in the first decade of the twenty-first century. First, the steady growth in fiscal capacity from around 2002 gave the central government the means to invest in social provisions. Second, major health and demographic problems – the SARS crisis of 2003 and population ageing – focused leaders' attention on health and old-age provisions and demonstrated their potential for political destabilization. Third, increasing political unrest in the countryside was perceived as resulting at least in part from high rural–urban inequality and continued rural deprivation. Major initiatives involved abolishing rural taxes and introducing rural *dibao* (a 'minimum livelihood guarantee' programme much like that introduced in the cities in the 1990s), improving access to health care in the countryside and setting up rural pensions schemes. In the cities, the focus was on extending social health and old-age insurance to dependants and those without formal work who had been excluded from the social insurance programmes set up in the 1990s.

Abolition of Rural Taxes

From 2000, the Chinese central government made serious efforts to reduce rural taxes, which had long been a source of grievance in the countryside and were thought to be an important cause of rural protest and anti-government violence (Bernstein and Lü 2003). In 2000, during the tenure of leaders Jiang Zemin and Zhu Rongji, the central government initiated a policy of reducing rural fees and taxes (Yep 2004). But from 2002, under their successors Hu Jintao and Wen Jiabao, the policy evolved rapidly until in 2006 rural taxes were abolished completely. The abolition of rural taxes is often considered to be a significant policy initiative in terms of reducing inequality and rural poverty.

Although abolishing rural taxes was not a social security and welfare reform, it did have some impact upon rural social security and welfare. First, it increased rural dwellers' disposable income, meaning they had more resources to invest in joining pension and health schemes. Second, spending on rural poverty relief, *dibao* and compulsory education, which were previously funded primarily through taxes and fees directly collected from rural residents, were now to be a responsibility of higher-level governments. Research shows, however, that after the reduction and abolition of rural taxes, the income of township governments in some poorer areas fell, negatively impacting on the performance of public services including the funding of social security and welfare for rural dwellers (Li and Wu 2005).

Extending the *Dibao* Programme to the Countryside

Although the Ministry of Civil Affairs had begun by developing rural *dibao* in the early 1990s, at the same time as urban *dibao*, until Hu and Wen came to power in 2003, the rural system was piloted mainly in the rural counties of a few economically developed major cities and provinces, notably Beijing, Shanghai and Guangdong. It thus provided in the early twenty-first century for only around 4 million people (Wang 2011).

From 2004, however, the Chinese central government began to push forward the establishment of rural *dibao* and dramatically increased the number of people able to receive it. By 2005 population coverage had doubled to 8 million, and by 2006 it doubled again to 16 million (Ministry of Civil Affairs 2012b). In early 2007, the central government then announced its plan to establish and expand rural *dibao* across the whole country. And by June 2007, the Ministry of Civil Affairs had declared that it was established in all China's 31 provinces (Guo 2007). The number of rural dwellers receiving *dibao* then increased rapidly from 35 million in 2007 to 53 million in 2012 (Ministry of Civil Affairs 2012b). In 2010, the central government declared in its 'No. 1' document that all those entitled to rural *dibao* should be actually included in the scheme, indicating that some people had been denied benefits despite meeting the income criteria for support (Party Central Committee and State Council 2009).

Under the *dibao* programme, the minimum living standard is determined by the local government (usually county-level government) based on 'local conditions', meaning the local cost of living, local incomes and local government spending capacity. The standard thus varies significantly between different locales. For example, according to Ministry of Civil Affairs figures in February 2014, the highest level of payment (meaning the monthly household average per capita income level that the rural *dibao* helps people achieve) was found in Beijing (where it was 340.70 yuan) and the lowest standard was in Tibet (where it was 70.39 yuan) (Ministry of Civil Affairs 2014).

New Rural Co-operative Medical Schemes

The 2002 central party-state Decision promoting the NRCMS envisaged it as voluntary and locally organized, with a limited role for central government, but it soon evolved to become more ambitious and, crucially, to be backed by more central state spending. The Severe Acute Respiratory Syndrome (SARS) epidemic spread across China and then beyond its borders from late 2002 to mid-2003, just as new leaders Hu and Wen took over from Jiang and Zhu. The epidemic thrust China's problem-stricken health system into the limelight, as it became apparent that SARS would be difficult to contain if it spread to rural areas, because farmers were unable to afford treatment and would not seek diagnosis for fear of incurring high costs for tests and treatments. Although the crisis was contained by summer 2003, it had put health system problems, including the gap between rural and urban health provision, high on the policy agenda. The government began local experiments in 2003 and then in 2006 rolled out the NRCMS programme nationally, with central government fiscal transfers to aid poorer regions.

The NRCMS programme is broadly viewed as having successfully established a nationwide scheme with mass participation (around 90 per cent of the rural population) that has been welcomed by rural dwellers. It is expected to provide a platform for development and improvements, perhaps even a merger of rural and urban health insurance systems in the longer run. But the NRCMS is also widely seen as underfunded as well as undermined by health cost inflation. At the same time there are major problems with local poor capacity to administer the schemes (Zhang 2013). The NRCMS is therefore still in need of political support for its development. It remains unclear how high a political priority it will be for top leaders Xi Jinping and Li Keqiang.

Rural Pensions

Rural pensions are a very recent innovation in China. Traditionally, old-age care was the responsibility of individual families, and elderly rural dwellers relied on their children – and especially their sons, with whom they often lived – to look after them as they grew old and needed more care. Into the twenty-first century, however, rural elderly care became more and more important for two key reasons. First, with the strict implementation of family planning policies since the late 1970s, the nuclear family had become smaller, and China's population structure shifted to an inverted triangle shape, with more elderly, and fewer younger people. A rural family now usually had many fewer children than before (often only one or two), which meant that sources of family support for elderly relatives had declined. Second, increasing numbers of young and middle-aged rural dwellers now migrated to cities to find work, often leaving the older generation without adequate care.

For these two reasons, old-age support in the countryside became recognized as a serious social problem.

Although during the 1980s and the 1990s the Chinese central government had permitted some local governments to carry out experimental rural pension scheme pilots, and had made efforts to establish a nationwide rural pension scheme, this 'Old Rural Pension Scheme' failed due to insufficient government funding; by 2001, only 60 million rural dwellers had joined it, and its funds were only 22 billion yuan (Ministry of Labour and Social Security and National Bureau of Statistics 2006). In 2009, however, the Hu and Wen administration announced a 'New Rural Pension Scheme' (NRPS, at first known as the Rural Pension Pilot Programme), which spread quickly and by 2011 had 326 million participants, 85 million pension recipients, and 120 billion yuan in funding (Ministry of Human Resources and Social Security and National Bureau of Statistics 2012). It had been set up nationwide by 2012.

The State Council's stated principle for the NRPS was that it should provide 'basic insurance, broad coverage, flexibility and sustainability' (*baojiben, guangfugai, youdanxing, kechixu*). The scheme is organized locally and funded through a combination of personal payments, village collective contributions and government subsidy. In principle, every person aged over 60 is qualified to enjoy a basic government-backed pension. Contributions each month for the basic pension are 55 yuan per person, a figure set by the central government and government-funded. The central government shoulders the entire cost of basic pensions for central and western provinces. For the richer eastern provinces, the costs are shared equally between central and local governments. In addition to the basic pension, the scheme sets different payment levels according to rural residents' ability to pay (from 100 yuan per year to 5000 yuan per year). In order to encourage people to join the scheme, the government offers subsidies so that, in theory, the more the individual pays, the more benefits they are able to enjoy. The subsidy is provided by the government and all the money (both the money paid by individuals and the money subsidized by the government) goes into individual residents' accounts.

Consolidation and Expansion of Urban Welfare and Social Security

While the central party-state clearly focused on rural welfare and social security during the first decade of the twenty-first century, it also extended provision in the cities, building on programmes created the decade before. Urban poverty assistance was no longer on the agenda, however, with the Ministry of Civil Affairs announcing in 2004 that with 22.5 million urban *dibao* recipients by the end of 2003, the programme had attained full coverage (despite its still low levels of assistance) (Chinanews 2004). Instead, attention had turned again to social insurance. In 2007 the centre introduced Urban Residents' Health Insurance for the non-working population, addressing criticisms that 1990s social health insurance for urban employees neglected dependants and the many others without formal employment (Lin et al. 2009). In 2011 it then announced trial Social Pension Insurance for Urban Residents (Dorfman et al. 2013), and claimed by the end of that year to have 5.4 million participants (Ministry of Human Resources and Social Security and National Bureau of Statistics 2012). Across social insurance programmes, there was also some improvement – though locally very variable – in the rights of rural migrant workers (Watson 2009).

During the Hu and Wen period there was much greater effort to extend the reach of the social security system, particularly in rural areas. The NRCMS, rural pension schemes, rural *dibao*, urban residents' basic medical insurance and urban residents' pension schemes, as well as rural and urban medical assistance schemes, were all established and significantly improved during this period, covering almost the whole Chinese population and constituting the largest social security network in the world. Also during this period, the government invested huge resources into social security and welfare programmes (both rural and urban), and increased spending on social security from 199 billion yuan (10.5 per cent of total government spending) in 2001 to 1536 billion yuan (14.1 per cent of total government spending) in 2011 (Shi 2012: 14). The central government in particular now plays a much bigger role and shoulders more responsibility for funding the social security system. Overall, in terms of welfare and social security, the Hu–Wen period was one of success, in terms of increasing the flow of resources and significantly expanding provision. These successes are sometimes overlooked in analyses of the period.

WELFARE AND SOCIAL SECURITY ISSUES FOR CHINA'S NEW LEADERS

Despite the achievements of the Hu and Wen period in extending welfare and social security, serious problems remain. First, the whole social security system is highly fragmented, with different social groups participating in different schemes (Zheng, B. 2009). Not only are the rural and urban social security systems still dualized, but also urban enterprise workers on the one hand, and public servants and public sector employees on the other, belong to different systems. Meanwhile a large number of migrant workers are enrolled in different locally designed social security systems. The social security schemes and programmes are, moreover, mainly managed at county level, meaning that the whole country thus has more than 2000, each operating independently. Social security funds are the responsibility of the county government, which must run them as appropriate to the level of local economic development and its own fiscal capacity. Such a highly fragmented social security system is not only politically unfair but also seriously hinders the portability of social security provisions for migrant workers and people who move from one occupational group to another (for example, a public sector worker who chooses to work in an enterprise) (Zheng 2008).

Second, the rapidly ageing population and serious fund deficits undermine the long-term sustainability of the social security system. The rapidly ageing population in China threatens to bankrupt the current social security system, further reducing pension payments or postponing the retirement age. In 2010, pension schemes in 15 provinces were in deficit and required central government fiscal transfers of nearly 200 billion yuan to fill the gap (Zheng 2012).[3] And by 2011, the total hidden debt of the urban workers' pension scheme reached 2.25 trillion yuan (Geng 2012).

Third, funds and services are often badly managed. Local government capacity to manage funds is often weak, so that although large sums have been accumulated for future payments, local social security managers have few ways of investing to maintain or increase their value. Instead the majority of the funds are simply deposited in banks, and lose value. At the same time, systems for managing and delivering social security are poor, despite the rapid expansion of coverage. In 2002, the ratio between the number of employees in social security service institutions and the numbers of participants in the schemes was 1:2645, but by 2012 it had more than tripled to 1:9692 (Zheng 2013). The social security system is thus overloaded.

Other challenges remain as negative legacies of the Hu and Wen period. These include the serious inequalities that still exist between rural and urban social security provisions; the rapidly ageing population and the pension fund deficit that threaten the sustainability of the pension system; migrant workers' social security coverage; and poor management of the social security system. Finally, the level of government spending on welfare and social security is still low. In 2012, according to the National Bureau of Statistics, total government spending on social security and employment was almost 1.3 trillion yuan, while the gross domestic product (GDP) for that year was 52 trillion yuan and total government spending was 13 trillion yuan. Thus spending on welfare equalled 2.4 per cent of GDP and 10 per cent of total government spending (National Bureau of Statistics 2013).

Although it is true that, as commonly argued, rising living standards have supported the CCP's development strategies, the important role that welfare and social security played in reducing opposition among those strategies' losers is often neglected. That role became more evident under Hu Jintao and Wen Jiabao, however, because these two leaders explicitly focused their efforts on promoting 'harmony' and social fairness by extending social security. With so many problems still evident, continued improvement of welfare and social security may now be critical to the CCP's survival as it seeks to reduce inequalities and the perceived discontent they generate by balancing the relative roles of state and market.

But what will be the priorities and approach of China's current leaders, Xi Jinping and Li Keqiang? They seem committed to some form of social justice with equalization of basic services, and it is likely that welfare and social security will continue to play an important role in reducing political opposition. In the Decision issued by the Third Plenum of the 18th CCP Central Committee, social security reform remained high on the policy agenda. The Decision stressed the need to 'establish a more equal and sustainable social security system', to realize nationwide coordination (*quanguo tongchou*) of basic pensions, to push forward the pension system reform of public servants and public sector workers, to integrate rural and urban social security schemes, to carry out policy research and policy-making on gradually delayed retirement, as well as to enhance the management of social security (Party Central Committee 2013). But while Xi and Li appear committed to social justice and the 'equalization' of basic services, they will have to tackle entrenched vested interests if they are to create a fairer and more equal society. While their efforts to reduce public sector privilege and develop sustainable social security for an ageing society are likely to be popular with the public, they are likely to meet strong opposition from within the elite that supports the party-state itself. To find a path through both popular and elite challenges to the party-state will take both courage and political skill.

ACKNOWLEDGEMENT

This work was supported by the United Kingdom's Economic and Social Research Council (grant numbers ES/J012629/1, ES/J012688/1). Information on how to access research materials is available at the project web pages: http://www.gla.ac.uk/schools/socialpolitical/research/sccr/research/.

NOTES

1. This work was supported by the United Kingdom's Economic and Social Research Council [grant numbers ES/J012629/1, ES/J012688/1]. Information on how to access research materials is available at the project web pages: http://www.gla.ac.uk/schools/socialpolitical/research/sccr/research/.
2. We focus here on work published in English. Research on social policy by scholars in mainland China has, since it appeared in the late 1980s, also tended to describe rather than explain, or has explained policies as rational responses to the problems of 'marketization' (see for example the work translated in Yang 2003).
3. Although 15 provinces were in deficit, the rest were in surplus, with Guangdong having the largest (40 billion yuan in 2010). However, because the funds were managed and operated at county level rather than at national level, surpluses could not be transferred to deficit regions.

PART III

POLITICAL ECONOMY AND SOCIAL CHANGE

15. Corruption and anti-corruption
Dali L. Yang and Yan Xu

Official corruption, defined as the exchange of official power for private gain through violation of laws and regulations, has been a serious socio-political issue in China. As it sought to displace the ruling Guomindang (GMD, or Nationalist Party), the Chinese Communist Party (CCP) and its friends such as Edgar Snow successfully attacked the GMD as largely dominated by four corrupt families. The attack chiselled away at the GMD's legitimacy and helped to win over supporters for the CCP as a clean and disciplined new political force seeking to liberate the people from domestic and foreign oppressors (Snow 1938; Tsou 1963).

As the CCP took over national power, Mao Zedong and his colleagues took aim at corruption and numerous other forms of what they considered to be political deviances, including launching the Great Proletarian Cultural Revolution, one of the goals of which was to combat those pursuing 'revisionism' and 'capitalism' (Wilson 1977).

Following Mao's death, China turned its attention from class struggle to economic construction, and corruption has grown alongside the economy. Public discontentment with corruption, then known as 'official profiteering', was an important factor fuelling the massive student demonstrations in 1989. Successive Chinese leaders from Deng Xiaoping to Jiang Zemin, Zhu Rongji, Hu Jintao and Xi Jinping have repeatedly emphasized that fighting against corruption is crucial to the survival of Communist Party rule.

With one-party rule, poorly compensated officialdom, limited press freedom and a weak legal framework, the CCP's efforts to contain corruption and achieve clean government have so far produced only limited success. In numerous public opinion surveys, the Chinese public have consistently ranked corruption as one of their top concerns. Such public dissatisfaction with corruption is a major threat to the legitimacy of the Party.

This chapter focuses on corruption and the Party's efforts to contain it. It will first show that corruption is not a new problem for the CCP but had received attention shortly after 1949. Subsequent campaigns against bureaucratism and official misconduct put huge pressure on cadres and reined in corruption. However, with China's opening up to the outside world and domestic market-oriented reforms since the 1980s, corruption has reached new heights in terms of form and scale. The next section will focus on anti-corruption work. Several agencies are involved in anti-corruption, but the CCP's Central Discipline Inspection Commission (CDIC) and local Discipline Inspection Committees (DICs) stand at the centre of the anti-corruption establishment, directly dealing with most cases and coordinating the work of other agencies. This chapter will then review the massive anti-corruption initiatives launched since Xi Jinping became the CCP's General Secretary and Wang Qishan the head of the CDIC in 2012.

CORRUPTION IN THE PRC: HISTORY AND REALITY

Corruption has been a major concern for Chinese leaders ever since the People's Republic of China was formed in 1949. Throughout human history, and repeatedly in Chinese dynastic history, spoils have gone to the victors. As the CCP took control of the country and entered cities, its political and military leaders, most of whom hailed from the countryside and had been fighting under spartan conditions in guerrilla areas for many years, faced enormous material temptations to enjoy the spoils of victory. Mao Zedong was acutely aware of this danger and the arrogance that was likely to arise as the Party achieved total victory. Therefore, before the CCP's leadership moved into Beijing, he famously warned against 'sugar-coated bullets' and called on Party members to maintain a thrifty and plain lifestyle.

Mao's worries were not unwarranted. Before long, local authorities started to report rising number of corruption cases. Prompted by these reports, Mao Zedong and his colleagues launched the Three-Anti Campaign in 1951. Aimed at combating graft, waste and bureaucratism, the Three-Anti Campaign was intended to bring discipline to officialdom and was one of many campaigns and movements that terrorized Chinese society in the Mao era. About 3.85 million cadres took part in the campaign and it soon went beyond acceptable limits as the participants needed to fulfil their quotas of corrupt cadres. Almost a third of those participating were found to have committed graft, although most cases involved insignificant sums and were exempted from punishment (Lü 2000). The two most well-known cases were those of Liu Qingshan and Zhang Zishan, two prefecture-level officials working in areas near Tianjin. Both survived torture in GMD prisons and had done important work for the CCP during the Civil War. They were found to have embezzled over 37 000 yuan of local funds, a huge sum at the time, and were executed with Mao's personal approval.[1] Mao clearly wanted to make an example of these cases. Apart from Liu and Zhang, 40 other officials were also given the death penalty and roughly 10 000 were put behind bars (Bo Yibo 1991).

With heavy-handed campaigns aimed not only at Party cadres and government employees but also at capitalists and landlords, corruption and bribery in the PRC was largely contained by the mid-1950s. Yet subsequent campaigns and mass movements continued to include elements designed to combat graft and bureaucratism (White 1989a). These campaigns included the 1957 Rectification Movement, the 1960 Three-Anti Campaign in rural areas[2] and the Four Clean-Ups Movement between 1963 and 1966. While the Cultural Revolution was much more complex, there was some element of anti-graft and anti-bureaucratism in it as well. Systemic examination of corruption during the Mao era is scarce, but declining disciplinary violations and crime rates suggest that corruption went down in the 1960s and early 1970s (Kwong 1997). Yet with the dysfunction of the Party apparatus including its disciplinary organs, and the lack of supervision of the rebels and the revolutionary committees, the real picture might be more complex. Taking large bribes might be rare, but anecdotal stories about officials' helping people to enter college or obtain scarce commodities in exchange for gifts were abundant. In an era of material shortages, the proliferation of personal exchange relationships was not surprising. Nonetheless, it was so pervasive that scholars who study China have tended to refer to Chinese society as one based on informal relations and the practice of *guanxi* or special relationships (Yang 1994).

Corruption in the Post-Mao Era

Magnitude and changing forms

It is widely acknowledged that corruption in China has increased rapidly following the start of economic reform and opening up in the late 1970s. Both the number of cases handled by the authorities and ordinary people's perceptions support this observation. Data released by the Ministry of Supervision, the DIC system and the Procuratorate show dramatic increases in the number of cases and amounts involved per case. The Corruption Perceptions Index (CPI), compiled by Transparency International using various surveys, also shows a declining trend (Table 15.1), with the CPI dropping from more than 5 in the first half of the 1990s to a nadir of 2.2 in 1992 (a score of 10 means corruption-free). Rampant corruption, particularly the alleged profiteering activities by 'princelings' (children of senior officials), raised public ire and was a major factor in rallying students to Tiananmen Square in 1989.

As the Chinese economy further diversified and the scale and scope of the Chinese reform programme have expanded, the incidence, forms and complexity of corruption have continued to evolve, partly in response to institutional reforms designed to improve governance and curb corruption, and partly in order to take advantage of new opportunities that have emerged.

The most obvious indicator of the severity of corruption is the total sums involved in corruption cases. He Zengke (2000), a senior researcher at the CCP's Compilation and Translation Bureau, notes that both the number of cases involving large sums and the ratio of senior officials exposed rose significantly. Wedeman (2004) concluded that corruption in China intensified and underwent a qualitative change in the 1990s. Guo Yong (2008) analysed about 600 corruption cases involving officials at county and division level or above and found that the average sum involved in a corruption case of provincial and

Table 15.1 China's Corruption Perceptions Index

Year	Score	Year	Score
1980–85	5.1	2004	3.4
1988–92	4.7	2005	3.2
1995	2.2	2006	3.3
1996	2.4	2007	3.5
1997	2.9	2008	3.6
1998	3.5	2009	3.6
1999	3.4	2010	3.5
2000	3.1	2011	3.6
2001	3.5	2012	3.9
2002	3.5	2013	4.0
2003	3.4	2014	3.6

Note: The score indicates the perceived level of corruption on a scale of 0–10, where 0 means highly corrupt and 10 means very clean. Transparency International started to use a 0–100 scale in 2012. The scores for 2012 and 2013 are transformed for consistency.

Source: Transparency International, available at http://www.transparency.org/research/cpi/.

ministerial officials ballooned from 17 000 yuan in the 1980s to more than 3 million yuan in the early 2000s. Today it is common to read about multi-million dollar cases in the Chinese media. In addition, the latency period of corruption – the period from the time when an official first commits a corrupt act to the time when the case is discovered – has lengthened.

The forms of corruption have also changed, as the Chinese economy and the amount of wealth have both grown enormously. While in the 1980s corrupt officials often engaged in graft by taking advantage of the price discrepancies that existed in the dual-price system, such opportunities had largely withered away by the mid-1990s as a result of the advent of buyers' markets for most products. Instead corruption migrated to other areas where regulatory power existed over scarce and valuable resources, such as stock listings, land sales, government-funded projects and procurements, and state or collective-owned assets that were being privatized (Sun 2004; Yang, Dali 2004).

Causes

To account for widespread corruption in transitional China, researchers have provided a wide variety of explanations. We review some of the major arguments here.

The overall policy of economic reform and opening up is perhaps the most important backdrop to the surge of corruption since the 1980s. Indeed, many view rising corruption as a direct but unintended consequence of reform, or more precisely, of the gradualist and imbalanced approach to reform (Gong 1994; He 2000; Pei 2006). As China made the transition from central planning to market economy, bureaucratic power remained entrenched and unchecked, leaving cadres with much discretionary power and huge opportunities for rent-seeking. In the words of Jean Oi, 'the reforms did not take power away from cadres so much as they merely redistributed power among cadres and modified the list of resources they control' (Oi 1989a: 226). This is evident in the real estate sector, where decentralization of the industry has increased the number of official players who can share the spoils of the booming housing market (Zhu 2012). In fact, the combination of a freer market environment and continued bureaucratic control especially at the local level meant that officials can easily find opportunities to enrich themselves and their families from the growing economic pie. More specifically, officials can: (1) make power-for-money deals using their power to intervene in market activities; (2) prey on public property by taking advantage of the adjustment of property rights in the transition period and their access to power and information; or (3) directly or through family relationships engage in business activities to take advantage of institution loopholes and lack of supervision.

Accompanying the era of reform is a profound shift in public values and social morality (White 1996). Prior to reform, officials were encouraged to lead a thrifty and even puritan lifestyle; otherwise they would be deemed as enjoying a 'capitalist' and 'corrupt' lifestyle. The reform made it a glorious thing to get rich and brought about dramatic increases in the standard of living as well as a transformation in social values. Hedonism replaced asceticism for many, and Chinese society has repeatedly been swept up in 'fevers' for material possessions of one kind or another. At the same time, the state's capacity for setting ideological and moral standards has declined (Sun 2004). All too often 'get-rich-quick' mentalities have taken over, and those with political clout are no exception.

Another explanation of rising corruption focuses on the institutional flaws that not only fail to contain corruption but may have even fostered it. On this account, the failure to rein in corruption is not so much because the CCP has become weaker, but because the institutional designs to combat corruption were so problematic that they have in fact sustained corruption. Melanie Manion (2004) provides an insightful comparison between Hong Kong and Mainland China. Hong Kong was once beset by serious corruption, especially widespread graft in the territory's police force. Following the escape of a corrupt senior police officer in 1973, the Hong Kong governor responded to the boiling public anger and created the Independent Commission against Corruption (ICAC) the following year. A major turning point was reached. The ICAC not only enjoyed the independence and resources to catch offenders, but also introduced reforms in government agencies to increase the cost of and reduce the opportunities for corruption. These efforts have made Hong Kong's civil service one of the cleanest in the world. In contrast, while the CCP revived the disciplinary agencies in the 1970s and 1980s, both the local DICs and procuratorates are in the thrall of the Party and are constrained by Party committees. This institutional configuration means that the DICs are incapable of independently supervising officials in their respective localities. The deficiencies of such a system will be further explored when we discuss recent reforms of the discipline inspection system that have been introduced since Wang Qishan became head of the CDIC in 2012.

Finally, researchers have focused on the inherent contradictions of Communist Party rule for corruption control. Xiaobo Lü (2000) argues that corruption among Communist cadres is not only a phenomenon of the post-Mao reform period. Rather, it is the result of a long process of what he calls organizational involution, in which the CCP gradually lost its ability to sustain officialdom with either the Leninist-cadre or the Weberian-bureaucratic mode of integration. Instead, the CCP has unintentionally created and sustained a set of neo-traditional ethos, mode of operation and authority relations among its cadres. Such neo-traditionalism has served to foster official corruption.

Consequences
Whereas earlier research, in particular Samuel Huntington (1968) and Joseph Nye (1967), suggested that some forms of corruption might facilitate development, today's researchers on China generally accept that corruption results in economic losses in the long run. Yet because they use different definitions of what constitutes corruption, and because of uncertainties with the data used, researchers have produced widely different estimates or 'guestimates' of the costs of corruption in China. Using data on kickbacks, entertainment expenditure by officials and illegal use of public funds, Minxin Pei (1999) estimated that corruption cost about 4 per cent of China's gross domestic product (GDP). In contrast, Hu Angang (2001) included into his consideration tax evasion, the underground economy and monopoly in highly regulated industries in reaching his conclusion that corruption cost between 13.2 per cent and 16.8 per cent of GDP in the late 1990s.

Regardless of the estimated welfare losses caused by corruption, it is perhaps more interesting that China has maintained high growth rates for more than three decades. This juxtaposition of rapid growth with corruption has prompted Yan Sun (1999, 2004) to argue that corruption is less destructive in China than elsewhere. For Sun, corruption in the early stages of the reform era might be characterized as more of the Huntingtonian development-enabling type: it turned political forces hostile to reform into participants, and enabled social forces otherwise excluded from power to 'buy their way in', thereby helping to propel reform forward. On Sun's account, corruption in the post-1992 period has tended to be primarily counterproductive and to become a bottleneck for reform. Wedeman (2012) also offers nuanced observations on the incidence and nature of corruption in China. He notes in particular that: (1) corruption in China only intensified after many growth-enhancing reforms had been put in place; and (2) much corruption in Chinese is linked to the commodification of undervalued resources (such as land and natural resources). He argues that these factors help to explain why China has enjoyed robust growth despite suffering from predatory forms of corruption commonly associated with economic decline or stagnation.

Corruption has also contributed to rising income inequality and social discontent, thus undermining the legitimacy of CCP's rule. Charges of corruption, such as those related to land acquisition, have frequently featured in protests and mass incidents. Corruption of state-owned enterprise managers was also an important cause of large-scale worker protests (Chen, F. 2000). During the student protests in the 1980s, fighting against corruption, especially corruption by the 'princelings', was a key demand made by the student protesters. Resentment against corruption has been particularly detrimental to CCP rule not only because of the sheer scale of corrupt behaviour but also thanks to the CCP's earlier appeal to class struggle, equality and clean government. Indeed, Maoist propaganda has contributed to the fact that accusations of official malfeasance have often been framed in class terms, the very concept that the CCP had relied upon (Perry 1999). Although many people may not have experienced corruption directly, and the government keeps a tight control over media coverage on corruption, 'grapevine' rumours can still allow the public to obtain information about venality and may have magnified public perception of how serious the problem is, thereby reducing people's trust in the CCP's rule (Zhu et al. 2013).

From a more positive perspective, the severity of corruption has acted as a catalyst for more efforts to contain it, such as improvement of the legal system (Hao 1999). Indeed, as corruption became more rampant, CCP leaders ratcheted up the intensity of anti-corruption work. While corruption has remained one of the leading public concerns in China, these efforts helped to bring China's Corruption Perception Index back in the 3 range, where it has stabilized. The next section will examine China's anti-corruption organizations and recent efforts.

ANTI-CORRUPTION

The Anti-Corruption Establishment

Anti-corruption in China involves multiple agencies, including the Central Discipline Inspection Commission (CDIC) and local discipline inspection committees (DICs), the procuratorates, the courts and the National Audit Office. The CDIC plays the central role in leading anti-corruption investigations, coordinating the work of relevant agencies, and conducting inspection work in the provinces, central ministries and key organizations. The Secretary of CDIC is simultaneously a member of the powerful Standing Committee of the CCP Central Ccommittee (CC) Politburo and can thus work closely with the top

Party leader. The CDIC and the local DICs have their own investigators and are empowered to detain suspected officials using extralegal procedures (Sapio 2008).

The Chinese government used to have its own supervision agency. When the central government was formed in 1949, it included a People's Supervision Committee that oversaw the conduct of government employees. The committee was renamed the Ministry of Supervision in 1954 and was merged into the CCP's Central Supervisory Commission in 1959. The Ministry of Supervision and local supervision bureaus were re-established in 1986 but were again incorporated into the Party's discipline inspection system in 1993. While the ministry retains its name, partly to make it easier for Chinese anti-corruption officials to engage in international exchanges through official government channels, all of the operating departments merged with those of the CDIC. In other words, the CDIC and the Ministry of Supervision became one institution with two nameplates. Following China's ratification of the United Nations Convention against Corruption, the government also established the National Bureau of Corruption Prevention in 2007, which is embedded in CDIC/Ministry of Supervision. The bureau's major duties include domestic coordination and international cooperation related to corruption prevention (Xinhua 2007).

The Supreme People's Procuratorate and the provincial and sub-provincial procuratorates include anti-corruption-and-bribery departments for handling corruption cases. They are responsible for formally investigating and prosecuting officials who have been investigated by the CDIC or local DICs. (For enforcement figures by the DICs and the procuratorates, see Table 15.2.) Legally speaking, confessions extracted by the CDIC or local DICs are not admissible in court, and thus prosecutors are often invited to join the CDIC investigations from early on so that the same evidence extracted during the CDIC investigations can also be counted as prosecutorial evidence to be presented in court. The procuratorates may launch their own investigations against graft but generally they tend to take over cases that have already gone through investigation by the discipline inspection commissions. Compared to those in the Party's discipline inspection committees, staff of the procuratorates tend to have had more formal education in law and are thus regarded as more professional in following legal procedures when handling corruption cases.

The courts are where corruption cases are tried and sentences meted out to culpable officials. In theory the procuratorates and the courts are independent of each other and of the DICs, but they all fall under Party leadership. Indeed, the police (public security), the procuratorates and the courts are all supervised by the Party's Political and Legal Affairs Commissions (PLCs). In the provinces and municipalities, the budgets for all these organizations are funded out of the provincial or municipal government budgets and are thus more easily susceptible to local influence. Since prior to the Beijing Summer Olympics of 2008, the Chinese authorities have increasingly prioritized the maintenance of stability under the rubric of harmonious society. As a result, police chiefs increasingly took over the leadership of the PLCs and they have tended to prize order at the expense of law, although the percentage of PLC secretaries that are concurrently provincial police chiefs has gone down more recently (Wang and Minzner 2015).

The National Audit Office and the audit offices in the localities have gradually developed capacities for conducting financial audits of government departments, state-owned

260   *Handbook of the politics of China*

Table 15.2   Key corruption-related figures since 1998

Year	Party members given disciplinary sanctions	Criminal cases of public employees filed by procuratorates*
1998	158 000	35 084
1999	132 447	38 382
2000	136 161**	45 113
2001	175 364	45 266
2002	N/A	43 258
2003	174 580***	43 490
2004	164 831***	43 757
2005	115 143***	41 447
2006	97 260	40 041
2007	N/A	40 752
2008	133 951	41 179
2009	138 708**	41 531
2010	146 517	44 085
2011	142 893	44 506
2012	160 718	47 338
2013	182 038	51 306

Notes:
*   Criminal cases of public employees (职务犯罪) include not only corruption cases such as embezzlement and bribe-taking but also malpractice and infringement which account for roughly 20 per cent of the total number. Data for 1998–2002 are in number of cases, the rest are in number of people.
**   From January to November.
***   From December of the previous year to that year's November.

Sources: Work reports and press conferences of CDIC and the Supreme People's Procuratorate of various years.

enterprises (including financial institutions), and social security funds (Yang, Dali 2004). Of particular interest are audits conducted at the time of the promotion or retirement of Party and government officials. Whether in conducting routine audits or in audits related to promotion and retirement, the audit offices may provide key information, especially on financial irregularities, to the discipline inspection commissions. Such audits have thus played an important role in uncovering corruption cases. The auditing of railway contractors, for example, led to the investigation and eventually downfall of the former Minister of Railways Liu Zhijun.[3]

The Evolution of the CCP's Disciplinary Organs

The CCP leadership, then led by Chen Duxiu, established a Central Supervisory Committee to oversee party discipline in 1927, when the CCP was still a small insurgent group facing suppression from the GMD and the warlords. Modelled on the Central Control Committee of the Communist Party of the former Soviet Union, the Central Supervisory Commission did not last long; in fact, its first Chairman was arrested and executed just months after being elected. A year later, the CCP leadership convened its Party Congress in Moscow and set up a Central Review Committee to supervise finance

Table 15.3   Leadership of CDIC since 1949

Period	Secretary	Concurrent positions
1949–55	Zhu De	Member of the Politburo and the Secretariat
1955–69*	Dong Biwu	Member of the Politburo
1978–87	Chen Yun	Member of the Politburo Standing Committee (PBSC)
1987–92	Qiao Shi	Member of the PBSC and the Secretariat, Secretary of Central Political and Legal Affairs Commission
1992–2002	Wei Jianxing	1992–97: member of the Politburo and the Secretariat; 1997–2002: member of the PBSC and the Secretariat
2002–07	Wu Guanzheng	Member of the PBSC
2007–12	He Guoqiang	Member of the PBSC
2012–	Wang Qishan	Member of the PBSC

Note: * The CDIC was renamed the Central Control Commission in 1955 and kept the name until it was formally abolished in 1969, although it ceased to function in 1967.

Source: CDIC website, available at http://www.ccdi.gov.cn/xxgk/lsyg/201308/t20130826_9195.html.

and accounting. Under war conditions, this Review Committee played a subsidiary role at best.

Shortly after it took national power in 1949, the CCP leadership established discipline inspection commissions extending from the central level down to the counties, with the mission of uncovering and imposing sanctions upon disciplinary violations in the Party. Initially led by Marshall Zhu De, the Central Discipline Inspection Commission (Table 15.3) worked directly under the CCP's Politburo, while the local discipline inspection committees were under the leadership of the respective Party committees. By the end of 1954, there were about 7200 full-time discipline inspection cadres nationwide. In 1955, following the Gao Gang–Rao Shushi affair, the CCP leadership decided to further enhance Party discipline and replaced the CDIC with a new Central Supervisory Commission to handle 'any cases of Party members violating party constitutions, party discipline and state laws and rules'.[4] By the end of 1956, the CSC system had 14000 staff members nationwide. In 1962, the purview of CSC was enlarged and the CSC dispatched permanent supervisory teams to ministries and commissions of the State Council. These teams were directly led by the CSC and the team leader could attend the party group or committee meeting of the ministry or commission.

As Mao and other CCP leaders unleashed waves of political campaigns in the 1950s and 1960s, the disciplinary inspection system and later the supervisory committees were also heavily engaged. They not only handled cases of cadre corruption but also dealt with those who were deemed to have gone astray politically in one way or another, depending on the prevailing political trend. Between 1950 and 1964, around 2.75 million Communist Party members received disciplinary sanctions. In the years 1952 and 1958, the number of those punished accounted for more than 3 per cent of the total party members, reflecting the intensity of those campaigns.

However, the CSC itself became a victim when the Cultural Revolution started in 1966. Many CSC officials, especially those who had worked in the organization *xitong* or in Northern China under Liu Shaoqi, were purged. As Mao became 'demigod', the CSC was abolished altogether in 1969. The Chinese Communist Party Constitutions of 1969 and 1973 omitted any reference to discipline inspection within the Communist Party.

Following the death of Mao, discipline inspection was again included in the Party Constitution adopted at the Eleventh Party Congress in 1977 and the Central Discipline Inspection Commission came into being at the historic Third Plenum of the 11th Central Committee held at the end of 1978. Veteran revolutionary Chen Yun, a Standing Committee member of the Politburo, became the Secretary of CDIC and he was joined by Deng Yingchao, widow of Zhou Enlai, and Hu Yaobang, a rising star who also headed the Party's Organization Department, as the second and third secretaries.

The CDIC was immediately a major player in the rehabilitation of the Communist Party. It led the investigation of Lin Biao as well as the radical Gang of Four and their associates. Together with the Central Organization Department headed by Hu Yaobang, the CDIC was involved in the rehabilitation of numerous Party veterans who had been purged and persecuted during the Cultural Revolution, including Liu Shaoqi who died in infamy in 1969. These efforts helped the CCP to recover from the ravages of the Mao era and contributed to the strategic shift from class struggle to economic development and reform.

Soon the CDIC shifted its attention to Party working methods and corruption. In 1982, it launched a major campaign against economic crimes including bribe-taking, embezzlement and smuggling in the coastal areas that were the vanguard for China's opening up to the outside world. Between 1982 and 1986, disciplinary sanctions were imposed upon more than 67 000 Party members and more than 25 000 were expelled from the Party. While ostensibly against corruption, the campaign allowed Chen Yun, a conservative leader who was famous for arguing that market forces must be kept bound 'like a bird in the cage', to slow down the pace of reform and opening up. Ren Zhongyi and Xiang Nan, the reform-minded Party secretaries of Guangdong and Fujian, were forced to make self-criticism to the CDIC for not doing their best to combat rising corruption (Vogel 2011). Premier Zhao Ziyang (2009) concluded in his memoir that the campaign was essentially against opening up.

The severity of corruption and the rising public sentiment against it exhibited during the 1989 demonstration pressed the CCP to treat the issue more seriously. Just a month after the crackdown at Tiananmen, the Party centre issued a decision that required several major state-owned companies – particularly Kanghua, where sons and daughters of Party leaders worked – ought to be closed and that spouses and sons and daughters should be prohibited from business activities.[5] In the post-Tiananmen years, corruption has remained highly visible on the political agenda of successive national leaders from Jiang Zemin to Hu Jintao and Xi Jinping. During the 1990s, the transition to the market for products and the divestiture of commercial businesses and operations owned by or affiliated with the People's Liberation Army, the Armed Police, judicial organs, and Party and government agencies helped to level the playing field for businesses of all types, and reduced the possibilities of corruption in these areas. Yet new opportunities quickly emerged in construction, banking, initial public offerings (IPOs), the regulation of resource industries and pharmaceuticals, as well as government procurement, land allocation and social security fund management. Personnel appointments, masterminded by the Party, have always been opaque and thus often open to the exchange of influence for personal gain.

With persistent public discontent about the scourge of corruption, the Chinese leadership has repeated vowed to crack down on corruption. By the 1990s, senior party leaders had recognized that they needed to combine anti-corruption campaigns with institutional reforms that reduced the incentives for officials to become corrupt in the first place.

The CDIC/Ministry of Supervision gradually enhanced its leadership and institutional capacity in dealing with corruption. In 1994, the discipline inspection system was authorized to detain and order those concerned to account for matters related to cases under investigation at a specific time and place. This extrajudicial measure, deployed by the Party's discipline inspection establishment against officials who are also Party members, is now known as *shuanggui* and has become a powerful tool for the discipline inspection system, although the legal basis of *shuanggui* as a form of extralegal detention is disputed (Sapio 2008). Moreover anti-graft laws were strengthened and real-name financial services were adopted to make it harder for corrupt individuals to hide their financial assets (Yang, Dali 2004).

The CDIC has also gained greater institutional clout over government ministries and localities. While CDIC/ Ministry of Supervision officials seconded to other government ministries and agencies were initially largely part of the host ministries and agencies, they are now required to report to the CDIC/Ministry of Supervision. The CDIC/Ministry of Supervision also introduced and institutionalized the use of roving inspection teams to monitor provincial leaders.

In 1998, the central leadership convened the Central Anti-Corruption Coordination Group, with Wei Jianxing, then a member of the PBSC and the Secretary of CDIC, as Chair and Luo Gan, Secretary of the Central Political and Legal Affairs Commission, as Deputy Chair.[6] The Director of the Central Organization Department was later included in the group so that officials in question can be transferred, suspended or removed in a timely fashion (Jiang Lai 2008). Such coordination groups allow the top leadership to steer anti-corruption work across a broad spectrum of agencies, including the police, the courts, the procuratorates and the audit office.

The reforms of the anti-corruption establishment have been accompanied by significant public management reforms. In addition to the divestiture of businesses operated by the armed forces, the armed police and other state institutions, the Chinese leadership downsized the size of government dramatically in 1998 and has undertaken various initiatives to rationalize the administrative approval regime. Local governments have set up one-stop government service centres and introduced competitive bidding, tendering and auctions in government procurement and the allocation of commercial land use rights. In addition, government financial audits have been strengthened in tandem with extensive government budget management reforms (Yang, Dali 2004).

THE ANTI-CORRUPTION STORM UNDER XI JINPING AND WANG QISHAN

Following the installation of Xi Jinping as Party General Secretary and Wang Qishan as CDIC Secretary in late 2012, Xi and Wang have made anti-corruption a top priority. In his first Politburo speech, Xi warned that the continuing spread of corruption would 'doom the Party and the state', and vowed to take serious measures (Wong 2012).

Led by Wang Qishan, a charismatic troubleshooter who had previously tackled troubled finances in Guangdong and the Severe Acute Respiratory Syndrome (SARS) outbreak in Beijing, the Xi–Wang anti-corruption crusade has drawn worldwide attention with the arrest or investigation of dozens of 'big tigers', officials ranked at the vice-ministerial level or above. The most prominent cases include:

- Bo Xilai: Politburo member and Chongqing Party Chief Bo Xilai was removed in advance of Xi's ascension to the position of General Secretary but Bo was put on trial in 2013 and sentenced to life in jail, partly for corruption.
- Zhou Yongkang: China's internal security czar between 2007 and 2012, a member of the Politburo Standing Committee (PBSC) and Secretary of the Central Political and Legal Affairs Commission, Zhou was put under formal investigation in mid-2014 and became the first member of the Politburo Standing Committee to have been investigated for corruption. Media reports have revealed a huge business empire built by Zhou Yongkang's son and relatives under Zhou's influence (Forsythe et al. 2014),[7] and in June 2015 Zhou was sentenced to life in prison for taking bribes, abuse of power and leaking state secrets. A significant number of Zhou's former secretaries and followers who had risen to high positions in the Ministry of Public Security, Sichuan province and the China National Petroleum Corporation (CNPC) have also been taken into custody for corruption.
- Xu Caihou: A former Vice-Chairman of the Central Military Commission and member of the Politburo, Xu became the highest-ranking military leader taken down for corruption. A large number of other corruption cases have also been uncovered in the military.
- Ling Jihua: Formerly a member of the Central Committee Secretariat and Director of the Central Committee (CC) General Office, Ling was the Chief of Staff of Hu Jintao. In 2012, Ling's son died in a mysterious car crash when driving a Ferrari (Ansfield 2012). Ling's efforts to cover up the accident sparked suspicions and investigations that ended with his eventual downfall in December 2014.

Besides catching these 'big whales' the Xi-Wang anti-corruption drive has also caged dozens of 'big tigers' in the provinces such as Sichuan, Shanxi, Jiangsu, Yunnan and Inner Mongolia as well as in the central government and major state-owned enterprises (see Table 15.4). The total number of cases filed by the national discipline inspection system surged from 137 859 in 2011 to 155 144 in 2012, and 172 532 in 2013 (Xinhua 2012a, 2013a, 2014a).

Yet the anti-corruption drive is part of a broader initiative to reshape Party style and strengthen discipline. Codified in 'eight stipulations' announced by the Politburo in December 2012, this initiative has imposed strict guidelines on how officials live (five-star hotels are generally off limits), meet, travel (no easy access to first class) and eat (no luxury dining, with dramatic declines in the consumption of shark fin soup) (Xinhua 2012b). The efforts to discipline the Party have been accompanied by initiatives led by Premier Li Keqiang to enhance government budget transparency and reduce the number of government approval requirements.

These efforts have touched upon every aspect of public life in China and made officials lose sleep. There are various reports of officials committing suicide to avoid disgrace and

Table 15.4 High-level officials investigated since the 18th Party Congress, as of December 2014

Name	Time of announcement	Positions held
Li Chuncheng	Dec 2012	Deputy Party Secretary of Sichuan, Alternate CC Member
Liu Tienan	May 2013	Deputy Director of National Development and Reform Commission, Director of National Energy Administration
Ni Fake	Jun 2013	Deputy Governor of Anhui
Guo Yongxiang	Jun 2013	Deputy Governor of Sichuan
Wang Suyi	Jul 2013	Member of Inner Mongolia Party Committee Standing Committee
Li Daqiu	Jul 2013	Vice-Chairman of CPPCC Guangxi Committee
Wang Yongchun	Aug 2013	Vice-General Manager of CNPC, Alternate CC Member
Li Hualin	Aug 2013	Vice-General Manager of CNPC
Jiang Jiemin	Sep 2013	Director of SASAC, General Manager of CNPC, CC Member
Ji Jianye	Oct 2013	Mayor of Nanjing
Liao Shaohua	Oct 2013	Member of Guizhou Party Committee Standing Committee
Chen Baihuai	Nov 2013	Vice-Chairman of CPPCC Hubei Committee
Guo Youming	Nov 2013	Deputy Governor of Hubei
Chen Anzhong	Dec 2013	Deputy Director of Jiangxi People's Congress
Tong Mingqian	Dec 2013	Vice-Chairman of CPPCC Hunan Committee
Li Dongsheng	Dec 2013	Vice-Minister of Public Security, CC Member
Yang Gang	Dec 2013	Deputy Director of General Administration of Quality Supervision, Inspection and Quarantine
Li Chongxi	Dec 2013	Chairman of CPPCC Sichuan Committee
Zhu Zuoli	Feb 2014	Vice-Chairman of CPPCC Shaanxi Committee
Jin Daoming	Feb 2014	Deputy Director of Shanxi People's Congress
Shen Peiping	Mar 2014	Deputy Governor of Yunnan
Xu Caihou	Mar 2014	Vice-Chairman of Central Military Commission, Member of the Politburo
Yao Mugen	Mar 2014	Deputy Governor of Jiangxi
Shen Weichen	Apr 2014	Party Group Secretary of China Association for Science and Technology, Member of CDIC
Song Lin	Apr 2014	Chairman of China Resources Group
Mao Xiaobing	Apr 2014	Member of Qinghai Party Committee Standing Committee
Tan Qiwei	May 2014	Deputy Director of Chongqing's People's Congress
Yang Baohua	May 2014	Vice Chairman of CPPCC Hunan Committee
Zhao Zhiyong	Jun 2014	Member of Jiangxi Party Committee Standing Committee
Su Rong	Jun 2014	Vice-Chairman of CPPCC
Du Shanxue	Jun 2014	Deputy Governor of Shanxi
Ling Zhengce	Jun 2014	Vice-Chairman of CPPCC Shanxi Committee
Wan Qingliang	Jun 2014	Member of Guangdong Party Committee Standing Committee, Alternate CC Member
Ji Wenlin	Jul 2014	Deputy Governor of Hainan
Tan Li	Jul 2014	Deputy Governor of Hainan
Han Xiancong	Jul 2014	Vice-Chairman of CPPCC Anhui Committee

Table 15.4 (continued)

Name	Time of announcement	Positions held
Wu Changshun	Jul 2014	Vice-Chairman of CPPCC Tianjin Committee
Chen Tiexin	Jul 2014	Vice-Chairman of CPPCC Liaoning Committee
Zhou Yongkang	Jul 2014	Member of Politburo Standing Committee, Secretary of Central Political and Legal Affairs Commission
Chen Chuanping	Aug 2014	Member of Shanxi Party Committee Standing Committee, Alternate CC Member
Nie Chunyu	Aug 2014	Member of Shanxi Party Committee Standing Committee
Bai Yun	Aug 2014	Member of Shanxi Party Committee Standing Committee
Ren Runhou	Aug 2014	Deputy Governor of Shanxi
Bai Enpei	Aug 2014	Party Secretary of Yunnan
Pan Yiyang	Sep 2014	Member of Inner Mongolia Party Committee Standing Committee, Alternate CC Member
Qin Yuhai	Sep 2014	Deputy Director of Henan People's Congress
Sun Zhaoxue	Sep 2014	General Manager of Aluminum Corporation of China
He Jiacheng	Oct 2014	Executive Vice-President of Chinese Academy of Governance
Zhao Shaolin	Oct 2014	Member of Jiangsu Party Committee Standing Committee
Liang Bin	Nov 2014	Member of Hebei Party Committee Standing Committee
Sui Fengfu	Nov 2014	Deputy Director of Heilongjiang's People's Congress
Zhu Mingguo	Nov 2014	Chairman of CPPCC Guangdong Committee, Alternate CC Member
Ling Jihua	Dec 2014	Member of the Secretariat, Director of the General Office, Vice-Chairman of CPPCC
Wang Min	Dec 2014	Member of Shandong Party Committee Standing Committee
Han Xuejian	Dec 2014	Member of Heilongjiang Party Committee Standing Committee
Sun Hongzhi	Dec 2014	Deputy Director of State Administration of Industry and Commerce

loss of assets. Indeed, even thieves are known to prey on the residences of officials on the assumption that these officials would be reluctant to report their loss of ill-gotten valuables and cash to the police (Xinhua 2014b). The harsh crackdown and the simultaneous tightening of cadre behaviour have also had a palpable impact on the economy and businesses. Luxury retailers and high-end restaurants and hotels have reported a sharp decline in sales, implying that officials are at least becoming more cautious, if not cleaner. Some economists have suggested that the newest anti-corruption campaign may have also contributed to the slowdown of the Chinese economy, because officials worry that initiating new projects might be perceived as seeking kickbacks.[8] The campaign has also implicated foreign companies operating in China, which are often seen as more law-abiding than Chinese firms. For example, pharmaceutical giant GlaxoSmithKline has been found bribing hospitals, doctors and industry associations in China in order to charge higher prices for its drugs and make more revenue. Chinese authorities arrested executives of Glaxo's China unit and fined the company 3 billion yuan (Bradsher and Buckley 2014). In addition, it seems the anti-corruption drive has encouraged the public to report corrupt officials. The number of reports received by CDIC surged to almost 2 million in 2013, a 45 per cent increase from the figure in 2011. Some of these reports contributed to the downfall of high-level officials. For example, prior to the investigation of Liu Tienan, former Director of the National Energy Administration, and Song Lin, former Chairman of the central state-owned China Resources Group, both were reported by real-name whistleblowers who provided information to the CDIC and posted evidence of corruption online.

Practitioners and scholars of corruption are agreed that corruption cannot be controlled using bursts of anti-corruption campaigns alone. Wang Qishan has repeatedly noted that the struggle against corruption will be long-term, complex and arduous. For him, the anti-corruption drive is needed to treat the symptoms of corruption in order to win time for a fundamental cure.[9] Such a cure requires the design and building of anti-corruption institutions that are both capable and effective (Manion 2004).

In its late 2013 Decision on various major issues in 'comprehensively deepening reforms' (hereafter: the Decision), the CCP Central Committee laid out key aspects of reforms to strengthen the supervision of power and curb the abuse of power (Xinhua 2013e). While emphasizing the need for greater transparency in Party and government work, the discipline inspection system led by Wang Qishan has significantly augmented its authority and capacity. In terms of leadership, organizational structure and interagency coordination, the CDIC has unquestionably become the most powerful in its history.

The institutional reforms in the CDIC are designed to curb centrifugal forces and strengthen central leadership and thus build on previous efforts going back to the Jiang Zemin era (Yang, Dali 2004). To begin with, in order to be able to handle the growing caseload, the CDIC under Wang Qishan has increased the number of discipline inspection and supervision offices from eight to 12, including one dedicated to anti-corruption work in central Party organs and three additional ones targeted at the provinces. It also established an organization department to assume the CDIC's increasing role in appointing provincial DIC secretaries (more on this below). The Foreign Affairs Bureau merged with the Corruption Prevention Office to form the International Cooperation Bureau that helps coordinate the work of pursuing officials that have fled overseas. To monitor anti-corruption officials, the CDIC also set up the Office for Supervision of Discipline Inspection Cadres, which is overseen by Zhao Hongzhu, the first-ranking Deputy Secretary of CDIC and a member of the CCP Secretariat (Figure 15.1).

The Decision emphasized the importance of top-down hierarchical leadership in the investigation of cases, noting in particular that cases at a particular level of the Party or government should primarily be led by the DIC at the superordinate level rather than by the DIC Secretary in the same locality. Moreover, the CDIC has drastically strengthened its involvement in the appointment of provincial-level DIC secretaries and deputy secretaries. In particular, the CDIC uses its power to directly appoint provincial-level DIC secretaries to curb local influence. Prior to 2005, most of the provincial DIC secretaries had worked in only one province, which means they were deeply connected with

```
                    ┌── General Office                    ┌── Discipline Inspection
                    │                                     │   and Supervision
                    │                                     │   Offices 1–12
                    ├── Organization
                    │   Department                        ├── Case Reviewing
                    │                                     │   Office
                    ├── Propaganda
                    │   Department                        ├── Office for Supervision
                    │                                     │   of Discipline
                    ├── Research Office                   │   Inspection Cadres
     CDIC ──────────┤                                     │
                    │                                     ├── International
                    ├── Laws and Regulations              │   Cooperation Bureau
                    │   Office
                    │                                     ├── Administrative
                    ├── Party/Government                  │   Affairs Office
                    │   Ethics Office
                    │                                     ├── Commission Party
                    ├── Petition Office                   │   Committee
                    │
                    └── Office for Central                └── Retired Cadres
                        Inspection Work                       Bureau
                        Leading Group
```

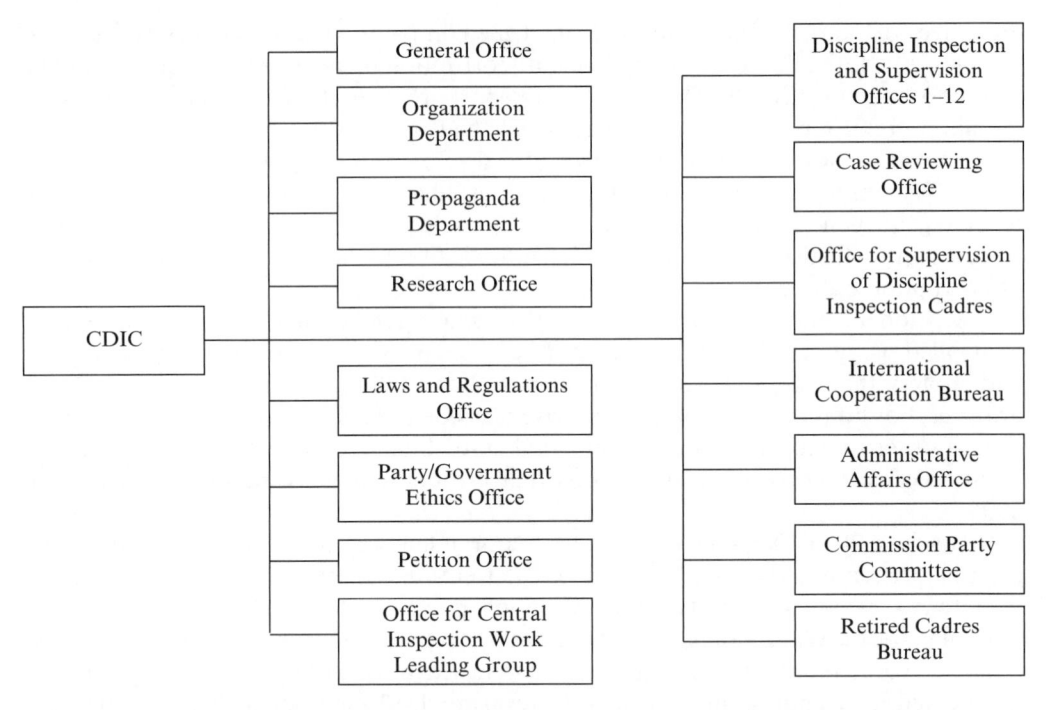

Note: Discipline Inspection and Supervision Offices 1–5 are responsible for disciplinary work in central party organs, State Council ministries, Central SOEs and other centrally affiliated institutions. Offices 6–12 are responsible for disciplinary work in provinces.

Source: CDIC website, available at http://www.ccdi.gov.cn/xxgk/zzjg/201403/t20140314_20114.html.

Figure 15.1 Organization chart of CDIC, as of September 2014

local interests and thus were more susceptible to local interference. By the end of 2013, over 80 per cent of provincial DIC secretaries had worked either in another province or in the Center before assuming their DIC position, enabling the CDIC to hold a tighter grip on provincial DICs (see Figure 15.2).

Furthermore, the CDIC has continued to strengthen its presence in central government ministries and Party departments. Prior to the reform, discipline inspection groups were primarily set up in government ministries, but not in Party departments such as the Central Organization Department or the Central Propaganda Department. The Decision requires that discipline inspection groups will be embedded in these central Party organs as well. The systematic and intense dispatch of roving inspection teams has especially attracted attention. In the first two years since the 18th Party Congress, the CCP sent out 46 inspection teams that covered all 31 provinces and multiple ministries, leading state-owned enterprises (SOEs) and major universities. These inspection teams are given heavier duties. Wang Qishan, who also heads the Central Inspection Work Leading Group, told team leaders that they could be held responsible if the team fails to find existing major problems or fails to report irregularities that have been found.[10] With stronger incentives, inspection teams are now more serious, and in

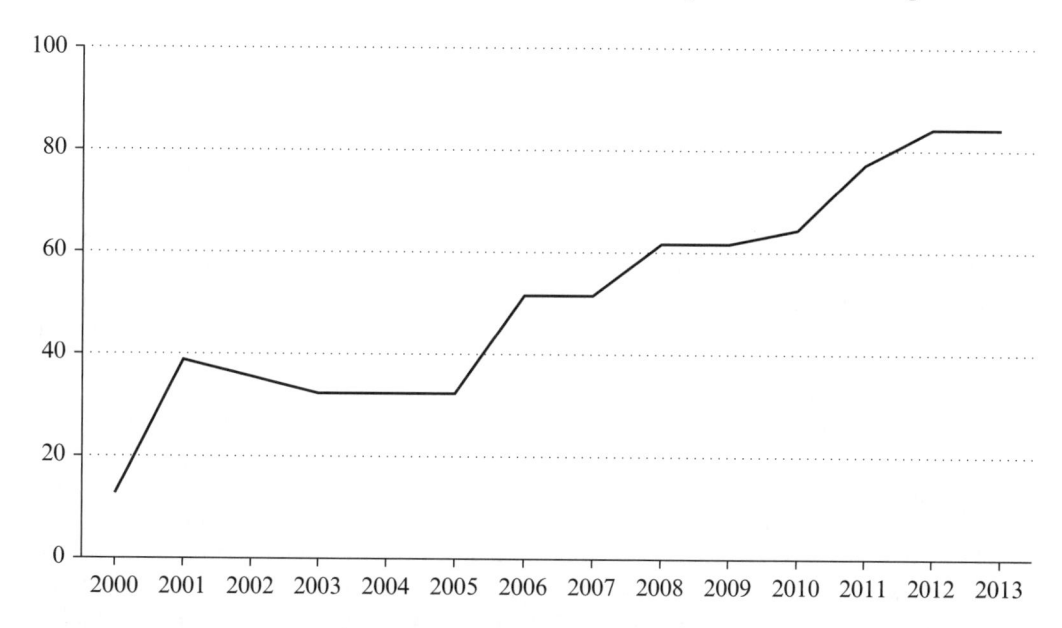

Figure 15.2 The percentage of provincial DIC Secretaries who started their careers outside their current provinces

several instances inspection was followed by investigation of high-level officials at the inspected units.

Finally the CDIC has increasingly made use of its authority for interagency coordination to strengthen anti-corruption work and launch new initiatives. Formerly, this often simply meant gathering information on bank accounts and property ownership from the relevant parties. In May 2014, the CDIC convened a meeting on pursuing fugitives overseas by bringing together representatives from the Supreme People's Court, the Supreme People's Procuratorate, the Ministry of Public Security, the Ministry of State Security, the Ministry of Foreign Affairs and the People's Bank of China. In July, the Ministry of Public Security announced Operation Fox Hunt 2014 to repatriate officials who have absconded (Wu Mengda and Chen Fei 2014). By September, the operation had brought back 88 suspects from over 40 countries, including 11 fugitives who had hidden for more than ten years (Zhang Yang 2014).

In addition, Wang Qishan and the anti-corruption leadership have sought to reconfigure the incentives for local leaders who have tended to prioritize the economy. Wang Qishan stated in early 2014 that the Party chiefs were to be responsible for building a clean government, and they would be held accountable if major corruption cases took place in their units.[11] For instance, in September 2014, the Party Secretary of Shanxi Province (Yuan Chunqing) was removed because several other top provincial officials were detained or arrested for corruption (Shang Huihui 2014). Changed incentives might induce local Party bosses to be less preoccupied with generating GDP, and to pay more attention to the conduct of cadres under their jurisdiction.

ANTI-CORRUPTION AND SUSTAINABILITY

Corruption is not a recent problem for the People's Republic of China and the CCP leadership, and like the GMD it displaced, the CCP has wrestled with corruption in one form or another ever since it took power. Since the late 1970s China has oriented itself to economic development and seen the introduction of profit incentives, while the system of governance has been characterized by a strong party-state presence and weak rule of law. This evolving hybrid system has proved to be fertile ground for corruption even while the Chinese leadership has launched waves of anti-corruption campaigns and efforts to improve public management. Judging by the scores for China's Corruption Perceptions Index, China has so far been able to tolerate a certain degree of corruption without derailing the official focus on economic development.

Since Xi Jinping became the top Chinese leader in late 2012, he and CDIC Secretary Wang Qishan have launched the most audacious anti-corruption crusade in the PRC's history, and have already brought about remarkable changes in how officials behave. Wang has also strengthened the anti-corruption institutions and made efforts to change local officials' incentives so that they focus more on clean government and less on growth. Nonetheless, it remains to be seen whether the anti-corruption efforts can be sustained over time, and whether the institutional reforms for anti-corruption will be matched by reforms in the legal system and in institutions for political accountability.

NOTES

1. In terms of the old currency, the absolute sum was 370 million, which was equivalent to 37 000 yuan.
2. The 'three antis' are anti-corruption, anti-waste and anti-bureaucratism. This campaign needs to be distinguished from the Three-Anti Campaign launched in 1951 and the New Three-Anti Campaign launched in 1953.
3. *Zhonghua renmin gongheguo shenjishu shenji jieguo gongbao* No. 30, 2013, available at http://www.audit.gov.cn/n1992130/n1992150/n1992500/3352942.html.
4. *Zhongguo gongchandang quanguo daibiaohuiyi guanyu chengli dangde zhongyang he difang jiancha weiyuanhui de jueyi* (Decision on Establishing CCP Supervisory Commissions), 31 March 1955, available at http://fanfu.people.com.cn/GB/143349/165093/165095/9888936.html.
5. *Zhonggong zhongyang guowuyuan guanyu jinqi zuojijian qunzhong guanxin de shide jueding* (CCP Central Committee and State Council Decision on Accomplishing a Few Things That the Masses Care For), 28 July 1989, available at http://dangshi.people.com.cn/GB/146570/198300/200214/200216/12449252.html.
6. See http://www.scopsr.gov.cn/zlzx/zlzxlsyg/201203/t20120323_35157_10.html.
7. And reports by Caixin, available at http://china.caixin.com/2014/zykaqjl/index.html.
8. See *The Economist* (2014) and Davis (2014).
9. Caixinwang, 'Wang Qishan: Dangqian fanfu yao yi zhibiao wei zhu wei zhiben yingde shijian' (Wang Qishan: The current anti-corruption should give priority to cure the symptoms to gain time for a fundamental cure), 25 January 2013, available at http://china.caixin.com/2013-01-25/100486367.html.
10. Zhong jiwei wangzhang (CDIC website), 'Zhang jun tan gaijin xunshi gongzuo, qianghua xunshi jiandi' (Zhang Jun speaks on improving inspection work and strengthening supervision through inspections), available at http://v.mos.gov.cn/zhibo03/index.shtml.
11. Wang Qishan (13 January 2014), 'Jujiao zhongxin renwu chuangxin tizhi jizhi shenru tuijin dang feng lianzheng jianshe he fan fubai douzheng – zai Zhongguo gongchandang di shiba jie zhongyang jilu jiancha weiyuanhui di sanci quanti huiyi shangde gongzuo baogao' (The central task of focusing innovative institutional mechanisms to further promote clean government and combat corruption – Report of the 3rd Plenum of the Central Discipline Inspection Committee to the Chinese Communist Party 18th Central Committee).

16. The class politics of the Chinese Communist Party
Yingjie Guo

Class politics was a centrepiece in the decades-long revolution of the Chinese Communist Party (CCP) and has had a major impact on the nature, constitution and direction of the Party and the People's Republic of China (PRC). The significance of the politics derives from the CCP's class identity and the centrality of class in its stated ideology. As defined in the constitutions of the CCP and the PRC, the former is 'the vanguard of the Chinese proletariat', and the latter, 'a socialist state under the people's democratic dictatorship (or proletarian dictatorship), led by the proletariat and based on the alliance of the workers and peasants'. This Party line on the class nature of the CCP and PRC has been consistently affirmed since the CCP was founded as a political party. In the post-Mao era, the Party's propaganda continues to insist on its class identity even after it abandoned class struggle in favour of economic development relying in part on capitalist modes of production together with capitalist forms of property ownership.

'Class politics' as used in this chapter comprises three overlapping subtypes or dimensions. The first is class-based political activities which are conducted through the agency of some classes in opposition to others and whose aim is to advance the interest of some classes at the expense of others. This notion encompasses 'class struggle' as it is commonly understood by CCP ideologues and social analysts in China. The second is the battle of ideas which is integral to class struggle insofar as every struggle between classes, as Stuart Hall (1981) observes, is always also one between cultural modalities, and winning the struggle of ideas is as important to class struggle as are economic and political struggles. The third is distinct from the second in that it revolves around the construction of class, class relations and class experience as social realities instead of centring on positive or negative evaluations of established classes. At the centre of this kind of class politics is the contestation over what constitutes classes, how they are related to each other, and what role they are believed to play in society.

This latter form of class politics deserves particular attention as social classes, like every other kind of social phenomena, cannot be conceived independently of the volition and representation of social agents (Althusser 1971). Indeed, classes are better seen as products of the very cognition and intellectual or political processes through which they are observed, classified, described and explained. The shifting significance of class, competing class schemes and constructed status orders, for example, are tied to paradigm shifts in representation and analysis in particular, and prevailing ideas, beliefs, values and practices in society in general, which are part and parcel of socio-political change as a whole. Important linkages thus emerge between class concepts, methodologies of class analysis and theoretical explanations of class structure, consciousness and action.

It is therefore imperative for analysts of class politics to bear in mind that '[a] large part of the chequered history of the concept of class has to be understood in terms of the changing concerns of those who have made use of the notion, concerns which reflect changing directions of emphasis within sociology itself' (Giddens 1977: 99). It is noteworthy too that descriptions and explanations of class, like every other kind of knowledge about the social world, are 'an act of construction implementing schemes of thought and expression', that between conditions of existence and practice or representations there intervenes the structuring activity of the agents (Bourdieu 1984: 467). The principal agents involved in this process, most notably political activists, social analysts and other participants, help to produce the meaning of their social world. Consequently, the overlapping and interrelatedness between the three types of class politics are only to be expected; the tripartite distinction in this chapter merely serves analytical purposes.

In fact, the CCP's class politics has not been confined to the advancement of class interests but also focused, during the greater part of its history, on examining individuals' attitudes, instilling the right consciousness in them, turning them into loyal followers of the Party and new Chinese with a socialist outlook, and mobilizing them for 'revolutionary' action (Guo, Yingjie 2008, 2013). That said, the significance of class in the CCP's political thinking and its commitment to class struggle have fluctuated over time in accordance with ideological swings and frequent shifts in political goals and priorities. The fluctuations are probably best seen from the alternating prominence of the aforesaid types of class politics in various historical periods, and the general patterns and definitive characteristics – if not the nuances – of the politics can be encapsulated in three explanatory models: the mobilizing model, the normative model and the symbolic model. The first predominated from the early 1920s to 1956, although the CCP continued to resort to it sporadically till 1978, especially during the Cultural Revolution; the second, between 1956 and 1978; and the third, in the post-Mao era.

Class politics in the first model is meant, first and foremost, to create a political and military force with the capacity to overthrow the party-state of the Kuomintang (KMT). The second is characterized by attempts to control the thinking and behaviour of CCP members and ordinary citizens. To this end, the Party employed a hegemonic discourse where a frontier was drawn between desirable and undesirable ideas, beliefs, values and practices, which were respectively labelled proletarian and bourgeois, Marxist and revisionist, progressive and reactionary, or revolutionary and counter-revolutionary. Class in the third model has little more than symbolic significance, whilst class politics centres on the construction of class and status in line with or in opposition to out-of-date class-based ideologies and attendant political symbols.

These dimensions of the Chinese Communists' class politics raise fundamental questions about both Marxian class theory and criticisms of the theory, especially their contrasting viewpoints about whether classes are social actors. From a Marxist perspective, classes are social forces capable of transforming human societies, and the struggle between the two 'great classes' of capitalist society – the proletariat and bourgeoisie – is the motive force of history propelling societies from capitalism to socialism and communism, whereas other classes, such as the peasantry, have insignificant or negligible roles to play in the process. By 'class' Marx meant a social category conceived on the basis of relations to the means of material production. He further made a distinction between 'class in itself' and 'class for itself', the difference being that the former is an objective grouping, and the latter is aware of its conditions, identity, interests and relations with other classes, and takes actions against class exploitation and domination.

Central to Marx's class theory is the unity of structure, consciousness and action, or the S–C–A chain. The logic of the theory is that (economic) class existence determines class consciousness and leads to class activism. But it is unclear how the S–C–A chain actually unfolds, how a 'class in itself' becomes a 'class for itself', and why economic structure inevitably determines consciousness and leads to action. That has prompted critics to accuse the theory of economic determinism and logical reductionism. Pahl (1989), for example, believes that the major weakness of Marxian class theory lies in its assumption of correspondence between social structure, group consciousness and group action. According to Hindess (1986, 1987), classes are not collective actors since the objectivity of class interests that are pursued by diverse actors in various sites of struggle cannot be confirmed either theoretically or empirically. Indeed, aside from the theoretical-ideological mediation of conceptions of class and class struggle, it is not hard to fathom the likelihood of disruption of the S–C–A chain and the linear transformation of societies by multiple intervening factors, such as human agency and historical contingencies.

The Chinese Communists' use of class casts doubt on the Marxian conception of class consciousness, class action and class struggle as something that inevitably arises from objective economic structures. It draws attention to the impact of political mobilization on the content and course of political action as well as on the contours and intensity of the political agents' consciousness. The question that arises as a result of due recognition of the role of political mobilization in the development of class consciousness is whether the latter can be thought to be a simple and even predominant effect of objective, economic causes such as relations to the means of production. These observations are applicable in varying degrees to every phase of the CCP's class politics from 1921 to 1978, but that time span is obviously too long to be covered in this chapter. What can be done here is to illustrate how the three models worked by focusing on critical moments in the CCP's history instead of trying to present a detailed overview. The section that follows will concentrate on the early years of the Party.

CLASS MOBILIZATION IN THE EARLY DAYS

The influence of Marxism and Soviet Communism on the class thinking of the early Chinese Communists was apparent. Among their first publications were the booklets entitled *Historical Materialism* and *Class Struggle*. They agreed early that the CCP to be founded in 1921 would be the vanguard of the Chinese proletariat and that their goal was the establishment of a proletarian dictatorship. Nonetheless, the top priority at the beginning of the Chinese Communist movement was to find a foothold and figure out how to proceed with political activism. For a long time, the Communists were divided over the goals of their movement and consequently over which classes to mobilize and how to mobilize them. Their leadership decided at its first national congress in 1921 that the Party's long-term goal was to take China into Communism, but its immediate goals – defeating imperialism and feudalism – were not clarified until the second and third national congresses (1922 and 1923).

These goals were later contextualized in and legitimated by a grand narrative of staged revolution, where the 'Chinese revolution' is divided into the 'bourgeois revolution' (1840–1949) and the 'socialist revolution' (post-1949). The former comprises two stages: the 'old democratic revolution' (1840–1919) and the 'new democratic revolution' (1919–49).

Each of the constructed revolutions is invariably represented as class struggles despite the chaotic socio-political situation in China and the complexity of mainstream Chinese politics over that long period. The 'old democratic revolution' is a struggle between the Chinese people under the leadership of the bourgeoisie on the one hand and feudalist classes and imperialists on the other, which aims to rid China of imperialism and feudalism and set up a bourgeoisie dictatorship. The 'new democratic revolution' is a struggle of the revolutionary classes under the leadership of the proletariat against imperialists, the comprador-bourgeoisie, bureaucratic capitalists and feudalists. Its objective is the transformation of relations of production under the domination of those classes and the rotting superstructure of Chinese society. The struggle between the working classes and the bourgeoisie constitutes the 'socialist revolution' that seeks to replace capitalism with socialism. As the articulated nature and goals of the revolutions differ, the CCP's mobilization strategies vary during each revolution.

It is safe to assert that in the early days of the Chinese Communist movement, the long-term goal was largely irrelevant except for discursive purposes, and that the goal allowed for enormous flexibility. And there is no evidence to suggest that the CCP was wholeheartedly committed to its short-term goal of defeating imperialism and feudalist warlordism. Though the 'feudalist class of landlords' was a consistent target of the Communists' political activity, the struggle against landlords and rich peasants was not simply meant to 'liberate' the poor peasants; it was also a mobilization strategy which enabled them to acquire the support of the vast majority of poor peasants and the capacity to bring down the party-state of the KMT. Unsurprisingly, 'the most important questions for the revolution' were which class was its primary force, which class was that force's chief ally, and which classes were 'our' friends and enemies (Mao 1991b). The answer of the majority of early Communist leaders was to mobilize the industrial workers ahead of the peasantry.[1]

Their answer was by no means based on the objective strength and class consciousness of the Chinese proletariat. This was compounded by the practical difficulty of separating industrial workers from peasants. In the CCP's early experience of mobilization in Anyuan, for instance, what was presented in Party historiography actually included both workers and peasants (Perry 2012). There was certainly much disagreement on the strength and class consciousness of the proletariat among the pioneers of the Chinese Communist movement, and the proletariat's readiness for revolution was the subject of a heated debate at the first national congress of the Party (He et al. 1986: 47). There was a strong view that the proletarian class was still in its infancy and that the CCP's priority was therefore to concentrate on educating them and enhancing their class consciousness so that they would join the revolution. But some leaders contended that it was a better idea to immediately start recruiting workers and increasing the number of workers loyal to the Party. At any rate, nobody suggested that the proletariat was ready to participate in, let alone lead, the revolution, and those on each side of the debate stressed the need for the CCP to educate the workers and enhance their consciousness.[2] In the end, the second view prevailed at the congress, although its final decision to focus on proletarian mobilization incorporated the emphasis on education and inculcation.[3] The emphasis was to be reiterated consistently in the CCP's thought work all the way till the end of the Mao era and beyond.

What had more bearing on the CCP's decision were no doubt Marxian assumptions about the superior revolutionary capacity of the proletariat in comparison with the peasantry and the leading role that Russia's industrial workers played in the October Revolution. The assumptions were arguably accountable for the Party line in the greater part of the 1920s that, although this class was small in number – totalling around 2 million in 1925 by Mao's estimation – it 'represented the new force of production in China' and was 'the most progressive class in modern and contemporary China' (Mao 1991a: 213). Its importance was said to derive from its concentration, low social status, the deprivation of its means of production, and its despair and suffering at the hands of imperialists, warlords and capitalists.

Hence, starting from 1920, the Communists set up a large number of trade unions and workers' clubs, and organized strikes in Shanghai, Guangzhou, Wuhan and numerous other major Chinese cities. Thirty-one trade unions had emerged by the end of the year in Guangzhou alone, and by early 1923, over 30 had been established in Hunan. Equally worth mentioning were the Communists' intensified efforts in launching magazines targeting proletarian readers and establishing evening schools for workers. The magazines and schools became critical media and forums for spreading Marxist ideas, educating the workers, enhancing their revolutionary consciousness and galvanizing them for action. Activities of agitation and education like these increased dramatically between 1920 and 1927, allowing the CCP to achieve unexpected development and expansion. This was accompanied by the rapid expansion of the CCP's military force, especially during the united front, thanks to the KMT's incredible tolerance.

It is now hard to ascertain the actual impact of Communist agitation and mobilization on the class consciousness and political activism among China's industrial workers in the 1920s, but the latter cannot simply be seen as an inevitable result of economic structures or objective class relations. Elizabeth Perry's (2012) detailed case study of the Communist mobilization in Anyuan, for example, finds that many workers, through participation in mass education, acquired an unprecedented appreciation of the economic importance and political potential of the proletariat and consequently transferred their loyalties from the local secret society to the workers' club. The case study also demonstrates that the workers' growing participation in schools, literacy and vocational training classes, reading rooms, libraries, consumer co-operatives, drama and lecture troupes and other grassroots organizations developed under Communist supervision was a concrete expression of the shift in collective identity. For this reason, explanations of the development of class consciousness among the Anyuan miners, and elsewhere, must take account of the CCP's agitation and mobilization. If class consciousness and action can be enhanced or fermented through agitation and mobilization by various social forces such as political parties, and if mobilization is indispensable to consciousness formation, it follows that economic structures are at best necessary conditions but not sufficient conditions for consciousness. If so, Marx's 'materialist' theorization of class struggle will not hold. By the same token, it is a fallacy for critics of Marxian class theory to assert that classes are not collective actors at all; whether they are or not depends on education and mobilization, among other things, as the CCP's experience suggests.

The CCP's pressing task of political mobilization and military expansion obviously favoured pragmatism instead of dogmatism. This can certainly be seen from the CCP's shift in focus from the cities to the countryside and from the proletariat to the peasantry, which represented a clear departure from orthodox Marxian class theory and the revolutionary practice of the Soviet Communist Party.[4] It ensued from the CCP's severe setback in 1927 as a result of the break-up of the KMT–CCP united front and Chiang Kai-shek's massacres of Communists, which caused considerable loss of personnel and made it difficult for the CCP to operate in the cities. It was more immediately related to the Party's unsuccessful military uprisings in urban and rural areas between 1927 and 1928. These setbacks forced the CCP to revise the prevailing view within the Party that the peasantry was not a progressive class representing the most advanced force of production; peasants were now represented as the most trustworthy ally of the proletariat.

Although small-scale and isolated attempts at mobilizing peasants had already started in the early 1920s, massive mobilization began only after 1927, following Stalin's speech at the executive committee of the Comintern in Moscow in November–December 1926 on the future of the Chinese revolution (Hao and Duan 1984: 90). Stalin stressed that the peasant question was the most urgent question for the revolution. In the months that followed, eminent Communists such as Li Daozhao, Zhou Enlai and Mao Zedong published articles to call attention to the urgent need for mobilizing the peasants. In his report on the peasants' movement in Hunan, Mao urged the CCP organizations to 'go all out to mobilize the masses' in rural areas, and reiterated that only by mobilizing the peasants without constraint and supporting their revolutionary action could the proletariat and its vanguard obtain leadership in the Chinese revolution, and only by doing so could the revolution succeed (Mao 1991a).

Education was once again a key component in the CCP's peasant mobilization when it began to accelerate in 1927. The CCP branches set up large numbers of peasants' study centres, as well as peasants' associations. However, of even more importance in the CCP's rural strategy was the establishment of bases which allowed the Party to maintain its troops after their withdrawal from the cities and to gain a stable power base. Reduction of rents and interest and land redistribution were placed squarely at the centre of its mobilization strategy to facilitate the development and expansion of the CCP-controlled bases. The strategies changed over time but it was a consistent practice to confiscate all or part of the land owned by major landowners and to give it to the poor peasants. The property of small landowners was not confiscated, but the interest they received from poor and middle peasants for money and land on loan was reduced. The rich peasants were allowed to keep their property so that they would not be alienated. Much attention was paid to the alliance between the poor and middle peasants, who were considered to be of pivotal importance to the success of the agrarian revolution. And businesses in the base areas were protected and investment was encouraged to ensure the supply of essential goods and economic growth, although businesspeople were discouraged from profiteering and providing high-interest loans to poor and middle peasants.

The objective of the CCP's agrarian revolution was simple: it was intended to win over the poor and middle peasants, who made up the overwhelming majority of the rural population, at the expense of a small number of landlords. With the participation and support of the majority of the peasants in the base areas secured, and resistance neutralized, the CCP was able to exercise *de facto* governmental authority over the areas under its control, obtain sufficient resources to support its political and military operations, and expand its army. In this process, financial and material resources were extracted from the landlords on a compulsory basis and from the poor and middle peasants on a voluntary basis. Human resources were also extracted from the poor peasants to expand the CCP's military force.

All in all, the mobilization of the peasantry was an essential link in the CCP's course of action and the key to its success. As Benjamin Schwartz (1951) observes, Communist victory in China could be understood only in terms of their leadership of a social revolution based on peasant discontent.[5] The most crucial link between the peasants' discontent and activism was the CCP's mobilization strategy, which empowered the peasants and gave them material and symbolic incentives for rallying behind the Communist forces while building up the CCP's capacity for extracting material and human resources for armed struggle. This strategy was employed again and again in the land reforms during the war against Japan and in the first years of the PRC, and was undoubtedly instrumental in achieving Communist victory and establishing a state socialist system in China.

NORMATIVE CLASS IN THE MAO ERA

Class struggle was reiterated sporadically between 1949 and 1978, although more so at times of leftist influence, and class mobilization remained useful for the party-state during this era, especially for leftist leaders of the CCP. Still, starting from 1949 and particularly after 1956, the meaning and significance of class and class struggle were beginning to change dramatically. Three views on class and class struggle in the Mao era can be found in the existing literature, as Stuart Schram (1984: 29–30) notes. The first suggests that, with the passing of years, Mao Zedong came to define class according to increasingly subjective criteria; until during the Cultural Revolution the quality of 'proletarian' was attributed only to those who were loyal to his person or had thoroughly mastered his thought. The second view contends that, with the turn to the left at the Tenth Plenum in September 1962, which was symbolized by the slogan 'Never forget the class struggle!', Mao moved back to a more objective definition of the protagonists in this struggle, stressing the harmful influence of the remnants of old exploiting classes. In the third view, in Mao's last years class struggle primarily meant for him the struggle against the 'new class' elements in the CCP.

Schram's dismissal (1984: 30) of all these views as one-sided to the extent of being largely misleading is rather heavy-handed, although some aspects of the views are indeed debatable. Especially disputable is his notion of subjective and objective criteria with reference to Mao's definitions of class. It is unclear whether he believes that Mao used subjective or objective criteria to identify classes under the new circumstances, or that Mao's class thinking focused on the subjectivities and objectivities of the existing or emerging classes. The primary question here is whether or not the exploiting and exploited classes identified before Liberation continued to constitute objective classes, or classes in themselves, after Liberation, following the socialist transformation of productive property. They were certainly not classes in themselves in the Marxian sense of the term; Mao's notions of class were largely ideological constructs which were neither exactly based upon Marxian conceptions nor substantively grounded in the PRC's class actualities.

But then Marx's conceptions of class and class struggle were developed on the basis of capitalist modes of production and productive relations and are therefore not applicable to class and struggle under the conditions of state socialism in the PRC. Mao and other CCP leaders had thus entered unchartered territories and had to 'cross the river by groping for pebbles' when handling questions of class. On the one hand, the CCP leadership had little reason to play down class struggle after it came to power in 1949, not least because its authority had not reached every part of China. The Party continued to insist on class struggle as a social reality, and the need to carry on the struggle, even after the completion of the 'land reform movement' (1950–53), the 'suppression of counter-revolutionaries' (1950–51) and 'the socialist transformation of the ownership of the means of production' (1953–56). On the other hand, China's reconstruction and economic development in the early years of the PRC made it necessary for the CCP not to engage in protracted, disruptive class warfare.

By 1956, all the classes that the CCP identified during the 'bourgeois revolution' with reference to their relations to the means of production had already ceased to exist as classes and been transformed into something else. The landlords and bourgeois classes, including the comprador-bourgeoisie, bureaucratic capitalists and national bourgeoisie, were no longer exploitative classes or classes per se for the simple reason that they had been deprived of their productive property, while many had been physically eliminated or jailed. The poor peasants owned land now, and the proletariat had turned from a propertyless class into the collective owners, at least nominally, of all the urban productive property of the PRC. Hence, the CCP declared at its eighth national congress in September 1956 that:

- the struggle between the proletariat and bourgeoisie had basically ended in the PRC;
- the exploiting classes had disappeared as classes in themselves in the PRC;
- the PRC had basically become a socialist system;
- the principal contradiction in the country was no longer between the proletariat and bourgeoisie, but between the people's aspirations for an advanced industry and the reality that China had a backward agrarian economy, and between the people's needs for rapid economic and cultural development and the failure of the current economic and cultural development to meet their needs; and
- the focus of the CCP's work was no longer the liberation of the force of production under old productive relations but the protection and advancement of the force of production under the new productive relations.

That was an unmistakable shift from class struggle to economic and cultural development, although the CCP added later that class struggle would continue for a long time, as the remnants of the old exploiting classes would linger on under socialism. Now that class struggle had 'basically come to an end' in China, that the principal contradictions in Chinese society were the contradictions among the people,[6] it was logical to conceive class struggle as a war of ideas, beliefs, values and practices. Certainly, the totalitarian party-state's 'social engineering' programme sought not only to fulfil its constitutional function as an instrument of class suppression but also to create a new status order in accordance with the stated goals of the Communist revolution and to redistribute economic, political, social and cultural resources amongst the designated classes (Parish 1984). All the same, class struggle no longer took the form of class antagonism; rather, the focus of class politics had shifted to the totalitarian control of Party members' and citizens' thought and behaviour. To this end, the party-state imposed class labels on its citizens and resorted to ideological indoctrination.

Hence, the party-state continued to classify Chinese citizens in terms of their source of economic support during the three years immediately preceding 1949, using labels which were originally assigned during the first years of Communist revolution (Watson 1984: 4; Unger 1984). This was in part to perpetuate the myth of class struggle and in part to mark the varying degrees of trustworthiness and differentiated need for surveillance. Citizens' classified categories combined *chengfen* (social role) and *chushen* (social origin). *Chushen* designated a person's status as determined by their early experience or their family's economic circumstances, while *chengfen* was defined as a person's most important background or occupational status before entering upon revolutionary work or being assigned to a job (Kuhn 1984: 28). The resulting *chengfen* categories in the rural areas included landless labourers, poor peasants, lower middle peasants, middle peasants, upper middle peasants, rich peasants, and landlords. City dwellers were classified as workers, staff, bogus staff, petit bourgeoisie, and so on. Those who were born after 1949 inherited these labels in the patriline from their fathers and grandfathers (Watson 1984: 4). Whilst most of the class labels were ascribed, a handful could be earned, although such cases were rare (Watson 1984; Unger 1984). It was possible, for example, for a son of a landlord who had distinguished himself during the revolutionary struggles against the Japanese and Kuomintang to receive the label of 'revolutionary cadre'. This practice lasted well into the 1980s, affecting millions of Chinese, although discrimination gradually eased in the reform era. Those who carried bad class labels, including many who had done no wrong at all, were singled out for mass criticism when leftist radicalism prevailed in the CCP and when class struggle was revitalized. They were also relegated to the bottom of the PRC's status order, deprived of a broad range of civil and political rights, and had less favourable life chances in terms of education, employment, promotion, career paths, social networking, marriage choice, and so on.

The CCP's ideological indoctrination of Party members and Chinese citizens was extended way beyond Marxism, Leninism and Mao Zedong Thought to include a broad range of normative ideas, beliefs, values and practices. The prescribed and condemned ideas, beliefs, values and practices were respectively ascribed to the 'good' and 'bad' classes and labelled proletarian and bourgeois or feudalist, Marxist and revisionist, progressive and reactionary, or revolutionary and counter-revolutionary. The frontier in the CCP's class discourse shifted as the Party's ideological pendulum swung left and right, and quite often it was not grounded in objective classes at all, so that class and class struggle became floating signifiers to be fixed arbitrarily in line with political imperatives of the day, or tropes to be manipulated for political purposes.

Just as those labels were produced artificially and applied arbitrarily, so were subjectivities identified and attributed to various classes without sociological analysis or empirical verification. Thus, the party-state constructed a proletarian value system consisting of Marxist, socialist, internationalist, patriotic and other progressive ideas, beliefs and norms of social and individual conduct. The values and norms were spelt out further in practice and divided into three components: consciousness, epistemology and behaviour (Zhang Weiping 1995: 870). The first comprised outlooks on humankind, happiness, life and death, suffering and pleasure, politics, religion, morality, glory and shame, beauty and ugliness, love and hate, marriage, family, and so forth. The second included judgements on self and others as well as on events and situations, analytical capacity, and cognitive and practical methodologies in general. The third referred to facial expressions, language and bodily dispositions.

In each and every case, the proletarian and the bourgeois or feudalist was clearly differentiated. Religious belief and superstition, for example, was labelled bourgeois or feudalist, while the proletarians were atheists. More concrete proletarian attributes included diligence at school, industriousness at work, discipline, collectivism, selflessness, frugality, modesty, the willingness and ability to bear hardships, and everything else that the party-state promoted; whereas laziness, individualism, selfishness, poor discipline, extravagance, wasteful habits, attention-seeking and pleasure-loving behaviours, and many other things that the party-state wished to discourage were described as bourgeois. Even different ways of talking, walking, eating, drinking and dressing were differentiated in class terms, as was most visibly demonstrated in posters, movies and the Peking operas. Those in the ranks of the proletariat who were guilty of bourgeois or feudalist ideas, beliefs, values and conduct were not seen as true proletarians and must be politically proletarianized through education and 'thought work'. The task of proletarianization was carried out through a combination of propaganda and regular group 'political study' sessions in the schools and work units, citizens' criticism of others and themselves at group meetings, and regular political performance reviews.

The pivotal role of the CCP's 'thought work' in the process is highlighted in its standard conceptualization by the Party. In a manual for conducting Party affairs, 'thought work' is described as the 'purposeful activity of classes and political groups which aims to exert ideological influence on people, transform their consciousness and guide their conduct', and the CCPs skilful 'thought work' is singled out as one of the most critical factors contributing to its success in its revolutionary struggle and socialist construction (Zhang Weiping 1995: 18, 869). What is most striking about it is not just its underlying assumption of the class categorization of various norms of thinking and behaving but also the conviction that the right norms must be instilled in the targeted subjects. The assumption and conviction do not conform to the Marxian notion that social existence determines social consciousness, that class consciousness and the superstructure of a society more broadly are reflections of economic class structures and the economic base. Indeed, CCP ideologues disagree with Marx and agree with Lenin that socialist consciousness does not arise naturally or inevitably from objective economic structures or class relations but must be induced externally (Zhang Weiping 1995: 72).

Not surprisingly, then, CCP theoreticians made little attempt to establish the unity of class structure, consciousness and action despite their avowal to adhere to Marxism; on the contrary, while the unity was assumed, consciousness and action were detached from structure or ignored altogether to allow the arbitrary labelling of classes. Neither the ascribed subjectivities of the reactionary classes nor that of the proletariat and peasantry was something to be sociologically discovered and verified; rather, these were largely products of the CCP's construction which was nothing but an act implementing its schemes of thought and expression. In other words, class was taken for granted rather than being treated as a problem to be analysed (Watson 1984: 2). A result of this was the creation of classes or class elements without the matching class consciousness, and class consciousness independent of class structures.

This discursive practice was advantageous to the CCP in that it enabled the Party to deal with class conditions and consciousness separately so that class membership could be manipulated in such a way that it functioned as an incentive structure, with individuals being rewarded and punished with membership in the 'good' and 'bad' classes on the basis of putative consciousness or 'political performance' alone.[7] Instead of locking individuals into classes so that members of the 'good' classes did not have to exert themselves, while the rest despaired of ever escaping from the 'bad' classes, the CCP made class membership elastic and flexible enough to allow for its manipulation. Furthermore, as ascribed class consciousness was unrelated to class structures, and as class struggle had been transformed into a battle of ideas, the Party was able to liberate itself from the shackles of objective economic structures and to have a free hand in its endeavour to create a new species of 'socialist' men and women who looked, talked, behaved and thought according to the party-state's prescribed norms, and to cleanse the new society of undesirable ideas, beliefs, values and practices. In this exercise, class struggle, as in the case of intra-Party politics, was employed as a trump card.

The battle of ascribed subjectivities was extended into the CCP as well, as was particularly the case during the 'socialist education campaign' and the Cultural Revolution. Not only was there a bourgeoisie in Chinese society, Mao reiterated repeatedly, but there was also a bourgeoisie or bureaucratic bourgeoisie in the Party, and the class struggle within the CCP was one between socialist and capitalist roads. As a matter of fact, however, what was called a class struggle was essentially a factional power struggle or line struggle over different courses of action in economic development. Party leaders who dissented from Mao's thinking were called capitalist roaders, representatives of the bourgeoisie, secret agents of the enemy classes or traitors, while their alternative developmental blueprints were labelled revisionist or capitalist. No verification was needed; accusations alone were sufficient for sealing their identity. This hegemonic discursive practice allowed Mao and his followers to trump their competitors and opponents in the Party more easily than would have been possible had the intra-Party conflict been treated as merely a matter of different opinions amongst fellow CCP members.

SYMBOLIC CLASS IN THE POST-MAO ERA

The 'reform and opening up' since 1978 can be simply characterized as the replacement of class struggle and 'continuous revolution' with economic development through partial marketization and privatization. This profound transformation has brought with it a different economic logic, different ways of distributing material and symbolic rewards to society, and a different political organizing principle. It has thus drastically altered the class map and status order of the PRC. Class has consequently taken on different meaning and significance; it has now become little more than a symbol. Not only is there no need to mobilize classes or regulate citizens' thinking and behaviour in accordance with normative standards articulated in class terms, but the mobilization of classes for class struggle is actually a bad thing so far as the Party is concerned.

The key notes of the social blueprint of Deng Xiaoping, Jiang Zemin, Hu Jintao and Xi Jinping, be it '*xiaokang* society' ('a prosperous society'), 'harmonious society' or 'Chinese Dream', are economic development, prosperity, high living standards, social harmony and people's happiness. Thus, class and conflictual social relations, as well as analytical methodologies that capture such relations, have little place in the party-state's scheme of things because they will undercut images of harmony or add to the challenge of building a prosperous and harmonious society or realizing its dreams. Still, class remains a political reality in the PRC due to its place in the CCP's ideology. The Party's allegiance to Marxism, albeit spurious, prevents it from openly rejecting Marx's class concept and class theory, and it remains important for the CCP to make believe that it has not betrayed its class base, which is central to its identity and *raison d'être*. In addition, the class structures, class composition, class relations and status order in Chinese society have changed dramatically over the last three decades, and these changes must be understood, explained and reconciled with the CCP's stated ideology.

An undeniable political reality is the class identity of the CCP and the PRC embedded in their constitutions as well as the class symbols in the national flag and state emblems. In official conceptions, the 'people' include the CCP, the proletariat, the peasantry, the petit bourgeoisie and the national bourgeoisie. These classes and the Party have been represented by the five stars in the national flag and state emblems. Yet, those state symbols are out of date, as they were introduced in the early 1950s. The national bourgeoisie ceased to exist in 1956 and the petit bourgeoisie has not been considered to be an existing category in official communications since the beginning of the reform era, after its mainstream, the intellectuals, was elevated into the working class. That notwithstanding, the symbols have been left unchanged despite the CCP's emphasis on political correctness. Its dilemma is that state symbols need to remain stable, while socio-political change is constant. The party-state therefore cannot update the symbols every time they become obsolete for fear of creating impressions of ideological-political instability and inconsistency. The fear becomes even more acute in light of entrenched perceptions in China that associate modifications of state symbols with the collapse of dynasties.

Hence, instead of revamping the national flag and emblems, the Party has chosen to obliterate their original symbolism and to give them a new meaning. The five stars are now said to stand for the CCP and the 'whole Chinese people': The class connotation of these symbols is thus erased and replaced by nationhood (Guo 2004). But the class identity of the CCP and PRC as defined by their constitutions cannot be erased as easily or unnoticeably; it is therefore downplayed and diluted through the introduction of Jiang Zemin's theory of 'three represents', which, through a sleight of hand, transforms the 'vanguard of the proletariat' into a national party representing advanced productive forces, the whole nation and advanced culture. Now that the advancement of productive forces has become its overriding objective, the CCP is freed from the shackles of socialist relations of production, or the basic principles of Chinese socialism, because productive forces, or the ability to use tools to act upon nature, define individuals' relations with nature instead of class relations and are therefore ideologically neutral. It is also able to sever its ideological bond with the working class. Non-socialist forms of ownership then become acceptable, and the new clarion call is 'to get rich is glorious', as advanced over three decades ago by Deng Xiaoping.

The transformation of the PRC's status order is most apparent in the declining status of the proletariat and peasantry. In the Mao era, they were the 'masters of the country' and constituted 'the regime's only, or surely, most legitimate, political actors' (Solinger 2004: 54–55). In the post-Mao era, they are 'masters of the country' in name only, but consumers with limited purchasing power in reality. Large sections of the working class have even joined the new poor and the underclass since losing their 'iron rice bowl' and becoming detached from the CCP's historical mission. In the eyes of the new poor among the workers and peasants, socialism and the leadership of the proletariat have become meaningless, except as a reminder of the CCP's ideological apostasy or as grounds for challenging the Party. They have good reason to hold the CCP responsible for maintaining the social contract and demanding that it live up to its own claims as articulated throughout the revolutionary era. After all, it was the Party which set in motion and presided over a reform that has taken away the job security and guaranteed social welfare of the industrial working class, and paved the way for the rise of propertied classes. Their best prospect is to move out of poverty and get rich; a route available, at best, to a small minority of workers. Unless they do so, their status in society will remain low, in contrast to the new masters of the country and the new historical subject in the 'socialist market economy'.

From the Party's perspective, it matters little whether the proletariat loses its status as the most progressive force in history; all the better that it no longer constitutes the mainstream – and future – of society. For the Party's new mission of wealth creation and the marketization of the economy requires efficient creators of wealth and consumers with ample purchasing power, rather than a revolutionary working class. The mission therefore entails a fundamental shift from a primary concern with the working class to the principal creators of wealth, namely those who own, finance or even monopolize the enterprises that produce and market goods and services, including, in particular, capitalist classes and well-off middle classes. The latter's growing prominence in society contrasts with the decline of the proletariat and peasantry and is indicative of a new status order that finds no parallel in Maoist China.

Equally dramatic as the changes in the PRC's status order is the transformation of its class map. As social and political commentators in the PRC agree, the destratified Chinese society before 1978, which in official descriptions comprised two classes (workers and peasants) and one stratum (intellectuals), has evolved into a much more complex structure as a result of over three decades of reform. But they are divided over how to analyse the emerging social structure and patterns of stratification, and over whether stratification is creating relations of conflict. The debate over terminology and approaches to social analysis has added a complex political dimension to the description of social groupings and structures, with descriptions entangled in webs of theories, paradigms and ideological positions as well as prescriptions for idealized social configurations (Guo, Yingjie 2008).

The party-state continues to stick to its traditional two-class scheme, although it has eliminated the stratum of intellectuals by promoting it into the working classes as part of its relaxation of ideological and political control over society and mobilization strategy. Whilst the CCP acknowledges the emergence of new social groups in the reform era, it does not treat these groups as classes separate from the working class, but as part of the latter or as transitional groups that do not belong to any existing class (Jiang 2001: 169). Even those who work with large volumes of capital and rank among the richest in the country and in the world are placed in the working class instead of being classified as exploiting classes. In this milieu, the CCP has thrown open its doors to private entrepreneurs and businesspeople and, indeed, prioritized their interests (Jiang 2001).

The CCP's current class scheme is not in the least convincing and it is refuted by many.

If the elimination of the old exploiting classes of landlords and capitalists meant the deprivation of their means of production, the possession of productive property in the reform era must have given rise to new exploiting classes. Indeed, classes, as defined with Marxian or other criteria, can be readily identified in China today. It is certainly possible to find a bourgeoisie with a considerable amount of productive property, a proletariat deprived of the means of production, and class exploitation and class antagonism. Such a class map is not something that the CCP wants to highlight or acknowledge, for it cannot be squared with the Party's claims about its adherence to Marxism or the socialist nature of the PRC. The Party can only deny the emergence of a bourgeoisie, for 'if a bourgeoisie has emerged, we must have gone astray' (Deng 1993b: 110–111).

The party-state's stated adherence to Marxism is one reason why most Chinese social scientists and commentators refrain from using the concept of class struggle and delving into social conflict in their analysis. Another reason is that they have carried on the 'farewell to revolution', a clarion call that rang loud amongst Chinese intellectuals in the late 1980s and early 1990s. The revolution they had in mind, above all, was the CCP-led violent class struggle which caused the loss of countless lives and suffering to millions of Chinese. The rejection of revolution was no doubt a rejection of Marxian class theory and has been translated into specific ways of reconceptualizing social structure and analysing social classes which break with Marxist approaches, so that it is no longer possible to conceive of society as comprising warring classes and of class struggle as the motor of history. Yet, despite animated debate about class and common rejection of Marxist class theory, few Chinese analysts go so far as to explicitly challenge officially endorsed class schemes.

Two approaches predominate in class analysis in the PRC, both of which are based on occupational structures and stay clear of class consciousness and class relations. One is the party-state's two-class framework, which many scholars employ as well (Guo 2008, 2013). It has two variants. The first takes all social strata to be constituent groups of the two existing classes; the second treats some strata as free-floating or transitional groupings which neither belong to the classes nor form separate classes. Either way, the identified categories are either dismissed or largely confined within the proletariat and peasantry and are therefore counted as members of the working class. Consequently, the constitutional polity of the PRC gains a measure of credibility and consistency, while social stratification, regardless of its scope and extent, can only be conceived to be intra-class stratification.

The other approach breaks up the two-class structure and rearranges all the identified groupings into a new hierarchy of strata. The approach is best exemplified by the work of Lu Xueyi and some 20 colleagues of his at the Chinese Academy of Social Sciences (CASS) (Lu et al. 2002, 2005, 2010). In an influential series of three volumes on social stratification, mobility and structure in Post-Mao China, Lu et al. divide China's 'occupied population', totalling 700 million, into ten occupational strata. These are: state and social administrators, managerial personnel, private entrepreneurs, professional and technical personnel, clerical personnel, individual-operated business proprietors, commercial and service personnel, industrial workers, agricultural labourers, and the unemployed and partially unemployed. In this scheme, occupation determines their group membership, whilst other causal components of life chances, such as income, education or political, economic and cultural capital, mainly affect the individuals' ranking within the groups and the groups' ranking in the overall hierarchy of strata. The identified strata are not 'classes' in a Marxian sense, but largely objective groupings devoid of subjectivities. The social reality that emerges from the analysis is one without conflicting class consciousness or antagonistic class relations. It is therefore consistent with the Party line and well attuned to the leitmotif in the post-Mao China of social harmony and political stability.

THE FUTURE OF CLASS

The evolution of class politics in the CCP's history is evidently characterized by flux and inconsistencies. The inconsistencies are no doubt attributable to the tension between the Party's instrumental use of class and its fluctuating faith in Marxism. On the one hand, it is clear that the Chinese Communists have drawn on Marxian class theory for theoretical-ideological guidance, and conceived and articulated their revolution within a Marxist and Leninist framework. It is equally clear, on the other hand, that the framework is broad and elastic enough to allow for a large measure of creative interpretation and flexibility, that the CCP's adherence to Marxism has often been tempered by pragmatism. The extent of the flexibility of the framework and the Party's creative interpretation is demonstrated by its dramatic shift from concentrating its political activity on the industrial workers to the peasants in its early days and from carrying out class struggle in the Mao era to embracing market capitalism in the post-Mao era. The shifts notwithstanding, the CCP denies it has departed from the framework or no longer believes in Marxism, proletarian dictatorship or the Leninist state as an instrument for the oppression of some classes by others.

What has been remarkably consistent throughout the CCP's history is its instrumental use of class. Its decision to prioritize the mobilization of industrial workers before 1927 had much to do with the influence of Marxian class theory and the Soviet Communists' successful revolutionary experience. The CCP was badly served by the influence not just because its mobilization was frustrated but more importantly because it proved unfeasible under the 'white terror' in the Chiang Kai-shek era. It was forced to overcome the influence and turn its attention to the mobilization of the peasants against orthodox Marxist wisdom. Indeed, political mobilization was a task of much greater importance than strict adherence to Marxism and it must be accomplished whether the means to do so conformed to its tenets or not. The instrumental use of class was even more apparent between 1956 and 1978, when the CCP's ascribed class qualities and attributes in this period were not objectively related to the actualities of class structures; nor were they the result of sociological investigation. What mattered to the CCP was not only the creation of a socialist party-state but also the transformation of Chinese citizens into loyal subjects.

While the CCP's mobilization strategy in the early days was consistent with the Party's goal of 'liberating the Chinese people', that goal was not just an end in itself but also a means to another end, namely the seizure of state power. Cynicism about either end is unnecessary as the two can be seen as mutually dependent rather than mutually exclusive. For the CCP must mobilize the peasantry in order to overthrow the KMT and replace its rule with its own, and it must seize power in order to liberate the Chinese people. Analogously, the normative use of class from 1956 to 1978 was consistent with the CCP's goal of building a socialist society together with a new generation of proletarian, socialist men and women. What was represented as proletarian or socialist subjectivities included everything that the Party wished to see in society, and the purpose of its 'thought work' was not so much the proletarianization of citizens as ideological-political control.

What was most striking about the CCP's instrumental use of class was that the right consciousness and actions were not just the criteria by which the progressive classes were defined, nor did these derive automatically from relations to the means of production, but they were to be created through education, indoctrination or coercion. In other words, the idea of inevitability underpinning the S–C–A chain in Marx's class theory was simply ignored. From the Party's point of view, whether classes were social actors and whether class subjectivities would inevitably arise from objective economic structures were irrelevant questions to ask. The Chinese Communists had neither the time nor the patience to wait for the proletariat and the peasantry to become classes for themselves spontaneously; instead, they set about creating class consciousness where it was missing and prompted action through education and mobilization. In this, they followed Lenin instead of Marx.

Not that Marx neglected the role of political parties in fermenting class consciousness and action. But his emphasis on the objectivity and inevitability of consciousness and action contrasted with Lenin's proposition that the right consciousness for class action can only stem from political mobilization. The contrast betrays the tension not only between Marx's theory of 'scientific socialism' and Lenin's theory of revolution, but also in the Marxian class theory. If political parties' agitation and mobilization have a decisive role to play in the progression of the S–C–A chain, the latter can hardly be construed to be inevitable, while the materialist conception of class and class struggle will become much less meaningful and incapable of grounding the Marxian class theory.

The fact that the CCP has abandoned class struggle and reduced class to a problematic symbol in the post-Mao era further illustrates the instrumentality of class in its political thinking. There can be no doubt at all that to renounce class struggle is to renounce the social scientific core of Marxism and the cornerstone of Marx's systematic account of socio-political change, for Marx's account of social progress from capitalism to socialism proceeds from the premise that the struggle between the warring classes of society is the motive force of history. Thus, faith in Marxism must include adherence to class struggle. As loyalty to Marxism remains one of the CCP's 'four cardinal principles', and given its need for ideological consistency, the Party is compelled to retain the dated class symbols which highlight the contradiction between the CCP's stated ideology and its daily practices, thereby undermining the credibility of the ideology and taking away its capacity to legitimize or guide the practices. The Party's way out of the dilemma is either to live up to its class-based ideology or to revise it.

NOTES

1. The resolution that the CCP adopted in Shanghai in July 1921 stated that 'The basic mission of this party is to establish industrial unions'. See All-China Federation of Trade Unions (1985: 1).
2. There is sufficient evidence to suggest that examples in CCP legend of pure proletarian awakening and activism in the 1920s are actually questionable. During the Anyuan Great Strike in September 1922, for instance, intellectuals, local gentry, government officials, military officers,

merchants, Red Gang 'dragon heads', church clergy and capitalists also contributed to its success. See Perry (2012: 71).
3. The CCP's founding resolution stressed the importance of workers' schools as an essential stage in the process of organizing industrial unions and made it clear that the main task of these schools was 'to raise workers' consciousness'. See All-China Federation of Trade Unions (1985: 2).
4. This is not to suggest that the CCP turned away from the industrial proletariat entirely or that the latter stopped playing an important role in the Communist revolution. As Perry (2012, especially Chapter 4) notes, politicized former Anyuan miners later played a central role in the transformation of the revolutions from a proletarian to a peasant movement. The most reliable troops in the Autumn Harvest Uprising of September 1927 were former workers from Anyuan.
5. Chalmers Johnson (1962) rejects Schwarz's view, arguing that the CCP's agrarian revolution had in fact failed in 1934, when the Communist forces went on the Long March; that Communist victory in China was due rather to their ability to harness spontaneous peasant nationalism, which asserted itself after the Japanese invasion; and that the strategy of utilizing peasant nationalism was neither in accordance with any principles nor was it the result of any consciousness formulations. It may be contended that Johnson overstates the role of peasant nationalism in the CCP's victory and does not recognize the incentive structure that the CCP created for the peasants through land reform.
6. Mao stated flatly in his speech on 27 September 1957, in line with the CCP's resolution at its eighth congress, that class struggle had basically come to an end. Mao did not state explicitly that contradictions among the people had replaced class struggles, but that is the conclusion that leading analysts of Mao's speech have drawn. See Su Shaozhi (1981: 8); Klaus (1982) and Schram (1984) agree with Su.
7. This practice in the CCP can be traced back to the late 1920s, when Mao Zedong put forward the view that an individual's objective class nature could be modified as a result of subjective transformation, brought about by ideological indoctrination or participation in revolutionary struggle. For discussions of this point see, for example, Stuart Schram (1981, 1984).

17. From Xianglin's Wife to the Iron Girls: the politics of gender representation
Wang Zheng

The six-decade history of the People's Republic of China (PRC) has witnessed drastic changes in gender discourses and practices. Contentions over gender norms and gendered power relations have intimately interconnected with political, economic, social and cultural changes, constituting a prominent realm of power struggles entangled with shifting class alignments and infused with ideologies vying for dominance. While the lives of women and men have been deeply implicated in such a realm of power that generates conflicting and contradictory gender prescriptions and regulations, its very pervasiveness poses challenges to analytical scrutiny. This chapter focuses on the politics of gender representation to narrow down the vast field of gendered power struggles in the PRC[1] while presenting a historical narrative with some coherence over grave historical ruptures in the past six or so decades.

Selecting two well-known signifiers of historically distinct gender discourses in the PRC, Xianglin's Wife and the Iron Girls, I trace the historical processes through which these gendered symbols were produced and investigate the changing political contexts within which their meanings were contested and altered. Examining multiple forms of artistic representation of Xianglin's Wife, a quintessential victim of 'feudal oppression' originally portrayed in a classic New Cultural literary text of the 1920s, I establish a tangible linkage between May Fourth feminism and socialist state feminism by identifying specific cultural producers and analysing their agendas. The heritage of May Fourth feminism in the socialist period has rarely been noticed in Chinese scholarship on the PRC, which reflects a reductionist tendency as well as gender bias in studies of socialist China.[2] Bringing Xianglin's Wife, which was a household name in the PRC, into analytical focus, this chapter examines gender politics in socialist feminist cultural transformation in the early PRC and presents a reinterpretation of the socialist period from a gender perspective.

While the symbolic meanings of Xianglin's Wife have remained more or less consistent, the drastic changes in the symbolic meanings of the Iron Girls offer a highly productive site for an exploration of historical ruptures in the short history of the PRC. The Iron Girls were not fictional figures but real young women who took on physically demanding work in either agriculture or heavy industry during socialist construction. This name was initially chosen by a brigade of adolescent girls in a model village of collective agriculture, Dazhai. The Iron Girls Brigade was emulated nationwide from the mid-1960s, when it was promoted by the socialist state, and then denounced soon after the end of the Cultural Revolution in 1976. Glorifying or demonizing Iron Girls epitomizes entangled ideological and political struggles in both the socialist and postsocialist periods. Delineating the complex contests behind contending representations of the Iron Girls allows me to probe the production of dominant discourses in changing political milieus. The Chinese elite's condemnation of this socialist symbol of working-class women emerged immediately after the Chinese Communist Party (CCP) decided to abandon the socialist planned economy and socialist equalitarian ideology, providing a revealing case of how class and gender power relations started to shift in the collaboration between the educated elite and the state.

Ultimately, my interrogation of the construction and deconstruction of Xianglin's Wife and the Iron Girls as cultural symbols illuminates the politics of post-socialist knowledge production through a double lens of gender and class. I argue that denigrating and erasing a socialist feminist history with a May Fourth feminist heritage premised on cultural transformation was an integral part in the production of a post- (and anti-) socialist hegemonic discourse that enabled China's dramatic turn to capitalism, a process marked by the naturalization, legitimation and reproduction of class and gender hierarchies.

XIANGLIN'S WIFE: TRANSMITTING A NEW CULTURE AGENDA

The emergence of Xianglin's Wife as a quintessential symbol of victims of feudal oppression in the dominant gender discourse of the socialist period has a complicated history. Xianglin's Wife is the protagonist in the short story, 'New Year's Sacrifice', written by the prominent May Fourth New Cultural writer Lu Xun (1886–1936) in 1924. A widow who ran away from her mother-in-law's scheme to sell her into a second marriage, Xianglin's Wife worked as a servant for a wealthy family before she was kidnapped by men sent by her mother-in-law. After resisting capture through a futile suicide attempt, Xianglin's Wife accepted the second marriage, even though it stigmatized her as an unchaste woman according to the gender norms of her time. After a few years of married life, new tragedy befell her: an illness killed her hardworking husband, and a wolf devoured her young son. She returned to her old master's home to resume her service, only to find that as an unchaste widow who had lost two husbands she was forbidden to serve food at the New Year's sacrifice. Even her devoted Buddhist practice could not cleanse her unclean soul. Driven to insanity, she became a homeless beggar and died in the street on a snowy New Year's Eve.

Lu Xun created the poignant fictional character as an indictment of the inhumane cultural norms and oppressive institutions that were seen as characteristic of Chinese society, a typical critique launched by a leading cultural rebel during the May Fourth New Cultural era (1915–1925). Victimized women and oppressive gender practices served as common literary tropes in New Culturalists' writings, becoming a hallmark of their feminist stance. Critiquing gender oppression under the 'old' Confucian culture was a major performative act constitutive of a 'new' identity of modern intellectuals for that generation's educated elite. Similar or even sharper feminist critiques of Chinese patriarchal culture had been articulated by a leading feminist, He-Ying Zhen, at the end of the Qing dynasty.[3] Now, with the New Culturalists' discursive power, critical feminist voices entered the mainstream discourse of the early Republic era. Denouncing a patriarchal gender system based on *nan/nü* (male/female) the differentiation between men and women, became a prominent theme in the elite's pursuit of modernity through most of the twentieth century. Xianglin's Wife, who was mired in 'traditional' cultural practices and social institutions, represented cultural radicals' burning desire to create a new culture in an ancient land.

Lu Xun's short story was first turned into a performance in 1946, when underground CCP members in Shanghai worked with left-oriented artists to stage an adaptation of 'New Year's Sacrifice' called *Xianglin's Wife* as a Yue opera, a form of opera that originated in Shengzhou, Zhejiang Province.[4] As a commemoration of the tenth anniversary of Lu Xun's death, the Yue opera *Xianglin's Wife* became a rallying point of left-wing artists in Shanghai when they were facing intense persecution from the ruling Nationalist Party. In the context of the political battles between the Nationalist Party and the Communist Party in the post-World War II period, the staging of the Yue opera *Xianglin's Wife* gained new political meanings of resisting Chiang Kai-shek's dictatorship and critiquing social ills under the reign of the Nationalist Party. In 1948 the Yue opera *Xianglin's Wife* appeared on the silver screen for the first time, indicating the success of its adaption of Lu Xun's famous short story.

After the PRC was founded, many adaptations of 'New Year's Sacrifice' were performed by local operas. The Yue opera *Xianglin's Wife* went through several revisions, gaining increasing popularity. Once the CCP was the state power holder, production of local operas based on Lu Xun's short story were no longer gestures of political protest. Rather, many leading CCP cultural producers were expressing their youthful New Culture visions with their newly acquired political authority and material resources in the socialist state. Among the cohort of CCP artists who had been baptized in the New Cultural movement, Xia Yan (1900–1995) played the most prominent role in continuing New Culture agenda and transmitting New Culture feminism via film production in socialist China.

A prolific essay writer, screen playwright and translator, Xia Yan had demonstrated his interest in feminism since the 1920s by contributing many essays to women's magazines and translating socialist feminist texts, including August Bebel's *Women and Socialism* (1879 [1910]). Before the Nationalist government's official ban on left-oriented books and authors in 1934, *Women and Socialism* had already gone through several printings. It soon became a foundational text for the development of socialist feminism of the CCP. In 1954, Xia Yan became the top official of the film industry of the PRC. His record as the underground CCP leader of a group that infiltrated the Shanghai film industry in the early 1930s made him well qualified for this position. He managed to continue writing scripts while leading the development of China's film industry. The first screen script he produced after he became the Deputy Minister of Culture was his adaptation of 'New Year's Sacrifice'. The decision to produce a feature film based on Lu Xun's short story was made to commemorate the twentieth anniversary of Lu Xun's death.

The first feature film in colour produced in China was an instant hit on its release in 1956. Directed by the talented Sang Hu (1916–2004), who had risen to fame before 1949, and with a top-ranked cast, the film won a special prize at the Karlovy Vary International Film Festival in Czechoslovakia in 1957 and a Silver Cap prize at the Mexico International Film Festival in 1958.[5] The wide circulation of the film made Xianglin's Wife a household name in the PRC. The high illiteracy rate in the 1950s made printed media an ineffective way of reaching the masses. But the general public could easily recognize an oppressed woman in feudal society, brilliantly portrayed by the famous movie star Bai Yang

(1920–96). Xia Yan's adaptations of 'New Year's Sacrifice' and other literary classics of the New Culture period provided a concrete link for the transmission of the New Culture heritage of feminist critiques of Chinese patriarchal culture into the public discourse of the PRC.

Making a cinematic adaptation of a New Culture classic in socialist China was not only a matter of artistic creativity. The changed historical context demanded reworking the New Culture text, which could alter its meanings. As a renowned New Culturist who had an intimate knowledge of Lu Xun and his works, as well as the historical and cultural context of his literary creativity, Xia Yan strove both to be faithful to the original story and to address the demands of the contemporary period. A prominent change in socialist cultural production was in the representation of women. In New Culturalist literary representations, the trope of women victims had been deployed to express modern elite men's condemnation of feudal culture. Now, with the participation of Communist women, socialist cultural production developed very different artistic representations of women. Upon the founding of the PRC, one of Xia Yan's predecessors, a dynamic feminist leader of the film industry, Chen Bo'er (1907–1951), had pioneered a paradigm of Communist heroines based on life stories to celebrate women's contribution to the Communist Revolution and the founding of the PRC. Full of agency and political consciousness, revolutionary heroines in socialist films were antithetical to Xianglin's Wife, a quintessential image of the abused and powerless woman who suffered under feudal oppression. The new paradigm was in accordance with the CCP's line in cultural production, articulated in Chairman Mao's Yan'an talk in 1942: that is, representing the workers, peasants and soldiers as major historical actors, although the general principle was ungendered in Mao's formulation. Devoting substantial state resources to the production of such a symbol of women's oppression as Xianglin's Wife was anomalous in that context. Some justifications were necessary even with the legitimacy lent by the film's commemoration of Lu Xun's death.

As the top official of the film industry, Xia Yan was keenly aware of the paradigm shift in visual representation. In fact, the whole film industry had recently emerged from a severe political crisis. Indeed, the first political campaign in the cultural realm was launched by Mao's critique of the film *The Life of Wu Xun*, based on a late Qing historical figure, which was released in 1950 in Shanghai when Xia Yan was in charge of cultural production in the city. Mao criticized Communist leaders for applauding a film that represented a supporter of feudal rulers instead of extolling the new class forces, new characters and new ideas that fought against the old socio-economic systems and political culture.[6] The critique of *The Life of Wu Xun* in 1951 had frozen film production for almost two years as confused cultural producers were frantically reviewing their own aesthetic standards and political positions in order to adjust to the demands of socialist cultural production (Wu 1993: 79–227). Although Xianglin's Wife was not a supporter of feudal rulers, but rather a victim of the feudal society, the theme had nothing to do with 'extolling new class forces' as Mao advocated. It required political courage for the new Deputy Minister to take on the task of making *New Year's Sacrifice* in 1955, the first adaptation of a modern literary classic in socialist film. Understanding the political context is crucial to our understanding of the changes Xia Yan made in his adaptation.

Three important changes are relevant to this discussion. First, the film presents an honest, kind and hardworking man as Xianglin's Wife's second husband, He Laoliu.

After Xianglin's Wife's suicide attempt failed at her wedding, she was touched by He Laoliu's kindness and gave up her resistance. In the original story, Xianglin's Wife hinted that her second husband took her by his superior physical strength, which led to her final submission. Xia Yan's explanation for the alteration was that he wanted to portray some 'sympathy and understanding between the poor'. Her momentary enjoyment of a good marital life, in Xia Yan's view, would contrast more sharply with her subsequent tragedy. Besides, Xia Yan revealed, 'I think it would be difficult to depict his "physical power" on screen. It could easily appear vulgar; and it would impair the character of an honest and kind hunter, He Laoliu' (Xia 1996: 712). The erasure of sexual violence committed by a poor man reveals not only Xia Yan's artistic taste but also his political astuteness. Xianglin's Wife could be presented as the victim of feudal systems, but not of the sexual violence of a proletarian man. Rather, socialist cultural representations should highlight the fundamental goodness of labouring people. Operating within the political parameters of the time, the film reduced the penetrating sharpness on the relationship between gender and class in Lu Xun's original story, but simultaneously advocated new ideals of marital relations.

The second major change was that Xia Yan added a dramatic act of resistance by Xianglin's Wife that was not in the original short story, to suggest this downtrodden woman's revolt against the oppressive institutions. In the film, after Xianglin's Wife had realized that donating her hard-earned money to the Buddhist temple did not help to wash away the stigma of marrying twice, she chopped the threshold of the temple with a knife in desperate indignation. This addition became highly controversial among film critics, who argued that such a rebellious action did not follow the logic of the protagonist's character and instead reflected the playwright's political considerations. The criticism implied that Xia Yan followed the rising paradigm in socialist cultural production that extolled oppressed classes' agency and rebellious spirit at the expense of realism. It certainly revealed some critics' belief that for a lowly woman like Xianglin's Wife, an expression of revolt was inconceivable. Answering this criticism in an essay published in the magazine *Chinese Films* in 1957, Xia Yan explained that the resistant act was not his invention. It had first appeared in the film of the Yue opera *Xianglin's Wife* in 1948, and then in many other local operas on stage as well. This evidence implicitly refuted the charge that he was conforming to the socialist principles of cultural production by adding the act of revolt. More significantly, he emphasized that when he had watched those operas, the scene of Xianglin's Wife's rebellion never failed to move him, which was why he decided to keep this scene in his film adaptation. He cited a passage from Lu Xun's original story depicting Xianglin's Wife's ferocious physical fight against her kidnappers that ended with her banging her head into the corner of a table in a suicide attempt, which he argued showed that Xianglin's Wife's rebellious character had been depicted in the original story. He contended that 'On the surface, Xianglin's Wife is obedient, timid, and believing in gods and ghosts. But these should never become the grounds for one to conclude that a timid soul would never have thoughts and commit actions of revolt' (Xia 1996: 711).

Xia Yan perceived correctly that at the heart of this debate was the question of whether an oppressed woman like Xianglin's Wife was capable of any expression of agency. He obviously differed from some of the male critics in his cohort. His prolific literary production consistently demonstrated his appreciation of strong female characters. In an essay on Chinese women written in 1944, he explicitly stated that from his early childhood on he had been attracted to heroines who violated gender norms in Chinese operas and literature, and was impatient with passive or conformist female characters (Xia 1996: 644). Although Xianglin's Wife's resistance to a second marriage could easily be interpreted as her thorough conformity to the gender norm of chastity, Xia Yan's decision to take it as an externally meek woman's expression of her strong character did not depart from Lu Xun's multifaceted depiction of Xianglin's Wife.

Still, Xianglin's Wife was not a revolutionary heroine, and the story certainly did not celebrate women's agency even with the addition of the act of revolt. What was the justification for the cinematic production of *New Year's Sacrifice* in socialist China? The third major change reveals some clues to the answer. Xia Yan added a voiceover by a male narrator at the beginning and end of the film, who was not the authorial 'I' in Lu Xun's story. When the opening scene of a rural mountain area unfolds, a male narrator's voice emerges: 'For the youth today, the story happened long, long ago. It was more than forty years ago, around the time of Xinhai Revolution, in a mountain village of east Zhejiang.' Explaining the story's historical context and location in plain language was Xia Yan's strategy to make the film accessible to the large audience who had not read the story, especially those who were illiterate. The second time the male narrator's voice emerges is when the final scene depicts Xianglin's Wife collapsing in the snow: 'A diligent and kind woman, Xianglin's Wife dropped dead after having endured numerous miseries and mistreatments. This happened over forty years ago. Yes, this was an event in the past. Fortunately, those times have finally passed and will never return.'

Conflating a literary fiction with a historical event, the narrator cum screenwriter presented a visual memory of what constituted the 'old' feudalist China to the younger generations who were thought to be ignorant of the gender and class oppressions of the past. But the conflation was inconsistent with Xia Yan's decision not to include Lu Xun, the writer, in the adapted film as the short story did. He decided to drop the first-person narrative structure in his film adaptation 'because if Mr Lu Xun appeared in the film, it would cause confusion between real people and events and fictionalized literature' (Xia 1996: 709). The tension in his representing Xianglin's Wife as simultaneously both fictional and real reveals the complex goals of this Communist artist who wanted to create an artistic film that had high educational value for the masses. Adding an upbeat voiceover to the film's tragic ending left ample room for interpretation.[7] Taking it at face value, we may say that the superfluous comment on the visual image was meant to remind the audience that the CCP was the liberator that ended the misery of Chinese women, thus lending legitimacy to the Party's rule. With the wide circulation of the film *New Year's Sacrifice*, Xianglin's Wife was solidly established in the public discourse as *the* symbol of women's oppression in 'the old feudal society' or 'before liberation', two common phrases demarcating the historical era before the CCP took state power in 1949. In this sense, we may say that Xia Yan made a major contribution to the hegemonic gender discourse in the Mao era that represented Chinese women as victims of a feudal society who were liberated by the CCP in 1949. As feminist scholars outside China have correctly argued, portraying Chinese women before 1949 as mere victims of feudal oppression erased women's agency as well as their crucial economic, social and cultural contributions throughout China's long and complex history.[8]

A rich and powerful literary text visualized by such sophisticated artists as Xia Yan and other filmmakers, however, necessarily contains multiple complex meanings. The film does more than inscribe a vivid image of an oppressed woman of the old feudal society in the public's mind. It illustrates in painstaking visual detail what the abstract term 'feudalism' meant, and in what specific ways and sites the oppression of labouring women was enacted. Indeed, the film could be read as a didactic visual text to teach the general public what institutions, social norms and power relations were feudalistic and were responsible for Xianglin's Wife's tragic life. Arousing emotive sympathy from the audience necessitates a rational rejection of all the inhumane institutions and practices so powerfully represented in the film.

The film's passionate indictment of feudalism, in fact, makes Xia Yan's Pollyanna-like declaration that all those inhumane practices had now entirely vanished sound highly disingenuous. To say the least, as a high official of the CCP, he would have an intimate knowledge of the ferocious patriarchal resistance to the implementation of the new Marriage Law drafted by state feminists and passed in 1950. In 1953, an investigation by the Ministry of Justice estimated that nationally, 70 000 to 80 000 women had 'been murdered or forced into suicide' annually since 1950 as a result of family problems and mistreatment.[9] Many women were persecuted and punished either by their husbands' families when they demanded a divorce or by their natal families when they resisted an arranged marriage. In the early 1950s, when a feminist marriage law profoundly shook the patriarchal society and exposed the persistent power of deeply entrenched patriarchal institutions, norms and practices, the decision to make a film of *New Year's Sacrifice* had more implications than simply commemorating Lu Xun. Fundamentally, it was a camouflaged attempt to continue the feminist agenda of anti-feudalism rather than a celebration of the CCP's supposed eradication of feudalism. The film introduced to the general public a highly gender-inflected definition of feudalism and confirmed the legitimacy of a feminist agenda of transforming a patriarchal culture in the PRC. The feminist significance of the symbol of Xianglin's Wife can be found in state feminists' frequent invocations of the term 'remnants of feudalism' in their speeches and publications when insisting on the necessity of a continuous struggle against misogynist and discriminatory gender practices in socialist China.[10]

The tremendous popularity of *New Year's Sacrifice* effectively exerted its discursive power to represent the oppression of labouring women as the Other of socialism. A poignant condemnation of a feudalist past was in this sense simultaneously a clear demarcation of what a socialist today was not – or should not be. Xianglin's Wife discursively delegitimized any ways in which the experiences of women under socialism resembled hers. The feminist implications of a transformative Xianglin's Wife cannot be recognized in the popular, yet crude concept of 'the Communist Party's propaganda' for understanding socialist cultural production. Assuming a monolithic entity called the Party that monopolized the cultural apparatus in the service of an authoritarian state, this stereotypical concept glosses over the complex political agendas of cultural producers while dismissing all efforts at cultural transformation, including those by socialist feminists. This re-examination of the political significance of socialists' reproduction of the New Culture movement's symbol of women's oppression in feudal society suggests complex dynamics in cultural representation. Now I turn to those dynamics as they shaped contentions over the symbol of women's liberation in socialist society, the Iron Girls.

THE IRON GIRLS: AN UNSTABLE SYMBOL OF CONTENTIOUS POLITICS

A glorified term widely disseminated in the official media from the mid-1960s to 1976, the 'Iron Girls' came to symbolize the masculinization of Chinese women by Maoist gender policies immediately after the CCP's Third Plenary of the Eleventh Congress in 1978, a political event that marked the end of Maoist socialist revolution. Responding to the CCP's call for ideological emancipation, Chinese intellectuals and artists began to voice their condemnation of the Cultural Revolution and the CCP's 'ultra-leftist line' with a proliferation of literature, films, artistic performances and polemical essays. In 1979 a comic dialogue performance entitled *The Iron Girls* gained instant popularity as it relentlessly mocked those young women who had excelled at physical labour and enjoyed prominent media attention until the end of the Cultural Revolution. Attacking a model of socialist womanhood that was promoted by the state powerfully demonstrated the spirit of ideological emancipation from the constraints of the Mao era. Signifying a dramatic shift in the public discourse of women's liberation, the comic dialogue ushered in a powerful backlash against the official gender ideology of equality between men and women in the socialist period, and advocated the replacement of so-called gender sameness with gender differentiation (Honig and Hershatter 1988: 23–31).[11] Gender again loomed large as a pivot at a major historical turning point.

Why did the Iron Girls become one of the first targets of post-Mao condemnations of the Cultural Revolution and the socialist state? A review of the rise of the Iron Girls illuminates the complex entanglement of gender, class, conflicting visions of Chinese modernity, and power politics in the PRC. The first Iron Girls Brigade appeared in Dazhai, Shanxi Province, in 1963 when the village suffered severe destruction by a flood (Sun and Liu 2008).[12] Twenty-three adolescent girls ranging in age between 13 and 16 formed a youth task force to join male villagers, old and young, in salvaging crops, rebuilding collapsed cave houses and restoring destroyed terraced farmland around the mountain village. On an exceptionally cold day when they were fixing the terraced land, their village head, Chen Yonggui (1915–86), told the girls to go home early. But the girls replied, 'Since the men do not go home, we will not go home, either. Why should we go back first?' Their strong determination and their remarkable ability to endure hardship won them a compliment from Chen Yonggui: 'You girls are made of iron!'[13] The praise circulated among the villagers, and the girls proudly named themselves the Iron Girls Brigade.

Long recognized as a local model village in socialist collectivized agriculture, Dazhai rose to national prominence in 1964 after the Shanxi provincial head reported to Chairman Mao on Dazhai's stunning accomplishments. Mao was deeply impressed with Dazhai farmers' self-reliance in transforming the poor mountainous village into a thriving collective community without material support from the state, as well as the remarkable leadership capacity of their illiterate leader, Chen Yonggui. Mao announced that developing agriculture should rely on the spirit of Dazhai, that is, self-reliance (Sun and Liu 2008: 127, 129). When Dazhai became the national model for agriculture, it was featured in national publicity. The stories of the Iron Girls Brigade played a prominent part in these depictions. The 17-year-old brigade leader Guo Fenglian instantly became a national celebrity, and photos of energetic adolescent girls engaging in various physically demanding farming tasks defined the phrase 'Iron Girls' in the public mind.

Official publicity praising rural women's extraordinary productivity had been a prominent theme since the early 1950s. Socialist state feminists played a pioneering role in using media to acknowledge rural women's contribution to socialist construction and to promote women's entrance in traditionally masculine spaces and occupations. Before the emergence of the term 'Iron Girls', women's task forces in rural collective agricultural work commonly adopted the names of legendary heroines who had excelled in the performance of male roles, mostly in military affairs, such as Hua Mulan and Mu Guiying. This practice was often reported by *Women of China*, a magazine run by the All-China Women's Federation.[14]

As Gail Hershatter's work on rural women in northern China during the 1950s demonstrates, poor women often had to take on tasks normally reserved for men when abled-bodied men were drafted in large numbers in times of war.[15] But, because traditional gender norms associated women's domestic seclusion with chastity, poor women who had to work in the fields were doubly degraded by the intertwined social hierarchies of class and gender. Across China's vast geographic area and its diverse ethnic cultures, the gender division of labour varied tremendously. But physical labour performed either by women or by men historically marked a lower class standing, especially among the majority Han Chinese.

Socialism transformed the meanings of women's involvement in agricultural work by glorifying their participation in collectivized agriculture, and rewarding those who demonstrated the capacity and skills to take on tasks that were locally defined as male. State endorsement and promotion combined the state's need for female labour in rural development with the socialist feminist vision of breaking down gender barriers and transforming gender hierarchies through women's full integration into all spheres of life. Mobilizing rural women's participation in agriculture was a key pillar of state policy, especially during the Great Leap Forward when many rural men moved into industrial work. As Hershatter emphasizes, rural women's labour continued to be an indispensable part of socialist construction through the Mao years, as well as the foundation of economic growth in the post-Mao era. In short, by 1963 rural women commonly took on strenuous physical labour without being stigmatized, and this important aspect of rural women's lives entered socialist cultural representation in a way that celebrated their agency as well as the value of their contribution.

Dazhai had historically been afflicted by wars, so there had been a persistent shortage of able-bodied men since the war of resistance against Japanese invasion. One of the Iron Girls, Jia Cunsuo, recalled:

> Why were the Iron Girls so famous? What happened to male youth? Historically Dazhai had a situation of a flourishing yin and a weak yang. It was all caused by history. Those whom the Japanese killed and drafted were all young men. After the liberation, those who joined the army or went out to work were also mainly male comrades . . . Therefore, female comrades in Dazhai seemed more prominent than male comrades. Actually, most male comrades left the village for employment outside. (Sun and Liu 2008: 89)

In this village women had long been playing the major role in farm labour as well as all kinds of economic activities in and outside the household.

The remarkable strength and tenacity that Dazhai women exhibited in performing physically demanding farm work made a vivid impression on county officials who had been required to work in the fields for one month each year during the 1950s. Zhao Mancang recalled leading a team of male county officials in 1959. They followed men in the fields for about ten days but then became physically unable to continue. So Chen Yonggui suggested that they move to work with women. 'Originally we thought working with women in the fields would be less strenuous,' Chao recalled:

> but actually women's labor was more intense ... Dazhai women had a particular habit while working in the fields. They did not talk and often went on without any break. So following women in the fields for one week was even worse than before. Some in our team had such severe bodily pains that they could not sleep at night. Our county judge did not even have the strength to hold his bowl after a day's work in the fields. He dropped his bowl in the canteen. (Sun and Liu 2008: 235)

Performing challenging physical labour in the fields was the norm for Dazhai women who were responsible for their family's survival in the poor mountainous area. Decades later, the leader of the Iron Girls Brigade, Guo Fenglian, recalled their goals at that time: 'To work hard to produce more grain so that we would be able to fill up our stomachs; and that would also be our contribution to socialism.'[16]

What made the Iron Girls special was the national attention bestowed upon them by the socialist state. In line with the socialist feminist goal of transforming gender and class hierarchies, Guo Fenglian was rapidly promoted, especially after the Cultural Revolution began. When the head of their village, Chen Yonggui, was promoted to be the Vice-Premier of the State Council, Guo succeeded him as the head of Dazhai in 1973 and then was placed on the county, provincial and national leading bodies. She was received by Chairman Mao three times and met Premier Zhou Enlai many more times. Letters of admiration from all over China flooded her home, and she had to ask her team members to join her in replying to each of them. Signifying the new, socialist identity as a rural woman who was no longer confined by her traditional kinship obligations or her lowly peasant social position, but defined by her superb contribution to collective agriculture and her excellent leadership capacity, the Iron Girl Guo Fenglian became a symbol of rural women's double liberation from gender and class constraints and the antithesis of Xianglin's Wife, the symbol of women's oppression in feudal society. Other groups of women, including those in industry, emulated the Iron Girls Brigade (Jin 2007),[17] consolidating the theme of challenging gender boundaries and transforming gender and class hierarchies that had been promoted by socialist state feminists since the founding of the PRC.

Gayatri Chakravorty Spivak, in her famous essay 'Can the Subaltern Speak?', delineates the power dynamics involved in 'muted women's' entry into the system of signification and suggests the many barriers that subaltern speech encounters (Spivak 1988). The representation of Chinese rural women in the socialist period also involved multiple power relations and heterogeneous agendas. While I do not claim that socialist representations of rural women conveyed the unmediated voices of subaltern subjects, I do contend that the positive representation of labouring women in the official media empowered women who had previously been absent from cultural representations of China's drive for modernity. The difference between the image of a female victim of feudal oppression like *Xianglin's Wife*, which stood as the Other of the modern, and the Iron Girls, who signified women's agency and prominent role in a socialist society, is significant. So is the fact that the story of *Xianglin's Wife* was written and rewritten by men to represent their desire to modernize Chinese society, while the Iron Girls inscribed rural women's bodies with socialist collectivism and socialist feminist ideology. The representation of the Iron Girls embodied new socialist feminist gender subjectivity in the pursuit of socialist modernity. The transformation in socialist cultural representation and gender practices is most visibly displayed by a juxtaposition of the two cultural symbols: Xianglin's Wife and the Iron Girls.

GENDER AND CLASS IN POST-SOCIALIST CRITIQUES OF SOCIALIST WOMEN'S LIBERATION

The post-socialist discursive shift from glorifying the Iron Girls as a model of working-class women's capability and strength to disparaging them as a disreputable symbol of women's masculinization is a visible manifestation of a profound political rupture. Yet in the name of condemning the Maoist 'ultra-leftist line', the attack on the Iron Girls conceals the intense contentions over gender and the class realignment that marked China after 1979. Seemingly initiated by intellectuals and artists on their own, the attack on the Iron Girls was nevertheless a response to political changes mandated by the Communist Party's Central Committee. Deng Xiaoping's call to 'thoroughly negate the Cultural Revolution' and abandon rural collectivization, including the flagship village of Dazhai, gave a green light to the expression of such gender sentiments against socialist feminist pursuits. At no time did the party condemn the Iron Girls, although Guo Fenglian was removed from all her leading positions in 1980 as an implementation of the 'thorough negation' of the Cultural Revolution and disappeared from the limelight for almost two decades.[18] The choice of a specific gendered target and the denunciation of women's masculinization were certainly creative works of the intellectuals of the post-Mao era. What motivated their particular discursive manoeuvres in that social-historical context?

The image of the Iron Girls aroused fear and anxiety in many urban elite men. As the man in the comic dialogue *The Iron Girls* declared, he would never dare to marry an Iron Girl because he would be afraid that she might flatten him with a random swing of her overdeveloped biceps (Honig and Hershatter 1988: 25).[19] Proclaiming their aversion, rather than attraction, to the strong women depicted in socialist visual and literary culture soon became a popular theme in urban men's writings. Literary men would proudly confess that while watching socialist films or reading socialist novels they had never been attracted to the revolutionary heroines who could perform extraordinary tasks but whose sexual appeal was downplayed. Instead, they found themselves attracted to the sexy female spies or other counter-revolutionaries, which made them feel uncomfortably guilty. One even claimed that being unable to openly express his attraction to sexy women, who were represented as reactionaries or degenerates, was a form of sexual repression by the socialist state (Hinton 2003).[20]

Historians Emily Honig and Gail Hershatter point out in their study of changing gender discourses during the 1980s that the backlash against the Iron Girls was partly 'man-made'. A group of male scholars attending a meeting on the status of women in

1986 declared themselves particularly revolted by the idea that women should be masculinized and become 'iron woman'. According to these male scholars, 'A woman who becomes masculine is a mutant. Capable women should be different from men. They have their own special charm, for example exquisiteness and depth of emotions, and well-developed imagistic thinking' (Honig and Hershatter 1988: 25). Urban educated men's heterosexual desire was not merely unfulfilled but seemingly threatened by prevailing images of strong women who could outperform men. Condemning the Iron Girls is thus only a sign of the entangled dynamics of sexual, gender and class politics set in motion by socialist revolution. In contrast with elite men's call for strong women 'with the character of men' in their pursuit of modernity at the turn of the twentieth century (Liu et al. 2013: 250), we may treat late-twentieth-century elite men's openly articulated fear of strong women as an index of historical change in which a critical mass of strong women emerged in the public realm rather than merely existing in men's fantasies about modern women.

Elite men's critique of socialism's masculinization of women went hand in hand with a widely circulated claim that men had been emasculated by the socialist state. Literary scholar Xueping Zhong, in her path-breaking study of Chinese elite men's representation of masculinity in the 1980s, analyses the myth of *yinsheng yangshuai*, that is, a widespread discursive construction of a 'women-are-too-strong-and-men-are-too-weak phenomenon' and identifies a male 'marginality complex' (Zhong 2000). In the 1980s, literary men's writings centred on their painful experience of 'castration' by the Maoist regime, which made intellectuals 'impotent' politically, economically and sexually (Zhong 2000). Male intellectuals' protest against a Maoist authoritarian political system was often charged with sexual imagery, and pursuing sexual potency became a major performative act in the effort to achieve a masculine identity. In fact, because the Maoist state monitored the sexual mores of citizens, taking on a sexual libertarian stance also indicated an avant-garde, anti-authoritarian and anti-socialist position. Elite men's newly found freedom of heterosexual expression was never free of gender ideologies, however. Absent any serious challenge or any critical framework to examine the nature of their assertion of masculinity and prescription for femininity, Chinese male intellectuals reproduced problematic gender discourses that had been rejected by Chinese feminists at the turn of the twentieth century. Ironically, with the mandate of dismantling Maoism in the name of moving China towards modernity, elite men's blatantly misogynist language and sexist proposals were justified as a progressive stance against the so-called ultra-leftist imposition of gender equality on the Chinese people by an authoritarian regime. Literary men's condemnation of the putative masculinization of Chinese women and assertion of a naturalized masculinity charged with sexual potency as righteous moves redressing the ills of the socialist state soon extended from the cultural realm to economic fields when a state-commanded market economy accelerated.

Starting in the 1980s, many male sociologists and economists engaged in concerted attacks on equal employment policies and promoted a restoration of gender differentiation (*nannü youbie*), which posits that women's roles as mother, wife and daughter are expressions of their 'natural femininity' (Meng 1986).[21] The double deployment of a key principle in Confucian social hierarchy – that is, gender differentiation, and a Western sexological notion of an essentialized 'femininity' translated into China in the early twentieth century – epitomizes the reactionary outlook of many male intellectuals in the late twentieth century. But these conservative and outdated gender ideologies were repackaged as bold challenges to an egalitarian socialist state ruled by the dictator Mao, gaining them an avant-garde status in 'ideological emancipation'. In an article published in the prestigious academic journal *Sociological Studies*, Zheng Yefu argued that contemporary China is falling far behind developed countries in terms of the level of a knowledge economy in determining power and productivity, as well as the level of social and material wealth. However, Chinese women's liberation surpassed all countries in the world in terms of women's equal employment and equal pay. Deploring this strange situation, Zheng offered a critique that condensed key elements in the backlash against socialist women's liberation:

> The immediate consequence of such an 'outpaced' (chaoqian) women's liberation that deploys administrative power is messed up family relations . . . We have failed to explore a new gender division of labor in family life because, through supporting the weak and suppressing the strong, a strong administrative power has interfered and destroyed the normal division of labor between the strong and the weak in family. It has even made the weak mistakenly think they are not weak, but made the strong lose confidence in themselves. Ultimately, it has deprived Chinese society of 'real men.' . . . A women's liberation promoted by politics has also made China lost its own females [*sic*]. (Zheng 1994: 112)

Zheng Yefu was among a large number of vociferous male intellectuals who expressed strong interest in reviving 'normal' gendered power relations that had been disrupted by socialism. Widely circulated arguments condemning gender equality include: 'equality of outcome should be the natural consequence of equality of opportunity and its realization should not rely on social movements' (Pan 1988); socialist women's liberation 'outpaced' the low level of productivity; because women's physical characteristics made them less adaptable to various job requirements, excessive employment of women reduced enterprise efficiency; the helping that women took from the socialist 'big rice pot' exceeded the value of the quantity and quality of their work (Chang 1988); the 'egalitarian' ideal of equality between men and women violated the law of value, thus it ought to be abandoned in the commodity economy; a new equality between men and women should not be expressed in rights and distribution but should be in the exchange of value between men and women; females could best express their values in the service sector, as secretaries and in public relations (Zhang Xiaosong 1988); the role of men was suppressed in exchange for a relative increase in women's status; for the sake of national development, Chinese women should learn from Japanese women to return home and sacrifice themselves for the nation.[22] Male elites' concerted demand to restore pre-socialist gender norms compelled a male sociologist, Pan Suiming, to give this explanation: 'Since 1980 the society has promoted a good-wife-and-virtuous-mother and harmonious family ideal because during the past thirty years, especially under the societal attack in the Cultural Revolution, Chinese men tenaciously guarded the family and protected women; now they request compensation from women' (Pan 1987).

Just as Xueping Zhong's analyses of novels written by men in the 1980s demonstrate that critiques of the authoritarian state were saturated by men's desires for a problematic imagined masculinity, condemnations of socialist equalitarian ideology and gender equality policies by male sociologists and economists were also unavoidably charged with their desires to restore elite men's gender and class privileges. Pan Suiming's self-aggrandizing claim for 'compensation' from women for men's gallant deeds under socialism presents a rare contradiction to the usual bemoaning of the loss of masculinity. That view was expressed unambiguously by Zheng Yefu, who used the US economist George Gilder's (1981) *Wealth and Poverty* to echo his own ultimate concern: 'In the welfare culture, money has become not something earned by men's hard work but a right to women offered by the state ... Nothing can be more damaging to men's value than increasingly recognizing that his wife and children could live better without him.' Resisting the 'damage' inflicted by a socialist welfare state legitimized a righteous condemnation of a draconian form of women's liberation that 'beat men back into the family to become "housewives" and drove women into society to become "strong persons," and eventually destroyed men's masculinity and women's tenderness, degenerating both into a "neutered" or "asexual" state' (Zheng 1994: 111). Restoring women to domesticity would not only improve productivity but, more importantly, guarantee the strengthening of masculinity.

The dominant masculinist sentiment unabashedly propagated since the 1980s advocates the revival of Confucian spatial gender differentiation: men should manage 'the outside' or public space, while women are in charge of 'the inside' domestic space. This end would be accomplished by removing women from gainful employment and sending them back to the kitchen. According to its advocates, the proposal to rearrange the gender order is not only crucial to restoring men's and women's innate human natures, but also promises to enhance China's potency in the world. 'Where are the Masculine Men', the theme song of a popular TV show *An Overview of Shanghai Husbands* written by a famous male playwright, Sha Yexin, in 1990, declared that taking on any household chores diminished Chinese men's masculinity. 'If a country has no masculine aspiration, how can it shake the world?' (Wang 1991: 17). Thus, the rise of China is premised on 're-feminizing' Chinese women whose 'natural femininity' was tragically destroyed by socialism. While none of these intellectuals had any concept of gender as an analytical category, their grand schemes of a powerful China were nevertheless imbued with gender ideologies. Professing similar nationalist sentiments, Chinese male elites at the end of the twentieth century rejected the vision of Chinese modernity with gender equality at its core, which their forefathers had advocated a century before. A new nationalist dream modelled after the superpower, the United States, was charged with a desire for a hypermasculine sexual and political potency, as well as for gender privileges as male elites eagerly immersed themselves in global capitalism. As an inconvenient symbol that signified the dismantling of both gender and class hierarchies, the Iron Girls acutely disturbed this elite masculine dream, so it was abandoned together with an equalitarian social and economic system permeated by socialist feminist practices.

Perplexingly, some urban women intellectuals also condemned the Iron Girls and Chinese women's masculinization, although their critique of socialist women's liberation was not a wholesale negation. Urban educated women in the late twentieth century generally insisted that Chinese women were more socially advanced than women in Western capitalist countries and admitted that they were the beneficiaries of socialist gender equality policies.[23] Their critiques centred on the measurement of women's liberation against male standards, as the often-quoted saying of Mao illustrates: 'The times are different now. Whatever male comrades can do, female comrades can do, too.' As these women saw it, socialist gender equality was defined as gender sameness to the extent that women's 'natural femininity' was suppressed. As a consequence, women were no longer feminine, but became desexualized and neutered. Moreover, what injured delicate female bodies was not only the double burden of paid labour and household chores but also the demanding – and demeaning – physical labour required of women as epitomized in the campaigns promoting emulation of the Iron Girls.

A popular short story by a woman writer, Zhang Xinxin, entitled 'Where Did I Miss You?' and published in 1981, depicts an urban educated woman's painful realization of her 'masculinization' through the eyes of the man she loved but failed to attract. In this story of complex and contradictory meanings, the author unambiguously attributed her process of 'masculinization' to her social experience of shouldering multiple responsibilities and performing physically demanding work in a rural village. Contrary to Pan Suiming's claim that men gallantly protected women, Zhang deplores the lack of 'strong men'. Alluding to her experience of being sent down to a mountain village during the Cultural Revolution, Zhang gave these vivid flashbacks as the protagonist reviewed her 'masculinizing process':

> She carries water on the tortuous path by the mountain cliffs, and a little imbalance would spill the water into yellow dirt without any trace . . .
> She carries a gunnysack over fifty kilos heavy toward a stack, moving up step by step with all her efforts, with her teeth set . . .
> In a decade when one was most attentive to one's appearance she only had a few blue clothes to change; and worrying about growing increasingly busty, she deliberately folded her shoulders. (Zhang Xinxin 1981)

If Guo Fenglian and her team members were reading these memories in 1981, they would recognize them as a realistic description of their daily hard work and poverty during the 1960s. Guo Fenglian even did not have decent clothes without patches in 1965 when Premier Zhou Enlai made the first visit to Dazhai. She had to borrow a new blouse from her friend in order to host the national leader. These Iron Girls might also agree with Zhang's description of the sexual norm at the time, which reflected a traditional notion of women's chastity that demanded concealing both women's bodies and their expressions of sexuality. But they would not imagine the cultural meanings Zhang gave to these realistic 'flashbacks', although their meanings and implications would nonetheless be instantly recognizable to urban educated women.

Literary scholar Li Xiaojiang articulates the significance in such literary representations:

> The image of masculinized women often appears in contemporary women writers' works. They do not eulogize it, but express their secret anguish. On the one hand they interrogate the tendency toward women's masculinization; and on the other hand they imply condemnation of the ultra-leftist ideologies and an era of no-females. (Li 1988: 32)

Here we discern a criticism shared by women and men writers of the supposed 'ultra-leftist masculinization of women'. In strikingly similar language to that used by Zheng Yefu, Li follows Zhang's argument to critique the 'damage done to a whole generation of women' in a 'twisted era'. The similarity stops there, however. The damage to women was not to their sense of value, like the damage to men's self-esteem in Zheng Yefu's portrayal. Rather, it was that 'women experienced their adolescence without youth, and experienced a hardened life without pursuing beauty and without experiencing tenderness. Now the loss of youth and emotional life was imbedded in their deep psychological structures, affecting their courtship, marriage and even family life' (Li 1988: 103).

Educated women's critique of socialist women's liberation, interpreted as 'native women's voices', has gained wide circulation among feminist scholars outside China, especially among those in the field of China studies, since the 1990s. Feminist academics in the US were making conscious efforts to deconstruct Euro-centric or US-centred knowledge production, paying special attentions to the voices of 'Third World women'. Informed by post-colonialist critiques, this well-intentioned feminist agenda overlooked the specific historical context within which women's 'native' voices were articulated and the locally situated power relations in knowledge production in the so-called Third World. With neither a critical awareness of the historical context in which the Chinese elite produced knowledge, nor a critical framework to delineate the intense class reconfiguration going on in China's historical turn from socialism to capitalism, a feminist respect for what were imagined as native voices from the Third World led to an uncritical facilitation of the global circulation of urban educated women's critiques implicated in masculinist discursive manoeuvres. The thesis that women have been masculinized by a state-led strategy for women's liberation that adopted male standards became an accepted truth both inside and outside China, constituting a major theme in the public memory of socialism. English-language scholarship on women in China often adopted problematic terms such as 'gender erasure' and 'the masculinization of Chinese women' to define the effects of socialist gender policies, rather than treating them as signs of discursive manoeuvres that emerged in an era of intensely contested power relations between and among gender and class that needed to be unpacked and interrogated.[24]

What was the historical context within which some urban women literary scholars and novelists embraced the notion of masculinization? On what grounds can I claim that these concepts were an urban elite's discursive construction? The original Iron Girls, Guo Fenglian and her team members, have never used the term 'masculinization' to describe the effects of their heavy manual labour. In fact, agriculture in China has long been feminized, in the sense that women have constituted the major labour force, beginning with the Great Leap Forward and continuing into the twenty-first century as large numbers of able-bodied rural men have migrated to cities or joined the military. Women shouldering physical labour in the fields as well as domestic toil has long been a norm of Chinese rural society in the PRC. Their physical labour has been associated with their earning capacity (earning more or fewer work points in the era of collectivization, or producing more or fewer agricultural commodities in the recent era of privatization and marketization), and hence an important factor contributing to their family's financial status, rather than their gender identity.[25] Rural women and men have never worried that women would be masculinized by performing physical labour, even though they have increasingly taken on previously male tasks out of sheer necessity in a changing economic environment.

Indeed, the evidence shows that rural women have continued to express their pride in being able to do 'whatever men can do', in total unawareness of the urban elites' discourse of masculinization. A 1995 feminist intervention project in Yunnan distributed digital cameras to village women so that they could take photographs of scenes and subjects that interested them. The resulting photo album powerfully conveys Yunnan rural women's demanding physical work in both agricultural production and domestic reproduction. Most agricultural tasks women performed in this region demand great physical strength but are obviously regarded as women's normal work. The captions of several photos specifically note that now women can do things that previously only men were allowed to do, such as fishing, threshing grain and driving an ox cart. There is no trace of worrying about being masculinized, but full recognition of rural women's hardship, endurance and tremendous contribution to the rural economy and family livelihoods (Ou 1995). The outcry against women's masculinization by taking on men's jobs definitely was not shared by, or even transmitted to, millions of rural and urban Iron Girls.

Even more revealingly, urban elite women and men have not expressed any concern about rural women's 'masculinization' during the accelerated feminization of agriculture in recent decades, with the privatization of rural economy and out-migration of rural men. The silence on rural women's burdensome responsibilities in a privatized economy contrasts sharply with the outcry against the 'masculinization of women' by the socialist state policy of gender equality in the 1980s. This odd contrast has two possible explanations. First, the intensity of rural women's physical labour may never have been the concern of those urban elite who worried about women's masculinization, so there is no contradiction in their current silence. Second, the thesis of the masculinization of women was situated in the political context of anti-socialism, and the decisively changed political and economic milieu in twenty-first century China had eliminated the motivation to continue this discursive device. In any case, the 1980s discourse protesting against the masculinization of Chinese women should be situated and interpreted in relation to early debates regarding gender and class relations in the elite pursuit of modernity.

Chinese women's bodies have always been a focal point of elites' contention at moments of drastic social change. From the late Qing reformers' agitation against footbinding, the early Republic-era feminists' endorsement of physical education as a way to strengthen women's bodies, the 1930s feminists' and nationalists' advocacy of robust beauty, to the PRC socialist state feminists' promotion of strong, heroic women that culminated in the celebration of the Iron Girls in the mid-1960s, physically strong women remained the ideal type in dominant discourses of Chinese modernity. Moreover, after the initial eugenic emphasis on producing healthy sons, the primarily rationale for building up women's physique was to enable them to enter what had been exclusively men's world, according to the historical convention of gender segregation that prevailed in 'respectable families'. If qualms about women's 'masculinization' were expressed after this alien term entered Chinese via the translation of 'Western scientific knowledge' in the early twentieth century, they never became widespread or serious enough to appear in the dominant discourses.[26]

What, then, made the post-Mao urban elite women reject this heritage by deploying a pseudo-scientific and essentialist notion of sex to disparage women's performance of physically demanding tasks? If the discursive device was directed at an authoritarian state's monopoly of gender policies, why were other lines of analysis of the shortcomings of socialist women's liberation foreclosed? What political context enabled this particular critique, rather than other narratives about socialist women's liberation that were available at the same time, to gain traction domestically and transnationally? We must take a closer look at the political context of women intellectuals' discursive practices at that time.

Women intellectuals in the 1980s certainly shared the political agenda of deconstructing the Maoist state with their male counterparts. The 'ideological emancipation' campaign was a discursive manoeuvre by which post-Mao intellectuals broke free from a class categorization that had placed intellectuals among the 'class enemies' during the Cultural Revolution. Critiquing the CCP dictatorship under Mao became a material passage to social ascendancy for many senior or newly minted intellectuals, who offered various proposals to steer China away from authoritarian socialism. While their condemnations of the damage caused by Mao's (mis)use of class in political struggles were mostly pertinent, their total rejection of the utility of class as an analytical category for examining deeply entrenched social hierarchy and power relations in Chinese society, coupled with their passionate commitment to demolishing an equalitarian ideology and redistribution system, reveals their class standing and their desire to revive intellectuals' privileges as a social elite. In place of the now notorious Maoist class struggle, intellectuals propagated a myth of a value-free scientific knowledge as the panacea to cure the ills of a socialist system and to move China onto the track of 'global' – or, rather, capitalist – modernity. Demonstrating their full collaboration with the new CCP leadership's agenda to depoliticize a severe political rupture, intellectuals' massive deployment of 'scientific theories' in all fields successfully reinstated their elite position as experts, while camouflaging a historical process of class realignment replete with power dynamics of gender and ethnicity.[27] It was against this particular background that naturalizing femininity and masculinity emerged as a scientific truth from biology and psychology (constituted largely of translated texts published before 1949 and discredited in the West in the second half of the twentieth century) that would help the Chinese to recover the 'human nature' that had been distorted by the Maoist dictatorship.

For some women intellectuals, theorizing a biologically determined femininity prior to and beyond the realm of the social and political was also a political strategy to detach gender issues from a Maoist class analysis. Masculinist authority in the CCP did use a Maoist class label to denigrate or suppress state feminists' concerns over gender inequalities,[28] although in the post-Mao conceptual framework of a party-state such contentions went unrecognized. But by condemning the party-state's suppression of gender issues with a theoretical pillar of a naturalized femininity, women critics produced a discourse of universal womanhood bound by biology. Joining male intellectuals in abandoning class as a valid analytical category, women intellectuals also had no qualms about presenting natural femininity as well as their discursive claim on it as free of class inflection. The hallmark of achieving this natural femininity, however, was a rejection of masculinization symbolized by the Iron Girls whose rural and working-class identity was openly displayed.

Women intellectuals' complicity with male elites in redefining the Iron Girls as the symbol of socialist masculinization of women did not simply pry open a discursive space to discuss gender issues free from Maoist class hegemony. It also became part of the process of class realignment at that moment of profound political rupture. Class tensions and power dynamics in the socialist period were conveniently glossed over by a 'scientific' accusation of masculinization. Urban elite women's aversion to the recent experience of being sent to villages or factories to take on manual labour found an elevated feminist expression in denouncing the patriarchal socialist state's suppression of women's femininity and erasure of gender difference. The ability to claim a delicate and tender natural femininity has signified a privileged social status that shields a woman from physical labour, conventionally a prominent marker of lower-class status. Co-opted by a market economy, that naturalized femininity has been expressed in women's ability to consume dazzling feminine products. In post-socialist China, gender differentiation has resumed its historic function as a marker of class distinctions.

CODA

When being interviewed by a Beijing TV talk show host in 2012, Guo Fenglian, now the chief executive officer (CEO) of Dazhai Conglomerates with assets of over 1.7 billion yuan, attempted to refute urban elites' denigration of the Iron Girls by saying, 'We are also made of flesh and bones, not iron.' She never deploys the term 'masculinization', which meaningfully signifies her rural identity or her conscious rejection of the hegemonic gender discourse in the post-socialist era. With an ironic twist, the Iron Girl who was silenced for over 20 years has returned to the limelight with a new identity as the CEO of a major enterprise. Owing much to the cultural capital of Dazhai gained in the socialist period as well as to her personal reputation and leadership capacity honed since her adolescence, Guo led Dazhai from a rural village of collective agriculture to a diversified conglomerate owned by Dazhai villagers collectively. Hailed by the media as accomplishing a 'magnificent turn from an Iron Girl to an Iron Lady',[29] Guo's success in the market economy enabled her to resume her membership in the Standing Committee of the National Congress and gain discursive power in an era when power is the prerogative of the rich.[30] In interviews on TV and in print media, she has consciously utilized her regained discursive power to inform the public of the glorious history of Dazhai's collectivization and the Iron Girls' tremendous contribution to the village's development. Even when the young TV host, cast in the typical image of sexualized modern femininity, exclaims with a tinge of condescending sympathy about Guo's hardened and coarse hands, Guo is not apologetic about this proof of the hard physical labour she performed in her youth. With full dignity and pride, she presents a powerful narrative of a meaningful youth among the Iron Girls.[31] The re-emergence of the real Iron Girl with discursive power presents a significant crack in the long-solidified discursive sediment regarding the 'socialist masculinization of women'.

By the time Guo Fenglian reappeared in public, both gendered discursive terrains and social practices had changed in significant ways. Gender differentiation has become the hallmark of a market economy in which abundant feminine commodities lavishly package a hegemonic modern femininity embodied in omnipresent images of young sexy women celebrities. Gender differentiation has also been prominently displayed in gender stratification in employment, with millions of young rural women at the bottom toiling in sweatshops for the global market, and men dominating managerial positions. While a rapidly expanding and feminized service industry has provided new employment opportunities, the lack of opportunity for women to rise to positions of power and wealth has led to a dramatically enlarged gender gap in average incomes. The ratio between women's and men's incomes has declined from 0.84 to 1 in 1988, to 0.65 to 1 in 2011; women now earn just two-thirds of what men do.[32] Although the result of complex factors, the increasingly gendered class disparity indicates the concrete socio-economic effects of the elite's discursive demolition of socialist gender equality ideology and practices since the 1980s.

The masculinist discursive manoeuvre in the 1980s also paved the way for the emergence of a hegemonic masculinity in China's merger with global capitalism. The rapidly rising economic power of China has relieved the male elite from its previous inferiority complex. The dramatic amassing of power and resources in the hands of elite men – party and state officials, entrepreneurs and intellectuals – has made the elite men's dream of 'potency' come true. One visible indicator of masculine potency is the booming sex industry, as well as the new norm (or rather a revival of polygamy) of keeping multiple mistresses as a sign of success. Such expressions of hegemonic masculinity in contemporary China inadvertently acquired negative connotations through Xi Jinping's recent anti-corruption campaign. All fallen officials are exposed as possessing not only massive amounts of wealth but also numerous women. Male commentators, either from the right or the left, all express a sense of disgust toward those corrupt officials. But relevant questions about the formation of this type of hegemonic masculinity have not yet emerged in any analysis of the pattern of corruption among male officials.

Critical reviews of the intense discursive struggles in the 1980s have recently emerged among some Chinese literary scholars. While examinations of the shortcomings of intellectual debates and agitations in the 1980s express serious efforts to engage with intellectual legacies of a recent past, it is still rare to see a self-reflective interrogation of the politics of post-socialist knowledge production in and outside China with critical lenses of both gender and class (Zha 2006).[33] To open up that line of inquiry, this chapter has examined the politics of making cultural symbols of Xianglin's Wife and the Iron Girls to illuminate a history of intense discursive struggles that were professedly over visions of modernity, but were replete with power dynamics of gender and class. The impressive success of elite men's discursive manoeuvres at the historical turn from socialism to capitalism is evidenced in the fact that severe class and gender polarization is the hallmark of China today. A critical review of the rise of hegemonic discourses in post-Mao China is therefore imperative.

NOTES

1. Gendered power struggles can take place in high politics, within the party's power structure, in the processes of state formation and the formulation of laws and public policies, as well as in everyday life, ranging from education and employment, and the gendered division of labour in production and reproduction, to the decision to keep or abort a female foetus. They can be manifested intensely in organized feminist activities, either within or outside the official system, on or off the internet, and within or outside the media's attention.
2. In the English-speaking academy, the relationship between feminism and socialism in China became a focus in feminist scholarship in the 1970s. Davin (1976), Croll (1978), Johnson (1983), Stacey (1983) and Andors (1983) all recognized the legacy of May Fourth feminism for the Chinese Communist Party and in the Chinese Communist Revolution. But none of these works has been translated into Chinese. The marked lack of interest among Chinese academics in these feminist scholarly works is symptomatic of an intellectual aversion to the whole subject of the Chinese revolution, compounded by a reluctance to approach the subject from a feminist perspective. Overall, these works share a critical assessment that the CCP did not do enough to liberate Chinese women, which presents a sharp contrast to the dominant assessment produced by the post-Mao male elite: that Chinese women's liberation under the CCP had outpaced what the material condition permitted in that historical era, that is, the CCP overdid it.
3. See Liu et al. (2013).

4. Jin Jiang's work on the history of Yue opera gives a detailed account of the adaptation of Lu Xun's short story to a Yue opera. See Chapter 4 in *Women Playing Men: Yue Opera and Social Change in Twentieth-Century Shanghai*, Seattle: University of Washington Press, 2009. My translation of the character Xianglin Sao differs from hers as Xianglin was the name of her husband and the nameless character only acquired a name as Xianglin's Wife. Lu Xun's penetrating understanding of Chinese gender system was also expressed in the naming of his character. Also see http://www.yizhuge.com/nwxq2.asp?ID=7 (accessed 23 August 2013). The Yue opera is one of many operas based on local dialects in China. Yue opera was the first to adapt Lu Xun's short story, as his hometown is in Zhejiang and the story was situated in his hometown. If the short story had an audio version, Xianglin's Wife would speak the Shaoxing dialect on which the Yue opera developed.
5. http://i.mtime.com/4020546/blog/7374617/ (accessed 15 August 2014). To view the film online, access https://www.youtube.com/watch?v=Q3gXI4Zw6HU.
6. The film's portrayal of Wu Xun is much more complex and subtle than characterized by Mao. The director of the film added many scenes to depict Wu Xun as a man of a low class who did not identify with the dominant Confucian values. It is very likely that Mao did not finish the long film in which scenes of Wu Xun's refusal to identify with the ruling class were concentrated in the last half hour.
7. Contemporary critics think the voiceover is an evidence of Xia Yan's sacrificing artistic standards in compliance with the political demand of the time. See Wei Jiankuan, 'Xia Yan xiansheng gaibian Zhufu de baibi' (Failures in Xia Yan's adaptation of *New Year's Sacrifice*), http://www.xiexingcun.com/dushu/ShowArticle.asp?ArticleID=11294, accessed 18 August, 2014.
8. This critique of the May Fourth New Culturalist portrayal of women as victims of feudal society was first made in Ko (1994); see her introduction for a critical analysis of the rise of the 'May Fourth story' of the Chinese tradition. See also Wang (1999) which also challenges the CCP's dominant representation of women pre-1949 as victims without agency.
9. For a detailed study of the implementation of the 1950 Marriage Law in the PRC in English, see Johnson (1983: esp. 132). For Chinese studies and sources on the contentions over of the Marriage Law, see Deng (1993b), Duan (2000: 119–121), Huang (2004: 33–54), Deng (1988: 49–54) and Luo (2007: 427–428).
10. For analyses of socialist state feminists' deployment of the concept of feudalism, see Wang, Z. (2005: 519–551) and Wang (2010: 827–849).
11. Honig and Hershatter (1988) vividly capture the discursive shift in that historical moment; for their discussion of the Iron Girls, see pp. 23–31.
12. The most valuable source material on the history of the Iron Girls Brigade in Dazhai is in a two-volume collection of oral histories of 150 villagers (Sun and Liu 2008). Several websites also provide valuable visual and written sources on the leader of the Iron Girls Brigade, Guo Fenglian: http://space.tv.cctv.com/video/VIDE1229948499008452; http://tv.sohu.com/20130510/n375487819.shtml; and http://www.globalview.cn/ReadNews.asp?NewsID=24337.
13. CCTV (2009); see also, Sun and Liu (2008: 99, 102–104).
14. See Bao and Gao (1958: 4), Jing (1958: 5) and Corresponding Group of the Xu County Committee (1958: 3).
15. Hershatter (2011). The renowned poet in the Tang Dynasty, Du Fu [杜甫] (712–770), wrote about how robust women ploughed the fields in the times of war. See Binche Xing [兵车行], http://www.interactivetech.ca/ref/baijia/dufu.htm.
16. See CCTV talk show featuring Guo Fenglian, http://tv.sohu.com/20130510/n375487819.shtml (accessed 20 September 2013).
17. Jin presents the mixed assessments of former participants. Complaints of damage to some women's health because of heavy physical labour were common, especially in urban industries. Yet Jin emphasizes that the spirit of the Iron Girls, taken as a challenge to traditional gender divisions of labour, was emulated by many women of that generation, including those who did not join Iron Girls brigades.
18. See http://www.china.com.cn/economic/zhuanti/xzgjjlsn/2009-07/24/content_18200659.htm and http://tv.sohu.com/20130510/n375487819.shtml (accessed 13 May 2014). The course of Guo Fenglian's career constitutes a fascinating account of China's history over the past five decades.
19. Guo Fenglian, however, had many suitors, including some men who were urban residents. Some Iron Girls of Dazhai even married men from other villages who came to live there, reversing the usual pattern of patrilocal residence.
20. See the interview with a male writer in the documentary film *Morning Sun*.
21. This summary of public debates and surveys on women's roles comments that women confront three choices: the choice of the state that requires women's contribution to the society; the choice of men that demands women's good appearance, gentle personality and strong ability in domesticity; and women's own choice. The author emphasizes that many women's rejection of just being a good wife and mother is in sharp conflict with men's expectations. For a discussion of increasing gender conflicts in the economic reform, see Wang (2003).

22. At a banquet during my lecture tour in China in July 2013 my host, a high-level male university administrator, asked me to explain 'gender studies'. After hearing my brief explanation, he offered his solution to tensions in gender relations: 'To maintain harmony and balance in conjugal relations, wives should return home and their salaries should be paid to their husbands.'
23. For an early examination of how socialist women's liberation benefited women, written by one of the beneficiaries, see Li (1988). Her assessment shares the prevailing male intellectuals' concept that the level of women's liberation outpaced socio-economic conditions, and that gender equality was bestowed on Chinese women by the state.
24. Examples of English-language scholarship that circulated the thesis of 'the masculinization of Chinese women' include Yang (1999), Cui (2003) and Yang (1997).
25. Rural men highly value women with a strong physique. In some rural areas in Fujian, bride price was determined by her body weight, a practice that persisted even through the Cultural Revolution.
26. For discussions of changing gender discourses in the twentieth century China, see Ko and Wang (2007).
27. For a critical examination of the relationship between the post-socialist ascendancy of the discourse of 'scientific modernity' and the rapidly increasing political power of scientists, see Greenhalgh (2008).
28. See Wang (2006) and Wang (2010).
29. The 'Iron Lady' was a nickname for the UK Prime Minister, Margaret Thatcher.
30. Guo Fenglian was first appointed to the Standing Committee of the Fifth National Congress in 1978. She was removed from all her official positions in 1980 after Deng Xiaoping's decision to abandon collectivization of the rural economy. She resumed her membership of the Standing Committee of the National Congress in 2003.
31. http://tv.sohu.com/20130510/n375487819.shtml (accessed 20 August 2014).
32. http://www.wageindicator.cn/main/salary/753759735de58d445dee8ddd and http://www.baike.com/wiki/ (accessed 25 August 2014).
33. The literary scholars and artists included in the volume present fascinating memories of and comments about what they experienced during the 1980s. Tellingly, neither gender nor class is deployed as an analytical category in their narratives.

18. Rural development*
Jean C. Oi

One of the more noteworthy features of China's development is the degree to which poverty was reduced by broad-based economic growth that raised peasant incomes.[1] This is not to say that China has solved its development problems. Poverty has not been eradicated, some areas are still extremely poor (Unger 2002), inequality is growing, and the demographic challenge may mean that China will grow old before it grows rich. Nonetheless, China's development experience illustrates how a country, even one with limited resources, and without large outlays of investment from the state itself, has the potential to increase production and growth by providing sufficient incentives for producers and agents of the state who are tasked with implementing reform policies.

The Chinese case is also instructive for understanding who are the key actors in economic development. The answer to this question says much about what it would take to generate similar growth in other developing countries. Much of the earlier scholarship highlighted the efforts of the local state in rural China's take-off, although that work also recognized the incentives for and efforts of the peasants who responded to state-led policies. Others take a contrary view, to argue that it was due to the entrepreneurial spirit of the peasants themselves; some adamantly deny that this was done with any support from the local state (Zhou 1996). A less extreme view of bottom up reform sees the state following, rather than leading (Kelliher 1992). More recent work, while less strident about the ability of the peasants to reform on their own, nonetheless, sees the engine of China's growth as primarily due to the private sector in the 1980s (Huang 2008, 2010). These debates will be addressed in the discussion below as I examine how China managed to lift so many out of poverty.

A lesson of China's rural reforms is that institutional change can promote economic development, regardless of regime type, if the necessary incentives are provided and resources can be mobilized. This applies regardless of whether one thinks China's growth was due primarily to the peasants themselves, private entrepreneurs, or local cadres. Unlike other efforts at reform, and contrary to what one might predict about officials in an authoritarian one-party state, China's cadres, regardless of whether they were leading the effort or simply following, found it in their interests to promote the reforms. But as will be seen, this did not mean that they supported all types of reform, only certain reforms; yet, these were sufficient to generate significant economic growth. That is a distinguishing feature of China's reform efforts.

There is no need to accept the notion that communist officials would obstruct or fail to respond to incentives, simply because they are in a one-party, Leninist system. In the case of rural China during the 1980s, it is possible to understand what prompted rapid economic development by examining those factors that affected the behaviour of peasants and the local officials who oversaw development when China began its reforms. By examining key institutional changes and the incumbent incentives for peasants and cadres, insights can be gained into the development process that led to the dramatic rise in rural incomes in China. This chapter asks: what caused the change in previous patterns of behaviour? How did they mobilize the necessary resources? It also asks: what are the limitations of such strategies? Answers to these questions may provide lessons for other countries in their efforts to reduce poverty, both about the incentives needed, as well as some cautionary notes about what can go wrong.

INSTITUTIONAL CHANGE AND ECONOMIC DEVELOPMENT

A feature of China's reform experience is that large parts of its centrally planned economy were dismantled without local officials necessarily losing power. Unlike the situation in Russia or Eastern Europe where there was a revolution and adherence to the 'big bang' approach to reform, China purposely used many of the existing personnel and kept its core institutions even as reforms were also being put in place. This was part of what Naughton termed 'growing out of the plan', or what the Chinese see as 'groping for stones to cross the river' model of change. The key to China's reforms was not so much what was dismantled, but what was left of the old system, and how these institutions were adapted and how new institutions were added. Contrary to earlier theories about how communist officials would react to reform,[2] China's peasants and officials responsible for implementing reform responded to incentives because they were crafted in such a way as to benefit their economic and political well-being, obviating a key obstacle to change.

Perhaps because reform strategies were politically constrained, particularly in the 1980s and into the 1990s, China chose to work largely within the confines of existing institutions, more than most developing countries. Reform leaders were extremely cognizant of the need to protect certain ideological tenets; to legitimize Deng Xiaoping's claims that China would remain a socialist system. Up until 1988, it was illegal for a private business to employ more than seven workers. In the case of agriculture, the household responsibility system gave peasant households the right to the surplus from the harvest, but the ownership of land, that is, the right of alienation, remained with the collective. To this day, the ownership of farmland has not been privatized.

Below, I examine key institutional changes to highlight the unique aspect of these policies and how they contributed to China's rapid rural development and rising incomes, as well as the problems they created. This discussion will be divided into three sections. The first section considers the causes of increased incomes beginning in the late 1970s. This reveals something about what drives peasant behaviour. The second considers how rural industry, which contributed the most to increased peasant incomes, was developed, as well as why it eventually declined. This reveals why local officials spearheaded development and how resources were secured to achieve such rapid growth. It also examines why China then adjusted its development strategy to incorporate the private sector. The third section considers how the regime has tried to create a more 'harmonious society' to deal with the problems that have come with reform and to help those who are still poor. The final section explores lessons from China's reform.

SOURCES OF INCREASED PEASANT INCOME TO SPUR ENTHUSIASM FOR PRODUCTION

The decollectivization of agriculture and the return to household farming represent significant departures from the Mao period. Each peasant household gained the right to farm a piece of land and enjoy the right to the surplus, i.e., the profits, from that land. The collective no longer stood between the peasant producer and the harvest. Decollectivization was in many ways akin to a second land reform (Unger 1986). Like the original land reform in the early years of the People's Republic of China (PRC), this was a terribly contentious process that sometimes took months, with many charges of cadre corruption (Oi 1989b). Sometimes disputes could only be settled by drawing straws to determine who should get what piece of land. At stake was, of course, the quality and character of the primary means of production for peasant families. How rich was the land? How far was it from the family house? How far was it from sources of water for irrigation?

Equal land distribution gave each family the resources to think that they, too, could benefit from Deng Xiaoping's dictum that it was acceptable for some to 'get rich first'. However, the household responsibility system, while important, would not have been enough by itself to explain the increased enthusiasm for production. The answer to why peasants started to work harder to grow more grain cannot simply be attributed to a change in property rights. Only part of Demsetz's bundles of rights were changed (Demsetz 1983): decollectivization transferred the right of management and the residual from the land to the peasant households, but the right of alienation, i.e., the right to sell the land, remained with the collective. This was not privatization. The ownership of the land remained in collective hands. Individual families had the right to the surplus from the use of the land and the right to manage the land, but did not have the right to sell or transfer the use of the land.

Some have argued that a far more important and necessary development that spurred production was the dramatic increase in state procurement prices (see Putterman 1988; Mcmillan et al. 1989; Oi 1989b). Starting in 1979, the state increased the price it paid to peasants by as much as 50 per cent for all grain procurement sales sold over the basic quota amount. This meant that the reopening of free markets, while important, was not the driving force assumed in the Washington Consensus.

In the case of China's transitional economy, there was both plan and market. During the early reform period, the market was not always the first choice for either the sale or the procurement of goods. In the late 1970s and early 1980s, state procurements provided peasants with a secure government market for their output at guaranteed prices, not the free market. Guaranteed state procurements at pre-set high prices made it exceedingly lucrative for peasants to work harder to grow more and sell more to the state, without worry that market prices would fall. The impact of price incentives is further reflected in the fact that when the government no longer guaranteed high over-quota procurement prices and peasants were forced to go to the open market, harvests declined and the state again faced problems with grain production. Peasant productivity responds to price signals and economic incentives, whether these are given by the market or by the state. Eventually, one also sees that there was the beginning of the commercialization of agriculture (Zhang and Donaldson 2008).

An accompanying change was the increased value of money. The structure of China's economy was modified so that more consumer goods were being produced. In contrast to the Mao period when everything was rationed and one needed not only money but ration tickets, with these various reforms, peasants had new reasons to want money to buy the increasing number of goods that were now available in state stores and on the free market.

Expanding Options for Increasing Incomes

Along with decollectivization of agriculture and the opening of markets, the state allowed diversification of production. No longer did everyone have to grow grain; no longer was production dictated entirely by the state set plan. The peasants who had the knowledge and the skill required to grow cash crops, such as vegetables and fruit, could reap much higher returns than those who stayed only in grain production. In the long run, grain production has not been the route to increased incomes.

While cash cropping brought peasants more income than grain production, those who stay in agriculture were still at a disadvantage in terms of income. Economists have shown that the greatest income disparity in rural China can be seen in wages from off-farm income (Rozelle and Boisvert 1994; Naughton 2007a). Along with the structural changes in the production of agriculture and new incentives for farming, peasants also started taking different routes to earn their livelihood.

Migration and Non-Farm Income

Migration to the cities is the most common route taken by rural residents in search of higher incomes. In developing countries, millions of poor who leave their villages end up in dire situations, living in the shanty towns of Latin America or on the streets of cities like Calcutta. In China, too, the same dreams of more opportunity and higher incomes have taken hold of the young, both male and female. The number of migrants has grown dramatically since the reforms began in the late 1970s.[3] Even early in the reforms, the building boom served as a source of higher wages for peasants who worked in collectively organized construction teams.

While China has its share of migrants, including beggars, China differs from India or the Latin American countries in its ability to control the influx of rural people. During the Mao period the combination of rationing of basic necessities, most importantly grain, and the household registration system (*hukou*) kept those without urban household registration in the countryside. Once the reforms began, migration controls were undermined as free markets were opened and peasants had a way to secure food and housing. More and more peasants found it possible to venture into the cities (Solinger 1999). However, their fate is at the mercy of local authorities, who periodically engage in sweeps to clear out the makeshift communities that are set up in cities like Beijing.[4]

While China mirrors other developing countries in its flow of workers from rural to urban areas, the pattern of the flow differs. As in other countries, peasants seek industrial jobs, often far from their villages, in different parts of the country. We know that peasants in other developing countries rely on networks to find jobs in cities. However, organization is taken to another level in China. Local officials often act as labour brokers.

Entrepreneurial officials seek out factories, work out contract terms with the firms, sign a contract for a set number of workers, set out the wages and benefits, and so on, and then recruit local peasants for these jobs. Assuming that a fairly large number go to one factory or locality, even buses are designated to bring peasants home for the holidays. For example, officials in a relatively poor county in Henan found jobs for locals in much more developed provinces like Guangdong. When local officials act as agents, peasants are assured of a job before they leave their home villages. This may explain the relatively low number of homeless and jobless migrants in China's cities.

Wages from Rural Industry

Peasants did not have to migrate to increase incomes. Diversification of the rural economy included industrialization. Peasants became workers in rural industry, known as township and village enterprises (TVEs), located in the countryside, often in the peasant-workers' home village or in their township. These firms included both privately owned as well as local collectively owned firms started by townships and villages.[5] It was this rural industrialization that allowed China's economy to take off and greatly increase rural incomes.

Rural industry existed during the Mao period, mostly in the form of commune-level enterprises (Wong 1988). However, the industrialization that occurred starting in the early to mid-1980s went beyond anything that could be explained by these limited numbers of commune-level enterprises. Between 1978 and the mid-1990s, employment in TVEs grew by 9 per cent annually, from 28 million in 1978 to a peak of 135 million in 1996. TVE value added went from 6 per cent of gross domestic product (GDP) in 1978 to 26 per cent of GDP in 1996. Along with this growth came the creation of new jobs that were essential in explaining how China managed to get so much of its population out of poverty after the decollectivization of farming. Rural industry absorbed a large amount of the surplus labour created after the move to household farming.

Some peasants simply started their own household enterprises. Huang is correct in terms of sheer numbers, privately owned firms dominated.[6] However, the importance of these privately owned firms varied. It is well known that in the more developed coastal provinces like Zhejiang and Fujian the private sector was at the core of economic development.[7] Work by Huang shows that the private sector was also at the heart of the economic growth and lifting the peasantry out of poverty in the very poor, land-locked provinces like Guizhou (Huang 2010). In these poor, less industrialized areas, these private enterprises were essential for increasing peasant incomes.

However, for China as a whole, in terms of the ability to employ large numbers of peasants and provide the scope for substantial output, it was collectively owned township and village enterprises that were the key sources of increased wage income. Moreover, these were not just existing factories from the commune period. Townships and villages that never previously had industry established factories, producing goods ranging from simple agricultural-based items like tofu and soap, to more industrial items like steel piping and chemicals. Both the scale and the rapid rise of these firms were impressive, especially at the village level, which saw the growth of the largest number of collectively owned firms.

RAPID RURAL INDUSTRIALIZATION

The economic history of most countries suggests that industrialization is the route out of rural poverty. Industrialization is usually accompanied by urbanization, where large numbers of those who had previously farmed for a living become workers and move from rural to urban areas. By the time the post-Mao reforms began, China had major industries in its many large cities. The process of rural industrialization that emerged during the 1980s was very different from what had occurred earlier in China and, for that matter, the rest of the world.

China's story of successful rural industrialization was a combination of institutional innovation and path-dependence. As counter-intuitive as it may seem, China's Maoist legacy and particular form of central planning were key, and allowed for rapid growth in rural industry (Oi 1999).[8] The rise of rural industry is one of the clearest examples of how China's policy regime affected its development strategy and subsequent outcomes.

The problems of state-led growth are well known. The cases of China before reform and the Soviet Union are prime examples of the failures of centrally planned economies. While the centrally planned system of the Mao period can be blamed for the disappointing performance of China's economy before reform, the legacy of the Maoist system, coupled with changes in the incentives for those overseeing development, became a key variable that allowed rural industry to develop rapidly once reforms began (Oi 1999). In many areas local officials facilitated and/or spearheaded the rapid growth of TVEs. For both collectively owned township or village-owned enterprises or privately owned enterprises, local officials played a determining role, either in directly leading development or in allowing and facilitating development. A new set of powerful incentives for the local state made the difference and prompted localities to seek new sources of revenue, whether from collective or private sources.

Local Cadre Incentives for Pursuing Rural Industry

If any country wants to replicate China's experience, it must give those responsible for overseeing local level development – the local agents of the state – sufficient incentives to support reform and pursue development. The underlying premise is that when officials are presented with the right set of incentives, they will be enticed to change their behaviour. I hold this to be true in the case of China, despite operating in what is still a communist system. China's officials, like those in any political system, 'are rational actors who respond to incentives and existing constraints within the limits of their cognitive ability to evaluate alternatives and process information' (Oi 1999: 7).

To understand policy outcomes, especially in China, one also needs to disaggregate the 'state'. Local governments, while under the control of the upper levels, are also entities distinct from the central state and society, with their own agendas. The centre formulates policies, but the policy outcomes, regardless of how well intentioned the policy, depend on how these policies will be received by those at the lower levels. Key is whether there are sufficient incentives, positive and negative, to encourage those at the local levels to implement these policies. Policy formulation and implementation are two entirely different things (Grindle 1980).

Incentives for township-level officials to develop rural industry

The reassignment of property rights over increased revenues generated at the local levels prompted local cadres to be entrepreneurial and foster the development of rural industry. The fiscal reforms in 1980 instituted a revenue-sharing system that extended down to the townships.[9] Localities only had to give the upper levels a set portion of the taxes, which was the quota amount; the residual, which was the over quota tax revenue, was theirs to keep and use. Moreover, there was a separate category of taxes that were exempt from revenue-sharing, which were designated as extra-budgetary revenues. These extra-budgetary revenues belonged entirely to the localities. Thus, under the 1980s fiscal reforms, the rights to all over-quota revenues and the extra budgetary revenues generated at the local level belonged to the locality.

These increased revenues not only went into the local coffers for administrative expenses, and so on, but these funds could also be used as bonuses to be given to individual cadres within that administrative level. This meant that local coffers had more funds to make administration easier, affording officials the ability to provide more public goods or make further investments in the local economy. Equally, if not more importantly, cadres who worked hard to generate increased revenues also personally benefited from bigger pay cheques. The reassignment of property rights to those who successfully implemented reforms explains why the China case goes against established wisdom that says cadres in Leninist systems will not support reform (Kornai 1992). Unlike the case of Russia, where the power of cadres was threatened by reform, there was little reason for most Chinese cadres to oppose reforms like the revenue-sharing system and the development of TVEs. The two in tandem allowed cadres to increase their take-home pay and public funds to carry out their administrative duties.

Moreover, cadres were willing to promote the development of TVEs because these collective enterprises were owned by the townships or villages; not independent private businessmen. The logic is easy to grasp: these were firms that were still under the control of local officials. Again, the rise of these enterprises would only add to rather than detract from their sources of power.

Some recent work has argued that it was privately owned rural industry, not collective, that accounted for China's economic miracle (Huang 2008, 2010). Existing scholarship has long acknowledged that private firms always outnumbered the collectively owned ones (Oi 1999; Oi and Walder 1999). In the 1980s, in areas where local officials were supporting the development of the collective sector, the private firms while numerous often remained small because they were not allowed access to the capital needed to develop industry of any scale. There were areas, however, where private firms were dominant from the start, such as in Wenzhou and parts of Fujian. In those areas even though local officials did not directly control these firms, those who did worked closely with local officials so that all benefited. In some of these areas, many of these privately owned firms were 'given red hats to wear', that is, disguised as collectively owned enterprises, in order to share in the preferential access to inputs and services given to collectively owned firms. Huang's research adds to our knowledge about the variation that exists in China by showing that in very poor places like Guizhou, the private sector also was dominant from the start. However, unlike other places, local officials never bothered to hide this private ownership with 'red hats' (Huang 2010). This last finding begs the question of why Guizhou felt confident enough not to hide its private sector and to provide preferential allocation which, at least in theory, should have only been given to collectively owned firms. For the country as a whole, open support for and the rise of privately owned firms only occurred in the 1990s, after the collectively owned ones started having problems.[10]

This progression of ownership forms, starting with the collectively owned, is another reason why the China case goes against established notions about the likely response of communist officials to reform. The development of collectively owned enterprises not only did not threaten cadre power, but it enhanced it. Moreover, as the reforms took hold, the route to political success and to bureaucratic promotion was to successfully develop one's locality. Over time, in most areas, regardless of whether collective firms were previously dominant or not, this development encompassed helping privately owned firms. Thus, officials who wanted to get ahead politically also had an incentive to pursue rural industry and generate increased revenues regardless of the ownership structure.

Incentives for village-level officials to develop rural industry

Villages are not a level of government and thus were not subject to the 1980s fiscal reform and its revenue-sharing system. However, for villages the incentive for developing rural industry boiled down to a similar revenue imperative. Except in the case of village cadres, it was prompted by the need for new sources of collective income and resources when the household became the unit of production after the communes were abolished and the rights to agricultural revenue were taken away from the collective – that is, the village – and given to the households. Individual households gained the right to decide the disposition of the surplus after state taxes and sales were made. The collective, instead of giving peasants their share of the harvest, now was dependent on each peasant household to get its only source of revenue, which was a surcharge, the *tiliu*, that the household paid to the collective (Oi 1989b). Moreover, these fees were only a small sum tied to a percentage of peasant incomes. If a village had no other sources of collective revenue, there were few or no funds to provide public goods; sometimes there was not even enough to meet the most basic expenditures. Some village coffers became so poor that village cadres were incapable of governance; some villages became known as 'paralyzed villages', where peasants refused to listen to the cadres and the cadres were devoid of power because they had little hold over peasants and were incapable of providing services due to their lack of resources. Ironic as it may be, successful decollectivization became the root cause of the 'peasant burden' problem, which led to protests and substantial discontent in China's countryside. Villages devoted primarily to agriculture found themselves in a situation where the only way to fund the local coffers was to increasingly demand more surcharges and fees from their peasant households.[11]

In contrast, those villages that were able to successfully mount a village collective enterprise were able to generate and use profits from these collectively owned firms to more than make up for the loss of revenue from the sale of the collective harvest. Furthermore, the creation of a village-owned enterprise meant that a village leader could mobilize new resources to create a new power base; this consisted of profits from the firms but also the newly created jobs, which could be doled out to village members. Again, the incentives were such that promoting development enhanced rather than hurt the power of officials. Some of the most successful village leaders were promoted to the township level. At minimum these high-achieving village cadres received accolades; some attained a seat in the local people's congress and some were named national models. Thus, both economic and political incentives at the village level also were geared toward promoting growth.

The Business Model: Local State Corporatism

How did village and township enterprises develop and expand so quickly in China's countryside, where there was little in terms of savings and the necessary technical skills and industrial experience? By the 1980s China was no longer entirely under the plan. The growth in TVEs was neither centrally planned nor directed. In fact, Deng Xiaoping expressed surprise at their success. These factories were collectively owned but they were not under the plan; they were not given planned allocations of low-priced inputs; markets had to be found, rather than being predetermined by the state. It should be noted that this differed from the model in Japan or Korea, where a central level bureaucracy like the Ministry of International Trade and Industry (MITI) or the Economic Planning Board led development. Overall, in China the rise of TVEs was a decentralized, local state-led economic development that occurred at the lowest level of formal administrative bureaucracy, townships, and the villages below them.

China's reformers created new institutions that provided incentives for local cadres to support development, but these incentives, while necessary, were insufficient. They were complemented by a rather unique set of circumstances created by China's political economy, which allowed rural firms to develop and grow much more quickly than one might expect. This changed the development situation in a number of respects.

First, because these were collective rather than privately owned firms, one should not ask how individuals raised funds and grew their firms; instead, one should ask how townships and villages, as collective entities, developed their local enterprises. Second, collectively owned township and village enterprises were part of a much larger entity that acted as both the source of inputs and the bearer of risks and responsibility.

In China, government and economy were essentially one, resulting in an institutional development that I have written about elsewhere and labelled 'local state corporatism' (Oi 1992, 1999). It refers to the strategy and manner by which local governments ran and developed local industry. Local governments ran their collectively owned firms as diversified corporations, redistributing profits and risks, thereby allowing the rapid growth of rural industry with limited resources. Local governments took on many characteristics of business corporations, with local officials serving a role equivalent to that of a board of directors. Over time, local governments extended their influence and assistance to encompass private firms. In some localities, local governments worked and supported the private sectors from the start to grow the local economy.

Under local state corporatism, a collectively owned firm was managed by an individual, who was often contracted to run the firm for a fixed profit, but this manager, much like a manager in a state-owned enterprise, was not responsible for either the funding or the risks if the firm failed. The ability to grow these firms was dependent neither on an individual having sufficient savings nor on his or her ability to get loans. It was state agents in the local bureaucratic agencies who mobilized resources, sought out loans, technical assistance, and bureaucratic approvals for licences, and so on. This is in stark contrast to situations of predatory local officials taking resources out of firms in other developing contexts. China's TVEs were created and grew thanks to local official entrepreneurs who mobilized resources to invest in local firms. This is not to say that there was no corruption or abuse of power by local officials. In some villages, these collectively owned firms were essentially assets of local officials (Lin and Chen 1999). To underscore a point made earlier, the growth was due to the fact that even without corruption, local officials could routinely and legally receive large bonuses from successful rural industry and increase their power base. Leaders of rich industrialized villages could use the profits of their factories to give their peasants paved roads and street lamps as well as subsidies to cover various fees, including for education. The wages from factory jobs greatly increased the income of peasant families and support for the village cadres. Villages that successfully developed rural industry catapulted into the ranks of the richest in China. Moreover, taxes and fees from these village-owned enterprises filled township and county coffers.

Adapting the Maoist Legacy to Mobilize Resources

Accepting that local officials were the real entrepreneurs who spearheaded growth, one still needs to understand how it is that they could mobilize sufficient resources to achieve such high rates of growth. A few examples will illustrate how it was that firms could get started when there was little savings, either in the hands of individuals or in collective coffers.

The capital essential to get firms off the ground could be raised from within the collective by the village cadres, most likely, the Party Secretary. Using his position as a cadre, he could mobilize individual peasant households within the village to contribute funds. While the amounts were not large, they often sufficed to start a low-level factory. For the early TVEs, such as those producing tofu or soap, the entry costs were fairly low: the required inputs, technology, and so on were often minimal.

Aside from raising the necessary initial capital, cadres also had the power to take profits from a factory to pool capital for collective use. If the first factory effort was successful, then the profits from that factory could be used either to fund a technology upgrade or to expand the operation. In some cases, when a factory was highly profitable the excess funds could be pooled to start a second factory. The crucial point was that the cadres in China's villages had the power to mobilize whatever resources were available within the community. Cadres could raise funds even in a relatively poor village from small amounts contributed by numerous individual villagers to start a small enterprise that could quickly grow and then help fund new village firms.

One might question whether this type of villager contribution has been entirely voluntary. Local cadres have been criticized for this type of forced 'fundraising' from its rural households. While there was no doubt that some peasants would have preferred not to give up their modest savings, one can also see how they could be persuaded to contribute to a collective effort that promised to bring new jobs, non-agricultural jobs and collective revenue.

Moreover, because China did not follow the big bang approach there was a unique situation where both plan and market operated side by side. As a result, local officials became the entrepreneurs who spearheaded rural industry and could capitalize on their bureaucratic position to access state-allocated goods, to the extent that they still existed. At a minimum, they would have access to the negotiated priced goods that existed as China transitioned from a planned to a market economy.[12] Most importantly, this included essential inputs such as credit from the local banks and credit co-operatives. Thus, instead of throwing the old institutions out (what one might expect of a country trying to reform), the Maoist bureaucratic structure provided critical support to the rapid development of China's TVEs. This included a hierarchical banking system and access to information and technology. Officials at the lowest levels had access to the full array of resources at the disposal of China's entire bureaucratic hierarchy, all the way to Beijing. Lower-level officials were connected to higher levels by going through bureaucratic channels. Each successive level had access to more and more goods and services. This was the sinew of local state corporatism.

In the context created by local state corporatism, unlike firms in a market setting, no single individual had to bear the risks of starting a company. The risks were borne by the collective. This collective strategy thus overcame two huge barriers to development in poor countries: the lack of individual savings and the fear of failure. Each collectively owned township and village enterprise was part of the larger corporation. Those at the village level could seek help from the township and the county. The ladder extended all the way up the bureaucracy to Beijing.

Pitfalls of Rapid Industrialization

The TVEs, as successful as they were in the 1980s, were not without problems, some of which plagued villages for a decade after. During the period between the late 1980s and into the early 1990s, TVEs began to suffer from inefficiencies and soft budget constraints (Kung 1999) as well as changing market conditions with increased competition, higher consumer demands, and decreasing profits. The take-away message from the Chinese model is not that collectively owned firms are superior to privately owned ones. Local state corporatism allowed rapid economic growth at a specific point in time within China's particular political economy, but this does not mean that collectively owned enterprises were the most economically efficient. As economic and political conditions changed, the benefits of the collective model began to be outweighed by its costs.

The point that needs to be remembered about the China case is that collectively owned township and village enterprises were the most economically and politically feasible in the context where there was both little private savings and deep-seated, ideologically driven distrust of the private sector. If China had at the beginning of the reforms promoted a strategy supporting the rapid development of a private sector, which was capable of challenging local officials, the outcome would likely have been much more like that predicted by Kornai. Communist officials would have either blocked reform or preyed heavily upon private business. Instead, in China, only later, when the collectively owned firms began to be a financial burden and private ones turned into a viable revenue source, did the state rethink its options and embrace the private sector. Perhaps equally important, by that point, after almost a decade of market reforms, local officials realized that they could still have power with the rise of private business.

The Chinese case, while offering hope for other developing countries, with limited resources, also serves as a caveat that there may be huge costs when these collectively owned enterprises fail. More than a few TVEs saw hard times by the 1990s, leaving villages with rusting factories and heavy debt.[13] We now know that rural industry became one of the most common sources of village debt (Ong 2006; Oi and Zhao 2007). This was even true of those that were seemingly very successful in the 1980s. The financial toll from TVE failures was heavy, both for the individual villages and ultimately for the individual peasant families who had to pay the bill. The rural credit co-operatives, which lent the money for the factories, were mired in red ink. Using survey data to arrange villages along an agricultural dependence continuum, one finds that a wide range of villages, including those that had industrialized, faced a situation where debt was going up rapidly while incomes were slowing or decreasing.[14] Although the sources of the debt were different, there are large increases in debt at both ends of the agricultural dependence spectrum. Villages that were highly industrialized and those most dependent on agriculture accrued increasing debt.

The extent of the problems with collectively owned TVEs is evident in the decision by local officials to switch their support to private firms. The private sector had begun to equal or outpace collective firms in generating increased revenues. Bankers and local officials began to consider loans to the private sector more secure. Collateral was required in loans to private firms, and it was clear who was responsible for paying back the loans. This was in sharp contrast to the situation for the collectively owned firms, where no collateral was required. Local governments simply signed as the guarantor for a loan, which meant that there was no single person clearly named as being legally responsible for repayment. When there was a market downturn and TVEs faced problems, the number of bad loans to collectively owned TVEs mounted with no relief in sight. In response to problems with public ownership and heavy debt, many localities engaged in state-sponsored privatization, selling village and township enterprises. By the mid-1990s an increasing number of collectively owned firms were sold as local officials decided that they were too costly and other sources of revenue generation became available, that is, private firms.

Aside from serving as a cautionary tale, the China case also suggests that too many assumptions have been made about the course of development, and industrialization in particular. Development is not a linear process. Villages that started down the road towards industrialization can and did suffer setbacks, even those that seemed to have been initially successful. Some failed attempts were so costly that the village finances could not recover. The negative experience of some villages with rural industrialization brings attention to an interesting possibility. Some villages that never attempted to industrialize actually found themselves in a better economic condition than the ones that attempted to industrialize but failed, accruing heavy debt in the process. Contrary to common assumptions, survey evidence reveals that the financially troubled villages in the 1990s include those that never attempted to industrialize and those that attempted to industrialize but failed (Oi and Shimizu 2010). Moreover, privatization of these firms does not necessarily improve performance (Li and Rozelle 2003).

The failure and debt from TVEs reveals the flip side of the successful collective model of development. The Maoist legacy allowed rural industry to develop very rapidly, more rapidly than would probably have been the case if the private entrepreneur model had been followed. However, this also meant that unsustainable firms were established because officials could mobilize the necessary resources, at least in the short run. A national retrenchment in the late 1980s created havoc with credit freezes and resulted in a market shake-up. While a market shake-up was ultimately necessary, those that were relatively weak and produced lower-quality goods found themselves unable to compete and fell more quickly than might have otherwise been the case with the retrenchment policies. Exports were increasingly an important part of the market, but only firms that employed more highly skilled workers or could upgrade their equipment to produce the higher-quality products could compete.

But even in rich areas that have enjoyed growth and still have high incomes, new problems have emerged as consequences of successful industrialization and development. Farming land is requisitioned but some peasants fail to receive adequate compensation. Moreover, rural industry continues to pollute farmland and water supplies. In some places rural industry has spoiled rivers to the point where water is no longer potable or even suitable for irrigation.[15]

NEW POLICIES TO BUILD A 'HARMONIOUS SOCIETY'

If the 1980s was a highpoint of China's rural development, throughout the 1990s the countryside was plagued with problems. The numerous challenges came to be summed up by the phrase 'three agricultural problems': the general malaise in agriculture, stagnant rural development along with increasing debt from failed TVEs, and those who work the land fail to get ahead. Statements by China's top leaders that these problems could threaten the core of the regime suggest that the state recognized the need to become more proactive as fear increased over the consequences of the unresolved problems emerging over the course of reform (Oi 2004). These fears were stoked by the increasing numbers of peasant protests surrounding burdens and cadre corruption (Bernstein and Lu 2000; O'Brien 1996; Li and O'Brien 1996; O'Brien and Li 2004; O'Brien and Li 2006). As the literature on village protests documents, villagers became increasingly bold in openly articulating their discontent about these problems (O'Brien 1996; Li and O'Brien 1996; Li and O'Brien 2008; Cai 2008; Bernstein and Lu 2000). In some instances they made official complaints to higher levels. In other instances they took to the roads to protest, sometimes resulting in violence.

The centre, long aware of the farmer burdens and rising discontent, issued many 'red-letter directives' that ordered local officials to reduce peasant burdens. But these edicts largely fell on deaf ears (Bernstein and Lu 2000; Oi 2004; Oi and Shimizu 2010). If the 1994 tax reform was driven by the desire to gain control over more revenues, the recentralization over cadres was driven by fears of increasing peasant discontent and charges of cadre corruption, after earlier, indirect control mechanisms failed. In the troubled context of the 1990s the central state started to consider more direct action, both with regard to making further changes in the fiscal system and in tightening controls over grassroots cadres.

By the early to mid-2000s, China's leaders had a newfound awareness as to the degree of discontent and problems that had developed over the course of the reforms. Simply promoting economic growth was not sufficient. China's ability to reduce poverty slowed over time. New efforts needed to be made to address problems of inequality and the excesses including environmental degradation and pollution.

The Double-Edged Sword in Reducing Peasant Burdens

The state in 2001 finally abolished fees and surcharges at the township and village levels to eliminate key sources of peasant burdens. By 2006 it took the unprecedented step of also abolishing the remaining agricultural tax. By 2006 peasants were for the first time in China's history free from all taxes and surcharges. The positive impact of these policies on peasant incomes was further heightened by good harvests.

However, the state's well-intentioned policies have created a new set of problems for those at the lowest level of the administrative bureaucracy. While the tax-for-fee reform and abolition of the agricultural tax were good for peasant incomes, these substantially cut revenues of villages and townships. The waves of debt that researchers have found in China's rural areas are attributed to the efforts to develop TVEs, unfunded education improvement mandates, and the failure of credit associations, among others. The effort made by the central authorities to reduce peasant burdens through these well intentioned policies only aggravated the problem begun by the 1994 fiscal reforms, which took much of the extra budgetary funds out of the localities, pushing some localities over the fiscal edge into debt (Liu, Y.L. 2012; Ong 2012; Kennedy 2007; Li 2007; Oi and Zhao 2007).

Localities are expected to make up lost revenue through increased economic development. In some areas where there are relatively abundant development possibilities, this may be manageable. The difficulty exists in those areas that lack easy development opportunities. It is not hard to imagine that the same syndrome that drove cuts in one levy only to increase another is going to re-emerge. This time the solution is the turn to land finance, where localities are selling land to obtain needed revenues.

Fiscal Transfers to Fill the Gap

The central state did try to provide aid to the localities by granting fiscal transfers after the abolition of the agricultural tax. The central state is providing some fiscal safety nets, as it did when it implemented its 1980s fiscal reforms, to stem political opposition from the localities. These fiscal transfers are intended to compensate the localities for the revenue shortfalls and allow localities to meet basic expenditures. The centre allocates funds to provinces that then disburse them to counties and eventually to townships, which will then use the money to help their villages and to supplement their own revenues.

The problem is that the fiscal transfers may be insufficient to make up for the lost revenues. Interviews in selected counties suggest that the localities are still very short of past revenues generated, in part, no doubt, because the transfers are only based on the legal amount of fees that localities were able to collect.

Regardless of whether the transfers are sufficient, surveys since the policy change suggest that many infrastructural projects have been granted to localities through fiscal transfers. Overall, the upper levels now fund more of local infrastructural development. However, some research suggests that the disbursement of these funds is not uniform (CCAP/UC Davis/University of Toronto Research Team 2007; Oi et al. 2012). Moreover, while considerable money is flowing into poor areas to provide public goods, there is also evidence that grants are not always used in the most efficient manner.

There is also the long-term question of whether this system of fiscal transfers is sustainable. Beijing is currently flush with revenues, but what will happen if there is a

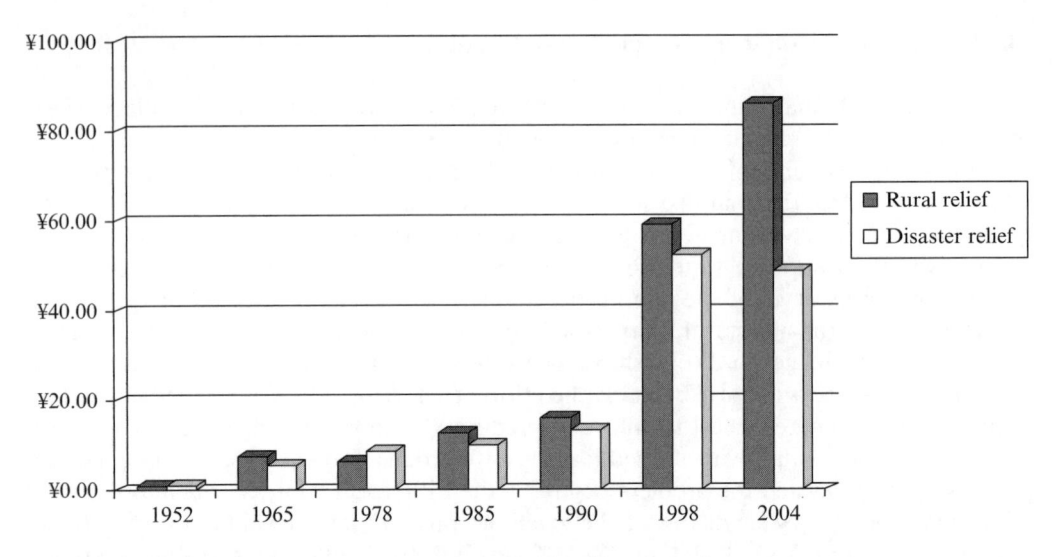

Figure 18.1   Rural welfare expenditure (in 100 million yuan)

downturn in central-level coffers? How will such policy changes affect the incentives of local officials? Some local officials complain that the cuts in fiscal and political resources have 'hollowed out' township administration, leaving it as nothing more than 'fake government'. The various policies implemented by the central state to reduce peasant burdens and improve peasant–state relations have left many townships in a very precarious position.

New Social Policies and Funding

In addition to relieving peasants of burdens, China has been increasing its earmarked spending on rural welfare, as Figure 18.1 shows.

Since 2000, the Development Orientated Poverty Alleviation Programme in Rural China (2001–10) has been implemented to solve the subsistence problems of the remaining poor and to help the low-income group. The goal is to improve infrastructure, technology, education, public health care and cultural development to achieve all-round community development and improved living standards (Rural Survey Organization of National Bureau of Statistics 2007).

This upward trend in peasant assistance received a further boost when President Hu Jintao declared the need to create a 'harmonious society', which explicitly recognizes the problems that have come with China's rapid growth.[16] Among these are tensions resulting from the lack of social welfare policies and the increasing income inequalities that have emerged in China. Some of the poor have fallen into difficult economic straits as a result of the reforms. Increasing income inequalities stemming from the reforms have created new tensions in society as China's Gini coefficient has increased. Based on data from the National Bureau of Statistics (NBS) Rural and Urban Household Surveys, the Gini coefficient without adjustments for urban–rural cost of living has risen (Ravallion and Chen 2007; World Bank 2009). See Figure 18.2.

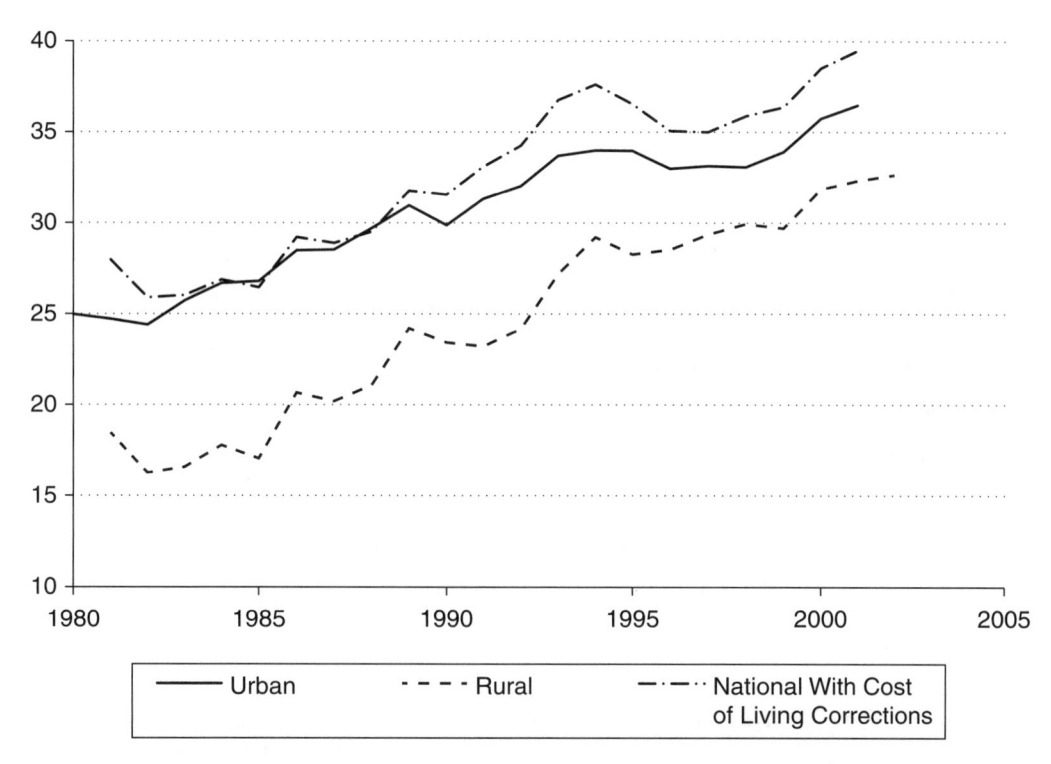

Sources: Ravallion and Chen (2007) and World Bank (2009).

Figure 18.2 Gini indices of income inequality

While China's income inequality has been rising, even by the mid-2000s, as Figure 18.3 shows, it was not particularly high, particularly when compared to other countries.[17] However, by 2013 China had a higher Gini coefficient than the USA (*The Economist* 2013a). It is not so much that there is inequality, but that inequality has risen dramatically since the reforms began in China.

Stubborn pockets of long-term poverty will require new and sustained efforts aimed at new growth policies that target the remaining poor segments of the population (see Huang et al. 2007). Relieving tensions and reducing inequalities caused by the reforms were given special attention at the 17th CCP Congress. Reports were given of progress made, and pledges were made to guarantee future key expenditures and accelerate the development of all social programmes. It was reported that 13.7 billion yuan in poverty relief funds was used in 2006 from the central budget for 'infrastructural development in poor villages, job training for poor farm labourers looking for urban employment and industrialization' (Ministry of Finance 2007). The central and western regions received support for the development of a rural medical assistance system. Under the new co-operative health care system, farmers are responsible for just one-third of insurance costs while central and local governments share the remaining two-thirds.

The government acknowledges problems in the fiscal transfer system and has pledged to improve the mechanism for ensuring a stable increase in general transfer payments.[18]

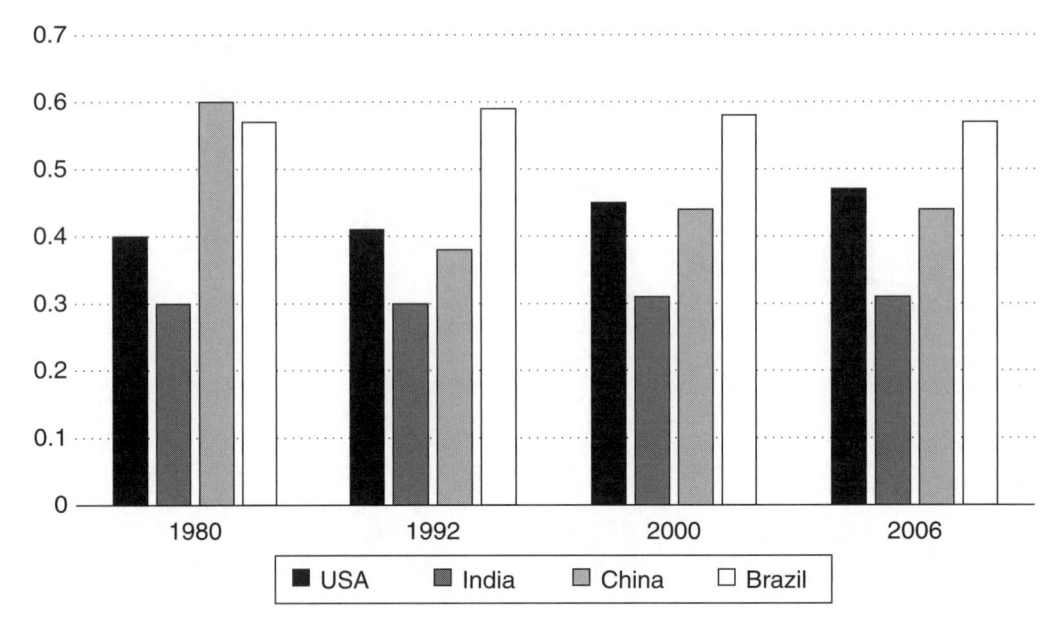

Sources: Watkins (2006), DeNavas-Walt et al. (2007) and Ahluwalia (2007).

Figure 18.3 Comparative changes in inequality

Measures were also taken to expand the transfer payments to ethnic minority areas, providing a total of 15.563 billion yuan in 2006. Ethnic autonomous counties that are not located in an ethnic autonomous region or prefecture were included in the scope of these payments. Improvements were also noted for the rules regarding transfer payments to financially strapped areas such as old revolutionary areas, border areas and Tibet. Wen Jiabao, in a visit to Shanxi province, promised to spend 339.7 billion yuan (US$41.9 billion) for 'peasants, agriculture and rural areas this year – a record high and an increase of 14.2% over last year's funding' (Xinhua 2006b).

The Ministry of Finance Report also stated that the 2007 budget further increased allocations to address problems in the countryside, including new efforts toward poverty alleviation. A total of 14.4 billion yuan, an increase of 700 million yuan over the total for 2006, was allocated for poverty relief. Perhaps most important is the extension of a basic living allowance programme, which was introduced in the 1990s for urban areas, to rural residents across the country. The central government will allocate 3 billion yuan to fund basic cost of living allowances for rural residents (Ministry of Civil Affairs 2007). However, it will leave localities to determine the scope of the entitled group and the basic allowance amount based on local conditions. The central government will then assist poor areas as needed (Ministry of Finance 2007).

The problems related to transfer payments were also addressed. Pledges were made to increase transfer payments to improve the ability of local governments to provide basic public services. Regular transfer payments from the central budget to local governments in 2007 were set at 192.4 billion yuan and were mainly to the central and western regions. Regular transfer payments to ethnic minority areas were set at 21 billion yuan, an increase of 39.7 billion yuan and 5.4 billion yuan, respectively, over the 2006 figures. In addition, there were more general allocations to ease the financial problems of counties and townships (Ministry of Finance 2007).

China's new social policies suggest that the leadership has come to the decision that broad-based growth policies are no longer enough. It now seeks sustainable development. China made great strides early in its reform efforts, but the ability to quickly increase incomes has diminished. It has been much harder to maintain the high rates of increase since the huge rises in income in the early to mid-1980s. The recent rise in rural incomes suggests that the situation may begin to change for the better, but the state is now enacting policies that will provide a stronger safety net, social security and increased health care provisions. The new policies suggest that China realizes the need to reinforce its efforts at poverty alleviation in addition to trying to help the poor achieve economic growth in their localities. This assessment is supported by the research by western economists who have looked at causes of poverty and income increases and concluded that just following broad-based growth policies will no longer be sufficient (Zhang et al. 2003).

Further resources were committed to help the poor in the wake of the global financial crisis in 2008. The central government has mandated a minimum subsistence level safety net (*dibao*) for all citizens, both urban and rural, although the amounts will vary by regions and locality. In addition, as an aid to migrants who lost their jobs and had to return to their home localities, some local governments provided financial assistance and helped workers get back wages. Some have established retraining and placement programmes and help to start small businesses. Fortunately, for China, many of the migrants have since found new jobs, both in coastal areas but also increasingly in the hinterland, closer to the homes of many of the migrants, as factories have moved inland in search of cheaper production costs. In some coastal areas there is now a shortage of labour, especially skilled labour.

Building a New Socialist Countryside

The state's direct intervention in the countryside, abolishing fees and taxes to solve problems, has continued and a new recentralization of authority is emerging. This followed the decisive turn towards more centralized administrative control of towns and villages beginning in the mid-1990s, after fears of potential rural instability linked to peasant discontent and the perception of cadre corruption. We see this in increased administration and oversight of village- and town-level fiscal revenues, expenditures and public-goods investments. The state has adopted a bifurcated approach toward households and cadres: it has allowed markets to boom as the state has remained out of the decision-making calculus of farm households; at the same time, however, it has tightened its grip over township and village cadres and has moved fiscal and administrative controls up the bureaucracy, limiting the authority of township or village cadres. This development has evolved over time with the increasing fiscal capacity of the central state in a broad shift in the central state's agenda to recentralize control, both fiscal and administrative (Oi et al. 2012).

China's continued urbanization has resulted in a dramatic demographic shift in the rural areas, often resulting in only the old and the very young left in villages. Driven in part by this shift and the need to find more efficient ways to provide public goods, since the mid-2000s the state has embarked on an ambitious plan to reorganize the countryside – part of the 'new socialist countryside' policy – to create what are called new 'rural communities'. While the implementation is still limited and uneven across the country, some villages are being merged or divided to create these new rural communities. In some areas, peasants are being resettled from sparsely populated villages into new rural communities. Even in those villages where there are no mergers with other villages or boundary changes, villagers are being located to new residential areas, often to apartment buildings, leaving their traditional courtyard homes.

The creation of these new rural communities has also been accompanied by significant rural discontent. While peasants may get new and better housing, there are issues of whether the move is voluntary, especially for the old who do not want to leave the family's ancestral home. But more contentious have been the disputes that have arisen as the authorities have had to compensate the peasants for the houses and the land that they lost in the process. Land conflicts have turned into the most common source of discontent in China. More recently under Xi Jinping these efforts seem to have slowed as the policy is being rethought.

LESSONS FROM CHINA'S REFORM

China has a long way to go before it solves its many problems, both old and new. Some are still in poverty, but China's growing economy, even if slowing, bodes fairly well for its ability to meet the fiscal challenges the solutions will entail. Clearly, the social and welfare policies of the Maoist era, the 'iron rice bowl' and security of the unit (*danwei*) system, are mostly memories of the past. China needs to build and fund new welfare institutions and fund social policies suitable to a market economy.

In spite of the incompleteness and problems of China's reforms, the transformation of the economy in the last decades of the twentieth century may serve as an attractive model for poor countries to try to replicate. Dramatic increases in agricultural output were achieved without dramatic investments of resources, other than procurement price increases. Rural industrialization occurred with limited resources and technical know-how, and again with limited investment by the central state. Thus, the early stage of China's reforms was the ultimate low-cost development model, requiring little from central coffers.

But such a model had problems, as the discussion above has highlighted. The increases in grain production were relatively short-lived and very much tied to prices. Local-led rural industrialization had its negative consequences. Nonetheless, China's development experience suggests that countries, even those with limited resources, have the potential to increase enthusiasm for production and output by providing sufficient incentives for producers and those in charge of overseeing development.

It is unclear whether there is a Chinese model and whether it can be exported. A key part of the success of China's reforms, especially its rural industrialization, is the infrastructural support that was embedded in a strong Maoist state from which the reforms emerged. Local state corporatism with its institutions of support for credit, technology and technical know-how are key in understanding how a backward economy could quickly mobilize so many resources to develop industry in previously unindustrialized areas. The existence of a unified and effective state that runs from the centre to the localities is thus the key element of the Chinese experience.

Having a strong central state, however, is not inconsistent with agents at the local level who pursue development to advance their own discrete set of interests. China's reform experience illustrates how the right set of incentives can be deployed to mobilize local officials to push economic reform. China's reform experience is a clear illustration of the importance of historical context and institutions. This suggests path-dependence but it also stresses the ability to spur change by embedding incentives into institutions. There was a specific political economy of reform in China that dictated a particular path of change and development. The model was not one that always stressed economic efficiency. The decision to promote collectively owned enterprises is a good case in point. Collectively owned rural industry was the one option that was both economically and politically feasible. Ignoring the political constraints would have been disastrous. Instead, only gradually, were private firms promoted as the context changed. Such examples suggest that there is much to be said for China's more gradual route to development. 'Growing out of the plan' or 'groping for stones to cross the river' may seem to some only to prolong well-known problems of the old regime. But in some cases, it may be the most feasible and thus the only successful strategy. In the case of China, one must also remember that there was the overarching political constraint of ideological justification and keeping the Chinese Communist Party in power.

NOTES

* Parts of this chapter draws on my 'Development Strategies and Poverty Reduction in China', in Bangura (2015).
1. I discuss the strengths and limitations of China's poverty relief policies in my 'Development Strategies, Welfare Regime and Poverty Reduction in China', paper for the UNRISD Project on Poverty Reduction and Policy Regimes (Oi 2008). Also see Asian Development Bank (2004).
2. See, for example, the classic work by Kornai (1992), which argues that Leninist officials would obstruct reform if reforms threatened the planned economy.
3. See, for example, Rozelle et al. (1999) and Rozelle et al. (2002); also Woon (1999).
4. This has been best documented for Zhejiang village in Beijing. See Zhang, L. (2001).
5. This term, TVE, is shorthand for the four types of firms that developed rapidly as a consequence of the reforms: two forms of collectively owned firms – township or village-owned enterprises; and two types of privately owned firms – jointly owned firms and individually owned firms.
6. Yasheng Huang (2010) has argued that this point has not been sufficiently appreciated. However, scholars such as Oi (1999) noted that while the private (*geti*) firms were the largest in number, their overall scope, employment and output were surpassed by the collectively owned firms.
7. See chapters in Oi and Walder (1999).
8. We now know that there were differences in the way central planning worked in different Leninist systems. It is unclear that Russia would have had similar success if it had followed similar policies. For a discussion of some key differences see Goldstein (1996: 143–169).
9. Revenue-sharing stopped at the township level because villages are not a level of government.
10. See Oi (1999) and Oi and Walder (1999), especially the chapter by Chen (1999: 49–70). Huang (2010) argues the opposite, saying that the 1990s saw the decline of the private rural enterprise. The problem may in part be one of definition. Without question the privatization of previously collectively owned enterprises took place in the 1990s. The fact that rural enterprises as a whole declined during that period is a separate issue.
11. The peasant burden problem was made worse by the 1994 fiscal reforms that took much of the extra budgetary funds from the localities, leaving localities with insufficient revenues (see below).
12. These were goods that were less than market price but more than the allocated state price.
13. There are early signs of this in studies such as Sargeson and Zhang (1999). Also see Oi (1999).

14. Author survey. Also see Oi and Shimizu (2010).
15. For pollution problems from TVEs see Warwick (2003) and Economy (2004).
16. This is most evident in the hesitant pattern of reform seen in its state-owned enterprises (SOEs).
17. The closer to 1, the more unequal is the distribution of income.
18. The central government allocated 152.7 billion yuan in 2006 for general transfer payments to local governments, mainly those in the central and western regions. This represents an increase of 40.7 billion yuan over the 2005 figure (Xinhua 2006b).

19. Non-governmental organizations
Jennifer Y.J. Hsu

Non-governmental organizations (NGOs) have become increasingly important stakeholders in the transformation of Chinese society over the course of the last 20 years, and this has radically impacted upon the literature on the topic. Publications on the rise of Chinese NGOs, and to a lesser extent Chinese civil society, have attracted the interest of a range of scholars across the social sciences. The study of Chinese NGOs is important to the field of Chinese politics because of the insights provided to understand state–society relations in contemporary China. Furthermore, research in this area indicates how various Chinese stakeholders (state and non-state) are managing a range of social concerns, significant because of the implications for socio-political changes. As a result this chapter will first focus on a general overview of NGOs and their functions in society. The second section will discuss the emergence of Chinese NGOs from a civil society perspective. I will then look at the implications of NGOs' presence on state–society relations in China. While the development of Chinese NGOs is affected by the political context, not all NGOs have had the same developmental experience. The following section will look at four different NGO sectors to demonstrate that the rules and regulations governing NGOs, formal and informal, have had varying effects on NGO developments. I will then consider some of the latest trends affecting Chinese NGOs and how that has impacted on scholarly work on NGOs. The conclusion will draw together final thoughts on the transformative effects of NGOs.

A systematic analysis of the activities of NGOs provides insight into the claims of the progressive transformative potential of NGOs. Adopting a broad perspective on the points of connection (and disconnection) in state–NGO relations illuminates the process by which social and political stakeholders utilize NGOs as an arena to produce, articulate and reconstruct ideas (and ideologies) of progress and development. NGOs possess material, symbolic, interpretive and geographical power (Hasmath and Hsu 2014) and thus, have been pushed forth as agents of social and political change by NGOs themselves and international organizations such as the United Nations (UN) and World Bank, and to a lesser extent national governments through their respective development agencies.[1] Scholars have cast NGOs in myriad ways, including as alternate service providers to the state (e.g Green and Matthias 1995; Henderson 2002; Leonard 2002) and as facilitators of citizen participation and democratic change (e.g. Bratton 1989; Diamond 1994).[2] Here, NGOs are seen as opponents to the state and as a proxy for future democratization. Recent NGO literature does provide an alternative to reorient our focus and understanding of NGOs as potential partners with the state. It is in this context that we may derive new scholarship, through the investigation of the intricacies of state–NGO relations. Doing so provides detailed insights into state behaviour.

When the state and NGOs interact with one another, the process is likely to impact upon and transform both actors. Before further conceptualizing their interactions, it would be appropriate to first define 'NGO'. The heterogeneity of the sector means that as an analytical category, 'NGO' remains imprecise and complex.[3] The difficulty of pinpointing a precise definition of 'NGO' is reflective of the diversity of organizations with varying sizes, organizational structures and goals. Moreover, a nation's legal and cultural contexts will inevitably have an effect on the definition of the term. The origins of the term can be traced back to the 1945 charter of the United Nations in which the label 'non-governmental organizations' was given to international non-state organizations that received the privilege of a consultative status to be included in the UN's work (Lewis and Kanji 2009: 8). A more tangible definition of NGOs is provided by the World Bank, which outlines the following common characteristics of NGOs:

> NGOs comprise a wide variety of associations, societies, foundations, and charitable entities that are (i) entirely or largely independent of government; (ii) not operated for profit; and (iii) exist to serve humanitarian, social or cultural interests, either of their memberships or of society as a whole. (World Bank 1998: 2)

The United Nations Department of Public Information (2012) defines NGOs in similar terms, but it also notes the voluntary nature of NGOs, where participation is not coerced. Furthermore, the UN observes that the institutional structure of NGOs enables them to be accountable to their members and donors (UN Economic and Social Council Resolution E1996/96).

Although NGOs can be active in a wide array of activities, the nature of their interaction with the state has been succinctly categorized by Lewis (2009) into three primary roles: implementer, catalyst and partner. As implementers, NGOs are responsible for mobilizing resources for the delivery of social services to those in need. This role is becoming increasingly common (and in China too), since governments and donors are contracting out the delivery of goods and services to NGOs as part of government reforms and privatization plans. As catalysts, NGOs can act as facilitators of social transformation through their 'ability to inspire, facilitate or contribute to improved thinking and action' (Lewis and Kanji 2009: 13). Such actions may target specific individuals, groups, organizations, communities or governments. As partners, NGOs may partner with the government, donors, private sector or communities to achieve specific goals in mutually beneficial relationships (ibid.). Through engaging and partnering with one another, the process is likely to transform both the state and NGOs.

The central question concerns the type of relationship that NGOs have with the state as it unveils the motivations and agendas of the state. While state–NGO relations are important to understand, at the same time, NGOs are credited for bringing an array of important issues to the attention of the public, and therefore have the chance to elevate certain issues to the agendas of national governments such as environmental sustainability, climate change, poverty reduction and income inequality. Most scholars and activists agree that the work of many NGOs is vital to communities around the world. However, this more positive assessment is also often linked to the observation that NGOs can take on the role of 'democratizing' in 'non-democratic' societies (e.g Hadenius and Uggla 1996; Demirovic 2003) by invigorating the growth of a strong civil society. The Philippines is an oft-cited example of the power of NGOs in facilitating the transition to democracy and of strengthening civil society and citizen participation in the political process. Despite the success of the Philippine NGO sector in facilitating democratic transition, issues regarding the level of institutionalization of NGOs in the political system and their level of democratic accountability and representation (Clarke 2001; Wurfel 2004), as well as the effectiveness of NGOs, remain in doubt. All these questions are applicable to NGOs around the world. Nevertheless, instead of speculating on the democratizing effect of NGOs in China, the focus of this chapter is to provide an insight into the Chinese NGO sector and current state–NGO interactions. Given the myriad factors that are likely to play a role in shaping China's political transition, it is unlikely that making direct predictions of the likelihood of democratic reforms within the context of NGOs will increase our understanding of the complex nature of state–NGO relations, nor will it uncover the dynamics of NGO sectoral development.

FRAMING THE RISE OF CHINESE NGOs

The emergence of Chinese NGOs has been correlated with a strengthening of civil society (see, e.g., *The Economist* 2014). In addition, such perspectives have also added to the debate of whether this means a retreat of the state. However, the question we should be asking is not whether NGOs equate with a weakened state, rather: how does the emergence of NGOs alter the state? Of equal importance is to assess the work of Chinese NGOs within their own terms, that is, to analyse their work and the impact they have on their constituents and the broader society. The separation between state and society is often regarded as a crucial factor for non-state stakeholders such as NGOs to emerge and represent the interests of citizens. China's political environment, where a one party-state exists, has opened up questions of whether a civil society exists and the viability of a Chinese civil society. While it is not my intention to conflate NGOs with civil society, as an analytical tool, civil society is particularly useful in reframing our focus on the non-state elements that are facilitating change. Nonetheless, the political environment in China does restrict the activities and effectiveness of NGOs.[4]

The scholarship on Chinese civil society from the late 1980s and early 1990s, prompted by the student protests in Tiananmen in June 1989, considered whether the student movement represented an emerging civil society agitating for socio-political change (see e.g. Østergard 1989; Gold 1990; McCormick et al. 1992). Subsequent investigation into Chinese civil society focused on whether the strength of the Chinese state should result in an exploration of a public sphere within the context of a Habermasian model (Rankin 1993; Wakeman 1993), given that many non-China specialists emphasize the requisite of state–society separation in order for civil society to exist. For Philip C. Huang (1993), the Habermasian model of public sphere may yet be unsuitable for China because of its historical roots in Europe and subsequent values attached to the 'public sphere', although one could potentially say the same for civil society. Hence, he resolves this dilemma by using the term 'third realm', which allows us to 'talk about those changes in terms of the expansion and institutionlization of a third space, without being drawn into a simplistic dichotomization between state and society' (Huang 1993: 225). Studies conducted by Mary B. Rankin (1990, 1993), William T. Rowe (1989, 1993) and David Strand (1989) drew upon evidence from China's late Qing and early Republican period to suggest that civil society and the public sphere did emerge in China's modern history. The debate over the existence of Chinese civil society has subsided and been replaced by an acknowledgment of the need to interpret the pluralization of Chinese society.

More recent studies have sought to apply the concept of civil society loosely in the context of China. Timothy Brook and B. Michael Frolic (1997: 8) argued in their edited volume that civil society is a useful heuristic device 'for thinking through certain changes that China is currently undergoing, but neither reproduces nor fully explains that reality'. Brook and Frolic (1997) outlined an analytical framework to survey Chinese civil society, beginning with the assumption that civil society is voluntary and comprised of social organizations. Brook followed these assumptions by suggesting that aside from kinship ties, Chinese society is organized by locality, occupation, fellowship and common cause. However, Heath B. Chamberlain (1998: 81) argued that we need not embark on an extensive exercise to find a Western-style civil society in China, and further amending the concept will only lead to confusion. David Yang (2004: 3), on the other hand, believed in the utility of the civil society framework, for it is 'in fact sufficiently nuanced to accommodate many key elements of traditional Chinese political thought'. Editors of *Urban Spaces in Contemporary China* (Davis et al. 1995) were less hesitant on conceptual issues; they deemed the public sphere a relevant concept to the study of China. One of the major contributions of the book is the interrelationship between changes to urban public and private life as a result of transformation in the physical environment and how social spaces emerge from social practices in physical spaces. The approach taken by Gordon White et al. (1996) does not assume that the existence of civil society will lead to political change in China. In later writings on Chinese civil society, a shift becomes discernible: an acceptance that the dynamics of China's economic transition has changed the relationship between state and society, and the undoubted emergence of social groups of all sorts, gives indication of a pluralization of Chinese society, if not a civil society. Studies since the mid- to late 1990s shifted towards a study of social groups. The debates on civil society of the 1990s provided subsequent studies with a framework to understand the emergence of NGOs, whereby the discussion of Chinese civil society ought not to be confined to a search for a separation between state and society, but rather to see civil society as a normative concept (Hsu 2012a). Thus the remainder of this chapter will focus on NGOs in China.

STATE–SOCIETY RELATIONS

Recent literature on Chinese NGOs has sought to focus attention on the rise and development of NGOs and their implication for state–society relations. Scholars have approached this development from different but overlapping perspectives. One can argue that the growth of NGOs is an indication of the growing strength of civil society; however, a more nuanced understanding is required. The growth of the NGO sector can in part be attributed to the failure of the Chinese state to address the social challenges that have come to the fore as a result of economic transition and decentralization (e.g. Ho 2001; Qin 2004; Schwartz 2004). Policy failures and the withdrawal of the state (J. Hsu 2009; Ma 2002; Yin 2009) are key elements in the emergence of NGOs. Nonetheless, those studies that I have categorized as falling under the state–society banner – bearing in mind the paucity of such categorization, as it clearly overlaps with other subheadings of this chapter – have tended to focus on the regulations that govern Chinese NGOs and also the level of autonomy of NGOs, despite the strength of the state. The focus on regulation is understandable as it is a clear indication of how the Chinese state views and engages with NGOs. Entwined with this exploration of regulations is the scholarly concern regarding the independence of NGOs, again reminiscent of the civil society debate. Others have chosen to focus on developing a more nuanced framework for understanding state–NGO relations, thus moving from the earlier civil society and public sphere frames. Relatedly, studies of the most recent nature not only seek to develop new frameworks but also call attention to the greater need to differentiate the 'central' from the 'local' state, when addressing state–NGO relations. This section will uncover the differing strands of research that have emerged under the state–NGO category.

While the growth of Chinese NGOs has been rapid, it is also marked by stringent regulations. Importantly, but in brief, for NGOs to obtain legal status, all organizations must register with the Ministry of Civil Affairs and have a sponsoring government agency. These procedures are burdensome and difficult to complete, particularly finding a sponsoring agency. Thus, many NGOs circumvent the process by not registering at all or by registering with the Industry and Commerce Bureau where a sponsor is not required. The regulatory framework for Chinese NGOs has drawn the attention of scholars because it signals state behaviour toward NGOs. Karla Simon (see, e.g., Simon 2013) has written extensively on the NGO regulatory frameworks in China. Her works provide those unfamiliar with the legal territory and the resulting challenges to NGOs with a good grasp of the current and evolving situation for NGOs. Timothy Hildebrandt (2011: 987) explores the complicated process of registration of NGOs where he argues that registration is not necessarily the end goal for all NGOs, especially as an unregistered status may actually provide more opportunities: for example, to secure financial support from international sources, which a registered organization may not otherwise receive. Whether NGOs are registered or not, they are ultimately bound by the state; however, even within this circumscribed space, there is a range of dynamics at play with substantial impact on the NGO sector.

The question of autonomy is one explored by Lu Yiyi (2007) where she challenges the notion that autonomy is a significant issue for NGOs. She believes that it is much more fruitful for us to analyse how NGOs negotiate with the state to shed light on the institutional environment for NGOs. In an earlier article by Ma Qiusha (2002), she observes that autonomy is defined along the lines of regulations relating to NGO registration and this is significant for the types of NGOs we see emerging in China (e.g. social service, welfare and cultural organizations). The types of NGOs emerging are also related to the diminishing state involvement in such realms. Nonetheless, Tony Saich (2008: 198) suggests that the closeness between state and NGOs is important because the state prefers that 'the sector be dominated by organizations in which the government plays a strong role'. If observed from the perspective of state regulations, we may conclude that the state is strong and NGOs are relatively weak, due to the tangible aspects of state power. But such analysis tells us very little about the dynamics and strategies at play. This binary of state and NGO, strong and weak, is not very helpful in dissecting the strategies that both state and NGOs employ to engage with one another for mutual benefit. Chris King-chi Chan (2013) argues that creative solutions are needed in the face of stringent regulations. The labour NGOs detailed in Chan's study indicate that informal partnerships with local branches of mass organizations give the NGO a level of independence to conduct their work. Fulda et al. (2012) observe that once NGOs are able to identify issues of mutual interest for both NGOs and local authorities, collaborations are much more likely; collaboration with government authorities is one of the keys to an NGO's success and possible longevity. Despite all of this, how might we explain and predict state behaviour across different NGO sectors? The answer may be that Chinese NGOs have developed relatively unevenly across different sectors, as seen in the next section.

Frameworks for interpreting state behaviour vis-à-vis NGOs have ranged from corporatism back to civil society (see Ma 2006). Regimes that are highly institutionalized, as is the case with China, are more likely to develop institutions to govern NGOs (Heurlin 2010). Thus, in the case of China, the state has shown that transition to a market economy has provided an opportunity to co-opt new actors to further its goals, here in the case of NGOs, to deliver a range of social services.[5] This notion of corporatism also resonates with Jennifer Hsu and Reza Hasmath (2014), who further suggest that local states are increasingly important to our analysis of the state behaviour. They suggest that there is a 'noticeable adaptation of corporatist measures – namely, the local state is utilizing subtle or tacit forms of approval to manage the sector' (Hsu and Hasmath 2014: 517). Corporatism may have its limitations in interpreting the nature of associational life in China because corporatist regulations fail to achieve the goal of social control (Howell 2012); however Hsu and Hasmath (2013: 8) argue that a 'corporatist lens allows the observer to investigate the opening up of social space while acknowledging the continued control of the state of various realms'. Carolyn Hsu (2010) proposes the framework that considers state and NGO institutional interdependence using organizational theories. The alliances developed between the two stakeholders, she demonstrates, are mutually beneficial, where both parties are able to secure much-needed resources. Despite these new or refashioned frameworks, the civil society framework persists (see Deng and Shieh 2011; J. Hsu 2012b; Jia and Sun 2009; Teets 2009), quite possibly because it highlights the role of NGOs; that is, NGOs are given the 'spotlight' in understanding changes to state–society relations. Nevertheless, the process of NGO development has been an uneven one.

NGOs BY SECTOR

The Chinese NGO sector as a whole has grown substantially over the last decade, with 462 000 organizations registered with the Ministry of Civil Affairs at the end of 2011, an increase of 3.7 per cent since 2010 (Ministry of Civil Affairs 2012a). The number reflects only NGOs registered with the Ministry of Civil Affairs. Estimates of unregistered organizations and those registered with the Industry and Commerce Bureau range from 200 000 to 1.4 million, with as high an estimate as 2.7 million (Deng 2010). Deng Guosheng (2010) contends that the state's informal or hidden rules govern the operations and future development of NGOs, similar to Hildebrandt's (2011) analysis. Rules, whether formal or informal, have led to uneven expansion of NGOs across China and, relatedly, across sectors. The following sections provide an insight into four NGO sectors: environmental, migrant, HIV/AIDS, and general service delivery to demonstrate the heterogeneity of the sector and also that each sector's experiences with the state differ substantially.

Environmental NGOs (ENGOs)

The literature on NGOs in the environmental sector is perhaps the most extensive in comparison to other sectors. It is also this sector where we see the greatest potential for Chinese NGOs to impact state policies. To understand why environmental NGOs are more likely to affect policies and mobilize collective action, it is necessary to look at the confluence of economic development on the environment, reduced state capacity due to decentralization to address social issues, and greater tolerance for NGOs which has led to the proliferation of ENGOs. Large-scale infrastructural dam projects – signalling China's modernization and development – such as the Three Gorges dams, have displaced 1.4 million people with insufficient compensation. The recent central government decision to revive the Nu River hydroelectric project in Yunnan has galvanized environmentalists to protect the last of China's major rivers that has not yet been dammed. In part, the Nu River dam project is a reflection of China's development conundrum of how to adequately deal with the rapid consumption of resources in a more sustainable and environmentally friendly way. The dam, according to the government, is a greener solution to power the future of China's development, rather than relying on coal. However, the lack of environmental safeguards and compensation for displaced residents and farmers, as demonstrated in other dam projects, has heightened tension and conflicts between the state and local communities. The central government is no doubt concerned with the costs of environmental damage. According to the World Bank (2007c), the cost of water and air pollution to health and non-health sectors (e.g. damages to crops and fisheries) is about 5.8 per cent of gross domestic product (GDP). Thus, the huge environmental costs and their impact on China's future development have enabled ENGOs to emerge and operate with a certain degree of freedom. The public education campaigns that ENGOs have engaged in since the mid-1980s, as a result of the Three Gorges Dam, have created alliances between environmentalists, scientists and ENGOs, representing an important moment for the environmental movement (Wu, F. 2009). The Three Gorges Dam construction 'alerted the general public, for the first time after 1949, [to] large-scale environmental problems hidden beneath the booming economy in China' (Wu, F. 2009: 4). By the mid-1990s, environmental activism had picked up pace with the establishment of Friends of Nature[6] in 1994, the first environmental group to actively recruit members, disseminate environmental research and engage with the public on a range of environmental issues. This activism can also be found in the fertile ground of universities today. In 2006 there were some 500 mature university and college ENGOs (Shao 2010).

Considerations of ENGOs' effectiveness in influencing environmental policy changes have not averted discussion on the prospects for democratization. Peter Ho (2001) argues that while ENGOs have increased in quantity and strengthened Chinese civil society, this is largely a function of the 'greening' of the state, where environmental laws and related agencies have been established to monitor and protect the environment. Institutional constraints, such as registration, have severely limited the opportunities of ENGOs. Moreover, Ho (2001) maintains that the inability to mobilize nationally on environmental issues leaves the majority of ENGOs fragmented and localized. ENGOs, despite their activeness and, to an extent, success in public education and environmental policies, clearly have not brought about political transition. Thus, enquiries into the potential for Chinese NGOs to affect political transition cannot elucidate the changes that are occurring at the local level, largely the interaction between local authorities, NGOs and communities. To gain real insight, focus ought not be directed at the potential for ENGOs to take contentious actions but at their ability to persuade local authorities to change their attitudes regarding environmental issues (see e.g. Wu, F. 2009: 5; Cooper 2006). Tang Shui-Yan and Zhan Xueyong (2011), in their examination of ENGOs' advocacy and collective petition activities, found that personal connections to the party-state played an important role in an ENGO's ability to have influence in policy creation. The case of anti-dam movements is no exception (Lin 2007). Regardless of whether ENGOs are effective in impacting policy change or not, ENGOs can operate as both sites and agents of local political change. We are unlikely to see large-scale political change as a result of the relationship between communities and ENGOs, but ENGOs can offer citizens the means to 'practise political skills, organize and participate in civic action, and test political limits' (Yang 2005: 65). Setsuko Matsuzawa (2012) concludes in similar fashion with a study on a dam-affected village, noting that citizens' engagement with environmental activism has helped citizens gain more opportunities to exercise their rights and forge new social space. Most recent research on ENGOs focuses on the use of technology and media to strengthen grassroots environmental activism (see, e.g., Liu 2011; Sima 2011; Sullivan and Xie 2009; Yang 2010; Yang and Taylor 2010). ENGOs may not have transformed China's political structure, but the impact on local community and political responses to environmental issues, as well as the fostering of citizen activism in community issues, clearly cannot be gleaned from an interpretative position of democratization or large-scale political transformation. The case of Chinese ENGOs indicates that to interpret the transformative potential of NGOs, analysis must be centred at the local level.

HIV/AIDS NGOs

The developments in the ENGO literature have paved the way for other sectoral studies. While some of the trends in the literature on HIV/AIDS reflect that of ENGOs, such as the role of changing government policies, two trends are unique to the issue of HIV/AIDS. The first is the role of HIV/AIDS NGOs in working with specific sub-population groups, such as sex workers, drug users, men who have sex with men (MSM), and infected blood donors (see Xu et al. 2005) – groups considered in the high risk category – and the delivery of services to these groups, whether it be needle exchanges or HIV screening tests. The work of HIV/AIDS NGOs in China is largely localized, working in a specific geographic area with certain subgroups. Therefore, to recognize and appreciate the impact of HIV/AIDS NGOs, again, our attention and analytical lens needs to align with the empirical realities, given that the vast majority of NGOs, regardless of sector, cannot operate at the national level, let alone the provincial level. At the local level, NGOs are often challenged in their work by law enforcement agencies, for example the criminalization of sex work makes it difficult for NGOs to reach sex workers, a key target group in HIV prevention (Kaufman 2011); or by the political responses to health interventions for MSM (Zhang and Chu 2005). While government attitudes have started to change with regards to HIV/AIDS, as evidenced by the increasing numbers of NGOs working and delivering services in this sector (Li et al. 2010), NGOs, such as those continuing to work with sub-population groups, are hampered not only by slow-to-change attitudes, but also by poor social capital (Lau et al. 2011). A range of factors have come to the fore with regard to NGOs' ability to respond to the HIV/AIDS challenge, aside from the difficulties all NGOs have to face in relation to registration status and their relationship with the state. Organizational structure is a key to understanding the capacity of NGOs, including the inexperience of staff, employment of non-health professionals and unstable funding (ibid.: 263). Consequently, to understand the effectiveness of HIV/AIDS NGOs on their constituents, it is necessary to recognize the constraints they face and the strategies adopted to navigate such environments, which leads directly to the second strand that is particular to this sector: transnational activism.

This transnational activism is in part shaped by researchers' call for greater collaboration between the Chinese state, domestic NGOs and international NGOs to combat the effects of HIV/AIDS. Gu Jing and Neil Renwick (2008: 100) echo this call, writing: 'the fight against HIV/AIDS can only be successful if there is full engagement between government, civil society, and international agencies'. Positive signs are starting to emerge in the collaboration between domestic and international NGOs (Wu 2011), where we are starting to see transference of new norms and practices in dealing with HIV/AIDS in China, but the offshoot of such collaboration is that Chinese NGOs are more effective when connected to global civil society actors (Kaufman 2012). Such evaluation does call into question the sustainability of such collaborations and the eventual effectiveness of domestic NGOs when partnerships or projects end. While international cooperation has brought substantial funding to HIV/AIDS-related work in China, Hildebrandt (2011) cautions against being too optimistic, as it has led to substantial misuse of funds and corrupt practices by both NGOs and government agencies who are recipients of international financial support. Nonetheless, international partnerships have transferred knowledge and skills in the treatment and management of HIV/AIDS to China, and they are now active in delivering HIV/AIDS programmes to other nations (Sun et al. 2010).

HIV/AIDS NGOs are challenged and restricted by the institutional environment, but if we shift our attention to the strategies that NGOs are adopting, we see the transformation potential of Chinese NGOs. Therefore, the study of NGOs cannot be framed within the language of political change. What is emergent in the literature on the HIV/AIDS NGOs is the active attempts by NGOs to reshape the discourse and perception of people living with HIV/AIDS (PLWHA) and breaking stereotypes of 'high-risk groups' (Wan et al. 2009; Wilson 2012). This activeness in (re)framing is nowhere more evident than in the plight of rural–urban migrant workers.

Migrant Workers' NGOs

Migrant NGOs have not followed the same trajectory as that of the environmental or HIV/AIDS sectors – often marked by a significant event such as the building of the Three Gorges Dam, or the Henan blood scandal – a clear sign of the heterogeneity of Chinese NGOs. However, a point of similarity with the previous two sectors is the inability to discount the role of the state in the development of migrant NGOs. The emergence of migrant groups and organizations in China's urban areas is largely due to the lack of social provision by urban authorities and the *hukou* (household registration), where one's entitlements from the state are tied to an individual's registration. The influx of migrant labourers into China's wealthy modern coastal areas in search of paid employment has led to sharp tensions between urban and rural residents. Among visions of China's economic modernization, the Chinese state has had an active role in shaping the discourse on migrants, through improving their *suzhi* (quality) (see, e.g., Jacka 2009; Murphy 2004) in line with the state's vision of China. Scholarly work on labour and migrant NGOs demonstrates that the focus on defending migrant workers' legal rights in the workplace has started to shift perceptions and treatment of migrants, starting from the state (Cheng et al. 2010; Croucher and Miles 2010; Lee 2008: 16). Labour-focused NGOs have gone a long way in assisting migrants in defending their working rights, but as Friedman and Lee (2010: 524) write, 'most labour NGO attention is focused on providing workers with after-the-fact advice on how to attempt to resolve grievances through the officially administered processes of mediation, arbitration and litigation'. Despite its many flaws and a government mass organization, the All-China Federation of Trade Unions has made significant headway in working more effectively to represent migrant workers' rights and labour rights in general (see Chan 2007, 2009).

Rather than focusing on labour or workers' rights, broader aspects of 'rights', particularly those associated with citizenship, have also drawn the attention of scholars (see e.g. Solinger 1999; Zhang 2002). Again, the impact of Chinese NGOs in the migrant sector and on the discourse on migrants' rights can only be understood if we steer our analytical lens to understanding the localized actions of these NGOs. According to Ren Xuefei (2011), NGOs are challenging the current urban citizenship regime. NGO service delivery has helped to expand social rights to migrant workers. She notes that despite the legalistic approach of NGOs, the different legal aid programmes have done a lot to empower migrant workers by raising awareness of their rights and by fostering a sense of collective identity. It would appear that the discourse on rights is no longer solely within the confines of the state. Research in the migrant NGO sector demonstrates the positive contributions NGOs have made in advancing migrants' rights and also in opening up space for civil society. However, both Jennifer Hsu (2012a) and Chloe Froissart (2006) argue that migrant NGOs are not only circumscribed by the political environment, but also by their own internal capacity and desire to maintain the status quo for fear of government reprisals. Shifting analysis to interpret the organizational capacity of NGOs and strategies engaging with the local authorities will bear fruit for understanding the transformational potential of Chinese NGOs.

General Social Service Delivery NGOs

Experimentation and changes in the way central and local authorities deliver social services have recently generated new scholarly works in understanding these changes and their impact on NGOs. Jessica Teets (2012) argues that the social delivery model has transitioned to a social innovation model where the government contracts with non-profits and private firms in order to reduce costs for social service delivery. This has two important implications for governance, according to Teets. First, including citizens in the provision of services, the hierarchical relationship between state and society is changed to a more supervisory one, in line with corporatism. Second, the changes to service delivery may very well empower the non-profit sector in China, but they also create difficulties in ensuring accountability and transparency of government services. Karen Fisher et al. (2012) share similar misgivings with regards to the service delivery transformation in disability services. The authors found that NGOs' understanding and application of accountability processes were rudimentary. As the Chinese authorities move further ahead with the contracting out of service delivery to NGOs, issues of accountability will become ever more pertinent, especially where it come to ensuring the most effective care for China's marginalized population groups. Responsibility for developing transparency, accountability and good governance lies in part with the NGOs (Ma 2012), but lack of experience may present a serious challenge in dealing with these issues. Hasmath and Hsu (2008) suggest that international NGOs can have a greater role in improving the capacity and skill sets of NGOs, whereas Anthony Spires (2012) believes that capacity training offered by foreign NGOs needs to incorporate the lessons and experiences of local NGOs in order to resonate with its participants. While research into the role of NGOs in contracted service delivery is an emerging field of enquiry, a word of caution is in order. We must ask whether a move to a neoliberal market-based model of service delivery will lead to a homogenization of the Chinese NGO sector, because as NGOs compete for limited contracts and resources, they reshape themselves into models that are accepted by the state to win contracts. The government is praised for its experimentation with contracting out social services to NGOs, but research into this new area will need to adopt a more critical lens in order to identify the influence on NGOs and their future work.

TRENDS IN THE NGO SECTOR

Chinese NGOs have demonstrated their ability to approach a variety of societal issues with innovation, but their capacity to respond is also dictated by the formal and informal arrangements as set out by the state. Trends affecting the NGO sector include not only central-level authorities but those at the local level too. Moreover, understanding NGOs' engagement strategies with the state and organizational capacity is critical if we are to recognize the potential impact of NGOs on Chinese society. Using institutional theories, Carolyn Hsu (2010) demonstrates that organizational strategies of NGOs are shaped both by external conditions and by the institutional experiences of their members. New organizations will usually adopt the institutional experiences that their members are familiar with. In an analysis of first-generation Chinese NGOs, Carolyn Hsu observed that founders utilized their experiences that were deeply rooted in working with and through party-state agencies to manage their organizations. Carolyn Hsu (2009) also notes that an institutional interdependence framework can highlight the symbiosis (although unequal) where NGOs are able to use the resources and freedom granted to them by the state with greater efficacy, and the state is able to use its alliance with NGOs as a signalling device to other state actors of social problems. Similarly, Paul Thiers (2009: 161) writes that the variety of state and NGO engagements has led to semi-state pluralism and that we should expect 'mixed politics' as a result. Spires (2011: 12), on the other hand, notes that this symbiotic relationship is both 'fragile and contingent'. Given the pluralization of state–NGO relationships, juxtaposed against the dominance of the state, scholars have repeatedly returned to the corporatist framework to interpret and make sense of the pluralization of state–NGO relations (see e.g. Heurlin 2010; Kojima et al. 2012; Unger and Chan 2008). While acknowledging the shortcomings of state corporatist approach, noting that it may not interpret the full extent of state–society relations and that it obscures the hegemonic agenda of the state in certain realms, Hsu and Hasmath (2013: 140) argue that the party-state will need to adopt more effective corporatist strategies with NGOs to ensure its legitimacy to rule. Clearly, the claims of progressive transformation on the part of Chinese NGOs must be analysed within the context of the state. As noted previously, the insistence on separating state and civil society and NGOs will not bring about fruitful analysis of how state and NGOs engage with one another or the subsequent outcomes. Thus, studies that acknowledge the reality of the Chinese state and their ensuing focus on strategies of engagement demonstrate that NGOs can and do push the boundaries of the state, but not necessarily in areas where one might expect, for example towards democratization. Nonetheless, opportunities are available to NGOs to engage in transformative practices.

Events such as the Wenchuan earthquake of 2008 have opened up substantial space for NGOs to assist in disaster relief (Deng and Shieh 2011; Menefee and Nordtveit 2012; Teets 2009), demonstrating the social capital of NGOs in mobilizing resources and volunteers. Jessica Teets (2013: 14) further develops the civil society framework by suggesting that pluralization of society is not leading to democratization, or even an autonomous civil society, but rather to 'consultative authoritarianism' as characterized by 'a pluralistic society participating in policy formation and implementation, and the use of multiple indirect tools of state control'. Along comparable lines to consultative authoritarianism is the idea of 'graduated control'. Within this system the state, out of self-interest, uses different control strategies for different social organizations. These different strategies are dependent on the social organization's proficiency as well as the goods or services it offers (see Kang and Han 2011; Wu and Chan 2012).

Focusing on patterns and strategies of engagement between state and NGOs underscores the development potential of NGOs. Such potential, as studies reviewed in this chapter demonstrate, is predicated upon the NGO's know-how in interacting with the authorities, requiring persistence and proactiveness on the part of the NGO (Fulda et al. 2012). In Chloe Froissart's (2010) research, strategies of state–NGO engagement are explored on the lines of geography, where local conditions and politics will impact upon how NGOs deliver their services as well as their future trajectory. Along similar lines of geography, but focusing on the spatial arrangements of the state, Hsu (2012b) provides a systematic analysis of the different layers of the state and their engagement with migrant NGOs to emphasize the analytical need to differentiate between local and central states when analysing state–NGO relations, as each level of the state will impact on the development of NGOs in varying ways. The development of new frameworks and theories is critical in order to understand the pluralization of state–NGO relations in China.

The management of Chinese NGOs has occurred through formal regulations; however, new trends including the resurgence of government-organized NGOs (GONGOs) and Party-organized NGOs (PONGOs) demonstrate the methods by which both Party and state have sought to engage and supervise NGOs. The growth of the NGO sector has prompted a Party-building drive to establish local grassroots Party branches in over 403 000 social organizations (Thornton 2014). The Chinese Communist Party's comprehensive drive to cover the civil society sector has drawn both caution and accolades. The emergence of PONGOs suggests a new hybrid form of social organization sponsored and funded by local Party committees. Such developments demonstrate an active attempt and a rethinking of strategy from the Party's perspective to understand and interact with the flourishing civil society sector. According to Patricia Thornton (2014), having Party branches within a social organization may be both a benefit and a burden to the organization in question. The benefit could come in the form of assistance in administrative costs of running the organization. However, the presence of the Party may prevent attempts to professionalize, whereby frequent reporting to the Party will drain existing resources dedicated to the organization's constituents, irrespective of Party assistance. Furthermore, the presence of the Party may reinforce perceptions that such organizations are mouthpieces of the Party. Relatedly, GONGOs are regarded as the social arm of the party-state. Major GONGOs include the All-China Federation of Trade Unions, the All-China Women's Federation and the Communist Youth League of China. Such organizations enjoy special political status and receive funding from the state. Given their status and funding, GONGOs have wide coverage and access to the community, which ensures breadth of the project, although not necessarily depth. GONGOs are working and delivering services to a range of constituents from women to impoverished school children. Carolyn Hsu (2014) in her study of the China Youth Development Foundation shows that the GONGO has successfully exploited the agencies of the party-state to achieve organizational goals. GONGOs have worked co-operatively with NGOs to deliver social services; however, as with PONGOs there is the potential for NGOs to be sidelined by their party-state partners for the sake of a carefully managed NGO sector by the state.

NGOs AND TRANSFORMATION

Chinese NGOs face a range of institutional constraints due to the nature of the Chinese state. Acknowledging this reality and adopting an appropriate framework to interpret the rise of Chinese NGOs will lead to rich analytical enquiry but will also introduce new areas of inquiry. NGOs are not synonymous with democracy or democratization, as the Chinese case has clearly shown. But that does not make Chinese NGOs any less transformative than their Western counterparts. Instead the transformation that is taking place is the impact that Chinese NGOs have on state attitudes, behaviour and policy at the local level towards a range of social issues. Given the political realities Chinese NGOs must contend with, large-scale transformation at the national level is out of the question. Indeed, Chinese NGOs have had substantial impact in terms of the environment and large-scale infrastructural projects, reshaping the national discourse on migrant workers and a host of other issues. Thus, transformation needs to be understood in terms of not only political change, but also social change: that is, the impact on communities.

On a final note, the future of scholarship in this area will be enriched by further interdisciplinary work. Discipline-bound research on Chinese NGOs can only highlight a proportion of the NGO sector. Literature from the environmental and HIV/AIDS sector shows the possibility for scientists to engage with social science researchers to explain the social, political, environmental, economic and health-related drivers for the precipitous growth of NGOs. Furthermore, interdisciplinary collaboration can enhance our frameworks for interpreting state–NGO relations. What this chapter has revealed is the greater need to further develop theories and frameworks to interpret the pluralization of state–NGO relations in China. Scholars reading this chapter are encouraged to consider what implications the proliferation of NGOs may have for the Chinese party-state. Are current frameworks of civil society and corporatism sufficient for understanding state–NGO relations? These questions are crucial to avoid being blindsided by the intricacies of each of our own research projects. An interdisciplinary approach can potentially inform the work of NGOs. The emergent bio-social approach to understanding epidemics such as HIV/AIDS (see e.g. Sutherland and Hsu 2012) – whereby a medical explanation is insufficient to explain the spread of diseases, but requires a combination of social explanations – can help to shape the work of NGOs to better utilize their often limited resources. It is hoped that research and practice are two-way streets, where practice can inform scholarship, for a truly engaged and relevant scholarship.

NOTES

1. For example, the United States Agency for International Development (USAID) in 2011 dedicated US$17 billion to the programme areas under its Strategic Goal of Governing Justly and Democratically. Programmes include promoting human rights, democratic governance, civil societies and broad-based economic growth, amongst others (USAID 2012).
2. See Claire Mercer's (2002) review and critique of the NGO literature that equates and/or associates NGOs with democratization.
3. Najam (1996) has identified at least 47 different acronyms in reference to NGOs. This list has since been modified by Lewis and Kanji (2009). For a concise treatment of the term 'NGO' and its history, see Lewis (2009).
4. Despite such restrictions, what is interesting to note is that government-organized NGOs (GONGOs) and Party-organized NGOs (PONGOs) have emerged to be important stakeholders in the broadly defined realm of 'NGO' development. These organizations have sought to embed themselves in grassroots NGOs as a way for the party-state to better manage the sector. See the section on 'Trends in the NGO Sector' in this chapter for further details.
5. I thank Deborah Davis for noting the need to incorporate the market into the consideration of NGOs, as the state is no longer the only factor impacting upon the rise and development of NGOs. Please see Howell (2012) for further exploration of the role of the market in the development of Chinese NGOs.
6. Friends of Nature was registered as a secondary organization with affiliation to Beijing Municipal Government's Department of Culture.

20. Reports of social unrest: basic characteristics, trends and patterns, 2003–12
Lynette H. Ong

A persistent question that preoccupies scholars who study authoritarian China is social stability and durability of the communist regime. The authoritarian government, obsessed with social stability, looks for any sign of unrest which may pose a threat to the regime. It invests hundreds of millions of renminbi every year in stability maintenance, propaganda, and internet monitoring to root out would-be protestors.

Despite that, and gleaning from various media reports, it can be surmised that the number of social unrest cases – a major threat to the Communist Party's rule – has risen. While that may be true, details of the frequency, size, scope, grievances giving rise to, and impact on the regime of social unrest are still rather elusive. Publicly available official figures indicate a total of 8700 'mass incidents' in 1993, increasing tenfold to 87 000 in 2005. However, the authorities have ceased issuing any official figures since then. A frequently cited estimate by Sun Liping, a researcher at Tsinghua University, suggests that there were 180 000 incidents in 2010 (Orlik 2011).

This chapter addresses these important issues by analysing a dataset of social unrest in China constructed from more than 2500 cases during 2003–12. The dataset is constructed based on coding of unrest cases reported in the Chinese-language and English media.

The chapter begins by analysing official definitions of the term 'mass incidents', which is used in China to describe social unrest cases. Despite its frequent usage, the meaning of 'mass incidents' is shrouded in confusion and little understood. I underline three important characteristics in the official definitions, which are illegality, mobs and the public order disturbance nature of 'mass incidents'. Next, the chapter introduces the Social Unrest In China (SUIC) event dataset I have built which covers a ten-year period from 2003 to 2012. The chapter will introduce definitions, basic characteristics, trends and patterns of the cases included in the dataset. Land-related grievances, namely those that have arisen due to land expropriations, demolitions, evictions and relocations, account for nearly 40 per cent of all cases. Labour disputes in state-owned enterprises, and private and foreign-owned firms, are the next major motivators of social unrest. I highlight the saliency of 'social anger-venting incidents' due to their magnitude, frequent violence and ability to mobilize a large number of participants who are not directly impacted upon by the events.

OFFICIAL DEFINITIONS OF 'MASS INCIDENTS'

The Chinese concept of social unrest is rather dissimilar to Western notions. While the Western conception of social unrest typically connotes some forms of political actions, be they collective actions, social movements, social resistance, riots or revolutions, the

Chinese understand the term to mean a congregation that is not sanctioned by the authorities, and commitment of an act that disturbs public order. Granted, genuine political revolutions, social resistance or movements are rare events in authoritarian China. Therefore, the Chinese concept is a much broader umbrella concept that encompasses a large number of scenarios and activities that do not fall within the Western confines. That is why the Chinese have used the term 'mass incidents' (*quntixing shijian*) to describe 'social unrest' as understood in the West.

However, the official lexicon had evolved over time. In the 1990s and early 2000s, the term 'mass incidents' was often used in conjunction with 'troublemaking' (*naoshi*), 'outburst' (*tufa*) or 'security' (*zhi'an*). The official terms used to describe incidents of these nature included 'mass outbursts' or 'mass spontaneous incidents', 'mass troublemaking' and 'mass security incidents'. It was only from 2003 onwards that 'mass incidents' became the single unified official terminology for these events (Xiao 2012).

In addition, the authorities have never provided an unambiguous definition for the term. According to the *Dictionary of Party Building* 'mass incidents' refers to:

> events that are triggered by social conflicts, which involve groups of people who come into formation spontaneously, form congregations that lack a legal basis, engage in behavior that creates verbal or physical clashes, in order to express their own demands or advocate their own interests, or to vent their dissatisfaction, the outcome of which is a serious adverse impact on social order and social stability. (Ye and Lu 2009)

According to Xiao (2012), relevant public security regulations issued in the 1990s and in 2000 underscored two common characteristics of these events: unlawfulness (*weifa*), and involvement of a mass of people (*qunti*) or a mob (*juzhong*). All congregations are deemed unlawful in China unless organizers have successfully secured approval from the authorities. By definition, this renders unlawful any sort of rallies, marches, demonstrations, strikes, sit-ins and protests. Collective petitioning involving more than five people is also considered an unlawful assembly. A mob obviously involves a group of people, though the number required for it to pass the threshold of a 'mass incident' has never been explicitly spelt out.

In 2000, the Public Security Bureau issued a regulation on 'mass incidents' that included the following examples: (1) unlawful rallies, marches and demonstrations that involve a large number of people; (2) any rally, march, demonstration and collective petitioning that seriously disturbs public order or endangers public security; (3) any socially destabilizing strike action; (4) large-scale congregations organized by any illegal organization or cult; (5) mobbing or attacks on any government agency, party or military unit, radio or television station, foreign embassy or consulate; (6) mobbing or attacks on any public transportation hub or public place; (7) mobs or riots in large-scale events or celebrations; (8) mobbing or looting of any government or private warehouse or logistic hub; (9) large-scale mob fights; and (10) any group act that seriously endangers public security and social order (Public Security Bureau 2000).

The exhaustive list underlines the fact that any event that poses a threat to public order or public security could be officially deemed a 'mass incident'. This broadens the scope considerably to cover incidents such as attacks on private property, football hooliganism, drunken fights, and other events that lack any social grievance as a cause. They fall within the ambit owing to their unruly nature, and threat due to 'public order disturbance'.

Additionally, a 2004 central government-issued work document underlined 'mass incidents' as events that have arisen from 'conflicts between and among private individuals', as opposed to the anti-system or anti-regime protests. In my view, this central document provides an additional dimension to the definitions instead of giving it a strict qualification. In other words, official definitions of 'mass incidents' may be understood to include all unlawful and mob-like activities, driven by anti-system or anti-government sentiments, as well as by conflicts among private individuals. It is worth emphasizing that 'mass incidents' go beyond what are commonly perceived as anti-government or anti-regime group actions.

EVENT IDENTIFICATION IN THE SUIC DATASET: SOURCES, CRITERIA AND DEFINITION

The SUIC is a hand-coded dataset. The coders scoured the English- and Chinese-language internet sites and media databases for reports on 'mass incidents'. English sources were particularly useful for incidents that occurred in the first half of the 2000s when the Chinese-language internet sites were relatively undeveloped. A number of incidents in the earlier years were obtained from the Lexis-Nexis database that collects media reports from the *South China Morning Post*, Agence France-Presse (AFP) and Associated Press (AP). In the second half of the 2000s, several human rights organizations based in China and overseas began reporting and documenting incidents on a regular basis. The SUIC dataset has benefited tremendously from the emergence of 64Tianwang, Molihua, Radio Free Asia and the *China Labour Bulletin*. The dataset has also drawn cases from national and local Chinese-language newspapers, such as *Xinhua Daily* (New China News Agency Daily), *Fazhi Ribao* (Legal Daily), *Southern Weekend* and *Caijing* (Finance), among others. When certain reports lack details or present conflicting details, the coders made an attempt to cross-check facts from other news sites.

As criteria for inclusion in the dataset, I followed the official definitions of the Chinese authorities, because one of the SUIC dataset's objectives is to capture a snapshot of what qualify as 'mass incidents' in China. The search terms included '*kangyi*' (protests), '*jingzuo*' (sit-ins), '*saoluan*' or '*baoluan*' (riots), '*shiwei*' (demonstrations), '*jihui*' (rallies), '*youxing*' (marches), '*minyuan*' (grievance), '*quntixing shijian*' (mass incidents) and '*raoluan shehui zhixu*' or '*raoluan gonggong zhixu*' (public order disturbance). That notwithstanding, incidents of a public order disturbance nature that occur on a daily basis could be countless. We were therefore quite selective in including these events, especially if they inform little about underlying social grievances.

As mentioned, the authorities have never made clear about the threshold for the number of participants in a 'mass incident'. Some Chinese scholars suggest that incidents involving 10 or 15 or more participants should be considered 'mass incidents'. An overwhelming majority of the events in the SUIC dataset consist of more than ten participants. For collective petitioning, I adhered to the official definition of more than five individuals for an event to qualify as a 'mass incident'. However, I also included self-immolation cases often involving a single individual, because I perceive that as a protest of desperation. Self-immolation cases have increased in number in recent years, owing to the increased salience of land-related and religious reasons.

The SUIC dataset contains a total of 2528 cases from 2003 to 2012. Though many of them occurred for more than one day, subsequent events were not counted, but coded as a different duration. Despite that the SUIC dataset captures only a snapshot of the frequently cited 180 000 'mass incidents' annually; I believe that repeated cases may partly account for the disparity. Public order disturbances that do not exhibit an anti-government tendency, which are largely excluded from the current dataset, could be another reason for the discrepancy. The SUIC dataset is also subject to the following caveats. To the extent that media reports are biased towards larger incidents, and those that create more damage to property and result in more casualties, our dataset is predisposed to those cases. A potentially significant drawback is development of the internet and independent journalism in China, which resulted in a higher density of cases reported in the second half of the period covered in the dataset. These caveats should be borne in mind when interpreting the data, particularly the time series trends.

DESCRIPTIVE STATISTICS: TRENDS AND PATTERNS

The number of incidents increased steadily throughout the period from 2003 to 2012, as Figure 20.1 illustrates. Notably, it increased steadily from 2003 to 2011, and rose sharply in 2012. However, the trend over time should be interpreted with caution. The internet in China was more developed in 2012 than was the case in the early 2000s. Most independent journalism organizations, from which most of the cases in the dataset were drawn, did not even exist in the earlier period. Thus, I had to rely on traditional newspaper outlets,

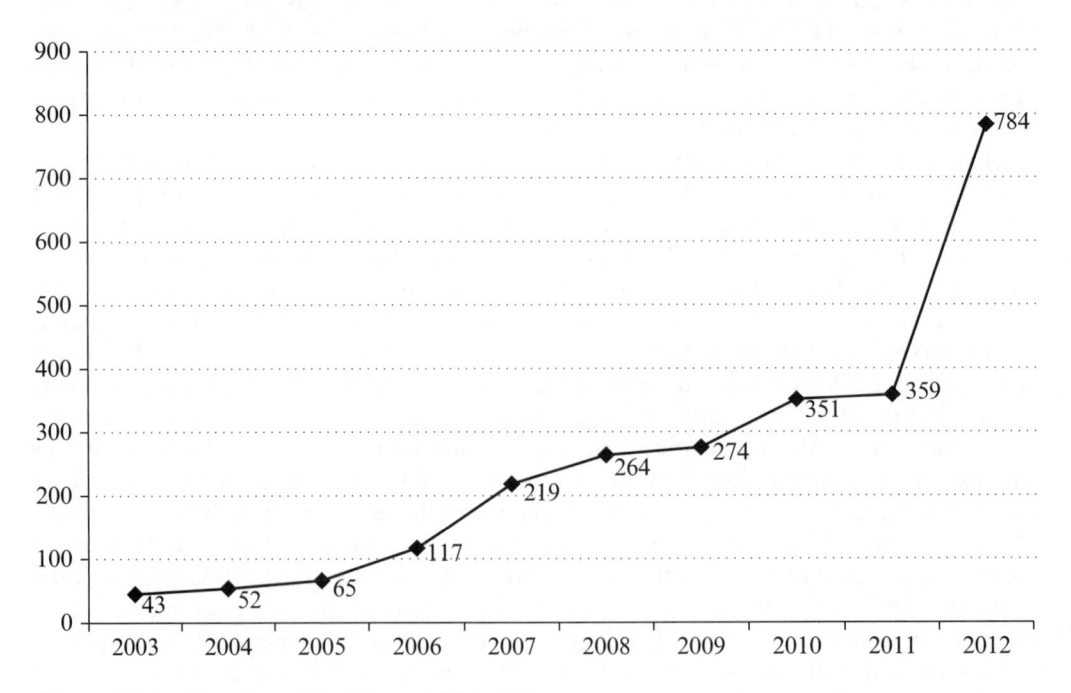

Figure 20.1 Number of incidents, 2003–12

Table 20.1   Duration of cases (N = 2528)

Duration	Number of cases	% of total
1 day	2263	89.5
2–7 days	229	9.1
>7 days	36	1.4
Total	2528	100

Table 20.2   Size of protests (N = 2528)

No. of people involved	No. of incidents	%
1–10	109	4.3
11–100	421	16.7
101–1000	967	38.2
1001–10 000	605	23.9
>10 000	71	2.8
NA	355	14.0
Total	2528	100

such as *South China Morning Post* and the *People's Daily*, for notification of incidents that happened in the earlier period.

Two-thirds (67 per cent) of the cases happened in urban areas, referring to prefecture-level cities, provincial capitals, and municipalities, according to official definitions. The other one-third (33 per cent) happened in rural areas, which are county-level cities, townships and villages. In terms of duration, 90 per cent of cases occurred for only a single day, 9 per cent occurred for between two and seven days, while the remaining 1 per cent were long-term incidents that persisted for more than seven days, as shown in Table 20.1.

Size of protest is measured by the number of people involved in the actions, not including the police or security personnel sent to maintain order or contain the actions. Protest size seems to be normally distributed. As Table 20.2 suggests, the largest category is 101–1000 people (38 per cent), followed by 24 per cent in the 1001–10 000 category, and 17 per cent in the 11–100 category. Four per cent of the cases involved fewer than ten people, and 3 per cent involved more than 10 000 people (Table 20.2).

Cases related to land expropriation, demolition and relocation were the single largest category, accounting for more than one-third of the total (36 per cent). We decided to group these three categories together because it is often challenging to disentangle them: land expropriation is usually followed by demolition, and demolition and relocation usually go hand in hand. The second-largest category is labour disputes in private or foreign-owned companies, most frequently involving migrant workers (14 per cent), labour disputes in state-owned enterprises (11 per cent), environment-related incidents (6 per cent), and cases instigated by brutality of the police or city patrols (5 per cent). See Table 20.3 for categories of various grievances, and Table 20.4 for their frequencies.

As I have argued elsewhere (Ong and Göbel 2014), most of the protests in China are aimed at gaining redress for material grievances. Factory workers protest because they

Table 20.3 Types of grievances and examples

Abbreviations	Grievances	Examples
ED	Education-related	Incidents staged by teachers over low wages and poor working conditions; parents against shoddy construction that killed children during Sichuan earthquake
ET	Ethnically motivated	Incidents staged by the Uighurs and Tibetans, or disputes between the Hans and ethnic minorities
EV	Environment	Paraxylene plants and other chemical factories; dams and hydropower plants; air pollution; contaminated drinking water
FD	Freedom and human rights	One-child policy, human rights, religions, Falun Gong, etc.
HE	Health-related	Disputes taking place in hospitals, and over health issues, such as AIDS and food safety
HO	Homeowners	Incidents staged by urban homeowners
IV	Investment	Investors' protests over fraud and Ponzi schemes
LR	Land rights	Related to land expropriations, demolition, relocation in rural and urban areas, often over low compensation, corruption, violence, etc.
MD	Labour disputes in private firms	Labour disputes in private and foreign-owned firms, often involving migrant workers' complaints of low wages, owed wages and poor working conditions
MJ	Miscarriage of justice	Incidents triggered by what participants saw as a miscarriage of justice, even though they are not directly affected by the incidents
MS	Miscellaneous	Incidents that do not come under any other category, such as collective petitions for unknown or unreported reasons
NP	Nationalist	Connected to nationalism, such as anti-Japan protests
PB	Police brutality	Incidents caused by brutality and unjustified use of force by the police and city patrol (*chengguan*)
PM	Private matters	Disputes between and among private individuals, but not against the state
SD	State-owned enterprise labour disputes	Labour disputes in state-owned enterprises, often over enterprise restructuring, inadequate retrenchment packages and pension schemes, etc.
TB	Taxi and pedi cabs	Incidents staged by taxi and pedi cab drivers, often over low fares
TX	Tax-related	Incidents triggered by high taxes in rural and urban areas
VE	Veterans	Veterans' displeasure over low or inadequate pensions

are paid low wages or are owed wages, or they suffer poor working conditions. Peasants resist because they receive inadequate compensation for giving up their land and houses. People take environmental grievances to the street because their drinking water has been contaminated, or the air will be polluted by the construction of a chemical plant. These grievances have not been generally framed as advocacy for improvement of labour or peasants' rights, even though they could have been that way. Following this logic, participants are restricted to the individuals whose material interests have been directly affected; those who are not direct victims have no reason to coalesce. Therefore, most protests tend

Table 20.4 Grievance type and frequency (N = 2528)

Grievance	Number of cases	% of total
Education (ED)	75	3.0
Ethnic (ET)	69	2.7
Environment (EV)	142	5.7
Freedom/rights (FD)	72	2.9
Health (HE)	27	1.1
Homeowners (HO)	30	1.2
Investment (IV)	31	1.2
Land expropriation, demolition and relocation (LR)	900	35.6
Labour disputes in private and foreign-owned companies (MD)	362	14.3
Miscarriage of justice (MJ)	38	1.5
Miscellaneous (MS)	91	3.6
Nationalist (NP)	35	1.4
Police and city patrol brutality (PB)	137	5.4
Private matters (PM)	48	1.9
State-owned enterprise labour disputes (SD)	281	11.1
Taxi and pedi cabs (TB)	141	5.6
Taxes (TX)	9	0.4
Veterans (VE)	37	1.5
Total	2528	100

to be relatively small in size, and in contained or localized areas, with no mobilization across regions or segments of the population.

However, there are some exceptions to these trends, as SUIC data have revealed. The exceptions are grievances such as miscarriage of justice cases, police or city patrol brutality, and freedom or human rights cases, which are contestations of certain values or rights. Miscarriage of justice cases are incidents the immediate causes of which do not fit squarely into other categories. They often attract participants and onlookers who are sympathetic over injustice in such cases, rather than those directly impacted upon by the events. In 2006, hundreds of people in Shaoyang, Hunan staged a protest because a local reporter who exposed corruption of a government official was given a jail sentence. In 2007, the death of a student in Guang'an, Sichuan provoked more than 1000 people, including students and residents in the city, to protest because the alleged killer escaped justice because he was related to the head of the local police. It is noteworthy that these cases are capable of mobilizing sympathizers across different segments of the populations, although the participants are still locality-specific.

Another similar grievance capable of marshalling a large number of participants who are direct victims is the brutality of the police or city patrols (*chengguan*). City patrols are para-municipal officials tasked with enforcing local urban management bylaws, and maintaining urban management order. They are notorious for using unjustified force and violent tactics in their dealings with street vendors, hawkers and migrant workers. These incidents are typically stories of some disadvantaged groups or societies, such as migrant workers, who die in police custody or are beaten to death by city patrol. Oppressive acts

Table 20.5 Proportions of grievance types, 2003–12 (N = 2528)

Grievance	2003	2004	2005	2006	2007	2008	2009	2010	2011	2012
ED	0.0	0.0	0.0	6.0	1.8	5.7	3.7	3.1	2.5	2.4
ET	0.0	3.9	0.0	0.9	1.8	8.0	3.7	1.7	1.1	2.7
EV	0.0	3.9	7.7	3.4	5.9	7.2	6.9	5.4	4.2	6.3
FD	2.3	0.0	3.1	2.6	1.8	1.5	1.1	0.9	0.6	6.4
HE	0.0	0.0	0.0	0.9	1.8	0.4	0.7	1.1	1.7	1.2
HO	2.3	0.0	0.0	1.7	0.5	1.9	2.2	0.3	0.6	1.5
IV	2.3	1.9	1.5	2.6	0.5	3.0	2.2	0.3	0.0	1.2
LR	32.6	26.9	30.8	39.3	38.4	24.6	41.2	52.4	41.8	26.8
MD	0.0	9.6	7.7	5.1	12.3	11.7	8.0	10.3	20.3	20.0
MJ	2.3	1.9	1.5	2.6	1.8	1.1	1.5	1.7	1.1	1.4
MS	4.7	3.9	3.1	7.7	0.5	2.7	3.7	3.4	1.4	5.2
NP	0.0	0.0	0.0	0.0	0.5	1.1	0.0	2.9	0.0	2.7
PB	11.6	5.8	4.6	9.4	6.4	6.8	5.1	2.6	2.5	6.5
PM	2.3	0.0	0.0	3.4	2.7	3.0	1.1	4.0	1.4	0.9
SD	37.2	32.7	24.6	12.0	16.4	11.4	14.6	6.3	6.7	8.4
TB	0.0	7.7	6.2	2.6	4.1	8.7	2.2	2.6	12.5	4.9
TX	2.3	1.9	4.6	0.0	0.0	0.0	0.4	0.0	0.3	0.3
VE	0.0	0.0	4.6	0.0	2.7	1.1	1.8	1.1	1.4	1.4
Total	100	100	100	100	100	100	100	100	100	100

by those who misuse their powers against the weak often provoke widespread public anger, especially among migrant societies who feel they share the same plight. However, these cases are also typically contained within the localities, and have no cross-regional mobilization effect.

Freedom and human rights cases, such as protests over the one-child policy and the Falun Gong cult, which could mobilize a large number of people across the society and geographical boundaries, are rare. Since they are typically targeted at the central government, they are promptly suppressed and the participants are prosecuted. The 1989 Tiananmen protests are classic examples of resistance in the cause of freedom and human rights.

There are several striking trends in the changes in proportion of grievances over time, as Table 20.5 illustrates. The percentage of land-related cases rose steadily throughout the 2000s, but peaked in 2010. At that point, land-related issues accounted for more than half of all cases. Worker disputes in private and foreign-owned companies, which were almost non-existent in the early 2000s, climbed steadily to 20 per cent of cases in 2011 and 2012; on the other hand, the proportion of state-owned enterprise worker disputes fell steadily throughout the period, from 37 per cent in 2003, to 6–8 per cent in 2010–12. Taken together, the last two trends reflect the growing importance of private and foreign-owned companies in the economy, and the decline of the state-owned enterprises, with the accompanying trends in labour unrest.

In terms of the provincial distribution of incidents, Guangdong and Sichuan have the highest proportion of cases, followed by Beijing, Hubei, Zhejiang, Jiangsu and

Table 20.6 Per capita income ranking and number of incidents (N = 2528)

Province/municipality	Ranking of provincial/ municipal disposable income per capita	Number of incidents	Number of incidents per million people
Shanghai	1	112	4.9
Beijing	2	173	8.8
Zhejiang	3	143	2.6
Guangdong	4	527	5.1
Jiangsu	5	133	1.7
Tianjin	6	28	2.2
Fujian	7	70	1.9
Shandong	8	96	1.0
Liaoning	9	22	0.5
Inner Mongolia	10	17	0.7
Chongqing	11	64	2.2
Hunan	12	86	1.3
Guangxi	13	83	1.8
Yunnan	14	52	1.1
Anhui	15	51	0.9
Hainan	16	34	3.9
Hubei	17	146	2.6
Shaanxi	18	89	2.4
Hebei	19	30	0.4
Henan	20	95	1.0
Shanxi	21	37	1.0
Sichuan	22	233	2.9
Jilin	23	20	0.7
Jiangxi	24	39	0.9
Ningxia	25	5	0.8
Guizhou	26	38	1.1
Tibet	27	12	4.0
Xinjiang	28	9	0.4
Heilongjiang	29	29	0.8
Qinghai	30	20	3.6
Gansu	31	35	1.4

Shanghai, respectively. These seven provinces and municipalities combined account for over 50 per cent of total reported cases.

Are social unrest cases more likely to happen in economically developed regions? The number of incidents per se does not appear to be correlated with the ranking of provincial or municipal income per capita. However, if the number of incidents on a per capita basis are taken into account, this appears to be positively correlated with the per capita income ranking. If income per capita increases by 1 per cent, the number of incidents per million people rises by 0.016. Beijing, Guangdong and Shanghai manifest the highest number of incidents on a per capita basis (Table 20.6).

Table 20A.1 (in the Appendix) provides details of reported grievances in provinces and municipalities. In Guangdong, 38 per cent of the cases were labour disputes in private and foreign-owned companies; another nearly 30 per cent were related to land. In Sichuan, 34 per cent of the cases were land-related, while 17 per cent were state-owned enterprise labour disputes. In Beijing, 36 per cent were due to land issues, and about 19 per cent fall under the 'miscellaneous' category, which most commonly reflects collective petitioning. In Hebei, while 43 per cent of the cases were land-related, 27 per cent were labour disputes in state-owned enterprises. In Zhejiang and Jiangsu provinces, half of the cases were related to land-related issues. Taken together, these patterns suggest that land-related issues were the primary grievance across most regions, regardless of income level. Labour disputes in private and foreign-owned firms, which commonly involve migrant workers, were most frequent in Guangdong, Shanghai and Jiangsu, where most of these firms are sited. High proportions of labour disputes in state-owned enterprises could be found in the provinces of Jilin, Chongqing, Hubei, Hebei and Shandong. Unsurprisingly, regions with the highest proportion of ethnic-related conflicts were those with significant minority populations, namely Tibet, Qinghai and Xinjiang.

VIOLENCE, PROTEST SIZE AND 'SOCIAL ANGER-VENTING' INCIDENTS

Roughly half of the cases involved violence.[1] In particular, police or city patrol brutality (90 per cent of which were violent), taxes (89 per cent), ethnic (72 per cent), land-related (64 per cent), miscarriage of justice (61 per cent), and environment (57 per cent) cases. Conversely, violence was noticeably absent in a significant proportion of these cases: taxi or pedi cabs (84 per cent), veterans (81 per cent), education-related (83 per cent), nationalist (77 per cent), state-owned enterprises (75 per cent), and private or foreign enterprises (71 per cent), as shown in Table 20.7.

Size of protest is defined as the number of people involved, not including armed police or security personnel sent to repress the crowd or maintain order. As shown in Table 20A.1, size of protest is divided into five categories: (0) 1–10 people; (1) 11–100 people; (2) 101–1000 people; and (3) 1001–10 000 people; and (4) more than 10 000 people. Most of the grievances have a normally distributed protest size, as Figure 20.2 illustrates. However, notably, close to half of these categories involved more than 1000 people, that is, they fall into protest size categories (4) and (5). These cases are nationalist protests (51 per cent), and driven by grievances such as ethnicity (45 per cent), miscarriage of justice (48 per cent), failed investment schemes (48 per cent), police or city patrol brutality (50 per cent), and taxes (89 per cent, but with only nine cases).

ANGER-VENTING INCIDENTS

'Social anger-venting incidents' (*shehui xiefen shijian*) have entered the official lexicons of social stability and control. The term, first coined by prominent Chinese Academy of Social Science researcher Yu Jianrong, has the following characteristics: (1) spontaneous events caused by chance (*ouran*), rather than premeditated; and their exact causes are

Table 20.7 Use of violence by grievance type (N = 2528)

Grievance	Violence involved?				
	No (number)	No (%)	Yes (number)	Yes (%)	Total number
ED	62	82.7	13	17.3	75
ET	19	27.5	50	72.5	69
EV	63	43.5	82	56.6	145
FD	42	58.3	30	41.7	72
HE	13	48.2	14	51.9	27
HO	22	73.3	8	26.7	30
IV	18	58.1	13	41.9	31
LR	327	36.3	573	63.7	900
MD	258	71.3	104	28.7	362
MJ	15	39.5	23	60.5	38
MS	61	67.0	30	33.0	91
NP	27	77.1	8	22.9	35
PB	13	9.5	124	90.5	137
PM	21	43.8	27	56.3	48
SD	212	75.4	69	24.6	281
TB	119	84.4	22	15.6	141
TX	1	11.1	8	88.9	9
VE	30	81.1	7	18.9	37
Total	1323	52.3	1205	47.7	2528

often unclear; (2) no distinct organizers, as most participants have no direct relationship with the incident's victims; (3) text messaging and social media aiding transmission of information and rumours to potential participants; (4) compared to other incidents, 'social anger-venting incidents' have a greater likelihood of criminal conduct such as beating, smashing, looting and burning. This could turn them into riots, that often result in significant damage to private and public property (Yu, J. 2009).

These incidents are anger-venting because most of the people who take part in the actions are venting their anger, against the authorities, government officials who are known for unjustified use of violence, such as the police and city patrols, or against rich and powerful individuals who escape justice because of their social status or resources.

An incident that happened in Chizhou, Anhui in 2005 is a good example of such cases. An Anhui student who was riding a bicycle home from school was hit by a sedan with a Jiangsu registration plate. While the car sustained some paint scratches, the student suffered injuries from the accident. The student requested the driver to take him to the hospital. The owner refused. The driver and his passengers got into an argument with the student and some bystanders, who sided with the student. During the ensuing heated argument, the driver uttered, 'If I were to beat an Anhui person to death, it would only cost me 300 000 yuan in compensation'. That provoked a fight between the two sides, and resulted in injuries. The police came and took all of them into custody. Later, a crowd of friends and supporters from both sides started gathering outside the police station. Rumours began flying around that the police had let the driver go free because of his *guanxi*, and that the student had died from his injuries. The rumour about his death was

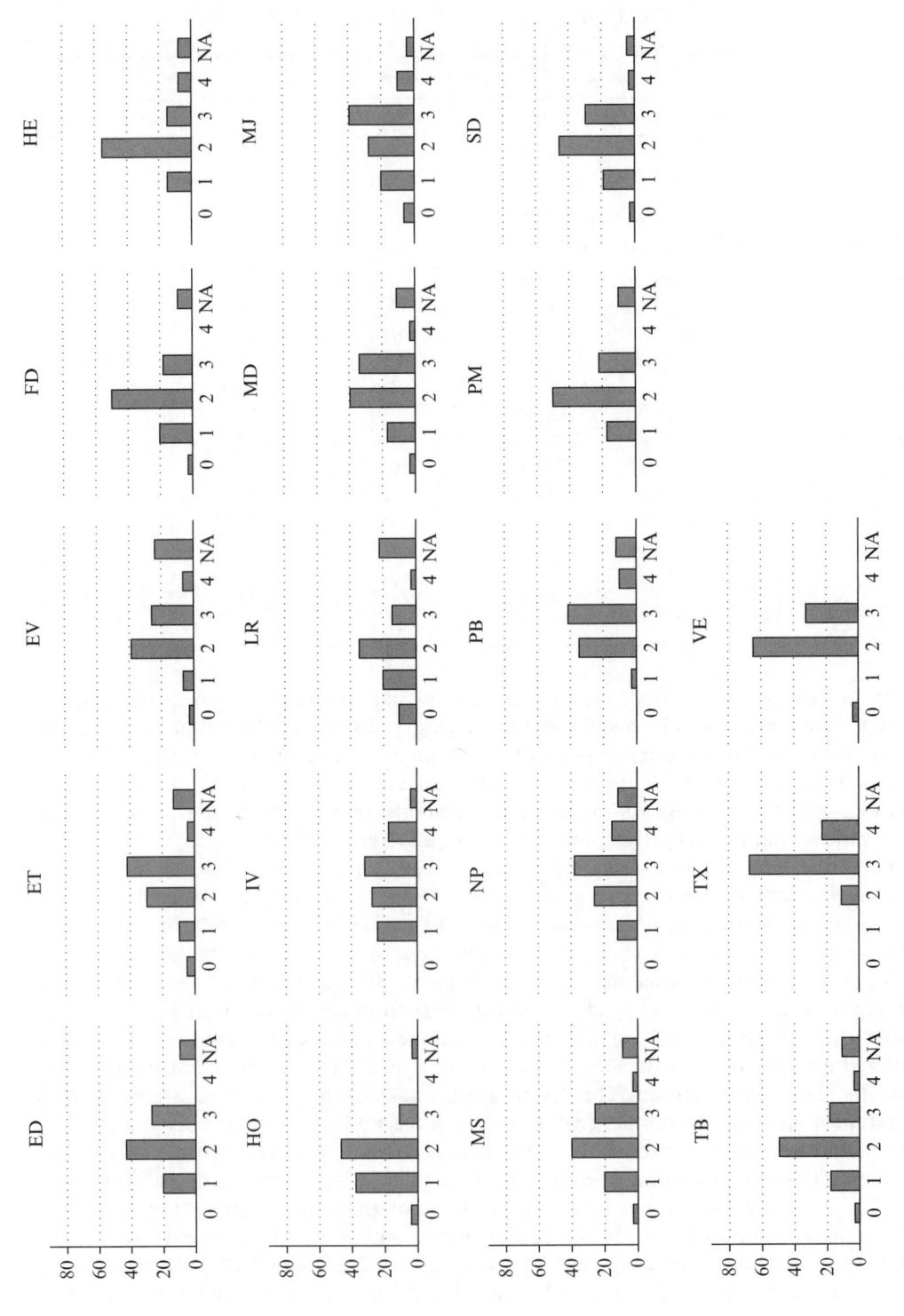

Figure 20.2 Grievances and their protest size

untrue, but the other rumours could not be proved or disproved. Meanwhile, as many as 10 000 spectators began to gather outside the police station. The crowd became emotionally charged and began smashing the sedan and setting fire to some police vehicles. The two sides got into a stand-off, with the crowd throwing rocks at armed police officers. More riot police were sent to the scene and the mob was finally rounded up.

This case underscores various common elements of 'social anger-venting incidents'. Most of the people who took part in the actions were not directly affected by the incident in the first place. Their participation was largely motivated by underlying public distrust of the police, and societal tensions between ordinary people and the rich and powerful. Put simply, the incident provided an opportunity for the 'have-nots' in the society to vent their deep-seated discontentment and anger towards the 'haves'. The lightning rod of the incident, which was the traffic accident in this case, became relatively insignificant. Information transmission was aided by modern technology. Though some of this comprised rumours that turned out to be untrue, they inflamed the public and helped to gather more sympathetic onlookers.

What types of cases exhibit the characteristics of 'anger-venting incidents'? Our data analysis, as shown in Table 20.8, suggests that cases motivated by miscarriage of justice (74 per cent), and police or city patrol brutality (76 per cent) are most likely to be 'anger-venting'. This is unsurprising, because while these cases often lack an unambiguous cause, they are capable of evoking deep-seated sentiments among some segments of the population, and provoke them to rally irrespective of the immediate cause. The sentiments could

Table 20.8 'Anger-venting incidents' by grievance type (N = 2528)

Grievance	No (number of incidents)	No (%)	Yes (number of incidents)	Yes (%)	Total
ED	75	100.0	0	0.0	75
ET	48	69.6	21	30.4	69
EV	143	98.6	2	1.4	145
FD	65	90.3	7	9.7	72
HE	18	66.7	9	33.3	27
HO	30	100.0	0	0.0	30
IV	31	100.0	0	0.0	31
LR	860	95.6	40	4.4	900
MD	343	94.8	19	5.3	362
MJ	10	26.3	28	73.7	38
MS	88	96.7	3	3.3	91
NP	34	97.1	1	2.9	35
PB	33	24.1	104	75.9	137
PM	38	79.2	10	20.8	48
SD	278	98.9	3	1.1	281
TB	136	96.5	5	3.6	141
TX	7	77.8	2	22.2	9
VE	36	97.3	1	2.7	37
Total	2273	89.9	255	10.1	2528

be social wrath against the rich and powerful, and local authorities, disdain for the police and public officials, or animosity towards certain ethnic groups. It does not take a great deal to ignite this flame in the society. If the breakdown of 'anger-venting' incidents is taken together with those of violence and protest size, it is discernible that these cases tend to be violent, and involve a large number of people, typically more than 1000 people.

SOCIAL UNREST CASES

Despite various caveats about the dataset, there are clear signs that the number of social unrest cases rose from 2003 to 2012. Land-related cases are the single largest grievance source, accounting for about half of all cases. That said, protests by migrant workers in private and foreign-owned factories rose rapidly. There is some degree of positive correlation between regional per capita income and frequency of incidents, with Beijing, Guangdong and Shanghai registering the highest number of incidents. Violent cases are mostly caused by grievances such as police and city patrol personnel brutality, land claims, miscarriage of justice and ethnic imbalance. Some kinds of protest are likely to involve more than 1000 people: nationalist protests, ethnic claims, miscarriages of justice, failed investment schemes, and police or city patrol brutality. In particular, cases caused by miscarriage of justice, and police or city patrol brutality, are most likely to be 'anger-venting', attracting a large number of participants who are unrelated to the actual incidents.

ACKNOWLEDGEMENT

The team of research assistants involved in the project to construct the SUIC dataset includes Menglu Cai, Tony Zhang, Zhe Yuan, Pujan Modi from the University of Toronto, Jin Shi from Peking University, Ken Zeng and Yi'ang Zhang from Renmin University of China. The author is particularly grateful for excellent research assistance provided by Menglu Cai and Ken Zeng, but takes final responsibility for the quality of this chapter.

NOTE

1. A case is coded as a 'violent' incident when the Chinese term *baoli* is mentioned. This involves the use of violence by protestors or the armed police, or both.

APPENDIX

Table 20A.1   Number of people involved (% in each category) (N = 2528)

Grievance	1–10	11–100	101–1000	1001–10000	>10001	N/A	Total cases
ED	0.0	20.0	44.0	26.7	0.0	9.3	75
ET	4.4	8.7	29.0	40.6	4.4	13.0	69
EV	1.4	6.2	37.9	24.8	6.2	23.5	145
FD	1.4	20.8	50.0	18.1	0.0	9.7	72
HE	0.0	14.8	55.6	14.8	7.4	7.4	27
HO	3.3	36.7	46.7	10.0	0.0	3.3	30
IV	0.0	22.6	25.8	32.3	16.1	3.2	31
LR	9.7	19.9	33.2	14.2	1.6	21.4	900
MD	1.7	15.2	38.1	33.2	1.1	10.8	362
MJ	5.3	18.4	26.3	39.5	7.9	2.6	38
MS	3.3	20.9	39.6	25.3	2.2	8.8	91
NP	0.0	11.4	25.7	37.1	14.3	11.4	35
PB	0.0	2.9	35.0	41.6	8.8	11.7	137
PM	0.0	16.7	50.0	22.9	0.0	10.4	48
SD	0.7	18.5	45.2	28.8	2.5	4.3	281
TB	0.7	18.4	49.7	17.7	2.1	11.4	141
TX	0.0	0.0	11.1	66.7	22.2	0.0	9
VE	2.7	0.0	64.9	32.4	0.0	0.0	37

PART IV

INTERNATIONAL RELATIONS

21. China on the world stage
Shaun Breslin

In an era when China is widely regarded as one of the major actors on the world stage, it is salient to remember that this role is a relatively recent phenomenon. To be sure, China was never really wholly absent from the world stage, even during the relatively isolationist days of the Maoist era. The People's Republic of China (PRC) was, after all, a nuclear power from the mid-1960s,[1] a willing pawn in power-balancing between the superpowers during the Cold War, and a permanent member of the United Nations Security Council (UNSC) with veto power from 1971. Nevertheless, the scope and depth of China's global presence and power today is markedly different from the first decades of the PRC, and the way in which China exercises its rising power has been identified as one of the most important 'great dramas' of the twenty-first century which will help to determine the fate of the Western global liberal order (Ikenberry 2008: 23).

The primary purpose of this chapter, then, is to trace the way in which China has emerged from relative isolation to become an actor on the world stage with the potential to influence the trajectory of global politics. A key determinant of this journey is the way in which Chinese perceptions of both the nature of the world order, and the nature of China as a global actor, have changed along the way; sometimes in response to changing material circumstances and sometimes in response to changing Chinese priorities and actions. To date, as it has become a global actor, China has tended more to accept the existing order and adapt to it, rather than pushing for fundamental and/or radical reform. But this is not a wholesale and unquestioning acquiescence. China's privileged position in the United Nations (UN) has made it able to frustrate the ambitions of the Western liberal powers (though not able to stop them pursuing their objectives through other ways). Along with other rising powers, China has expressed its dissatisfaction with the distribution of power within the major institutions of global governance, and how the preferences of Western liberal states are often pursued via these institutions. And at times, China has not just expressed dissatisfaction, but also pushed for actual concrete change.

Although the primary focus of this chapter is on politics at the global level, it is impossible to entirely avoid considerations of bilateral relations along the way, and there is inevitably some overlap with other chapters in this volume. China's rise, for example, is typically analysed in combination with the perceived and/or relative decline of the power of the USA. More recently, it is in China's growing financial relations with other developing states (and the political consequences of them for the nature of the global order) that many see the signs of a shifting balance of global authority. As this increasing spread of Chinese interests and influence across the world is often being led by commercial actors, albeit frequently with the support and encouragement of the Chinese state, the first task is to briefly outline the growing complexity and plurality of interests and actors in order to understand China's international interactions.

CONTEXTUALIZING THE STUDY OF CHINA AND THE WORLD

Who is 'China'?

When China's international interactions were dominated by official diplomatic relations, and relatively minimal and state-controlled trade policies, it was relatively easy to identify who spoke and acted for China. This was an elite project where the China that appeared on the world stage was manifest by the words and actions of the political elite. To be sure, different agencies were responsible for different arenas of interaction, but speaking in terms of 'China says' and 'China thinks' and 'China wants' was not particularly problematic.

After China began to re-engage with the global economy, this situation became less clear-cut as more actors and interests began to interact with external partners both within China and (particularly more recently) overseas. This has led to a focus on new foreign policy actors (Jakobson and Knox 2010) and, in particular, the growing significance of Chinese companies which are motivated simply by the pursuit of profits, rather than acting on behalf of the state in pursuit of state-defined strategic objectives (Brautigam 2009). It is broadly accepted that the Foreign Ministry is relatively weak within the Chinese bureaucratic hierarchy, and the State Councillor in charge of foreign affairs is not even a member of the Politburo (let alone the more powerful Standing Committee).[2]

This increasing plurality is somewhat less important when it comes to considering the global level than it is for bilateral relations. Even if the interests of Chinese companies are taken into account in the formulation of Chinese policy, the task of articulating these interests and exercising Chinese power at places like the UN or the International Monetary Fund (IMF) remains the responsibility of politicians and diplomats. What they say and do in these fora really can be considered to represent an official Chinese position, and when this chapter refers to a 'Chinese' position, it is in this sense of the dominant preferences of the Chinese elites as manifest in policy pronouncements and initiatives in the specific policy arena at hand.

But even here, there are two reasons why care needs to be exercised in talking in terms of a single Chinese position – the idea of 'China Inc.' (Fishman 2005). First, bureaucratic agencies have different positions on China's place in the world, and the best way to attain what they think are China's national interests. For example, the People's Bank of China and the Ministry of Commerce hold very different positions on exchange rate policy and the wisdom and consequences of internationalizing the renminbi (Freeman and Wen 2013). Second, whilst action in global institutions might be the preserve of officialdom, this is not the case when it comes to the annunciation of different opinions on what China's role should be (Foot 2006). These include different voices of Chinese officials from various ministries and agencies, from Chinese think tanks and academics, comments and editorials in the press, and the ever-growing online Chinese community of netizens. Of course, there remain limits on what can be said in public. But within these constraints there is a very lively debate. As with many national polities, extreme but relatively unrepresentative voices can often generate more 'noise' and interest then more moderate ones. And for those who are looking for a Chinese threat to the global order, it is not hard to find voices calling for an assertive or even aggressive Chinese position, that are then taken as representative of what 'China' wants.

The Past in China's Present

Although this chapter focuses on China on the global scale in the contemporary era, it is built on an understanding that where China is today is influenced by where it came from. The next section of the chapter briefly traces how Chinese views of the world order and China's position on the world stage have evolved under Chinese Communist Party (CCP) rule. However, it is also important to recognize that China's place in the world today still contains within it elements of China's past that go further back in time. Memories of the subjugation of China's interests (and sovereignty) to the Western powers in the nineteenth century have been kept alive and utilized to inspire a strong nationalist sentiment. So too have memories of war with Japan, and the imperial objectives of China's neighbour and arguably major competitor for regional leadership and influence. And throughout these stories about the past, the role of the CCP's heroic actions in saving China from a 'century of humiliation' remains at the fore. Having achieved initial salvation from foreign subjugation, the Party also then restored Chinese borders and sovereignty – well, more or less; this remains an unfinished task – and continues to protect China's interests in a hostile international environment where major (Western) powers are largely opposed to and/or fearful of China's return to its 'rightful' position of global power (if not supremacy).

The way in which an understanding of the nature of the global order is explained to the Chinese people forms part of a broader project of legitimating one-party rule through ideological means. In many respects, this use of history has an important domestic role and is primarily for internal consumption. Importantly for this chapter, domestic discourses can be more nationalistic, more critical of the West, and more forceful in asserting a Chinese revisionist agenda than when the audience is an international one. And the rhetoric of (extreme) disaffection has not been matched by Chinese action in international organizations (or not yet at least).[3] A number of in-depth studies have concluded that participation in international institutions has largely 'socialized' China into abiding by the existing established rules and norms of the global order.[4] This can result in a disjuncture between those analyses that focus on the assertive rhetoric of some Chinese on the one hand, and studies of China's largely accommodative approach to participating on global governance fora on the other. It is important to keep this potential divergence in mind when considering the evolution of Chinese policies and preferences.

FROM (RELATIVE) ISOLATION TO GLOBAL ACTOR

From the very moment that the PRC was established, China's international actions and ambitions had firm global consequences. Military involvement in the Korean War, border wars and 'skirmishes' with India and the Soviet Union (Union of Soviet Socialist Republics, USSR), and the ever-present possibility of a military campaign to 'reunite' Taiwan, ensured that China remained an issue of some importance. But in many ways it was just that: an *issue* that concerned others, rather than a key actor on the world stage in its own right. The transition from issue to actor was to come later.

Note that this relative absence from the world stage was not all of China's own choosing. A US-led diplomatic embargo of China after 1949, as Washington gave its full diplomatic support to the Kuomintang on Taipei, not only kept the PRC outside the UN system but also prevented formal diplomatic recognition by the majority of Western states and their Asian allies (Zhang 1998). It also meant that international agreements, treaties and conventions signed or joined by 'China' before 1949 did not automatically pertain to the new PRC regime.

Arguably China's first appearance as a truly global actor was at the Geneva conference of 1954, called by the USSR to search for a settlement to the Korean War, and to promote peaceful resolution of conflicts in Indochina. Although still outside the UN system, the PRC participated alongside the USA, France, the Soviet Union and the UK for the first time as part of what would become 'the big five'.[5] While the USSR was instrumental in organizing the conference in the first place, and helping to socialize the PRC's largely inexperienced representatives into the world of big power diplomacy, Geneva also showed that China had interests and objectives of its own that did not always chime with Moscow's. Geneva was also important in establishing a view of a less than united Western world in the eyes of Chinese representatives. The USA was seen as more reluctant than Britain and France to respond to the Soviet initiative in the first place, and was blamed for obstructing the emergence of a working peace proposal. The conference showed that the Western 'bloc' was not always a single actor, and that Chinese diplomacy might exploit the different interests and preferences of Western states (Zhai 1992).

The Bandung conference of 1955, although not a truly global affair as such, provided a quick opportunity for the PRC to further establish itself as an actor on the world stage (and in particular, beyond its own specific security concerns in the region). China's leaders were very much aware that not just Chinese revolutionary rhetoric, but action in Korea and Vietnam, had generated concern about Chinese (revolutionary) foreign policy. China, in the person of Zhou Enlai, used Bandung as an opportunity to signal a 'marked change of attitude'; to present China as a force for peace and to try to reassure other states (not least Indonesia, as host) that it was not interested in interfering in the internal affairs of other states (Fitzgerald 1955: 113). Although China was only ever to participate in the Non-Aligned Movement as an observer, this also allowed China to promote its credentials as an independent Third World power, rather than a mere adjunct to Soviet foreign policy.

This approach was encapsulated in the 'Five Principles of Peaceful Coexistence', which remains the theoretical cornerstone of China's world view today. First developed to guide negotiations with India in 1953–54,[6] the principles are:

1. Mutual respect for each other's territorial integrity and sovereignty.
2. Mutual non-aggression.
3. Mutual non-interference in each other's internal affairs.
4. Equality and mutual benefit.
5. Peaceful co-existence.

However, this formal fundamental bottom-line respect for state sovereignty was not always fully followed through, as China both provided 'ideologically inspired support for violent insurrectionary movements' overseas and also deployed 'relatively peaceful agitation' designed to influence policy change in (and thus interfere with the internal affairs of) other sovereign states (van Ness 1970: 8). Not for the last time, different identities occasionally clashed as China tried to establish itself as a global power. On the one hand, there was the identity of China as a fellow developing state, a former victim of colonialism, trying with other developing states to resist the hegemony of the global superpowers. And on the other hand, there was China as a supporter of the oppressed people throughout the world, committed to promoting socialist alternatives to the dominant and aggressive capitalist global agenda.

This dual identity was complicated as relations with the USSR deteriorated from the late 1950s. Rather than a socialist ally, the USSR came to be identified as a 'Soviet revisionist renegade clique' that was practising 'social-imperialism and social-fascism', at times in 'collusion with US imperialism' to oppress the people of the world. It had also become a real and present threat to China's territorial integrity (and the survival of the revolution) in an echo of 'tsarist Russian imperialist aggression against China'.[7]

As the Soviet Union increasingly became identified as a real and present danger, then the logic of realpolitik took over and influenced the way that the Chinese acted on the global stage. The logic of 'my enemy's enemy is my friend' meant that whether China was a supporter of the status quo or revolutionary insurgents in other states could be determined by that country's relations with the Soviet Union. For example, in the protracted Angolan Civil War, China provided training and support for the National Union for the Total Independence of Angola (UNITA) against the Soviet and Cuban-backed Popular Movement for the Liberation of Angola (MPLA), which ultimately saw China supporting the same side in the conflict as the Republican-led US administration and apartheid-era South Africa (Jackson 1995).

This position of supposed equidistance from both of the superpowers became enshrined in the 'Theory of the Three Worlds'. Identified with Mao Zedong, but articulated by Deng Xiaoping at the UN in 1974, this world view placed the USSR and the USA as the joint First World superpowers intent on dominating as much of the globe as possible. The Second World consisted of developing countries which, while sometimes still exercising colonial-type relations with developing countries, were also subject to being 'controlled, threatened or bullied' by the superpowers, or had even effectively become 'dependencies' of them: 'In varying degrees, all these countries have the desire of shaking off superpower enslavement or control and safeguarding their national independence and the integrity of their sovereignty.'[8]

The developing countries of Asia, Africa and Latin America made up the Third World. And with China the only Third World state that was a permanent member of the UNSC, this gave it a special position in the fight to resist the superpowers and their allies (Yee 1983: 241).

China's Emergence as a Global Actor

That China had this position of privilege was a result of UN General Assembly resolution 2758 of 25 October 1971, which saw the Taipei regime of the Republic of China lose its seat on the UN to Beijing, and its replacement by the PRC as the sole representative of one China. Whilst the US voted against the resolution to switch authority in this way, Washington had been taking steps towards rapprochement since 1969 via diplomatic representatives in Poland, and through Romanian and Pakistani interlocutors (Xia 2006a). Kissinger's secret trip to China in 1971, and Nixon's much more public visit the following year, laid the foundations for China to gradually re-establish itself as a global actor. And in many ways, the basic underpinnings of China's global role remained more or less in place until the end of the Cold War.

The primary policy focus, particularly after Mao's death in 1976 (and even more particularly after the acceleration of reform under Deng's de facto leadership in 1978) was on domestic economic (and political) reconstruction. And foreign policy was more or less designed to support this focus, as China's leaders utilized the space created by Cold War bipolarity to develop better relations with former enemies and potential (Western capitalist) enemies, and to participate in the capitalist global political economy. China was not given anywhere near the same levels of aid, military support and the 'free ride' into the global political economy that the US granted its earlier Asian Cold War allies.[9] But until 1989 and the Tiananmen incident at least, perceptions of China in the US as a common enemy of the USSR helped to provide a 'favourable international environment' for China's (re)engagement with the capitalist global economy (Pearson 1999: 174).

As the 1980s progressed, China's view of the fundamental nature of the global order changed. Despite residual tensions with the Soviet Union, the threat of war was much diminished. This allowed the underlying drive in Chinese diplomacy and international relations to make the subtle but important shift from preventing war (in an inherently conflictual international order) to promoting peace (Zhao 1995b: 54). And rather than resist exploitation from the capitalist global economy, China increasingly sought to (selectively) join it. As part of this process of global re-engagement, China increasingly 'conformed to the implicit norms of the international financial system' and became part of existing institutions created and designed to govern global capitalism (Lardy 1999: 207). China 'joined' the World Bank (WB) and IMF in April 1980 – organizations which it had previously officially vilified as agents of global capitalism – and became an active participant in both.[10] In the 1980s and 1990s, this participation largely entailed China being in a receptive mode, becoming the biggest beneficiary of WB development loans and utilizing IMF reserves to support the domestic financial system in 1986. Notably, while both organizations did provide technical advice and help to support domestic marketization strategies, they did not place pressure on China to go for quick and full 'shock therapy' liberalization as they had done elsewhere, instead supporting China's incremental reform (Bottelier 2006). China, it seems, was undergoing a process of 'socialization and . . . integration into the society of states' (Zhang 1998: 73).

What happened in Tiananmen Square in June 1989 provided a turning point of sorts. Although in hindsight the period and extent of China's 'punishment' might seem relatively short and minor, at the time the possibility of China becoming isolated was very real. The end of the Cold War created a wider context of changing conceptions of China's global role. As Roger Sullivan (1992: 3) argued at the time, there was no longer any need for the US (and the broader West) to accommodate China's interests with limited conditions, as the need to build alliances against the Soviet Union had disappeared: 'it was not so much that China had changed, but that the world had changed'.

It was in this (changed) global context that China's attempts to join the third pillar of global economic regulation, the World Trade Organization (WTO),[11] faced a number of difficulties through the 1990s. There was considerable concern in the West, most notably but not only in the United States, about the way in which China was using access to the global economy to grow, while not allowing the global economy reciprocal access to the Chinese economy. Economic concerns became intertwined with other debates: discussions about the nature of the Chinese political system, whether it was ethical to deal with a country with China's human rights record, and the wisdom of facilitating the economic rise of a country that might one day want to change the global order. An increasingly economically powerful China might even be a threat to security; if not of global security, at least of security in Southeast and East Asia (Roy 1994). As there was an annual vote in Washington over whether to extend China access to the US market, there was ample opportunity for these suspicions and doubts to be aired in very public ways.

Despite these concerns, the importance of promoting liberalization and what the White House later called empowering reformers in China led the US to sign a new trade agreement in November 1999 which paved the way for Chinese entry (White House 2000). Even though the WTO is a multilateral organization, securing entry entails numerous separate bilateral negotiations with any existing member that requests it. It took two more years before everybody was either happy with the terms of Chinese entry, or negotiated specific terms that allowed them to retain restrictions on trade with China in specific areas. And in order to get there, Chinese negotiators made commitments to liberalization that went much further than previous countries at China's level of development had gone. But in December 2001, what had become a 15-year road to WTO membership was finally achieved.

CHINA VIEWS ITSELF AND CHINA VIEWS THE WORLD

The annual debates in Washington over trade relations with China fed into a pre-existing feeling within China that it was was being 'demonized' (Liu and Liu 1997). As a result, what became known as 'the China threat thesis' gained increasing purchase. The basic idea here was that foreign forces hostile to China were deliberately trying to establish a vision of China as a threat to the West and the global order. Their aim, according to this approach, was to encourage policies and alliances designed to prevent China from rising and getting what it not so much wanted, but needed, to continue to develop (Wang 1996). Note here that in addition to the importance of exports in generating Chinese growth, China became a net oil importer in 1993, increasing the significance of the outside world for China's development.

Whilst a popular response was to assert that China did not need the world,[12] China's leaders were more circumspect. Although it is difficult to pin down the exact provenance for the origin of the *taoguang yanghui* principle,[13] it became widely accepted to be the guiding principle of China's global role (Tang 2011: 179). Literally meaning 'hide brightness, nourish obscurity', *taoguang yanghui* was part of what is often referred to as a 24-character phrase, but in its full version somewhat confusingly has 28 characters which can be translated as 'calmly observe, secure your position, deal with things with composure, hide brightness and nourish obscurity, protect our advantages, never seek leadership and accomplish some achievements'.

This phrasing has led some to focus on 'hide' as a sign that Chinese policy is all about pretence: pretending to be a force for peace and stability and hiding China's real intention to change the global order. At the very least, it seems that the Chinese leadership were aware that if they clearly articulated what they wanted from and for the global order, this could lead to others trying to make sure that they did not get it (Johnston 2008). And as Medeiros and Fravel (2003) point out, while Chinese perceptions were that its power in the global order was increasing, there was little enthusiasm to be identified by others as a global power for fear that China might then be expected to take the leadership roles and global responsibility that go with Great Power status.

If China was to become a Great Power – and all available evidence suggested that this was increasingly the case – then China's leaders had to think how this would be received in other states, and how perceptions of China would generate policies. Chinese strategy was built, then, on a very firm understanding that how Chinese demands and objectives were framed would be a crucial determinant of whether these goals could be attained. The same understanding and impulse informed the promotion of the idea that China was and would remain a 'responsible great power' that will not threaten the interests of others, will not challenge the existing global order, and whose continued rise is the best bet for continued regional and global economic prosperity (Xia 2001).

The transition of this self-defined national identity[14] into a more formalized understanding of the nature of the world, and China's role in it, began with the articulation of a 'new security concept' in 2002 in a Foreign Ministry position paper (FMPRC 2002) and defence White Paper (State Council 2002). Whilst the threat of some form of military conflict had not gone away, the post-Cold War era meant that war was increasingly unlikely. Moreover, the Asian financial crisis and the events of September 11 in the USA showed that there were now a myriad of other challenges to all countries; challenges which were best met by multilateral cooperation, partnership and dialogue rather than through unilateral action. The new world order had to be built not on competition, but on mutual trust, mutual benefit, equity and cooperation (Fu 2003).

This understanding travelled through an early iteration in the form of the 'Peaceful Rise of China' (*heping jueqi*) concept to become a quasi-official ideology in two different forms. The first is the concept of 'Harmonious World', identified with the leadership of Hu Jintao. First used in 2005, the Harmonious World is in many respects an update of the five principles of peaceful coexistence, and shares a number of its basic features. It emphasizes consultation, mutual respect and equality in political relations and the promotion of a democratic global order; cooperation, 'win–win' relations and balanced development in economics; respect for diversity and mutual learning in cultural or 'civilizational' affairs; mutual trust and cooperation and the peaceful resolution of security issues rather than resorting to war; and cooperation to solve common environmental problems (Hu 2005). The second is the expanded reassertion that China's rise will not destabilize the global order, as previous rising powers had done, in the shape of the 2011 White Paper on Peaceful Development:

China's peaceful development has broken away from the traditional pattern where a rising power was bound to seek hegemony ... With a keen appreciation of its historical and cultural tradition of several thousand years, the nature of economic globalization, changes in international relations and the international security landscape in the 21st century as well as the common interests and values of humanity, China has decided upon peaceful development and mutually beneficial cooperation as a fundamental way to realize its modernization, participate in international affairs and handle international relations.

Low Profile No More?

Not surprisingly, the debate over whether a low profile could be, should be, or indeed had been maintained became a major focus of debate and scholarship. Under Hu Jintao, the expansion of China's international economic relations – in terms of both the amount of money involved and the number of partner countries – also resulted in the need to adopt a form of 'diplomatic activism' to protect expanded interests (Zhao 2010a). Having a low profile simply makes no sense if this leaves others to make decisions on global affairs that will have a profound impact on what China needs and wants (Gao and Wang 2007). And as Wang Yizhou (2011) argued, China had, in fact, for a number of years been finding ways of 'creatively' becoming a proactive global citizen in dealing with transnational issues that impacted on China. Particularly as the West struggled to overcome financial crisis, the time seemed right to change not just global polity, but also some of the norms and principles that underpin the global order, to support Chinese interests and ambitions (Economy 2010).

But not everybody agreed. The problem in being more proactive and having a higher profile is that this might reignite the fear of a 'China Threat', and ultimately make it harder for China to get what it wants. Moreover, as already noted, there is a reluctance for China to take global responsibility commensurate with the expectations of being a Great Power (Li, M. 2011: 21). Although China might be a Great Power, or on the verge of Great Power status, it is still a relatively poor power (in per capita terms) with limited capabilities. As such, China's primary responsibility must be to its domestic internal constituency rather than to a vaguely defined global order (Chen, Z. 2009: 26).

So when the idea that a 'G2' (Group of Two) was emerging as the world's dominant alliance first came into prominence in 2005, it was treated with some suspicion in China. The idea, as proposed by Bergsten (2005), was that as the two biggest global economies and quasi-representatives of the developed and developing worlds, respectively, there was a responsibility on China and the US to try and reach a prior understanding on key issues so that they could be taken forward effectively through the existing institutions of global governance. Whilst this external recognition of China's new-found global status was welcomed in China, there was a suspicion that China was being flattered into taking on more global burdens and responsibilities; that China was being encouraged to sacrifice domestic responsibilities for a place at the global top table next to the US (Li, M. 2011: 21). There was also concern that this might be an attempt to tie China into a subservient role to maintain US unipolar hegemony, or to force China to break its promises and take on a hegemonic position itself (An 2013).

The debate over whether or not to take a more active role was partly taken out of China's hands by events elsewhere. The nominally 'global' financial crisis might have had global consequences, but was seen in China as originating from Western (neo) liberal forms of economic governance and US global leadership (Kang 2010). With China overtaking Germany to become the world's biggest exporter, and Japan to become the world's second-biggest economy, some Chinese analysts saw the onset of a 'post-American age' (Chen, Y. 2009); or at least the beginning of the end of American unipolarity, which might take some time still to unravel (Jiang 2011).

As leaders of crisis-hit economies sought for solutions, the understanding that China should be an integral part of this search became broadly accepted, as symbolized by the invitation to become a member of the new G20 in 2008. Some even saw China as the West's 'economic saviour', through its ability to replace existing powers as an engine of global growth by sucking in (European) exports and increasing its outward investment to major economies (Baker 2011). This idea was symbolized by the failed attempt by the EU to gain Chinese financial support for its euro rescue package in the autumn of 2011, a policy that was widely reported by using the analogy of Europe taking a 'begging bowl' to China.

Finding neat start and end dates for different eras is never easy, and China's changing role on the world stage did not simply start with the collapse of Lehman Brothers. The 2008 Beijing Olympics, for example, had been planned for many years as a key means of placing China back at the centre of global attention; a Chinese version of 'shock and awe' (Cha 2011) that would show the world what China could do. But the global crisis and the transition to a new generation of China's leaders do seem to have combined to result in a more confident expression of Chinese interests. For the influential Chinese scholar Yan Xuetong (2014), Xi Jinping's assumption of power in 2012 marked the transition from the era of keeping a low profile to a new one of 'striving for achievement' (*fenfayouwei*). This includes coming up with China's own version of the G2, the 'new type of major power relations' first articulated by Xi Jinping during a trip to Washington in 2012. Whilst not marking a rejection of the dominance of domestic issues in Chinese considerations and policy-making, I suggest that the concept marks an official recognition that China is not just a 'normal' global power, but one that occupies a special position in the global order.

CHINA AND GLOBAL GOVERNANCE REFORM

As China has become an ever more prominent actor on the world stage, its leaders have become enthusiastic and high-profile participants at multilateral forums. This not only includes working in and with existing institutions, but also entails initiating or joining new initiatives in collaboration with non-Western partners; with the other BRICS (Brazil, Russia, India, China, South Africa) countries through leaders' meetings, with Asian developing countries though Association of Southeast Asian Nations (ASEAN)–China (and ASEAN+3) summits and the Shanghai Cooperation Organization, with African states through the Forum on China–Africa Cooperation (FOCAC), in America's back yard through the China–Caribbean Economy and Trade Cooperation Forum, and in the Middle East and North Africa through the China–Arab Nations Cooperation Forum (Sohn 2011). The annual Bo'ao Forum for Asia has also become a means of articulating Chinese interests and objectives (although the audience is wider than just non-Western states here).

The Chinese leadership has become adept at using international meetings of various sorts to explain to the world how China sees itself and to outline what sort of great power China will be and is. This is supported by a well-orchestrated and well-funded state project to promote a preferred image of what China is and what it stands for to the rest of the world. It does this through the expansion of Confucius Centres, through the spread of foreign-language TV and radio stations, and perhaps also through becoming an important destination for overseas students. This ongoing process of what Xi Jinping called 'disseminating modern Chinese values' (*China Daily* 2014b) is typically referred to in China (and often from external observers as well) as promoting or wielding China's 'soft power'; although a concerted state-led effort to promote a preferred national self-image seems something other than 'soft', and the concept of 'international political marketing' (Sun, H. 2007) might be more appropriate.

Whatever it is called, this project entails establishing China's difference: China as a different type of Great Power that will never try to seek hegemony, and will treat other countries as partners rather than exploit them. Unlike Western powers, China will not link economic aid to political conditionalities. And China's own state-led developmental model might provide an example for others: that there are different paths to modernization than following the preferred Western free market capitalist model. Put all of these together, and the result is a China that provides an alternative to the Western liberal global order.

What this suggests, then, is that there is something wrong with the status quo that needs to be remedied by this Chinese alternative. And with the financial crisis cementing the idea in China that it had returned as a 'Great Power', the time was right to express Chinese dissatisfaction: dissatisfaction with both the distribution of global power, and the norms and philosophies that have built the global order. But this dissatisfaction was tempered by an acknowledgement that the liberal global order – the liberal economic order at least – had actually served Chinese interests very well; initially through the growth of inward investment and Chinese exports, and more latterly through the increase in Chinese outward investment and the resulting spread of Chinese economic interests across the globe. Maintaining state controls to protect key sectors and actors at home, and providing support for individuals and companies overseas, remain important components of a Chinese form of (state) capitalism. But a desire to create an uneven playing field that gives China whatever advantage is possible within the existing order is not the same thing as seeking to destabilize or overthrow it.

So despite the sometimes rather loud articulation of a radical vision of a dissatisfied China wishing to build a new order – either from within China or outside – the agenda seems more to be about how to make the existing system work to better suit Chinese interests. To this end, China's ambition is to work to 'democratize international relations' and create a multipolar world order (Foot 2006: 91). In some iterations, reform is not so much an ambition as a 'duty' that China owes the world; or the rest of the unfairly disadvantaged developing world at least (Yeophantong 2013). Exercising this duty, and achieving this objective, requires proactive Chinese strategies and partnerships with other like-minded dissatisfied states to reform institutions of global governance to ensure that they reflect the changing balance of authority between existing (Western) powers and emerging and developing states (Chin and Thakur 2010: 119). Such a rebalancing by its very definition entails undermining the authority of the existing privileged global powers and, most clearly, trying to undermine the dominance of the USA.

Perhaps the highest-profile attempt, rhetorically at least, to do so was when the Governor of the People's Bank of China called for a new 'super-sovereign reserve currency' to replace the dollar as the global reserve (Zhou 2009). A more concrete sign of this 'power shift' was the 2010 change in quota shares at the IMF and the World Bank. The decision was largely negotiated at the preceding G20 Finance Ministers meeting, and China's leaders have continued to use the G20 as a forum for pushing for further reform and the creation of a 'fair and inclusive international financial system' (Huang and Yao 2013). Recalibration of rights resulted in an overall transfer of 6 per cent of quota shares towards China, Brazil, India and Russia, with China emerging as the third-biggest member country.

But IMF reform also shows the challenges ahead in promoting a democratizing agenda. The reforms only left the BRICS countries collectively with about half of the voting share of European countries, even though the BRICS countries' combined gross domestic product (GDP) was roughly double that of Europe at the time. Moreover, although voting reforms were accepted in one part of Washington, DC at the IMF, they were not ratified in another part of the city by the US Congress.[15] Frustration with the progress of reforms appears to be one of the reasons that the BRICS countries pushed ahead with establishing their own 'New Development Bank' in the official Fortaleza Declaration in 2014.[16] And when combined with Japan's continued predominance in the Asian Development Bank, this frustration also perhaps partially explains the decision to create the Asian Infrastructure Investment Bank. Although primarily designed as a regional organization, the inclusion of non-Asian members on the Bank's board of directors points to a new emerging leadership role of sorts for China in global financial governance.

The WB also provides an example of how China's role is changing in ways that challenge the status quo in subtle 'responsible' ways, rather than through radical transformation. The main significance of the WB for China was originally as a recipient: a recipient of development aid financing and a recipient of policy advice and recommendations. But this situation has changed. The WB still works with China to produce reports and predictions, and funds development projects in China. But in addition to the shift in voting rights, China has started to pay off its credits earlier than originally planned, and actually became a WB donor state in 2008.

In many respects, though, it is not so much what China has done in and with the WB that is important here, as what it has done bilaterally, and the emergence of China as a major provider of development and aid-related finance to others (Figure 21.1). It is necessary to exercise some caution here as it is easy to exaggerate the significance of Chinese financial flows because they are new or rising rapidly (or because they are in some ways feared). Outward investment from China is still less than outward flows from Europe and Japan, for example (Reilly 2013a).

Nevertheless, as Chin (2012) points out, this growth of outward investment is important for global governance in three ways. First, Chin shows how the growth of alternative Chinese development funding has led the WB to rethink its own position and to seek to build partnerships with China as a co-donor. In the process, Chinese preferences for the non-imposition of liberalizing conditionalities on financial relationships with developing states is in part internalized by the WB. Second, by providing an alternative source of finances for countries seeking developmental support, China undermines the ability

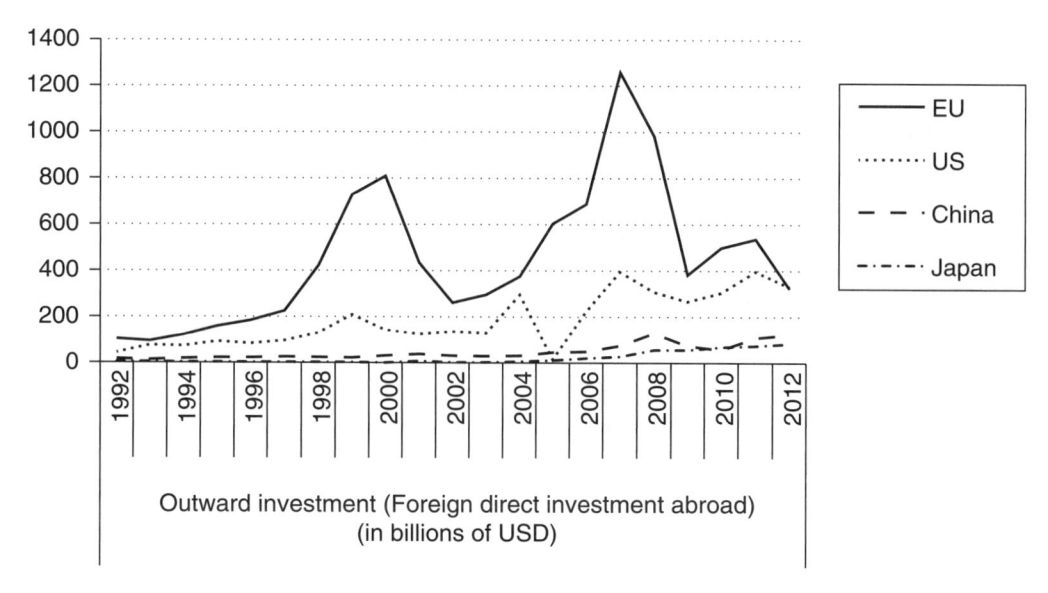

Figure 21.1   The growth of outward investment in comparative perspective

Source: UNCTAD, unctad.org/Sections/dite_dir/docs/WIR2013/WIR13_webtab02.xls.

of others to enforce their preferences by imposing 'good governance' conditions on the provision of finance and aid. This might not entail the strengthening of Chinese preferences for forms of global governance, but at the very least undermines the ability of existing powers to promote and defend the existing liberal global order. This challenge to the existing global aid infrastructure has a multilateral dimension as well, in the form of the above-mentioned BRICS 'New Development Bank' headquartered in Shanghai (BRICS 2014).

Third, despite the fact that China has become an active participant in almost all institutions of global governance, it is still not a member of all of them. China remains excluded, for example, from the G7/G8 process. Nor is it a member of the Organisation for Economic Co-operation and Development (OECD) which, through its Development Assistance Committee (DAC), is a major global aid actor. Although there is a China–DAC study group to 'share knowledge and exchange experiences',[17] China does not record and report its overseas financial flows in ways that conform to DAC standards. Moreover, much of what other countries received from China for development-related projects is not counted as being 'aid' as such (officially, overseas development assistance) due to the nature of Chinese development loans. This is because it is not clear that the recipient country is the main 'beneficiary' of these financial flows (as DAC definitions insist must be the case for 'aid'), as Chinese companies typically win the contract to carry out development projects overseas, and source equipment, services, technology and materials from domestic Chinese sources. What this means is that money from one of the major providers of finance that has developmental consequences for a number of countries is not considered to be 'aid' because it does not fit in with pre-existing standards, practices and understandings that have been developed by others. Global standards are increasingly out of step with the global reality.

There seems to be an assumption that that there is no need to change DAC definitions because China will eventually come round and conform to existing practices. And there are good reasons for this. As Scott Kennedy (2012) has shown, the record shows that China has indeed tended to conform with existing standards, particularly when doing so means that Chinese companies increase their ability to compete with others and become global actors. But he also notes that: 'China is generally more passive and reactive in governance of labor, climate change, and competition policy. Promotion of these latter areas typically means constraining industry, something China seeks to avoid' (Kennedy 2012: 15).

It is worth remembering, then, that despite a largely accommodational approach, there are issue areas where China is more prepared to challenge the status quo, propose Chinese alternatives and/or go its own way. China's policy on providing development-related finance is one example of where it is doing just this.

CHINA AND THE UN

China's position on democratizing the UN has been somewhat less forceful; at least, when it comes to the democratization of the UNSC where China, of course, holds a privileged position as a permanent member. To be sure, China's official position is one of supporting what is typically referred to as 'rational' UN reform, which includes expanding the UNSC to bring in more developing nation representatives 'and African countries in particular' (Wang, G. 2005). However, there seems little desire, to say the very least, to see reform that might see countries like Japan and India being granted the same global privileges as China itself. The more pressing need for UN reform for China is to make it more powerful as *the* arbiter of international power politics, and a brake on US power. In particular, if decisions need to be taken over acts that might infringe state sovereignty, then this should only ever be done with the proper approval of the UN. The West and/or the US simply have no right to make decisions on their own, through the North Atlantic Treaty Organization (NATO), or through ad hoc coalitions of the willing.

As already noted, respect for sovereignty and non-interference are cornerstones of the Five Principles of Peaceful Coexistence which are in turn the basis of China's position on global politics. Over the years, China has used its veto in the UNSC to block UN resolutions that would or could lead to breaches of sovereignty. This is often done alongside Russia, which shares with China many of these basic understandings of the nature of the global order, and the need to balance US/Western power.

Note, though, that China has in fact (at the time of writing in July 2015) only exercised its veto sparingly since joining the UN in 1971: blocking action against Syria (four times), Zimbabwe and Myanmar. It also used its veto to block resolutions supporting peace proposals for countries that recognized Taiwan (the Former Yugoslav Republic of Macedonia in 1999, and Guatemala in 1997) and to support its ally Pakistan's objection to Bangladesh membership of the UN in 1972 (which it did not oppose two years later). By comparison, over the same period, the USA has used its veto on 73 occasions,

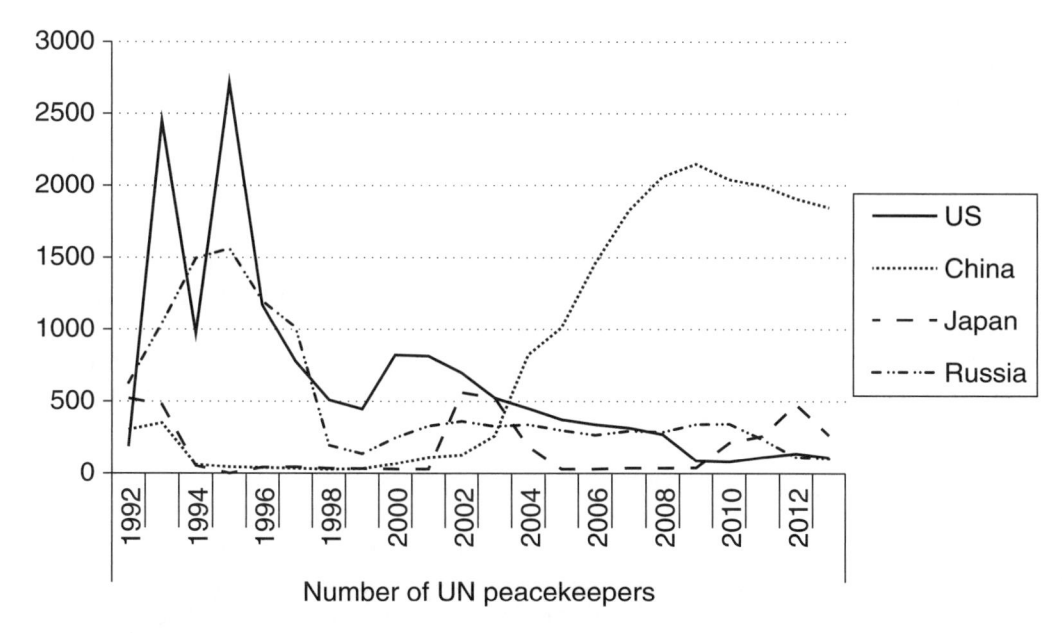

Source: UN, http://www.un.org/en/peacekeeping/resources/statistics/contributors.shtml.

Figure 21.2 Chinese UN peacekeepers in comparative perspective

Moscow 19 times (nine as Russia, and ten as the Soviet Union),[18] the UK 24 times, and France 14 times. Looking at voting behaviour, though, is only a very blunt instrument. There is also the 'hidden veto' to consider, where the simple threat (or certainty) of expectation of a veto means that the resolution is either not tabled, or is diluted through rewriting in ways that avoid it being vetoed (Nahory 2004).[19] Thus, for example, attempts to draft a resolution condemning North Korea were abandoned in 2010, and proposed resolutions calling for sanctions on Iran and Sudan had to be modified and 'diluted' to ensure that they did not incur a Chinese veto (Wuthnow 2011: 21).

Despite this concern with sovereignty, China is prepared to responsibly protect human rights in other countries (Figure 21.2) and even to sanction intervention to do so – but only under certain circumstances. Action is only sanctioned when it has the support of the relevant local regional organizations, and it has to take place under the authority of the UN system (that is, rather than being pursued independently by the Western powers) (Liu, T. 2012). Perhaps not surprisingly, China is happiest supporting activities that are welcomed by the relevant sovereign government: where the government concerned accepts external help to keep the peace. But there have been times when China has been prepared to support more peacemaking initiatives as well, including those that impinge on the supposed sovereignty of existing governments. For example, China supported sanctions against the Ivory Coast in 2011, and did not oppose the imposition of a no-fly zone over Libya in the same year. Perhaps more surprisingly, it actually voted in favour of a prior resolution which referred to 'the outrageous violence perpetrated by Muammar Qadafi on the Libyan people' to the International Criminal Court (Sceats and Breslin 2012).

There are clear tensions in Chinese policy. On the one hand, there is a desire to be seen as a responsible global actor, committed to promoting peace and ending suffering. But this commitment is tempered by a deep reluctance to let the West set the rules of the game and get its own way. And the Libyan case highlighted this dilemma. Although the vote was simply for a no-fly zone, this no-fly zone helped to bring about regime change in Libya. And by not exercising the veto, the popular view in China was that its diplomats had been partially complicit in allowing the Western powers to get what they wanted. To this quandary must be added material interests and the question of whether Chinese economic and/or security interests might be harmed by action or inaction (Zhao 2012). So it might be suggested that the more Chinese economic interests spread, and spread to parts of the world that might be politically unstable, then principle might have to be balanced by pragmatism when it comes to thinking about what is best for Chinese interests.

China, Human Rights and 'Universal' Norms

There is more, though, to the UN than just the UNSC. In financial terms, China's transfers to the UN regular budget have increased from 0.74 per cent of the total in 1997 (which put it nineteenth in a list of contributors) to 3.2 per cent in 2012 (which placed it eighth) (Chen 2014). And it is not just about money. China has, for example, become a rather active participant on the Human Rights Council (HRC). The HRC is just the sort of international organization that China says that it favours. It is elected by the General Assembly with the 47 seats based on geography rather than global power: 13 for Africa, 13 for the Asia-Pacific, eight for Latin American and the Caribbean, six for Eastern Europe, and seven for Western Europe and 'others' (including the USA). China has been very active in the Commission in three main ways. First, by ensuring that it had enough support in the General Assembly to be re-elected as one of the Asia-Pacific representatives in 2013. Second, in trying to get others to accept Chinese understandings and definitions of which human rights should be prioritized (socio-economic above political) when it comes to deciding what needs to be protected (Sceats and Breslin 2012). Third, starting from 2011, China began to make statements on behalf of not just itself, but also 30 other states, and has emerged as the effective leader of a caucus of developing states within the HRC (Muller 2014).

It seems, then, that Chinese strategic thinking concludes that it is better to be on the inside of an organization, trying to influence the way it works and evolves, rather than standing on the outside and criticizing without influence. The same thinking seems to have been at least part of the reason for seeking WTO entry. But once inside the organization, Chinese actors are not just passive acceptors of the status quo but seek to change the way it operates; not through promoting radical change in destabilizing ways, but by pushing for moderate change at the margins. And if this does not yet entail establishing a dominant Chinese view of the world and the way that it should be organized, the minimum aim is to ensure that Chinese alternatives become a way of undermining the legitimacy of Western preferences and thus weaken 'Western global dominance' (Pan 2010: 14).

CHINA ON THE WORLD STAGE

The PRC has played three different roles on the world stage. It started out as a global issue, became a global actor, and is now a global power; not *the* predominant global power, but a country whose actions and interests have an impact across the world. And this evolution in Chinese roles and power has not so much emerged alongside the decline in authority and legitimacy of the 'Western way', but has in some way been facilitated by it. China's rise would have occurred with or without the invasion of Iraq, and the financial turmoil in the USA and much of Western Europe in and after 2008. But these two very different types of crises created a space that alternative visions and alternative global actors could seek to occupy. And at times and on some issue areas, China has moved into this space; either though a concerted strategy to do so (for example, through China's emergence as an aid provider), or because others have willed it to (for example, in the external identification of a 'China Model').

What this will ultimately mean for the global order remains to be seen. It is easy to find expressions of Chinese dissatisfaction with the existing order. China cannot be considered to be a status quo power because there is a very real desire to change some of the rules of the game, to increase Chinese power (Buzan 2010) and to provide an alternative for other developing states to following the Western liberal way. And there has been a transition over the years from just being a critic of the existing order (and sometimes perhaps critical simply for the sake of being critical) to coming up with active solutions to perceived problems (Pang 2006). Yet China has to date been more of an accommodator than a challenger. And where it has challenged, it has done so in a rather responsible manner, in ways that do not destabilize an international system that has been an important component in facilitating Chinese growth.[20]

Although China has been reluctant to take on global leadership roles, and a focus on first meeting domestic demands remains at the centre of Chinese discourses and policies, it has become a leader of some, on some global issues. In some respects it was as the self-declared leader (of the 'Third World') that China first emerged as a key global actor (in the UN at least). More recently, it has become a leader in terms of airing dissatisfaction with the current global order. But agreeing on what is not wanted is not the same as agreeing on alternatives, and there is a recognition in China that actively articulating clear policy preferences might harm Chinese interests if it raises concerns in others about what China wants (Zhu 2011). How China's leaders exercise this new-found global power and make the transition from keeping a low profile to 'striving for achievement' (Yan 2014) will have a profound impact on how others view Chinese intentions. It will thus also have a profound impact on how easily it will be for China to act as a global power and potential or partial leader (of some) on the world stage.

NOTES

1. Testing its first atom bomb in 1964 and hydrogen bomb three years later.
2. Neither the current incumbent, Yang Jiechi, nor his predecessor, Dai Bingguo.
3. As Kang (2003) points out, it is impossible to win the argument that China is a status quo power, as sceptics will always reply that once China has the real power to change the world, it will do so.
4. The most influential work in this vein is Johnston (2008).

380 *Handbook of the politics of China*

5. Although other countries participated, the Chinese Foreign Ministry notes that only these five attended all sessions. See FMPRC (2000a).
6. Although the Foreign Ministry suggests that the basic principle of respect for other sovereign states was first established and enunciated by Mao in 1949 (FMPRC 2000b).
7. These quotes are all taken from Lin Biao's (1969) report to the Ninth Party Congress in 1969.
8. These quotes are taken from Deng Xiaoping's (1974) speech at the UN, on 10 April 1974.
9. For example, Japan, South Korea and Taiwan were given access to the US market without demands for reciprocal market opening. See Cumings (1987).
10. China, in the form of the post-World War II leadership of the Kuomintang, had been an original member in 1946, so technically the PRC 'assumed responsibility' for 'China's' relations with the IMF and WB rather than 'joining'. The major study of this early period was provided by Jacobson and Oksenberg (1990).
11. When China made its first bid to enter in 1986, this organization was still called the General Agreement on Tariffs and Trade. By the time China got in in 2001, it had been transformed into the WTO. This chapter will refer to the WTO throughout for convenience.
12. This popular rejectionist position is explored in detail in des Forges and Luo (2001).
13. The first use of the concept, if not the exact terms, seems to date from 1989. See Chen and Wang (2011).
14. Although it should be noted that Robert Zoellick's reference to China as a 'responsible stakeholder' (*fuzerende liyi guangguanzhe*) in 2005 also inspired debates within China about China's global role. For the original speech, see Zoellick (2005).
15. And at the time of writing in July 2015, still had not been ratified.
16. Although not specifically linked to the creation of the bank, Article 18 of the declaration (which also announced the new bank's creation) noted that the BRICS countries 'remain disappointed and seriously concerned with the current non-implementation of the 2010 International Monetary Fund reforms, which negatively impacts on the IMF's legitimacy, credibility and effectiveness'. See BRICS (2014).
17. According to its own webpage, http://www.oecd.org/dac/povertyreduction/thechina-dacstudygroup.htm.
18. Though this tends to underplay the massive dominance of Moscow's use of the veto before 1971.
19. The 'hidden veto' can also refer to persuading enough of the non-permanent members to vote against a resolution that it fails, and the permanent member itself does not have to use its veto (Schindlmayr 2001: 224).
20. Hence, my previous categorization of China as a 'dissatisfied responsible great power' (Breslin 2010).

22. Economic statecraft
James Reilly

Since 1978, China has repeatedly used foreign policy tools to advance its economic interests. Beijing is now beginning to reverse this equation, deploying its vast economic wealth to support foreign policy goals. China is flexing its economic muscle more frequently and on a wider range of issues, often backed up by nationalist sentiments at home. The strategic use of China's financial resources causes anxiety in Asia and around the world, and with good reason. Never in world history has one government had so much control over so much wealth. China's leaders govern a country that has the world's largest capital surplus and its second-largest economy, a highly coveted domestic market, and a currency with growing regional appeal. The temptation to deploy China's economic might for strategic benefit has proven irresistible. China today is using economic statecraft more frequently, more assertively, and in more diverse fashion than ever before.

Economic statecraft is the use of economic resources by political leaders to exert influence in pursuit of foreign policy objectives. There are three main strategies: providing capital through foreign aid or direct investment; expanding trade via preferential trade agreements or state procurements; and altering monetary policies such as purchasing foreign bonds or intervening in currency markets. These tools can be deployed either as incentives or as punitive measures. In recent years, for instance, Beijing has mixed economic rewards and punishments to expand its influence in Southeast Asia, deter arms sales to Taiwan, isolate the Dalai Lama, eviscerate criticism of China's human rights policies, and defend its maritime claims. Given China's economic heft and political determination, Beijing's expanding use of economic statecraft is of considerable strategic significance in Asia and around the world.

This chapter provides an overview of China's economic statecraft. It begins with existing studies on China's economic statecraft, followed by a historical and comparative perspective. The next section describes how Chinese scholars have become more active in promoting the use of economic statecraft. The chapter then examines the institutions and actors involved in China's economic statecraft, followed by the various techniques Beijing employs. The concluding section details several limitations and highlights looming challenges.

REVIEWING THE FIELD

Defined simply, economic statecraft is the use of economic resources by political leaders to exert influence in pursuit of foreign policy objectives. Economic statecraft seeks to either increase political affinity, where the target state identifies with the sending state's interests and preferences, and/or to achieve policy accommodation, whereby the target state adopts measures desired by the sending state. Three main strategies predominate: providing capital through foreign aid or direct investment; expanding trade via preferential trade agreements or state procurements; and altering monetary policies such as purchasing foreign bonds or intervening in currency markets.

Academic approaches to economic statecraft have changed considerably in recent years. In contrast to landmark works (Hirshman 1945; Baldwin 1985), scholars today tend to disaggregate the tools of economic statecraft into discrete topics: foreign aid (Holden 2009), sanctions (Taylor 2010), trade (Gowa 1994) and currency (Cohen 2006). Faced with the puzzle of dominant states unable to compel the compliance of weaker states, scholars have begun to examine domestic political conditions in targeted 'rogue regimes' (Nincic 2005). However, domestic politics within sending states have received less attention. Furthermore, most studies still focus on a rather narrow dynamic: a sending state using economic inducements or coercion to secure concessions by a target state (Ninic 2010). This approach downplays another strategy used by sending states: providing economic benefits unconditionally in order to build diplomatic ties and foster trust. Finally, most scholars still focus on the wealthy West (Solingen 2012), though efforts to develop a more inclusive framework examining how regional powers such as India, Brazil and Russia also engage in economic statecraft are emerging (Armijo and Katada forthcoming).

Economic statecraft often begins with the purposeful creation of economic dependence, creating the potential for a larger state to use economic resources to exert influence over a smaller, target state (Hirschman 1945). Economic leverage is often exercised through reciprocity: 'in which the actions of each party are contingent on the prior actions of the others in such a way that good is returned for good, and bad for bad' (Keohane 1986: 8). An alternative approach is the structural linkage strategy, which relies upon:

> a steady stream of economic benefits to reconfigure the balance of political interests within a target country. Structural linkage tends to be unconditional; the benefits are not turned on and off according to changes in target behavior. The sanctioning state expects instead that sustained economic engagement will eventually produce a political transformation and desirable changes in target behavior. (Mastanduno 1999: 304)

For instance, by providing aid, investment and trade benefits, Beijing signals its benevolent intent to countries worried about China's rise. For all these reasons, economic statecraft is an increasingly attractive policy tool for Beijing.

Assessing China's global economic power is one of the most prominent topics in world politics today (Shambaugh 2013a). Of particular interest has been China's use of economic resources to secure strategic energy resources overseas (Lee 2012). Experts have also examined the structures, actions and motivations of China's major state-owned economic entities, including state-owned enterprises (SOEs) and banks (Liou 2009; Downs 2011; Bell and Feng 2013). An alternative approach is to focus upon techniques in China's economic statecraft, including financial statecraft (Drezner 2009), sanctions (Reilly 2012a), foreign aid (Reilly 2012b) and free trade agreements (Ravenhill and Yang 2009). Finally, some scholars have adopted a regional approach, examining China's use of economic resources for political purposes toward Taiwan (Kastner 2009), Southeast Asia (Goh 2011), Africa (Brautigam 2009) and Latin America (Gallagher et al. 2012).

From within this rich and burgeoning literature, several themes emerge. Most significantly, zero-sum assessments of 'China, Inc' as either coherent or fragmented are being jettisoned in favour of more nuanced depictions of complex relations among the diverse political and economic actors engaged in China's economic activities overseas (Brødsgaard 2012). One benefit has been less attention to the simplistic debate over whether China's overseas economic expansion is driven more by market-based drivers or by mercantilist, state-based calculations (Smith and D'Arcy 2013). Instead, scholars increasingly acknowledge that China's overseas economic activities involve a range of economic actors who each pursue their own interests, while central leaders play crucial roles though coordination (Downs 2011) or in setting policy objectives and monitoring firms' alignment with central objectives (Haglund 2009). Norris (2010) applies a similar approach in his PhD dissertation by assessing the state's ability to manipulate commercial transactions to advance its strategic interests.

Such approaches foster a renewed appreciation for the ways in which domestic structural factors can shape China's economic interactions abroad. Earlier work highlighted the prevalence of a 'principal–agent' dilemma constraining China's influence in Africa (Gill and Reilly 2007). When a lead actor (principal) delegates authority to a subordinate (agent), the agent's own preferences, greater access to information and autonomy of action limit the principal's ability to control the agent (Laffont and Martimort 2001). This principal–agent dilemma is familiar to any manager or worker in a large firm. The dilemma, Alden and Large (2011: 31) suggest, is now 'at the heart of the problem of developing sustainable Chinese ties' with developing countries worldwide. Similarly, Brautigam and Tang (2012) argue that China's special economic zones in Africa reproduce key aspects of China's domestic economic developmental model.

A third trend is greater attention to how powerful domestic actors can shape central state preferences and thus influence the formation of policy objectives. Chen, Shaofeng (2011), for instance, shows how powerful SOEs acting in their own self-interest shaped China's energy policy in ways that do not necessarily advance China's energy security. Li (2014) suggests that province-level officials can have a similar effect upon Chinese policy toward neighbouring countries through a process of 'local liberalism'. The field would benefit from further studies examining how domestic actors shape China's economic statecraft at the stage of policy implementation. Such work could usefully build upon recent scholarship examining such dynamics within China's domestic politics (Huang 2012).

Finally, a number of studies have taken up the challenge of measuring the degree to which China has been successful in translating its economic prowess into political influence abroad. Intriguingly, findings suggest that Beijing is often unsuccessful. Tanner (2007) argues that political factors have limited China's use of economic pressure toward Taiwan despite its overwhelming economic influence. Medeiros et al. (2008: 239) conclude that 'China does not appear to have had much success in translating economic interactions into political influence' across Asia. Goh (2011) argues that Beijing has exploited convergent interests among its smallest and weakest Southeast Asian neighbours, but has been unable to significantly alter states' preferences or influence major policy decisions. Drezner (2009) shows that despite China's vast holdings of US government debt, Beijing had scant financial influence over the US during the global financial crisis.

While studies of China's economic statecraft have proliferated, the field still lacks a concise study that lays out the main objectives, actors, techniques and challenges facing China's economic statecraft. This chapter is designed to fill this gap.

A HISTORICAL AND COMPARATIVE PERSPECTIVE

China's use of economic statecraft is neither new nor unique. All countries seek to utilize economic resources for strategic benefits. The United States has been the most consequential user of economic statecraft since World War II, most notably with the Marshall Plan in Europe and its economic assistance to Japan, South Korea and Taiwan in the early stages of the Cold War. The US remains the world's most prevalent and powerful user of unilateral economic sanctions (Flowe and Gold 2000). Noting the top five recipients of US foreign aid in 2011 highlights its strategic motivations: Afghanistan, Israel, Iraq, Pakistan and Egypt. Nor is the US alone in its pragmatism. As de Mesquita and Smith (2009: 310) conclude: 'OECD members have little humanitarian motivation for aid giving.'

The People's Republic of China has engaged in economic statecraft since its inception, beginning with its aid programme. China's aid programme began on 23 November 1953 with the signing of the 'PRC–DPRK (Democratic People's Republic of Korea) Economic and Cultural Cooperation Agreement' (*People's Daily* 1953: 1). In this agreement, China cancelled North Korea's wartime debt of 729 million RMB (US$362.5 million) and provided a grant of RMB 800 million (US$400 million) for the period between 1954 and 1957, of which RMB 300 million (US$125 million) was made available during the first year. China also offered the free labour of nearly 0.5 million Chinese soldiers, who helped to restore or build bridges, dams, roads, rail lines, factories and apartments, as well as plant rice fields, provide medical services and deliver food. The aid programme's scale was extraordinary, equivalent in 1954 to 3.4 per cent of China's national budget (Shen and Xia 2012). From 1950 to 1970, China provided US$614 million worth of aid to North Korea, some 30 per cent of all aid provided to North Korea, just slightly under Soviet support levels. China enjoyed a favourable balance of trade during this period, eventually turning its trade surplus into loans that Beijing later forgave (Lin and Quan 2011).

As relations with the Soviet Union worsened in the 1960s, Beijing also leveraged the lure of its domestic market to exert political influence, most notably toward Japan. While valuing Japan as an alternative source of technology and investment, Sino-Japanese 'Friendship Trade' was constrained by a political litmus test imposed on Japanese companies by Beijing. China also used the trade for political pressure, such as halting trade in 1958 until Beijing received an apology for attacks on a Chinese flag at a Nagasaki trade fair (Mitcham 2005).

In the 1960s, as China found itself at loggerheads with both the Soviet Union and the United States, it rapidly expanded its aid programme in support of new nations 'fighting against colonialism and hegemony' (Shang 2010). By 1973, Beijing found itself providing aid to seven countries in Asia, six in the Middle East, three in Latin America, and 29 in Africa (Brautigam 2009: 41). The costs skyrocketed. From 1955 through to 1979, China's foreign aid expenditures averaged 0.87 per cent of gross domestic product (GDP) and 2.98 per cent of total government expenditures. By 1973, overseas development aid (ODA) spending reached 2.052 per cent of China's GDP, taking up an astonishing 6.9 per cent of total government expenditures; more than 25 per cent larger than the educational budget in that year. China had aid projects in more countries in Africa than even the United States (Brautigam 2009).

In reviewing these early days of China's aid programme, Chinese scholars admit that 'foreign aid was an important strategic tool for implementing China's concept of a peaceful foreign policy' (Wang Chenyan 2009: 44). As Mao Zedong noted: 'We were lifted into the UN by our African brothers' (Shang 2010: 57). Aid to countries such as Albania and Mongolia also encouraged them to 'at least remain neutral' in the Sino-Soviet split, and helped China to counter the isolation imposed by Western sanctions (Zhang 2012). Yet the broad consensus is that Mao-era aid was ineffective and excessive: 'The individuals who designed China's aid policies primarily considered political and security interests, but ignored economic interests', explains a Peking University professor. 'Because of this, China's true national interests suffered' (Sun, L. 2007: 9).

Clearly, the scale of the programme was unsustainable. A 1975 State Council conference signalled a drawdown in assistance by urging that aid recipients 'rely on themselves' in developing their economies (Brautigam 2009). Aid levels began to fall, while Chinese leaders started prioritizing 'mutual benefits'. In July 1979, Deng Xiaoping told a Politburo working group: 'we must ensure that both the donor and the recipient country can receive benefits' (Bin 2008: 36). Three years later, Premier Zhao Ziyang declared that China's economic relations with developing countries would be guided by an emphasis upon 'equality and mutual benefit' (Brautigam 2009). Over the next two decades, Chinese leaders focused upon using diplomatic and strategic policies to support China's own economic development. Yet as China's economy boomed in the 2000s, the temptation to deploy economic resources for strategic benefit grew stronger.

China's New Thinking on Economic Statecraft

China's more proactive approach toward economic statecraft is grounded in its scepticism toward Western morality claims. The United States, one scholar argues, uses sanctions to 'interfere in developing countries, promote American values, and try to sustain US global hegemony' (Yan 2005: 45). Foreign aid is seen in a similar light. As two Ministry of Commerce (MOFCOM) experts explain: 'For major powers, ODA is an important foreign policy tool. While promoting the social and economic development of recipient countries, it also serves the national interests of the donor country' (Nie and Zhou 2008). A conference report puts it bluntly: the West uses aid as 'as a tool of economic, political and military control over recipient countries' (*Ouzhou* 2002: 104).

This Realist perspective pervades Chinese strategic thinking. As Tsinghua University's Zhao Kejin wrote in the *Study Times*: 'China's economic advantage has not been translated into strategic advantage. We still lack a diplomatic strategy that focuses on increasing our international political influence – this is a very urgent task' (Yu, V. 2010). Professor Zhang Shuguang agrees that 'China has accumulated a great deal of strategic capital' which it should use as an economic 'weapon' to counter the US, Japan, India, Russia and Vietnam, while offering economic incentives toward countries in the Middle East, Africa and Latin America (Zhang 2012). A major study from the China Institute for Contemporary International Relations (CICIR), an influential think tank associated with the Ministry of State Security, concludes: 'Given the fact that our nation has increasing economic power, we should prudently use economic sanctions against those countries that undermine world peace and threaten our country's national interests' (Liu and Liu 2009: 36).

Experts have explored a variety of measures by which Beijing could exert influence:

limiting investments, imposing trade restrictions, freezing financial assets, punishing or rewarding corporate groups, and shifting foreign currency holdings. MOFCOM expert Liu Wei (2008: 32) argues that China should also expand the economic dependence of Western Europe, Japan and the US upon China, 'to ensure that if they try to sanction China, that they too will suffer economic consequences'. Noting that eight of the top ten trading partners that China runs a trade deficit with are in Asia, and that five of China's top ten sources of foreign direct investment (FDI) are in Asia, Liu and Zheng (2005: 13) add: 'China could have a major effect on these economies by shifting its policies via economic sanctions.' For instance, Taiwan's 'economic marginalization' due to its dependence upon China 'provides an opportunity for [using] economic sanctions' and creates a 'bargaining chip' for Beijing (Xue and Wang 2006: 150).

Similar discussions surfaced amidst the 2012 consumer boycott of Japanese products. Professor Zhou Yongsheng urged Chinese consumers to 'use the market economy as a tool' to advance Chinese interests (Xinhua Forum 2012). Others called for the boycott to target companies that support Japanese right-wing groups (*Global Times* 2012a). Feng Wei, from Fudan University, insisted that China should use economic measures to 'push Japan back to the negotiating table' (Wang 2012). Jin Baisong (2012), a Ministry of Commerce researcher, insisted:

> China should work out a comprehensive plan which should include imposition of sanctions and taking precautionary measures against any Japanese retaliation. China should also have several rounds of policies ready to undermine the Japanese economy at the least cost of Chinese enterprises. Furthermore, in case Chinese enterprises suffer because of the sanctions, the Chinese government should be prepared to compensate them. And once China imposes sanctions on Japan, the government should ensure that all enterprises in the country, domestic and foreign, obey the rules.

CHINA'S POLITICAL INDUSTRIAL COMPLEX

The combination of a socialist legacy and a state-led developmental model has left Beijing with the institutional capacity for directing economic resources for political purposes. At the apex of China's political industrial complex are powerful economic planning and regulatory agencies. The Ministry of Commerce (MOFCOM) oversees policies and companies involved in foreign trade and investment, and directly administers China's foreign aid programme through its Department of Foreign Aid (DFA). The National Development and Reform Commission (NDRC) sets China's industrial policy and overall economic policy directions. NDRC also administers national-level development projects, including cross-border infrastructure projects. The State-owned Assets Supervision and Administration Commission (SASAC) is the 'owner' of China's large state-owned enterprises and is tasked with increasing the value of these state assets. In aggregate, these agencies enjoy expansive power to shape China's overseas investments, trade, and foreign aid.

In the financial sector, three government entities play critical roles. The Ministry of Finance (MOF) oversees the financial sector, manages the national budget, sets fiscal policy, issues economic regulations, and dominates macroeconomic policies. The People's Bank of China (PBoC) is China's central bank. It manages the flow of currency, sets banking policies, and along with the China Banking Regulatory Commission (CBRC), oversees all banks. Under the PBoC, the State Administration of Foreign Exchange (SAFE) manages China's foreign exchange reserves, heavily influencing exchange rates. All Chinese banks are required to clear their foreign exchanges and convert all foreign currency to RMB through SAFE, leaving SAFE in control of most of China's $3 trillion in foreign currency reserves.

The supply of capital for China's economic statecraft comes primarily not from the government budget, but rather from China's policy and commercial banks, as well as its sovereign wealth funds. The two policy banks used in China's economic statecraft are the China Development Bank (CDB) and the Export-Import Bank (Ex-Im Bank). CDB has played a crucial role in financing infrastructure and energy projects in China and abroad; the Ex-Im Bank provides the subsidized loans for China's aid programme. China's commercial banks are also owned by the state and subject to an array of state regulations, though they are expected to be profitable. The four largest commercial banks are the Bank of China (BOC), the China Construction Bank (CCB), the Agricultural Bank of China (ABC), and the Industrial and Commercial Bank of China (ICBC). Smaller commercial banks abound, including the Bank of Communications, China CITIC Bank, and China Everbright Bank. Finally, China also has sovereign wealth funds, most importantly the China Investment Corporation (CIC), created in 2007 by the MOF to invest China's foreign currency reserves more aggressively than the low returns provided by SAFE's investments into US treasury bonds.[1]

These are massive institutions. The ICBC is the world's largest bank; three other Chinese banks are in the top ten (*BBC News* 2013). The nation's leading foreign-currency lender, the CDB's total assets exceed US$900 billion, more than the World Bank and Asia Development Bank combined (Norris 2010: 265). Over the past decade, Ex-Im Bank's loans to sub-Saharan Africa vastly exceeded funds lent by the World Bank (Rabinovitch 2012). SAFE is ranked as the world's third-largest sovereign wealth fund, with US$568 billion; the CIC is fifth, with US$482 billion in assets (http://www.swfinstitute.org/fund-rankings/). The state dominates the entire sector: 98 per cent of China's banking assets are state-owned (Chiu and Lewis 2006: 205).

These institutions collectively control much of China's vast national wealth. China's agricultural and industrial output is the world's largest. It is the world's second-largest exporter (US$2 trillion) and its third-largest importer (US$1.7 trillion). This economic heft confers considerable trading leverage. China is the largest trading partner for over 100 countries, including Australia, Japan, South Korea, Vietnam, Malaysia, Indonesia and India.

China's overall trade surplus has enabled it to run up the world's largest current account surplus (US$213.8 billion) and amass foreign exchange reserves of US$3.3 trillion. China holds one-fifth of all foreign-owned US Treasury securities. According to OECD data, China's overseas FDI stock of US$502 billion is less significant: only the fourteenth-largest. In 2012, China's FDI outflows of US$62.4 billion lagged behind the UK and Germany, and were only half of Japan's outward FDI, although China's investments have risen sharply since 2005. I turn now to consider how the Chinese government seeks to deploy these resources to advance foreign policy objectives, beginning with foreign aid.

PROVIDING ASSISTANCE

Foreign aid is a key resource for China's economic statecraft. By its own account, China had distributed aid to 161 countries by the end of 2009, including 123 developing countries: 30 in Asia, 51 in Africa, 18 in Latin America and the Caribbean, 12 in Oceania and 12 in Eastern Europe. Like all donors, China's aid is used to help bolster important diplomatic relationships, particularly among African countries and in Southeast Asia. Approximately 80 per cent of all Chinese aid goes to Asia and Africa (*China Review News* 2012).

China's aid projects generally originate from recipient country requests and are overwhelmingly oriented toward infrastructure projects, generally undertaken by Chinese firms. The recipient country obtains a new road or building, but rarely any cash transfers. Seeking to address recipients' domestic political concerns, Beijing often finds itself supporting prestige projects such as the Tonchan Palace, a five-star hotel in Vientiane, or the Lao National Stadium, built for the 2009 Southeast Asian Games (Zhu 2010).

China also relies upon selective 'purchasing diplomacy', in which Chinese state-owned enterprises make or forgo purchases of prominent commercial goods to either reward or punish foreign states for their diplomatic policy. Such purchases help to temper domestic disquiet over China's rising power. US diplomats, for instance, have quietly encouraged Beijing to expand its purchases of Boeing airplanes to bolster public support for Washington's engagement policy (Bader 2012: 75). Similarly, on his May 2013 visit to Germany, Premier Li Keqiang faced mounting German criticism over Chinese subsidies of solar panels. In response, Li opened his chequebook, overseeing major commercial deals and dangling the possibility of German firms obtaining contracts as a part of China's transition to a 'green economy' (China.org.cn 2013).

Purchasing diplomacy has also buttressed Beijing's struggle to discourage foreign leaders from meeting with the Dalai Lama. In 2009, after French officials announced that President Nicolas Sarkozy (who at the time also held the rotating European Union Presidency) would meet the Dalai Lama, China postponed the eleventh annual EU–China summit, to be held in Paris, and froze an order for 150 Airbus planes. Two Chinese trade delegations quickly crossed France off their travel agendas; the first delegation alone signed $15 billion worth of trade deals in other European countries. Before his January 2009 European tour, Premier Wen Jiabao noted: 'I looked at a map of Europe on the plane. My trip goes around France . . . We all know why' (She 2009). In response, Paris issued a strong statement recognizing Tibet as part of China's integral territory. A Chinese trade delegation soon landed in Paris. As a *China Daily* (2009) article chortled, 'France Goes Back on China's Shopping List'.

Another example emerged in December 2009, when Cambodia agreed to deport 20 ethnic Uighurs back to China to be prosecuted in connection with the July 2009 violent anti-government protests in Xinjiang province. Several weeks later, Chinese Vice-President Xi Jinping arrived in Cambodia bearing gifts: US$1.2 billion in grants and loans. The US State Department responded to Cambodia's decision to deport the Uighurs by cancelling a shipment of 200 surplus military trucks to Cambodia. Three weeks later, China donated 257 trucks (Pomfret 2010). By 2012, Chinese loans and grants to Cambodia reached US$2.7 billion. This benevolence seemed to pay off in July 2012, when Cambodia used its power as Chair of the Association of Southeast Asian Nations

(ASEAN) Summit to block a joint statement criticizing China's approach to territorial disputes in the South China Sea (Pheakdey 2013).

In delivering economic benefits, Chinese leaders pay careful attention to timing. 'Sending coal in the midst of a snowstorm', as the Chinese saying goes, maximizes political benefits. The global financial crisis was a major snowstorm, an opportunity for Beijing to purchase political capital cheaply. In April 2009, Premier Wen Jiabao announced a US$10 billion investment fund for regional infrastructure in Southeast Asia, along with a US$15 billion line of credit for poorer ASEAN states and US$40 million in 'special aid' for Cambodia, Laos and Myanmar (McCartan 2009). In Athens the following October, Wen promised to purchase Greek government bonds, encourage investment and tourism, and establish a US$5 billion fund to help Greek shipping companies buy Chinese ships. In exchange, Wen explained, 'we hope the EU recognizes as soon as possible China's full market-economy status, and will relax restriction on high-technology exports to China and oppose trade protectionism' (Skrekas and Batson 2010).

For wealthier nations, Chinese leaders rely upon the lure of their domestic market and the potential of Chinese investment to sway reluctant leaders. Canadian Prime Minister Stephen Harper, for instance, skipped the Beijing Olympics while promising Canadian voters that he would never sell out Canadian values for the 'almighty dollar'. Yet when he finally visited Beijing in 2009, after a four-year hiatus, Harper signed a joint statement acknowledging that 'differing histories and national conditions can create some distinct points of view on issues such as human rights'. In exchange, Chinese leaders promised to send trade and investment delegations, fund research centres and promote Chinese tourism to Canada. As Wenran Jiang (2010) explains, Harper's visit provides 'a clear example of how political engagement with China at the highest level can deliver tangible economic benefits'.

STRATEGIC INVESTMENTS

The most direct way for Chinese political leaders to utilize China's overseas direct investments for foreign policy purposes is to create a dedicated investment fund. For instance, on 14 August 2012, MOFCOM Vice-Minister Chen Jian pledged to 'support Chinese enterprises ... to advance the establishment of enhanced bilateral trade and investment structures [in the DPRK]' (*China Review News* 2012). A month later, the China Overseas Investment Federation announced a new RMB 3 billion (US$470 million) Fund for Investment into North Korea. One billion RMB was made available immediately for mining, real estate and infrastructure-related projects. In exchange, the DPRK Investment Office promised to 'protect the interests of Chinese investors' (*Xinjingbao* 2012b).

Chinese officials also use corporate investments to advance specific diplomatic objectives. In 1997, for instance, Chinese diplomats encouraged China Nonferrous Metals Co. (CNMC) to purchase a UK-owned copper mine in northern Zambia before a Taiwanese company could do so. With NDRC backing, CNMC was able to obtain low-cost investment capital, while Chinese embassy staff successfully encouraged the Zambian side to favourably consider the Chinese investment (interviews in Zambia 2008).

Nepal provides a clear example of strategic investments. Deeply concerned with the activities of Tibetan exile groups in Nepal, Beijing has showered Kathmandu with economic benevolence: building new roads, railways and border posts, and providing military assistance. One of the most ambitious projects has been Chinese support for a US$3 billion effort to transform the tiny Nepalese town of Lumbini where the Buddha was born 2500 years ago into the premier place of pilgrimage for Buddhists worldwide. Lumbini will have an airport, highway, hotels, convention centre, temples and a Buddhist university, all in addition to the installation of water, electricity and communication lines it currently lacks. The project is worth nearly 10 per cent of Nepal's entire GDP (Ranade 2011). Most importantly, China's investment seems to have paid off. The Dalai Lama has not been allowed to visit Lumbini since the late 1980s, and the Nepalese government's restrictions on political activism by Tibetan refugees have increased in recent years (Human Rights Watch 2014).

BEIJING'S ENMESHMENT STRATEGY

As the Nepal example suggests, China's economic statecraft has been particularly active with its 14 land neighbours. Promoting greater trade and investment offers Beijing a classic 'win–win' opportunity: drawing nearby countries into China's economic orbit while bolstering its diplomatic leverage and creating commercial opportunities for Chinese firms. China's push for regional infrastructure is at the heart of this effort. In recent years, Beijing has funded a thickening network of cross-border railways, roads, and oil and gas pipelines across mainland Asia (Holslag 2010). These projects enhance Chinese access to strategic natural resources, while meeting pressing infrastructure requirements among China's poorer neighbours. China has also ramped up its support for new regional institutions to fund cross-border projects, including President Xi Jinping's 2013 call to establish an Asian Infrastructure Bank.

To further facilitate economic integration and encourage domestic constituencies to support closer relations with China, Beijing has also offered preferential trade deals to key regional partners. As of 1 June 2015, China had signed 12 free trade agreements, with seven more under negotiation. While driving a hard bargain in trade talks with large, wealthy nations, Beijing has been surprisingly magnanimous toward smaller but strategically important economic partners. To assuage concerns over political integration, Beijing offered both Hong Kong and Macao generous Closer Economic Partnership Arrangements in 2003. China also included a generous Early Harvest Programme in the 2002 China–ASEAN Free Trade Agreement (CAFTA), opening Chinese markets to ASEAN agricultural imports. As Camarena and Dosch's Chapter 25 in this volume demonstrates, China's engagement in Southeast Asia has relied heavily upon these economic inducements. Instead of exacting the best deal possible for China, Beijing structured CAFTA to reassure China's Southeast Asian neighbours and give them a stake in China's economic success, striving to present itself as a 'benevolent regional hegemonic power' (Ravenhill and Yang 2009). CAFTA also bolstered Beijing's pursuit of WTO recognition as a market economy; a status ASEAN accorded China in September 2004.

In the case of Taiwan, Beijing has used the lure of its domestic market and manufacturing capacity to attract Taiwan's investors. Beijing's blandishments were finally reciprocated after Kuomintang (KMT) Party leader Ma Ying-jeou won the March

2008 presidential election. In 2010, Ma signed the Economic Cooperation Framework Agreement (ECFA), the first FTA between WTO members with a territorial conflict. Like CAFTA, ECFA strongly favours agricultural interests in Taiwan's 'green South', a traditional stronghold of anti-mainland sentiment. By 2020, Taiwan expects to send some 62 per cent of its exports to the mainland, bolstering its substantial trade surplus with China. An estimated 2 million Taiwanese businesspeople now live in China; 1 million Chinese tourists visit Taiwan annually (Cabestan 2010). For Beijing, its reward came when Ma was re-elected on 14 January 2012, aided by Taiwan's business community's support for deepening cross-Strait economic ties.

CHINESE SANCTIONS

While China has increased its use of economic sanctions in recent years, these are rarely openly declared. Instead, Beijing prefers to use vague threats, variation in leadership visits, selective purchases (or non-purchases) and other informal measures. Such informal measures enhance the leadership's flexibility, since they can be removed without an embarrassing policy reversal. They also provide Chinese leaders with credible deniability, thus minimizing diplomatic fallout.

Most countries impose international sanctions to place high costs upon the target country through sustained economic isolation. China's sanctions, in contrast, are more bark than bite. Beijing uses the threat of sanctions to signal its frustration: a warning that if a country does not reverse a certain action, stronger repercussions will come. China's threat of sanctions also signals that if other states take similar actions, they too will face economic costs.

This signalling strategy was on display in January 2010, following the US announcement of a US$6.4 billion arms sales to Taiwan. Vice-Foreign Minister He Yafei threatened Ambassador Jon Huntsman that China would 'impose sanctions against [US] companies that will engage in arms deliveries to Taiwan' (*RIA Novostiat* 2010). While no overt sanctions were implemented, China has already successfully deterred other countries from selling arms to Taiwan. The last major European sale to Taiwan was France's 1992 sale of Mirage fighter jets. It prompted Beijing to close the French consulate in Guangzhou and cost French companies the opportunity to help build the Guangzhou subway (Bräuner 2012).

Beijing's 'virtual sanctions' often rely upon disproportionate leverage: China combines highly focused, short-term economic threats with diplomatic pressure on a country or company to resolve an issue of limited significance to the sanctions target. In theory, the target will value its economic relationship with China more highly than the issue of limited significance. Chinese sanctions also tend to be rather short-lived. For instance, countries such as France, the United States and Japan, whose leaders met with the Dalai Lama – something China reacts strongly against – on average saw only a two-year drop in their exports to China.

China has also threatened economic sanctions to counter criticism of its human rights policy, such as the 2010 awarding of the Nobel Peace Prize to jailed dissident Liu Xiaobo. After the award was announced, China promptly cancelled a ministerial trade delegation to Norway (Chen 2010). Over the next two years, the Chinese Foreign Ministry refused to receive Norway's Ambassador to Beijing, while the bilateral human rights dialogue and free trade negotiations were postponed indefinitely (Jakobson and Peng 2012). Norwegian salmon exports to China also dropped by half in early 2011, though overall bilateral trade between China and Norway experienced 'no Nobel effect' according to Statistics Norway. Instead, bilateral trade rose sharply over 2011 (Deshayes 2011).

China has also imposed sanctions upon its erstwhile ally, North Korea. Following its February 2013 nuclear test, Chinese banks closed North Korean bank accounts and suspended their trading rights. Customs officials tightened border controls and tourism was officially discouraged ('In rare event' 2013). On 23 September 2013, China released a 236-page list of potential dual-use items that Chinese companies and individuals are proscribed from trading with North Korea (MOFCOM 2013).

Even the Chinese public has got into the sanctions game. Hollywood film studios, French supermarkets, Italian car manufacturers and British universities have all apologized for 'hurting the feelings of Chinese people', in hopes of avoiding consumer boycotts. The most recent example emerged during the 2012 anti-Japan protests in response to the Japanese government's purchase and 'nationalization' of the contested Senkaku/Diaoyu Islands. As emotions swelled, Chinese consumers declined to buy Japanese-brand electronics and cars, and began cancelling visits to Japan. As one blogger put it: 'the boycott of Japanese goods begins with me' (http://forum.home.news.cn/thread/103614758/1.html).

Yet as the examples of Japan and North Korea suggest, China's sanctions have often proven ineffective. Pyongyang continued its pursuit of nuclear weapons; Japan refused to back down in the territorial dispute. Such resistance points to some of the constraints facing China's economic statecraft.

BEIJING'S ROCKY ROAD

The very factors that have encouraged Chinese leaders to expand their application of economic statecraft can also limit its effectiveness. Despite the state's expansive economic influence, tensions between economic and strategic objectives are often stronger than most Chinese strategists recognize. The scale of state involvement in the economy also creates coordination problems across the diverse array of actors involved in economic statecraft. Furthermore, the scale of China's economy exacerbates anxiety about Chinese influence, undermining China's incentive strategy and instead encouraging backlashes and balancing efforts, particularly among China's Asian neighbours.

Is Win–Win Really Possible?

China's trade sanctions can undermine investor confidence and hurt domestic manufactures. The majority of China's massive trade surplus still involves processing trade: importing intermediate materials and exporting finished products. Selective trading bans disrupt these complex production chains, chasing investors to alternative manufacturing locations such as Vietnam. China also relies upon market access, technological transfer and capital provision from many of the wealthy nations in Europe, East Asia and North America that it may seek to sanction. As Chinese experts pointed out in 2012, consumer boycotts against Japanese cars primarily hurt Chinese workers (Gao 2012). China's leaders can ill afford to undermine their export-driven manufacturing sector amidst global economic uncertainty.

Trade sanctions can also spark economic disputes, undermining confidence in China's support for an open trading regime. For instance, media reports that China was blocking shipments of Rare Earth Elements (REE) to Japan during the September 2010 dispute over Japan's arrest and holding of a Chinese boat captain exacerbated concerns on Beijing's tightening export controls over REE, formally declared in July 2010 and aimed primarily at consolidating China's REE domestic sector (Areddy 2011). In response, on 13 March 2012, the US, the European Union (EU) and Japan filed separate but coordinated complaints with the WTO charging that China was limiting its export of rare earths (Associated Press 2012). China's actions thus stimulated a surge in rare earth element production elsewhere and sparked a backlash by its three top trading partners.

Offering preferential trading terms for political reasons also entails economic costs. The generous 'early harvests' that Beijing proffered to ASEAN and Taiwan, expanding their access to Chinese markets, generated grumbling at home. In the case of CAFTA, Chinese leaders assuaged provincial leaders' resentments through side-payments, offering investment capital and policy autonomy to Yunnan and Guangxi provinces (Ravenhill and Yang 2009). As China transitions toward a more advanced, higher-cost economy, domestic pressures for protectionist measures are likely to grow, limiting Beijing's ability to offer such generous terms in subsequent trade deals while increasing the costs of such side-payments.

Domestic Discontents

China's foreign aid is also facing sharper public scrutiny. In mid-November 2011, a minibus overloaded with over 60 nursery-age children travelling in rural Gansu province collided with a truck, leaving 19 children dead. Less than two weeks later, China's Foreign Minister announced that it was donating 23 brand-new school buses to Macedonia. Chinese netizens exploded in anger, with over 480 000 entries on *weibo* (a Chinese form of social media) in only a few days (*BBC News* 2011). 'If the Chinese government has excess school buses', one netizen fumed, 'they should first provide them to our own domestic students' (Pcbaby.com.cn 2011). An editorial in the *Global Times* urged the Foreign Ministry to 'reflect' (*fansi*) on the donation, warning: 'All China's government departments should strengthen their sensitivity to public opinion. Before undertaking any task, they should first carefully consider the judgment of public opinion' (*Global Times* 2011).

In his 2012 work report to the National People's Congress, Premier Wen Jiabao insisted that the government would 'guide Chinese enterprises under various forms of ownership in making overseas investments ... in an orderly manner'. However, by promoting overseas investments for political purposes, the Chinese government is creating a classic moral-hazard problem. Chinese corporations may feel free to act in a fiscally irresponsible manner because they can depend upon state-controlled banks for financial support. Indeed, a 2008 PBoC report estimated that Dandong companies alone have lost some US$20 million investing in North Korea (Zhou 2012).

Domestic actors may even hijack the policy process, manipulating strategic concerns to advance their own interests. The oil and gas pipelines built through Myanmar are a good example. Yunnan Province officials and experts collaborated with national oil companies (NOCs) to feed fears of a 'Malacca Dilemma' and promote the pipelines as a solution, despite their US$2.5 billion price tag and vulnerability to domestic instability. In this case, 'the preferences of the Chinese government and the NOCs do not coincide' (Chen 2008). Professor Zhang Shuguang (2012) warns that such 'special interest groups . . . should stand on the side of long-term overall national interests, not just advancing their own interests'. Yet the difficulty in enforcing such cohesion is exacerbated by a deepening principal–agent dilemma.

China's Principal–Agent Dilemma

Beijing's strategy of relying on state-owned corporations for strategic purposes engenders a principal–agent dilemma. Whenever a lead actor, or principal, designates another actor, an agent, to advance certain goals on their behalf, a number of conditions can impede effective coordination and oversight. In this case, China relies heavily on coordination among a complex array of corporations and government bureaucracies to achieve its policy objectives overseas. However, the combination of China's priority on economic development, the dizzying array of government principals and corporate agents with different bureaucratic rankings, and the scarcity of reliable and timely information, undermine effective government control over Chinese companies abroad.

The difficulty of controlling commercial actors is clear on the open seas. While Beijing has utilized fishing boats to demonstrate its maritime claims, ambitious fishermen are also causing diplomatic headaches. In May 2012, for instance, North Korean soldiers seized three Chinese fishing boats, demanding a 1.2 million RMB 'fine' for illegal fishing in North Korean waters. Negotiations stagnated until the dispute leaked online. China's netizens exploded in anger, denouncing North Korea's 'lawless behavior' and asking: 'What have we received for all of our foreign aid to North Korea?'[2] After Chinese diplomats finally got the boats released, the *Global Times* quickly urged Chinese citizens to 'remain calm and be more understanding of our friendly neighbor' (*Global Times* 2012c).

Seeking a more coherent approach, in March 2013 Beijing established the State Oceanic Administration, bringing law enforcement and economic regulatory agencies together under one roof. Yet the fishing boat incident points to an intensifying challenge for Beijing as more private enterprises go abroad; one unlikely to be resolved through bureaucratic reshuffles. Private firms are likely to be more aggressive than SOEs. They have few obligations to Chinese diplomats or national bureaucracies, relying instead upon a carefully cultivated local base of support. Successful local private entrepreneurs in China must cut corners to succeed. Commonplace acts such as bribing officials, falsifying contracts and evading laws are unlikely to decline as they move far from home. Instead of serving as reliable agents for Beijing's economic statecraft, such firms exacerbate anxiety over China's rise.

Spawning Backlashes and Balancing

Beijing has struggled for decades to cultivate a reputation as a responsible member of the international economic system, as Breslin's Chapter 21 in this volume shows. Beijing has also sought to ease fears of a 'China threat', particularly among its Asian neighbours.

Indeed, survey data shows that, fair or not, Asian citizens tend to blame China when their own economies turn downward (Linley et al. 2012). In Zambia, for instance, Michael Sata rode a populist wave of anti-China sentiments to his 2011 election, even though China has invested more than $300 million and employed more than 10 000 Zambians (Sata 2011). Such popular anxiety encourages policy reversals, such as Mongolia's recently tightened restrictions on foreign investment (Hook 2012).

China's aid, investment and trade benefits are designed to signal Beijing's benevolent intent and highlight the benefits of accommodation. Yet China's generosity also exacerbates fears of overdependence, particularly among its smaller Asian neighbours. As US Secretary of State Hillary Clinton told a Cambodian audience, 'I think it's smart for Cambodia to be friends with many countries. Look for balance. You don't want to become too dependent on any one country.' A number of Southeast Asian states, including Beijing's erstwhile ally Myanmar, have taken Clinton up on the offer, welcoming the US's 'pivot' back to Asia as a hedge against rising Chinese influence (Reilly 2013b). On US concerns over China's rise, see Gill's Chapter 24 in this volume. Similar anxieties are apparent within Taiwan as economic ties have deepened in recent years, most notably with the 2014 'Sunflower' movement. University students frustrated with the KMT's rapid passage of the controversial Cross-Strait Services Trade Agreement occupied Taiwan's Legislative Yuan for several weeks in March 2014, forcing the KMT to pledge tighter scrutiny of economic accords with China (Sunflower 2014).

Even North Korea has begun to reach out beyond Beijing. In May 2012, Kim Young Nam, the nominal head of state, visited Singapore and Indonesia seeking greater economic ties, reportedly to reduce North Korea's 'over-dependence on China' (*Global Times* 2012b). In April 2013, an article in North Korea's *Journal of Economic Research* criticized local 'trade companies for focusing on only one or two countries', warning that, 'the whole nation may experience political and economic pressure from trade companies that restrict foreign trade to only one country' (NKeconwatch 2013). Pyongyang's 2008 decision to award its exclusive cellphone rights to an Egyptian rather than a Chinese firm reflects this effort to minimize its dependence upon China.

IMPACT AND CONSTRAINTS

China is using economic statecraft more frequently, more assertively, and in more diverse fashion. Expansive state influence over vast economic resources, combined with a widespread presumption that economic and strategic objectives can be advanced simultaneously, encourages Beijing's greater application of economic statecraft. China relies primarily upon positive incentives to advance its strategic interests: directing aid, trade and investment for political benefit. As the case of Taiwan shows, Beijing's preference for delivering economic benefits is far more pacific than flexing its military muscles; although Chinese leaders have not shied away from using sanctions when core national interests are threatened.

However, the very factors that lead Beijing to expand its application of economic statecraft also undermine its effectiveness. Economic and strategic objectives do not always marry up, particularly given conflicting preferences across China's vast government bureaucracy. Expansive state influence across the economy also creates coordination problems across the diverse array of government and corporate actors involved in China's economic statecraft. Finally, the scale of China's economy exacerbates anxiety about Chinese influence, sparking populist backlashes and encouraging balancing efforts among China's Asian neighbours. While economic statecraft has emerged as an important element in China's foreign policy, these considerable constraints will continue to limit Beijing's influence abroad.

NOTES

1. The preceding overview draws in part from Norris (2010) and is based upon Reilly (2013a).
2. Postings at: http://finance.stockstar.com/SS2012052000000343.shtml (20 May 2012) and http://stock.jrj.com.cn/hotstock/2012/05/17172213166714.shtml (17 May 2012).

23. East Asia
Shogo Suzuki

The People's Republic of China's (PRC) recent rise to becoming a global power has meant that there has been an increasing interest in China's growing role in Africa and Latin America. However, one of Beijing's most important geographical areas in its foreign relations has been East Asia, and will continue to be so. Its regional neighbours, Japan and the Republic of Korea (ROK; or South Korea), are economic powerhouses that enjoy a much higher level of economic development than China. While still constricted by its constitutional constraints, Japan also has a formidable military. Furthermore, both Japan and South Korea are key allies of the United States (US), and act as important stations for the projection of American power in East Asia. Simply put, East Asia contains two regional powers that both have the ability to influence the regional distribution of power, and thus factor in Beijing's strategic calculations (Buzan 2004).

East Asia is also important for China because it is one of its most challenging areas of foreign policy. The region contains Taiwan, the last refuge of Chiang Kai-shek's Nationalist Party. Taiwan has since evolved into a thriving democracy, decreasing emotional and nationalistic ties with the communist Chinese mainland. The PRC regards Taiwan as an integral part of China, and lists reunification with the island as one of its key long-term national goals. Any unilateral declaration of Taiwanese independence is likely to invite Chinese military intervention, and thus constitutes a major flashpoint for the regional security dynamic. In addition, the region also contains the Democratic People's Republic of Korea (DPRK; or North Korea), one of the last remaining Stalinist regimes in the world and frequently regarded as a 'rogue regime' (see, e.g., Bush 2002). China has traditionally supported North Korea, regarding it as a useful buffer against South Korea. However, in recent years the DPRK has tested nuclear weapons, and attacked South Korea and its military assets, causing a series of regional crises. The regime has become something of a liability, placing Beijing in an awkward position.

Adding to this already complicated picture is the issue of history and nationalism. The expansion of the European international order into East Asia in the nineteenth century ended Chinese regional hegemony, and resulted in the loss of multiple territories. In addition, it spawned the rise of a new imperialist power, Japan, which proceeded to invade China in both the late nineteenth and early twentieth centuries (Suzuki 2009). The ensuing sense of national crisis and 'national humiliation' has been the basis on which modern Chinese nationalism has been constructed (Harrison 2001; see Smith, A.D. 2000). Thus, China has been embroiled in a series of emotionally charged disputes with Japan over the interpretation of 'history'. Furthermore, disputes with Tokyo have the potential to become highly politicized: emotional anti-Japanese demonstrations have regularly erupted in China whenever there is a perceived slight to Chinese nationalist sensibilities.

In short, East Asia matters - and matters tremendously - in Chinese foreign policy. Understanding how the PRC deals with the dynamics of this region gives us an insight into various challenges Beijing faces as it rises to power, and is of great utility to gain a broader perspective on Chinese foreign policy.

SINO-JAPANESE RELATIONS

Japan is China's most powerful and important neighbour, and relations with Japan constitute one of the most important bilateral relations of China's foreign policy. The two states enjoy a long history of economic and cultural interactions, and Chinese culture and civilization have been hugely influential throughout the history of Japan. Unfortunately, contemporary Sino-Japanese relations are characterized by frequent cycles of disputes, which take place alongside close trading relations. This dynamic has been called 'cold politics, hot economics' (*zhengleng jingre*). International relations theories that argue that dense, complex interdependence serves to make interstate relations more predictable and stable (Keohane and Nye 2001) have some trouble in explaining why Sino-Japanese relations remain so riddled with mutual antipathy. It is therefore worth spending some time to explore this seemingly contradictory dynamic.

Why China and Japan are Economically Very Close...

China and Japan have long enjoyed close economic relations with one another. Japan managed to maintain its trading ties with the PRC immediately after 1949, despite the fact that the two states had no diplomatic relations with one another. The Japanese side were well aware of the vast potential the 'China market' would offer to Japanese businesses, and in the context of the Cold War considered trading as an effective way to drive a wedge between China and the Soviet Union. Even during the height of the PRC's 'international isolation' during the Cultural Revolution, Japan remained one of China's biggest trading partners (Tanaka 1991: 43–60; see Zhang 1998: 39–41).

Economic relations developed rapidly once Deng Xiaoping came to power in 1978. Deng's ultimate aim was to consolidate the Chinese Communist Party's (CCP) rule by linking regime legitimacy to economic growth (Shue 2004). Foreign direct investment (FDI) was seen as a crucial part of this goal, and Japanese investment was welcomed by and flowed quickly into China. For the Chinese, Japanese foreign investment helped to introduce new technology and provided funding for new infrastructure. Furthermore, it provided valuable employment opportunities for locals, something which became increasingly important as the state-run business sector in China contracted. Meanwhile, for the Japanese, FDI to the PRC represented a means to penetrate the vast Chinese market for their products, as well tapping into the abundant cheap labour.

While rising costs in China mean that the Japanese today are increasingly looking to Southeast Asia as their main regional targets of investment, a substantial proportion of Japanese FDI flows into Asia are still designated for the PRC. Between the years 1995 and 2013, China claimed an average of 34.1 per cent of Japanese FDI flows into Asia. Even during times of political tension, Japanese investment has remained steady. For instance, during the tenure of Japanese Prime Minister Koizumi Jun'ichirō (2001–06) Sino-Japanese relations were dogged by controversies surrounding Koizumi's persistent visits to the controversial Yasukuni Shrine (see below). Yet, China's share of Japanese

FDI flows into Asia actually increased during 2001–03, and never went below the level of 2001 during the years 2003–06 (JETRO various years).

In addition, China and Japan's economies are highly complementary. The Japanese rely heavily on China for the import of agricultural products (such as soy beans, a staple of the Japanese diet) and light industrial products (which have often been produced by Japanese factories based in the PRC). China, for its part, imports Japanese machinery and mechanical parts that are often crucial for sustaining the Chinese manufacturing sector. This has resulted in highly dense trading relations between the two countries: China has been Japan's largest trading partner since 2004, while Japan 'was China's top trade partner for 11 years, only falling slightly behind the EU [European Union] and US since 2004' (He 2008: 164). If the EU is not counted as a single actor, Japan was China's second-largest trading partner after the US in 2011–12 (China Statistical Bureau 2013).[1]

... But Politically Far Apart

In spite of these close economic relations, relations between the PRC and Japan remained mired by bilateral tensions. As pointed out earlier, this may challenge some assumptions made by liberal theorists of international relations. According to Ikenberry and Mastanduno (2003: 17), it is often argued that:

> interdependence decreases the incentives for conflict and war, in part because states become reluctant to disrupt or jeopardize the welfare benefits of open economic exchange, and in part because domestic interest groups with a stake in interdependence constrain the ability of the state to act autonomously.

The main reason that Sino-Japanese relations remain those of 'cold politics, hot economics' is the existence of the so-called 'history issue', which is a term used to denote controversies arising from the legacy of Japan's invasion of China. Japan's aggression towards China had arguably begun in full in the first Sino-Japanese War of 1894–95, when it colonized Taiwan. Japan launched a full-scale invasion of China between 1931–45. The Japanese committed numerous war crimes (Mitter 2014): the Nanjing Massacre is perhaps the most notorious, but the Japanese also engaged in chemical warfare, and their medical research unit (known as Unit 731) carried out experiments on live human beings. Survivors of the second Sino-Japanese war are still alive, and combined with the sheer scale of Japanese atrocities, it is perhaps not surprising that this particular period of Japanese aggression remains vivid in both individual and collective memory in China.

Yet, memories of Japan's unsavoury past did not initially come to the forefront of Sino-Japanese relations when Japan and the PRC normalized diplomatic relations in 1972. The Chinese government waived their right to seek reparations from Japan, and appeared to be willing to embark on 'future-oriented' relations with the Japanese. However, it is important to note that China's initial decision to not raise the 'history issue' was not based on a deep sense of forgiveness towards the Japanese, and was rather a product of strategic convenience. At the time, the PRC was embroiled in a bitter ideological dispute with its neighbour, the Soviet Union. The two countries had also experienced a military skirmish over a territorial dispute in 1969. Moscow had even threatened China with nuclear attack as a result. Unsurprisingly, the Chinese designated the Soviet Union as its most dangerous adversary. In the context of improving Sino-US relations, the

Chinese leadership was keen to use Japan and the US as key 'allies' in their confrontation with the Soviets, and their intentions as such were visible in their insistence in including an 'anti-hegemony' clause in both the 1972 Sino-Japanese communiqué and the 1978 Sino-Japanese Treaty of Peace and Friendship (Ogata 1988; Tanaka 1991). It was for this reason that Beijing effectively swept the 'history issue' under the carpet, and decided not to make the history of Japan's invasion of China a bilateral issue. The many survivors of Japanese war crimes were thus denied their biggest chance to seek some form of restitution from Japan, and under the PRC's authoritarian political system they had no say in the matter either. The two countries subsequently enjoyed something of a 'honeymoon period', where Sino-Japanese friendship was stressed, and victims' voices were ignored by both governments.

However, once Japan's value as a strategic counterweight had diminished, the Chinese became less hesitant about bringing up the 'history issue'. As Caroline Rose (1998: 141) has noted with reference to the 1982 'textbook issue', China's protests against the reported contents of Japanese history textbooks were intimately linked to China's reassessment of its strategic dependence on the US and Japan. Given that a '[c]ommon theme running through China's bilateral relations with the USA, USSR [Union of Soviet Socialist Republics] and Japan' in the early 1980s was 'a shift away from the PRC–USA–Japan "alliance" of the 1970s, and an increasingly independent stance', the textbook issue 'was used as a clear signal, to both foreign and Chinese domestic audiences, of a fundamental shift in Chinese foreign policy'.

In addition, China's 'reform and opening up' policy had the effect of eroding popular support for the CCP, prompting the regime to attempt to bolster its legitimacy by utilizing memories of the Japanese invasion. Deng Xiaoping's reforms brought about an unprecedented rise in the living standards of Chinese citizens, but at the same time they brought about a rise in corruption and increasing income disparities. Such popular dissatisfaction erupted in the form of the mass demonstration at Tiananmen Square in 1989, which had to be put down by force. In response, the Chinese leadership decided to link the Party's legitimacy with its historical legacy of fighting the Japanese invaders (Johnson 1962). The 'Patriotic Education Campaign' was thus launched. History lessons emphasized Japanese brutalities and Chinese suffering, as well as the heroic exploits of the CCP-organized resistance. School excursions to historical sites of 'patriotic' importance were organized. The clear message behind this was that it was the CCP that saved China from the Japanese imperialist yoke, and without the CCP, China would never have become the independent and powerful state that it is today. Supporting the Chinese state and supporting the CCP were treated as the same thing.

All of this indicates that the Chinese had never 'forgotten' the painful memories of the Japanese invasion. In fact, these memories were recycled and used for the construction of a collective memory, and the younger generation were actually being continuously reminded of this particular historical period. Furthermore, as communism as an ideology diminished in importance in Chinese society, the CCP regime was forced to rely ever more on promoting 'patriotism' to maintain its legitimacy. While the Chinese government denies that its 'patriotic education campaign' is anti-Japanese, it is difficult to deny that it does result – regardless of intentions – in producing citizens that have negative images of the Japanese, and are highly sensitive to any perceived Japanese slights to Chinese sensitivities (Kitaoka 2010: 237). With a series of long-standing disputes and grievances, coupled with the effects of China's 'patriotic education' in recent years, it is hardly surprising that Chinese antipathy towards Japan remains strong. While systematic surveys of Chinese popular opinion are not always readily available, surveys taken by the Tokyo–Beijing Forum indicate that in 2013 (one year after the Senkaku/Diaoyu Island dispute erupted again) 92.8 per cent of those polled professed to having 'negative impressions' of Japan, and this figure only fell to 86.8 per cent in 2014. With regard to Sino-Japanese relations, in the 2014 survey 49.8 per cent expected Sino-Japanese relations to 'worsen' in the future (15.1 per cent thought relations would improve) (Tokyo–Beijing Forum various years). It is telling that the enduring image of Japanese society and politics remains 'militarism' (*junguo zhuyi*).[2] As a consequence, the PRC has witnessed a number of popular anti-Japanese demonstrations taking place at times of Sino-Japanese tensions. At times, even seemingly minor incidents are enough to spark off a massive outburst of anti-Japan sentiments. One of the more recent examples of this took place in 2003, when reports alleging that some Japanese students had performed a risqué skit at a student event in Xibei University in Xi'an resulted in massive anti-Japanese protests (Mizutani 2005: 9–24).

Given this societal dynamic, the Chinese government has to be seen to be taking a strong stance towards Tokyo if it is to maintain its image as a 'patriotic' force and sustain its legitimacy. This has ensured that the 'history issue' becomes a regular irritant in Sino-Japanese relations. Since the normalization of relations in 1972, China has lodged strong protests to Japan over controversies on how the history of Japan's invasion is depicted in textbooks, or whenever there are 'slips of the tongue' where prominent Japanese politicians make 'revisionist' remarks, such as denying the Nanjing Massacre. However, the most prominent 'history issue' in recent years has been Prime Ministerial visits to Yasukuni Shrine, which enshrines the tablets of the seven Class A war criminals who were sentenced to death by the Tokyo War Crimes Tribunal. Beijing regards such visits as highly inflammatory, akin to German leaders paying their respects at Hitler's grave. The problem first surfaced in 1985, when then Prime Minister Nakasone Yasuhiro's visit to the Yasukuni Shrine prompted demonstrations in China. For the sake of stable Sino-Japanese relations, Nakasone refrained from visiting the shrine, and his successors generally followed this practice. However, Koizumi Jun'ichirō persisted in making repeated visits to the shrine, and his actions resulted in massive anti-Japanese protests in 2005, as well as the freezing of Sino-Japanese top-level meetings.

It is, however, undeniable that the Chinese have also used the 'history issue' as a diplomatic bargaining chip when it suits them. Most of the Japanese elite at the time of normalization had experiences of the war, and harboured a sense of guilt towards the Chinese, and treated China as a 'special case' whose wishes needed to be accommodated. Thus, at times of Sino-Japanese disputes the Chinese would regularly make references to the past in order to draw out diplomatic concessions from the Japanese. For instance, in the 1987 Kokaryō controversy, where the Osaka High Court angered Beijing by ruling that the Republic of China in Taiwan had legal ownership of the Kokaryō student dormitory in Kyoto, Deng Xiaoping criticized the rise of 'Japanese militarism', Japanese chauvinism, and warned that foreign elements – a fairly obvious reference to Japan, considering that the Japanese had colonized Taiwan from 1895 to 1945 – were plotting to take over Taiwan once more (Ijiri 1996: 74). More recently, Beijing has attempted to link the 'history issue' with the territorial dispute surrounding the Senkaku/Diaoyu

Islands. The PRC has claimed that the Japanese government's refusal to acknowledge Chinese ownership of the islands is a failure to acknowledge that the islands were 'stolen' from China, and therefore is yet another example of Japan's incorrect attitude towards 'history' (*China Daily* 2014a).

Yet, there are increasing signs that such tactics are becoming increasingly counterproductive. The generation who fought the war have now faded from the political scene, and the Japanese elite now consists of the post-1945 generation. Furthermore, the progressive camp, which tended to take a pro-PRC political line and remained sympathetic to China's criticisms of the 'history issue', have now declined significantly as a political force. This is not to suggest that younger Japanese are somehow less repentant for their negative past: a poll conducted by the *Yomiuri Shinbun* in October 2005 (when Sino-Japanese relations had hit another low after Koizumi's visits to Yasukuni Shrine and massive anti-Japan demonstrations had taken place in China) indicated that 68.1 per cent agreed that the war against China was a 'war of aggression'. Furthermore, a comparison of opinion surveys taken in the 1970s and 1980s suggest that there is an increasing awareness of Japanese brutalities committed during the war (Yoshida 2005: 222–225). Previous Japanese narratives of the Asia-Pacific War tended to concentrate more on Japanese suffering (epitomized by the dropping of the atomic bomb on Hiroshima and Nagasaki) (Yoshida 2005: 243), so this increasing awareness of Japan as a perpetrator does demonstrate that Chinese claims to victimhood are broadly accepted in Japanese society today.

At the same time, however, there is a growing sense of exasperation towards frequent (and arguably cynical) uses of the 'history card' by the Chinese government, which means that the Japanese are no longer inclined to treat the PRC as a 'special case'. China's image in Japan was badly damaged by the former's violent suppression of the Tiananmen demonstrators in 1989, and the repeated bilateral tensions over the past years have made the PRC deeply unpopular among Japanese citizens. The annual survey on public perceptions on foreign policy taken by the Japanese Cabinet Office indicate that feelings of 'affinity towards China' fell sharply in 1989 following the violent crackdown of the student demonstrations in Tiananmen Square, and since 2003 Japanese citizens who harbour such sentiments have been consistently outnumbered by those who have 'no feelings of affinity'. In 2013, 80.7 per cent of those polled held 'no feelings of affinity towards China', while those who did amounted to only 18 per cent. The change in Japanese sentiments is starker when we compare these figures to 1988, where 68.5 per cent professed to hold 'feelings of affinity' towards China, while only 26.5 per cent did not (Cabinet Office, various). Such negative sentiments have meant that Beijing's use of the 'history card' is increasingly rebuffed by the Japanese (see, e.g., *Asahi Shinbun* 2013: 12), and is now less effective as a political tool.

The Senkaku/Diaoyu Territorial Dispute

In addition to the festering problems stemming from memories of the Asia-Pacific War, Sino-Japanese relations are further complicated by the existence of an increasingly bitter territorial dispute over the ownership of the Senkaku/Diaoyu Islands in the East China Sea. China's claims are based on the claim that historical documents show that the islands were discovered by and named by the Chinese in the fifteenth century, and that both the Ming and Qing dynasties had recognized the islands as part of their spheres of defence.

The PRC accuses Japan of 'stealing' the islands from China by taking advantage of their victory in the 1894–95 Sino-Japanese War. Furthermore, the Chinese consider the islands to be part of the Penghu Islands, which were seized along with Taiwan in the 1895 Treaty of Shimonoseki and ought have been returned to China after Japan's defeat in 1945 in accordance with the San Francisco Treaty of 1951 (Ministry of Foreign Affairs, People's Republic of China 2012).

The Japanese, for their part, claim that the Senkaku/Diaoyu Islands were *terra nullis:* uninhabited territory with no evidence of effective Chinese control over the islands. They dispute the PRC's claims that the islands are part of the Penghu Islands, stating that they are part of the Ryūkyū Islands and therefore fall beyond the scope of the San Francisco Peace Treaty. As further evidence they argue that the islands were administered by the United States and returned to Japanese control in 1972 as part of Okinawa prefecture. Tokyo also questions the motives of Chinese claims to the islands, pointing out that the PRC did not make claims to possession of the islands until the 1970s, when the possibility of potential oil reserves in the surrounding seas emerged. They have also produced Chinese-published maps which indicate that the Senkaku/Diaoyu Islands are Japanese territory as further proof of this (Ministry of Foreign Affairs, Japan: 2014; Okada 2012).

Whichever position one takes, the two claims are so fundamentally different that there is very little room for compromise. To date, the two states have sought to diffuse any potential territorial disputes by shelving the issue. The Japanese side does not allow any of its own citizens to land on the islands without prior permission. Whenever Chinese nationalist activists landed on the islands or entered the disputed waters, they were swiftly repatriated so as not to cause unnecessary friction with the PRC. The Chinese side, for its part, did not seek to overtly challenge Japanese control of the islands even though they disputed it. The PRC did not send any coastguard or naval vessels into the waters surrounding the Senkaku/Diaoyu Islands.

This tacit agreement has eroded in recent years, however. In December 2008, Chinese vessels first entered the disputed waters. Japan also departed from its normal practice of immediately repatriating Chinese citizens who entered Japanese-controlled waters in 2010, when it arrested and detained the captain of a fishing boat that had rammed Japanese coastal guard vessels. By detaining the Chinese captain in accordance with Japanese domestic law (rather than treating this as a 'special case' where relations with China needed to be taken into account), Japan was arguably reasserting both its 'effective control' of the islands and its official position that 'there exists no territorial dispute' over the Senkaku/Diaoyu Islands.

However, the biggest Sino-Japanese crisis over the islands to date has taken place since 2012, when the Japanese government decided to nationalize the islands, which had previously been in the possession of a private citizen in Japan. The move came after the controversial populist-nationalist Mayor of Tokyo, Ishihara Shintarō, announced that the Tokyo Metropolitan Government was planning to purchase the islands. Ishihara, who has been vocal in his antipathy towards the PRC, had also floated the idea of building structures on the islands, a move that would have been seen as highly provocative by Beijing. The Japanese government's nationalization plans were an attempt to forestall this and maintain some level of stability in Sino-Japanese relations. Beijing, however, saw this as an irreversible altering of the status quo with regard to the Senkaku/Diaoyu Islands. It has since sent Chinese coastguard vessels to the disputed waters on a regular basis, a move that is designed to gradually erode Japan's 'effective control' of the islands and challenge Japanese claims that there is 'no territorial dispute'. Chinese vessels' entry into the disputed waters has abated somewhat in recent years (at its peak in August 2013, 28 vessels were counted entering territorial waters) (Japan Coast Guard n.d.), and it is worth noting that neither the People's Liberation Army Navy nor the Japanese Maritime Defence Force have been involved in these confrontations. All of this suggests that both sides – while taking vigorous steps to assert their claims to the Islands – do not wish to escalate the confrontation. However, there is still no sign of either side being willing to compromise over these issues, and it appears that the naval cat-and-mouse game between China and Japan is set to continue for some time.

TAIWAN

If Sino-Japanese relations are one of the most significant medium- to long-term challenges for the stability of East Asia, the 'Taiwan issue' is the most immediate and potentially dangerous factor that could spark a military conflict in the region. Taiwan was made a Japanese colony after the 1895 Treaty of Shimonoseki, and reverted back to Chinese control in 1945. Following the civil war between the Nationalists (Kuomintang, KMT) and the CCP, Chiang Kai-shek fled to Taiwan with his Nationalist troops and many mainlanders. The KMT have remained there since, and Taiwan – which calls itself the Republic of China (ROC) – has managed to remain a separate, de facto independent state with a different political system from the communist-controlled mainland.

Initially, the two sides maintained highly confrontational relations with each other. Chiang Kai-shek remained committed to the retaking of the Chinese mainland, and claimed to be the sole representative government of China. Following the Korean War of 1950, the US committed itself to the defence of Taiwan in order to prevent the spread of communism in Asia, ensuring the KMT regime's survival and the continued division of China. Both sides engaged in fierce diplomatic rivalry to garner recognition from other states and shore up their claims to being the sole legitimate government of 'China'. A number of states, including the US, Japan and South Korea, recognized the KMT regime over the CCP regime in Beijing, and this support was crucial in helping the ROC to maintain its seat in the United Nations (UN) as the representative of China. At times both sides engaged in military conflict, the most notable being the PRC's bombardment of the ROC-controlled islands of Quemoy (Jinmen) and Mazu in 1958.

In some aspects, the confrontation between China and Taiwan is less tense than it was in the past. For a start, as separation from the mainland became a long-term one, it has become increasingly clear (and accepted, albeit with reluctance from some quarters) that the political goal of the ROC's reunification of the mainland was unrealistic. Furthermore, the diplomatic war between the ROC and the PRC has ended in Taiwan's defeat. The PRC's diplomatic situation improved significantly in 1971, when it took over Taiwan's seat in the UN as the representative of China. In 1972, the US moved to establish diplomatic relations, which automatically resulted in the severance of official interstate relations with Taiwan in 1979, when the US–PRC Joint Communiqué was announced. The Japanese quickly followed suit, dealing another severe blow to Taiwan's diplomatic standing. The Taiwanese have attempted to maintain their claims to being a legitimate sovereign state by maintaining as many official diplomatic relations as possible. Their key tactic has been dubbed 'dollar diplomacy', where Taipei promised to hand out a significant amount of aid to a particular country – usually a relatively small country in the developing world – in return for diplomatic recognition. However, the increasing economic power of the PRC means that Beijing can now not only match, but also better Taipei's offers of aid to entice states to switch their diplomatic allegiances to the PRC. Furthermore, the recipients of Taiwanese aid quickly learnt to play the PRC and ROC off against one another, resulting in ever-increasing demands for aid that even the Taiwanese found burdensome (Taylor 2002). As a result, Taipei has had to reconcile itself with the political reality of its own diplomatic isolation, and this means that there are fewer diplomatic battles fought between the PRC and Taiwan.

Taiwan's Democratization and the Emergence of New Tensions over Taiwan

In spite of Taiwan's abandonment of its goals of reuniting the Chinese mainland, potentially dangerous tensions remain between Taipei and Beijing. One cause of these is the democratization of Taiwan, which began in the late 1980s when Lee Teng-hui (Li Denghui) became President of Taiwan. Prior to this, Taiwan was under martial law. Chiang Kai-shek, his son Chiang Ching-kuo (Jiang Jingguo) and the mainlanders dominated Taiwanese politics, despite the fact that they were vastly outnumbered by the native Taiwanese. This political elite maintained that the island was an inalienable territory of China, and stuck rigidly to the goal of eventual reunification. Yet, the native Taiwanese population did not necessarily share the same views. For a start, Taiwan has an indigenous population (about 0.5 million people) of Malayo-Polynesian descent who may not always subscribe to the Han-centric view of Taiwan as part of China.

In the case of the Taiwanese, who number 14.5 million and are the largest ethnic group, 50 years of Japanese colonial rule had separated Taiwan from the Chinese mainland, and resulted in the emergence of a somewhat different identity, even though they were 'descendants of immigrants from Fujian province who came over to Taiwan in the late Ming and early Qing dynasties (17th century)' (Cook and Meer 2005: 50). Their sense of alienation from the mainland was made more acute by the brutal rule of the KMT shortly after the departure of the Japanese colonial rulers. The KMT elite frequently looked upon the Taiwanese with contempt, regarding them as ideologically corrupted by Japanese rule and lacking in loyalty towards China (Rigger 1997: 316). Corruption and misgovernment led to riots, culminating in the notorious February 28 Incident (usually known as the 228 Incident) in 1947. Between 20 000 and 40 000 Taiwanese are reported to have been murdered by the regime (Cook and Meer 2005: 51).[3]

These historical events, coupled with memories of PRC bombardments and military threats against the island, have resulted in an increasing sentiment of 'separation' and antipathy towards the Chinese mainland, as well as mainlander politicians who continue to advocate eventual reunification with China. Crucially, the democratization of Taiwan and the rise of native Taiwanese within the political elite has allowed such feelings – previously suppressed ruthlessly under martial law and the so-called 'White Terror' by the KMT – to be articulated widely. This has had an increasing impact on how Taiwanese citizens view themselves. While quantifying and measuring identity is notoriously difficult (Rigger 1999–2000), surveys carried out by the Election Study Centre of the National Chengchi University in Taipei on Taiwanese attitudes towards their identity show interesting results: whereas only 17.6 per cent of Taiwanese polled in 1992 identified themselves as exclusively 'Taiwanese', this figure had increased to 60.4 per cent in June 2014. Crucially, this number was larger than those who thought of themselves as both Chinese and Taiwanese (32.7 per cent). Taiwanese who thought of themselves as 'Chinese', in contrast, only accounted for 3.5 per cent of the population in the same year (Election Study Centre, National Chengchi University n.d.).

The democratization of Taiwan and the introduction of competitive elections mean that this political dynamic is utilized by politicians. As a result, the political system of Taiwan turns on an 'externally derived' primary axis that is 'concerned with the islands' sovereignty and their relationship to their sibling rival, the People's Republic of China' (Cook and Meer 2005: 23). Taiwanese politics is thus split broadly into the 'pan-blue' camp (consisting of the KMT and the People First Party) that aims for eventual reunification or political integration with China; and the 'pan-green' camp (consisting of the Democratic Progressive Party and the Taiwan Solidarity Union) which is more interested in Taiwan remaining separate, or even independent from the mainland. The presidential elections of 2000 saw the election of the first ever pan-green president, Chen Shui-bian of the Democratic Progressive Party (DPP). It is important to note that the overwhelming majority of Taiwanese citizens do not wish for immediate independence: 55 per cent of those polled in the 2003 survey on Taiwan's national security preferred the continuation of the status quo, as opposed to 6 per cent who wanted independence and 6 per cent who wanted unification (Rigger 2005: 419). However, such political developments do indicate that the PRC cannot take it for granted that the Taiwanese will be amenable to its goals of reunification with the Chinese mainland.

China Eyes Taiwan

Such developments in Taiwan are naturally looked upon with considerable suspicion by Beijing. The CCP regime has consistently maintained a 'one China' policy, which sees Taiwan as a province of China and an inherent part of the Chinese state, and in this sense it is in agreement with die-hard 'pan-blue' politicians in Taiwan. The CCP regime has also maintained that the reunification of China is one of its most important political goals, and insists that reunification must take place on Beijing's terms.

Beijing's position on the Taiwan issue is spelt out in its 2000 White Paper, 'The One-China Principle and the Taiwan Issue' (Gov.cn n.d.). The paper reiterates the PRC's 'one China' position, and states that reunification can take place under the 'one country, two systems' formula currently practised in Hong Kong and Macau, with the additional proviso that 'the Central Government [in Beijing] will not send troops or administrative personnel to be stationed in Taiwan' in the event that unification takes place. It is telling that the paper uses considerable space lambasting then Taiwanese President Lee Teng-hui, who gradually moved to a position more sympathetic to Taiwanese independence. The paper claims that Lee 'connived at and provided for the separatists who advocate "Taiwan independence" and their activities', and accuses him of becoming 'the general representative of Taiwan's separatist forces, a saboteur of the stability of the Taiwan Straits'. Given that the reunification of Taiwan is a non-negotiable goal for the PRC, it is perhaps not surprising to find bombastic texts in official pronouncements concerning

Taiwan. However, the language used is also indicative of the worry that the increasing ideological 'separateness' of Taiwan inflicts upon the Chinese leaders. More recently, Beijing has attempted to intensify the pressure on Taiwan by adopting the Anti-Secession Law in 2005, when the DPP's Chen Shui-bian was the incumbent President of Taiwan. Article Eight of this law, which comes across as a thinly veiled threat aimed towards the 'pan-green' camp, states:

> In the event that the 'Taiwan independence' secessionist forces should act under any name or by any means to cause the fact of Taiwan's secession from China, or that major incidents entailing Taiwan's secession from China should occur, or that possibilities for a peaceful reunification should be completely exhausted, the state shall employ non-peaceful means and other necessary measures to protect China's sovereignty and territorial integrity.

The Future of the Taiwan Issue

These dynamics mean that Taiwan remains a potential flashpoint within the Asia-Pacific region. At present, it appears that the 'red line' for the PRC that would result in military conflict is a unilateral declaration of independence. Yet, the Taiwan issue is not a purely bilateral matter (or 'internal' matter, as the Chinese government would like to have us believe), as any military clash between China and Taiwan has the potential to involve the US as well. Although the US terminated official relations with Taiwan in 1979 and acknowledged China's 'one China' principle,[4] it committed itself to the island's protection through the 1979 Taiwan Relations Act (US Government Printing Office). The Act states explicitly that 'peace and stability in the area are in the political, security, and economic interests of the United States, and are matters of international concern'. It states that it is US policy 'to provide Taiwan with arms of a defensive character', and 'maintain the capacity of the United States to resist any resort to force or other forms of coercion that would jeopardize the security, or the social or economic system, of the people on Taiwan'. This, Cook and Meer (2005: 2) argue, 'purposefully leaves a question mark over if and when the United States would intervene in a cross-strait conflict'.

This 'strategic ambiguity' of the US works both ways: on the one hand, it could create a false sense of security and embolden pro-independence politicians to use the 'Taiwan identity' card to score cheap political points. This has the potential to provoke the PRC, and could even drag the US into a confrontation with the Chinese; something that it will be keen to avoid. On the other hand, Washington's 'strategic ambiguity' serves as a powerful deterrent against Beijing and Taiwan. As the PRC cannot be entirely sure whether or not the US will come to the military aid of Taiwan, it has to be careful not to resort to force against any perceived provocations from Taiwan. In some cases, the US has indeed demonstrated its commitment to defending Taiwan: when Beijing decided to conduct live missile drills off the coast of Taiwan in 1996 to intimidate the Taiwanese electorate on the eve of the first ever democratic presidential election, the US was quick to despatch carriers to the region. In the case of Taiwan, a degree of uncertainty helps to rein in any populist attempts to declare independence and crossing the 'red line' that Beijing has set. In this sense, then, the ambiguous political stance of the US vis-à-vis Taiwan has played a crucial role in ensuring that cross-Straits relations between the PRC and Taiwan do not boil over into military confrontation. However, with Taiwanese domestic politics complicating the picture and eroding the traditional 'one China' consensus that was previously adhered to by both Taiwan and China, we are likely to see tensions flare up from time to time.

KOREA

China's already complicated foreign policy in East Asia is made even more complex by the divided state of Korea. China is one of the very few countries that enjoy strong relations with both the Democratic People's Republic of Korea (DPRK, or North Korea) and the Republic of Korea (ROK, or South Korea). Because of this rather special position, Beijing also has the difficult task of managing and balancing its diplomatic interests in both Koreas, which are at times at odds with one another.

The PRC's initial foreign relations with the Korean peninsula were largely limited to North Korea. Mao Zedong committed Chinese troops to aid the DPRK during the Korean War of 1950–53. This decision 'almost single-handedly rescued Kim Il Sung's regime from extinction' (Kim 2006: 51), but in the subsequent context of the Cold War, there was little scope for China to establish diplomatic relations with South Korea. PRC–ROK relations remained frosty: Seoul recognized Taiwan as the sole legitimate government of China, while the 'Chinese leaders reiterated the immutability of their "militant friendship" in North Korea' (Kim 2006: 51). The strategic importance of PRC–DPRK relations was frequently referred to as similar to the relations between 'lips and teeth', and was solidified in the 1961 PRC–DPRK Treaty of Friendship, Cooperation, and Mutual Assistance.

PRC–ROK Relations: From Confrontation to Close Partner

This situation changed with the inauguration of South Korean President Roh Tae Woo's 'Nordpolitik', as well as the thawing of the Cold War (see Chung 2007: 56–74; Kim 2006: 58–63). Seoul was keen to expand its international standing (particularly vis-à-vis the DPRK) by establishing diplomatic relations with (the then) socialist countries. In reality, both states had already established increasingly robust trading relations with one another: by 1984, Sino-ROK trade had reached $434 million, a figure close to China's trade with North Korea ($498 million) (Kim 2006: 55; also see Jia and Zhuang 1992: 1146). Strategic considerations stemming from the capitalist–communist ideological divide, as well as the Sino-Soviet split, prevented both states from entering into formal diplomatic relations with one another. With the ending of the Cold War, this situation changed. China, which had regarded the ROK as a positive role model for development, had been keen to consolidate its 'reform and opening up' policy by attracting South Korean investment (Chung 2003–04: 558–559). Furthermore, the Soviet Union's successful establishment of diplomatic relations with the ROK meant that that Soviet political influence (and prestige) in the DPRK had weakened considerably. The Chinese could thus embark on normalization with South Korea without fear of the North Koreans abandoning them for Moscow (Jia and Zhuang 1992: 1140; Cha 1999: 76). The two states finally achieved this in 1992.

Since then, Sino-ROK relations have gone from strength to strength. Bilateral trade has flourished between the two states. China enjoys a relatively favourable image within

South Korean society, particularly among the younger generation, who even choose China over the US (Japan tends to be the most unpopular) (Chung 2007: 96–100). Geographical proximity and economic complementarity have resulted in China becoming the ROK's largest destination for FDI in 2001, and its largest export partner in 2003. Indeed, as Kim (2006: 77) notes, 'a 48 percent rise in exports to $35.1 billion accounted for a startling 98 per cent of South Korea's GDP growth in 2003. Without China as an export market, South Korea's economic growth would have been virtually flat.' Not all has been smooth sailing, for sure: China and Korea engaged in a brief but intensive trade war over Korea's import of Chinese garlic. In this case, the Chinese were able to draw out favourable concessions from South Korea by introducing retaliatory measures against key Korean exports to China. Seoul was thus made painfully aware of the pitfalls of excessive dependence on the China market (Chung 2003–04; see Kim 2006: 80). As China's own technological industry begins to take off, there is also a possibility that South Korean firms will find themselves in increasing competition with China (Cha 1999: 92).

On the security front, both the PRC and the ROK have shared common interests with regards to the Korean peninsula, despite the fact that China still remains a key ally of North Korea. Both sides support the notion of a nuclear-free Korean peninsula (Cha 1999: 74), and during the US–DPRK nuclear stand-off between 2003 and 2005, both Beijing and Seoul found themselves opposing the US's highly confrontational policy towards North Korea, which was labelled as part of the 'Axis of Evil' by President George W. Bush. Both sides were in agreement that rhetoric and policies that would corner Pyongyang would be counterproductive, and China played a key part in bringing the North Koreans to the negotiating table. However, such agreements between Seoul and Beijing also took place during South Korean administrations that were relatively committed to a more conciliatory policy towards the DPRK (Kim Dae Jung and Roh Moo Hyun). At times when South Korea has chosen to adopt a tougher stance towards the North Koreans, Beijing's views may have not necessarily matched those of Seoul. When the ROK and the US engaged in naval exercises in response to the North Korean's sinking of a South Korean naval vessel in 2010, Beijing stuck closely to its 'long-standing policy of not openly criticizing North Korea for its role in border skirmishes', and condemned the exercises (Jerdén 2014: 63).

PRC–DPRK Relations: From Close Ally to Distant Partner?

If relations between China and the ROK have generally gone from strength to strength in recent years, the same cannot be said for Beijing's relations with its traditional ally, the DPRK. According to Shambaugh (2003a: 44), Beijing's strategic goals vis-à-vis North Korea (and the Korean peninsula as a whole) are sixfold: the PRC seeks to ensure the survival of the DPRK regime; encourage political and economic reforms in North Korea; 'maintaining and developing more comprehensively robust relations between China and South Korea'; 'establishing China's dominant external influence over the Korean peninsula (North and South)'; 'integrating north and south, through economic and social means, leading to political unification over time'; and bringing about 'unprovocative and responsible North Korean behavior on security issues ranging from its nuclear weapons program to proliferation of other weapons of mass destruction and their means of delivery to the deployments of DPRK conventional forces'.

In order to fulfil the first goal, the PRC has shielded the DPRK regime from US pressure at times of confrontation (although this is also motivated by the fear that the unpredictable North Korean regime could prove to be even more destabilizing for regional security if provoked). It has also provided extensive economic aid to the DPRK regime, which reportedly 'accounts for 70–90 percent of North Korea's fuel imports . . . and about one-third of the DPRK's total food imports' (Shambaugh 2003a: 46). Such desires to prolong the life of the North Korean regime are motivated by a number of factors. First, there is a possibility that Beijing would prefer to maintain the DPRK as a buffer zone, rather than have the ROK, a US ally, absorb the North and directly face its borders. Second, and more importantly, the Chinese fear the potential instability that the collapse of the regime would bring about to its borders. There are already a sizeable number of North Korean refugees who live clandestinely in Chinese territory neighbouring the DPRK. Nowadays, Beijing's biggest fear is the possibility of North Korean refugees flooding over into the Chinese border, leaving Beijing with a large humanitarian crisis in its territory.

However, it is worth keeping in mind that such goals are motivated more by China's national interest, rather than a form of fraternity based on ideology or the historical legacy of fighting the Korean War alongside the DPRK. Nowadays, relations between the two states are best described as distant. Security relations 'have given way to symbolism and ceremony', and 'the strained relationship is also reflected in the appreciable decline in the frequency and level of mutual visits' between the leaders of the two states (Kim 2006: 71). As noted by Kim (2006: 87), 'China does not, to its frustration, receive as much North Korean gratitude as it would like nor does it wield as much leverage as Washington would believe, precisely because Pyongyang knows that China's aid is in its own self-interest.' Furthermore, there is, to date, limited evidence to suggest that the North Korean regime is about to embark on political and economic reforms along China's own 'reform and opening up' lines in order to facilitate its own survival. This means that the North Koreans are likely to continue their dependence on Chinese aid, much to the exasperation of Beijing. It is thus hardly surprising that there are reports that:

> Chinese officials . . . speak with disdain, despair, and heightened frustration when discussing the DPRK and China's relations with it. These critics deplore the sycophantic cult of personality surrounding the Kim dynasty, the Stalinist security state, the command economy, the poverty of the populace . . . and so forth (Shambaugh 2003a: 45)

In sum, China's Korea policy – of simultaneously pursuing closer relations with South Korea, while propping up the latter's adversary, the DPRK – presents the PRC with something of a 'Goldilocks problem' of striking the right balance between its two bilateral relations. On the one hand, it does not wish to find itself 'entrapped' in its alliance with the DPRK, and find itself in a confrontation with South Korea and jeopardize its highly lucrative economic relations with the latter. While Beijing currently maintains its policy of not overtly taking sides in military skirmishes between the North and South Koreans, this policy can be strained considerably in the event of North Korean provocations. Apart from harming Beijing's relations with Seoul and driving the ROK closer to America, it also has the potential to sour Sino-US relations. This, of course, could prevent the PRC from achieving its goal of enhancing its influence over the Korean peninsula, which it views 'as its natural sphere of influence – much as the United States views Latin

America and Russia views Central Asia' (Shambaugh 2003a: 50). On the other hand, its own domestic concerns mean that it is unable to let the North Korean regime collapse. The DPRK's unpredictability has been made even more acute due to the fact that the country now has a relatively young and inexperienced leader, Kim Jong Un. Unlike his father Kim Jong Il, who was gradually groomed to be Kim Il Sung's successor, Kim Jong Un succeeded his father unexpectedly. It remains to be seen as to whether or not Kim Jong Un will embark on the path of reform or abandon the DPRK's nuclear weapons programme. Under such circumstances, Beijing's dilemma of managing its triangular relations between the two Koreas seems set to continue.

CHINA AND EAST ASIA

As we have seen, China faces a myriad of challenges in its foreign relations with East Asia. The region includes an important regional power which China views with antipathy (Japan), a divided state (Korea) with a nuclear crisis, and what Beijing regards as an illegitimate regime with potential 'revisionist' intentions of overturning its sacrosanct 'one China' principle, which could compel China to resort to force (Taiwan). Most states would find this regional dynamic a significant challenge in itself. However, in the case of China, its own rise – a long-held aspiration ever since the so-called 'hundred years of humiliation' – will bring about additional challenges in its East Asian foreign policy (and already has done so).

Until recently, China had been fairly successful in getting its East Asian neighbours to accept its rise and accommodate it (with the obvious exception of Taiwan). Both Japan and South Korea adopted a policy of seeking to enmesh China into the international community and facilitate China's rise as a 'responsible great power' that sought to uphold the normative fabric of the international community. Seoul and Tokyo were key supporters of China's multilateral diplomacy, and played an important role in inviting or backing Chinese participation in a variety of multilateral fora, such as the Asia-Pacific Economic Cooperation meetings or the World Trade Organization (Cha 1999: 78; Jerdén and Hagström 2012). The thinking behind this strategy was that it would be counterproductive to treat China as a 'threat', as it would only foster a siege mentality on the part of the PRC. Given that China's rise to power was already a political fact, it would be better to accept this and ensure that the PRC would become a stakeholder in the existing international order. China's main foreign policy goal in the early 2000s, dubbed 'peaceful rise' (*heping jueqi*) was broadly compatible with this goal.[5] Beijing joined an unprecedented number of multilateral organizations, and showed evidence of increasing acceptance and compliance with international norms (Foot and Walter 2010). Its attempts to mediate in the US–DPRK nuclear stand-off were broadly welcomed by the region. At a time when the Bush administration's unilateralism was seen as having detrimental effects on international order, China's actions were seen as another signal of it becoming a 'responsible great power'.

Since 2009, however, we are seeing some signs that the policy of 'peaceful rise' may have become less of a priority in Chinese foreign policy. China's actions in the Senkaku/Diaoyu territorial dispute with Japan have been seen as disproportionate, and only serve to escalate the tensions that exist between the two states. Similarly, Beijing's reluctance to send out strong words of condemnation in the face of North Korea's sinking of the ROK naval vessel *Cheonan* or the shelling of Yeongpeong island in 2010 has also been seen as a signal of a more 'assertive' or 'revisionist' foreign policy emerging (Shambaugh 2010; Friedberg 2011). Whether or not this is true remains a matter of debate (Johnston 2013; Jerdén 2014). However, there is no doubt that some of China's regional neighbours – notably Japan – are becoming increasingly wary of China's rise, and are seeking to strengthen their alliance relations with the US. Japan's China policy has become increasingly politicized in Diet debates, and the more accommodative policy has come under increasing criticism (Hagström and Jerdén 2010). Since the eruption of the 2012 Senkaku/Diaoyu dispute, Japan has engaged in a proactive diplomatic offensive, criticizing the PRC in international fora and seeking to strike up a 'strategic partnership' with India, which has long been suspicious of China's rise.

Fears of an assertive China could also bring about an enhanced US presence in East Asia. With the notable exception of North Korea, the PRC's most important neighbours, Japan and the ROK, are both key allies of the US and play a crucial role in Washington's global security policy. While PRC–ROK relations may have succeeded in weaning Seoul off Washington to some extent, if China mismanages its rise to power, there is a possibility that its neighbours would choose the *Pax Americana*, blunting China's regional political influence. Such developments can only bring about an unwelcome layer of complexity in China's already complicated East Asia foreign policy. Put differently, China's foreign relations in East Asia are not simply a series of bilateral relations: they are, to different degrees, intimately connected to Sino-US relations, China's most important area of foreign policy. It is therefore crucial that Beijing gets its East Asia policy right. And while there is no doubt that the shifts in the US–China power balance will (rightly) continue to preoccupy many analysts and foreign policy practitioners in China, it could be East Asia that proves to be the biggest challenge for Chinese foreign policy in the near to mid-term future.

NOTES

1. In 2012, Hong Kong actually overtook Japan as the PRC's second-largest trading partner after the US, but if we exclude Hong Kong (which is a Special Administrative Zone with a separate political system, but nevertheless a part of the PRC) as a foreign trading partner, then Japan remains the PRC's second-largest single-country trading partner.
2. The survey asked respondents to give up to three answers, so it is important to note that this is not the only image that Chinese polled by the Tokyo–Beijing Forum. The less negative term 'capitalism' (*ziben zhuyi*) also scores consistently highly.
3. Fleischauer (2007), however, puts the figure at 10 000 to 25 000.
4. The 1979 US–China Communiqué states that 'The Government of the United States of America acknowledges the Chinese position that there is but one China and Taiwan is part of China' (Embassy of the United States 1979).
5. The term 'peaceful rise' was later changed to 'peaceful development' (*heping fazhan*).

24. Admiration, ambivalence, antipathy: the past and future for US–China relations
Bates Gill

The history of foreign relations between the United States and China is often dated to the voyage of the *Empress of China* which set sail from New York on George Washington's birthday in February 1784 – just a few months following the Treaty of Paris formally ending the American Revolutionary War – and became the first American merchant vessel to enter Chinese waters.[1]

Now some 230 years later, the two Pacific nations look back on a complex and all-encompassing relationship; respectful and raucous, complex and calculating, aloof and attentive, at times close and at times bitterly hostile, a mix of admiration, ambivalence and antipathy. And the future looks to be no different, with the bilateral relationship between the United States and China already defining the future of the twenty-first century, for better or for worse.

All the more reason, then, that a search of 'WorldCat', the online world library catalogue, turns up more than 26 000 books and articles on the topic of 'United States – Foreign relations – China'. Remarkably, this is more than for 'United States – Foreign relations – Soviet Union' (16 730), and several times more than for US foreign relations with Great Britain, France, Canada or Australia.[2] These works on US–China ties reflect the breadth of this remarkable relationship; even narrowing the search to only English-language books published since 2005 returns nearly 3400 citations, covering the full gamut of US–China relations, including cultural relations; climate change; economic issues of trade, finance and intellectual property protections; global and regional security; human rights; espionage; non-proliferation; education; energy; public opinion and nationalism; counterterrorism; outer space; media relations; and corporate experiences from Huawei to Walmart. Even a 'short' bibliography of relatively recent books proves daunting: Michael Swaine (2011) in his recent work *America's Challenge* lists nearly 300 'books, chapters and pamphlets' relevant to his study.

With this in mind, it is not possible in this brief chapter to provide a full assessment of the literature on US–China relations. Thankfully, there have been a number of excellent bibliographic surveys on this topic in the past, including those by Warren Cohen (2010) in his stand-out *America's Response to China*. In that bibliographic work, Cohen also helpfully points us to the 'comprehensive survey of the Chinese literature on Chinese–American relations' authored by Chen Jian (1996). Wang Dong (2013), in her historical study of US–China relations, provides a bibliography which is as extensive as it is helpful, and includes references to additional bibliographic surveys in English, Chinese and Japanese.

Instead, this modest chapter will draw the reader to a range of major English-language works, by Westerners, Chinese and others, which focus primarily on the official, government-to-government relationship between the two countries. Again, bowing to space constraints, the chapter will not spend much time in reviewing official government publications from either side, but rather will take up more scholarly assessments by experts of US–China relations as well as book-length memoirs.

If there is a consistent framework for understanding US–China ties running through these works it is the conclusive sense of schizophrenia characterizing the relationship. US–China relations, certainly at the level of official interactions, but also in terms of public perceptions, are consistently described as 'waxing and waning', a mix of 'cooperation and competition', akin to a 'pendulum' swinging between positive and negative relations, a constant cycle of exuberance, then disappointment, dashed expectations and eventual rapprochment, or as Isaacs (1958) described it, a mix of respect, contempt, benevolence, disenchantment and hostility, and all the while full of misperceptions on both sides.

Arkush and Lee (1993) also compile an interesting collection of not always flattering first-hand Chinese accounts of America spanning many decades, while Jespersen (1999) details the idealized and hopeful images Americans had of China in the run-up to the Communist revolution, coinciding with the 'age of admiration', before the ensuing 'disenchantment', in Isaacs's typology. An interesting and much-needed Chinese perspective is provided in Jing Li's (2011) *China's America*. David Shambaugh's (1993) *Beautiful Imperialist* was a groundbreaking work when it appeared and remains a valuable read. In a turning of the tables, he examined the institutions and individuals in China concerned with America-watching. In so doing, he revealed a large, misinformed and troubling perception gap about America amongst China's leading experts.

In a more recent volume Turner (2014), in his *American Images of China*, speaks to a familiar set of themes in discussing four basic images of China in America: idealized, uncivilized and threatening, and an opportunity. But he also asserts an active American choice to draw on those images for policy reasons: 'US China policy has always been active in the production and reproduction of imagery and in the reaffirmation of the identities of both China and the United States' (Turner, 2014: 8). The dean of American China-watchers in the twentieth century, John King Fairbank (1975), also grappled with these issues, arguing that misperceptions, misunderstandings and wilful ignorance about what Americans want China to be will – absent a much deeper historical perspective – plague the Sino-American relationship as China (re)enters the world stage.

Interestingly, more than 230 years of intensive exchanges, including the deeply intertwined US–China ties of today, have not succeeded in overcoming what continues to be a fundamentally ambivalent and ambiguous relationship. As a result – and particularly as the United States and China become closer to co-equals across many dimensions of power and influence – the two countries today continue to grapple with questions of strategic mistrust and an uncertain future in spite of their best efforts to the contrary.

HISTORICAL RELATIONS

From its first publication in 1948, until its fourth enlarged edition appearing in 1983, the work by the venerated China scholar John King Fairbank (1983), *The United States and China*, stood for decades as the standard work in English to understand US–China ties.

With a strong emphasis on the Chinese historical and cultural context shaping its encounter with the West overall and the United States in particular, the book provides Western readers with the necessary understanding of China's perspective and how it shapes relations with America. Coming to terms through this work with the sweep of Chinese history, the depth of Chinese culture, and their impact on the Chinese socio-political system and its dealings with the outside world would leave a profound impression on generations of China scholars about the thorny difficulties and contradictions inherent to US–China relations.

Saying that he did 'not presume to compete' with Fairbank, Warren Cohen (2010: xv) looks at the other side of the coin, and focuses his attention on 'the American response to China'. Updated on a regular basis and now in its fifth edition, *America's Response to China* is the gold-standard textbook, both for its diplomatic history from the mid-nineteenth to mid-twentieth centuries and for its placement of more contemporary developments within their historical context. In the concluding paragraphs to the fourth edition (published in 2000), Cohen presciently foresaw the future challenge for Americans in their dealings with China:

> Given the realities of China's new role in the world, it is apparent that Americans are going to have to do what they do least well: learn to live with uncertainties and unresolved issues. They will have to keep talking to people they do not like and accept the fact that those people will continue to do things that Americans find intolerable. They will have to recognize that although their country will enter the Twenty-First Century as the most powerful nation in the world, it will not be able to control the actions of other peoples. In due course, they may even understand the need for engagement with China . . . As the new millennium approached, most Americans were not so sure. (Cohen, W.I. 2010: 242)

In the words of one reviewer (Woo 2011: 173), 'Cohen confirms the apparent schizophrenic nature of US foreign policy in the facile friend or foe pendulum swing that Harold R. Isaacs . . . wrote about more than half a century ago.' In another work appearing in an edited volume by the great China scholars Michel Oksenberg and Robert Oxnam, Cohen (1978: 55) also goes further to highlight this cyclical dynamic in US–China relations with a more detailed chronology.

Michael Hunt (1983) wrote what remains one of the great studies of America–China relations over their first century and a half, up to the early 1900s. His *Making of a Special Relationship* broke significant new ground in accessing both English- and Chinese-language sources to demonstrate that the 'special relationship' was actually not so special in the positive sense of the word. Rather, both Americans and Chinese treated one another with ill-hidden contempt, whether through the persecution and expulsion of American missionaries or the anti-Chinese Exclusion Act of 1882; reflecting not the commonly held benevolence invoked in the narrative of the 'Open Door', but rather the long-held suspicions and misunderstandings inevitably part of these two nations' interactions.

A more current and comprehensive study by the respected China-watcher Robert Sutter (2013) reviews the twists and turns over 200 years of US–China relations up to the present day, and finds – similarly to other authors reviewed here – that in spite of such a long history, mutual misperceptions and mistrust persist and very much shape current policies. This book is particularly helpful in drawing together the historical record, the contemporary situation, and future prospects for US–China relations. In looking at that history, his overall assessment is sobering:

> It shows enormous changes over time, with patterns of confrontation, conflict and suspicion much more prevalent than patterns of accommodation and cooperation ... That the base of cooperation is incomplete, thin and dependent on changeable circumstances at home and abroad is evident, as the societies and governments more often than not show salient differences over a variety of critical issues involving security, values, and economics ... [T]he review in this book also shows officials, elites, and public opinion on both sides demonstrating persisting suspicion and wariness of the other country and its possible negative intentions or implications affecting Sino-American relations. (Sutter 2013: 3)

Among the few Chinese scholars publishing major works in English on the history of US–China relations (see below), Dong Wang (2013) makes a very important contribution with her *The United States and China*. This work offers a comprehensive sweep of the entire relationship, from 1784 to the beginning of the twenty-first century. Different from Cohen's approach, she attempts to give equal weight to both US and Chinese perspectives and responses. This well-researched and highly readable work puts forward three over-arching 'propositions', all of which fit squarely within the meta-narrative of the literature on the historical nature of US–China relations. These propositions are:

> US–Chinese relations constitute an ongoing contest between two states in a changing global context...
> Economically, China has been catching up, clashing with America's capability and desire to control change...
> While the United States is an important model for China, America's role has been challenged from the beginning. (Wang 2013: 2–13)

An eminent historian of China and China's interaction with the outside world, Jonathan Spence, also underscores in some of his work the often troubled US–China relationship, replete with misperceptions driving overly hopeful expectations. In addition to his extensive discussion of Sino-American relations in his magnum opus, *The Search for Modern China* (Spence 1990), these themes are particularly well drawn and striking in one of Spence's earliest works, the classic *To Change China* (Spence 1969). In this book which every would-be China expert must read, he describes the 'curious continuity' of 16 different Western 'advisors' to China, over a span of three-and-a-half centuries, and how they all had similar dreams but met with similar frustrations and, ultimately, similar failures in their attempts to 'change China'. The amazing tales of remarkable Americans – Peter Parker, Frederick Townsend Ward, William Martin, Edward Hume, Oliver Todd, Claire Chennault, Joseph Stilwell and Albert Wedemeyer – trenchantly but intimately depict the larger saga of hopes, fears, vexations and disappointment which infuses the history of US–China relations.

CONTEMPORARY PERIOD

The opening of formal diplomatic ties between the two countries in 1979 also opened the floodgates for a rush of new insights and angles on their relationship, but the tale of ambiguity and ambivalence continued. One of the early standard-setters was Harry Harding's (1992) *Fragile Relationship*, which provides a detailed description of the events and policy developments in US–People's Republic of China (PRC) relations from 1972 to the tragic events of June 1989 in China. Noting the mixed record for US–China relations in that period, he observes that '[a]n oscillating pattern of progress and stagnation, crisis and consolidation has characterized the relationship between China and the United States during the past twenty years' (Harding 1992: 5). In looking ahead and calling for a 'new' and more 'normal' relationship with China, Harding argues that America needs to move away from the 'cycle, by which hostility gave way to reconciliation, and euphoria yielded to disenchantment' (Harding 1992: 358). If, on the other hand, Washington chooses to 'cling to these familiar caricatures of China – as ally or adversary, as willing student or as ideological antagonist', such views will 'merely doom the United States to repeat the cycles of euphoria and disillusionment that have been so costly in the past' (Harding 1992: 361).

An excellent companion volume to *Fragile Relationship*, David M. Lampton's (2001b) *Same Bed, Different Dreams* picks up where Harding left off by covering the period 1989 to 2000 in US–China relations. Beginning with the very title of the book, Lampton recognizes the big and growing challenges facing US–China relations and seeks to answer the questions, 'Why is the relationship between the United States and China so difficult for Washington and Beijing to manage?' and 'How can it be handled more effectively?' His final conclusions are cautiously optimistic, but at the same time he reckons that US–China ties 'will always be characterized by a complex mix of cooperation and contention, at best' (Lampton 2001b: 1–2).

Another important work in the decade following the Tiananmen crisis was by the former journalist turned scholar-analyst, James Mann (1999). *About Face* provides excellent detail on the causes, consequences and inner workings of China policy decision-making for the Nixon, Ford, Carter, Reagan, George H.W. Bush and Clinton administrations. But the work also sharply critiques American policy on two important levels and underscores once again the often conflicted US approach toward Beijing. The first critique concerns a repeated pattern of American 'high politics' vis-à-vis China: how several American presidents post-Nixon – including Ford, Carter, Reagan and Clinton – took office 'with the intent of altering the style or the substance of American policy toward China', but in the end, they 'tended to preserve far more than they changed' (Mann 1999: 175). Second, Mann observes that Americans – from presidents to the general public – have never fully reconciled the contradiction which lies at the heart of US–China relations: how can a nation which upholds the ideals of freedom and democracy have a truly strategic and constructive relationship with one which shuns these ideals? 'The events of 1989 shattered this uneasy accommodation. These questions could no longer be submerged. The Tiananmen massacre reminded Americans of the basis on which the Chinese regime held power ... We are still grappling today with this history, and we will continue to do so for some time' (Mann 1999: 376). This latter critique would form the core of Mann's (2007) later book, *The China Fantasy: How Our Leaders Explain Away Chinese Repression*.

The opening chapters in both Harding's *Fragile Relationship* and Mann's *About Face* offer excellent summations of the circuitous and difficult pathways which led to the Nixon–Mao breakthrough of 1972. More detailed accounts of this critical period – 'the week that changed the world' in Richard Nixon's famous phrase – are available most prominently from the two Americans who were at the centre of these events, Nixon (1979) himself and Henry Kissinger (1979), Nixon's national security advisor at the time. On the lighter side, at least two books explore the role which ping-pong diplomacy played in bringing the two nations together in the early 1970s (Griffin 2014; Itoh 2011).

Margaret MacMillan's (2007) *Nixon and Mao* provides a more objective and analytical account of the transformative opening of US–China relations. Reflecting on this momentous period and its aftermath, she notes how the US and China have their 'ups and downs':

> Perhaps they are bound to be rivals, for each in its own way aspires to be a model for others. Each has a tendency to think it is right, that it is more moral than other nations. They have come to know each other well, but they do not always understand each other. The Americans hope that the Chinese are becoming more like them; repeatedly they have been disappointed. The Chinese are repeatedly surprised by and suspicious of American concerns for democracy and human rights. American protests, notably after Chinese authorities brutally put down the pro-democracy movement in Tiananmen Square in 1989, strike them as interference on a par with that of the Western imperialists during the century of humiliation. (MacMillan 2007: 335)

John Garver's (1982) work, *China's Decision for Rapprochement with the United States* attempts to tell the Chinese side of the story, an issue to which I will return below.

Other interesting insights into the history of the US–China relationship come from the advisors, diplomats and analysts who were engaged on a day-to-day basis in crafting and implementing policy. There are numerous such examples and they form a critically important resource for understanding the twists and turns of US–China relations. Among the most important and useful are those by John Paton Davies (2012), Zbigniew Brzezinski (1983), George Shultz (1993), James Baker (1995), George W. Bush and Brent Scowcroft (1998) and, more recently, works by James Lilley (2005), Robert Suettinger (2003) and Jeffrey Bader (2012). Suettinger's work in particular emphasizes the domestic pressures and complexities which complicate the formulation of America policy in Beijing and China policy in Washington. Showing how the exigencies of such pressures, rather than grand strategic design, are more often at the heart of policy development, he argues that conflict between the United States and China is not inevitable. Nevertheless, he points out, 'the routine misperception of each other's goals and policies . . . is leading to increasing hostility and distrust that could eventually have tragic consequences' (Suettinger 2003: 6).

Of particular importance in capturing the insights and views of US officials, Nancy Bernkopf Tucker's (2001) *China Confidential* is essential reading. Based on first-hand accounts from some 35 China experts who served as diplomats and policy-makers, the book provides rare insights into the challenges of US–China relations over five decades. Tucker finds that as these veteran public servants reflect on their experiences and look ahead, they worry about 'the nature of future Sino-American relations: cooperative or contentious? constructive or destructive? wary or warm? Again, American diplomats who continue to worry about the interaction, even though they have left their official posts, think about issues that will certainly complicate the ability of their successors in Washington to adopt a clear and productive China policy.' These issues include pervasive suspicion and distrust on the Chinese side, as well as contentious issues such as

Taiwan, economic tensions, and China's steady military modernization (Tucker, 2001: 497 *et seq.*).

In surveying the English-language literature on US–China relations, a major drawback soon arises: the relative paucity of Chinese perspectives as compared to American. Gaining true insight into the thinking of top PRC leaders will always be difficult if not impossible given the hagiography and secrecy which clouds official Chinese accounts. But some works, such as Ezra Vogel's (2011) intensively researched biography of Deng Xiaoping, shed light on what the paramount Chinese leader thought of relations with the United States. But this work is still not truly a 'Chinese perspective'.

Fortunately, recent years have seen an increasing number of Chinese scholars producing serious research on US–China relations which is accessible to readers of English. Dong Wang (2013) was noted above for her work covering the full history of US–China relations from the late eighteenth to the early twenty-first centuries. In addition, one of the leading and long-standing Chinese scholars of US–China relations is Chen Jian whose research in Chinese archives has opened new insights into Chinese policy-making vis-à-vis America at critical turning points in the relationship; his *China's Road to the Korean War* (1994) and *Mao's China and the Cold War* (2001) are standouts in this regard. Xia Yafeng (2006b), a former Chinese junior diplomat, and now a professor in the United States, in *Negotiating with the Enemy* tells the fascinating tale of how the United States and China kept channels of communication open even in times of bitterest rivalry during the early Cold War years. Other important contributions on US–China relations are made by Hao Yufan (2010, 2013; and Hao and Su 2005) and Zhao Suisheng (2008, 2013), who through their work have encouraged a range of Chinese scholars to publish their research in English.[3] Interestingly, such Chinese perspectives are often even more conflicted about relations with the United States, revealing a pervasive wariness and distrust about long-range American intentions.

LOOKING AHEAD

Given this often troubling background of history and contemporary developments, there is no shortage of authors – particularly centred within the world of Washington, DC public policy think-tanks – who put forward ideas and recommendations about the future of US–China relations. There is general agreement that the relationship between these two powers will, more than any other bilateral relationship, define the twenty-first century, for better or for worse. Most, but not all, of these authors tend to believe that continued 'engagement', leavened with prudent 'hedging' and combined with careful 'management' of the relationship, is the only realistic course to avoid a conflict which neither side wants. Others disagree and see inevitable competition and contentiousness hardwired in to US–China relations, and point to the failure of engagement to bring about the changes in their relationship that either side had hoped.

Several authors have tried to soften the sharp edges of misunderstanding and misperception by making more information about China and US–China relations more widely available to a broader interested public. For example, Robert Sutter's (2010) *The A to Z of United States–China Relations* is typical of this useful genre. In a similar vein, *China: The Balance Sheet* (Bergsten et al. 2007) was an attempt to provide fact-based analysis in a relatively compact format, primarily targeting officials, members of Congress, and other private and public policy elites who were not necessarily China experts, but needed a concise, reliable and policy-relevant guide to thinking about China and the future of US–China relations.

In another important effort to authoritatively inform policy deliberations, Nina Hachigian (2014) takes an innovative approach in her *Debating China*. She draws together a collection of prominent Chinese and American experts on the US–China relationship, puts them into pairs – one Chinese and one American – and asks each pair to discuss a key issue of US–China ties through exchanges of 'collegial letters' to one another. It is especially helpful to have the Chinese perspective. The result – covering a range of topics from economics, to human rights, to the media, to Taiwan, Tibet and military power – is a readily accessible and level-headed set of discussions. Still, it is clear that considerable disagreement exists between US and Chinese perspectives on most of the key issues between the two countries.

Another approach, particularly useful for students and other newcomers to the field of US–China relations, is that of China experts such as Orville Schell and David Shambaugh (1998) and Scott Kennedy (2003), who have very helpfully pulled together key texts, documents, articles, statements and other parts of the public record which provide a basic foundation to understanding China and US–China relations. Kennedy's book is more directly relevant to US–China relations and demonstrates the breadth and combativeness of opinion in the United States about China. The volume also includes two interesting contributions by two leading Chinese scholars who reflect on the fractious US debate.

But even as more Americans are coming to learn more about China, and the same is true for Chinese about America, the expert community seems increasingly troubled about the 'new normal'. As David Shambaugh writes in the opening pages of his thoughtful and well-structured edited volume *Tangled Titans*, 'the principal theme of the relationship at present and into the medium term future, is that the United States and China are inextricably tied together, that they cooperate extensively, but that there is also rising competition in the relationship' (Shambaugh 2013b: 4). The principal reasons behind this conundrum involve, on the one hand, the remarkable forces of globalization which have driven the intensive interdependence we see today between China and America; and on the other hand, the steady accumulation of comprehensive national power by China such that it can assert its interests more effectively in areas where the United States once held singular sway. Underneath this conundrum, not far below the surface, lies the historical experience of the relationship and its mix of hopes, fears, misperceptions and mistrust.

Looking ahead, what does the scholarly literature tell us about the future of US–China relations? In simplest terms, two basic visions are foreseen but neither is all that encouraging about peaceful outcomes for US–China relations. The first foresees a US–China relationship which will almost inevitably become more contentious, not less, even allowing for deepening interdependence between the two. Mearsheimer (2014a), in his *Tragedy of Great Power Politics*, most prominently advocates this view. He writes in the concluding chapter to that work: 'If the Chinese economy continues growing at a brisk clip in the next few decades, the United States will once again face a potential peer competitor, and great-power politics will return in full force' (Mearsheimer 2014b). Drawing on the theory of 'offensive realism', Mearsheimer summarizes his argument:

> [I]f China continues to grow economically, it will attempt to dominate Asia the way the United States dominates the Western Hemisphere. The United States, however, will go to enormous lengths to prevent China from achieving regional hegemony. Most of Beijing's neighbors, including India, Japan, Singapore, South Korea, Russia, and Vietnam, will join with the United States to contain Chinese power. The result will be an intense security competition with considerable potential for war. In short, China's rise is unlikely to be tranquil. (Mearsheimer 2014b)

In response to what is likely, in his view, to be an intensified security competition over time, Mearsheimer calls for the 'optimal strategy' of containment of China in order to preserve American interests. But in the end, the picture he paints of what will happen if China continues to rise is, in his words, 'not a pretty one' (Mearsheimer 2014b). Prior to the publication of the first edition of *Tragedy* in 2001, these same basic arguments were put forward by Richard Bernstein and Ross Munro (1997) in *The Coming Conflict with China*. This book argues that China's return to great power status on the one hand, and America's long-held determination to prevent any single country from dominating Asia, means the two 'are bound to collide'.

Aaron Friedberg (2012) comes to similar conclusions in his *Contest for Supremacy*. He shares the Realist assumption about increasing geopolitical competition between an America determined to maintain its primacy in Asia, and a rising China aiming to oust America from its front yard as it seeks to expand its sphere of influence. In addition, and echoing many past analyses which point to this fundamental weakness in US–China relations, Friedberg argues that the different ideologies and political systems of the two countries only further divide the two and actually make rivalry even more likely. On this latter point, he and James Mann (2007) share common ground. Mann concludes, in *The China Fantasy*, that a 'huge, permanently undemocratic, enduringly repressive China ... persisting in to the mid-twenty-first century, would cause large problems for American policy elsewhere in the world' (although he argues that American leaders are not preparing the American public for such a potential outcome) (Mann 2007: 112).

The other basic vision for future US–China relations represented in the literature recognizes the ongoing changes in the power dynamic between China and the United States, and is not sanguine about the possibilities for democracy in China in the near to medium-term future. However, at the same time, this view tends to see more constraints on Chinese power and on US–China security competition more broadly. Regarding constraints on China, proponents of this view would point to the country's deepening interdependence with the outside world, including the United States; a demonstrated willingness to become more integrated in and accept the norms of the international community; and its continuing need for relatively stable and constructive set of external relationships in order to address a range of domestic challenges and maintain the leadership of the Chinese Communist Party. These points are stressed by a number of authors, including by Rosemary Foot and Andrew Walter (2010) in their *China, the United States, and Global Order*, and in this author's (Gill 2010) *Rising Star*.

G. John Ikenberry (2011, 2014) goes even further to argue that the international system itself is actually another critical factor in alleviating the likelihood of US–China conflict. Referring to views which see China (and other powers) seeking to undermine the global liberal order, he writes:

> [T]his panicked narrative misses a deeper reality: although the United States' position in the global system is changing, the liberal international order is alive and well ... China and other emerging great powers do not want to contest the basic rules and principles of the liberal international order; they wish to gain more authority and leadership within it. Indeed, today's power transition represents not the defeat of the liberal order but its ultimate ascendance. (Ikenberry 2011)

And, more to the point, he argues:

> Ultimately, even if China and Russia do attempt to contest the basic terms of the current global order, the adventure will be daunting and self-defeating. These powers aren't just up against the United States; they would also have to contend with the most globally organized and deeply entrenched order the world has ever seen, one that is dominated by states that are liberal, capitalist, and democratic. This order is backed by a US-led network of alliances, institutions, geopolitical bargains, client states, and democratic partnerships ... The prosperity of nearly every country – and the stability of its government – fundamentally depends on this order. In the age of liberal order, revisionist struggles are a fool's errand. (Ikenberry 2014)

A slightly different take on this latter argument is found in Geoff Dyer's (2014) book, *The Contest of the Century*. He argues that while US–China relations will certainly become more competitive, and China in many ways more assertive, the United States – assuming it can get its fiscal and political house in order – will, through its fundamental strengths and ability to lead, continue to hold sway globally, in spite of China's rise.

Others take the argument further still to state that too many observers overlook the fundamental factors of strategic stability which have defined the US–China relationship for four decades and will continue to do so in to the foreseeable future. Writing in the journal *Washington Quarterly*, Tom Fingar of Stanford University and Fan Jishe of the Institute of American Studies, Chinese Academy of Social Sciences, point to such factors as mutual nuclear deterrence, shared strategic priorities, and 'mutually reinforcing political and economic interdependencies' as forming three powerful 'pillars' for strategic stability between the two countries (Fingar and Fan 2013). While recognizing the challenges to these pillars – potentially destabilizing enhancements to their respective political-military positions vis-à-vis one another, and 'realist fatalism' in both countries – their recommendation is to continue shoring up the pillars of stability in spite of these potentially corrosive effects.

According to this approach, these forces, combined with astute leadership and management of the relationship on both sides of the US–China relationship, can do much to alleviate inevitable tensions and deflect expected competitive tendencies away from outright conflict. Suettinger (2003), in *Beyond Tiananmen*, argues 'management is the key – management of complex goals, multiple disagreements, sensitive emotions, cumbersome bureaucracies, countervailing pressures, unrealistic expectations, and imperfect information' (Suettinger 2003: 441). Given the options, this set of literature argues the necessity for continued engagement between the two powers, and persistent and careful management of the relationship, as the best future course.

Interestingly, the view that the current 'power transition' can evolve relatively peacefully, unlike such transitions in the past, is also shared by a number of Chinese scholars in the edited volume by Ross and Zhu (2008) and in the book by Zhu Zhiqun (2006), *US–China Relations in the 21st Century: Power Transition and Peace*.

But at the same time, such analysts cannot be overly optimistic. To begin with, as Foot and Walter (2010) conclude, adherence to international norms by China is often patchy (as is the case at times with the United States), opening the door for tensions and trouble. For the long term, can analysts always count on the leaders of the United States and China to exercise judicious leadership and wise management of relations, ever aiming to bolster the foundations of strategic stability between the two? Can they be certain that America will be able to fully recover from its current fiscal woes and political dysfunction? How can advocates of this approach be so sure that international institutions and norms will suffice to constrain the world's two most powerful nations from marching inexorably toward conflict? More immediately, what of the challenge of inadvertent crises, sparked not intentionally but as the result of unintended incidents which devolve quickly into confrontation, or worse?

SAME AS IT EVER WAS?

The literature on the future of US–China relations is not particularly reassuring on these questions. On the one hand, many analysts are at best pessimistic about the future (though they might not use that term, preferring instead to say they are 'realistic' about what is to come). On the other hand, the other principal group of analysts are, at best, only cautiously optimistic.

As such, from a real-world policy perspective, we are left primarily with variations on the theme 'engage but hedge', an approach pursued by both China and the United States. But, as Evan Medeiros (2005) writes:

> [S]uch hedging is fraught with complications and dangers that could precipitate a shift toward rivalry and regional instability. It is a delicate balancing act that, to be effective and sustainable, requires careful management of accumulating stresses in US–China relations, of regional reactions to US and Chinese hedging policies, and of the domestic politics in each country. (Medeiros 2005: 145–167)[4]

Coming out of the policy communities of both sides are a wide range of recommendations on how to proceed through this thicket. One of the most exhaustive and elaborate efforts is Michael Swaine's (2011) *America's Challenge*. In this work he provides extensive detail and analysis in examining all the key facets of US–China relations today through the lens of three key variables: 'US policymakers' basic beliefs and underlying assumptions' regarding US and Chinese strategic interests and how they interact; 'recent legacy and logic of US and Chinese policy practices' across a range of key issue sets relevant to US–China relations; and 'those possible factors that will have the most direct impact on the ability and willingness of a future US administration to sustain or modify policy approaches to China' (Swaine 2011: 15). In addition, he incorporates in this analysis extended interviews with more than 50 current and former policy practitioners from the US government. From this work, he concludes there is a need for the United States to 'consider alternatives' to US predominance:

> US policy toward China must continue to incorporate the two closely related approaches [of] cooperative engagement balanced with hedging ... However, the new challenges of the

twenty-first century, combined with many long-standing strategic and policy problems [with China] – often involving growing levels of mutual distrust – will place unprecedented demands on US policymakers, requiring them to take a more proactive stance on many issues, adopt a longer-range perspective, and consider alternatives to the current emphasis on predominance in the Western Pacific as the basis of US strategy toward China. (Swaine 2011: 15)

He continues later in the book that, especially for America, reducing strategic distrust, creating new types of interstate relations and multilateral fora, and resolving major economic problems will require:

> thinking in more farsighted ways, making hard choices and sometimes even abandoning long-standing policy beliefs and assumptions. None of this is beyond the grasp of US leaders. But their success will almost certainly depend on recognizing that, in dealing with China in the twenty-first century, the status quo will not suffice. (Swaine 2011: 380)

In another valuable book coming out of the Washington policy community, two strategic thinkers – like Mearsheimer and Ikenberry, not specialists in US–China relations – also point to the potential for significant problems ahead for the bilateral relationship. But the authors, James Steinberg and Michael O'Hanlon (2014), look to the types of mechanisms which helped keep the US–Soviet rivalry from erupting into open conflict. Their book, *Strategic Reassurance and Resolve*, is less about accommodation and altering the status quo than introducing known methods for alleviating security competition, with a particular focus in such areas as arms control, crisis stability, military spending, modernization and deployments, and cybersecurity. Hence their recommendations to both sides to work toward a clear communication of core interests ('resolve') and a concerted joint effort to introduce even greater self-restraint, transparency and confidence-building ('reassurance') into their security relationship.[5]

Many of these and other nuanced policy approaches are a part of the ongoing interaction between the United States and China and will continue to be debated in the years ahead, many of them gaining traction and many going unimplemented. All the while, such pragmatic efforts to forge greater long-term stability will continue to confront innumerable challenges.

Perhaps the most persistent of these challenges in the past, at present and going forward into the foreseeable future, is strategic mistrust. To highlight and help to address this problem, Kenneth Lieberthal and Wang Jisi (2012) – the former one of America's leading China-watchers, and the latter one of China's leading America-watchers – make a unique and critically important contribution in their jointly authored work, *Addressing US–China Strategic Distrust*. As the authors write, in spite of an extensive history of US–China relations and the current set of intensive bilateral relations:

> This history and these extensive activities have not, however, produced trust regarding long-term intentions on either side, and arguably the problem of lack of such trust is becoming more serious. Distrust is itself corrosive, producing attitudes and actions that themselves contribute to greater distrust. Distrust itself makes it difficult for leaders on each side to be confident they understand the deep thinking among leaders on the other side regarding the future US–China relationship. (Lieberthal and Wang 2012: iv)

To address this challenge, each author independently and candidly details the sources for their country's distrust of the other and then puts forward a cogent joint analysis and range of specific ideas – including in such areas as economics and trade, military strategy, cybersecurity, 'minilateral' dialogues and popular sentiment – for their governments to pursue in order to alleviate the risks arising from this core problem and put the relationship on a more trustful and stable long-term footing. They express the hope that their 'candid explication of the substance and internal narratives of distrust in each government may help policy makers on each side to understand the underlying context in which their policies are seen', and that their policy suggestions, if implemented, might 'erode the bases for deep distrust over longterm intentions and facilitate greater mutual understanding' (Lieberthal and Wang 2012: 49). But as well-intentioned and carefully considered as this work might be, its authors recognize the challenges ahead:

> The above analysis is both candid and sobering. It does not bode well for the long-term ability of the US and China to maximize cooperation for mutual benefit. Looking to the future, it is possible that growth in strategic distrust cannot be avoided and that the two countries can, at best, strive to develop means to limit the resulting damage to their respective interests. Both sides should prepare to do this if efforts to reduce strategic distrust prove ineffective. (Lieberthal and Wang 2012: 39)

The history and current developments of US–China relations clearly tell us the relationship will continue to be burdened with serious and difficult challenges. These range from the perceptual, cultural, ideological and historical, to the tensions of today and tomorrow over great power interests, prerogatives and mistrust. For the future, scholars, experts and policy-makers need to tackle these imperative questions: Given these abiding and looming problems embedded in the very nature of US–China relations, how have the two countries managed to avoid outright conflict for more than half a century? And how can that success be sustained, if it can be at all?

ACKNOWLEDGEMENT

The author wishes to acknowledge the very helpful research assistance of Elizabeth Ingleson in the early stages of this chapter.

NOTES

1. Smith (1984) provides a history of the ship and its voyage. Dolin (2012) offers a more comprehensive history of American maritime engagement with China in the nineteenth century.
2. Search undertaken at https://www.worldcat.org, on 16 May 2014.
3. Suisheng Zhao Suisheng is also the founder and long-time editor of the *Journal of Contemporary China*, known for its success in publishing Chinese scholars in English.
4. Dr Medeiros has been on the White House National Security Council (NSC) staff since 2009 and, from 2013 to 2015 served as the Senior Director for Asia at the NSC.
5. 'Strategic reassurance' was a term Steinberg attempted introduced into the lexicon of US–China relations when he was US Deputy Secretary of State in 2009.

25. Southeast Asia
Alberto Camarena and Jörn Dosch

Ever since the 'rise of China' has captured the public and academic imagination, Southeast Asia has taken centre stage in this debate because of the region's proximity to China (Chong and Li 2011; Yeoh 2009; Storey 2011; Percival 2007; Kurlantzick 2007). If the People's Republic of China (PRC) was to establish itself as a leading and possibly hegemonic power on the international stage, such a development would surely manifest itself first in the nation's immediate neighbourhood, or so the mainstream argument goes. At one end of the spectrum, some argue that China's rise provides manifold opportunities for Southeast Asia, which nicely matches China's official 'win–win' rhetoric: since the Association of Southeast Asian States (ASEAN)[1] 'collectively established official contact with China in 1991, the two sides have made remarkable progress in forging a strategic partnership for peace and prosperity' (Yang and Heng 2011: 126). At the other end of the spectrum, a smaller group proposes that the emergence of an expansionist China is a threat to a stable regional order (for example Grieco 2002; Sokolsky et al. 2001). Most of the studies in this latter category were published in the early 2000s and written against a backdrop of growing concerns about the future role of the United States in Southeast Asia: a zero-sum scenario for big power hegemony in which 'the Chinese are now eating the Americans' lunch in the region' (Cox 2008: 310). The key argument is aptly summarized by Thomas Christensen:

> China's diplomatic accommodation of its neighbours . . . can be seen as parts of a strategy to drive the United States out of the region. The danger is that regional actors will bandwagon with and accommodate a rising China, rather than balance against it by drawing closer to the United States. (Christensen 2006: 98)

As Martin Stuart-Fox (2002: 240) concludes his outline of some two millennia of contact between China and Southeast Asia:

> The ASEAN ten will do all in their power not to provoke China. What they want is to both slow and ease the changing power balance. They want the United States to remain a powerful presence, serving as a balancing force in the regional power equation, and have made this known; but they do not want to be part of any balance-of-power coalition. At the same time, they also want to make room for China.

This chapter takes a different approach. It does not follow the popular trend of analysing China–Southeast Asia relations through the lens of Washington's role, interests and strategies in the region, or against the backdrop of relations between the US and China. Nor does it intend to contribute to the 'rise of China hype' by presenting the PRC's role in and towards Southeast Asia as a largely new and recent phenomenon. Instead we aim to provide a sober discussion which traces the history of modern diplomatic relations (from the late 1940s to the present) between China and Southeast Asia, and to show how both domestic developments in China and exogenous factors have deeply affected these relations and thereby also shaped the regional order. At the same time the following analysis gives justice to the fact that there has never been one, homogeneous Southeast Asian approach towards China. While some periods have seen more unified regional strategies than others, overall each of the Southeast Asian states have followed a different path in their respective relations with China because of 'an eclectic mix of elite perceptions, state ideology, geography, security concerns, economic aspirations and responses to changes in the geographical environment' (Storey 2011: 286).

For the purposes of convenient analysis, China's foreign policy vis-à-vis Southeast Asia will be divided into three broad periods. The first period extends from the birth of the People's Republic until Mao Zedong's death (1949–1976); the second covers Deng Xiaoping's rule (mid-1970s to early 1990s); and the third begins with the fall of communism in Eastern Europe and the collapse of the Soviet Union. From the outset it is important to stress that each of these periods has had a profound impact on the manner in which China has interacted with both individual Southeast Asian states and ASEAN as an organization.

ASEAN was founded in 1967 and today comprises all Southeast Asian states with the exception of Timor Leste. Since ASEAN has almost become a synonym for Southeast Asia and both terms are used interchangeably in many publications, it is difficult to draw exact lines between, first, Southeast Asia as a region and ASEAN as an organization, and second, the states of Southeast Asia as individual nation states and in their capacity as ASEAN members. While this chapter tries to distinguish between Southeast Asia and ASEAN, overlaps are not always unavoidable.

THE MAO PERIOD, 1949–76

Before focusing on China's relations with individual Southeast Asian states, we will first take a look at China's response to the formation of ASEAN, which in many ways set the stage for the PRC's perception of, and policies towards, the region. The foreign policies of the superpowers, the structure of the international system, China's calculation of its relative power and interests within this global order and the weight of ideology played critical roles in Beijing's strategic decisions towards Southeast Asia. The Cold War's reach in the region resulted in most Southeast Asian countries having to side with one of the two superpowers, or else attempting to adopt a non-aligned stance, which was much more difficult to achieve. In the 1950s and 1960s in particular, relations between China and Southeast Asia were best described as stressful and characterized by a high degree of caution and distrust which emerged between the respective political elites and peoples (Shao 1996).

This negative milieu adversely affected relations between China and ASEAN mainly because of most member states' alignment with Western powers. Singapore and Malaysia had signed security pacts with their former colonial master, the UK; Thailand and the Philippines were closely aligned with the United States, providing military bases and, in the case of Thailand, having direct military involvement in the Vietnam War. Against the backdrop of the (at the time) seemingly irreversible deterioration of Sino-Soviet relations on the one hand, and Sino-American hostility on the other, Beijing described ASEAN as a 'puny counter-revolutionary alliance' promoting the interests of 'American imperialism' and 'Soviet revisionism'.[2] Initially, only Jakarta had cordial relations with Beijing, since Indonesian President Sukarno promoted an independent foreign policy and wanted to distance the country from collaboration with ex-colonial forces (Leifer 1983). Thus, China's initial reaction to the formation of ASEAN expressed a profound ideological and practical distrust against its members, and the Association came to be seen with suspicion and as a front for further attempts to contain China. This was indeed almost inevitable, since ASEAN's members found common ground in a real (if veiled) fear of China and close interactions with the US. Yet, the founding members of ASEAN did not pursue the creation of a regional organization to actively contain China, but rather to protect their non-communist political systems from outside interference (Connors et al. 2011).

The architects of Southeast Asian regionalism were intimately aware that ASEAN should not be perceived by external regional actors as a military alliance or any other sort of organization aiming to contain China (Gurtov 1975). However, the formation of ASEAN had been preceded by several attempts at regional groupings, involving at least part of the newly formed ASEAN partnership, of which some clearly followed anti-communist objectives. Previous regional groupings included the South East Asia Treaty Organization (SEATO), Association of Southeast Asia (ASA), Maphilindo (Malaysia, the Philippines and Indonesia), the Asian and Pacific Council (ASPAC), and the Five Power Defence Arrangements (FPDA). SEATO and the FPDA for example were explicit in their objective to serve as defence pacts and military alliances sponsored by major Western powers, with SEATO led by the US and the FPDA guided by the UK and Australia (Wah 1983, 1991). Beijing saw ASEAN primarily as yet another incarnation of pro-Western regional bloc-building. In the minds of the Chinese leadership, there was little reason to construe ASEAN as anything fundamentally different from SEATO or any other regional organization with a similar membership. Chinese commentators at the time noted that 'China is to bravely resist the ominous threat coming from imperialistic and revisionist cliques in the form of regional pacts'.[3]

China's relations with individual Southeast Asian states were also affected by the influence of ideology and the international regional and global factors characteristic of the Cold War. According to Khaw Hoon, to be considered by China as a friendly Southeast Asian neighbour it was necessary to meet at least some of the following criteria:

- A willingness to recognize the government of the PRC as the sole government of China and to establish relations with it based on the Five Principles of Peaceful Coexistence.
- Disavowal of the concept of two Chinas and respect for China's position that Taiwan is an integral part of Chinese territory.
- Disallowance of foreign, especially US, military bases in their territories.
- Repudiation of American policies in Southeast Asia in general and Vietnam in particular.
- The adoption of a non-aligned orientation of their foreign policies (Khaw 1977: 13).

These conditions left no significant room for improving Sino-Southeast Asian relations during the Mao period, as all ASEAN members recognized Taiwan as the sole government of China. Thailand, Singapore and the Philippines openly supported US policies in the region and even contributed troops and bases during the Vietnam War. The individual foreign policies of the ASEAN states heavily tilted towards US interests in the region and did not sustain an independent, non-aligned stance. China and ASEAN would have to wait some years in order to be able to improve their relations.

Relations with Indonesia

Sino-Indonesian relations got off to a good start as the two regimes found common ground in their respective armed struggles for national independence. In July 1950, Jakarta and Beijing established diplomatic relations soon after Indonesia obtained full independence from the Netherlands in December 1949. Both governments were eager to develop diplomatic recognition as a means to improve their international standing and a significant contribution towards securing their survival in the new global post-World War II order. Furthermore, both nations considered themselves part of the Third World and were strongly opposed to the power politics of the superpowers (Suryadinata 1996). Both Sukarno and Mao perceived imperialism, colonialism and capitalism as the main enemies confronting their respective nations and the developing world (Weinstein 1976). Where Mao spoke about imperialism and revisionism as the eminent dangers for China and the world, and the role of the Chinese Communist Party (CCP) in the fight against them, Sukarno identified the 'Old Established Forces' as the reactionary camp, and his 'New Emerging Forces' as the progressive forces of the world, which were meant to lead revolutionary-like changes within countries and the international system (Mozingo 1976). However, bilateral relations eventually began to deteriorate. The Indonesian government became increasingly wary of China's connections with the Communist Party of Indonesia, which were perceived as Beijing's attempt to interfere in Indonesia's national affairs through interactions with the ethnic Chinese minority living in the country. The New Order regime remained vigilant and wary of any communist activity within the country, and was hostile towards China throughout the 1970s.

Relations with Burma and Indochina

Burma's historic concern to remove tensions in relations with China – particularly due to the country's vulnerable 1350-mile land border – made the question of diplomatic recognition of the young PRC in the late 1940s a priority. Furthermore, the Burmese government also feared the possibility of China attempting to annihilate the remnants of the Nationalist army stationed in the country, thus facilitating an excuse for military intervention in Burma's territory (Johnstone 1963). Formal relations were established on 8 June 1950 and initially remained generally stable but relatively distant, characterized by official declarations of friendship which served to cover and contain significant underlying tensions. In 1954, China, Myanmar and India jointly proclaimed the Five Principles of Peaceful Co-existence that were subsequently adopted by the Non-Aligned Movement as the basis for international relations and also found their way into the Sino-Burmese Joint Declaration of 29 June 1954 (Pettman 1973). Overall, Sino-Burmese relations experienced ambivalent peaceful coexistence (1949–1961), and a period of temporary setbacks (mid-1960s–1970), leading eventually to improved relations from the early 1970s (Gurtov 1975; Appadorai 1982).

China's relations with Indochina during the Mao period centred on its support for the Vietnamese independence and later North Vietnam's reunification efforts. The PRC followed two main strands of policy towards Vietnam during the first two Indochina wars: cooperation and containment. Beijing provided considerable support to Ho Chi Minh in the independence war against France (1950s) and later supported the Vietminh in its fight against South Vietnam and the US in the 1960s–1970s. China's support for Vietnam's war effort served geopolitical and ideological interests. On the one hand, Mao could eliminate 'hostile imperialism' from its southern border; and on the other, Beijing could spread revolution in Indochina and contain Vietnam's attempts to dominate in Laos and Cambodia. From the 1950s until the late 1960s, China's cooperation with Vietnamese revolutionaries was predominant. Nevertheless, by the early 1970s Beijing's containment policy became more conspicuous. This was due to the intensification of the Sino-Soviet rift at the same time as Hanoi and Moscow were deepening their ties. Thereafter, the leadership in China became increasingly concerned with the prospects of a post-war Indochina dominated by Vietnam in alliance with the Union of Soviet Socialist Republics (USSR) (Zhai 2000: 217).

Relations between the countries further deteriorated when Vietnamese troops invaded Cambodia on 25 December 1978, removing the Khmer Rouge regime – an ally of Beijing – from power (Lawson 1984). The nadir of Sino-Vietnamese relations came shortly thereafter, when China decided to invade Vietnam in order to 'teach the Vietnamese a lesson'. The war was brief (17 February – 5 March 1979) and had mixed results for China, as Beijing did not achieve the victory needed in order to force Vietnam to retreat from Cambodia. After this brief military interlude, relations between both countries remained hostile and China would often refer to Vietnam as a stooge of revisionist powers (referring to Moscow); in the meantime Hanoi considered China as its most serious threat until the improvement of relations during the early 1990s (Ang 1998).

Relations with Thailand, the Philippines, Malaysia and Singapore

Apart from Indonesia the original ASEAN members did not express a radical anti-colonial, anti-imperialist foreign policy which could have eased relations with the PRC. On the contrary, the governing political elites within these countries all developed strong ties with Western countries, particularly with the US, rejecting communism as a viable option for their own societies and supporting the American war effort in Indochina (Tarling 1999; Yim 1990: 137). Furthermore, China reacted adversely to the formation of Malaysia and Singapore (formerly Malaya), as Beijing thought of them as 'stooge states' serving colonialist and imperialist designs from their previous masters (that is, the United Kingdom). China bitterly argued that 'Malaysia is a dagger thrust in the heart of Southeast Asia by the US and British imperialists. It is an implement of old and new colonialism.'[4] The ASEAN members became very aware of the potential dangers that the PRC could pose to their own national security and survival, and their support of the US in Indochina was at least partly driven by the strategic considerations to strengthen and increase their level of security in the face of a perceived expansionist and aggressive communist Vietnam (van Canh and Cooper 1983: 222–257). If Beijing feared an active policy of containment orchestrated by the US and the USSR with the help of Southeast Asian states, Thailand, the Philippines, Malaysia and Singapore were greatly concerned about China's interference in their national affairs, mostly in the way of giving support to communist parties and maintaining close links with ethnic Chinese minorities in these countries.

China's Support for Communist Parties and Movements

In Southeast Asia China proactively established links with communist parties and revolutionary movements across the region, providing support in all its forms: material, military, financial and propagandistic. The underpinnings of such relations were based on Mao's thesis of contradictions and the need to create united fronts. A fundamental contradiction was to be found between the oppressed and imperialist nations of the world. Therefore, the main goal of all oppressed nations would be to 'break the yoke' of imperialist rulers and then move towards new forms of socio-political organization such as communism (Yee 1983). Beijing's support for communist parties in the region had the ultimate task of helping them achieve this objective. For this reason, Southeast Asia's political elites viewed with trepidation Beijing's efforts to establish and fortify its relations with communist parties within their territories; even more so as these communist parties were also in many cases instrumental in forming and organizing armed anti-government movements, as happened in Malaya, Thailand, Vietnam, the Philippines and Borneo; and it was also suspected China played a role in the failed coup attempt of the 30 September Movement (Gerakan 30 September) on 1 October 1965 in Indonesia which the armed forces and the emerging Suharto regime immediately blamed on the Indonesian Partai Komunis Indonesia (PKI; Communist Party of Indonesia) triggering the killing of an estimated 500 000 actual and alleged PKI members in 1965 and 1966 (Steinberg 1987).

THE DENG XIAOPING PERIOD, MID-1970s–EARLY 1990s

Most of the factors just outlined remained in place after the death of Mao in 1976 and during Deng's tenure. In the sphere of domestic politics, the most important transformation was replacing Mao's ideological radicalism with Deng's pragmatism, and a corresponding shift from the primacy of politics to the primacy of economics. China's foreign policy began to incorporate calculations about what could serve the country's economic development (or in Marxist–Leninist language, the development of the productive forces) and downplayed the importance of the previous ideological contents. Thus, access to foreign markets and goods, and technology transfers, became a crucial objective of China's foreign policy. Beijing's new foreign policy was summed up by the fundamental objectives of promoting peace and security, both at the national and the international level. A peaceful international setting should become most conducive to uninterrupted growth and the promotion of the four modernizations, whereas war would run against China's opportunity to catch up with the developed world (Evans 1995). Furthermore, propagandistic opposition to Western nations and values lost its emphasis as the campaigns against spiritual corruption and bourgeois influence were left aside (Meisner 1996). All these measures facilitated the justification of deeper relations with capitalist states and a vast number of changes within the economic, administrative and legal spheres in the country, and greatly contributed to radical changes in Chinese foreign policy.

At the same time, international events played a fundamental role in shaping Beijing's relations during this period. The first stage of foreign policy design during the Deng period was still dominated by Cold War logic. Deng also put a great emphasis on the so-called Third World, although China's previous policies had alienated too many Third World states by, in some cases, cooperating with their opponents or fostering domestic opposition groups. One of the obvious reasons to stress the importance of the Third World was that many developing nations were potential markets for Chinese goods, or were places where Chinese soft power could purchase influence (Sutter 1986). A number of events later marked the transition from the Deng period towards a new and the most recent phase in China's foreign policy: first, a domestic factor, the Tiananmen incident in the summer of 1989; and second, the massive international structural change triggered by the collapse of the Soviet Union and the demise of communism in Eastern Europe. These different stages of China's foreign policy under Deng also manifested themselves in Beijing's relations with both ASEAN and individual Southeast Asian countries.

Relations before 1989

As the result of the Open Door policy and the promotion of the four modernizations, Deng expressed the need for a peaceful international environment in which China could develop. He concluded that China had to stop supporting insurgencies in Southeast Asia if Beijing wanted ASEAN to support the resistance to Vietnam's invasion of Cambodia. Furthermore, the improvement in relations with the US, which had progressed since the early 1970s, leading to the final full normalization of Sino-American diplomatic relations in 1978, helped to change Southeast Asia's perceptions of China. However, undoubtedly the most important factor affecting the nature of Sino-ASEAN relations during this period was Vietnam's invasion of Cambodia. Under Deng, China's relations with Southeast Asia varied in two main respects: on the one hand, Sino-Vietnamese relations reached a very low point; but, on the other, it was precisely because of this development that relations between China and the ASEAN members improved. Alice Ba referred to this as the 'second phase' of Sino-ASEAN relations. A critical factor affecting Sino-ASEAN relations during this period was the US withdrawal from Indochina which seemingly confirmed the need for the ASEAN states to address the matter of regional order on their own. However, ASEAN's voices were not homogeneous, as some members (for example, Malaysia and Indonesia) considered China the main threat, whereas others (for example, Thailand and Singapore) perceived Vietnam to be the more eminent challenge to regional peace and stability. Regardless of these differences ASEAN entered into a de facto alignment with Beijing, particularly as the US was not willing to get directly involved, and China had a strong interest in containing Soviet–Vietnamese influence in the region, just as much as ASEAN did (Ba 2003: 625; also Jones 2012). Moreover, due to Thailand's fears about Vietnamese expansionism, Bangkok decided to turn to China not just for diplomatic but also for military assistance. Thus, China went from being the primary antagonist to become Thailand's security guarantor. In sum, China's need for a globally peaceful international environment, the normalization of relations between the US and China, coupled with a sympathetic and common ground between ASEAN states and China directed against Vietnam's invasion of Cambodia, began to generate a new set of positive developments between the Association's members and Beijing (Chanda 1990: 66).

Relations after Tiananmen

The Tiananmen incident affected China's relations with the outside world by temporarily halting the reforms initiated by Deng, and bringing the ideological conservatives back to power. Yet, not all members of the international community condemned the Chinese government and applied sanctions. This was particularly the case for East Asian governments, which were evasive and unwilling to intervene in what they saw as the internal affairs of a third country. While Japan and South Korea expressed some mild criticism of Beijing's actions, Southeast Asian governments decided not to get involved at all, and stuck to a policy of considering the incident as a purely internal Chinese matter. 'While the rest of the world was doing its best to isolate China, ASEAN reached out to Beijing' (Shambaugh 2005: 26). In fact, China–Southeast Asia relations intensified in the wake of the Tiananmen incident. While China's relations with Southeast Asia had already improved since the early 1980s, the Tiananmen incident in June 1989 was the most significant turning-point.

The sanctions imposed by Western countries and the almost simultaneous collapse of the Soviet Union and East European communist regimes forced China into temporary international semi-isolation. Chinese leaders had to adjust their foreign policy, and one of their new initiatives was a more Asia-oriented outlook with Southeast Asia as a major focus (Zhao 1995a: 8–15). China also aimed at substituting as much as possible the loss of economic assistance and political support from European and American sources by trying to create new coalitions to protect itself from the US-led cluster of nations (Long 1992).

THE PERIOD SINCE THE END OF THE COLD WAR

The end of the Cold War and the settlement of the Cambodian conflict – which formally came to a conclusion with the Paris Peace Agreement of 1991 – opened a new episode in the development of relations between China and Southeast Asia. Throughout the Cold War period, China's interactions with ASEAN states were conducted solely on a bilateral basis. No institutionalized linkages existed between China and ASEAN as a regional organization. The withering of ideological barriers at the turn of the decade paved the way for the restoration or re-establishment of diplomatic ties between China and all ASEAN states by 1991 (Table 25.1).

Viewed in this light, the attendance by then Chinese Foreign Minister Qian Qichen at the opening session of the 24th ASEAN Ministerial Meeting in July 1991 as a guest of Malaysia was a significant event in Sino-ASEAN relations. He subsequently put forward proposals for a China–ASEAN Joint Committee on Economic and Trade Cooperation, a China–ASEAN Science and Technology Training Centre, and a Technology Development and Service Centre. At the invitation of Tang Jiaxuan, then Vice-Minister of Foreign Affairs of China, ASEAN Secretary-General Dato' Ajit Singh led an ASEAN delegation

Table 25.1   The establishment of diplomatic relations between China and Southeast Asian countries

Country	Diplomatic relations with China
Brunei	September 1991
Cambodia	July 1958
Indonesia	April 1950 – October 1967, re-established in August 1990
Laos	April 1961, normalized in 1989
Malaysia	May 1974
Myanmar (Burma)	June 1950
Philippines	June 1975
Singapore	October 1990
Thailand	July 1975
Vietnam	January 1950–79, re-established in October 1991

on a visit to China in September 1993. The two sides held exploratory talks in Beijing to strengthen China–ASEAN cooperation in the fields of trade, economic relations, science and technology, and reached broad understanding of these areas of cooperation.[5] This was followed, *inter alia*, by China's attendance at the inaugural meeting of the ASEAN Regional Forum in 1994, and finally the granting of 'ASEAN dialogue partner' status in 1996.[6] Together, these events marked the beginning of the multilateral impulse in China and the ASEAN states (Kuik 2005; Lee Lai To 2001). The emphasis on multilateralism was accompanied by a new Chinese understanding of security which highlighted the importance of dialogue and consultation instead of military alliances and pacts, and linked security with broader topics such as economic development and the environment. This way of thinking found its almost perfect mirror in ASEAN's approach to security as exemplified by the ASEAN Regional Forum (ARF) as a forum for the discussion of security-relevant regional issues in a non-confrontational setting. Former Chinese Defence Minister Chi Haotian described the ARF as 'a courageous effort in probing the ASEAN initiative to carry out open dialogue and consultation on regional and political and security issues'.[7]

Beijing's move to involve itself in ASEAN activities since the early 1990s has formed a central part of China's Good Neighbourliness Policy (GNP) which originated in the wake of the Tiananmen incident and followed the main objective to strengthen Beijing's ties with its neighbouring countries. Senior Chinese leaders also began promoting their country's policies through regular trips abroad. Throughout the 1990s, Jiang Zemin, Li Peng and Zhu Rongji travelled the world with increasing frequency, and were particularly keen to visit other Asian nations. This transformation in diplomacy began in the early 1990s, with Beijing's drive to expand its bilateral links and to establish various levels of 'partnership' to facilitate economic and security coordination, and to offset the United States system of regional alliances. During this period Beijing also gradually abandoned its previous aversion to multilateral institutions, which Deng had always feared could be used to punish or constrain China. Chinese leaders started to recognize that such organizations would allow their country to promote its trade and security interests and limit US leverage. For China's relations with Southeast Asia this strategy implied increasingly proactive contributions to regional order-building. In 1997, China helped initiate the ASEAN Plus Three mechanism, a series of yearly meetings among the ten ASEAN countries plus China, Japan and South Korea; followed by the ASEAN Plus One mechanism, exclusive annual meetings between ASEAN and China, usually headed by the Chinese premier (Medeiros and Fravel 2003).

Despite territorial disputes and other differences (see below), Chinese leaders have valued good relations with the ASEAN states. Likewise, in the perception of Southeast Asian governments, China was no longer seen as a power dissatisfied with the status quo and intent on exporting revolution. Shortly before Deng's death in 1997, Jiang Zemin reaffirmed the foreign policy line of the Deng era, characterized by 'avoiding the limelight and keeping a low profile', while concentrating on China's own affairs (Cheng 1999b: 86). Subsequent statements on Chinese foreign policy repeatedly emphasized continuity and peace and had the ASEAN states in mind as important targets. Chinese leaders perceived the early 1990s as a transitional period between bipolarity and multipolarity and expected this transition to last for a considerable length of time. Towards the end of the decade confidence in multipolar und multilateral structures had clearly grown.

The foreign policy of the so-called 'fourth generation' leadership (after those led by Mao, Deng and Jiang) has put strong emphasis on the fostering of friendly and mutually beneficial relations with neighbouring states (Xiao 2009: 306). As part of this process China has become increasingly involved in Southeast Asia's traditional security affairs as well. Particularly since the early 2000s, Beijing has established military links with Thailand, the Philippines, Indonesia, Singapore, Burma/Myanmar, Cambodia and Malaysia. This extends not only to military aid and loans, bilateral talks on military issues, joint production of military equipment and joint training exercises, but it also includes participation in regional security forums and the signing of defence memoranda of understanding (MOUs). The view has been growing among Southeast Asian elites that ASEAN and China share the profits of security management in an overall situation of a positive-sum game (or win–win situation, according to the official Chinese term) (Dosch 2007).

Since the end of the Cold War and the restructuring of the international order, one of the most debated aspects of the new international order has been whether the rise of China as a major regional and global power is to become a significant factor for stability or instability, both in East Asia and in the world in general. At this point in time it is important to underline that Southeast Asian governments and commentators alike do not view the so-called 'China Threat' in the same way as more distant observers, particularly Western nations. Most ASEAN states do not fear a non-democratic China, but would be concerned about one that might bully them within their region in political, security-related and economic ways. Furthermore, even though Chinese power is on the rise, China's particular approach to ASEAN and Southeast Asian countries has not shown a drift towards coercion but rather towards sustained and intense cooperation. David Shambaugh's observation of a decade ago is still valid: 'Even though some countries remain unsure of China's long term ambitions, and are thus adopting hedging policies against the possibility of a more aggressive China, the majority of Asian states currently view China as more benign than malign and are accommodating themselves to its rise' (Shambaugh 2004–05: 67). This is particularly true for the opportunities that closer economic relations between China and Southeast Asia seem to have in store.

The ASEAN-China Free Trade Area

Throughout the 1990s, trade between China and ASEAN grew at an annual rate of 16 per cent, and in 2000 the trade volume stood at US$29.6 billion (Xiao 2009: 309). Since then trade increased even more dramatically and reached US$443.6 billion in 2013, according to official Chinese statistics.[8] The most significant annual increase during this period has been achieved since the China–ASEAN Free Trade Agreement (CAFTA) officially came into full effect on 1 January 2010. At this point China and ASEAN-6 (Brunei, Malaysia, Indonesia, Singapore, Thailand and the Philippines) had reduced tariffs to zero on 90 per cent of traded goods (China Customs 2011). The four newer ASEAN members – Cambodia, Laos, Myanmar and Vietnam – negotiated a delayed and gradual entry into CAFTA. The FTA has a combined gross domestic product (GDP) of US$6.6 trillion and comprises 1.9 billion people (ASEAN Secretariat 2010; see also Storey 2011: 78–81).

Chinese Premier Zhu Rongji first proposed a trade agreement at the ASEAN+China meeting in November 2000 in response to the Asian economic crisis and regional concerns about the impact of China's then imminent World Trade Organization (WTO) membership. Yet, this proposal 'also arose out of an acute sensitivity toward the need to maintain relations with as many states as possible in order to constrain American power under a global system defined by the struggle between "one superpower, many great powers"' (Hughes 2005: 125). Against this backdrop the idea was one of the most visible materializations of China's 'charm offensive' in Southeast Asia. Joshua Kurlantzick and others have described the charm strategy as the energetic and effective use of soft power (Kurlantzick 2007). China's diplomatic charm offensive is the continuation of previous efforts to constructively engage other regions and countries in order to improve Beijing's bilateral and multilateral relations, and also improve China's access to coveted resources abroad. The charm offensive has gone beyond establishing diplomatic relations and initiating frequent high-level visits to and from the capitals in the region: China has augmented its aid and investment in many Southeast Asian countries and its own image has improved considerably.

Within ASEAN, China is perceived as an engine of growth, a distinction that previously belonged to Japan. Malaysia is a case in point. China became Malaysia's largest trading partner in 2011, and no other country has benefited as much from the China–ASEAN Free Trade Agreement (CAFTA) as Malaysia. The two-way trade volume between China and Malaysia has increased by more than 15 per cent on average since 2000 and reached US$106 billion in 2013. In recent years the Malaysian government has not once deviated from its approach of presenting relations with China as entirely trouble-free and beneficial for the country's development towards industrialized-nation status (Dosch 2014: 25).

Seen from this perspective, CAFTA – which had already been gradually implemented under the Early Harvest Programme (EHP) since 2003 – has strengthened China's status as a benevolent regional leader. China's proposal of a 'strategic partnership' with ASEAN, unveiled at the ASEAN foreign ministers' meeting in Phnom Penh in June 2003, has to be seen in the same context. ASEAN members enthusiastically supported the free trade initiative not only for economic reasons but also because it offered a golden opportunity to jump on the China bandwagon with general political-security intentions in mind. While not all ASEAN members benefit in the same way from the free trade area and, particularly in the case of Vietnam, even run rapidly growing deficits in their trade relations with China, studies on CAFTA regularly stress the 'longer-term strategic objectives of this trade agreement' (Chandra and Lontoh 2011: 2) as it is expected to make a significant contribution to the fortification of Sino-South Asian relations.

This strategy also includes the strengthening of the region's resilience and resistance vis-à-vis regional and global economic crisis. Hardship and disappointment in the aftermath of the 1997 financial crisis, when ASEAN in general and the most affected members Indonesia and Thailand in particular felt let down by the 'West' and were at the mercy of the International Monetary Fund (IMF), still form part of the collective memory (Dieter 2008: 5). Against this backdrop, ASEAN, China as well as Japan and South Korea – a loose grouping which soon came to be known as ASEAN+3 – began to design and develop its own approach to monetary governance. The result was the Chiang Mai Initiative (CMI), a self-managed network of bilateral swap agreements between the national central banks of most member countries. In 2009 the CMI was multilateralized and the new Chiang Mai Initiative Multilateralization (CMIM) took effect in March 2010. The CMIM is a foreign currency reserve pool with a current size of US$240 billion – to which China contributes roughly one-third, while ASEAN collectively contributes 20 per cent – which can provide funds to member states suffering from short-term liquidity problems (Loewen 2014: 51). While the CMIM is untested so far it has undoubtedly been a stepping stone towards the evolution of a regional governance system in which China plays a central role.

However, general concerns about China's regional role and ambitions remain in most ASEAN capitals, especially in those states which are involved in the South China Sea disputes – a significant thorn in the side of China–Southeast Asia relations.

The South China Sea Disputes

China, with the exception of the Mongol Yuan Dynasty and a short period in the early Ming Dynasty, was a land-oriented empire and not a maritime power. During most of Chinese history, the most dangerous threat came from nomadic powers in Inner Asia, which diverted Chinese strategic attention towards the northern and western frontiers. In addition, as agriculture provided the basis of Chinese economy in the pre-modern times, China did not need to develop a powerful navy or conquer maritime territories to secure its access to resources. All this has changed with the programmes of modernization following the defeat of Qing China at the hands of maritime powers. The largest threat now came from the southeastern coasts and a modernizing China's growth and stability would depend in large part on its connection with the world market and overseas resources, primarily through the East and South China Seas. It was in this context that in the early twentieth century Chinese authorities began to assert Chinese sovereignty over the Paracel Islands in the South China Sea. This triggered protest by the Vietnamese court at Hue, which had established its control over the islands well before the French conquests of Vietnam. In the 1930s, while China began to publish maps declaring its territorial claims in the South China Seas, French authorities in Indochina also began to set up weather stations on and send garrisons to the Paracel and the Spratly Islands (Chemillier-Gendreau 2000; Nguyen Nha 1975; Li and Li 2003).

The Spratly Islands are a collection of coral reefs, atolls, islets, islands and sand bars scattered over a sea zone of some 410 000 square kilometres. This area is claimed, in whole or in part, by China, Taiwan, Vietnam, Malaysia, Brunei and the Philippines. Although the total land mass of the islands does not exceed 10 square kilometres, the Spratly Islands' geostrategic and economic significance is invaluable. Linking the Pacific and Indian Oceans, the South China Sea sees passage of nearly 50 per cent of global merchant traffic and 80 per cent of crude oil transports en route to Japan, South Korea and Taiwan. Securing sovereignty over the Spratly Islands equates to direct control of some of the most important sea lanes of communication. Furthermore, the islands are set amid some of the world's most productive fishing grounds and may prove rich in undersea oil and gas resources (Dosch 2011).

The dispute only gained prominence in 1978, when the Philippines set out its EEZ (Exclusive Economic Zone), formally including the island of Kalayaan in the Spratlys.[9] However, the controversy itself remained relatively dormant until 1988, when China and Vietnam clashed at Johnson Reef and several Vietnamese boats were sunk, killing over 70 sailors. Since then hostilities in the South China Sea have regularly erupted, most prominently between China and the Philippines. The Philippines considers China's occupation of Mischief Reef in 1995, and its repeated incursions into Scarborough Shoal since 1997, as direct assaults on the Philippines' territory. In the first half of 2012, Chinese paramilitary ships confronted Philippine vessels in a two-month stand-off over a disputed shoal. In June 2012, the Philippines withdrew its presence due to the approaching typhoon season and China has effectively controlled the disputed area since then. Today, military forces from Vietnam, China, Taiwan, Malaysia and the Philippines occupy about 45 of the islands. Brunei has claimed an EEZ in the southeastern part of the region without maintaining a military presence. In recent years, the Chinese navy has intensified its patrols throughout the area and has shown an increasing readiness and willingness to confront other nations for control within the contested island chains (see Storey 2011: 89–94 for details). Carlyle Thayer has described China's current approach as 'aggressive assertion of sovereignty over the South China Sea' (Thayer 2011: 573).

The essential problem is simple: the claimants disagree about the territorial division amongst them of the South China Sea. While China has repeatedly stated that it owns sovereignty and jurisdiction over the islands and adjacent waters, other nations involved in the dispute contradict this claim, basing their responses on historical or legal arguments. The most important provision in this regard is the 1982 United Nations Convention on the Law of the Sea (UNCLOS). At the core of the sovereignty dispute lies the so-called 'nine-dash line' (since it is defined by nine dashes on Chinese maps). This U-shaped line indicates China's claims to over 80 per cent of the South China Seas. In May 2009, China issued an official note concerning the nine-dash line, formally bringing the nine-dash line map to global attention. Shen Hongfang summarizes recent Chinese discourses on the dispute and cites the allegedly popular view among almost all of Chinese senior military officials that 'China is legally entitled to take military actions to repel the invaders' and that it might be necessary to 'teach some countries a lesson' (Shen 2011: 592–594).

Official diplomacy is markedly more tamed. In April 2011, Chinese President Hu Jintao called on other Asian nations to forge better cooperation regarding security matters involving territorial claims over the Spratly Islands to avoid disagreements (Presidential

Communications Operations Office 2011). The idea of a cooperative approach to resolving the territorial dispute is not new and has been floating for some two decades. ASEAN has been at the forefront of diplomatic initiatives to approach the dispute from a multilateral angle. The ASEAN–China Declaration on the Conduct of Parties in the South China Sea (DoC) of 2002 is often praised as a first step toward a peaceful settlement.[10] On paper, the DoC commits the signatories to resolve their territorial and jurisdictional disputes by peaceful means and in accordance with universally recognized principles of international law, including UNCLOS. Though not binding, and dependent upon the goodwill of signatory states, government officials and scholarly observers alike hope that the agreement will nevertheless oblige the Southeast Asian claimants and China to avoid any activity that would damage or complicate their relations.

CHINA AND SOUTHEAST ASIA

Relations between China and Southeast Asia have seen a substantial transformation from the days of mutual hostility based on and driven by deep ideological cleavages and the structural dynamics of the early Cold War period, to cautious and gradual rapprochement during the post-Mao period, and finally the full normalization of relations since the early 1990s. This most recent phase has been accompanied by the strengthening of multilateral channels of cooperation and positive-sum games in economic and security relations, but also rivalry related to the territorial disputes in the South China Seas.

The defining characteristic of the Mao period was China's support of communist parties and movements across Southeast Asia, which was at least partly facilitated by geographical closeness and cultural and historical factors. However, this strategy did not prove successful over a sustained period of time. This became most visible in the case of Vietnam, which was eventually 'lost' to the Soviet camp. After the death of Mao Zedong and the consolidation of Deng Xiaoping's position within China's leadership, fundamental transformations within China at the economic, social and political levels began to take place. Furthermore, changes in the international environment – such as China's rapprochement with the US and, later, the demise of the Soviet Union and communism in Eastern Europe – also contributed to a drastic change in the way China designed its foreign relations with Southeast Asia. The Sino-ASEAN relationship improved, moving from a mainly antagonistic period under Mao and the strictly anti-communist governments of the then ASEAN members towards a more conducive environment for constructive relations under Deng, which allowed both entities to find common ground in their respective international outlooks.

The first wave of normalization of diplomatic relations between China and Southeast Asia was mainly induced by the Sino-American strategic rapprochement of the early 1970s, which sent a tacit signal at least to some Southeast Asian countries that approaching China could now be tried, even if such rapprochement was still to be characterized by a high level of suspicion. Thus, Malaysia, Thailand and the Philippines established diplomatic relations with Beijing soon after the US re-engaged with China. Roughly one and a half decades later, the Vietnamese withdrawal from Cambodia and the end of the Soviet–Vietnamese alliance brought about significantly altered structural determinants, which had a marked impact on the mode of relations between China and Southeast Asia as a whole. This triggered the second wave of normalization of diplomatic relations of the late 1980s and early 1990s, involving Laos, Indonesia, Vietnam, Singapore and Brunei.

With regard to the broader international order, the implications of the fall of the Berlin Wall and the subsequent events for China were considerable as the larger sociopolitical and economic conceptual underpinnings of China's political system and development model seemingly began to lose legitimacy, initially not from within China but from outside its borders (Segal 1994). On the one hand, China would need to learn to further interact with the victors of the Cold War and play along with their norms within a restructured international order, as the defeated few survivors of this ideological conflagration were only a small cluster of weak states with no significant power to dictate the way forward at the regional and global level. The process of learning how to cope with this new international order and with the capitalist powers did not pass off without a period of analysis, often indicative of the fears of the Chinese leadership at the prospects of having diminished legitimacy to maintain their tight grip on the country's political rule.

Particularly sensitive after the Tiananmen incident, China's leadership interpreted the disappearance of the Soviet Union and its European satellite states as having the possibility of contributing to an erosion of the CPC's legitimacy at home and abroad. Furthermore, Beijing also feared an increased US world dominance and the development of a unipolar world system which could easily translate into added American pressure on China's regime. This all provided China with the opportunity for forging a positive re-engagement with its periphery, particularly Southeast Asia.

Another factor of significant importance in fostering a rapprochement between China and Southeast Asia was the diminished interest of the US in supporting security arrangements during the late 1980s and early 1990s. Even though the US was still to maintain its role as the most important international partner of ASEAN, its members began to expand their horizons and diversify their foreign policies in order to find more suitable regional arrangements and relations through which they envisioned to address their own concerns and interests in a more relevant and immediate way. As part of this strategy virtually all Southeast Asian governments reconceptualized China as a regional actor and soon started to acknowledge that China's economic reforms were generating a great deal of dynamism and growth which could potentially also benefit the ASEAN states (Kim 2006). In more recent years, the China–ASEAN Free Trade Agreement (CAFTA), which entered into force in 2010, has become the most potent metaphor for the economic win–win setting in China–Southeast Asia relations, although individual ASEAN members have benefited to varied degrees, with Malaysia as the frontrunner and Vietnam as the most negatively affected economy.

At the same time the South China Sea disputes have developed into a central and largely disturbing issue in Sino-ASEAN relations since it emerged in the late 1970s and first escalated a decade later. Since then particularly the bilateral Sino-Philippine and Sino-Vietnamese strands of the disputes have seen several circles of escalation and de-escalation. ASEAN's attempts to multilateralize the conflict have been successful only as far as official diplomacy and government rhetoric are concerned. In terms of realpolitik China's unilateral and at best bilateral approach to securing sovereignty over the South China Sea has prevailed to date. Overall, it is hard to ignore that China increasingly exerts regional leadership in Southeast Asia by setting the rules and organizing a growing network of bilateral and multilateral relationships in economic and security fields as a way of promoting Beijing's national interests. At the same time, leadership in international relations can only emerge and be institutionalized if the dominant regional power is willing to assume the responsibilities associated with it, is capable (in material terms of both hard and soft power) of establishing primacy, and is acceptable as a regional leader in the eyes of the subordinated states. While China's prominent role in shaping relations with Southeast Asia is largely accepted within the region, most ASEAN states are not yet prepared to put all their eggs in the China basket at the expense of weakening their respective relations with the US, Japan and, to a lesser extent, the European Union (EU). It would be too early to speak of a 'Pax Sinica' in Southeast Asia.

NOTES

1. ASEAN was founded in 1967 by Indonesia, Malaysia, the Philippines, Singapore and Thailand, and later joined by Brunei (1984), Vietnam (1995), Laos and Myanmar (1997) and Cambodia (1999).
2. *Peking Review*, 22 March 1968; see also *Peking Review*, no. 35, 29 August 1969.
3. *Peking Review*, 10 February 1969, pp. 24–25.
4. 'Malaysia', *Peking Review*, 8(2), 1965, pp. 14–15.
5. See, for example: 'ASEAN Secretariat Enters into Cooperation Agreement with Guangdong Province, China', September 2008, http://www.aseansec.org/21923.htm; 'ASEAN Plus Three Cooperation: Revised until January 2009', ASEAN+3 Cooperation Database, http://www.aseansec.org/4918.htm.
6. 'Dialogue partners' – a group also comprising the US, the European Union (EU), Russia, Japan, Australia and other major powers – interact with ASEAN in annual summit meetings of the heads of states and government and other institutionalized contexts.
7. 'Chinese Defense Minister Lauds New Security Concept', 6 September 2000, http://english.peopledaily.com.cn/english/200009/06/eng20000906_49894.html.
8. General Administration of Customs of China as reported by the ASEAN China Center, http://www.asean-china-center.org/english/2014-03/06/c_133164797.htm.
9. An EEZ extends to a distance of 200 nautical miles (370 km) beyond a coastal state's 12-mile territorial sea, and grants sovereign rights over the natural resources and exploitation in the zone, while preserving the freedom of navigation. Several coastal states had claimed EEZs since the 1940s, but it was not until 1982 that the third UNCLOS (United Nations Convention on the Law of the Sea) codified the EEZ.
10. The DoC is based on the earlier ASEAN Declaration on the South China Sea of 1992. In 2009 the ASEAN Political-Security Community Blueprint committed the group to 'work towards the adoption of a regional Code of Conduct in the South China Sea [CoC]'. In September 2012, Indonesia circulated a draft CoC – which is intended as a mechanism to implement the DoC – to ASEAN's foreign ministers. However, so far any initiatives to negotiate a CoC have been restricted to intra-ASEAN dialogues, while China has not yet made any formal commitment to participate in any such deliberations.

26. China and the European Union
Kerry Brown

The relationship between the European Union (EU) and the People's Republic of China (PRC) is one of the most important in the modern world. It ranks alongside that of the much higher-profile relationship between the USA and China, and yet it is much less analysed and understood. Despite this mutual importance, the EU and China pose some hard questions for each other, particularly in terms of how they conceptualize each other and find a common framework for engagement. They are markets that are interlocked and deeply interdependent, and globally important economic partners. But this one area of huge success is undermined by an array of political and security areas where their relationship is complex and often contentious. Particularly as a result of a series of constitutional changes since the Maastricht Treaty of 1993, the EU has acquired a number of new political, moral and social ambitions. This places it in conflict and disagreement with a China committed, at least rhetorically, to principles of non-interference and non-intervention beyond the zone of economics. The clash of values between the EU and China is well established and often cited, and it is this area that will be the focus of the discussion that follows.

That there is a general perception that the EU lacks hard political cohesiveness as an actor is not a controversial statement. This is certainly the consensus in China, as some of the material later in this chapter testifies. On military matters, for instance, the standard benchmark of hard power prowess, the EU is seen as far less than the sum of its member state parts. If it has acted at all in recent times, it has done so in the shadow of the US. The eruption of conflict in the Former Yugoslavia in the late 1990s marked the nadir of this tendency. Despite the fact that this conflict happened on its back doorstep, the EU did not intervene until emboldened by the US and in their shadow. Events like the collapse of Yugoslavia led eventually to attempts to implement a more uniform political and security framework in the Treaty of Lisbon in 2009. Since 2010 the EU's response to the unrest and uprisings in Libya, Syria and Ukraine shows that dependency on the US is still strong. The EU demonstrates that it prefers the power of verbal lectures over action.

Additionally, existing difficulties are compounded by the nature of the relationship between the EU and the PRC being seriously understudied in terms of good-quality theoretical material either in Chinese or in European languages. There are numerous reasons for the lack of good-quality analysis. The EU's internal understanding of its own attributes and how they appear is often as problematic for itself as for outsiders. Scholar officials such as Robert Cooper have called the EU something akin to the ultimate collection of 'postmodernist' states. The philosopher Jürgen Habermas, perhaps the single significant intellectual European figure of his generation to seriously address the existential problems posed by the EU, has labelled this project of pooling sovereignty a 'faltering' one. For him, the critical issue is 'the finalite of the unification process', a question that also bewilders many of those who constitute the electorate within the EU member states but who are unclear where the whole Union project is going (Habermas 2009: 81). At the heart of this confusion is the issue of which competences should be transferred to the EU, and which should remain within the states. This question provides fundamental conflicts, as political scientist Perry Anderson shows when he writes about the different intentions amongst the founding fathers of the Union in the 1950s, who divided between those who dreamed of a superstate, and those who saw the EU and its predecessors as a free market and nothing more (Anderson 2010: 23–24). The tension between these views – between European idealists on the one hand and pragmatists on the other – remains as strong now as when the EU was formed.

In contrast, China superficially provides an elegant unified veneer. Thus a richer and more instructive corpus of material exists on the nature of the Chinese state and its constituent parts and their functions than the EU, which is regarded as unappealingly complex. These materials range from the discussions of fragmented authoritarianism to those on the nature of central and local rule in China and the power of officials at different levels (Shue 1986; Lieberthal and Oksenberg 1988). Comparing the volume and quality of this literature with that devoted to the EU is instructive. From quantity alone, it could be said that people inside and outside China have thought harder and longer and come up with more models for the nature of the Chinese state than they have for the nature of the EU, even in the last two decades.

If there is confusion within an entity about the nature of its identity, then it is not surprising that this also infects the ways in which it relates to and thinks about others around it, including China. Furthermore the core constitutive EU documents have evolved since the creation of the European Economic Community by the Treaty of Rome in 1957, to 1993 when this was replaced by the EU. Enlargement from a core six states in 1957 to today's 28 only complicated things. A theoretical model is needed to capture the meaning of these changes and accurately determine the nature of the entity that eventually arose from them. Only a very dynamic theoretical model would be able to determine this. This model has yet to be found.

This chapter will give a survey of material looking at the more narrow issue of the relationship between the EU and China, and how this manifests the cognitive mismatch between the ways in which the EU and China understand themselves and how this self-understanding then impacts upon the way in which they see each other. The chapter will look, firstly, into descriptions of policy statements, and secondly, at the framework documents from government, analytic studies, comparative studies and political commentary. The objective will be to see whether there are any common links and messages between these different sources that help us to better conceptualize the relationship in the twenty-first century between them.

THE OFFICIAL DISCOURSE

From the first group of policy statements, there are three key documents that can be cited. Amongst the Chinese documents there are two White Papers on China's relations with the EU, issued by the State Council, one in 2003 and the second over a decade later in April 2014. These are the most authoritative high-level statements by the Chinese national government on its macro-political understanding of and intentions towards the EU. The 2003 document sets out the Chinese central government's world view and consensus vision on what the EU should represent:

> Both China and the EU stand for democracy in international relations and an enhanced role of the UN. Both are committed to combating international terrorism and promoting sustainable development through poverty elimination and environmental protection endeavors. China and the EU are highly complementary economically thanks to their respective advantages. (State Council 2003)

This White Paper additionally lists a number of political objectives, amongst which are strengthening high-level dialogues and visits, making the EU 'enforce the One China principle' regarding Taiwan, 'promoting the EU's understanding of Tibet', continuing the human rights dialogue, and strengthening mutual understanding between legislative entities and political parties in the EU and China. The targets included under economic cooperation are much more explicit, embracing trade and finance expansion, environment and science cooperation, and educational exchange. The military angle barely merits two brief paragraphs, perhaps as a covert symbolic gesture of Chinese disdain for the EU's hard power legitimacy.

A decade later, the updated White Paper, produced during President Xi Jinping's first ever visit to the headquarters of the EU in March 2014 as head of state of the PRC, is different in tone and content. Marked by the often frustrating experience of a decade of largely rhetorical commitment to strategic partnership with few solid outcomes beyond booming trade volumes, there was a more circumspect tone: 'China and the EU, the world's most representative emerging economy and group of developed countries respectively, are two major forces for world peace as they share important strategic consensus on building a multi-polar world', the paper states. It continues by stating that the two are partners for peace, growth, reform and civilization:

> China stands ready to work with the EU to better align China's comprehensive deepening of reform with the EU's reform and readjustment, draw upon each other's reform experience, share reform dividends, jointly improve the ability of reform and governance, and actively participate in the formulation and reform of the rules of global governance.

The dense repetition of the word 'reform' is ambiguous: a sign that while China understands its own needs to change, however it also sees similar structural needs in the EU, an entity keen to pronounce its superiority before 2008 but which has been humbled by the eurozone trauma since 2009. Echoing the comments that Xi Jinping had made during his speech at the College of Europe in Bruges on 31 March, the 2014 White Paper also accorded the two partnership on the basis of being civilizations, supplying a new Chinese mandated framework for their relationship: 'China stands ready to work with the EU to bring the two major civilizations in the East and West closer and set an example of different civilizations seeking harmony without uniformity, promoting diversity, learning from each other and enjoying common prosperity.' This label of 'civilizations' is a striking one, as it appears to aim at capturing some of the diversity that both China and the EU embrace within themselves, while showing concurrently their very different ways of finding internal unity (Xinhua 2014c). Despite this stress on sharing in the 2003 and 2014 papers, the strategic relationship over this period on the part of the EU failed to deliver the lifting of the arms embargo that it had imposed on China after the 1989 Tiananmen

Square massacre, nor grant China market economy status. This partly explains why the later paper is cooler and, over issues seen as core to China like Tibet and Taiwan, much more assertive.

Over this period the key document issued by the EU was the Communication of the Commission to the European Parliament of 24 October 2006:'The EU–China: Closer Partners, Growing Responsibilities'. This document describes the EU as 'the largest market in the world'. It states that it 'is home to a global reserve currency' which 'enjoys world leadership in key technologies and skills' and further states that 'the EU plays a central role in finding sustainable solutions to today's challenges, on the environment, on energy, on globalisation'. The EU has 'proved capable of exerting a progressive influence well beyond its borders and is the world's largest provider of development aid'. In the document, the EU posits China as 'a major power' and 'an increasingly important political actor'. For these reasons, 'the EU needs to respond effectively to China's renewed strength' and is required to do this on the basis of 'engagement and partnership'. The document then sets out a series of broad policy areas where this might happen: supporting China's transition towards a more open and liberal society, encouraging sustainable development, expanding trade and economic relations, and strengthening bilateral cooperation. The first of these targets is treated at length, and contains the most contentious issues addressed in the document: 'The EU must consider how it can most effectively assist China's reform process, making the case that better protection of human rights, a more open society, and more accountable government would be beneficial to China, and essential for continued economic growth', the document states. It is perhaps here that the official discourse which the EU and China use in the highest-level documents about each other is most starkly differentiated. Whereas the Chinese White Papers have presented objectives where it can see a change in the EU's views of them, for the EU in its prime declaration its objective is to see a fundamental change in the nature of governance within China itself (Commission to the Council of the European Parliament 2006). This difference in standpoint is clear in the other genres of literature examined below.

ANALYTIC COMMENTARY

China and the EU: A Common Future, edited by the late Stanley Crossick and Etienne Reuter (2008), contains essays covering the core areas of mutual interest between the two entities. As one of the few comprehensive overviews of EU–China relations in English, this book is useful purely for giving lists of interests and modes of operation between the two. Referring to the 'strategic partnership' agreed in 2003, Crossick and Reuter state that that the EU's interests are 'in commerce and other non-geopolitical areas', relations between the two 'are steady and pragmatic', and have become 'structurally asymmetrical'.'While the EU can deal with China as a sovereign unit, China often finds the EU is hardly a unit', they state. According to their analysis, there is the paradox that while provinces in China have a high degree of autonomy in policy enforcement, the central government is able to offer the final decision on agreements, but in dealing with the EU on key issues of importance to it, China still has to swivel between member states rather than negotiating centrally. Market economy status is a good example of this: something China has required the EU to grant it for a number of years, and where it has been rebuffed at EU multilateral level. This had driven it to seek to leverage influence at national level to create change (Crossick and Reuter 2008: 4–6).

There has been much debate on the meaning of 'strategic partnership'. Crossick and Reuter argue that the EU and China have had a different understanding of what the term actually means. The consensus within the EU, they state, is that 'the strategic partnership seeks to build on the current economic and trade relationship with a country whose global political and economic influence and power have grown substantially and will inevitably grow in the future'. For the Chinese, however, there was the assumption of a deeper shared vision of the international order. One Chinese voice in this collection, Dai Bingran, exemplifies this, giving a Chinese perspective on the meaning of this 'strategic partnership'. For him, 'both China and the EU need a peaceful international and regional environment'. They also have 'the common responsibility to address the negative effects of globalization' (Crossick and Reuter 2008: 254–256). As two important international entities, both share stakes and responsibilities and it would be 'more beneficial for them to work closely together' (Crossick and Reuter 2008: 253). After stating this aspiration to a shared vision, Dai has to acknowledge however that there are clear areas of distinctive difference in the mindsets within them both, making this deeper unity hard to achieve. 'The old ideological shadows still hang over the China–EU relationship', he states, citing the attempts to lift the arms embargo. 'It really is an irony', he argues, 'for the two parties to talk about building a strategic partnership between them, while one is still imposing political sanctions on the other'. The failure of the EU to eventually lift the embargo has 'taught China a lesson that the so called European foreign and security policy is still very far away, nor is the EU ready or able to resist political pressure from the US and others' (Crossick and Reuter 2008: 256–257).[1]

This dissonant tone reappears in the discussion in the book over trade issues, particularly the arguments on China being accorded market economy status; on reform of the World Trade Organization (WTO); on geopolitical issues regarding Iran, North Korea and Syria; and on technological and military partnership. On market economy status, Li Jinshan says that 'most Chinese see the treatment [of China] as a political rather than an economic or trading issue for the EU' (Crossick and Reuter 2008: 175). He states that misunderstanding comes more from the EU side than the Chinese side. 'Most Chinese', the author continues, 'may be quite ignorant about what is taking place in Europe, but they generally have no bad feelings or prejudices towards Europe. The case in Europe, however, is different, and distorted allegories and assertions are often heard' (Crossick and Reuter 2008: 262). In reference to geopolitical issues, Zhang Jun states that 'The EU has so far not been sufficiently involved in the regional co-operation of China's neighbourhood', in a discussion of ASEAN (Crossick and Reuter 2008: 1067). On African issues, Zhang Tiejun writes that 'there are substantial differences between the Chinese and European approaches' (Crossick and Reuter 2008: 156). In all these areas, therefore, it is hard to see what 'strategic partnership' really means where there are so many clear differences in approach and objectives.

There is high-quality analytic material on very specific aspects of the EU–China relationship. These too offer insights into how their structural and ontological differences impact upon the way in which they relate to each other and the value of their dialogue at a very practical level. Katrin Kinzelbach and Hatla Thelle exemplify this by offering an analysis of the EU–China human rights dialogue process. 'Contrary to the EU's original expectations, the [expert human rights] seminars have not served to revitalize the bilateral human rights dialogue or to resolve differences', they state. Instead, they serve as more of an appeasement to public opinion, at least in the EU: 'Political leaders from both sides can avoid an exchange on highly sensitive concerns by reassuring each other at the regular EU China [high level political] summits that they place a 'high value on the EU China human rights dialogue'. Leaders are 'willing to accept tensions on human rights issues as long as they only play out at lower level meetings, leaving the high level political contacts unaffected' (Kinzelbach and Thelle 2011: 73).

Kinzelbach and Thelle concentrate on the way in which EU and China human rights expert and official dialogues have been conducted since the 1990s and identify a number of procedural and structural aspects that have made them increasingly less effective. They offer empirical evidence based on interviews with participants over how both the subject matter for the seminars and those participating drifted away from core areas considered sensitive, and where the objectives set at the start of the dialogues were largely unmatched by their subsequent conduct and outcomes.

Annabel Egan also studies the process of the human rights dialogue, and shows that the problems and challenges experienced in this sensitive area are symptomatic of the discourse clash between the EU and China more generally. In an unpublished PhD thesis she argues that 'the first task for the EU therefore, must be to identify its own priorities and distinguish between those that relate to violations which stem from capacity issues and those that relate to violations which stem from deliberate policy' in the human rights area (Egan 2013: 277). As a developing country, China has been able to excuse itself from meeting the international benchmark standards in terms of delivery of justice and other human rights because of sheer lack of capacity rather than an outcome of deliberate policy choices. However, the EU has to decide where division between these two – failure due to lack of capacity or due to deliberate intent – finally lies. Often the EU frames its approach to China on the moral basis that it feels the system is existentially committed to deliberate violations of human rights as a political tool to forge unity and fear by the government within China, but at other times uses a more tolerant, pragmatic acceptance that as a developing country China's demand to be held to less stringent standards at the moment and concern that its distinct current stage needs to be taken into account, is conceded to. This conceptual tension has yet to be cleared up within the member states in Europe, and because of this the EU has rarely had a powerful and consistent position across the member states on its approach to rights issues in China.

COMPARATIVE MATERIAL

The theoretically richest group of publications on the EU and China is contained in works which place the relationship in the context of their standing with the US. *US–China–EU Relations: Managing the New World Order* edited by Robert Ross, Oystein Tunsjo and Tuosheng Zhang in 2010 is perhaps the most sophisticated of these, largely because it places different attempts to framework the natures of the EU, China and US beside each other, and draws out contrasts that are useful in conceptualizing their relationships between each other. Labelling it as a 'civilian power', Hans Maull states that the EU aspires to be 'transformative', a model of 'the kind of international order to which the EU aspires'. In undertaking this mission, the EU has to have 'a specific portfolio of capabilities, instruments, and skills' which 'have the ability to shape international outcomes' (Maull 2010: 50–51). Recognizing that another way by which to describe this is 'normative', Maull draws up an impressive list of methods by which the EU seeks to promote a 'civilizational hegemon': a culture of non-violent conflict management, rule of law and strong institutions, participatory decision making, and social justice and sustainability. In terms of how these link to international objectives, Maull presents a subsidiary list of objectives. These embrace 'the development of a stronger international society, well functioning international institutions and a rules-based international order' and 'taming the passion of states and spreading the rule of law. To make power lawful and law powerful.' The summary of this is the statement in the European Security Strategy issued in 2003 in Brussels, which says that 'the best protection for our security is a world of well governed democratic states' (Maull 2010: 54–55). The EU does therefore have clear international policy objectives, but its means of finding influence and geopolitical capital are more abstract and more dispersed, based on moral rather than brute political influence. Eschewing its fractious, bloodshed past, in the postmodern world, the EU presents itself as 'non-threatening', an 'attractive pole for many member states who wish to join it' (Maull 2010: 57).

The EU's material assets in this context are only the means to an end. They are the advertisements for the superiority of its governance system and its respect for stability and the predictability that legality brings. They are also predicated on the EU being a source of experience and skills, a knowledge repository. These are the key weaponry in the EU seeking mitigation for its lack of hard power by claiming persuasive power, 'to offer superior solutions to shared problems'. 'Given its economic wealth and its emphasis on economic integration the EU is obviously in a good position to offer enticements', Maull says (2010: 58). Its economic power also gives it negotiation weight, allowing it to use the carrot-and-stick method where its key incentive is access to the world's largest market and the wealth that this contains. The power of desire for access to this market is also a major negotiation asset when the EU attempts to be able to secure global standards outside itself, which accord with its self-interest. But as Maull points out, the great weakness of the EU and one that China has managed to often highlight is 'lack of strategic flexibility'. When it meets partners that 'may not be inclined to be influenced, persuaded or socialized' its powers of persuasion suddenly appear very limited.

The nature of these limits is well outlined by Salvatore Finamore in a chapter in *The EU, the US and China: Towards a New International Order?*, edited by Jing Men and Wei Shen (2014).Comparing EU and US engagements with China, Finamore writes that 'The United States and Europe, along with most other western actors, share a long list of similar concerns with regard to China's resurgence as a great power' (Jing and Shen 2014: 107).These range from trade related issues, concern over trade deficits between the EU and US in their relations with China, and worries over political and security related fields. 'Although American and European approaches to China seem to overlap in the substance of their goals and values there are significant differences in degree and context,' Finamore explains. 'The main distinction between the United States and Europe is that between a superpower on the one hand and a great power on the other hand, which. . . is certainly not a key strategic player in the region' (Finamore 2014: 109–110). Finamore aligns with Maull in describing a world in which an EU bereft of the main indicators of hard power is left to rely on forms of persuasion, moral influence and socialization of the preferability of its own model as an inducement to getting a partner like China to want to work with it. The main elements of its armoury of persuasion are material incentives, which in effect means access to its market, and what Finamore calls 'social influence through politics of naming and shaming', along with dialogue (Finamore 2014: 107). Somewhat contentiously, Finamore argues that 'the EU and US today share the same long term policy goals with respect to China, as well as the overall strategy for achieving them' (Finamore 2014: 119). One could argue back that in fact, as market state actors, the EU and US are most definitely not harmonious towards each other and both want better access to the Chinese market. Their main task in the last decade since Chinese entry to the WTO in late 2001 has been to leverage the globalization and standardization of trade norms in order to extract market benefit for themselves, despite the fact that the latitude for doing unique bilateral deals has been limited, at least until the recent resurgence of free trade agreements since the late 2000s. The issue then is what sort of incentives the EU can offer to challenge the US in this area.

Comparing the EU and US strategic approaches to China, and their long-term objectives, at least in terms of recent scholarly literature, proves productive in teasing out a clearer idea of the specificities of EU behaviour. Once one strips away the similarities as sovereign states that the US and China have, one can then see more clearly where the EU is more unique as an actor, and how it differentiates itself from the US in terms of its political, economic and social engagement with China.

POLITICAL COMMENTARY

This stress on the privileging of moral and cultural persuasion mixed with market tactics is best represented by a report issued by the European Council for Foreign Relations in 2009, *A Power Audit of EU–China Relations*, co-authored by British diplomat John Fox and French analyst Francois Godemont. This states in its opening chapter that:

> The EU's China strategy is based on an anachronistic belief that China, under the influence of European engagement, will liberalise its economy, improve the rule of law and democratise its politics. The underlying idea is that engagement with China is positive in itself and should not be conditional on any specific Chinese behaviour. (Fox and Godemont 2009: 1)

Fox and Godemont aim to bring down to size the onus within the EU on persuasion and moral and cultural influence, for they see it ranged against a China whose 'foreign and domestic policy has evolved in a way that has paid little heed to European values, and today Beijing regularly contravenes or even undermines them'. They see a China that is increasingly powerful and able to resist foreign interference, a China with highly certain internal values and identity, which has immense control over the levers of its foreign policy in term of how it is articulated and how it is then delivered. Mocking EU policy towards China as 'unconditional engagement', they plot how the EU has allowed itself to open up to a country and polity that is able to exploit its vanity and internal divisions in order to maximize its gains, while largely ignoring the imprecations of the EU for change and reform.

Even in the areas of economic engagement and market relations, Godemont and Fox see asymmetry that has grown from a European naivety and softness:

> The EU allows China to throw many more obstacles in the way of European companies that want to enter the Chinese market than Chinese companies face in the EU – one reason why the EU's trade deficit with China has swollen to a staggering €169 billion, even as the EU has replaced the US as China's largest trading partner. (Fox and Godemont 2009: 2)

This seems to be a restatement of the commercial principle that turnover is vanity, and that concrete profit alone is the real measure to aim for. The EU has vast trade relations with China, but the real profit largely accrues to the Chinese side. The fundamental cause of the problem, as Fox and Godemont's audit seeks to show, is that the EU is divided within itself. It contains what they claim are four distinct groups of member states: assertive industrialists, such as Germany or Poland, who are willing to stand up to China politically and commercially; ideological free traders such as the UK and Denmark who are ready to pressure China on politics but not if it gets in the way of trade; accommodating mercantilists such as Greece, Finland and Hungary, who believe that good political relations with China will lead to commercial benefits; and lastly, European followers who 'prefer to defer to the EU when conducting their relations with China'. These include Belgium, Ireland, Estonia and Latvia.

'Europeans tend to treat China as a malleable polity to be shaped by European engagement. But the reality is that China is a skilful and pragmatic power that knows how to manage the EU', state Fox and Godemont (2009: 8). They draw on a number of areas from energy policy to trade to human rights where the EU's stated collective policies have led to little substantive change in China itself, despite the aspiration to be a partner in reform. The elegant framework that this fine piece of polemic offers, however, often trips up in the real world it is meant to be about. European countries do not fit so easily into the four groups they outline. The UK, in 2012, received the harshest reprisals for the meeting between Prime Minister David Cameron and the Dalai Lama in London, with a suspension of visits at ministerial level for over a year, despite belonging to a group put down as less assertive than Germany or Poland. Germany in many ways operated as the ultimate pragmatist, but could do this because it was the sole EU country with a trade surplus with China, giving it extra leverage. Fox and Godemont show little interest in these subtle existing nuances, nor in the question of how positive for Europe's overall image in China are Chinese evaluations of the values the EU says it represents, something proved by a major Nottingham University–Chinese Academy of Social Sciences report from 2010 to 2013 which showed that on the whole these values were admired, even if they were not felt to be directly applicable to China (China Policy Institute, 2010–2013).

One thing the audit did achieve was to attract the irritated attention of the Chinese leadership, with a bewildered Wen Jiabao referring to it in a speech in 2009. Even so, the power audit document was highly representative of a critique of EU–China relations on the European side which felt that a process of irresistible appeasement was occurring; that the strategy of the EU to seek influence based on its confidence in its values over China was the best bet; and that China was morally, politically and intellectually painted as a foe or lesser partner, in addition to an ideological and geopolitical threat that needed to be dealt with. The document was highly symptomatic therefore of an antagonistic political attitude towards China in the EU. Oddly enough, the premises of its critique only underlined just how deeply the EU and China approach each other with a values mismatch.

THE DISCOURSE OF EU–CHINA RELATIONS: AN AUDIT

Looking at the range of material from the four different genres described above, there are two striking commonalities. First, no matter what genre is looked at, the political identity issue is the hardest to obtain conceptual clarity about, and the one that causes the largest problems. It is not accurate to say that discussion between the EU and China of specific political issues is hard; it is a more fundamental issue. They clearly do not understand what framework to see each other in, and the material often offers evidence of a monumental exercise in talking at cross-purposes. The root of this is self-conceptualization, and it is evident that there exists a very stark contrast between the way each entity sees itself and the way it thinks the other should see it. The EU is more problematic than China because of its more complex internal nature, and its largely undecided self-identity. The failure of the EU to be clearer about its political nature vexes almost all the material that deals with the relationship. The introduction of the US as a comparator in fact only makes this issue clearer. It shows up sharply the mystery of final destination which still lies at the heart of the EU project, and the fact that this mystery is hardly soluble because of what Habermas referred to as a lack of consensus internally about whether this final destination is a superstate or a super-market.

Another facet that compounds the confusion on identity and the nature of the EU–China relationship is that while the EU is vague about its political identity, it frequently sounds very certain about its values, at least when its officials speak, or official documents such as the Commission Communication of 2006 quoted above. Going from these, and much of the commentary that has grown up around them, values are a core part of identity and evidently matter to the EU. But Fox and Godemont give a diagnostic of the mismatch between the role of values for the EU and how differently they appear for China in its external engagement. Looking at this a little more deeply, however, we can see that the larger problem is caused by the fact that beneath a strong rhetorical commitment to values, the EU is in fact itself deeply divided over what is the precise nature of these values. Within the EU member states, there is disagreement on what sort of emphasis needs to be given to human rights, to legal rights, and to other social and political freedoms, and on how they need to figure in the relationship with China. Some member states wish to adopt a pragmatic view of values, and others a more absolute tone. The Czech Republic, Poland and Slovenia, for instance, have a harsher view of how to prosecute the values dialogue with China and where to set the bar when public condemnations and formal diplomatic protest are necessary. Possibly this is linked to each of these three countries recently emerging from Communist systems, and having new freedoms and identities that they hold more dearly and more closely to themselves (if that is the case, then Romania, which is far more emollient towards these issues with China, subverts this pattern, despite its similar political past as a member of the Communist bloc). The UK and Germany, in comparison, might be ranked as pragmatic in their values. Pragmatic or absolute, however, the most one can conclude is that whatever the confusion over definitions and precise meanings, the notion of values and how contentious they are figures in almost all the discussion of

EU–China relations. This even makes an appearance in the seemingly most self-interested economic material, where some forms of material engagement are legitimized by the EU because of changes they might bring to China's political or cultural behaviour.

The search to find a means by which to fruitfully talk about the values without becoming hopelessly abstract or antagonistically preachy has taken up much time over the last two decades. So much time has been spent on it, and it figures so prominently, probably because in many ways the EU remains a highly idealistic creation, a victory of ideas with much promise but great failures so far as what it has actually delivered, and this idealism infiltrates its view of others and its relations with them. The tension between what it is and what it should be particularly infects its language towards China, the ultimate pragmatic, non-idealistic polity (at least in its post-Deng manifestation). A China where 'practice is the sole criterion of truth' and in which we 'seek truth from facts' is pitted against an EU where there are visions, hopes and aspirations for a better world despite the parlous nature of the present one. This is also a world in which, most bewilderingly of all, the EU seeks influence and persuasion through its standing by these as yet to be realized ideals. Ironically, this may well be the source of the distrust between China and the EU, where China feels itself being recruited into a speculative project about which it has no clearer idea about the final outcome than does the EU itself. The Chinese view may be: 'Why not just live in the here and now of the market, than start on some quest for fulfilling the ideals a partner has about your future which might never happen'.

A Chinese attempt to resolve this issue of how best to view the EU appeared in the formulation used by the Chinese President when visiting Brussels in March 2014,when he referred to the EU–China relationship as being between civilizational partners. But creeping towards a common value basis, or accepting the need to respect each other's values on relative equality, has yet to be achieved. China can be described as having embarked on an ongoing search for status and respect. The EU has to make a strategic choice between putting the main emphasis on political suasion so that it might see a China come into view more like itself – a highly idealistic endpoint – or to follow its more pragmatic nature and work with a China that wants to see values on both sides taken seriously. The strategy for the EU now should be to ask China to spell out in much more detail what its values are. That is the path that is likely to occur in the coming few years. The search for a common language not just of market relations but also of social, political and even spiritual ambitions therefore continues, and remains the underlying intellectual project between the EU and China.

ACKNOWLEDGEMENT

I am very grateful for comments and help with this chapter by Noel Kwon and Rebecca Fabrizi.

NOTE

1. Dai is referring to the fact that the EU attempts to lift the arms embargo in 2004 were brought to a halt by the US.

Glossary of Chinese terms

baoli	a violent incident
bianzhi	*nomenklatura*, table of names
chengfen	social position (class composition in class analysis)
chengguan	city patrol personnel
chushen	social origin (class origin in class analysis)
danwei	social unit (of life and production)
dibao	minimum subsistence level livelihood guarantee
gaokao	national university entrance examination
guanxi	special relationship
heping fazhan	(China's) peaceful development
heping jueqi	(China's) peaceful rise
hexie shehui	harmonious society
hukou	household registration (system)
kexue fashan	scientific development
quntixing shijian	mass incidents of social unrest
sheng	province
shengwei	CCP provincial party committee
shuanggui	arrest without trial
suzhi	(individual, personal) quality
taoguang yanghui	'hide brightness, nourish obscurity' (principle of foreign policy)
tiliu	allowed surcharge
weibo	Sina weibo – a Chinese form of social media akin to Facebook and Twitter
xian	county
xiang	village
xiaokang (*shehui*)	prosperous (society)
xitong	political and administrative system
yuan	dollar, renminbi (RMB) unit of currency
zizhi (*qu*)	autonomous area; minority nationality administrative (region)

References

Agnew, John (1990), 'The Regional Systems Approach to Agrarian Societies: A Critical Appreciation of the Work of G. William Skinner', Annual Meeting of the Association of American Geographers, Toronto.

Agnew, John (2009), *Globalization and Sovereignty*, Lanham, MD: Rowman & Littlefield.

Ahluwalia, I.J. (2007), 'Indian Economy Update. Addressing a Conference on The Future of India in the World Economy', OECD Development Centre, Paris, 22 June 2007, available at http://www.oecd.org/document/30/0,3343,en_2649_201185_38779998_ 1_1_1_1,00.html.

Ahn, Byung-joon (1976), *Chinese Politics and the Cultural Revolution: Dynamics and Policy Processes*, Seattle, WA: University of Washington Press.

Ahn, Byung-joon (1983), *Chinese Politics and the Cultural Revolution, 2, The Great Leap Forward, 1958–1960*, New York: Columbia University Press.

Alden, Chris and Daniel Large (2011), 'China's Exceptionalism and the Challenges of Delivering Difference in Africa', *Journal of Contemporary China*, 20(68): 21–38.

All-China Federation of Trade Unions (ed.) (1985), *Zhonggong zhongyang guanyu gongren yundong wenjian xuanbian* (Compilation of Central Communist Party documents concerning the labour movement), Beijing: Archives Press.

Althusser, L. (1971), 'Ideology and Ideological State Apparatuses', *Lenin and Philosophy and Other Essays*, London: New Left Books.

An, Gang (2013), 'Rejecting the G2: China's Rise Should Not Be Accompanied by Hegemony', *Beijing Review*, 40(29 September).

Anagnostou, Dia (2001), 'Breaking the Cycle of Nationalism', *South European Society and Politics*, 6(1): 99–124.

Anderson, P. (2010), *The New Old World Order*, London: Verso.

Andersson, Fredrik N.G., David L. Edgerton and Sonja Opper (2013), 'A Matter of Time: Revisiting Growth Convergence in China', *World Development*, 45: 239–251.

Andors, P. (1983), *The Unfinished Liberation of Chinese Women: 1949–1980*, Bloomington, IN: Indiana University Press

Ang, Cheng Guan (1998), 'Vietnam–China Relations since the End of the Cold War', *Asian Survey*, 38(12): 1122–1141.

Ang, Yuen Yuen (2009), 'Centralizing Treasury Management in China: The Rationale of the Central Reformers', *Public Administration and Development*, 29: 263–273.

Ansfield, Jonathan (2012), 'How Crash Cover-Up Altered China's Succession', *New York Times*, 4 December.

Anyang City People's Congress (2012), *Difang renda changweihui fazhan licheng zhong zhongda shijian* (Significant events in the development of standing committee of local People's Congresses), 2 January, available at http://www.anyangrenda.gov.cn/Article/ShowArticle.asp?ArticleID=1075.

Appadorai, A. (1982), *Selected Documents on India's Foreign Policy and Relations: 1947–1972*, Oxford: Oxford University Press.

Areddy, James (2011), 'China Moves to Strengthen Grip Over Supply of Rare-Earth Metals', *Wall Street Journal*, 7 February.
Arkush, R. David and Leo O. Lee (eds) (1993), *Land Without Ghosts: Chinese Impressions of America from the Mid-Nineteenth Century to the Present*, Berkeley, CA: University of California Press.
Armijo, Leslie Elliott and Saori N. Katada (eds), (forthcoming), *Financial Statecraft of Emerging Powers: Asia and Latin America in Comparative Perspective*, New York: Palgrave Macmillan.
Asahi Shinbun (2013), 'Shasetsu: senkaku ichinen, amari ni ōku o ushinatta', 7 September, p. 12.
ASEAN Secretariat (2010), *ASEAN–China Free Trade Area: Not a Zero-Sum Game*, available at http://www.aseansec.org/24161.htm (accessed 26 February 2013).
Asian Development Bank (2004), *Poverty Profile of the People's Republic of China*, Manila: Asian Development Bank.
Associated Press (2012), 'China's Rare Earth Quota Faces WTO Complaint', March, available at http://www.cbc.ca/news/business/story/2012/03/13/china-rare-earth.html.
Ba, Alice D. (2003), 'China and ASEAN: Renavigating Relations for the 21st-century Asia', *Asian Survey*, 43(4): 662–647.
Bachman, David (1991), *Bureaucracy, Economy, and Leadership in China: The Institutional Origins of the Great Leap Forward*, Cambridge: Cambridge University Press.
Bachman, David (1992), 'The Limits on Leadership in China', *Asian Survey*, 32(11): 1046–1062.
Bader, Jeffrey A. (2012), *Obama and China's Rise: An Insider's Account of America's Asia Strategy*, Washington, DC: Bookings Institution Press.
Baker, Dean (2011), 'China's Chance to Become our Economic Saviour', *Guardian*, 22 September.
Baker, James A., III (1995), *The Politics of Diplomacy*, New York: Putnam.
Baldwin, David A. (1985), *Economic Statecraft*, Princeton, NJ: Princeton University Press.
Bangura, Yusuf (ed.) (2015), *Developmental Pathways to Poverty Reduction*, Basingstoke: Palgrave Macmillan.
Bao, Shy and Gao Qi (1958), *Gege saiguo Mu Guiying* (Everyone surpasses Mu Guiying), *Women of China*, April: 4.
Barabantseva, Elena (2008), 'From the Language of Class to the Rhetoric of Development', *Journal of Contemporary China*, 17(56): 565–589.
Barnett, A. Doak (1964), *Communist China: The Early Years, 1949–1955*, New York: Praeger.
Barnett, A. Doak (1967), *Cadres, Bureaucracy, and Political Power in Communist China*, New York, USA and London, UK: Columbia University Press.
Baum, Richard (1994), *Burying Mao: Chinese Politics in the Age of Deng Xiaoping*, Princeton, NJ: Princeton University Press.
BBC News (2011), 'China Debate over Minibus Gift Following Deadly Crash', 28 November, available at http://www.bbc.co.uk/news/world-asia-china-15916190.
BBC News (2013), 'Chinese Bank Tops Global Ranking for the First Time', 1 July, available at http://www.bbc.co.uk/news/business-23122491.
Bebel, August (1879 [1910]), *Women and Socialism*, transl. Meta L. Stern, New York: Socialist Literature Co.

Becker, Jasper (2000), *The Chinese*, New York: Free Press.
Becquelin, Nicolas (1997), 'Trouble on the Marches', *China Perspectives*, 10: 19–28.
Beijing Review (1981), 'Resolution on Certain Questions in the History Of Our Party Since the Founding of the People's Republic of China', 27 June.
Béland, D. and K.M. Yu (2004), 'A Long Financial March: Pension Reform in China', *Journal of Social Policy*, 33: 267–288.
Bell, Stephen and Hui Feng (2013), *The Rise of the People's Bank of China: The Politics of Institutional Change*, Cambridge, MA: Harvard University Press.
Bergsten, C. Fred (2005), *The United States and the World Economy*, Washington, DC: Institute for International Economics.
Bergsten, C. Fred, Bates Gill, Nicholas R. Lardy and Derek Mitchell (2007), *China: The Balance Sheet: What the World Needs to Know Now about the Emerging Superpower*, New York: Public Affairs.
Bernstein, Richard and Ross H. Munro (1997), *The Coming Conflict with China*, New York: Alfred A. Knopf.
Bernstein, T.P. and X.B. Lü (2000), 'Taxation Without Representation: Peasants, the Central and the Local States in Reform China', *China Quarterly*, 163: 742–763.
Bernstein, T.P. and X. Lü (2003), *Taxation without Representation in Contemporary Rural China*, Cambridge: Cambridge University Press.
Bevir, M. (2010), *Democratic Governance*, Princeton, NJ: Princeton University Press.
Bevir, M. (2013), *A Theory of Governance*, Berkeley, CA: University of California Press.
Bi, Mingxin (2011), 'China, EU Hold Human-Rights Dialogue in the CCP', 18 June, available at http://english.people.com.cn/90001/90776/90883/7413769.html (accessed 6 July 2014).
Bian, Yanjie and J.R. Logan (1996), 'Market Transition and the Persistence of Power: The Changing Stratification System in Urban China', *American Sociological Review*, 61: 739–758.
Bian, Yanjie and Zhanxin Zhang (2004), 'Urban Elites and Income Differential in China: 1988–1995', *Japanese Journal of Political Science*, 5: 51–68.
Bianco, Lucien (1971), *Origins of the Chinese Revolution: 1915–1949*, Stanford, CA: Stanford University Press.
Bin, Ke (2008), 'Yi li xuanzhe yu zhongguo duiwai yuanzu de bianhua' (The choice between justice and virtue, and changes in China's foreign aid), *Xiangchao* (Hunan Tide), August: 36.
Bo, Yibo (1991, 1993), *Ruogan zhongda juece yu shijian de huigu* (Reflections on Certain Major Decisions and Events), 2 vols, Beijing: Zhonggong zhongyang dangxiao chubanshe.
Bo, Zhiyue (1996), 'Native Local Leaders and Political Mobility in China: Home Province Advantage?', *Provincial China*, 2: 2–15.
Bo, Zhiyue (2002a), *Chinese Provincial Leaders: Economic Performance and Political Mobility since 1949*, Armonk, NY: M.E. Sharpe.
Bo, Zhiyue (2002b), 'Economic Development and Corruption: Beijing Beyond "Beijing"', *Journal of Contemporary China*, 9(25): 467–487.
Bo, Zhiyue (2003), 'The Provinces: Training Ground for National Leaders or a Power in their Own Right?' in David M. Finkelstein and Maryanne Kivlehan (eds), *China's Leadership in the 21st Century*, Armonk, NY: M.E. Sharpe, pp. 66–117.

Bo, Zhiyue (2004), 'The Institutionalization of Elite Management in China', in Barry J. Naughton and Dali L. Yang (eds), *Holding China Together*, New York: Cambridge University Press, pp. 70–100.

Bo, Zhiyue (2007a), *China's Elite Politics: Political Transition and Power Balancing*, Singapore: World Scientific.

Bo, Zhiyue (2007b), 'The PLA and the Provinces: The Military District and Local Issues', in David M. Finkelstein and Kristen Gunness (eds), *Civil–Military Relations in Today's China: Swimming in a New Sea*, Armonk, NY: M.E. Sharpe, pp. 96–130.

Bo, Zhiyue (2008), 'The 17th Politburo Candidates: From Provinces to Beijing', in Te-sheng Chen (ed.), *Political Recruitment and Local Governance in the 17th Congress of the Chinese Communist Party*, Taipei: INK Publishing, pp. 133–185.

Bo, Zhiyue (2010a), 'China's Model of Democracy', *International Journal of China Studies*, 1(1): 102–124.

Bo, Zhiyue (2010b), *China's Elite Politics: Governance and Democratization*, Singapore: World Scientific.

Boden, J. (2008), *The Wall behind China's Open Door: Towards Efficient Intercultural Management in China*, Brussels: ASP-VUB Press.

Borg, C., J. Buttigieg and P. Mayo (eds) (2002), *Gramsci and Education*, Boulder, CO: Rowman & Littlefield.

Bottelier, Peter (2006), 'China and the World Bank: How a Partnership Was Built', Stanford Center for International Development Working Paper 277, available at http://www.stanford.edu/group/siepr/cgi-bin/siepr/?q=system/files/shared/pubs/papers/pdf/SCID277.pdf (accessed 19 February 2009).

Bourdieu, P. (1984), *Distinction: A Social Critique of the Judgement of Taste*, Cambridge: Cambridge University Press.

Bradsher, Keith and Chris Buckley (2014), 'China Fines GlaxoSmithKline Nearly $500 Million in Bribery Case', *New York Times*, 21 September.

Bratton, Michael (1989), 'The politics of NGO relations in Africa', *World Development*, 17(4): 569–587.

Bräuner, Oliver (2012), 'How Europe shies from Taiwan', *Diplomat*, 20 March.

Brautigam, Deborah (2009), *The Dragon's Gift: The Real Story of China in Africa*, Oxford: Oxford University Press.

Brautigam, Deborah and Tang Xiaoyang (2012), 'Economic Statecraft in China's New Overseas Special Economic Zones: Soft Power, Business, or Resource Security?', IFPRI Discussion Paper 01168, March.

Bray, M. and R. Koo (eds) (2004), *Education and Society in Hong Kong and Macau: Comparative Perspectives on Continuity and Change*, Aarhus, Denmark: Comparative Education Research Centre, University of Hong Kong, and Kluwer Academic Publishers.

Breslin, Shaun (1996), *China in the 1980s: Center–Province Relations in a Reforming Socialist State*, London: Macmillan.

Breslin, Shaun (2010), 'China's Emerging Global Role: Dissatisfied Responsible Great Power', *Politics*, 30(s1): 52–62.

Breznitz, Dan and Michael Murphree (2011), *Run of the Red Queen: Government, Innovation, Globalization, and Economic Growth in China*, New Haven, CT: Yale University Press.

BRICS (2014), 'Sixth BRICS Summit – Fortaleza Declaration', available at http://brics6.itamaraty.gov.br/media2/press-releases/214-sixth-brics-summit-fortaleza-declaration (accessed 20 July 2014).

Brødsgaard, Kjeld Erik (2001), 'China's Cadres: Professional Revolutionaries or State Bureaucrats? (I)', Singapore: East Asian Institute Background Brief, No. 94, 11 July.

Brødsgaard, Kjeld Erik (2002), 'Institutional Reform and the Bianzhi System in China', *China Quarterly*, 170: 361–386.

Brødsgaard, Kjeld Erik (2012), 'Politics and Business Group Formation in China: The Party in Control?', *China Quarterly*, 211: 624–648.

Brook, Timothy and B. Michael Frolic (1997), 'The Ambiguous Challenge of Civil Society', in T. Brook and B.M. Frolic (eds), *Civil Society in China*, Armonk, NY: M.E. Sharpe, pp. 3–16.

Brzezinski, Zbigniew (1983), *Power and Principle: Memoirs of the National Security Adviser, 1977–1981*, New York: Farrar Straus & Giroux.

Buckley, Chris (2013), 'Portrait of Deng as Reformer in 1978 Plenum Ignores History', 9 November, available at http://sinosphere.blogs.nytimes.com/2013/11/09/portrait-of-deng-as-reformer-in-1978-plenum-ignores-history/?ref=asia.

Bullard, Monte (1985), *China's Political–Military Evolution: The Party and the Military in the PRC, 1960–1984*, Boulder, CO: Westview Press.

Bullard, Monte (1997), *The Soldier and Citizen: The Role of the Military in Taiwan's Development*, Armonk, NY: M.E. Sharpe.

Burns, John P. (ed.) (1989), *The Chinese Communist Party's Nomenklatura System*, Armonk, NY: M.E. Sharpe.

Burns, John P. (1994), 'Strengthening Central CCP Control of Leadership Selection: The 1990 Nomenklatura', *China Quarterly*, 138: 458–491.

Bush, George W. (2002), 'The President's State of Union Address', 29 January, available at http://georgewbush-whitehouse.archives.gov/news/releases/2002/01/20020129-11.html (accessed 11 April 2014).

Bush, George and Brent Scowcroft (1998), *A World Transformed*, New York: Alfred A. Knopf.

Buzan, Barry (2004), *The United States and the Great Powers: World Politics in the Twenty- First Century*, Cambridge: Polity Press.

Buzan, Barry (2010), 'China in International Society: Is "Peaceful Rise" Possible?', *Chinese Journal of International Politics*, 3(1): 5–36.

Byron, John and Robert Pack (1992), *The Claws of the Dragon: Kang Sheng – The Evil Genius Behind Mao – and His Legacy of Terror in People's China*, New York: Simon & Schuster.

Cabestan, Jean-Pierre (2010), 'The New Détente in the Taiwan Strait and Its Impact on Taiwan's Security and Future', *China Perspectives*, 3: 22–33.

CADC (2014), 'Changes to the Administrative Divisions of China', unpublished database co-developed by the University of Technology, Sydney and East China Normal University, Shanghai', *China Quarterly*, 193: 24–42.

Cai, Yongshun (2008), 'Local Governments and the Suppression of Popular Resistance in China', *The China Quarterly*, 193, pp. 24–42.

Callahan, William (2009), 'The Cartography of National Humiliation and the Emergence of China's Geobody', *Public Culture*, 21(1): 141–173.

Callahan, William (2013), *China Dreams: 20 Visions of the Future*, New York: Oxford University Press.

Cao, Jianguang (2008), 'Guonei defang zhili yanjiu shuping' (Review on local governance studies in China), *Dongnan Xueshu* (Southeast Academia), 2: 65–71.

Cartier, C. (2001), '"Zone Fever," the Arable Land Debate, and Real Estate Speculation: China's Evolving Land Use Regime and its Geographical Contradictions', *Journal of Contemporary China*, 10(28): 445–469.

Cartier, C. (2002), 'Origins and Evolution of a Geographical Idea: The Macroregion in China', *Modern China*, 28(1): 79–142.

Cartier, C. (2005), 'City-Space: Scale Relations and China's Spatial Administrative Hierarchy', in L. Ma and F. Wu (eds), *Restructuring the Chinese City*, New York: Routledge, pp. 21–38.

Cartier, C. (2015a), 'Territorial Urbanization and the Party-State in China', *Territory, Politics, Governance*, 3.

Cartier, C. (2015b), 'A Political Economy of Rank: The Territorial Administrative Hierarchy and Leadership Mobility in Urban China', *Journal of Contemporary China*.

Castellino, Joshua and Elvira Domínguez Redondo (2006), *Minority Rights in Asia: A Comparative Legal Analysis*, Oxford: Oxford University Press.

CCAP/UC Davis/University of Toronto Research Team (2007), 'Tax-for-Fee Reform, Village Operating Budgets and Public Goods Investment: Report for the World Bank, Beijing Office'.

CCP Central Committee (1981), 'Resolution on Party History, 1949–1981', *Proceedings of the Sixth Plenary Session*, 27 June, Beijing: Foreign Languages Press, p. 32.

CCP Central Committee (1984), 'Decision on Economic System Reform', Third Plenum of Twelfth Party Congress, 20 October, available at http://www.gov.cn/test/2008-06/26/content_1028140_2.htm, accessed 9 October 2014.

CCP Central Committee (1993), *Guanyu jianli shehui zhuyi shichang jingji tizhi ruogan wentu de jueding* (Decision Concerning Some Questions in the Construction of a Socialist Market Economy), China.com.cn. Available at http://www.china.com.cn/policy/txt/2002-04/12/content_9407527.htm, accessed 5 April 2014.

CCP Central Committee (2013), 'Zhonggong Zhongyang Guanyu Quanguo Shenhua Gaige Ruogan Zhongda Wenti de Juede' (Decision of Central Committee of China Communist Party on some important issues on deepening reform), Third Plenum of the Central Committee of the China Communist Party, 15 November, available at http://news.xiuhuannet.com/politics/2013-11/15c_118164235.htm, accessed 15 November 2013.

CCP Central Committee and State Council (1997), *Guanyu weisheng gaige yu fazhan de jueding* (Decision Concerning Health Reform and Development), Peoplenet. Available at http://www.people.com.cn/item/flfgk/gwy/jkww/w970115.html, accessed 18 October 2014.

CCP Central Organization Department (2002), *Dangzheng lingdao ganbu xuanba renyong gongzuotiaoli* (Regulation on Selection and Appointment of Party and Government Leading Cadres).

CCP Central Organization Department and the Ministry of Personnel (2008), *Gongwuyuan zhiwu renmian yu zhiwu shengjiang guiding (shixing)* (Regulation on the Appointment, Dismissal, Promotion, and Demotion of Civil Servants (Trial)), 29 February.

CCP General Office (2009), *2010–2020 nian shenhua ganbu renshi zhidu gaige guihua gangyao* (The plan for deepening the cadre management system during the 2010–2020 period), 3 December.
CCTV (2009), *Interview with Guo Fenglian*, available at http://tv.cntv.cn/video/C10305/97ea6621ecff407747a2f58821e0b9c3.
Cha, Victor (1999), 'Engaging China: Seoul–Beijing Détante and Korean Security', *Survival*, 41(1): 73–98.
Cha, Victor (2011), *Beyond the Final Score: The Politics of Sport in Asia*, New York: Columbia University Press.
Chamberlain, Heath B. (1998), 'Civil Society with Chinese Characteristics?', *China Journal*, 39: 69–81.
Chan, Anita (2007), 'Organizing Wal-Mart in China: Two Steps Forward, One Step Back for China's Unions', *New Labor Forum*, 16(2): 87–96.
Chan, Anita (2009), 'Challenges and Possibilities for Democratic Grassroots Union Election in China: A Case Study of Two Factory-Level Election and Their Aftermath', *Labor Studies Journal*, 34(3): 293–317.
Chan, Chris King-Chi (2013), 'Community-based Organizations for Migrant Workers' Rights: The Emergence of Labour NGOs in China', *Community Development Journal*, 48(1): 6–22.
Chan, H.S. (2004), 'Cadre Personnel Management in China: The Nomenklatura System, 1990–1998', *China Quarterly*, 179: 703–734.
Chan, K.W. (2010), 'Fundamentals of China's Urbanisation and Policy', *China Review*, 10(1): 63–94.
Chanda, Nayan (1990), 'The External Environment for Southeast Asian Foreign Policy', in David Wurfel and David Burton (eds), *The Political Economy of Foreign Policy in Southeast Asia*, London: Palgrave MacMillan, pp. 62–93.
Chandra, Alexander C. and Lucky A. Lontoh (2011), *Indonesia – China Trade Relations: The Deepening of Economic Integration Amid Uncertainty?*, Winnipeg: International Institute for Sustainable Development (IISD).
Chang, Chiung-Fang (2003), 'Fertility Patterns among the Minority Populations of China', PhD dissertation, Texas A&M University.
Chang, Kou-t'ao (1972), *The Autobiography of Chang Kuo-t'ao. Vol. 1, The Rise of the Chinese Communist Party 1928–1938*, Lawrence, KS: University Press of Kansas.
Chang, Leren (1988), 'Youhua peizhi he zuijia fenpei' (Optimization and the best distribution), *Zhongguo funübao* (China Women's News), 11 July.
Chang, Parris H. (1975), *Power and Policy in China*, London: Pennsylvania State University Press.
Chang, Parris Hsu-cheng (1969), *Patterns and Processes of Policy-Making in Communist China 1955–1962: Three Case Studies*, New York: Columbia University.
Cheek, Timothy and Juan D. Lindau (1998), 'Market Liberalization and Democratization: The Case for Comparative Contextual Analysis', in Juan D. Lindau and Timothy Cheek (eds), *Market Economics and Political Change: Comparing China and Mexico*, Boulder, CO: Rowman & Littlefield, pp. 1–20.
Chemillier-Gendreau, Monique (2000), *Sovereignty over the Paracel and the Spratly Islands*, The Hague: Kluwer Law International.
Chen, C.-J.J. (1999), 'Local Institutions and the Transformation of Property Rights in

Southern Fujian', in J.C. Oi and A.G. Walder (eds), *Property Rights and Economic Reform in China*, Stanford, CA: Stanford University Press, p. xiv.

Chen, Dingding and Jianwei Wang (2011), 'Lying Low No More?: China's New Thinking on the Tao Guang Yang Hui Strategy', *China: An International Journal*, 9(2): 195–216.

Chen, Donglin (2003), *Sanxian Jianshe: Beizhan shiqi de xibu kaifa* (Third Front construction: war preparation and the development of the West), Beijing: Zhonggong zhongyang dangxiao.

Chen, Feng (2000), 'Subsistence Crises, Managerial Corruption and Labour Protests in China', *China Journal*, 44(July): 41–63. doi:10.2307/2667476.

Chen, Ian Tsung-yen (2014), 'Balance of Payments and Power: Assessing China's Global and Regional Interdependence Relationship', *International Relations of the Asia-Pacific*, 14(2): 271–302.

Chen, Jack (1976), *Inside the Cultural Revolution*, London: Sheldon Press.

Chen, Jerome (1965), *Mao Tse-tung and the Chinese Revolution*, New York: Oxford University Press.

Chen, Jian (1994), *China's Road to the Korean War: The Making of the Sino-American Confrontation*, New York: Columbia University Press.

Chen, Jian (1996), *Chinese Communist Foreign Policy and the Cold War in Asia: New Documentary Evidence, 1944–1950*, Chicago: Imprint Publications.

Chen, Jian (2001), *Mao's China and the Cold War*, Chapel Hill, NC: University of North Carolina Press.

Chen, Jie (2013), *A Middle Class Without Democracy: Economic Growth and the Prospects for Democratization in China*, New York: Oxford University Press.

Chen, Jie and B. Dickson (2010), *Allies of the State: China's Private Entrepreneurs and Democratic Change*, Cambridge, MA: Harvard University Press.

Chen, Ling (2011), *System, Elites and Consensus: In Search of a New Explanatory Framework for China's Policy Process (Zhidu, Jingying yu Gongshi: Xunqiu Zhongguo zhengce guocheng de jieshi kuangjia)*, Beijing: Tsinghua University Press.

Chen, Ling and B. Naughton (2014), 'A Policy Mechanism for Change: China's Return to Techno-Industrial Policy', draft, Tsinghua University, School of Public Policy and Management.

Chen, Ling, Zhao Jing and Xue Lan (2010), 'Optimize or Compromise? A Consensus-Centered Conceptual Framework of the Policy-making Process in Transitional China' (in Chinese), *Guanli Shijie* (Management World), 8: 59–72.

Chen, Minglu (2015), 'From Economic Elites to Political Elites: Private Entrepreneurs in the People's Political Consultative Conference', *Journal of Contemporary China*, 24(94).

Chen, Minglu and David S.G. Goodman (2012), 'The China Model: One Country, Six Authors', *Journal of Contemporary China*, 21(73): 169–185.

Chen, Minglu and David S.G. Goodman (eds) (2013), *Middle Class China: Identity and Behaviour*, Cheltenham, UK and Northampton, MA, USA: Edward Elgar Publishing.

Chen, Mingsheng, Chen Wen and Yuxin Zhao (2012), 'New Evidence on Financing Equity in China's Health Care Reform: A Case Study on Gansu Province, China', *BioMed Central Health Services Research*, 12: 466.

Chen, S. and L. Li (2009), '60 nian jiangou yu gaige: jianxing jianjin de nongcun shehui baozhang zhidu' (60 years of construction and reform: the looming rural social secu-

rity system), *Dangdai Zhongguoshi yanjiu* (Contemporary China History Research), 16(5): 137–44.
Chen, Shaofeng (2008), 'Motivations behind China's Foreign Oil Quest', *Journal of Chinese Political Science*, 13(1): 79–103.
Chen, Shaofeng (2011), 'Has China's Foreign Energy Quest Enhanced its Energy Security?', *China Quarterly*, 207: 600–625.
Chen, Shirong (2010), 'China warns Nobel Committee not to Honour Dissident Liu', *BBC News*, 28 September.
Chen, Yugang (2009), 'Jinrong weiji, meiguo shuailuo yu guoji guanxi geju bianpinghua' (Financial crisis, American decline and the levelling out of the international relations structure), *Shijie jingji yu zhengzhi* (World Economics and Politics), 5: 28–34.
Chen, Zhao and Ming Lu (2009), 'Is China Sacrificing Growth when Balancing Interregional and Urban-Rural Development?', in Yukon Huang and Allesandro M. Bocchi (eds), *Reshaping Economic Geography in East Asia*, Washington, DC: World Bank, pp. 241–257.
Chen, Zhaogang (1986), 'The Theories on the Government's Role Need to be Updated', *Reform*, 5: 18–21.
Chen, Zhimin (2009), 'International Responsibility and China's Foreign Policy', in Masafumi Iida (ed.), *China's Shift: Global Strategy of the Rising Power*, Tokyo: National Institute for Defense Studies, pp. 7–28.
Cheng, Joseph Y.S. (1999a), 'The Sino Russian Strategic Partnership in the Eyes of the Chinese Leadership's World View', in Peter Koehn and Joseph Y.S. Cheng (eds), *The Outlook for US–China Relations Following the 1997–1998 Summits*, Hong Kong: Chinese University Press, pp. 85–110.
Cheng, Joseph Y.S. (1999b), 'China's ASEAN Policy in the 1990s: Pushing for Regional Multipolarity', *Contemporary Southeast Asia*, 21(1): 176–204.
Cheng, Joseph Y.S., Kinglun Ngok and Zhuang Wenjia (2010), 'The Survival and Development Space for China's Labor NGOs: Informal Politics and Its Uncertainty', *Asian Survey*, 50(6): 1082–1106.
Cheng, Li (2014), 'China's Communist Party-State: The Structure and Dynamics of Power', in William A. Joseph (ed.), *Politics in China: An Introduction*, 2nd edn, New York: Oxford University Press.
Cheng, Zhensheng (2002), *Guanyu 'wenge' Zhongguo wuyuan yewu zu de ruogan qingkuang* (Examining cases of 'reform' in the State Council business group), *Dangde Wenxian* (Party papers), 3: 61–66.
Cheung, Peter T.Y. (1998), 'Introduction: Provincial Leadership and Economic Reform in Post-Mao China', in Peter T.Y. Cheung, Jae Ho Chung and Zhimin Lin (eds), *Provincial Strategies of Economic Reform in Post-Mao China: Leadership, Politics, and Implementation*, Armonk, NY: M.E. Sharpe.
Cheung, Peter T.Y., Jae Ho Chung and Zhimin Lin (1998), *Provincial Strategies of Economic Reform in Post-Mao China: Leadership, Politics, and Implementation*, Armonk, NY: M.E. Sharpe.
Chien, C. (2010), 'Prefectures and Prefecture-Level Cities', in J.H. Chung and T.C. Lam (eds), *China's Local Administration*, London: Routledge, pp. 127–148.
Chin, Gregory (2012), 'Two Way Socialisation: China, the World Bank, and Hegemonic Weakening', *Brown Journal of World Affairs*, 19(1): 211–230.

Chin, Gregory and Ramesh Thakur (2010), 'Will China Change the Rules of Global Order?', *Washington Quarterly*, 33(4): 119–138.
China Customs (2011), 'China's Imports from ASEAN Up 44.8 Pct in 2010', available at http://www.e-to-china.com/2011/0607/93626.html, accessed 9 August 2011.
China Daily (2009), 'France Goes Back on China's Shopping List', 29 October, available at http://www.chinadaily.com.cn/china/2009-10/29/content_8865307.htm.
China Daily (2014a), 'Japan approves new textbooks claiming Diaoyu Islands', available at http://www.chinadaily.com.cn/world/2014-04/04/content_17410087.htm, 4 April (accessed 27 August 2014).
China Daily (2014b), 'China to Promote Cultural Soft Power', *China Daily*, 1 January.
China Data Center (n.d.), 'China Data Online', available at http://chinadataonline.org/.
China Leadership Monitor (2002–), Stanford, CA: Hoover Institution.
China News Analysis (1953–98), Hong Kong, 1953–93, Taiwan 1994–98.
China Policy Institute (2009–2012), 'China Policy Institute Blog', Nottingham: Nottingham University.
China Policy Institute (2010–2013), 'Chinese Views of the EU', available at http://www.nottingham.ac.uk/cpi/research/funded-projects/chinese-eu/index.aspx.
China Review News (2012), 'Zhongguo shifang zhchi chaoxian jingji gaige xinghao' (China sends a signal of support for DPRK economic reform), 15 August, available at http://www.zhgpl.com/doc/1022/0/1/8/102201897.html?coluid=59&kindid=0&docid=102201897&mdate=0815120130.
China Statistical Bureau (Zhongguo tongji nianjian) (2013), 'Value of Imports and Exports by Country (Region), of Origin/Destination', available at http://www.stats.gov.cn/tjsj/ndsj/2013/html/Z0607e.htm (accessed 13 August 2014).
Chinanews (2004), 'Minzhengbu fubuzhang: Zhongguo chengshi dibao jiben shixian yingbao jinbao' (Vice-Minister for Civil Affairs: China's Urban Minimum Living Security basically reaches all those who are eligible), *Zhongguo xinwen wang* (Chinanews), available at http://www.chinanews.com/news/2004/200-09-18/26/485360.shtml (accessed 30 April 2014).
China.org.cn (2013), 'Chinese, German PMs Agree to Promote Cooperation', 27 May, available at http://www.china.org.cn/world/2013-05/27/content_28938423.htm.
Chinese People's Political Consultative Conference (1949), 'The Common Program of the Chinese People's Political Consultative Conference', 29 September, available at http://news.xinhuanet.com/ziliao/2004-12/07/content_2304465.htm.
Chinese People's Political Consultative Conference (2012a), 'Charter of the Chinese People's Political Consultative Conference', available at http://www.cppcc.gov.cn/zxww/2012/07/03/ARTI1341300912828101.shtml.
Chinese People's Political Consultative Conference (2012b), 'Brief Introduction to CPPCC', available at http://www.cppcc.gov.cn/zxww/2012/07/03/ARTI134130155718 7103.shtml.
Chiu, Becky and Mervyn K. Lewis (2006), *Reforming China's State-Owned Enterprises and Banks*, Cheltenham, UK and Northampton, MA, USA: Edward Elgar Publishing.
Cho, Young Nam (2002), 'From "Rubber Stamps" to "Iron Stamps": The Emergence of Chinese Local People's Congresses as Supervisory Powerhouses', *China Quarterly*, 171: 724–740.

Cho, Young Nam (2003), 'Symbiotic Neighbour or Extra-Court Judge? The Supervision over Courts by Chinese Local People's Congresses', *China Quarterly*, 176: 1068–1083.
Cho, Young Nam (2006), 'The Politics of Lawmaking in Chinese Local People's Congresses', *China Quarterly*, 187: 592–609.
Cho, Young Nam (2009), *Local People's Congresses in China: Development and Transition*, Cambridge: Cambridge University Press.
Chong, Guan Kwa and Mingjiang Li (2011), *China–ASEAN Sub-regional Cooperation Progress, Problems, and Prospect*, Singapore: World Scientific.
Chou, Bill (2011), 'Challenges for China's Reform of Government Procurement', *Journal of Contemporary China*, 15(48): 533–549.
Chow, Yung-Teh (1966), *Social Mobility in China: Status Careers Among the Gentry in a Chinese Community*, New York: Atherton Press.
Christensen, J. Thomas (2006), 'Fostering Stability or Creating a Monster? The Rise of China and US Policy toward East Asia', *International Security*, 31(1): 81–126.
Chung, Jae Ho (1995), 'Studies of Central–Provincial Relations in the People's Republic of China: A Mid-term Appraisal', *China Quarterly*, 142: 487–508.
Chung, Jae Ho (2003–04), 'From a Special Relationship to a Normal Partnership? Interpreting the "Garlic Battle" in Sino-South Korean Relations', *Pacific Affairs*, 76(4): 549–568.
Chung, Jae Ho (2007), *Between Ally and Partner: Korea–China Relations and the United States*, New York: Columbia University Press.
Chung, Jae Ho, Hongyi H. Lai and Jang-Hwan Joo (2007), *Assessing the 'Revive the Northeast' (zhenxing dongbei), Program: Origins, Policies and Implementation*, Singapore: Asian Network for the Study of Local China.
Chung, Jae Ho, Hongyi Lai and Jang-Hwan Joo (2009), 'Assessing the "Revive the Northeast" (zhenxing dongbei), Programme: Origins, Policies and Implementation', *China Quarterly*, 197: 108–125.
Chung, J.H. and T.C. Lam (eds) (2009), *China's Local Administration: Traditions and Changes in the Sub-national Hierarchy*, London: Routledge.
CIA (1990), *The World Factbook*, Washington, DC: Skyhorese Publishing.
CIA (2015), *The World Factbook*, Washington, DC: Skyhorese Publishing.
Clarke, Donald (2014), 'China's Stealth Urban Land Revolution', *American Journal of Comparative Law*, 62: 324–366.
Clarke, Gerard (2001), *The Politics of NGOs in South-East Asia: Participation and Protest in the Philippines*, London: Routledge.
Clothey, Rebecca (2001), 'China's Minorities and State Preferential Politics', available at http://www.eric.ed.gov/PDFS/ED453139.pdf (accessed 13 July 2014).
Cohen, Benjamin (2006), *The Future of Money*, Princeton, NJ: Princeton University Press.
Cohen, Paul (1984 [2010]), *Discovering History in China: American Historical Writing on the Recent Chinese Past*, New York: Columbia University Press.
Cohen, Warren I. (1978), 'American Perceptions of China', in Michel Oksenberg and Robert B. Oxnam (eds), *Dragon and Eagle: United States–China Relations: Past and Future*, New York: Basic Books.
Cohen, Warren I. (2010), *America's Response to China: A History of Sino-American Relations*, 4th edn, New York: Columbia University Press.

Collins COBUILD (2006), *Advanced Learner's English Dictionary*, Glasgow: Harper Collins Publishers.
Commission to the Council of the European Parliament (2006), 'China: Closer Partners, Growing Responsibilities', available at http://eur-lex.europa.eu/legal-content/EN/ALL/?uri=CELEX:52006DC0631 (accessed 24 April 2014).
Common Programme (n.d.), 'Common Programme of the Chinese People's Political Consultative Conference', available in Chinese at http://news.xinhuanet.com/ziliao/2004-12/07/content_2304465.htm
Cong, Jin (1989), *Quzhe fazhan de suiye* (The years of circuitous development), Zhengzhou: Henan renmin chubanshe.
Connors, Michael, Remy Davison and Jörn Dosch (2011), *The New Global Politics of the Asia-Pacific*, 2nd edn, London, UK and New York, USA: Routledge.
Constitution (1954), available in Chinese at http://www.npc.gov.cn/wxzl/wxzl/2000-12/26/content_4264.htm.
Cook, Malcolm and Craig Meer (2005), 'Balancing Act: Taiwan's Cross-Strait Challenge', Lowy Institute Paper 6, Sydney: Lowy Institute for International Policy.
Cooper, Caroline M. (2006), '"This is Our Way In": The Civil Society of Environmental NGOs in South-West China', *Government and Opposition*, 41(1): 109–136.
Corresponding Group of the Xu County Committee (1958), *Turang geming zhongde 'Hua Mulan' zhandouying* ('Hua Mulan' battalion in the soil revolution), *Women of China*, 14(October): 3.
Cox, Nigel (2008), 'Review of Bronson Percival. The Dragon Looks South: China and Southeast Asia in the New Century', *Asian Affairs*, 39(2): 310–311.
Croll, E. (1978), *Feminism and Socialism in China*, London: Routledge & Kegan Paul.
Crossick, S. and E. Reuter (eds) (2008), *China–EU: A Common Future*, Singapore: World Scientific Publishing.
Croucher, Richard and Lilian Miles (2010), 'Chinese Migrant Worker Representation and Institutional Change: Social or Centralist Corporatism?', *Asian Journal of Comparative Law*, 5(1): 1–26.
Cui, Shuqin (2003), *Women Through the Lens: Gender and Nation in a Century of Chinese Cinema*, Honolulu: University of Hawaii Press
Cumings, Bruce (1987), 'The Origins and Development of the Northeast Asian Political Economy: Industrial Sectors, Product Cycles, and Political Consequences', in Fred Deyo (ed.), *The Political Economy of the New East Asian Industrialism*, New York: Cornell University Press, pp. 44–83.
Dahl, R. (1961), *Who Governs: Democracy and Power in An American City*, New Haven, CT: Yale University Press.
Davies, John Paton (2012), *China Hand: An Autobiography*, Philadelphia, PA: University of Pennsylvania Press.
Davin, D. (1976), *Woman-Work: Women and the Party in Revolutionary China*, Oxford: Clarendon Press.
Davis, Bob (2014), 'Anti-Graft Push Could Have Big Impact on China's Economy', *Wall Street Journal*, 21 August.
Davis, B. and L. Wei (2013), 'Meet Liu He, Xi Jinping's Choice to Fix a Faltering Chinese Economy', *Wall Street Journal*, 6 October, available at http://online.wsj.com/news/articles/SB10001424052702304906704579111442566524958.

Davis, Deborah, Richard Kraus, Barry Naughton and Elizabeth J. Perry (eds) (1995), *Urban Spaces in Contemporary China: The Potential for Autonomy and Community in Post-Mao China*, New York: Cambridge University Press.

Delegation of the European Union to China (2011), 'EU–China Human Rights Dialogue', 16 June, available at http://eeas.europa.eu/delegations/china/press_corner/all_news/news/ 2011/20110616_01_en.htm (accessed 11 July 2014).

De Mesquita, Bruce Bueno and Alastair Smith (2009), 'A Political Economy of Aid', *International Organization*, 63(2): 309–340.

Demirovic, Alex (2003), 'NGOs, the State, and Civil Society: The Transformation of Hegemony', *Rethinking Marxism*, 15(2): 213–235.

Demsetz, H. (1983), 'The Structure of Ownership and Theory of the Firm', *Journal of Law and Economics*, 26(2): 375–390.

Demurger, Sylvie, Jeffrey D. Sachs, Wing Thye Woo, Shuming Bao, Gene Chang and Andrew Mellinger (2001), 'Geography, Economic Policy and Regional Development in China', *Asian Economic Papers*, 1(1): 146–197.

DeNavas-Walt, Carmen, Bernadette D. Proctor and Jessica C. Smith (2007), *Income, Poverty, and Health Insurance in the United States*: 2006, US Census Bureau.

Deng, Guosheng (2010), 'The Hidden Rules Governing China's Unregistered NGOs: Management and Consequences', *China Review: An Interdisciplinary Journal on Greater China*, 10(1): 103–206.

Deng, Guosheng and Scott Kennedy (2010), 'Big Business and Industry Association Lobbying in China: The Paradox of Contrasting Styles', *China Journal*, 1: 101–125.

Deng, Guosheng and Shawn Shieh (2011), 'An Emerging Civil Society: The Impact of the 2008 Sichuan Earthquake on Grass-Roots Associations in China', *China Journal*, 65: 181–194.

Deng, Liqun (2005), *Shierge Chunqiu 1975–1987* (12 years 1975–1987), Hong Kong: Bozhi Publishing House.

Deng, Xiaoping (1974), 'Speech By Chairman of the Delegation of the People's Republic of China, Deng Xiaoping, at the Special Session of the UN General Assembly', available at http://www.marxists.org/reference/archive/deng-xiaoping/1974/04/10.htm (accessed 23 January 2001).

Deng, Xiaoping (1979), 'Deng Xiaoping guanyu qicao guoqing sanshi zhounian jianghua gao de tanhua jiyao' (Summary of Deng Xiaoping's talk on the draft speech for the 30th Anniversary National Day Celebration), 4 September, in Song Yongyi (ed.), *The Chinese Cultural Revolution Database CD-ROM*, Hong Kong: Chinese University Press.

Deng, Xiaoping (1985), 'Party Committees and all Levels of Government should Take the Education Seriously: The Speech National Work Conference on Education', *People's Education*, No. 7, available at http://www.cnki.com.cn/Article/CJFDTOTAL-RMJY198507000.htm.

Deng, Xiaoping (1993a), *Deng Xiaoping wenxuan* (Selected works of Deng Xiaoping), Vol. 3, Beijing: Renmin chubanshe.

Deng, Xiaoping (1993b), 'Zai Wuchang, Shenzhen, Zhuhai, Shanghai dengdi de tanhua yaodian' ('Essential points from talks in Wuchang, Shenzhen, Zhuhai, Shanghai and other places'), *Deng Xiaoping wenxuan* (Selected works of Deng Xiaoping), Vol. 3, Beijing: Renmin chubanshe.

Deng, Xiaoping (2004), *Deng Xiaoping Nianpu 1975–1997* (Deng Xiaoping Chronology 1975–1997), Beijing: Zhongyang Wenxian.

Deng, Yingchao (1988), *Guanyu Zhonghua Renmin Gongheguo hunyinfa de baogao- 1950 nian 5 yue 14 ri zai Zhangjiakou kuoda ganbu huiyi shang de jiangyan* (A report on the Marriage Law of the People's Republic of China: a speech at the expanded cadres' meeting in Zhangjiakou on 14 May 1950), in Chinese Women Cadre Management College (eds), *Zhongguo funü yundong wenxian ziliao huibian* (An anthology of source materials on the Chinese women's movement), Beijing: Chinese Women's Press.

Des Forges, Roger and Luo Xu (2001), 'China as a Non-Negemonic Superpower? The Use of History among the China Can Say No Writers and Their Critics', *Critical Asian Studies*, 33(4): 483–507.

Deshayes, Pierre-Henry (2011), 'Norwegian Salmon Off the Menu in China', AFP, 4 October, available at http://www.google.com/hostednews/afp/article/ALeqM5i6sUVm RWA4sg4c4_ cJdzrR6vD08Q?docId_CNG.d9e59580b60b0632b53dfe695f1c18f0.321.

Diamond, Larry (1994), 'Rethinking Civil Society: Toward Democratic Consolidation', *Journal of Democracy*, 5(3): 4–17.

Dickson, Bruce J. (2003), *Red Capitalists in China: The Party, Private Entrepreneurs, and Prospects for Political Change*, New York, USA and Cambridge, UK: Cambridge University Press.

Dickson, Bruce J. (2008), *Wealth into Power: The Communist Party's Embrace of China's Private Sector*, New York, USA and Cambridge, UK: Cambridge University Press.

Dieter, Heribert (2008), 'Lehren aus der Asienkrise. Neue Formen der finanzpolitischen Kooperation in Südost- und Ostasien' (Lessons from the Asian financial crisis. New forms of financial cooperation in South-East and East Asia), SWP-Studien 2008/S 33, November.

Ding, X., F. Li and Y. Sun (2008), 'Thirty Years of the Reform of the Investment Systems of Higher Education in China', *China Higher Education Research*, 6: 1–5 (in Chinese).

Dixon, J. (1981), *The Chinese Welfare System, 1949–1979*, New York: Praeger.

Dolin, Eric Jay (2012), *When America First Met China: An Exotic History of Tea, Drugs, and Money in the Age of Sail*, New York: Liveright Publishing.

Domes, Jürgen (1984), 'Intra-Elite Group Formation and Conflict in the PRC', in David S.G. Goodman (ed), *Groups and Politics in the People's Republic of China*, Armonk, NY: M.E. Sharpe, pp. 26–39.

Donaldson, John A. (2007), 'Tourism, Development and Poverty Reduction in Guizhou and Yunnan', *China Quarterly*, 190: 333–351.

Donaldson, J. (2009), 'Provinces: Paradoxical Politics, Problematic Partners', in J.H. Chung and T.C. Lam (eds), *China's Local Administration: Traditions and Changes in the Sub-national Hierarchy*, London: Routledge, pp. 14–38.

Donaldson, John A. (2011), *Small Works: Poverty and Economic Development in Southwestern China*, Ithaca, NY: Cornell University Press.

Dong, Biwu (1985), *Dong Biwu xuanji* (Selected works of Dong Biwu), Beijing: Renmin chubanse.

Dong, Lisheng (2005), 'China's Drive to Revitalise the Northeast', *China Perspectives*, 58: 2–17.

Donnithorne, Audrey (1967 [2013]), *The Chinese Economic System*, London: George Allen & Unwin/Routledge.

Donnithorne, Audrey (1972), *The Budget and the Plan in China: Central–Local Economic Relations*, Contemporary China Papers, No. 3, Canberra: Australian National University Press.
Donnithorne, Audrey (1976), 'Comment: Centralization and Decentralization in China's Fiscal Management', *China Quarterly*, 66: 328–340.
Dorfman, M.C., R. Holzmann, P. O'Keefe, D. Wang, Y. Sin and R. Hinz (2013), *China's Pension System*, Washington, DC: World Bank.
Dosch, Jörn (2007), 'Managing Security in ASEAN–China Relations: Liberal Peace of Hegemonic Stability', *Asian Perspective*, 31(1): 209–236.
Dosch, Jörn (2011), 'The Spratly Islands Dispute: Order-Building on China's terms?', *Harvard International Review*, 18 August, available at http://hir.harvard.edu/the-spratly-islands-dispute-order-building-on-china-s-terms (accessed 9 May 2014).
Dosch, Jörn (2014), 'Mahathirism and Its Legacy in Malaysia's Foreign Policy', *European Journal of East Asian Studies*, 13(1): 5–32.
Dowdle, M.W. (1997), 'Constitutional Development and Operations of the National People's Congress', *Columbia Journal of Asian Law*, 11: 1.
Downs, Erica (2011), *Inside China, Inc: China Development Bank's Cross-Border Energy Deals*, China Centre Monograph Series 3 (March), Washington, DC: Brookings Institution.
Dreyer, June Teufel (1976), *China's Forty Millions*, Cambridge, MA: Harvard University Press.
Dreyer, June Teufel (2005), 'China's Vulnerability to Minority Separatism', *Asian Affairs: An American Review*, 31(2): 69–85.
Drezner, Daniel (2009), 'Bad Debts: Assessing China's Financial Influence in Great Power Relations', *International Security*, 34(2): 7–45.
Duan, Yongqiang (2000), *Luo Qiong fangtan lu* (Interviews with Luo Qiong), Beijing: Chinese Women's Press.
Duckett, J. (2001), 'Political Interests and the Implementation of China's Urban Health Insurance Reform', *Social Policy and Administration*, 35(3): 290–306.
Duckett, J. (2004), 'State, Collectivism and Worker Privilege: A Study of Urban Health Insurance', *China Quarterly*, 177: 155–173.
Duckett, J. (2011), *The Chinese State's Retreat from Health: Policy and the Politics of Retrenchment*, London, UK and New York, USA: Routledge.
Duckett, J. and B. Carrillo (eds) (2011), *China's Social Welfare Mix: Conceptualising State and Societal Responses to Evolving Social Problems*, London: Routledge.
Duckett, J. and A. Hussain (2008), Tackling Unemployment in China: State Capacity and Governance Issues, *Pacific Review*, 21: 211–229.
Dyer, Geoff A. (2014), *The Contest of the Century: The New Era of Competition with China – and How America Can Win*, New York: Alfred A. Knopf.
Eastman, Lloyd E. (1988), *Family, Fields and Ancestors: Constancy and Change in China's Social and Economic History, 1550–1949*, Oxford: Oxford University Press.
The Economist (2013a), 'Gini out of the Bottle', 9 October.
The Economist (2013b), 'Chasing the Chinese Dream', 4 May.
The Economist (2014), 'Beneath the Glacier', 12 April, available at http://www.economist.com/news/china/21600747-spite-political-clampdown-flourishing-civil-society-taking-hold-beneath-glacier.

Economy, Elizabeth C. (2004), *The River Runs Black: The Environmental Challenge to China's Future*, Ithaca: Cornell University Press.
Economy, Elizabeth (2010), 'The Game Changer – Coping with China's Foreign Policy Revolution', *Foreign Affairs*, 89(6): 142–152.
Egan, A. (2013), 'Constructive Engagement on Human Rights: The Case of the EU Policy on China', unpublished Ph D thesis, University of Limerick.
Election Study Center, National Chengchi University, Taiwan (n.d.), http://esc.nccu.edu.tw/course/news.php?class=203.
Elliott, M.C. (2001), *The Manchu Way: The Eight Banners and Ethnic Identity in Late Imperial China*, Stanford, CA: Stanford University Press.
Elmer, Franziska (2011), 'Tibet and Xinjiang: Their Fourfold Value to China', *Culture Mandala*, 9(2): 1–14.
Embassy of the United States (1979), 'Joint Communiqué on the Establishment of Diplomatic Relations between the People's Republic of China and the United States of America', available at http://beijing.usembassy-china.org.cn/uploads/images/9y7T9oJSIFpfgTW6cO2_5w/1979_Joint_Communique.pdf, (accessed 26 September 2014).
Etzioni, Amitai (1961), *A Comparative Analysis of Complex Organizations*, New York: Free Press.
Evans, Richard (1995), *Deng Xiaoping and the Making of Modern China*, London: Penguin.
Fairbank, John K. (1975), *China Perceived: Images and Policies in Chinese–American Relations*, New York: Random House.
Fairbank, John King (1983), *The United States and China*, 4th edn, Cambridge, MA: Harvard University Press.
Fan, C. Cindy (1995), 'Of Belts and Ladders: State Policy and Uneven Regional Development in Post-Mao China', *Annals of the Association of American Geographers*, 85: 421–449.
Fan, C. Cindy (1997), 'Uneven Development and Beyond: Regional Development Theory in Post-Mao China', *International Journal of Urban and Regional Research*, 21(4): 620–639.
Fan, C. Cindy and Mingjie Sun (2008), 'Regional Inequality in China, 1978–2006', *Eurasian Geography and Economics*, 49(1): 1–20.
Fan, Shenggen, Ravi Kanbur and Xiaobo Zhang (2011), 'China's Regional Disparities: Experience and Policy', *Review of Development Finance*, 1: 47–56.
Farer, Tom J. (2003), 'The Ethics of Intervention in Self-Determination Struggles', *Human Rights Quarterly*, 25(2): 382–406.
Fenby, Jonathan (2013), *The Penguin History of Modern China: The Fall and Rise of a Great Power 1850 to the Present*, 2nd edn, New York: Penguin Global.
Feng, Congyi and David S.G. Goodman (eds) (2000), *North China at War*, Lexington: Rowman & Littlefield.
Feng, Jianhua (2007), 'Endangered Ethnic Culture', 28 May, available at http://www.bjreview.com/nation/txt/2007-05/28/content_64791.htm (accessed 13 July 2014).
Fenwick, Ann (1984), 'Evaluating China's Special Economic Zones', *Berkeley Journal of International Law*, 2(2): 1–23.
Fewsmith, Joseph (1994), *Dilemmas of Reform in China*, Armonk, NY: M.E. Sharpe.
Fewsmith, Joseph (1996), 'Institutions, Informal Politics, and Political Transition in China', *Asian Survey*, 36(3): 230–245.

Fewsmith, Joseph (2001), *Elite Politics in Contemporary China*, Armonk, NY: M.E. Sharpe.
Fewsmith, Joseph (2008), *China Since Tiananmen: From Deng Xiaoping to Hu Jintao*, 2nd edn, Cambridge: Cambridge University Press.
Fewsmith, Joseph (2009), 'Participatory Budgeting: Development and Limitations', *China Leadership Monitor*, 29.
Fingar, Thomas and Fan Jishe (2013), 'Ties that Bind: Strategic Stability in the US–China Relationship', *Washington Quarterly*, 36(4).
Fisher, Karen, Jing Li and Lei Fan (2012), 'Barriers to the Supply of Non-Government Disability Services in China', *Journal of Social Policy*, 41(1): 161–182.
Fishman, Ted (2005), *China, Inc.: How the Rise of the Next Superpower Challenges America and the World*, New York: Scribner.
Fitzgerald, C.P. (1955), 'East Asia After Bandung', *Far Eastern Survey*, 24(8): 113–119.
Fitzgerald, John (1996), 'The Nationless State: The Search for a Nation in Modern Chinese Nationalism', in Jonathan Unger (ed.), *Chinese Nationalism*, Armonk, NY: M.E. Sharpe.
Fitzgerald, J. (2002), 'The Province in History', in J. Fitzgerald (ed.), *Rethinking China's Provinces*, London: Routledge, pp. 11–40.
Fleischauer, Stefan (2007), 'The 228 Incident and the Taiwan Independence Movement's Construction of a Taiwanese Identity', *China Information*, 21(3): 373–401.
Fleming, Michael (2002), 'The New Minority Rights Regime in Poland', *Nations and Nationalism*, 8(4): 531–548.
Flowe, Benjamin H. and Ray Gold (2000), 'The Legality of US Sanctions', *Global Dialogue*, 2(3), available at http://www.worlddialogue.org/content.php?id=98.
FMPRC (2000a), 'The Geneva Conference', available at http://www.fmprc.gov.cn/eng/ziliao/3602/3604/t18033.htm (accessed 13 June 2005).
FMPRC (2000b), 'China's Initiation of the Five Principles of Peaceful Co-Existence', available at http://www.fmprc.gov.cn/eng/ziliao/3602/3604/t18053.htm (accessed 13 June 2005).
FMPRC (2002), 'China's Position Paper on the New Security Concept', available at http://www.mfa.gov.cn/eng/wjb/zzjg/gjs/gjzzyhy/2612/2614/t15319.htm (accessed 12 June 2003).
Fong, V.L. and R. Murphy (2006), *Chinese Citizenship*, London, UK and New York, USA: Routledge.
Foot, Rosemary (2006), 'Chinese Strategies in a US-Hegemonic Global Order: Accommodating and Hedging', *International Affairs*, 82(1): 77–94.
Foot, Rosemary and Andrew Walter (2010), *China, the United States, and Global Order*, Cambridge: Cambridge University Press.
Forsythe, Michael, Chris Buckley and Jonathan Ansfield (2014), 'Investigating Family's Wealth, China's Leader Signals a Change', *New York Times*, 20 April.
Fox, J. and F. Godemont (2009), *A Power Audit of EU–China Relations*, London: European Council for Foreign Relations.
Frazier, M.L. (2010), *Socialist Insecurity: Pensions and the Politics of Uneven Development in China*, Ithaca, NY: Cornell University Press.
Freeman, Charles and Wen Jinyuan (2013), *China's Exchange Rate Policies: Decoding the*

Cleavage Between the Chinese Ministry of Commerce and the People's Bank of China, Washington, DC: Center For Strategic and International Studies.

Friedberg, Aaron (2011), 'The Coming Clash with China', *Wall Street Journal* (Asia Edition), 17 January, p. 15.

Friedberg, Aaron L. (2012), *A Contest for Supremacy: China, America, and the Struggle for Mastery in Asia*, New York: W.W. Norton & Company.

Friedman, Eli and Ching-Kwan Lee (2010), 'Remaking the World of Chinese Labor: A Thirty Year Retrospective', *British Journal of Industrial Relations*, 48(3): 3–17.

Froissart, Chloe (2006), 'Escaping from under the Party's Thumb: A Few Examples of Migrant Workers' Strivings for Autonomy', *Social Research*, 73(1): 197–218.

Froissart, Chloe (2010), 'Is There a NGO Model? Comparing NGOs Supporting Migrant Workers in Beijing and the Pearl River Delta', Sciences Po, Asia Centre Conference Paper.

Frolic, B. Michael (1994), *China's Second Wave of Development: The Yangtze River Region*, Toronto: University of Toronto–York University Joint Centre for Asia Pacific Studies.

Fu, Yong (2003), 'Shi Lun Lengzhan Hou de Feichuantong Anquan Wenti' (An examination of post-Cold War non-traditional security issues), *Shehui Kexue*, 10: 33–40.

Fulda, Andreas, Li Yanyan and Song Qinghua (2012), 'New Strategies of Civil Society in China: A Case Study of the Network Governance Approach', *Journal of Contemporary China*, 21(76): 675–693.

Gallagher, Kevin P., et al. (2012), 'The New Banks in Town: Chinese Finance in Latin America', *Inter-American Dialogue Report* (February).

Gao, Jie (2010), 'Hitting the Target but Missing the Point: The Rise of Non-Mission-Based Targets in Performance Measurement of Chinese Local Governments', *Administration and Society*, 42(1): 56–76.

Gao, Mei (2012), '"Dizhi rihuo" bing bushi lixing de zuofa' ('Boycott Japanese goods' is definitely not a rational action), *Xinjingbao* (New Beijing News), 14 September, available at http://finance.people.com.cn/n/2012/0914/c1004-19005598.html.

Gao, Minzheng (2011), *Chinese Politico-Military Theory: The Communists' Thought on Civil–Military Relations*, Beijing: Current Affairs Publishing House.

Gao, Mingxuan and Wang Junping (2007), 'Issues of Concern to China Regarding the International Criminal Court', paper prepared for the Symposium on the International Criminal Court, Beijing, available at http://www.icclr.law.ubc.ca/Site%20Map/ICC/IssueofConcern.pdf (accessed 8 May 2009).

Gao, Peiyong (ed.) (2007), *Wei Zhongguo Gonggong Caizheng Jianshe Gouhua 'Luxiantu': Zhongyao Zhanlu Jiyuqi de Gonggong Caizheng Jianshe*, Beijing: Zhongguo Caizheng Jingji Jianshe chubanshe.

Gao, Peiyong, Zhang Bin and Wang Ning (eds) (2013), *Zhongguo Gonggong Caizheng Jianshe Baogao 2013* (China public finance development report 2013), 2 vols, Beijing: Shehui Kexue Wenxian chubanshe.

Garnaut, John (2012), *The Rise and Fall of the House of Bo*, Penguin Special (eBook), Australia: Penguin Aus.

Garnaut, Ross, Ligang Song and Yang Yao (2006), 'Impact and Significance of State-Owned Enterprise Restructuring in China', *China Journal*, 55: 35–63.

Garside, Roger (1981), *Coming Alive!: China after Mao*, New York: McGraw-Hill.

Garver, John W. (1982), *China's Decision for Rapprochement with the United States, 1968–1971*, Boulder, CO: Westview Press.

Geng, Y. (2012), 'Shebao zhidu buneng zai suibianhua' (The social security system cannot become further fragmented), *21 shiji jingji baodao* (Twenty-First Century Economic Report), 9 October: 26.

Ghai, Yash and Sophia Woodman (2009), 'Unused Powers: Contestation over Autonomy Legislation in the PRC', *Pacific Affairs*, 82(1): 29–46.

Giddens, Anthony (1977), *Studies in Social and Political Theory*, London: Hutchinson of London.

Gilder, George (1981), *Wealth and Poverty*, New York: Basic Books.

Gill, Bates (2010), *Rising Star: China's New Security Diplomacy*, Washington, D.C.: Brookings Institution Press.

Gill, Bates and James Reilly (2007), 'The Tenuous Hold of China, Inc. In Africa', *Washington Quarterly*, 30(3): 37–52.

Gladney, Dru C. (1996), *Muslim Chinese*, Cambridge, MA: Harvard University Press.

Glassman, Ronald (1991), *China in Transition: Communism, Capitalism, and Democracy*, Boulder, CO: Praeger.

Global Times (2011), 'Sheping: Dui yulun tiaoti, zhengfu xu zhudong sheying' (Editorial: In facing picky public opinion, the government must proactively adapt), *Global Times*, 22 November, available at http://newspaper.dbw.cn/hljcb/bm/1/2011-11/29/00010/20111129 00010_pdf.pdf.

Global Times (2012a), 'Dizhi rihuo yidan mangmu rongyi zishang' (Boycott Japanese goods – one day of blindness and it's easy to injure oneself), 22 August, available at http://money.163.com/12/0822/14/89H3QJ4A00253B0H.html (accessed 6 November 2012).

Global Times (2012b), 'Rimei cheng chaoxian zhengxunqiu xinmaoyi huoban, bimian "guodu yilai" zhongguo' (Japanese Media declares DPRK is seeking new economic partners to avoid 'over-dependence' on China), *Huanqiu Shibao* (Global Times), 31 May, available at http://world.huanqiu.com/roll/2012-05/2775256.html.

Global Times (2012c), 'Sheping: Zhongguo yinggai kuoda "mulin" deliejie' (Editorial: China should expand its understanding of 'friendly neighbour'), *Huanqiu shibao* (Global Times), 22 May, available at http://opinion.huanqiu.com/1152/2012-05/2741988.html.

Göbel, Christian (2010), *The Politics of Rural Reform in China: State Policy and Village Predicament in the Early 2000s*, London: Routledge.

Goh, Evelyn (2011), 'Rising Power . . . To Do What? Evaluating China's Power in Southeast Asia', RSIS Working Paper 226, 30 March.

Gold, Thomas B. (1990), 'The Resurgence of Civil Society in China', *Journal of Democracy*, 1(1): 18–31.

Goldstein, Avery (1991), *From Bandwagon to Balance-of-Power Politics: Structural Constraints and Politics in China*, Stanford, CA: Stanford University Press.

Goldstein, S. (1996), 'China in Transition: The Political Foundations of Incremental Reform', in A. Walder (ed.), *China's Transitional Economy*, Oxford: Oxford University Press.

Goldstone, Jack, Ted Gurr and Farrokh Moshiri (1991), *Revolutions of the Late Twentieth Century*, Boulder, CO: Westview Press.

Golley, Jane (2010), 'Prospects for Diminishing Regional Disparities', in Ross Garnaut, Jane Golley and Ligang Song (eds), *China: The Next Twenty Years of Reform and Development*, Canberra: ANU E Press, pp. 127–150.

Gong, Ting (1994), *The Politics of Corruption in Contemporary China: An Analysis of Policy Outcomes*, Boulder, CO: Praeger.

Goode, Richard B. (1984), *Government Finance in Developing Countries*, Washington, DC: Brookings Institution Press.

Goodman, David S.G. (1980), 'The Provincial First Party Secretary in the People's Republic of China, 1949–78: A Profile', *British Journal of Political Science*, 10(1): 39–74.

Goodman, David S.G. (1981), 'The Provincial Revolutionary Committee in the People's Republic of China, 1967–1979: An Obituary', *China Quarterly*, 85: 49–79.

Goodman, David S.G. (1984a), 'Provincial Party First Secretaries in National Politics: A Categoric or a Political Group', in David S.G. Goodman (ed.), *Groups and Politics in the People's Republic of China*, Armonk, NY: M.E. Sharpe, pp. 68–82.

Goodman, David S.G. (1984b), 'The Methodology of Contemporary Chinese Studies: Political Studies and the People's Republic of China', in Y.M. Shaw (ed.), *Power and Policy in the People's Republic of China*, Boulder, CO: Westview Press, pp. 317–339.

Goodman, David S.G. (1986), *Centre and Province in the People's Republic of China: Sichuan and Guizhou, 1955–1965*, Cambridge: Cambridge University Press.

Goodman, David S.G. (1994), *Deng Xiaoping and the Chinese Revolution: A Political Biography*, London: Routledge.

Goodman, David S.G. (1995), 'Introduction' in David S.G. Goodman and Gerald Segal (eds), *China Deconstructs*, London: Routledge.

Goodman, David S.G. (ed.) (1997), *China's Provinces in Reform: Class, Community and Political Culture*, London: Routledge.

Goodman, David S.G. (2001),'The Interdependence of State and Society: The Political Sociology of Local Leadership', in Chien-min Chao and Bruce J. Dickson (eds), *Remaking the Chinese State: Strategies, Society and Security*, London: Routledge, pp. 132–156.

Goodman, David S.G. (2002), 'The Politics of the West: Equity, Nation-Building and Colonialisation', *Provincial China*, 7(2): 127.

Goodman, David S.G. (2004a), 'The Campaign to "Open Up the West": National, Provincial-Level and Local Perspectives', *China Quarterly*, 178: 317–334.

Goodman, David S.G. (ed.) (2004b), *China's Campaign to Open Up the West*, Cambridge: Cambridge University Press.

Goodman, David S.G. (2014a), 'New Economic Elites: Family Histories and Social Change', in Sujian Guo (ed.), *State Society Relations and Governance in China*, Lanham, MD: Lexington Books, pp. 15–38.

Goodman, David S.G. (2014b), *Class in Contemporary China*, Cambridge: Polity Press.

Goodman, David S.G. (2016), 'Locating China's Middle Classes: Social Intermediaries and the Party-state', *Journal of Contemporary China*, 25(97).

Goodman, David S.G. and Gerald Segal (eds) (1995), *China Deconstructs*, London: Routledge.

Gov.cn (n.d.), 'The One-China Principle and the Taiwan Issue', available at http://english.gov.cn/official/2005-07/27/content_17613.htm (accessed 26 September 2014).

Gowa, Joanne S. (1994), *Allies, Adversaries, and International Trade*, Princeton, NJ: Princeton Univ. Press.

Graham, Norman (1991), 'The Role of the Military in the Political and Economic Development of the Republic of Korea', *Journal of Asian and African Studies*, 26(1).

Green, Andrew and Ann Matthias (1995), 'NGOs – A Policy Panacea for the Next Millennium?', *Journal of International Development*, 7(3): 565–573.

Greenhalgh, S. (2008), *Just One Child: Science and Policy in Deng's China*, Berkeley, CA: University of California Press.

Grewal, Bhajan S. and Abdullahi D. Ahmed (2011), 'Is China's Western Region Development Strategy on Track? An Assessment', *Journal of Contemporary China*, 20(69): 161–181.

Grewal, Bhajan and Fiona Sun (2002), 'Extending the Frontier of High Growth Inland: Implications for China's Regional Policy', in Bhajan Grewal, Lan Xue, Peter Sheehan and Fiona Sun (eds), *China's Future in the Knowledge Economy: Engaging the New World*, Melbourne, Australia and Beijing, China: Centre for Strategic Economic Studies and Tsinghua University Press, pp. 212–233.

Grieco, Joseph M. (2002), 'China and America in the World Polity', in Carolyn W. Pumphrey (ed.), *The Rise of China in Asia*, Carlisle Barracks, PA: Strategic Studies Institute, pp. 24–48.

Gries, Peter Hays (2004), *China's New Nationalism: Pride, Politics, and Diplomacy*, Berkeley, CA: University of California Press.

Griffin, Nicholas (2014), *Ping Pong Diplomacy: The Secret History Behind the Game that Changed the World*, New York: Scribner.

Grindle, M.S. (1980), *Politics and Policy Implementation in the Third World*, Princeton, NJ: Princeton University Press.

Groot, G. (2004), *Managing Transitions: The Chinese Communist Party, United Front Work, Corporatism and Hegemony*, New York: Routledge.

Grossman, Leo (1984), *Essays on International Law and Organization*, Leiden: Brill.

Gu, Jing and Neil Renwick (2008), 'China's Fight Against HIV/AIDS', *Journal of Contemporary China*, 17(54): 85–106.

Gui, Tiantian (2014), 'Guojia buwei luoma guanyuan weihe fagaiwei zuiduo' (Why NDRC sacked ministers), *Beijing Qingnianbao* (Beijing Youth Daily), 25 September.

Guo, Boxiong (2010), 'Promoting Officers by Putting Them in Difficult and Emergency Situations', *People's Daily*, 24 July.

Guo, Gaozhoung (2004), 'Guowuyuan weihe quxiao zongli bangong huiyi' (Why the State Council cancelled a meeting for the Premier), *Liaowang dongfan zhoukan* (Outlook Eastern Weekly).

Guo, G. (2007), 'Quanmin dibao jingru gongjian jieduan' (Is the Chinese welfare system entering an unviable phase?), *Diyi caijing ribao* (The First Economic Daily), 1 August: A01.

Guo, Jingfu and Jingtao Wang (2010), 'Study on Development Policies of the Special Industries in Ethnic Minority Areas of China', *International Journal of Business and Management*, 5(2): 201–204.

Guo, Yingjie (2008), 'Class, Stratum and Group: The Politics of Description and Prescription', in David S.G. Goodman (ed.), *The New Rich in China: Future Rules, Present Lives*, London, UK and New York, USA: Routledge, pp. 38–52.

Guo, Yingjie (2013), 'The Role of Intellectual Elites in China's Political Reform: The Discourse of Governance', in Xiaowei Zang and Chien-wen Kou (eds), *Elites and Governance in China*, London: Routledge, pp. 34–54.

Guo, Yong (2008), 'Corruption in Transitional China: An Empirical Analysis', *China Quarterly*, 194(June): 349–64.

Gurtov, Melvin (1975), *China and Southeast Asia, the Politics of Survival: A Study of Foreign Policy Interaction*, Baltimore, MD: Johns Hopkins University Press.

Gustafsson, Bjorn and Ding Sai (2010), 'New Light on China's Rural Elites', UNU-WIDER Working Paper No. 2010/108.

Gustafsson, Bjorn and Li Shi (2003), 'The Ethnic Minority–Majority Income Gap in Rural China during Transition', *Economic Development and Cultural Change*, 51(4): 805–822.

Guy, R.K. (2010), *Qing Governors and Their Provinces: The Evolution of Territorial Administration in China, 1644–1796*, Seattle, WA: University of Washington Press.

Habermas, J. (2009), *Europe: The Faltering Project*, London: Polity.

Hachigian, Nina (2014), *Debating China: The US–China Relationship in Ten Conversations*, Oxford: Oxford University Press.

Hadenius, Axel and Frederik Uggla (1996), 'Making Civil Society Work, Promoting Democratic Development: What Can States and Donors Do?', *World Development*, 24(10): 1621–1639.

Haglund, Dan (2009), 'In It for the Long Term? Governance and Learning among Chinese Investors in Zambia's Copper Sector', *China Quarterly*, 199(September): 627–646.

Hagström, Linus and Björn Jerdén (2010), 'Understanding Fluctuations in Sino-Japanese Relations: To Politicize or to De-politicize the China Issue in the Japanese Diet', *Pacific Affairs*, 83(4): 719–739.

Hale, William (2003), 'Human Rights, the EU and the Turkish Accession Process', in Ali Carkoglu and Barry Rubin (eds), *Turkey and the European Union*, London: Frank Cass, pp. 107–126.

Hall, Stuart (1981), 'Cultural Studies: Two Paradigms', in T. Bennet, G. Martin, C. Mercer and J. Woollacott (eds), *Culture, Ideology and Social Process*, London: Batsford Academic and Educational.

Hannum, Emily (2002), 'Educational Stratification by Ethnicity in China', *Demography*, 39(1): 95–117.

Hansen, Mette Halskov (2005), *Frontier People*, Vancouver: University of British Columbia Press.

Hao Mengbi and Duan Haoran (1984), *Zhongguo Gongchandang liushi nian (The Chinese Communist Party's Past Sixty Years)*, Beijing: Jiefangjun chubanshe.

Hao, X. and Ren C. (1999), 'Analyses of Chinese Vocational Education's Reforms and Developments', *Journal of Northeast Normal University (Philosophy and Social Sciences)*, 6: 90–95 (in Chinese).

Hao, Yufan (ed.) (2010), *Sino-American Relations: Challenges Ahead*, Farnham: Ashgate.

Hao, Yufan (2013), 'Domestic Chinese Influences on US–China Relations', in David Shambaugh (ed.), *Tangled Titans: The United States and China*, Lanham, MD: Rowman & Littlefield.

Hao, Yufan and Lin Su (eds) (2005), *China's Foreign Policy Making: Societal Force and Chinese American Policy*, Farnham: Ashgate.

Hao, Yuqing (ed.) (2007), *The Building of the PLA*, Beijing: National Defense University Press.

Harding, Harry (1987), 'The PLA as a Political Interest Group', in Victor Falkenheim (ed.), *Chinese Politics from Mao to Deng*, New York: Paragon House.

Harding, Harry (1991), 'The Chinese State in Crisis', in R. MacFarquhar and J.K. Fairbank (eds), *The Cambridge History of China*, Cambridge: Cambridge University Press, pp. 105–217.

Harding, Harry (1992), *Fragile Relationship: The United States and China since 1972*, Washington, DC: Brookings Institution Press.

Harrison, Henrietta (2001), *China: Inventing the Nation*, London: Arnold.

Harrison, James Pinckney (1972), *The Long March to Power: A History of the Chinese Communist Party, 1921–72*, New York: Praeger.

Hartford, Kathleen and Steven M. Goldstein (eds) (1989), *Single Sparks: China's Rural Revolutions*, White Plains, NY: M.E. Sharpe.

Harvey, D. (2005), *A Brief History of Neoliberalism*, Oxford: Oxford University Press.

Hasmath, Reza and Jennifer Hsu (2008), 'NGOs in China and Issues of Accountability', *Asia Pacific Journal of Public Administration*, 30(1): 1–11.

Hasmath, Reza and Jennifer Hsu (2014), 'Isomorphic Pressures, Epistemic Communities and State–NGO Collaboration in China', *China Quarterly*, 220: 936–954.

Hayhoe, R. (1989), *China's Universities and the Open Door*, Armonk, NY, USA and London, UK: M.E. Sharpe.

He, Baogang (2003), 'Minority Rights: A Confucian Critique of Kymlicka's Theory of Nonassimilation', in Kim-chong Chong, Sor-hoon Tan and C.L. Ten (eds), *The Moral Circle and the Self*, Chicago, IL: Open Court Publishing Company, pp. 219–245.

He, Baogang (2004), 'Confucianism versus Liberalism over Minority Rights', *Journal of Chinese Philosophy*, 31(1): 103–123.

He, B. (2007), *Rural Democracy in China: The Role of Village Elections*, New York: Palgrave/Macmillan.

He, B. (2011), 'Civil Engagement through Participatory Budgeting in China: Three Different Logics at Work', *Public Administration and Development*, 31: 122–133.

He, Qin, Wang Jiaxun and Chen Mingxian (1986), *Zhongguo Gongchandang shigang* (A concise history of the Chinese Communist Party), Beijing: Beijing daxue chubanshe.

He, Yinan (2008), 'Ripe for Cooperation or Rivalry? Commerce, Realpolitik, and War Memory in Contemporary Sino-Japanese Relations', *Asian Security*, 4(2): 162–197.

He, Zengke (2000), 'Corruption and Anti-Corruption in Reform China', *Communist and Post-Communist Studies*, 33(2): 243–270. doi:10.1016/S0967-067X(00)00006-4.

Heberer, Thomas (1989), *China and Its National Minorities*, Armonk, NY: M.E. Sharpe.

Heilmann, S. (2005), 'Regulatory Innovation by Leninist Means: Communist Party Supervision in China's Financial Industry', *China Quarterly*, 181: 1–21.

Heilmann, S. (2008a), 'Policy Experimentation in China's Economic Rise', *Studies in Comparative International Development*, 43(1): 1–26.

Heilmann, Sebastian (2008b), 'From Local Experiments to National Policy: The Origins of China's Distinctive Policy Process', *China Journal*, 59: 1–29.

Heilmann, Sebastian (2009), 'Maximum Tinkering under Uncertainty: Unorthodox Lessons from China', *Modern China*, 35(4): 450–462.

Heilmann, Sebastian and Oliver Melton (2013), 'The Reinvention of Development Planning in China, 1993–2012', *Modern China*, 39: 580–628.

Henan Sheng Renmin Zhengfu (Henan Province People's Government) (2007), 'Guanyu "Zhengzhou shi chengzhen jumin jiben yiliao baoxian banfa (shixing)" de jiedu' (Interpretation of "Zhengzhou City basic medical insurance for urban residents (trial)), 9 February, available at http://www.henan.gov.cn/hdjl/system/2007/02/09/010022521.shtml.

Henderson, Keith (2002), 'Alternative Service Delivery in Developing Countries: NGOs and Other Non-Profits in Urban Areas', *Public Organization Review: A Global Journal*, 2(2): 99–116.

Hendrischke, Hans J. (1999), 'Provinces in Competition: Region, Identity and Cultural Construction', in Hans Hendrischke and Chongyi Feng (eds), *The Political Economy of China's Provinces: Comparative and Competitive Advantage*, London, UK and New York, USA: Routledge.

Hendrischke, H. and C. Feng (eds) (1999), *The Political Economy of China's Provinces: Comparative and Competitive Advantage*, London, UK and New York, USA: Routledge.

Henrard, Kristin (2001), 'The Interrelationship between Individual Human Rights, Minority Rights and the Right to Self-Determination and Its Importance for the Adequate Protection of Linguistic Minorities', *Global Review of Ethnopolitics*, 1(1): 41–61.

Hershatter, G. (2011), *The Gender of Memory: Rural Women and China's Collective Past*, Berkeley, CA: University of California Press

Hess, Stephen E. (2009), 'Islam, Local Elites, and China's Missteps in Integrating the Uyghur Nation', available at http://www.usak.org.tr/dosyalar/dergi/4EeTmxtDN ppkrrFTak6s43XcfD6i Hq.pdf (accessed 16 July 2014).

Heurlin, Christopher (2010), 'Governing Civil Society: The Political Logic of NGO–State Relations Under Dictatorship', *Voluntas*, 21(2): 220–239.

Hildebrandt, Timothy (2011), 'The Political Economy of Social Organization in China', *China Quarterly*, 208: 970–989.

Hillman, Arye L. (2009), *Public Finance and Public Policy: Responsibilities and Limitations of Government*, 2nd edn, Cambridge: Cambridge University Press.

Hindess, B. (1986), 'Actors and Social Relations', in M. Wardell and S. Turner (eds), *Sociological Theory in Transition*, London: Allen & Unwin.

Hindess, B. (1987), *Politics and Class Analysis*, Oxford: Basil Blackwell.

Hinton, C. (2003), 'Interview', *Morning Sun*.

Hirschman, Albert O. (1945), *National Power and the Structure of Foreign Trade*, Berkeley, CA: University of California Press.

Hishida, Masaharu (ed.) (2012), *Chugoku-kyousantou no Sabaibaru senryaku* (CCP's survival strategy), Sanwa.co.

Ho, Peter (2001), 'Greening without Conflict? Environmentalism, Green NGOs and Civil Society in China', *Development and Change*, 32: 893–921.

Holbig, Heike (2004), 'The Emergence of the Campaign to Open Up the West: Ideological Formation, Central Decision-Making and the Role of the Provinces', *China Quarterly*, 178: 335–357.

Holbig, Heike (2013), 'Ideology after the End of Ideology: China and the Quest for Autocratic Legitimation', *Democratization*, 20(1): 61–81.

Holbig, Heike and Bruce Gilley (2010), 'In Search of Legitimacy in Post-revolutionary China: Bringing Ideology and Governance Back In', GIGA (German Institute of Global and Area Studies), Working Paper, No. 127, March.

Holden, Patrick (2009), *In Search of Structural Power: EU Aid Policy as a Global Political Instrument*, London: Ashgate.

Holslag, Jonathan (2010), 'China's Roads to Influence', *Asian Survey*, 50(4): 641–662.

Hong, L. (2002), 'New Chongqing: Opportunities and Challenges', in J. Fitzgerald (ed.), *Rethinking China's Provinces*, London: Routledge, pp. 41–87.

Honig, E. and G. Hershatter (1988), *Personal Voices: Chinese Women in the 1980s*, Stanford, CA: Stanford University Press.

Hook, Leslie (2012), 'Chalco Abandons Mongolia Coal Mine Deal', *Financial Times*, 3 September, available at http://www.ft.com/cms/s/0/8f059d54-f5d2-11e1-a6bb-00144feabdc0.html#ixzz25VHKGLMd.

Howell, Jude (ed.) (2004), *Governance in China*, Lanham, MD: Rowman & Littlefield.

Howell, Jude (2012), 'Civil Society, Corporatism and Capitalism in China', *Journal of Comparative Asian Development*, 11(2): 271–294.

Howland, Douglas (2011), 'The Dialectics of Chauvinism', *Modern China*, 37(2): 1–32.

Hsing, You-Tien (2006), 'Land and Territorial Politics in Urban China', *China Quarterly*, 187: 570–590.

Hsu, Carolyn (2009), 'Chinese NGOs and the State: Institutional Interdependence rather than Civil Society', paper presented at American Sociological Association, San Francisco, CA, 8–11 August.

Hsu, Carolyn (2010), 'Beyond Civil Society: An Organizational Perspective on State–NGO Relations in the People's Republic of China', *Journal of Civil Society*, 6(3): 259–277.

Hsu, Carolyn (2014), 'The China Youth Development Foundation', in R. Hasmath and J.Y.J. Hsu (eds), *NGO Governance and Management in China*, New York and Oxford, UK: Routledge.

Hsu, Carolyn (2015), 'The China Youth Development Foundation: GONGO (Government-Organized NGO), or GENGO (Government-Exploiting NGO)', in R. Hasmath and J.Y.J. Hsu (eds), *NGO Governance and Management in China*, New York and Oxford, UK: Routledge.

Hsu, Immanuel C.Y. (2000), *The Rise of Modern China*, 6th edn, New York: Oxford University Press.

Hsu, Jennifer Y.J. (2009), 'A State Creation? Civil Society and Migrant Organizations', in R. Hasmath and J. Hsu (eds), *China in an Era of Transition: Understanding Contemporary State and Society Actors*, New York: Palgrave, pp. 127–143.

Hsu, Jennifer Y.J. (2012a), 'Layers of the Urban State: Migrant Organisations and the Chinese State', *Urban Studies*, 49(16): 3513–3530.

Hsu, Jennifer Y.J. (2012b), 'Spaces of Civil Society: The Role of Migrant Non-Go', 12(1): 63–76.

Hsu, Jennifer Y.J. and Reza Hasmath (2013), 'The Changing Face of State Corporatism', in J.Y.J. Hsu and R. Hasmath, R. (eds), *The Chinese Corporatist State: Adaptation, Survival and Resistance*, New York: Routledge, pp. 1–9.

Hsu, Jennifer Y.J. and Reza Hasmath (2014), 'The Local Corporatist State and NGO Relations in China', *Journal of Contemporary China*, 23(87): 516–534.

Hu, Angang (2001), *Zhongguo 90 niandai hou banqi fubai zaochengde jinji suanshi* (Post 90s bribery and corruption: its economic impact), *Guoji jingji pinglun* (International Economics Review), 3: 12–21.

Hu, Fox Z.Y. and George C.S. Lin (2010), 'Same Bed, Different Dreams: A Comparative Analysis of the Growth and Performance of SOEs in Northeast and South China', *Issues and Studies*, 46(2): 33–86.

Hu, Jintao (2005), 'Build Towards a Harmonious World of Lasting Peace and Common Prosperity', Statement at United Nations Summit, available at http://www.un.org/webcast/summit2005/statements15/china050915eng.pdf (accessed 27 October 2013).

Hu, Yaobang (2007), *Hu Yaobang sixiang nianpu (1975–1989)* (Chronology of Hu Yaobang's thought, 1975–1989), 2 vols, Hong Kong: Taide shidai chubanshe.

Huang, Chuanhui (2004), *Tianxia hunyin: gongheguo sanbu hunyinfa jishi* (Marriage under the heaven: three marriage laws of the PRC), Shanghai: Wenhui Press.

Huang, Jin and Yao Chun (2013), 'Xi Conveys China's Views and Confidence at G20 Summit', *People's Daily Online Edition*, 7 September, available at http://english.people.com.cn/90883/8392765.html (accessed 23 September 2013).

Huang, Jing (2000), *Factionalism in Chinese Communist Politics*, New York: Cambridge University Press.

Huang, J., L. Zhang, et al. (2007), 'Economic Growth, the Nature of Growth and Poverty Reduction in Rural China.'

Huang, Philip C. (1993), '"Public Sphere" / "Civil Society" in China? The Third Realm between State and Society', *Modern China* 19(2): 216–240.

Huang, Philip C.C. (2012), 'Profit-Making State Firms and China's Development Experience: "State Capitalism" or "Socialist Market Economy"', *Modern China*, 38(6): 591–629.

Huang, Ray (1981), *1587, A Year of No Significance*, New Haven, CT: Yale University Press.

Huang, Ray (1997), *China: A Macro History*, Armonk, NY: ME Sharpe.

Huang, Yasheng (1996), *Inflation and Investment Controls in China: The Political Economy of Central–Local Relations during the Reform Era*, New York: Cambridge University Press.

Huang, Yiqing (ed.) (1996), *Zhongguo guoku de fazhan yu gaige 1985–1995* (Development and reform of Treasury in China, 1985–1995), Beijing: Zhongguo jinrong chubanshe.

Huang, Y. (2008), *Capitalism with Chinese Characteristics: Entrepreneurship and the State*, Cambridge, UK and New York, USA: Cambridge University Press.

Huang, Y. (2010), 'China Boom: Rural China in the 1980s', available at http://chinaboom.asiasociety.org/essays/detail/212 (accessed 3 October 2014).

Hucker, C.O. (1998), 'Ming Government', in D.C. Twitchett and F.W. Mote (eds), *The Cambridge History of China, Vol. 8, The Ming Dynasty, 1368–1644, Part 2*, Cambridge: Cambridge University Press, pp. 9–105.

Hughes, Christopher R. (2005), 'Nationalism and Multilateralism in Chinese Foreign Policy: Implications for Southeast Asia', *Pacific Review*, 18(1): 119–135.

Hughes, Christopher R. (2006), *Chinese Nationalism in the Global Era*, Abingdon: Routledge.

Human Rights in China (2007), 'China: Minority Exclusion, Marginalization and Rising Tensions', available at https://archive.org/stream/229019-china-minority-exclusion-marginalization-and/229019-china-minority-exclusion-marginalization-and_djvu.txt (accessed 11 July 2014).

Human Rights Watch (2014), 'Under China's Shadow: Mistreatment of Tibetans in Nepal', 1 April, available at http://www.hrw.org/node/123804.

Hunt, Michael (1983), *The Making of a Special Relationship: The United States and China to 1914*, New York: Columbia University Press.

Huntington, Samuel (1968), *Political Order in Changing Societies*, New Have, CT: Yale University Press.

Huntington, Samuel (1985), *The Soldier and the State: Theory and Politics of Civil–Military Relations*, Cambridge, MA: Harvard University Press.

Hurst, William (2009), *The Chinese Worker after Socialism*, Cambridge: Cambridge University Press.

Hyer, Eric (2006), 'China's policy towards Uighur nationalism', *Journal of Muslim Minority Affairs*, 26(1): 75–86.

Hyer, Eric (2009), 'Sinocentrism and the National Question in China', in Susana Carvalho and Francois Gemenne (eds), *Nations and their Histories*, Basingstoke: Palgrave Macmillan, pp. 255–273.

Ijiri, H. (1996), 'Sino-Japanese Controversy Since 1972 Diplomatic Normalization', in Christopher Howe (ed.), *China and Japan: History, Trends and Prospects*, Oxford: Clarendon Press, pp. 60–82.

Ikenberry, G.J. (2008), 'The Rise of China and the Future of the West: Can the Liberal System Survive?', *Foreign Affairs*, 87(1): 23–37.

Ikenberry, G. John (2011), 'The Future of the Liberal World Order: Internationalism After America', *Foreign Affairs*, May/June, available at http://www.foreignaffairs.com/articles/67730/g-john-ikenberry/the-future-of-the-liberal-world-order.

Ikenberry, G. John (2014), 'The Illusion of Geopolitics: The Enduring Power of the Liberal Order', *Foreign Affairs*, May/June, available at http://www.foreignaffairs.com/articles/141212/g-john-ikenberry/the-illusion-of-geopolitics.

Ikenberry, G.J. and M. Mastanduno (2003), *International Relations Theory and the Asia-Pacific*, New York: Columbia University Press.

Information Office of the State Council of the PRC (2005), *White Paper 2005: Regional Autonomy for Ethnic Minorities in China*, February, available at http://www.china.org.cn/e-white/20050301/index.htm (accessed 13 July 2014).

Information Office of the State Council of the PRC (2010), 'China's Ethnic Policy and Common Prosperity and Development of All Ethnic Groups', available at http://english.gov.cn/official/2009-09/27/content_1427989.htm (accessed 13 July 2014).

Ingram, Catherine (2011), 'Echoing the Environment in Kam Big Song', *Asian Studies Review*, 35(4): 439–455.

International Commission on Intervention and State Sovereignty (2001), 'The Responsibility to Protect', December, available at http://responsibilitytoprotect.org/ICISS%20Report.pdf (accessed 12 July 2014).

Isaacs, Harold R. (1958), *Scratches on our Minds: American Images of China and India*, New York: John Day Company.

Israel, Jorh (1973), 'Continuities and Discontinuities in the Ideology of the Great Proletarian Cultural Revolution', in Chalmers Johnson (ed.), *Ideology and Politics in Contemporary China*, Seattle, WA, USA and London, UK: University of Washington Press.

Itoh, Mayumi (2011), *The Origin of Ping-Pong Diplomacy: The Forgotten Architect of Sino-US Rapprochement*, Basingstoke: Palgrave Macmillan.

Iwasaki, Ikuo (ed.) (1994), *Development and Politics: A Study of Development-Oriented Authoritarian Regimes in ASEAN Countries*, Institute of Developing Economies.

Jacka, Tamara (2009), 'Cultivating Citizens: Suzhi (Quality), Discourse in the PRC', *Positions: Asia Critique*, 17(3): 523–535.

Jackson, Steven (1995), 'China's Third World Foreign Policy: The Case of Angola and Mozambique, 1961–93', *China Quarterly*, 142: 388–422.

Jacobs, J.B. (1999), 'Uneven Development: Prosperity and Poverty in Jiangsu', in H. Hendriscke and C.Y. Feng (eds), *The Political Economy of China's Provinces*, London: Routledge, pp. 113–154.

Jacobson, Harold and Michel Oksenberg (1990), *China's Participation in the IMF, the World Bank, and GATT: Toward a Global Economic Order*, Ann Arbor, MI: University of Michigan Press.

Jacques, Martin (2009), *When China Rules the World*, London: Allen Lane.

Jakobson, L. and D. Knox (2010), *New Foreign Policy Actors in China*, Stockholm: SIPRI.

Jakobson, Linda and Jingchao Peng (2012), 'China's Arctic Aspirations', SIPRI Policy Paper No. 34, November.

Japan Coast Guard (n.d.), 'Senkaku shotō shūhen kaiiki ni okeru chūgoku kōsen nado no dōkō to waga kuni no taisho', available at http://www.kaiho.mlit.go.jp/senkaku/ (accessed 18 August 2014).

Jefferson, G.H. and T.G. Rawski (1992), 'Unemployment, Underemployment, and Employment Policy in China Cities', *Modern China*, 18: 42–71.

Jerdén, Björn (2014), 'The Assertive China Narrative: Why It Is Wrong and How so Many Bought Into It', *Chinese Journal of International Politics*, 7(1): 47–88.

Jerdén, Björn and Linus Hagström (2012), 'Rethinking Japan's China Policy: Japan as an Accommodator in the Rise of China, 1978–2011', *Journal of East Asian Studies*, 12(2): 215–250.

Jespersen, T. Christopher (1999), *American Images of China, 1931–1949*, Palo Alto, CA: Stanford University Press.

JETRO (various years), 'Japanese Trade and Investment Statistics', available at http://www.jetro.go.jp/en/reports/statistics/ (accessed 12 August 2014).

Jia, Hao and Zhimin Lin (eds) (1994), *Changing Central–Local Relations in China: Reform and State Capacity*, Boulder, CO: Westview Press.

Jia, Hao and Qubing Zhuang (1992), 'China's Polity towards the Korean Peninsula', *Asian Survey*, 32(12): 1137–1156.

Jia, Xinjin and Long Sun (2009), 'Measurement Indices of Civil Society and Exploration of Their Localization', *China Nonprofit Review*, 1(1): 37–57.

Jiang, Lai (2008), 'Zhonggong jiaqiang fan fubai heguoqiang liyuanchao lingxian' (CCP to strengthen anti-corruption), *Dagongbao*, 14 February.

Jiang, Shuxian (2011), 'Guoji jinrong weiji he shijie duojihua qushi shenru fazhan' (The deepening development of a multipolar world and the international financial crisis),

China Center for Contemporary World Studies Research Paper, available at http://www.cccws.org.cn/NewsInfo.aspx?NId=627 (accessed 14 November 2011).

Jiang, Wenran (2010), 'Canada Resumes Summit Diplomacy with China', *ChinaBrief*, 10(1): 7 January.

Jiang, Zemin (2000), 'Zai xinde lishi tiaojian xia women dang ruhe zuodao "Sange Daibiao"' (How can CCP achieve the 'Three Represents' under new historical circumstances), speech on 25 February, Guangdong Province, available at http://www.kxdj.com/kxdj2005/html/160/125.html.

Jiang, Zemin (2001), 'Zai qingzhu Zhongguo gongchandang chengli bashi zhouniandahu shang de jianghua' (Speech at the Celebration of the Eightieth anniversary of the Founding of the Chinese Communist Party), in Jiang Zemin, *Lun sange daibiao* (On the Three Represents), Beijing: Zhongyang wenxian chubanshe.

Jiang, Zemin (2006a), 'Realizing Generation Leap in PLA Modernization and National Defence', *Selected Works of Jiang Zemin*, Vol. 2, Beijing: Renminchubanshe.

Jiang, Zemin (2006b), *Selected Works of Jiang Zemin*, Vol. 3, Beijing: People's Publishing House.

Jin, Baisong (2012), 'Consider sanctions on Japan', *China Daily*, 17 September 2012, available at http://www.chinadaily.com.cn/opinion/2012-09/17/content_15761435.htm.

Jin, Yihong (2007), 'Rethinking the "Iron Girls": Gender and Labour during the Chinese Cultural Revolution', in D. Ko and Wang Zheng (eds), *Translating Feminisms in China*, Oxford: Blackwell Publishing.

Jing, Dao (1958), 'Jiaohua yaozuo Mu Guiying' (Jiaohua wants to be Mu Guiying), *Women of China*, May, p. 5.

Jing, M. and W. Shen (2014), *The EU, the US and China: Towards a New International Order?*, Cheltenham, UK and Northampton, MA, USA: Edward Elgar Publishing.

Jiu San Society Zhengzhou Committee (2007), 'Guanyu jiakuai jianli chengshi shequ weisheng fuwu tixi de jianyi' (Suggestions on accelerating the establishment of a urban community health system), 29 October, available at http://www.zzzxy.gov.cn/zzzx/html/32/81/2007-10-29/2146.html.

Joffe, Ellis (1997), 'How Much Does the PLA Make Foreign Policy?', in David Goodman and Gerry Segal (eds), *China Rising: Interdependence and Nationalism*, London: Routledge, pp. 53–70.

Johnson, Chalmers (1962), *Peasant Nationalism and Communist Power: The Emergence of Revolutionary China, 1937–1945*, Stanford, CA: Stanford University Press.

Johnson, Chalmers (ed.) (1973), *Ideology and Politics in Contemporary China*, Seattle, WA, USA and London, UK: University of Washington Press.

Johnson, Emily and Gregory Chow (1997), 'Rates of Return to Schooling in China', *Pacific Economic Review*, 2(2): 101–113.

Johnson, K. (1983), *Women, the Family and Peasant Revolution in China*, Chicago, IL: University of Chicago Press.

Johnston, Alastair Iain (2013), 'How New and Assertive is China's New Assertiveness?', *International Security*, 37(4): 7–48.

Johnston, Alistair Ian (2008), *Social States: China in International Institutions, 1980–2000*, Princeton, NJ, USA and Oxford, UK: Princeton University Press.

Johnstone, W. (1963), *Burma's Foreign Policy: A Study in Neutralism*, Cambridge, MA: Harvard University Press.

Jones, Lee (2012), *ASEAN, Sovereignty and Intervention in Southeast Asia*, Basingstoke: Palgrave Macmillan.
Joseph, W.A. (2010), *Politics in China*, Cambridge: Cambridge University Press.
Kang, David (2003), 'Getting Asia Wrong: The Need for New Analytical Frameworks', *International Security*, 27(4), 57–85.
Kang, J. (2009), 'Sanji suoyou, duiwei jichu' (Three levels of ownership with the production team as the basic unit), *Dang'an Tiandi* (Global Party), 4: 17–21.
Kang, Shaobang (2010), 'Jinrong weiji yu shijie duojihua' (The financial crisis and world multipolarity), *Zhonggong zhongyangxiao xuebao* (Journal of the Central Party School), 14(1): 107–112.
Kang, Xiaoguang and Han Heng (2011), 'Graduated Control: Research on State–Society Relationship in Contemporary Mainland China', in Z. Deng (ed.), *State and Civil Society: The Chinese Perspective*, Singapore: World Scientific, pp. 97–121.
Kastner, Scott L. (2009), *Political Conflict and Economic Interdependence Across the Taiwan Strait and Beyond*, Palo Alto, CA: Stanford University Press.
Kau, Michael Y.M. (ed.) (1975), *The Lin Biao Affair: Power Politics and Military Coup*, White Plains, NY: International Arts and Sciences Press.
Kaufman, Joan (2011), 'HIV Sex Work, and Civil Society in China', *Journal of Infectious Disease* 204(Suppl. 5): s1218–s1222.
Kaufman, Joan (2012), 'China's Evolving AIDS Policy: The Influence of Global Norms and Transnational Non-Governmental Organizations', *Contemporary Politics*, 18(2): 225–238.
Kaup, Katherine Palmer (2002), 'Regionalism Versus Ethnicnationalism in the People's Republic of China', *China Quarterly*, 172: 863–884.
Kelliher, D.R. (1992), *Peasant Power in China: the Era of Rural Reform, 1979–1989*, New Haven, CT: Yale University Press.
Kennedy, J.J. (2007), 'From the Tax-for-Fee Reform to the Abolition of Agricultural Taxes: The Impact on Township Governments in North-West China', *China Quarterly*, 189: 43–59.
Kennedy, Scott (ed.) (2003), *China Cross Talk: The American Debate over China Policy Since Normalization: A Reader*, Lanham, MD: Rowman & Littlefield.
Kennedy, S. (2005), *The Business of Lobbying in China*, Cambridge, MA: Harvard University Press.
Kennedy, Scott (2009), *The Business of Lobbying in China*, Cambridge, MA: Harvard University Press.
Kennedy, Scott (2012), 'China in Global Governance: What Kind of Status Quo Power?', in Scott Kennedy and Shuaihua Cheng (eds), *From Rule Takers to Rule Makers: The Growing Role of Chinese in Global Governance*, Bloomington, IN: Indiana University Research Center for Chinese Politics and Business, pp. 9–21.
Kent, Ann (2002), 'China's International Socialization: The Role of International Organizations', *Global Governance*, 8(3): 343–364.
Keohane, Robert O. (1986), 'Reciprocity in International Relations', *International Organization*, 40(1): 1–27.
Keohane, Robert O. and Joseph S. Nye (2001), *Power and Interdependence*, New York: Longman.

Kersting, Norbert, et al. (2009), *Local Governance Reform in Global Perspective*, Wiesbaden: Vrelag fur Sozialwissenschaften.

Khaw, Guat Hoon (1977), 'An Analysis of China's Attitudes towards ASEAN, 1967–76', Occasional Paper, Vol. 48, Singapore: Institute of Southeast Asian Studies.

Kim, Samuel S. (2006), *The Two Koreas and the Great Powers*, New York: Cambridge University Press.

King, K. (2013), *China's Aid and Soft Power in Africa: The Case of Education and Training*, Woodbridge: Boydell & Brewer.

Kinzelbach, K. and H. Thelle (2011), 'Taking Human Rights to China: An Assessment of the EU's Approach', *China Quarterly*, 205(March): 60–79.

Kiselycznyk, Michael and Phillip Saunders (2010), 'Civil–Military Relations in China: Assessing the PLA's Role in Elite Politics', *China Strategic Perspectives*, No. 2, National Defence University Press, Washington D.C.

Kissinger, Henry (1979), *White House Years*, New York: Little, Brown & Company.

Kitaoka, Shin'ichi (2010), 'Nitchū kyōdō rekishi kenkyū' o furikaeru', in Kasahara Tokuji (ed.), *Sensō o shiranai kokumin no tame no nitchū rekishi kenkyū: 'Nitchū rekishi kyōdō kenkyū "kingendaishi"' o yumu*, Tokyo: Bensei shuppan, pp. 227–238.

Klaus, Richard (1982), *Class Conflict in Chinese Socialism*, New York: Columbia University Press.

Ko, D. (1994), *Teachers of the Inner Chambers: Women and Culture in Seventeenth-Century China*, Stanford, CA: Stanford University Press.

Ko, Dorothy and Wang Zheng (2007), *Translating Feminism in China*, London: Blackwell Publishing.

Koenig, Matthias (2008), 'Institutional Change in the World Polity', *International Sociology*, 23(1): 95–114.

Kohn, Richard (1994), 'Out of Control: the Crisis in Civil–Military Relations', *National Interests*, 35(Spring): 3–17.

Kojima, Kazuko (2012), 'Party in Intellectual Elites: Based on the Questionnaire Survey 2008–2009', in Masaharu Hishida (ed.), *CCP's Survival Strategy*, Sanwa Co. (in Japanese).

Kojima, Kazuko, Jae-Young Choe, Takfumi Ohtomo and Yutaka Tsujinaka (2012), 'The Corporatist System and Social Organizations in China', *Management and Organization Review*, 8(3): 609–628.

Kornai, J. (1992), 'The Socialist System – the Political-Economy of Communism', *NewStatesman and Society*, 5(207): 23–23.

Koszorus, Frank (1982), 'Sixty Years After', available at http://www.hungarianhistory.com/ lib/tria/tria41.htm (accessed 11 July 2014).

Kou, Chien-wen (2000), 'Why the Military Obeys the Party's Orders to Repress Popular Uprisings: The Chinese Military Crackdown of 1989', *Issues and Studies*, 36(6).

Kou, Chien-wen (2011), 'The Political Mobility of PLA Leaders after 1987: The Impact on Professionalism and Institutionalization', *Mainland China Studies*, 54(2).

Kou, Jianwen and Zang Xiaowei (eds) (2013), *Elites and Governance in China*, London: Routledge.

Kuhn, Phillip (1984), 'Chinese Views of Social Stratification', in James Watson (ed.), *Class and Social Stratification in Post-Revolutionary China*, Cambridge: Cambridge University Press, pp. 16–28.

Kuik, Cheng-chwee (2005), 'Multilateralism in China's ASEAN Policy: Its Evolution, Characteristics and Aspiration', *Contemporary Southeast Asia*, 27(1): 102–122.
Kung, J. (1999), 'The Evolution of Property Rights in Village Enterprises: The case of Wuxi County', in J.C. Oi and A.G. Walder (eds), *Property Rights and Economic Reform in China*, Stanford, CA: Stanford University Press, p. xiv.
Kurlantzick, Joshua (2007), *Charm Offensive: How China's Soft Power is Transforming the World*, New Haven, CT: Yale University Press.
Kwong, Julia (1997), *The Political Economy of Corruption in China*, White Plains, NY: M.E. Sharpe.
Kymlicka, Will (1995), *Multicultural Citizenship: A Liberal Theory of Minority Rights*, Oxford: Clarendon Press.
Laffont, Jean-Jacques and David Martimort (2001), *Theory of Incentives: The Principal–Agent Model*, Princeton, NJ: Princeton University Press.
Lai, Hongyi (2002), 'China's Western Development Program: Its Rationale, Implementation and Prospects', *Modern China*, 28(4): 432–466.
Lai, Hongyi (2006), *Developing Central China: Background and Objectives (I)*, Singapore: East Asia Institute.
Lai, Hongyi (2009a), 'China's Ethnic Policies and Challenges', *East Asian Policy*, 1(2): 5–13.
Lai, Hongyi (2009b), 'The Evolution of China's Ethnic Policies', Background Brief No. 440, East Asian Institute, National University of Singapore, 12 March, available at http://www.eai.nus.edu.sg/BB440.pdf.
Lai, Hongyi (2010), 'Ethnic Autonomous Regions', in Jae Ho Chung and Tao-chiu Lam (eds), *China's Local Administration*, London: Routledge, pp. 62–85.
Lampton, David M. (ed.) (1987), *Policy Implementation in Post-Mao China*, London: University of California Press.
Lampton, David M. (2001a), 'China's Foreign and National Security Policymaking Process: Is It Changing, and Does It Matter?', in David M. Lampton (ed.), *The Making of Chinese Foreign and Security Policy in the Era of Reform*, Stanford, CA: Stanford University Press, pp. 1–36.
Lampton, David M. (2001b), *Same Bed, Different Dreams: Managing US–China Relations 1989–2000*, Berkeley, CA: University of California Press.
Landry, P.F. (2008), *Decentralized Authoritarianism in China*, Cambridge: Cambridge University Press.
Lardy, Nicholas (1976a), 'Centralization and Decentralization in China's Fiscal Management', *China Quarterly*, 61: 25–60.
Lardy, Nicholas (1976b), 'Reply', *China Quarterly*, 66: 340–354.
Lardy, Nicholas (1992), *Foreign Trade and Economic Reform in China, 1978–1990*, Cambridge: Cambridge University Press.
Lardy, Nicholas (1999), 'China and the International Financial System', in Elizabeth Economy and Michel Oksenberg (eds), *China Joins the World: Progress and Prospects*, New York: Council on Foreign Relations Press, pp. 206–230.
Lardy, Nicholas (2012), *Sustaining China's Growth: After the Global Financial Crisis*, Washington, DC: Peterson Institute.
Larson, Megali Sarfatti (1997), *The Rise of Professionalism*, Berkeley, CA: UC Press.
Lau, J.T.F, C. Lin, C. Hao, X. Wu and J. Gu (2011), 'Public Health Challenge of the

Emerging HIV Epidemic among Men Who Have Sex with Men in China', *Public Health*, 125(5): 260–265.
Law, W.W. (2011), *Citizenship and Citizenship Education in a Global Age: Politics, Policies, and Practices in China*, New York: Peter Lang Publishing.
Lawson, E.K. (1984), *The Sino-Vietnamese Conflict*, New York: Praeger.
Lee, Chin-Kwan (2008), 'Rights Activism in China', *Contexts*, 7(3): 14–19.
Lee, Dongmin (2006), 'Chinese Civil–Military Relations', *Armed Forces and Society*, 32(3).
Lee, John (2012), 'China's Geostrategic Search for Oil', *Washington Quarterly*, 35(3): 75–92.
Lee, J.Y. and X. Wang (2009), 'Assessing the Impact of Performance-Based Budgeting: A Comparative Analysis across the United States, Taiwan, and China', *Public Administration Review*, 69(S1): 60–66.
Lee, Lai To (2001), 'China's Relations with ASEAN: Partners in the 21st Century?', *Pacifica Review*, 13(1): 61–71.
Leibold, James (2008), *Reconfiguring Chinese Nationalism: How the Qing Frontier and its Indigenes Became Chinese*, Basingstoke: Palgrave Macmillan.
Leibold, James (2010), 'The Beijing Olympics and China's Conflicted National Form', *China Journal*, 63: 1–24.
Leifer, Michael (1983), *Indonesia's Foreign Policy*, London: George Allen & Unwin.
Leonard, Kenneth L. (2002), 'When Both States and Markets Fail: Asymmetric Information and the Role of NGOs in African Health Care', *International Review of Law and Economics*, 22(1): 61–80.
Leung, J.C.B. (1994), 'Dismantling the "Iron Rice Bowl": Welfare Reforms in the People's Republic of China', *Journal of Social Policy*, 23: 341–361.
Leung, J.C.B. (1995), 'The Political Economy of Unemployment and Unemployment Insurance in the People's Republic of China', *International Social Work*, 38: 139–149.
Leung, J.C.B. (2005), 'Social Welfare in China', in A. Walker and C.-K. Wong (eds), *East Asian Welfare Regimes in Transition*, Bristol: Policy Press, pp. 49–71.
Lew, Roland (2004), 'Existing Socialism under the Chinese Communist Party's Rule', *Le Monde diplomatique*, October, Japanese translation available at http://www.diplo.jp/articles04/0410-4.html.
Lewis, David (2009), 'Nongovernmental Organizations and History', in H.K. Anheier, S. Toepler and R.A. List (eds), *International Encyclopedia of Civil Society*, New York: Springer.
Lewis, David and Nazneen Kanji (2009), *Non-Governmental Organizations and Development*, London: Routledge.
Lewis, John Wilson (1963), *Leadership in Communist China*, Ithaca, NY: Cornell University Press.
Li, B. and L. Jiang (eds) (1996), *Jiuzai jiuji* (Social assistance), Beijing: Chinese Society Publishers.
Li, Chao and John Gibson (2013), 'Rising Regional Inequality in China: Fact or Artifact?', *World Development*, 47: 16–29.
Li, Cheng (2012), 'The End of the CCP's Resilient Authoritarianism? A Tripartite Assessment of Shifting Power in China', *China Quarterly*, 211(September): 595–623.
Li, Chunling (2010), 'Characterizing China's Middle Class: Heterogeneous Composition

and Multiple Identities', in Cheng Li (ed.), *China's Emerging Middle Class*, Washington, DC: Brookings Institution Press, pp. 135–156.

Li, Chunling (2013), 'Sociopolitical Attitude of the Middle Class and the Implications for Political Transition', in Minglu Chen and David S.G. Goodman (eds), *Middle Class China: Identity and Behaviour*, Cheltenham, UK and Northampton, MA, USA: Edward Elgar Publishing, pp. 12–33.

Li, F. and W.J. Morgan (2013), 'Private Higher Education in China: Problems and Possibilities', in W.J. Morgan and B. Wu (eds), *Higher Education Reform in China: Beyond the Expansion*, London, UK and New York, USA: Routledge, pp. 66–78.

Li, H. (2001), 'The Political Stalinization of China: The Establishment of One-Party Constitutionalism, 1948–1954', *Journal of Cold War Studies*, 3(2): 28–47.

Li, H.B. and S. Rozelle (2003), 'Privatizing Rural China: Insider Privatization, Innovative Contracts and the Performance of Township Enterprises', *China Quarterly*, 176: 981–1005.

Li, H., N.T. Kuo, H. Liu, C. Korhonen, E. Pond, H. Guo, L. Smith, H. Xue and J. Sun (2010), 'From Spectators to Implementers: Civil Society Organization Involved in AIDS Programmes in China', *International Journal of Epidemiology*, 39: ii65–ii71.

Li, Jing (2011), *China's America: The Chinese View the United States, 1900–2000*, Albany, NY: State University of New York Press.

Li, Jinming and Li Dexia (2003), *The Dotted Line on the Chinese Map of the South China Sea: A Note, in: Ocean Development and International Law*, 34: 287–295.

Li, Junpeng (2001), Zhengfu zhineng yaocong zhijie ganyu jingji zhuanxiang gonggong guanli (Changing the Government functions from direct intervention in the economy to public administration), *Lilun daokan*, 10: 23–25.

Li, Keqiang (2014), 'Guanyu Shenhua Jingji Tizhi Gaige de Ruogan Wenti' (On some issues on deepening economic system reform), *Qiushi*, 9: 3–10.

Li, Linda Chelan (1998), *Centre and Provinces: China 1978–1993: Power as Non-Zero-Sum*, Oxford: Clarendon Press.

Li, Linda Chelan (2003), 'Towards a Public and Comprehensive Budget: Public Finance Reform in Guangdong', in Joseph Cheng (ed.), *Guangdong: Preparing for the WTO Challenge*, Hong Kong: Chinese University of Hong Kong Press, pp. 51–80.

Li, Linda Chelan (2004), 'Differentiated Actors: Central and Local Politics in China's Rural Tax Reforms', *Modern Asian Studies*, 40(1): 151–174.

Li, Linda Chelan (2005), 'Understanding Institutional Change: Fiscal Management in Local China', *Journal of Contemporary Asia*, 35(1): 87–108.

Li, Linda Chelan (2007), 'Working for the Peasants? Strategic Interactions and Unintended Consequences in the Chinese Rural Tax Reform', *China Journal*, 57: 89–106.

Li, Linda Chelan (2012), *Rural Tax Reform in China: Policy Process and Institutional Change*, London: Routledge.

Li, Linda Chelan and Martin Painter (2013), 'Strategic Action and Local Fiscal Policy in Education: How Chinese Cadres Manage Abundance', paper presented at the international conference on Political Development in Time of Crisis: Democracy, State, and Governance, Fudan University Shanghai, China, 6–7 April.

Li, Linda Chelan and Wen Wang (2014), 'Pursuing Equity in Education: Conflicting Views and Shifting Strategies', *Journal of Contemporary Asia*, 44(2): 279–297.

Li, Linda Chelan and Zhenjie Yang (2014), 'What Causes the Local Fiscal Crisis in China: The Role of Intermediaries', paper presented at 2014 Conference of Association of Asian Studies, Philadelphia, USA.
Li, Mingjiang (2011), 'Rising From Within: China's Search for a Multilateral World and its Implications for Sino-US Relations', RSIS Working Paper No. 225, Singapore.
Li, Mingjiang (2014), 'Local Liberalism: China's Provincial Approaches to ASEAN', *Journal of Contemporary China*, 23(86): 275–293.
Li, Nan (ed.) (2006), *Chinese Civil–military Relations: the Transformation of the People's Liberation Army*, New York and Oxford, UK: Routledge.
Li, Nan (2010), 'Chinese Civil–Military Relations in the Post Deng Era', *China Maritime Studies* No. 4, US Naval War College.
Li, N. (2013), 'Policy towards Rural Vocational Education in China since the Reform and Opening-up', Northeast Normal University, MPhil thesis (in Chinese).
Li, Peilin (2004), *Chinese Social Stratification*, Beijing: Social Science Literature Press.
Li, Peng (1994), 'Speech on the National Education for Work Conference', *Beijing Education*, No. 9, available at http://www.cnki.com.cn/Article/CJFDTOTAL-BJYU 409.001.htm.
Li, Shushi (1992), 'Jiefang sixiang chengqing shifei zhuanbian guannian: xuexi Deng Xiaoping tongzhi nanshun zhongyao tanhua de jidian tihui' (Liberating thoughts, clarifying standards and transforming ideas: insights from Comrade Deng Xiaoping's Southern Tour talks), *Lilun xuexi yu yanjiu*, 4: 1–5.
Li, Xiaojiang (1988), *Xiawa de tansuo* (Eve's exploration), Zhengzhou: Henan People's Press.
Li, Z. and L. Wu (eds) (2005), *'Daobi' haishi 'fan daobi' – nongcun shuifei gaige qianhou zhongyang yu difang zhijiande hudong* (Pressure for change: central-local interactions in rural tax-for-fee reform), Shehuixue yanjiu (Sociological Studies), 20(4): 44–63.
Liaong, Donghai and Wang Heyan (2010), 'Kuang ye daquan cong he lai' (The source of everything), 21 June, available at http://magazine.caixin.com/2010-06-19/100153712.html.
Lieberthal, Kenneth (1978a), 'Sino-Soviet Conflict in the 1970s: Its Evolution and Implications for the Strategic Triangle', Rand Report R-2342-NA, Santa Monica, CA.
Lieberthal, Kenneth (1978b), 'The Politics of Modernization in the PRC', *Problems of Communism*, May–June.
Lieberthal, Kenneth (1995), *Governing China: From Revolution Through Reform*, 1st edn, New York: W.W. Norton.
Lieberthal, Kenneth (2003), *Governing China*, 2nd edn, New York: W.W. Norton.
Lieberthal, Kenneth and Wang Jisi (2012), *Addressing US–China Strategic Distrust*, John L. Thornton China Center Monograph Series, no. 4, Washington, DC: Brookings Institution, available at http://www.brookings.edu/research/papers/2012/03/30-us-china-lieberthal.
Lieberthal, Kenneth and David M. Lampton (eds) (1992), *Bureaucracy, Politics and Decision-Making in Post-Mao China*, Berkeley, CA: University of California Press.
Lieberthal, Kenneth and M. Oksenberg (1988), *Policy Making in China: Leaders, Structures and Processes*, Princeton, NJ: Princeton University Press.
Lilley, James (2005), *China Hands: Nine Decades of Adventure, Espionage, and Diplomacy in Asia*, New York: PublicAffairs.

Lin, Biao (1969), 'Report to the Ninth National Congress of the Communist Party of China', available at http://www.marxists.org/reference/archive/lin-biao/1969/04/01.htm (accessed 14 November 1997).
Lin, Jinshu and Quan Zhenan (2011), *Xiandai Chaoxian Jingji* (Modern North Korea Economy), Yanbian: Yanbian Daxue Chubanshe.
Lin, N. and C. Chen (1999), 'Local Elites as Officials and Owners: Shareholding and Property Rights in Daqizhuang', in J.C. Oi and A.G. Walder (eds), *Property Rights and Economic Reform in China*, Stanford, CA: Stanford University Press, pp. 145–170.
Lin, The-Chang (2007), 'Environmental NGOs and the Anti-Dam Movements in China: A Social Movement with Chinese Characteristics', *Issues and Studies*, 43(4): 149–184.
Lin, W., G.G. Liu and G. Chen (2009), 'The Urban Resident Basic Medical Insurance: A Landmark Reform towards Universal Coverage in China', *Health Economics*, 18: S83–S96.
Lin, Wanlong and Christine P.W. Wong (2012), 'Are Beijing's Equalization Policies Reaching the Poor? An Analysis of Direct Subsidies under the "Three Rurals" (Sannong)', *China Journal*, 67: 23–45.
Lin, Yunhui et al. (1989), *Kaige xingjin de shiqi* (The period of triumph and advance), Zhengzhou: Henan renmin chubanshe.
Linley, Matthew, James Reilly and Benjamin Goldsmith (2012), 'Who's Afraid of the Dragon? Asian Mass Publics' Perceptions of China's Influence', *Japanese Journal of Political Science*, 13(4): 501–523.
Liou, Chih-shian (2009), 'Bureaucratic Politics and Overseas Investment by Chinese State-Owned Oil Companies: Illusory Champions', *Asian Survey*, 49(4): 670–690.
Liu, Alan (1992), 'The Wenzhou Model of Development China's Modernization', *Asian Survey*, 32(8): 696–711.
Liu, Chengjun and Sijing Sun (2013), 'Building a Powerful Military is the Party's Endless Endeavor', *Qiushi* (Seeking Truth), 24: 12.
Liu, Guoguang, Na Bensi and Yang Xixian (eds) (1998), *Zhongguo kua shijide san da gaige* (China at the turn of the century, three great reforms), Beijing: People's Party Publisher.
Liu, G.G., S. Zhang and Z. Zhan (eds) (2010), *Investing in Human Capital for Economic Development in China*, Hackensack, NJ and London: World Scientific Books.
Liu, J.D. (1996), *Zhongguo xingzhengqu huade lilun yu shijian* (China's administrative divisions in theory and practice), Shanghai: East China Normal University Press.
Liu, J.D. (2002), *Zhongwai xingzhengqu hua bijiao yanjiu* (A comparative study of Chinese and foreign administrative divisions), Shanghai: East China Normal University Press.
Liu, J.D., R.C. Jin and K.Y. Zhou (1999), *Zhongguo gaiqu dili* (Administrative geography of China), Beijing: Sciences Press.
Liu, J.D. and N. Wang (2000), *Zhidu yu chuangxin: Zhongguochengshi zhidde fazhan yu gaige xinlun* (System and innovation: new theory on urban system development and reform in China), Nanjing: Southeast University Press.
Liu, J.D., Z.J. Yuan and C.P. Gu (2011), *Fenquan yu dangdai zhongguo bushiqu kongjianhuade lilun yu shijian: changzhoushi anlie yanjiu* (Decentralization in theory and practice: Changzhou in Jiangsu province), Nanjing: Southeast University Press.
Liu, Jianping and Liu Weishu (2009), *Meiguo duiwai jingji zhicai wenti yanjiu – dangdai guoji jingji zhengzhihua de gean fenxi* (Research on the US's use of economic sanctions:

a case study of the politicization of current international economic relations), Beijing: Renmin Publishers.
Liu, Jianping and Zheng Xutao (2005), 'Meiguo duiwai jingji zhicai fazhan chushi ji dui woguo de qishi' (Emerging trends in US sanctions and lessons for China), *Taipingyang Xuebao* (Pacific Studies), 5: 5–14.
Liu, Jiayi (2013), 'Liu Jiayi Shenji biaoqing' (Liu Jiayi on Audit Expression CCTV), *Yangshiwang*, 30 October, available at http://jingji.cntv.cn/2013/10/30/ARTI1383113516855602.shtml.
Liu, Jingfang (2011), 'Picturing a Green Virtual Public Space for Social Change: A Study of Internet Activism and Web-Based Environmental Collective Actions in China', *Chinese Journal of Communication*, 4(2): 137–166.
Liu, Jixian (2008), 'New Development of PLA Political Work: Study Hu Jintao's Military Thought', *Political work of the PLA*, No. 10.
Liu, L., Rebecca Karl and Dorothy Ko (eds) (2013), *The Birth of Chinese Feminism: Essential Texts in Transnational Theory*, New York: Columbia University Press.
Liu, Mingxing, Juan Wang, Ran Tao and Rachel Murphy (2009), 'The Political Economy of Earmarked Transfers in a State-Designated Poor County in Western China: Central Policies and Local Responses', *China Quarterly*, 200: 973–994.
Liu, Qian, Bin Wang, Yuyan Kong and K.K. Cheng (2011), 'China's Primary Healthcare Reform', *Lancet*, 377: 2064–2066.
Liu, Tiewa (2012), 'China and Responsibility to Protect: Maintenance and Change of Its Policy for Intervention', *The Pacific Review*, 25(1): 153–173.
Liu, Wei (2008), 'Guoji jingji zhicai xintedian ji woguo de yingdui zhengce' (New characteristics of international economic sanctions, and the countermeasures China should take), *Shangwu jingji yanjiu* (Commercial Economic Research), 28: 30–35.
Liu, X. (2012), *The Mirage of China*, New York, USA and Oxford, UK: Berghahn Books.
Liu, Xiguang and Liu Kang (1997), *Yaomohua Zhongguo de Beihou* (Behind the demonisation of China), Beijing: China Social Sciences.
Liu, Xingwu and Alatan (1988), 'China's Policy Towards Her Minority Nationalities', *Social Scientist*, 16(1): 136–59.
Liu, Xinru (2012), 'The Western model of the military under state control is not viable in China', *PLA Daily*, 29 June.
Liu, Yazhou (2010), 'Enhancing Strategic Planning and Coordination of National Defence and Force Modernization According to the New Features of National Security Situations', *Seeking Truth*, 16 June.
Liu, Y.L. (2012), 'From Predator to Debtor: The Soft Budget Constraint and Semi-Planned Administration in Rural China', *Modern China*, 38(3): 308–345.
Loewen, Howard (2014), 'Institutional Interplay between the Chiang Mai Initiative and the International Monetary Fund', *European Journal of East Asian Studies*, 13(1): 50–67.
Long, Simon (1992), 'The Tree that Wants to Be Still: The Chinese Response to Foreign Pressure Since June 1989', *Pacific Review*, 5(2): 156–161.
Lou, Jiwei (ed.) (2013), *Caishui Gaige Zhonglun 2013* (A compendium of research essays and survey reports on fiscal reform 2013), Beijing: Jingji Kexue chubanshe.
Lou, Jiwei and Shuilin Wang (2008), *Public Finance in China: Reform and Growth for a Harmonious Society*, Washington, DC: World Bank.

Lu, Elaine Yi (2013), 'Beginning to Unlock the Black Box of the Budgetary Performance Evaluation Practices in China: A Case Study of Evaluation Reports from Zhejiang Province', *Public Money and Management*, 33(4): 253–260.
Lu, Ning (2001), 'The Central Leadership, Supraministry Coordinating Bodies, State Council Ministries, and Party Departments', in David M. Lampton (ed.), *The Making of Chinese Foreign and Security Policy in the Era of Reform*, Stanford, CA: Stanford University Press, pp. 39–53.
Lu, T. (2011), 'Jiguan shiye danwei yanglao baoxian gaigede zhijue yinsu yu celuo xuanze' (The constraining factors and strategic choices in public sector work unit old-age insurance reform), *Lilun tansuo* (Theory Exploration), 5: 87–90.
Lü, Xiaobo (2000), *Cadres and Corruption: The Organizational Involution of the Chinese Communist Party*, Palo Alto, CA: Stanford University Press.
Lu, Xueyi, et al. (2002), *Dangdai Zhongguo shehui jieceng yanjiu baobao* (Social Stratification in Contemporary China), Beijing: Zhongguo shehui kexue chubanshe.
Lu, Xueyi, et al. (2005), *Social Mobility in Contemporary China*, transl. Xiaowen Bao, ed. Harold Bashor, Montreal: America Quantum Media.
Lu, Xueyi, et al. (2010), *Dangdai Zhongguo shehui jiegou* (Social structure of contemporary China), Beijing: Zhongguo shehui kexue wenxian chubanshe.
Lu, Yiyi (2007), 'The Autonomy of Chinese NGOs: A New Perspective', *China: An International Journal*, 5(2): 173–203.
Lu, Zheng and Xiang Deng (2011), 'China's Western Development Strategy: Policies, Effects and Prospects', MPRA Paper No. 35201, available at http://mpra.ub.uni-muenchen.de/35201.
Lundberg, Maria and Yong Zhou (2009), 'Regional National Autonomy under Challenge', *International Journal on Minority and Group Rights*, 16(3): 269–327.
Luo, Gan (1998), 'Gaunyu guowuyuan jigou gaige fang'an de shuoming' (Explanation of the State Council Reform Plan), 6 March, available at http://www.people.com.cn/GB/shizheng/252/10434/10435/20030306/937505.html.
Luo, Qiong (2007), *Kangzheng, jiefang, pingdeng – Luo Qiong wenji* (Resistance, emancipation, equality – an anthology by Luo Qiong), Beijing: Chinese Women's Press.
Ma, Doris and Tim Summers (2009), *Is China's Growth Moving Inland? A Decade of 'Develop the West'*, London: Chatham House.
Ma, Jun (2006), 'Zero-Based Budgeting in China', *Journal of Public Budgeting, Accounting and Financial Management*, 18(4): 480–510.
Ma, Jun (2009), 'If You Can't Budget, How Can You Govern? A Study of China's State Capacity', *Public Administration and Development*, 29: 9–20.
Ma, Jun (2012), 'The Rise of Social Accountability in China', *Australian Journal of Public Administration*, 17(2): 111–121.
Ma, Jun and Muhua Lin (2012), 'Policymaking in China: A Review of Chinese Scholarship', *China Review*, 12(1): 95–122.
Ma, Jun and X. Ni (2008), 'Towards a Clean Government in China', *Crime, Law and Social Change*, 49(2): 119–138.
Ma, Jun and M.L. Niu (2006), 'Modernizing Public Budgeting and Financial Management in China', in H.A. Frank (ed.), *Public Finance Management*, New York: Taylor & Francis, pp. 691–736.
Ma, Jun and L. Yu (2012), 'Why Money Cannot be Spent as Budgeted? Lessons

from China's Recent Budget Reforms', *Journal of Public Budgeting, Accounting and Financial Management*, 24(1): 83–113.
Ma, L.J. (2005), 'Urban Administrative Restructuring, Changing Scale Relations and Local Economic Development in China', *Political Geography*, 24(4): 477–497.
Ma, Liang and Jiannan Wu (2011), 'What Drives Fiscal Transparency? Evidence from Provincial Government in China', paper presented at the first Global Conference on Transparency Research, Rutgers University-Newark, 19–20 May, available at http://ssrn.com/abstract=1807767.
Ma, Qiusha (2002), 'The Governance of NGOs in China since 1978: How Much Autonomy?', *Nonprofit and Voluntary Sector Quarterly*, 31(3): 305–328.
Ma, Qiusha (2006), *Non-Governmental Organizations in Contemporary China: Paving the Way to Civil Society?*, London: Routledge.
Ma, Z.Q. and J.D. Liu (2009), '*Pudong xinqu' gongnengqu yude guanli tizhi yu yuanxingji* (Management system and operational mechanisms of 'functional districts' in the Pudong New Area)', *Chenshi wenti* (Urban Problems), 6: 14–23.
MacFarquhar, Roderick (1983), *The Origins of the Cultural Revolution 2: The Great Leap Forward, 1958–1960*, New York: Columbia University Press.
MacFarquhar, Roderick (1997), *The Origins of the Cultural Revolution 3: The Coming of the Cataclysm 1961–66*, New York: Columbia University Press.
MacFarquhar, Roderick and Michael Schoenhals (2006), *Mao's Last Revolution*, Cambridge, MA: Bellknap Press of Harvard University Press.
Mackerras, Colin (1992), 'Integration and the Dramas of China's Minorities', *Asian Theatre Journal*, 9(1): 1–37.
Mackerras, Colin (1994), *China's Minorities*, Hong Kong: Oxford University Press.
Mackerras, Colin (1995), *China's Minority Cultures*, New York: St Martin's Press.
Mackerras, Colin (2003), *China's Ethnic Minorities and Globalization*, London: RoutledgeCurzon.
Mackerras, Colin (2005), 'People's Republic of China: Background Paper on the Situation of the Tibetan Population', available at http://www.refworld.org/pdfid/423ea9094.pdf (accessed 11 July 2014).
Mackerras, Colin (2011), 'Ethnic Minorities', in Xiaowei Zang (ed.), *Understanding Chinese Society*, London: Routledge, pp. 111–126.
MacMillan, Margaret (2007), *Nixon and Mao: The Week that Changed the World*, New York: Random House.
Manion, M. (2004), *Corruption by Design: Building Clean Government in Mainland China and Hong Kong*, Cambridge, MA: Harvard University Press.
Manion, M. (2008), 'When Communist Party Candidates Can Lose, Who Wins? Assessing the Role of Local People's Congresses in the Selection of Leaders in China', *China Quarterly*, 195: 607–630.
Manion, M. (2014), 'Authoritarian Parochialism: Local Congressional Representation in China', *China Quarterly*, 218: 311–338.
Mann, James (1999), *About Face: A History of America's Curious Relationship with China, from Nixon to Clinton*, New York: Alfred A. Knopf.
Mann, James (2007), *The China Fantasy: How Our Leaders Explain Away Chinese Repression*, New York: Viking.

Mao, Zedong (1956), 'Lun Xida Guanxi' (On the Ten Contradictions), *Selected Works of Mao Zedong*, Vol. 5, pp. 267–288.

Mao, Zedong (1970), *Mao Zedong sixiang wansui* (Long live Mao Zedong Thought), (1967, 1969), 2 vols, Taipei.

Mao, Zedong (1987–98), *Jianguo yilai Mao Zedong wengao* (Mao Zedong's manuscripts since the founding of the state), 13 vols, Beijing: Zhongyang wenxian chubanshe.

Mao, Zedong (1991a), 'Hunan nongmin yundong kaocha baogao' (A report on the peasants' movement in Hunan), *Mao Zedong xuanji* (Selected Works of Mao Zedong), Vol. 1, Beijing: Renmin chubanshe.

Mao, Zedong (1991b), 'Zhongguo shehui ge jieji de fenxi' ('An Analysis of the Social Classes of China'), *Mao Zedong xuanji* (Selected Works of Mao Zedong), Vol. 1, Beijing: Renmin chubanshe.

Martin, Roberta (1981), *Party Recruitment in China: Patterns and Prospects: A Study of the Recruitment Campaign of 1954–56 and its Impact on Party Expansion through 1980*, New York: Columbia University East Asian Institute.

Marx, Karl (1985), 'The General Council to the Federal Council of Romance Switzerland', *Karl Marx Frederick Engels Collected Works, Vol. 21*, Moscow: Progress Publishers.

Mastanduno, Michael (1999), 'Economic Statecraft, Interdependence, and National Security: Agendas for Research', *Security Studies*, 9(1–2): 288–316.

Matsuzawa, Setsuko (2012), 'Citizen Environmental Activism in China: Legitimacy, Alliances, and Rights-based Discourses', *ASIANetwork Exchange*, 19(2): 81–91.

Maull, Hans (2010), 'The European Union as Civilian Power: Aspirations, Potential, Achievements', in R. Ross, O. Tunsjo and T. Zhang, *US–China–EU Relations: Managing the New World Order*, London: Routledge, pp. 48–75.

McCartan, Brian (2009), 'A Helping Chinese Hand', *Asia Times*, 30 April, available at http://www.atimes.com/atimes/Southeast_Asia/KD30Ae01.html

McCormick, Barrett L., Su Shaozhi and Xiao Xiaoming (1992), 'The 1989 Democracy Movement: A Review of the Prospects for Civil Society in China', *Pacific Affairs*, 65(2): 182–202.

Mcmillan, J., J. Whalley, et al. (1989), 'The Impact of China's Economic Reforms on Agricultural Productivity Growth', *Journal of Political Economy*, 97(4): 781–807.

Mearsheimer, John J. (2014a), *The Tragedy of Great Power Politics*, updated edn, New York: W.W. Norton & Company.

Mearsheimer, John J. (2014b), 'Can China Rise Peacefully?', *National Interest*, 8 April; and in J. Mearsheimer, *The Tragedy of Great Power Politics*, updated edn, New York: W.W. Norton & Company; available at http://nationalinterest.org/commentary/can-china-rise-peacefully-10204.

Medeiros, Evan S. (2005), 'Strategic Hedging and the Future of Asia-Pacific Stability', *Washington Quarterly*, 29(1).

Medeiros, Evan and Taylor Fravel (2003), 'China's New Diplomacy', *Foreign Affairs*, 82(6): 22–35.

Medeiros, Evan S., et al. (2008), *Pacific Currents: The Responses of U.S. Allies and Security Partners in East Asia to China's Rise*, RAND: Santa Monica, CA.

Mei, D. (2005), '60 niandai tiaozheng hou nongcun renmin gongshe ge ren shouru fenpei zhidu' (Individual income distribution system of the rural people's communes since the adjustment of the 1960s), *Xinan shipu daxue xuebao*, 31(1): 99–103.

Mei, Xinyu (2010), *Fangdi chan liyijituan de nenglaing* (The comparative strength of real estate interest groups), 21 Century Net, available at http://www.21so.com/HTML/21cbhnews/2010/5-21-44418.html.

Meisner, Maurcie (1996), *The Deng Xiaoping Era: An Inquiry into the Fate of Chinese Socialism, 1978–1994*, New York: Hill & Wang.

Menefee, Trey and Bjorn Harald Nordtveit (2012), 'Disaster, Civil Society and Education in China: A Case Study of An Independent Non-Government Organization Working in the Aftermath of the Wenchuan Earthquake', *International Journal of Educational Development*, 32(4): 600–607.

Meng, Xiaoyun (1986), 'Dangdai Zhongguo funü mianmian guan' (Perspectives on contemporary Chinese women), *People's Daily* (overseas version), 8–10 January.

Meng, Xin, Kailing Shen and Sen Xue (2013), 'Economic Reform, Education Expansion, and Earnings Inequality for Urban Males in China, 1988–2009', *Journal of Comparative Economics*, 41: 227–244.

Mercer, Claire (2002), 'NGOs, Civil Society and Democratization: A Critical Review of the Literature', *Progress in Development Studies*, 2(1): 5–22.

Miller, Alice (2011), 'Dilemmas of Globalization and Governance', in Roderick MacFarquhar (ed.), *The Politics of China*, 3rd edn, Cambridge: Cambridge University Press, pp. 528–600.

Miller, Alice (2014), 'How Strong Is Xi Jinping?', *China Leadership Monitor*, No. 43.

Ministry of Civil Affairs (1992), 'Xianji nongcun shehui yanglao baoxian jiben fang'an (shixing)', (County level rural social old-age insurance basic programme (provisional)), available at http://www.people.com.cn/item/flfgk/gwyfg/1992/213061199201.html (accessed 10 May 2014).

Ministry of Civil Affairs (2007), 'General Information on Natural Disaster Relief, Social Relief, Social Welfare and Preferential Treatment and Resettlement of Demobilized Servicemen in China'.

Ministry of Civil Affairs (2012a), '2011 Social Services Statistical Report', available at http://www.mca.gov.cn/article/zwgk/mzyw/201206/20120600324725.shtml.

Ministry of Civil Affairs (2012b), '2012 nian shehui fuwu fazhan tongji gongbao' (Statistical communique on the development of social services, 2012), available at http://www.gov.cn/gzdt/2013-06/19/content_2428923.htm (accessed 3 April 2014).

Ministry of Civil Affairs (2013), '2013 nian 7 yuefen quanguo xian yishang nongcun dibao qingkuang' (The status of rural minimum living standard security scheme at the county level and above in July 2013).

Ministry of Civil Affairs (2014), '2014 nian 2 yuefen quanguo xianyishang nongcun dibao qingkuang' (Situation of national county level and above rural minimum living guarantee in February 2014), available at http://files2.mca.gov.cn/cws/201403/20140319171106530.htm (accessed August 10 2014).

Ministry of Civil Affairs (various editions), *Handbook of the Administrative Divisions of the People's Republic of China*, Beijing: SinoMaps Publishing House.

Ministry of Finance (1980), 'State Budgetary Revenues and Expenditures since 1960', Beijing.

Ministry of Finance (2007), 'Report on the Implementation of the Central and Local Budgets for 2006 and on the Draft Central and Local Budgets for 2007', available at http://news.xinhuanet.com/english/2007-10/24/content_6938749.htm.

Ministry of Foreign Affairs, Japan (2014), 'Senkaku Islands', available at http://www.mofa.go.jp/region/asia-paci/senkaku/index.html, 15 April (accessed 17 September 2014).

Ministry of Foreign Affairs, People's Republic of China (2012), 'Diaoyu Dao, an Inherent Territory of China', 26 September, available at http://www.fmprc.gov.cn/mfa_eng/topics_665678/diaodao_665718/t973774.shtml (accessed 17 September 2014).

Ministry of Human Resources and Social Security and National Bureau of Statistics (2012), '2011 niandu laodong he shehui baozhang shiye fazhan tongji gongbao' (Statistical communique on the development of labour and social security work in 2011), available at http://www.mohrss.gov.cn/SYrlzyhshbzb/zwgk/szrs/ndtjsj/tjgb/201206/t20120605_69908.htm (accessed on 15 August 2014).

Ministry of Labour and Social Security and National Bureau of Statistics (1998), '1998 nian laodong he shehui baozhang shiye fazhan niandu tongji gongbao' (Annual statistical communique of Labour and Social Security Work Development, 1998), available at http://www.mohrss.gov.cn/SYrlzyhshbzb/zwgk/szrs/ndtjsj/tjgb/200602/t20060207_69891.htm (accessed 10 August 2014).

Ministry of Labour and Social Security and National Bureau of Statistics (2006), '2001 niandu laodong shehui baozhang shiye fazhan tongji gongbao' (Statistical communique on the development of labour and social security work, 2001), available at http://www.mohrss.gov.cn/SYrlzyhshbzb/zwgk/szrs/ndtjsj/tjgb/200603/t20060301_69897.htm (accessed 14 August 2014).

Minzu Tuanjie Jiaoyu Caibian Yuzu (Editorial Organization of Nationalities Education Organization) (ed.) (2009), *Minzu lilun changshi* (General knowledge and theory about nationalities), Beijing: Zhongyang guangbodianshi daxue chubanshe (Central Broadcasting University Publishing House).

Misra, Kalpana (1998), *From Post-Maoism to Post-Marxism: The Erosion of Official Ideology in Deng's China*, London: Routledge.

Mitcham, Chad J. (2005), *China's Economic Relations with the West and Japan, 1949–79: Grain, Trade and Diplomacy*, Abingdon: Routledge.

Mitter, Rana (2014), *China's War with Japan, 1937–1945: The Struggle for Survival*, London: Penguin.

Mizutani, Naoko (2005), *Han nichi' kaibō: yuganda chūgoku no 'aikoku'*, Tokyo: Bungei shunjū.

MOFCOM (2013), 'Jinzhi xiang chaoxian chukou liangyong wuxiang he jishu qingdan' (List of dual use items and technology prohibited for export to DPRK), MOFCOM statement, available at http://images.mofcom.gov.cn/cys/201309/20130924140410534.pdf.

Montinola, Babriella, Yingyi Qian and Barry R. Weingast (1995), 'Federalism, Chinese Style: The Political Basis for Economic Success', *World Politics*, 48(1): 50–81.

Morgan, W.J. (2003), *Communists on Education and Culture: 1848–1948*, London, UK and New York, USA: Palgrave Macmillan.

Morgan, W.J. (2013), 'Ethics, Economics and Higher Education: A Comment', *Citizenship, Social and Economics Education*, 12(2): 129–135.

Morgan, W.J. and I. White (2013), 'Education for Global Development: Reconciling Society, State, and Market', *Weiterbildung*, 1, 38–41.

Morgan, W.J. and B. Wu (eds) (2013 [2011]), *Higher Education Reform in China: Beyond the expansion*, London, UK and New York, USA: Routledge.
Mozingo, David (1976), *China Policy Toward Indonesia 1949–1967*, Ithaca, NY: Cornell University Press.
Mu, Song (2009), 'Mao Zedong and the Creation of the PLA General Cadre Department', *PLA Daily*, 14 September.
Mu, Xi (2013), 'Xinzhong de wumai' (Mental smog), *Zhongguo Jingji he xinxihua* (China Economy and Informatization), 25 February, p. 110.
Muller, Wim (2014), 'China's International Human Rights Practice in the Context of its General Approach to International Law', Chatham House paper.
Mulvenon, James (2001), 'China: Conditional Compliance', in Muthiah Apalagapa (ed.), *Coercion and Governance in Asia: the Declining Political Role of the Military*, Palo Alto, CA: Stanford University Press.
Murphy, Rachel (2004), 'Turning Peasants into Modern Chinese Citizens: "Population Quality" Discourse, Demographic Transition and Primary Education', *China Quarterly*, 177: 1–20.
Mushkat, Roda (2011), 'China's Compliance with International Law', *Pacific Rim Law and Policy Journal*, 20(1): 41–69.
Muthiah, Apalagapa (ed.) (2001), *The Professionalism of Asian Armed Forces*, Hawaii: East–West Centre Press.
Nahory, Celine (2004), 'The Hidden Veto, Global Policy Forum', 19 May 2004, available at https://www.globalpolicy.org/security-council/42656-the-hidden-veto.html (accessed 13 June 2013).
Najam, Adil (1996), 'Understanding the Third Sector: Revisiting the Prince, the Merchant and the Citizen', *Nonprofit Management and Leadership*, 7(2): 203–219.
Nathan, Andrew (2003), 'Authoritarian Resilience', *Journal of Democracy*, 14(1): 6–17.
Nathan, Andrew J. (1973), 'A Factionalist Model for CCP Politics', *China Quarterly*, 53: 34–66.
National Bureau of Statistics (2013), *2013 guojia tongji nianjian* (China Statistical Yearbook, 2013), Beijing: National Bureau of Statistics.
National Health and Family Planning Commission (2012), 'Guojia weisheng jisheng wei fabu 2012 nian xinnonghe jinzhan qingkuang ji 2013 nian gongzuo zhongdian' (The National Health and Family Planning Commission announces the progress of new rural co-operative medical scheme in 2012 and working focuses in 2013).
National People's Congress (2004), *Constitution of the People's Republic of China*, available at http://www.npc.gov.cn/englishnpc/Constitution/node_2825.htm.
Naughton, B. (1988), 'The Third Front: Defence Industrialization in the Chinese Interior', *China Quarterly*, 115: 351–386.
Naughton, B. (1996), *Growing out of the Plan: Chinese Economic Reform, 1978–1993*, Cambridge: Cambridge University Press.
Naughton, B. (2005), 'Economic Policy in 2004: Slipping behind the Curve?', *China Leadership Monitor*, 13(Winter).
Naughton, B. (2007a), *The Chinese Economy: Transitions and Growth*, Cambridge, MA: MIT Press.
Naughton, B. (2007b), 'The Assertive Center: Beijing Moves Against Local Government Control of Land', *China Leadership Monitor*, 20(Winter).

Naughton, B. (2008a), 'A Political Economy of China's Economic Transition', in Loren Brandt and Thomas Rawski (eds), *China's Great Economic Transformation*, New York: Cambridge University Press, pp. 91–135.
Naughton, B. (2008b), 'A New Team Faces Unprecedented Economic Challenges', *China Leadership Monitor*, 26(Fall).
Naughton, B. (2009), 'Understanding the Chinese Stimulus Package', *China Leadership Monitor*, 28(Spring).
Naughton, B. (2014), 'China's Economy: Complacency, Crisis and the Challenge of Reform', *Daedalus, the Journal of the American Academic of Arts and Science*, 143(2): 14–25.
Nee, Victor (1989), 'A Theory of Market Transition: From Redistribution to Markets in State Socialism', *American Sociological Review*, 54: 663–681.
Nee, Victor (1991), 'Social Inequalities in Reforming State Socialism: Between Redistribution and Markets in China', *American Sociological Review*, 56: 267–82.
Nee, Victor (1992), 'Organizational Dynamics of Market Transition: Hybrid Forms, Property Rights, and Mixed Economy in China', *Administrative Science Quarterly*, 37: 1–27.
Nee, Victor (1996), 'The Emergence of a Market Society: Changing Mechanisms of Stratification in China', *American Journal of Sociology*, 101: 908–949.
Nee, Victor and P. Lian (1994), 'Sleeping With the Enemy: A Dynamic Model of Declining Political Commitment in State Socialism', *Theory and Society*, 23: 253–96.
Nee, Victor and R. Matthews (1996), 'Market Transition and Societal Transformation in Reforming State Socialism', *Annual Review of Sociology*, 22: 401–435.
Nee, Victor and Sonja Opper (2012), *Capitalism from Below: Markets and Institutional Change in China*, Cambridge, MA: Harvard University Press.
Nee, Victor and S. Su (1998), 'Institutional Foundations of Robust Economic Performance: Public Sector Industrial Growth in China', in J. Henderson (ed.), *Industrial Transformation in Eastern Europe in the Light of East Asian Experience*, New York: St Martin's Press, pp. 167–187.
Nee, Victor and Cao Yang (1999), 'Path Dependent Societal Transformation: Stratification in Hybrid Mixed Economy', *Theory and Society*, 28: 799–834.
Nee, Victor and Cao Yang (2002), 'Postsocialist Inequality: The Causes of Continuity and Discontinuity', *Future of Market Transition*, 19: 3–39.
Newspaper of the PLAAF (2010), 'The PLAAF Announces the Regulation on Enhancing Promotion of Wing Commanders', 29 July.
Nguyen, Nha (1975), 'Thu dat lai van de Hoang Sa' (Reconsidering the Paracel Islands issue), *Su Dia* (History and Geography), No. 29.
Nie, Hongyi and Zhou Baogen (2008), 'Dangqian xifang guojia de duiwai yuanzhu guihua' (Current plans of Western countries' foreign aid), *Guoji jingji hezuo* (International Economic Cooperation), 10: 45.
Nincic, Miroslav (2005), *Renegade Regimes: Confronting Deviant Behavior in World Politics*, New York: Columbia University Press.
Nincic, Miroslav (2010), 'Getting What You Want: Positive Inducements in International Relations', *International Security*, 35(1): 138–183.
Ningbo Shi Renmin Zhengfu Fazhan Yanjiu Zhongxin (Development Studies Centre of Ningbo People's Government) (2007), 'Ningbo shi zhengxie xiang shehui gongkai

zhengji ti'an xiansuo gonggao' (Notice of Ningbo PPCC on publicly inviting ideas from society on formal proposals), 5 December, available at http://www.nbjczx.com/detail_16747_46.html.

Nixon, Richard (1979), *RN: The Memoirs of Richard Nixon*, New York: Grosset & Dunlap.

NKeconwatch (2013), 'North Korean Markets Heavily Filled with Chinese Products and Currency', Institute for Far Eastern Studies, 25 April, available at http://www.nkeconwatch.com/2013/04/25/north-korean-markets-heavily-filled-with-chinese-products-and-currency/.

Norris, William J. (2010), *Economic Statecraft with Chinese Characteristics: The Use of Commercial Actors in China's Grand Strategy*, PhD dissertation, MIT, Cambridge, MA.

Nye, J.S. (1967), 'Corruption and Political Development: A Cost–Benefit Analysis', *American Political Science Review*, 61(2): 417–27. doi:10.2307/1953254.

O'Brien, K. (1994), 'Agents and Remonstrators: Role Accumulation by Chinese People's Congress Deputies', *China Quarterly*, 138: 359–379.

O'Brien, K.J. (1996), 'Rightful Resistance', *World Politics*, 49(1): 31–55.

Ogata, Sadako (1988), *Normalization with China: A Comparative Study of US and Japanese Processes*, Berkeley, CA: Institute of East Asian Studies, University of California.

Oi, J. (1989a), 'Market Reforms and Corruption in Rural China', *Studies in Comparative Communism* 22(2–3): 221–233. doi:10.1016/0039-3592(89)90015-X.

Oi, J. (1989b), *State and Peasant in Contemporary China: The Political Economy of Village Government*, Berkeley, CA: University of California Press.

Oi, J. (1992), 'Fiscal Reform and the Economic Foundations of Local State Corporatism', *World Politics*, 45: 99–126.

Oi, J. (1995), 'The Role of the Local State in China's Transitional Economy', *China Quarterly*, 144: 1132–1149.

Oi, J. (1999), *Rural China Takes Off: Institutional Foundations of Economic Reform*, Berkeley, CA: University of California Press.

Oi, J. (2004), 'Old Problems for New Leaders: Institutional Disjunctions in Rural China', in Y. Zhu, Z. Luo and R.H. Myers (eds), *The New Chinese Leadership: Challenges and Opportunities After the 16th Party Congress*, Cambridge, UK and New York, USA: Cambridge University Press, pp. 141–155.

Oi, J. (2008), 'Development Strategies, Welfare Regime and Poverty Reduction in China', UNRISD Project on Poverty Reduction and Policy Regimes.

Oi, J.C., K.S. Babiarz, et al. (2012), 'Shifting Fiscal Control to Limit Cadre Power in China's Townships and Villages', *China Quarterly*, 211: 649–675.

Oi, J. and K. Shimizu (2010), 'Uncertain Outcomes of Rural Industrialization: A Reassessment', in T.-K. Leng and Y. Zhu (eds), *Dynamics of Local Governance in China During the Reform Era – Challenges Facing Chinese Political Development*, Lanham, MD: Lexington Books, pp. 11–32.

Oi, J.C. and A.G. Walder (1999), *Property Rights and Economic Reform in China*, Stanford, CA: Stanford University Press.

Oi, J. and S. Zhao (2007), 'Fiscal Crisis in China's Townships: Causes and Consequences', in E.J. Perry and M. Goldman (eds), *Harvard Contemporary China Series 14*, Cambridge, MA: Harvard University Press, pp. 75–96.

Okada, Tadashi (2012), *Senkaku shotō mondai: ryōdo nashonarizumu no maryoku*, Tokyo: Sōsōsha

Oksenberg, Michel and James Tong (1991), 'The Evolution of Central–Provincial Fiscal Relations in China, 1971–1984: The Formal System', *China Quarterly*, 125: 1–32.

Ong, L. (2006), 'The Political Economy of Township Government Debt, Township Enterprises and Rural Financial Institutions in China', *China Quarterly*, 186: 377–400.

Ong, L. (2012), *Prosper or Perish: Credit and Fiscal Systems in Rural China*, Ithaca, NY: Cornell University Press.

Ong, Lynette H. and Christian Göbel (2014), 'Social Unrest in China', in Kerry Brown (ed.), *China and the EU in Context: Insights for Business and Investors*, London: Palgrave Macmillan.

Onishi, Yasuo (2001), *China's Western Development Strategy, Issues and Prospects*, China: Institute of Developing Economies.

Organization Department, CCP (2012), *Statistical Report on China's Human Resources 2010*, Beijing: Zhongguo Tongji.

Orlik, T. (2011), 'Unrest On Rise as Economy Booms', *Wall Street Journal*, 26 September, available at http://online.wsj.com/article/SB10001424053111903703604576587070600504108.html.

Østergaard, Clemens (1989), 'Citizens, Groups and Nascent Civil Society in China: Towards an Understanding of the 1989 Student Demonstrations', *China Information*, 4(2): 28–41.

Ou, Yen Sheng (ed.) (1995), *Visual Voices: 100 Photographs of Village China by the Women of Yunnan Province* (Zhongguo Yunnan nongcun funü ziwo xiezhen ji), Kunming: Yunnan People's Publishing House.

Ouzhou (2002), 'Duiwai yuanzhu yu guoji guanxi chengguo fabuhui ji zongshu' (Summary of the results of the conference on foreign aid and international relations), *Ouzhou* (Europe), 2: 104.

Overholt (2009–10), 'China in the Global Financial Crisis: Rising Influence, Rising Challenges', *Washington Quarterly*, 33(1).

Oxford Dictionaries (n.d.), 'Governance', Oxford: Oxford University Press, available at http://www.oxforddictionaries.com/definition/english/governance.

Pahl, R.E. (1989), '"Is the Emperor Naked?": Some Questions on the Adequacy of Sociological Theory in Urban and Regional Research', *International Journal of Urban and Regional Research*, 13(4): 711–720.

Paine, Suzanne (1981), 'Spatial Aspects of Chinese Development: Issues, Outcomes and Policies 1949–1979', *Journal of Development Studies*, 17(2): 133–195.

Pan, Jintang (1988), 'Funü jiefang de shizhi yu biaozhi tanxi' (Analyzing the substance and sign of women's liberation), *Zhongguo funübao* (China Women's News), 27 May.

Pan, Suiming (1987), 'Zhongguo xinnüxing mianlin de xuanze yu deshi' (New choice and gain-and-loss confronted by Chinese new women), *Zhongguo funübao* (China Women's News), 19 January.

Pan, Wei (2010), 'Western System Versus Chinese System', University of Nottingham Contemporary China Centre Briefing Series, 61:14.

Pan, Yue (2013), 'Minying jingji zhan GDP bizhong chao 60%, zhuce sijingqiye yiguo qianwan jia' (Private economy counts for over 60% of China's GDP. There are over

10 million private enterprises registers), *People's Daily*, 3 February, available at http://finance.people.com.cn/n/2013/0203/c1004-20414645.html.

Pang, Zhongying (2006), 'Zhongguo zai guoji tizhizhong de diwei yu zuoyong' (The status and motive of China in the international system), *Dangdai guoji guanxi* (Contemporary International Relations), 4: 7–22.

Parish, William (1984), 'Destratification in China', in James Watson (ed.), *Class and Social Stratification in Post-Revolutionary China*, Cambridge: Cambridge University Press, pp. 84–120.

Parish, W.L. and E. Michelson (1996), 'Politics and Markets: Dual Transformations', *American Journal of Sociology*, 101: 1042–1059.

Parris, Kristen (1993), 'Local Initiative and National Reform: The Wenzhou Model of Development', *China Quarterly*, 124: 242–263.

Party Central Committee (2013), 'Guanyu quanmian shenhua gaige ruogan zhongda wenti de jueding' (Decision concerning some important questions on fully deepening reform), *Renmin ribao* (People's Daily), 16 November, p. 1.

Party Central Committee and State Council (2009), *Guanyu jiada tongchou chengxiang fazhan lidu, jingyibu hangshi nongye nongcun fazhan jichude ruogan yijian* (Some opinions concerning strengthening urban–rural pooling and further consolidating the basis for developing agriculture and the countryside), available at http://www.gov.cn/gongbao/content/2010/content_1528900.htm (accessed 4 May 2014).

Pcbaby.com.cn (2011), 'Zhongguo xiang maqidun yuanzhu xiaoche, heshi guangzhu women de haizi' (China provides Macedonia with school buses; how does it care for our own children?), 28 November, available at http://cmt.pcbaby.com.cn/topic/a0/r0/p1/ps30/t12878971.html.

Pearson, Margaret (1999), 'China's Integration into the International Trade and Investment Regime', in Elizabeth Economy and Michel Oksenberg (eds), *China Joins the World: Progress and Prospects*, New York: Council on Foreign Relations Press, pp. 161–205.

Pei, Minxin (1999), 'Will China Become Another Indonesia?', *Foreign Policy*, 116(October): 94–109. doi:10.2307/1149646.

Pei, Minxin (2006), *China's Trapped Transition: The Limits of Developmental Autocracy*, Cambridge, MA: Harvard University Press.

Peng, Zhen (1991), *Peng Zhen Wenxuan* (Selected Works of Peng Zhen), Beijing: Renmin chubanshe.

Pentassuglia, Gaetano (2005), 'Minority rights, human rights', in Council of Europe and European Centre for Minority Issues (ed.), *Mechanisms for the Implementation of Minority Rights Standards*, Strasbourg: Council of Europe Publishing, pp. 9–25.

People's Daily (1953), 'Zhonghua Renmin Gongheguo Zhengfe He Chaoxian Minzhu Zhuyi Renmin Gongheguo Zhengfu Daibiaotuan Tanpan Gongbao' (Statement of the discussions between the Government of the PRC and the DPRK delegation), *Renmin Ribao* (People's Daily), 24 November, p. 1.

People's Daily (2000), 'China's Geographical Center Marked', available at http://english.people.com.cn/english/200009/13/eng20000913_50419.html.

People's Daily (2004), 'Zeng Qinghong: A pivotal document on enhancement of CCP's ruling capacity' (*Zeng qinghong: jiaqiang dangde zhizhengnengli jianshe de ganglingxing wenxian*), 8 October, pp. 2–3.

People's Daily (2008), 'Hu Jintao zai quandang shenru xuexi shijian kexue fazhanguan huodong dongyuan dahui shang fabiao zhongyao jianghua' (Hu Jintao's important speech on deepening the Party's campaign of learning and practising the outlook of scientific development at the Mobilization Rally), 19 September, p. 1.

People's Daily (2010), 'A Blueprint for Educational Modernization', 31 July.

People's Daily (2012), 'Ideological Foundation of the CPC', 30 October, available at http://english.people.com.cn/206215/206216/7997750.html (accessed 28 March 2014).

People's Daily (2013), 'Caizhengbu fuzeren jiedu sanzhong quanhui shenhua caishui gaige zhongdian', (The Finance Minister elaborating on the reform priorities of fiscal-tax reform endorsed by the Central Committee Third Plenum), 21 November, available at http://politics.people.com.cn/n/2013.1121/c1001-23607867.html, accessed 21 November 2013.

People's Daily (2014a), 'Caizhengbu buzhang: zhongyang difang shiquan huafen shi xiayibu gaige neirong' (Minister of Finance: the clarification of responsibilities between central and local governments is the next step of reform), 6 March, available at http://lianghui.people.com.cn/2014npc/n/2014/0306/c376929-24544695.html, accessed 7 May 2014.

People's Daily (2014b), 'Caizhengbu buzhang tan yusuan gongkai: Yaoqing keren jinwu bu de xian dasao yixia?', (Minister of Finance talked about fiscal transparency: clean up house before welcoming guests), 6 March, available at http://lianghui.people.com.cn/2014npc/n/2014/0306/c376929-24546364.html, accessed 7 May 2014.

Pepper, S. (1996), *Radicalism and Education Reform in 20th Century China: The Search for an Ideal Development Model*, Cambridge: Cambridge University Press.

Percival, Bronson (2007), *The Dragon Looks South: China and Southeast Asia in the New Century*, Westport, CT, USA and London, UK: Praeger Security International.

Perdue, P. (2005), *China Marches West: The Qing Conquest of Central Eurasia*, Berkeley, CA: University of California Press.

Perlmutter, Amos and Willia LeoGrande (1982), 'The Party in Uniform: Toward a Theory of Civil–Military Relations in Communist Political Systems', *American Political Science Review*, 76(4): 778–789.

Perry, Elizabeth (1999), 'Crime, Corruption, and Contention', in Merle Goldman and Roderick MacFarquhar (eds), *The Paradox of China's Post-Mao Reforms*, Cambridge, MA: Harvard University Press, pp. 308–331.

Perry, Elizabeth (2012), *Anyuan: Mining China's Revolutionary Tradition*, Berkeley, CA: University of California Press.

Peters, Anne (2009), 'Humanity as the A and Omega of Sovereignty', *European Journal of International Law*, 20(3): 513–544.

Pettman, R. (1973), *China in Burma's Foreign Policy*, Canberra: Australian National University Press.

Pheakdey, Heng (2013), 'Chinese Investment and Aid in Cambodia: A Controversial Affair', *East Asia Forum*, 16 July, available at http://www.eastasiaforum.org/2013/07/16/chinese-investment-and-aid-in-cambodia-a-controversial-affair/.

Pi, D. (ed.) (1995), *Shiye baoxian jieda* (An explanation of unemployment insurance), Beijing: Gaige chubanshe.

Pierre, J. and B. Peters (2000), *Governance, Politics and the State*, Houndmills: Macmillan.

PLA Daily (2010), Editorial, 'Broadening and Deepening War Preparation', 3 March.
PLA Daily (2012a), 'The Change in the Composition of PLA Soldiers Reflects New Achievements in Scientific Development', 6 March.
PLA Daily (2012b), 'The Achievement of Grass-Roots Construction of the PLA and the PAP, Part 5', 18 June.
PLA Daily (2012c), 'Building a Talented Contingent to Win the Informatized War – Achievement of PLA, Part 7', 7 October.
PLA Daily (2013a), 'Achieving a Deep Comprehension of the Party's Objective to Strengthen the PLA in the New Era', General Political Affairs Department, 14 May.
PLA Daily (2013b), 'Professional Ability is Criteria for Selecting Generals', 12 August.
PLA Daily (2014), 'Implementing Chair Xi's recent important instructions', 30 August.
PLA Life (2009), 'Mao Zedong's Order to Swap Eight Military Region Commanders in 1972', 20 August.
Pomfret, John (2010), 'China's Billions Reap Rewards in Cambodia', *Washington Post*, 20 November, available at http://www.washingtonpost.com/wp-dyn/content/article/2010/11/20/AR2010112003850_pf.html.
Postiglione, G. (ed.) (2006), *Education and Social Change in China: Inequality in a Market Economy*, Armonk, NY, USA and London, UK: M.E. Sharpe.
Prantl, Jochen and Ryoko Nakano (2011), 'Global Norm Diffusion in East Asia', *International Relations*, 25(2): 204–23.
Preece, Jennifer Jackson (1997), 'National Minority Rights vs. State Sovereignty in Europe', *Nations and Nationalism*, 3(3): 345–364.
Preece, Jennifer Jackson (1998), *National Minorities and the European Nation-States System*, Oxford: Clarendon Press.
Presidential Communications Operations Office (2011), 'Philippines. PH Shares China's Position in Resolving Territorial Dispute over Spratly Islands', 16 April, available at http://www.pcoo.gov.ph/archives2011/apr16.htm (accessed 26 February 2014).
Pu, Jinbao (2008), 'Before and After the Military Ranks were Restored', *PLA Daily*, 14 February.
Public Security Bureau (Gongan Bu) (2000), *Gong'anjiguan Chuzhi Quntixingzhianshijian Guiding* (Gong'an Regulation on Mass Incidents).
Putterman, L. (1988), 'Group Farming and Work Incentives in Collective-Era China', *Modern China* 14(4): 419–450.
Pye, Lucien (1982), *The Dynamics of Chinese Politics*, Boston, MA: Oelgeschlager, Gunn & Hain.
Qi, Yiming (2013), 'How Did Jiang Zemin Describe his Leadership after Retirement?', *CCP News Internet*, 29 May.
Qin, Hui (2004), 'NGO in China: The Third Sector in the Globalization Process and Social Transformation', available at http://web.mit.edu/newmediaactionlab/www/papers/qinhui_ngo.pdf.
Qiushi (2013), 'Seven Differences between China Dream and American Dream' (Zhongguomeng qubieyu meiguomeng de qida tezheng), 20 May, available at http://www.qstheory.cn/zz/zgtsshzyll/201305/t20130520_232259.htm (accessed 16 August 2013).
Rabinovitch, Simon (2012), 'A New Way of Lending', *Financial Times*, 24 September, available at http://www.ft.com/intl/cms/c1628ce2-03a3-11e2-bad2-00144feabdc0.pdf.

Ramo, Joshua Cooper (2004), *The Beijing Consensus*, London: Foreign Policy Centre and New York: Cambridge University Press.

Ranade, Jayadeva (2011), 'China Strengthens Hold on Nepal, Comes to India's Doorstep', 24 June, available at http://www.dnaindia.com/world/column_china-strengthens-hold-on-nepal-comes-to-india-s-doorstep_1558386.

Rankin, Mary B. (1990), 'The Origins of a Chinese Public Sphere: Local Elites and Community Affairs in the Late Imperial Period', *Études chinoises*, 9(2): 13–60.

Rankin, Mary B. (1993), 'Some Observations on a Chinese Public Sphere', *Modern China*, 19(2): 158–182.

Ravallion, M. and S. Chen (2007), 'China's (Uneven), Progress Against Poverty', *Journal of Development Economics*, 82: 1–42.

Ravenhill, John and Yang Jiang (2009), 'China's Move to Preferential Trading: A New Direction in China's Diplomacy', *Journal of Contemporary China*, 18(58): 27–46.

Reilly, James (2012a), 'China's Unilateral Sanctions', *Washington Quarterly*, 35(4): 121–133.

Reilly, James (2012b), 'A Norm-Taker or a Norm-Maker? China's ODA in Southeast Asia', *Journal of Contemporary China*, 21(73): 71–91.

Reilly, James (2013a), 'China's Economic Statecraft: Turning Wealth into Power', *Lowy Institute for International Policy, Policy Analysis*, November.

Reilly, James (2013b), 'China and Japan in Myanmar: Aid, Natural Resources and Influence', *Asian Studies Review*, 37(2): 141–157.

Remick, Elizabeth J. (2004), *Building Local States: China during the Republican and post-Mao Eras*, Cambridge MA: Harvard University Press.

Ren, Mei'e, Renzhang Yang and Haosheng Bao (1979), *Zhongguo Ziran Dili Gangyao* (Outline of China's physical geography), Beijing: Shangwu Yinshuguan.

Ren, Weide and Qiao Dezhong (2010), 'Dangdai zhongguo defang zhili de zhengzhi shengtai fenxi' (An analysis of political ecology in local governance in contemporary China), *Neimengfu Daxue Xuebao* (Journal of Inner Mongolia University), 42(3): 46–50.

Ren, Xufei (2011), 'Dancing with the State: Migrant Workers, NGOs, and the Remaking of Urban citizenship in China', in M.P. Smith and M. McQuarrie (eds), *Remaking Urban Citizenship: Organizations, Institutions, and the Right to the City*, New Jersey: Transaction Publishers, pp. 99–109.

Renmin Zhengxie Bao (The Chinese People's Political Consultative Conference Daily) (2007), Ningbo shi zhengxie yaoqing shimin canyu zhongdian ti'an duban' (Ningbo PPCC invites citizens to supervise how key proposals are dealt with), 15 August, available at http://www.rmzxb.com.cn/jrmzxbwsj/zxtz/2007/08/15/93499.shtml.

RIA Novostiat (2010), 'China Threatens US Firms with sanctions over Taiwan Arms', 30 January, available at http://en.rian.ru/world/20100130/157723449.html.

Rigger, Shelley (1997), 'Competing Conceptions of Taiwan's Identity: The Irresolvable Conflict in Cross-strait Relations', *Journal of Contemporary China*, 6(15): 307–317.

Rigger, Shelly (1999–2000), 'Social Science and National Identity: A Critique', *Pacific Affairs*, 72(4): 537–552.

Rigger, Shelly (2005), 'Party Politics and Taiwan's External Relations', *Orbis*, 49(3): 413–428.

Rithmire, Meg (2014), 'China's "New Regionalism": Subnational Analysis in Chinese Political Economy', *World Development*, 66(1): 165–194.

Robinson, Thomas W. (ed.) (1971), *The Cultural Revolution in China*, Berkeley, CA: University of California Press.

Rose, Caroline (1998), *Interpreting History in Sino-Japanese Relations: A Case Study in Political Decision-Making*, London: Routledge.

Ross, R., O. Tunsjo and T. Zhang (eds) (2010), *China–EU–US Relations: Managing the New World Order*, London: Routledge.

Ross, Robert S. and Zhu Feng (eds) (2008), *China's Ascent: Power, Security, and the Future of International Politics*, Ithaca, NY: Cornell University Press.

Rostow, W.W. (1954), *The Prospects for Communist China*, New York: Technology Press of Massachusetts Institute of Technology and John Wiley & Sons.

Rowe, William T. (1989), *Hankow: Conflict and Community in a Chinese City, 1796–1985*, Stanford, CA: Stanford University Press.

Rowe, William T. (1993), 'The Problem of "Civil Society" in Later Imperial China', *Modern China*, 19(2): 143–148.

Roy, Denny (1994), 'Hegemon on the Horizon? China's Threat to East Asian Security', *International Security*, 19(1): 149–168.

Rozelle, S. and R.N. Boisvert (1994), 'Quantifying Chinese Village Leaders Multiple Objectives', *Journal of Comparative Economics*, 18(1): 25–45.

Rozelle, S., L. Guo, et al. (1999), 'Leaving China's Farms: Survey Results of New Paths and Remaining Hurdles to Rural Migration', *China Quarterly* 158: 367–393.

Rozelle, S., J. Huang, et al. (2002), 'Emerging Markets, Evolving Institutions, and the New Opportunities for Growth in China's Rural Economy', *China Economic Review*, 13: 345–353.

Rupnik, Jacques (2000), 'Eastern Europe: The International Context', *Journal of Democracy*, 11(2): 115–129.

Rural Survey Organization of National Bureau of Statistics (2007), 'Poverty Statistics in China', available at http://www.nscb.gov.ph/poverty/conference/papers/4_Poverty Statistics in China.pdf (accessed 25 October 2007).

Saich, Tony (2006), 'China in 2005: Hu's in Charge', *Asian Survey*, 46(1): 37–48.

Saich, Tony (2007), 'China in 2006: Focus on Social Development', *Asian Survey*, 47(1): 32–43.

Saich, Tony (2008), 'The Changing Role of Urban Government', in S. Yusuf and T. Saich (eds), *China Urbanizes: Consequences, Strategies and Policies*, Washington, DC: World Bank, pp. 181–206.

Saich, T. (2011), *Governance and Politics of China*, 3rd edn, Basingstoke: Palgrave Macmillan.

Saich, Tony and Biliang Hu (2012), *Chinese Village, Global Market: New Collectives and Rural Development*, New York: Palgrave Macmillan.

Sanderson, H. (2013), 'China's Xi Amassing Most Power Since Deng Raises Reform Risk', *Bloomberg News*, 31 December.

Sanft, C. (2014), *Communication and Cooperation in Early Imperial China: Publicizing the Qin Dynasty*, Albany, NY: SUNY Press.

Sapio, Flora (2008), 'Shuanggui and Extralegal Detention in China', *China Information*, 22(1): 7–37. doi:10.1177/0920203X07087720.

Sargeson, S. and J. Zhang (1999), 'Reassessing the Role of the Local State: A Case Study of Local Government Interventions in Property Rights Reform in a Hangzhou District', *China Journal*, 42: 77–99.
Sata, Michael (2011), 'Zambia's "King Cobra" Finally Strikes', *BBC News*, 23 September.
Sautman, Barry (1999), 'Ethnic Law and Minority Rights in China', *Law and Policy*, 21(3): 283–314.
Sautman, Barry (2000), 'Legal Reform and Minority Rights in China', in Stuart S. Nagel (ed.), *Handbook of Global Legal Policy*, New York: Marcel Dekker, pp. 71–102.
Sautman, Barry (2012), 'Paved with Good Intentions', *Modern China*, 38(1): 10–39.
Sceats, Sonya and Shaun Breslin (2012), *China and the International Human Rights System*, London: Chatham House.
Schaeffer, Robert K. (2012), *Red Inc.: Dictatorship and the Development of Capitalism in China, 1949–2009*, Boulder, CO, USA and London, UK: Paradigm.
Schell, Orville and John Delury (2013), *Wealth and Power: China's Long March to the Twenty-first Century*, New York: Random House.
Schell, Orville and David Shambaugh (eds) (1998), *The China Reader: The Reform Era*, New York: Vintage Books.
Schindlmayr, Thomas (2001), 'Obstructing the Security Council: The Use of the Veto in the Twentieth Century', *Journal of the History of International Law*, 3(2): 218–234.
Schluessel, Eric T. (2007), '"Bilingual" Education and Discontent in Xinjiang', *Central Asian Survey*, 26(2): 251–77.
Schram, Stuart (1965), *The Political Thought of Mao Tse-tung*, New York: Praeger.
Schram, Stuart (1966), *Mao Tse-tung*, Harmondsworth: Penguin Books.
Schram, Stuart (1981), 'To Utopia and Back: A Cycle in the History of the Chinese Communist Party', *China Quarterly*, 87(September): 407–439.
Schram, Stuart (1984), 'Classes, Old and New, in Mao Zedong's Thought', in James Watson (ed.), *Class and Social Stratification in Post-Revolutionary China*, Cambridge: Cambridge University Press, pp. 29–55.
Schrei, Josh (2002), 'The Dark Side of China's Western Development Plan', *China Brief*, 2(7).
Schurmann, Franz (1966), *Ideology and Organization in Communist China*, Berkeley, CA: University of California Press.
Schurmann, Franz (1968), *Ideology and Organization in Communist China*, 2nd edn, Berkeley, CA: University of California Press.
Schwartz, Benjamin (1951), *Chinese Communism and the Rise of Mao*, Harvard University Press.
Schwartz, Benjamin (1960), 'The Legend of the "Legend of 'Maoism'"', *China Quarterly*, April–June.
Schwartz, Benjamin I. (1964), *In Search of Wealth and Power: Yen Fu and the West*, Cambridge, MA: Harvard East Asian Series.
Schwartz, Benjamin (1968), *Communism and China: Ideology in Flux*, Cambridge, MA: Harvard University Press.
Schwartz, Jonathan (2004), 'Environmental NGOs in China: Roles and Limits', *Pacific Affairs*, 77(1): 28–49.
Scobell, Andrew (2006), 'China's Evolving Civil–Military Relations: Creeping Guojiahua', in Nan Li (ed.), *Chinese Civil–Military Relations*, New York: Routledge.

Seckington, Ian (2005), 'Nationalism, Ideology and China's "Fourth Generation" Leadership', *Journal of Contemporary China*, 14(42): 22–33.
Seeberg, V. (2000), *The Rhetoric and Reality of Mass Education in Mao's China*, Lewiston, New York: Edwin Mellen Press.
Segal, Gerald (1992), 'China and the Disintegration of the Soviet Union', *Asian Survey*, No. 9.
Segal, Gerald (1994), 'China Changes Shape: Regionalism and Foreign Policy', Adelphi Paper No. 287, London: International Institute for Strategic Studies.
Selden, Mark (1970), *The Yenan Way in Revolutionary China*, Cambridge, MA: Harvard University Press.
Shambaugh, David (1993), *Beautiful Imperialist: China Perceives America, 1972–1990*, Princeton, NJ: Princeton University Press.
Shambaugh, David (2003a), 'China and the Korean Peninsula: Playing for the Long Term', *Washington Quarterly*, 26(2): 43–56.
Shambaugh, David (2003b), *Modernizing China's Military: Progress, Problems, and Prospects*, Berkeley, CA: University of California Press.
Shambaugh, David (2004–05), 'China Engages Asia: Reshaping the Regional Order', *International Security*, 29(3): 64–99.
Shambaugh, David (ed.) (2005), *Power Shift: China and Asia's New Dynamics*, Berkeley, CA: University of California Press.
Shambaugh, David (2008), *China's Communist Party: Atrophy and Adaptation*, Washington, DC: Woodrow Wilson Center Press.
Shambaugh, David (2010), 'The Chinese Tiger Shows Its Claws', *Financial Times*, 17 February, p. 9.
Shambaugh, David (2013a), *China Goes Global: The Partial Power*, Oxford: Oxford University Press.
Shambaugh, David (ed.) (2013b), *Tangled Titans: The United States and China*, Lanham, MD: Rowman & Littlefield.
Shan, Wei and Chen Gang (2009), 'The Urumqi Riots and China's Ethnic Policy in Xinjiang', *East Asian Policy*, 1(3): 14–22.
Shang, Changfeng (2010), '"Wenge" shiqi zhongguode duiwai yuanzhu' (Chinese foreign aid in the era of the 'Cultural Revolution'), *Dangshi wenhui* (Party History Digest), 2: 56–57.
Shang, Huihui (2014), 'Shanxi shengwei zhaokai lingdao ganbu dahui Wang Rulin ren Shanxi shengwei shuji' (Shanxi Provincial Party Committee convenes meeting of leading cadres as Wang Rulin becomes Provincial Party Secretary), *Shanxi ribao* (Shanxi Daily), 2 September.
Shao, Kuo-kang (1996), *Zhou Enlai and the Foundations of Chinese Foreign Policy*, New York: St Martin's Press.
Shao, Xiaoxia (2010), 'University NGOs in China's Northwest: Taking Gansu Province as an Example', *Chinese Education and Society*, 43(2): 33–42.
She, Zhan (2009), 'Dalai wenti yu raofa zhilu' (The Dalai issue and 'circling France' trip), *Shijie jingji yu zhengzhi* (World Economics and Politics), 3(423): 45–46.
Shen, Hongfang (2011), 'South China Sea Issue in China–ASEAN Relations', *International Journal of China Studies*, 2(3): 585–600.
Shen, Zhihua and Yafeng Xia (2012), 'China and the post-war reconstruction of North

Korea, 1953–1961', Working Paper #4, North Korea International Documentation Project, Woodrow Wilson International Center for Scholars (May 2012).

Sheng, Yueh (1971), *Sun Yat-sen University in Moscow and the Chinese Revolution: A Personal Account*, Lawrence, KS: University of Kansas Center for East Asian Studies.

Sheng, Yumin (2005), 'Central–Provincial Relations at the CCP Central Committees: Institutions, Measurement and Empirical Trends, 1978–2002', *China Quarterly*, 182: 338–355.

Sheng, Yumin (2007), 'The Determinants of Provincial Presence at the CCP Central Committees, 1978–2002', *Journal of Contemporary China*, 16(51): 215–237.

Shi, H. (2012), 'Yi ren wei ben, kua yue fazhan: shehui baozhang tixi jianshe shinian chengjiu zongshu, (xia)' (Summary of the achievements noted at the tenth anniversary of the creation of the national insurance system in China, part 2), *Zhongguo shehui baozhang* (Chinese Social Insurance), 12: 14–17.

Shih, Victor C. (2008), *Factions and Finance in China: Elite Conflict and Inflation*, New York: Cambridge University Press.

Shirk, Susan L. (1993), *The Political Logic of Economic Reform in China*, Berkeley, CA: University of California Press.

Shirk, Susan (2002), 'The Delayed Institutionalization of Leadership Politics', in Jonathan Unger (ed.), *The Nature of Chinese Politics: from Mao to Jiang*, Armonk, NY: ME Sharp

Shue, V. (1986), *The Reach of the State: Sketches of the Chinese Body Politic*, Stanford, CA: Stanford University Press.

Shue, Vivienne (1988), *The Reach of the State: Sketches of the Chinese Body Politic*, Stanford, CA: Stanford University Press.

Shue, Vivienne (2004), 'Legitimacy Crisis in China?', in Peter Hays Gries and Stanley Rosen (eds), *State and Society in 21st Century China: Crisis, Contention and Legitimation*, Abingdon: RoutledgeCurzon pp. 59–89.

Shultz, George P. (1993), *Turmoil and Triumph: My Years as Secretary of State*, New York: Charles Scribner's Sons.

Sima, Yangzi (2011), 'Grassroots Environmental Activism and the Internet: Constructing a Green Public Sphere in China', *Asian Studies Review*, 25(4): 477–497.

Simon, Karla W. (2013), *Civil Society in China: The Legal Framework from Ancient Times to the 'New Reform Era'*, New York: Oxford University Press.

Skinner, G. William (1964), 'Marketing and Social Structure in Rural China (Part I)', *Journal of Asian Studies*, 24(1): 3–44.

Skinner, G.W. (ed.) (1977), *The City in Late Imperial China*, Stanford, CA: Stanford University Press.

Skrekas, Nick and Andrew Batson (2010), 'Beijing Offers Support to Greece', *Wall Street Journal*, 4 October, available at http://online.wsj.com/public/page/news-asia-business.html.

Smith, Anthony D. (2000), 'Theories of Nationalism: Alternative Models of Nation Formation', in Michael Leifer (ed.), *Asian Nationalism*, London: Routledge, pp. 1–20.

Smith, G. (2010), 'The Hollow State: Rural Governance in China', *China Quarterly*, 203: 601–618.

Smith, Graeme and Paul D'Arcy (2013), 'Global Perspectives on Chinese Investment', *Pacific Affairs*, 86(2): 217–232.

Smith, Neil (1984), 'Uneven Development and Location Theory: Toward a Synthesis', in Richard Peet and Nigel Thrift (eds), *New Models in Geography: The Political Economy Perspective*, Boston, MA: Unwin Hyman.

Smith, Phillip Chadwick Foster (1984), *Empress of China*, Philadephia, PA: University of Pennsylvania Press.

Smith, Warren (2004), *China's Policy on Tibetan Autonomy*, Working Papers, No. 2, East–West Center, Washington, DC.

Smith Finley, Joanne (2007), 'Chinese Oppression in Xinjiang, Middle Eastern Conflicts and Global Islamic Solidarities among the Uyghurs', *Journal of Contemporary China*, 16(53): 627–654.

Snow, Edgar (1938), *Red Star over China*, New York: Random House.

Sohn, InJoo (2011), 'After Renaissance: China's Multilateral Offensive in the Developing World', *European Journal of International Relations*, 18(1): 1–25.

Sokolsky, Richard, Angel Rabasa and C. Richard Neu (2001), *The Role of Southeast Asia in US Strategy Toward China*, Santa Monica, CA: RAND Corporation.

Solingen, Etel (ed.) (2012), *Sanctions, Statecraft, and Nuclear Proliferation*, Cambridge: Cambridge University Press.

Solinger, Dorothy J. (1991), *From Lathes to Looms: China's Industrial Policy in Comparative Perspective, 1979–1982*, Stanford, CA: Stanford University Press.

Solinger, Dorothy J. (1992), 'Urban Entrepreneurs and the State: The Merger of State and Society', in A.L. Rosenbaum (ed), *State and Society in China: The Consequences of Reform*, Boulder: Westview Press, pp. 121–141.

Solinger, Dorothy J. (1996), 'Despite Decentralization: Disadvantages, Dependence and Ongoing Central Power in the Inland: The Case of Wuhan', *China Quarterly*, 145: 1–34.

Solinger, Dorothy J. (1999), *Contesting Citizenship in Urban China: Peasant Migrants, the State, and the Logic of the Market*, Berkeley, CA: University of California Press.

Solinger, Dorothy J. (2004), 'The New Crowd of the Dispossessed: The Shift of the Urban Proletariat from Master to Mendicant', in Peter Gries and Stanley Rosen (eds), *State and Society in 21st-Century China: Crisis, Contention, and Legitimation*, New York, USA and London, UK: RoutledgeCurzon.

Song, S. (2003), '1949–1978 nian zhongguo nongcun shehui baozhang zhidu toushe' (Perspectives on China's 1949–1978 rural social security system), *Zhongguo jingjishi yanjiu* (Chinese Economic History Research), 3: 25–34.

Song, S. (2006), 'Zhongguo nongcun shehui baozhang zhidu jiegou yu bianqian toushi (1979–1992)', (Perspectives on structure and changes in China's rural social security system (1979–1992), *Zhongguo tese shehui zhuyi yanjiu* (Chinese socialism research), 1: 69–74.

Song, Yongyi (ed.) (2002), *The Chinese Cultural Revolution Database CD-ROM*, Hong Kong: Chinese University Press.

Spence, Jonathan (1969), *To Change China: Western Advisors in China, 1620–1960*, New York: Little, Brown & Company.

Spence, Jonathan (1990), *The Search for Modern China*, New York: W.W. Norton & Company.

Spires, Anthony J. (2011), 'Contingent Symbiosis and Civil Society in an Authoritarian State: Understanding the Survival of China's Grassroots NGOs', *American Journal of Sociology*, 117(1): 1–45.

Spires, Anthony J. (2012), 'Lessons from Abroad: Foreign Influences on China's Emerging Civil Society', *China Journal*, 68: 125–146.

Spivak, G. (1988), 'Can the Subaltern Speak?', in C. Nelson and L. Grossberg (eds), *Marxism and the Interpretation of Culture*, Urbana, IL: University of Illinois Press, pp. 271–313.

Stacey, J. (1983), *Patriarchy and Socialist Revolution in China*, Berkeley, CA: University of California Press.

State Council (1998), '1998 年国务院机构改革的情况', 中国机构编制网, available at http://www.scopsr.gov.cn/zlzx/zlzxlsyg/201203/t20120323_35152.html.

State Council (2002), *White Paper on China's National Defence in 2002*, Beijing: Information Office of the State Council.

State Council (2003), *China's EU Policy Paper*, available at http://china.org.cn/e-white/20050817/p2.htm (accessed 24 April 2014).

State Council (2007), *White Paper on China's Political System*, available at http://www.china.org.cn/english/news/231852.htm.

State Council (2013), 'Guowuyuan zai quxiao he xiafang 82 xiang xingzheng shenpi xiangmu gongji 221 xiang' ('The State Council Cancels 88 out of 221 measures'), *Renminwang* 10 December 2013, available at http://politics.people.com.cn/n/2013/1210/c1001-23802376.html.

State Council (2014a), 'Guowuyuan pizhuan fazhangaiweihui guanyu 2014 nian shenhua jingji tizhi gaige zhongdianrenwu yijian de tongzhi' (State Council approving the National Development and Reform Commission's notice on 'Some opinions on the 2014 priorities in deepening economic system reform'), available at http://www.gov.cn/zhengce/content/2014-05/20/content_8818.htm, accessed 20 May 2014.

State Council (2014b), 'Guowuyuan guanyu shenhua yusuan guanli zhidugaige de juede' (A decision of the State Council on deepening the budget management system), State Council No. 45 (2014), 26 September2014, available at http://www.gov.cn/zhengce/content/2014-10/08/content_9125.htm, accessed 1 November 2014.

State Council Secretariat (2013), 'Guowuyuan bangongting juanfa caizhengbu guanyu tianzheng he wanshan xianji jiben caili baozhang jizhi yijian de tongji' (A notice of the State Council Secretariat relaying a guideline from Ministry of Finance on adjusting and improving the basic fiscal security mechanism at the county level), State Council Secretariat Document 112 (2013), 30 December, available at http://www.gov.cn/zheng-wuxinxi/zhengcefabu/201401/t20140110_1034684.htm, accessed 20 May 2014.

Steinberg, David (ed.) (1987), *In Search of Southeast Asia: A Modern History*, Honolulu: University of Hawaii Press.

Steinberg, James and Michael E. O'Hanlon (2014), *Strategic Reassurance and Resolve: US–China Relations in the Twenty-First Century*, Princeton, NJ: Princeton University Press.

Steinberg, David A. and Victor C. Shih (2012), 'Interest Group Influence in Authoritarian States: The Political Determinants of Chinese Exchange Rate Policy', *Comparative Political Studies*, 45(11): 1405–1434.

Stoker, G. (1998), 'Governance as Theory: Five Propositions', *International Social Science Journal*, 50: 17.

Storey, Ian (2011), *Southeast Asia and the Rise of China: The Search for Security*, London, UK and New York, USA: Routledge.

Strand, David (1989), *Rickshaw Beijing: City People and Politics in 1920s China*, Berkeley, CA: University of California Press.
Stuart-Fox, Martin (2002), *A Short History of China and Southeast Asia: Tribute, Trade and Influence*, Short History of Asia Series, Crows Nest, NSW: Allen & Unwin.
Su, Shaozhi (1981), 'Shilun woguo xian jieduan de jieji zhuangkuang he jieji douzheng' (Tentative views on the class situation and class struggle in China at the present stage), Selected Writings on Studies of Marxism, 6 February, Beijing: Institute of Marxism–Leninism and Mao Zedong Thought, Chinese Academy of Social Sciences.
Suettinger, Robert L. (2003), *Beyond Tiananmen: The Politics of US–China Relations, 1989–2000*, Washington, DC: Brookings Institution Press.
Sullivan, Jonathan and Lei Xie (2009), 'Environmental Activism, Social Networks and the Internet', *China Quarterly*, 198: 422–432.
Sullivan, Roger (1992), 'Discarding the China Card', *Foreign Policy*, 86(3): 3–23.
Sun, Henry (2007), 'International Political Marketing: A Case Study of its Application in China', *Journal of Public Affairs*, 7(4): 331–340.
Sun, J., H. Liu, H. Li, L. Wang, H. Guo, D. Shan, M. Butlerys, C. Korhonene, Y. Hao and M. Ren (2010), 'Contributions of International Cooperation Projects to the HIV/AIDS Response in China', *International Journal of Epidemiology*, 39: ii4–ii20.
Sun, Jingzhi (1988), *Economic Geography of China*, Hong Kong: Oxford University Press.
Sun, Liping and Liu Xiaoli (eds) (2008), *Koushu Dazhai shi* (Oral histories of Dazhai), Guangzhou: South Daily Press.
Sun, Luxi (2007), *Cong guojia liyi shiyexia kan zhongguo jianguo yilai de duiwai yuanzhu zhengce* (Viewing China's foreign aid policy since China's establishment from the perspective of national interests), *Shidai jinrong* (Current Finance), 11(356): 9.
Sun, Yan (1999), 'Reform, State, and Corruption: Is Corruption Less Destructive in China than in Russia?', *Comparative Politics*, 32(1): 1–20. doi:10.2307/422430.
Sun, Yan (2004), *Corruption and Market in Contemporary China*, Ithaca, NY: Cornell University Press.
Sun, Ying (2013), 'Municipal People's Congress Elections in the PRC; A Process of Co-option', *Journal of Contemporary China*, 23(83): 183–195.
Sunflower, Sutra (2014), *The Economist*, 8 April, available at http://www.economist.com/blogs/banyan/2014/04/politics-taiwan.
Suryadinata, Leo (1996), *Indonesia's Foreign Policy Under Suharto: Aspiring to International Leadership*, London: Marshall Cavendish.
Sutherland, Dylan and Jennifer Y.J. Hsu (2012), *HIVAIDS in China – The Economic and Social Determinants*, London: Routledge.
Sutter, Robert G. (1986), *Chinese Foreign Policy: Developments after Mao*, New York: Praeger.
Sutter, Robert G. (2010), *The A to Z of United States–China Relations*, Lanham, MD: Scarecrow Press.
Sutter, Robert (2013), *US–Chinese Relations: Perilous Past, Pragmatic Present*, 2nd edn, Lanham, MD: Rowman & Littlefield.
Suzuki, S. (2009), *Civilization and Empire: China and Japan's Encounter with European International Society*, London: Routledge.
Swaine, Michael D. (2011), *America's Challenge: Engaging a Rising China in the Twenty-first Century*, Washington, DC: Carnegie Endowment of International Peace.

Szelényi, Ivan (1978), 'Social Inequalities in State Socialist Redistributive Economies', *International Journal of Comparative Sociology*, 19: 63–87.
Szelényi, Ivan (2008), 'A Theory of Transitions', *Modern China*, 34: 165–175.
Szelényi, Ivan and Eric Kostello (1996), 'The Market Transition Debate', *American Journal of Sociology*, 101: 1082–1096.
Szelényi, Ivan and Eric Kostello (1998), 'Outline of an Institutional Theory of Inequality: The Case of Socialist and Postcommunist Eastern Europe', in Mary C. Brinton and Victor Nee (eds), *The New Institutionalism in Sociology*, Stanford University Press, pp. 305–326.
Talhelm, T., X. Zhang, S. Oishi, C. Shimin, D. Duan, X. Lan and S. Kitayama (2014), 'Large-Scale Psychological Differences Within China Explained by Rice Versus Wheat Agriculture', *Science*, 244(6184): 603–608.
Tan, Jian (1985), 'The Theories on the Government's Role Need Further Development', *CASS Journal of Political Science*, 1: 16–18.
Tanaka, Akihiko (1991), *Nitchū kankei 1945–1990*, Tokyo: Tōkyō daigaku shuppankai.
Tang, James (2011), 'Chinese Foreign Policy Challenges: Periphery as Core', in Alan Carlson and Ren Xiao (eds), *New Frontiers in Chinese Foreign Relations*, Lanham, MD: Lexington, pp. 173–190.
Tang, Shui Yan and Zhan Xueyong (2011), 'Political Opportunities, Resource Constraints and Policy Advocacy of Environmental NGOs in China', *Public Administration*, 91(2): 381–389.
Tanner, Murray (2007), *Chinese Economic Coercion Against Taiwan: A Tricky Weapon to Use*, Santa Monica, CA: RAND.
Tanner, Murray (2009), 'How China Manages Internal Security Challenges and its Impact on PLA missions', in Roy Kamphamsen, David Lai and Andrew Scobell (eds), *Beyond the Strait, PLA Missions other than Taiwan*, Carlisle: US Army War College.
Tapp, Nicholas (2010), 'Yunnan: Ethnicity and Economies – Markets and Mobility', *Asia Pacific Journal of Anthropology*, 11(2): 97–110.
Tarling, Nicholas (1999), *The History of Southeast Asia*, Vols 1–4, Cambridge: Cambridge University Press.
Taylor, Brendan (2010), *Sanctions as Grand Strategy*, London: Routledge.
Taylor, Ian (2002), 'Taiwan's Foreign Policy and Africa: The Limitations of Dollar Diplomacy', *Journal of Contemporary China*, 11(30): 125–140.
Teets, Jessica (2009), 'Post-Earthquake Relief and Reconstruction Efforts: The Emergence of Civil Society in China', *China Quarterly*, 198: 330–347.
Teets, Jessica (2012), 'Reforming Service Delivery in China: The Emergence of Social Innovation Model', *Journal of Chinese Political Science*, 17(1): 15–32.
Teets, Jessica (2013), 'Let Many Civil Societies Bloom: The Rise of Consultative Authoritarianism in China', *China Quarterly*, 213: 19–38.
Teiwes, Frederick C. (1966), 'The Purge of Provincial Leaders, 1957–1958', *China Quarterly*, 27: 14–32.
Teiwes, Frederick C. (1967), *Provincial Party Personnel in Mainland China, 1956–1966*, New York: East Asian Institute, Columbia University.
Teiwes, Frederick C. (1971), 'Provincial Politics in China: Themes and Variations', in John M.H. Lindbeck (ed.), *China: Management of a Revolutionary Society*, Seattle, WA: University of Washington Press, pp. 116–189.

Teiwes, Frederick C. (1974), *Provincial Leadership in China: The Cultural Revolution and Its Aftermath*, Ithaca, NY: China–Japan Program, Cornell University.

Teiwes, Frederick C. (1979 [1993]), *Politics and Purges in China: Rectification and the Decline of Party Norms 1950–1965*, 1st edn, White Plains, NY: M.E. Sharpe; 2nd edn, Armonk, NY: M.E. Sharpe.

Teiwes, Frederick C. (1984), *Leadership, Legitimacy, and Conflict in China: From A Charismatic Mao to the Politics of Succession*, Armonk, NY: M.E. Sharpe.

Teiwes, Frederick C. (1987), 'Establishment and Consolidation of the New Regime', in Roderick MacFarquhar and John K. Fairbank (eds), *The Cambridge History of China*, Cambridge: Cambridge University Press, pp. 49–143.

Teiwes, Frederick C. (1988), 'Mao and His Lieutenants', *Australian Journal of Chinese Affairs*, 19–20: 1–80.

Teiwes, Frederick C. (1990), *Politics at Mao's Court: Gao Gang and Party Factionalism in the Early 1950s*, Armonk, NY: M.E. Sharpe.

Teiwes, Frederick C. (1995), 'The Paradoxical Post-Mao Transition: From Obeying the Leader to "Normal Politics"', *China Journal*, 34: 55–94.

Teiwes, Frederick C. (2014), 'Mao Zedong in Power (1949–1976)', in William A. Joseph (ed.), *Politics in China: An Introduction*, 2nd edn, New York: Oxford University Press, pp. 72–118.

Teiwes, Frederick C. and Warren Sun (eds) (1993), *The Politics of Agricultural Cooperativization in China: Mao, Deng Zihui, and the 'High Tide' of 1955*, Armonk, NY: M.E. Sharpe.

Teiwes, Frederick C. and Warren Sun (1996), *The Tragedy of Lin Biao: Riding the Tiger during the Cultural Revolution, 1966–1971*, London: C. Hurst & Co.

Teiwes, Frederick C. and Warren Sun (1999), *China's Road to Disaster: Mao, Central Politicians and Provincial Leaders in the Unfolding of the Great Leap Forward, 1955–1959*, Armonk, NY: M.E. Sharpe.

Teiwes, Frederick C. and Warren Sun (2007), *The End of the Maoist Era: Chinese Politics During the Twilight of the Cultural Revolution, 1972–1976*, Armonk, NY: M.E. Sharpe.

Teiwes, Frederick C. and Warren Sun (2013), 'China's Economic Reorientation after the Third Plenum: Conflict Surrounding "Chen Yun's" Readjustment Program, 1979–80', *China Journal*, 70: 163–187.

Thayer, Carlyle A. (2011), 'China's New Wave of Agressive Assertiveness in the South China Sea', *International Journal of China Studies*, 2(3): 555–584.

Thiers, Paul (2009), 'Stretching Away from the State: NGO Emergence and Dual Identity in a Chinese Government Institution', in R. Hasmath and J. Hsu (eds), *China in an Era of Transition: Understanding Contemporary State and Society Actors*, New York: Palgrave, pp. 145–163.

Thornton, Patricia (2014), 'The Rise of Party Organized NGOs', in R. Hasmath and J.Y.J. Hsu (eds), *NGO Governance and Management in China*, Abingdon: Routledge.

Tian, Qunjian (2004), 'China Develops its West: Motivation, Strategy and Prospect', *Journal of Contemporary China*, 13(41): 611–636.

Tian, S.S., H. Luo and W. Zeng (2006), *Introduction to China's Administrative Divisions*, Beijing: Beijing University Press.

Tilak, J.B.G. (2011), *Trade in Higher Education: the Role of the General Agreement on Trade in Services*, Paris: UNESCO.

Tisdell, C.A. (1993), *Economic Development in the Context of China: Policy Issues and Analysis*, New York: St Martin's Press.
Tong, Yanqi and Shaohua Lei (2013), *Social Protest in Contemporary China, 2003–2010: Transitional Pains and Regime Legitimacy*, Routledge.
Townsend, James R. (1969), *Political Participation in Communist China*, Berkeley, CA: University of California Press.
Townsend, James R. (1974), *Politics in China*, Boston, MA: Little, Brown, & Company.
Tsang, Shu-ki and Yuk-shing Cheng (1994), 'China's Tax Reforms of 1994: Breakthrough or Compromise?', *Asian Survey*, 34(9): 769–788.
Tsou, Tang (1963), *America's Failure in China, 1941–50*, Chigaco, IL: University of Chicago Press.
Tsou, Tang (1995), 'Chinese Politics at the Top: Factionalism or Informal Politics? Balance-of-Power Politics or a Game to Win All?', *China Journal*, 34: 95–156.
Tucker, Nancy Bernkopf (ed.) (2001), *China Confidential: American Diplomats and Sino-American Relations, 1945–1996*, New York: Columbia University Press.
Tung, William L. (1968), *The Political Institutions of Modern China*, The Hague: M. Nijhoff.
Turner, Oliver (2014), *American Images of China: Identity, Power, Policy*, London: Routledge.
Uhalley, Stephen, Jr (1988), *A History of the Chinese Communist Party*, Stanford, CA: Hoover Institution Press.
Unger, Jonathan (1984), 'The Class System in Rural China: A Case Study', in James Watson (ed.), *Class and Social Stratification in Post-Revolutionary China*, Cambridge: Cambridge University Press, pp. 121–141.
Unger, J. (1986), 'The Decollectivization of the Chinese Countryside – a Survey of 28 Villages', *Pacific Affairs*, 58(4): 585–606.
Unger, J. (2002), 'The Transformation of Rural China', *Asia and the Pacific*, Armonk, NY: M.E. Sharpe, pp. 95–118.
Unger, Jonathan and Anita Chan (2008), 'Associations in a Bind: The Emergence of Political Corporatism', in J. Unger (ed.), *Associations and the Chinese State: Contested Spaces*, Armonk, NY: M.E. Sharpe, pp. 48–68.
United Nations (1965), *The International Convention on the Elimination of All Forms of Racial Discrimination*, available at http://www.ohchr.org/EN/ProfessionalInterest/Pages/CERD.aspx (accessed 12 July 2014).
United Nations (2007), *United Nations Declaration on the Rights of Indigenous Peoples, General Assembly Resolution*, September, available at http://www.un.org/esa/socdev/unpfii/ documents/DRIPS_en.pdf (accessed 12 July 2014).
UN Department of Public Information (2012), 'About Us', available at http://outreach.un.org/ngorelations/about-us/.
USAID (2012), *Foreign Operations FY 2011 Performance Report, FY 2013 Performance Plan*, Washington, DC: USAID.
US Congressional-Executive Commission on China (2005), *China's Regional Ethnic Autonomy Law*, 11 April, available at http://www.gpo.gov/fdsys/pkg/CHRG-109shrg21045/pdf/CHRG-109shrg21045.pdf (accessed 12 July 2014).
Van Canh, Nguyen and Earle Cooper (1983), *Vietnam Under Communism: 1975–1982*, Stanford, CA: Hoover Institution Press.

Van Ness, Peter (1970), *Revolution and Chinese Foreign Policy: Peking's Support for Wars of National Liberation*, Berkeley, CA: University of California Press

Vermeersch, Peter (2003), 'EU Enlargement and Minority Rights Policies in Central Europe', *Journal of Ethnopolitics and Minority Issues in Europe*, 1: 1–32.

Vermeersch, Peter (2004), 'Minority Policy in Central Europe', *Global Review of Ethnopolitics*, 3(2): 3–19.

Vogel, Ezra F. (2011), *Deng Xiaoping and the Transformation of China*, Cambridge, MA: Belknap Press of Harvard University Press.

Wah, Chin Kin (1983), *The Defence of Malaysia and Singapore: The Transformation of a Security System, 1957–1971*, Cambridge: Cambridge University Press.

Wah, Chin Kin (1991), 'The Five Power Defence Arrangements: Twenty Years After', *Pacific Review*, 4(3): 193–203.

Wakeman, Frederic (1993), 'The Civil Society and Public Sphere Debate: Western Reflection on Chinese Political Culture', *Modern China*, 19(2): 108–138.

Walder, Andrew (1995), 'Local Governments as Industrial Firms: An Organizational Analysis of China's Transitional Economy', *American Journal of Sociology*, 101: 1060–1073.

Walder, Andrew (1996), 'Markets and Inequality in Transitional Economies: Towards Testable Theories', *American Journal of Sociology*, 101: 1060–1173.

Walder, Andrew (2002), 'Markets and Income Inequality in Rural China: Political Advantage in an Expanding Economy', *American Sociological Review*, 67: 231–253.

Walder, Andrew (2003), 'Elite Opportunity in Transitional Economies', *American Sociological Review*, 68: 899–917.

Walder, Andrew J., Li Bobai and Donald J. Treiman (2000), 'Politics and Life Chances in a Socialist Regime: Dual Career Paths into the Urban Chinese Elite, 1949–1996', *American Sociological Review*, 65: 191–209.

Walker, Richard L. (1955), *China under Communism: The First Five Years*, New Haven, CT: Yale University Press.

Wan, Yanhai, Hu Ran, Guo Ran and Linda Arnade (2009), 'Discrimination against People with HIV/AIDS in China', *Equal Rights Review*, 4: 15–25.

Wang, Chenyan (2009), 'Jiejin guoji jingyan: kexue tuijin duiwai yuanzhu' (Borrowing from international experience: scientifically advancing foreign aid), *Guoji jingji hezuo* (International Economic Cooperation), 6: 40–45.

Wang, Chenyan (2012), 'Japan Anniversary Events Postponed', *China Daily*, 24 September, available at http://www.chinadaily.com.cn/china/2012-09/24/content_15776399.htm.

Wang, Dong (2013), *The United States and China: A History from the Eighteenth Century to the Present*, Lanham, MD: Rowman & Littlefield.

Wang, Guangya (2005), 'Statement by Ambassador Wang Guangya, Permanent Representative of China to the UN, at the 60th GA Session on Security Council Reform', available at http://www.china-un.org/eng/hyyfy/t220921.htm (accessed 14 July 2013).

Wang, H. (2011), *Zhongguo chengxiang zuidi shenghuo baozhangzhidu: huigu yu pingjia* (China's rural and urban minimum living standard guarantee system: review and assessment), *Ha'erbin gongye daxue xuebao, shehui kexue ban* (Ha'erbin Industrial University Journal, Social Sciences edition), 13(2): 22–7.

Wang, Huaxin (1997), *Zonghe caizheng yusuan gailun* (Introduction to comprehensive budgeting), Beijing: Zhongguo caizheng jingji chubanshe.

Wang, Li (2001), *Wang Li fansilu* (Wang Li's reflections), Hong Kong: Beixing chubanshe.

Wang, Nianyi (1988), *Dadongluan de niandai* (The years of great turmoil), Henan: Zhengzhou renmin chubanshe.

Wang, N. and W.J. Morgan (2009), 'Student Motivations, Quality and Status in Adult Higher Education in China', *International Journal of Lifelong Education*, 28(4): 473–491.

Wang, N. and W.J. Morgan (2012), 'The Harmonious Society, Social Capital and Lifelong Learning in China: Emerging Policies and Practice', *International Journal of Continuing Education and Lifelong Learning*, 4(2): 1–15.

Wang, Shaoguang (1997), 'China's 1994 Fiscal Reform: An Initial Assessment', *Asian Survey*, 37(9): 801–817.

Wang, Shaoguang (2008), 'Changing Models of China's Policy Agenda Setting', *Modern China*, 34: 56–87.

Wang, Shaoguang and Fan Peng (2013), *The Chinese Model of Consensus Decision-Making: A Case Study of Healthcare Reform (Zhongguoshi Gongshixing Juece: 'Kaimen' yu 'Mohe')*, Beijing: Renmin University Press.

Wang, Wen, Xinye Zhang and Zhirong Zhao (2012), 'Fiscal Reform and Public Education Spending: A Quasi-natural Experiment of Fiscal Decentralization in China', *Journal of Federalism*, 42(2): 334–356.

Wang, Xia (1991), *Haipai zhangfu mianmianguan* (An overview of Shanghai husbands), Shanghai: Shanghai Social Sciences Press.

Wang, Yizhou (2011), *Chuangzaoxing jieru: zhongguo waijiao xin quxiang* (Creative involvement: a new direction in China's diplomacy), Beijing: Beijing University Press.

Wang, Yuhua and Carl Minzner (2015), 'The Rise of the Security State', *China Quarterly*, 222(June): 339–359.

Wang, Yunxiang (1996), 'Zhongguo weixi lun xi' (Analysing the China Threat theory), *Guoji Guancha* (International Survey), 3: 35–40.

Wang, Yuxiang and JoAnn Phillion (2009), 'Minority Language Policy and Practice in China', *International Journal of Multicultural Education*, 11(1): 1–14.

Wang, Zheng (1999), *Women in the Chinese Enlightenment: Oral and Textual Histories*, Berkeley, CA: University of California Press.

Wang, Zheng (2003), 'Gender, Employment and Women's Resistance', in Elizabeth J. Perry and Mark Seden (eds), *Chinese Society: Change, Conflict and Resistance*, 2nd edition, London and New York: RoutlegeCurzon, pp. 159–182.

Wang, Zheng (2005), '"State Feminism"? Gender and Socialist State Formation in Maoist China', *Feminist Studies*, 31(3): 519–551.

Wang, Zheng (2006), 'Dilemmas of Inside Agitators: Chinese State Feminists in 1957', *China Quarterly*, 188(December): 59–78.

Wang, Zheng (2008), 'National Humiliation, History Education, and the Politics of Historical Memory: Patriotic Education Campaign in China', *International Studies Quarterly*, 52: 783–806.

Wang, Zheng (2010), 'Creating a Socialist Feminist Cultural Front: Women of China 1949–1966',*China Quarterly*, 204(December): 827–849.

Warwick, Mara (2003), 'Environmental Information Collection and Enforcement at Small-scale Enterprises in Shanghai: The Role of the Bureaucracy, Legislatures and Citizens', Ph.D. Dissertation, Department of Civil Engineering, Stanford University.

Watkins, K. (2006), *Human Development Report 2006 Beyond Scarcity: Power, Poverty, and the Global Water Crisis*, United Nations Development Programme.

Watson, A. (2009), 'Social Security for China's Migrant Workers – Providing for Old Age', *Journal of Current Chinese Affairs*, 38(4): 85–115.

Watson, James (1984), 'Introduction', in James Watson (ed.), *Class and Social Stratification in Post-Revolutionary China*, Cambridge: Cambridge University Press, pp. 1–15.

Wedeman, Andrew (2000), 'Budgets, Extra-Budgets, and Small Treasuries: Illegal Monies and Local Autonomy in China', *Journal of Contemporary China*, 9(25): 489–511.

Wedeman, Andrew (2004), 'The Intensification of Corruption in China', *China Quarterly*, 180: 895–921. doi:10.1017/S0305741004000670.

Wedeman, Andrew (2012), *Double Paradox: Rapid Growth and Rising Corruption in China*, Ithaca, NY: Cornell University Press.

Wei, Jiankuan (n.d.), 'Xia Yan xiansheng gaibian Zhufu de baibi' (Failures in Xia Yan's adaptation of *New Year's Sacrifice*), available at http://www.xiexingcun.com/dushu/ShowArticle.asp?ArticleID=11294 (accessed 18 August 2014).

Wei, Liqun (2005), *Kexue Fazhan Guan he Xiandaihua Jianshe* (The scientific development concept and modern construction), Beijing: Renmin Chuban She (People's Publishing House).

Wei, X. (1994), *Zhongguo shehui baozhang zhidu yanjiu* (Research into the Chinese Social Security System), Beijing: Renmin Univesity Publishing.

Weinstein, Franklin B. (1976), *Indonesian Foreign Policy and the Dilemma of Dependence: From Sukarno to Suharto*, Ithaca, NY: Cornell University Press.

Weitzman, Martin and Chenggang Xu (1994), 'Chinese township–village enterprises as vaguely defined cooperatives', *Journal of Comparative Economics*, 18(2): 121–145.

Wen, Jiabao (2012), 'Report on the Work of the Government', delivered at the Fifth Session of the Eleventh National People's Congress, 5 March, available at http://online.wsj.com/public/resources/documents/2012NPC_GovtWorkReport_English.pdf.

White, Gordon (1996), 'Corruption and the Transition from Socialism in China', *Journal of Law and Society*, 23: 149.

White, G. (1998), 'Social Security Reforms in China: Towards an East Asian Model?', in R. Goodman, G. White and H.-J. Kwon (eds), *The East Asian Welfare Model: Welfare Orientalism and the State*, London: Routledge, pp. 175–197.

White, Gordon, Jude Howell and Xiaoyuan Shang (1996), *In Search of Civil Society: Market Reform and Social Change in Contemporary China*, Oxford: Clarendon Press.

White, Lynn T. (1989a), *Policies of Chaos: The Organizational Causes of Violence in China's Cultural Revolution*, Princeton, NJ: Princeton University Press.

White, Lynn, III (1989b), *Shanghai Shanghaide? Uneven Taxes in Reform China*, Hong Kong: Center of Asian Studies, University of Hong Kong.

White House (2000), 'The US–China WTO Agreement Will Help Promote Reform, Accountability, and Openness in China', White House Office of the Press Secretary, available at http://usinfo.state.gov/regional/ea/uschina/wtofact2.htm (accessed 3 June 2001).

Whiting, Susan (1999), 'The Regional Evolution of Ownership Forms: Shareholding Cooperatives and Rural Industry in Shanghai and Wenzhou', in Andrew Walder and Jean Oi (eds), *Property Rights and Economic Reform in China*, Stanford, CA: Stanford University Press, pp. 171–200.
Whiting, Susan (2000), *Power and Wealth in Rural China: The Political Economy of Institutional Change*, New York: Cambridge University Press.
Whyte, M. (1989), 'Who Hates Bureaucracy? A Chinese Puzzle', in V. Nee and D. Stark (eds), *Remaking the Economic Institutions of Socialism*, Palo Alto, CA: Stanford University Press.
Wildavsky, Aaron (1986 [1997]), *Budgeting: A Comparative Theory of Budgetary Process*, New Brunswick, NJ: Transaction Publishers.
Wildavsky, Aaron (1992), *The New Politics of the Budgetary Processes*, 2nd edn, New York: Harper Collins.
Williams, Erin Elizabeth (2008), 'Ethnic Minorities and the State in China', available at http://www.cpsa-acsp.ca/papers-2008/Williams,%20Erin.pdf (accessed 12 July 2014).
Wilson, Amy A. (1977), 'Deviance and Social Control in Chinese Society: An Introductory Essay', in Amy Wilson and Richard Wilson (eds), *Deviance and Social Control in Chinese Society*, New York: Praeger Publishers.
Wilson, Ian and You Ji (1990), 'Leadership by "Lines": China's Unresolved Succession', *Problems of Communism*, 39(January): 28–44.
Wilson, Scott (2012), 'Settling for Discrimination: HIV/AIDS Carriers and the Resolution of Legal Claims', *International Journal of Asia-Pacific Studies*, 8(1): 35–55.
Winichakul, T. (1994), *Siam Mapped: A History of the Geo-body of a Nation*, Honolulu: University of Hawaii Press.
Wittfogel, Karl A. (1960), 'Part 1: The Legend of "Maoism" Part 1 and Part 2', *China Quarterly*, January–March and April–June.
Wittfogel, Karl A., Benjamin Schwartz and Henryk Sjaardema (1960), 'Controversy', *China Quarterly*, October–December.
Womack, B. (2009), 'China between Region and World', *China Journal*, 61: 1–20.
Wong, Christine P.W. (1988), 'Interpreting Rural Industrial Growth in the Post-Mao Period', *Modern China* 14(1): 3–30.
Wong, Christine P.W. (1991), 'Central–Local Relations in an Era of Fiscal Decline: The Paradox of Fiscal Decentralization in Post-Mao China', *China Quarterly*, 128: 691–715.
Wong, Christine P.W. (1992), 'Fiscal Reform and Local Industrialization: The Problematic Sequencing of Reform in Post-Mao China', *Modern China*, 18(2): 197–227.
Wong, Christine P.W. (1997), *Financing Local Government in the People's Republic of China*, a publication for Asian Development Bank, Oxford: Oxford University Press.
Wong, Christine P.W. (2009), 'Rebuilding Government for the 21st Century: Can China Incrementally Reform the Public Sector?', *China Quarterly*, 200: 929–952.
Wong, Christine P.W., Christopher Heady and Wing T. Woo (1995), *Fiscal Management and Economic Reform in the People's Republic of China*, Hong Kong: Oxford University Press.
Wong, Edward (2012), 'New Communist Party Chief in China Denounces Corruption in Speech', *New York Times*, 20 November.

Wong, L. (1998), *Marginalization and Social Welfare in China*, London: Routledge.
Woo, Franklin J. (2011), 'America's Response to China: A History of Sino-American Relations (Review)', *China Review International*, 18(2): 173–179.
Woon, Y.F. (1999), 'Labor Migration in the 1990s: Homeward Orientation of Migrants in the Pearl River Delta Region and its Implications for Interior China', *Modern China*, 25(4): 475–512.
World Bank (1986), *International Experience in Budgetary Trends during Economic Development and its Relevance for China*, Washington, DC: World Bank.
World Bank (1987), *China: Finance and Investment*, Washington, DC: World Bank.
World Bank (1989), *Sub-Saharan Africa: From Crisis to Sustainable Growth*, Washington, DC: World Bank.
World Bank (1990), *Revenue Mobilization and Tax Policy*, Washington, DC: World Bank.
World Bank (1992a), *Intergovernmental Fiscal Relations in China*, Washington, DC: World Bank.
World Bank (1992b), *Reforming Intergovernmental Fiscal Relations*, Washington, DC: World Bank.
World Bank (1992c), *Governance and Development*, Washington, DC: World Bank.
World Bank (1993), *Budgetary Policy and Intergovernmental Fiscal Relations*, Washington, DC: World Bank.
World Bank (1995a), *Public Investment and Finance*, Washington, DC: World Bank.
World Bank (1995b), *Macroeconomic Management and Fiscal Decentralization*, Washington, DC: World Bank.
World Bank (1996), *China: Social Sector Expenditure Review*, Washington, DC: World Bank.
World Bank (1998), 'The Bank's Relations with NGOs', Social Development Papers No. 28, Washington, DC: World Bank.
World Bank (1999a), *China, Rural China: Transition and Development*, Washington, DC: World Bank.
World Bank (1999b), *Accelerating China's Rural Transformation*, Washington, DC: World Bank.
World Bank (2001), *China: Overcoming Rural Poverty*, Washington, DC: World Bank.
World Bank (2002), *Corporate Governance and Enterprise Reform in China: Building the Institutions of Modern Markets*, Washington, DC: World Bank.
World Bank (2004a), *Finance in China: Removing Ambiguity over Governments' Role*, Washington, DC: World Bank.
World Bank (2004b), *China's (uneven) Progress against Poverty*, Washington, DC: World Bank.
World Bank (2005a), *Public Expenditure and the Role of Government in the Chinese Health Sector*, Washington, DC: World Bank.
World Bank (2005b), *Land Policy Reform for Sustainable Economic and Social Development: An Integrated Framework for Action*, Washington, DC: World Bank.
World Bank (2006a), *The Fiscal Framework and Urban Infrastructure Finance in China*, Washington, DC: World Bank.
World Bank (2006b), *Land Leasing and Land Sale as an Infrastructure-Financing Option*, Washington, DC: World Bank.

World Bank (2007a), *Improving Rural Public Finance for the Harmonious Society*, Washington, DC: World Bank.
World Bank (2007b), *Public Services for Building the new Socialist Countryside*, Washington, DC: World Bank.
World Bank (2007c), *Cost of Pollution in China: Economic Estimates of Physical Damages*, Washington, DC: World Bank.
World Bank (2008), *Financing Rural Development*, Washington, DC: World Bank.
World Bank (2009), 'China – From Poor Areas to Poor People: China's Evolving Poverty Reduction Agenda. An Assessment of Poverty and Inequality in China', Washington, DC: World Bank.
World Bank (2010a), *Equity and Public Governance in Health System Reform*, Washington, DC: World Bank.
World Bank (2010b), 'Strengthening Subnational Debt Financing and Managing Risks: Policy Note', Washington, DC: World Bank.
World Bank and Organisation for Economic Co-operation and Development (2005), *Strengthening Procurement Capacities in Developing Countries*, Washington, DC, USA and Paris, France: World Bank and OECD.
Wu, Di (ed.) (1993), *Zhongguo dianying yanjiu ziliao 1949–1979* (Source materials for Chinese film studies, 1949–1979), Beijing: Culture and Art Publishing House.
Wu, Fengshi (2009), 'Environmental Activism and Civil Society Development in China', Harvard–Yenching Institute Working Paper Series, available at http://www.harvard-yenching.org/sites/harvard-yenching.org/files/featurefiles/WU Fengshi_Environmental Civil Society in China2.pdf.
Wu, Fengshi (2011), 'Strategic State Engagement in Transnational Activism: AIDS Prevention in China', *Journal of Contemporary China*, 20(71): 621–637.
Wu, Fengshi and Kin-man Chan (2012), 'Graduated Control and Beyond: The Evolving Government–NGO Relations', *China Perspectives*, 3: 9–17, available at http://chinaperspectives.revues.org/5928.
Wu, Guoguang (2008), 'From Post-Imperial to Late Communist Nationalism: Historical Change in Chinese Nationalism from May Fourth to the 1990s', *Third World Quarterly*, 29(3): 467–482.
Wu, Jinglian (2013), *Wu Jinglian: Voice of Reform in China*, ed. and with an Introduction and Preface by Barry Naughton, Cambridge, MA: MIT Press.
Wu, Mengda and Chen Fei (2014), 'Zhong jiwei xietiao zhihui 2014 woguo xianqi jingwai zhui tao fengbao' (The commission to coordinate the command of foreign fugitives sets off a storm in 2014), *Zhongguo jijian jiancha bao* (CCP Discipline Committee inspection report), 28 August.
Wu Wei (2013), *Zhongguo 80 niandai zhengzhi gaige de taiqian muhou* (On Stage and Backstage: China's Political Reform in the 1980s), Hong Kong: New Century Media and Consulting Co.
Wu, Y. and Wen Wang (2012), 'Does Participatory Budgeting Improve the Legitimacy of the Local Government? A Comparative Case Study of Two Cities in China', *Australian Journal of Public Administration*, 71: 122–135.
Wurfel, David (2004), 'Civil Society and Democratization in the Philippines', in Y. Sato (ed.), *Growth and Governance in Asia*, Honolulu: Asia-Pacific Center for Security Studies, pp. 215–224.

Wuthnow, Joel (2011), 'Beyond the Veto: Chinese Diplomacy in the United Nations Security Council', PhD thesis, Columbia University, New York.

Xia, Liping (2001), 'China: A Responsible Great Power', *Journal of Contemporary China*, 10(26): 17–25.

Xia, Ming (1997), 'Informational efficiency, organisational development and the institutional linkages of the provincial people's congresses in China', *The Journal of Legislative Studies*, 3(3): 10–38.

Xia, Ming (2000), 'Political Contestation and the Emergence of the Provincial People's Congresses and Power Players in Chinese Politics: A Network Explanation', *Journal of Contemporary China*, 9(24): 185–215.

Xia, Yafeng (2006a), 'China's Elite Politics and Sino-American Rapprochement, January 1969 – February 1972', *Journal of Cold War Studies*, 8(4): 3–28.

Xia, Yafeng (2006b), *Negotiating with the Enemy: US–China Talks During the Cold War, 1949–1972*, Bloomington, IN: Indiana University Press.

Xia, Yan (1996), 'Zatan gaibian' (On adaptation), in Li Ziyun (ed.), *Xia Yan qishinian wenxuan* (Selections from Xia Yan's seventy years of works), Shanghai: Shanghai Art and Culture Press.

Xiao, Ren (2009), 'Between Adapting and Shaping: China's Role in Asian Regional Cooperation', *Journal of Contemporary China*, 18(59): 303–320.

Xiao, Tangbiao (2012), 'Dangdai zhongguo de quntixingshijian: gainian, leixing yu xingzhi bianxi' (Mass incidents in contemporary China: concepts, types and nature), *Journal of Humanities* (Renwen Zazhi) 4.

Xie, Minggan (2014), 'The creation of (1984), 'Resolution on Economic Reform' (Zhonggong zhongyang guanyu jingji tizhi gaige de jueding' yansheng qianhou), in Ouyang Song and Gao Yongzhong (eds), *Gaige Kaifang Koushushi (An Oral History of Reform and Opening)*, Beijing: Zhongguo Renmin Daxue, pp. 270–294.

Xie, Yu and Emily Hannum (1996), 'Regional Variation in Earnings Inequality in Reform Era Urban China', *American Journal of Sociology*, 101: 950–992.

Xin, Y. (2001), 'Shilun renmingong shede lishi dili' (Tentative discussion of the historial place of the people's communes), *Dang dai zhongguo lishi yanjiu*, 3: 27–40.

Xinhua (2006a), 'China to Boost Rise of Central Region'.

Xinhua (2006b), 'Wen Hears Farmers' Concerns on the 11th Five-Year Plan', Xinhua News Agency.

Xinhua (2007), 'Ma Wenjiu chengli guojia yufang fubai ju redian wenti da jizhe wen' (Ma Wen-jeou answers questions on the established National Corruption Prevention Bureau), 18 September, available at http://news.xinhuanet.com/legal/2007-09/18/content_6745870.htm.

Xinhua (2009), '74% of PLA Cadres Possess University Qualifications', 5 January.

Xinhua (2012a), 'Zhongguo yi pi da an yai'an bei yisong sifa' (Number of cases in China transferred to juciial process), 6 January, available at http://news.xinhuanet.com/politics/2012-01/06/c_111388295.htm.

Xinhua (2012b), 'Zhonggong zhongyang zhengzhi ju zhaokai huiyi shenyi guanyu gaijin gongzuo zuofeng, miqie lianxi qunzhong de youguan guiding fenxi yanjiu 2013 nian jingji gongzuo' (CCP Politburo holds a meeting on improving workstyle and close ties with the masses in the amalysis of 2013 economic work), 4 December, available at http://cpc.people.com.cn/n/2012/1205/c64094-19793530.html.

Xinhua (2013a), '2012 nian quanguo jijian jiancha jiguan chaban anjian gongzuo qingkuang' (Conditions of the cases investigated by the national discipline inspection organs in 2012), 9 January, available at http://news.xinhuanet.com/politics/2013--01/09/c_124208047.htm.

Xinhua (2013b), 'Benjie zhengfu juxing zuihou yici guowuyuan changwu huiyi' (Last meeting of State Council Standing Committee), 20 February, available at http://www.gov.cn/jrzg/2013-02/20/content_2336417.htm.

Xinhua (2013c), 'Zhongyang bian ban fuze ren jiu guowuyuan jigou gaige he zhineng zhuanbian da renmin ribao, Xinhua she jizhe wen' (A responsible person of the Central Office of the State Council answers questions on functional transformation and institutional reform by reporters from *The People's Daily* and the New China News Agency), 10 March, available at http://news.xinhuanet.com/2013lh/2013-0/c_114967850.htm.

Xinhua (2013d), 'China's new premier presses reforms as "biggest dividend"', 17 March, available at http://news.xinhuanet.com/english/china/2013-03/17/c_132240248.htm.

Xinhua (2013e), 'Zhonggong zhongyang guanyu quanmian shenhua gaige ruogan zhongda wenti de jueding' (CCP Central Committee decision on certain important questions for all round reform), 11 November, available at http://news.xinhuanet.com/politics/2013-11/15/c_118164235.htm

Xinhua (2013f), 'China's Communist Party membership exceeds 85 million', 1 July.

Xinhua (2014a), 'Zhongjiwei: 2013 nian zhongyang jiwei li'an jiancha 31 ming zhong guan ganbu' (CCP Central Discipline Inspection Committee files 31 cases of central cadres in 2013), 10 January, available at http://news.xinhuanet.com/legal/2014--01/10/c_125985409.htm.

Xinhua (2014b), 'Caichan gongkai kao xiaotou guanggu?' (Do thieves visit public property?), 22 September, available at http://zgws.xinhuanet.com/info.aspx?id=67944&typeid=15.

Xinhua (2014c), 'Deepen the China–EU comprehensive strategic partnership for mutual benefit and win–win cooperation', available at http://news.xinhuanet.com/english/china/2014-04/02/c_133230788.htm (accessed 25 April 2014).

Xinhua Forum (2012), 'Congwo zuoqi dizhi rihuo aiwo zhonghua' (Boycott Japanese goods, love our China, it begins with me), available at http://forum.home.news.cn/thread/103614758/1.html.

Xinkuaibao (2012a), 'Zhanjinag gangtue xiangmu huo pi shi zhang qinwen wenjian' (Mayor approves Zhanjiang steel plant project), 29 May, available at http://www.ycwb.com/epaper/xkb/html/2012-05/29/content_1401224.htm.

Xinjingbao (2012b), 'Woguo yijia shehuituanti jiangxiang chaoxian touzi 30 yiyuan' (Chinese social organization will invest 3 billion RMB in DPRK), 24 September, available at http://news.sina.com.cn/c/2012-09-24/023925236400.shtml.

Xiong, Jue (2013), 'Zhongguo defang zhili zhong de zhengfu yu shehui' (Government and society in local governance in China), *Hunan Chengshi Xueyuan Xuebao* (Journal of Hunan City University), 34(6): 64–68.

Xu, Chenggang (2011), 'The Fundamental Institutions of China's Reforms and Development', *Journal of Economic Literature*, 49(4): 1076–1151.

Xu, Hua, Zeng Yi and Allen F. Anderson (2005), 'Chinese NGOs in Action against HIV/AIDS', *Cell Research*, 15(11–12): 914–918.

Xu, Y. (2000), *The Chinese City in Space and Time: The Development of Urban Form in Suzhou*, Honolulu: University of Hawaii Press.

Xu, Zhaoming (1986), 'Government's Role in Transition: A Discussion of the National Conference on the Theory of Government's Role', *CASS Journal of Political Science*, 5: 53–57.

Xue, Benhui and Wang Li (2006), 'Dalu dui Taiwan jingji zhicai de kenengxing fenxi' (Analysis of the possibility of mainland sanctions against Taiwan), *Falu yu shehui* (Law and Society), 11: 150.

Yan, Jianying (2005), 'Meiguo jingji zhicai yu fazhanzhongguojia de jingji anquan' (US economic sanctions and the economic security of developing countries), *Guoji luntan* (International Forum), 7(3): 43–48.

Yan, Jirong (2009), 'Fuwuxing Zhengfu de Yanjiu Luxiang' (A review of the studies on service-oriented government), *Xuehai*, 1: 191–201.

Yan, Xiaojun (2011), 'Regime Inclusion and the Resilience of Authoritarianism: The Local People's Political Consultative Conference in post-Mao Chinese politics', *China Journal*, 66: 53–67.

Yan, Xuetong (2014), 'From Keeping a Low Profile to Striving for Achievement', *Chinese Journal of International Politics*, 7(2): 153–184.

Yang, Aimei and Maureen Taylor (2010), 'Relationship-Building by Chinese ENGOs' Websites: Education, Not Activation', *Public Relations Review*, 36(4): 342–351.

Yang, Dali (1990), 'Patterns of China's Regional Development Strategy', *China Quarterly*, 122: 230–257.

Yang, Dali L. (1996), *Calamity and Reform in China: State, Rural Society, and Institutional Change Since the Great Leap Famine*, Stanford, CA: Stanford University Press.

Yang, Dali (1997), *Beyond Beijing: Liberalism and the Regions in China*, London, UK and New York, USA: Routledge.

Yang, Dali (2004), *Remaking the Chinese Leviathan: Market Transition and the Politics of Governance in China*, Stanford, CA: Stanford University Press.

Yang, David (2004), 'Civil Society as an Analytic Lens for Contemporary China', *China: An International Journal*, 2(1): 1–27.

Yang, Guobin (2005), 'Environmental NGOs and Institutional Dynamics', *China Quarterly*, 181: 46–66.

Yang, Guobin (2010), 'Brokering Environment and Health in China: Issue Entrepreneurs of the Public Sphere', *Journal of Contemporary China*, 19(63): 101–118.

Yang, Li and Geoffrey Wall (2009), 'Minorities and Tourism: Community Perspectives from Yunnan, China', *Journal of Tourism and Cultural Change*, 7(2): 77–98.

Yang Liyong and Zhou Yong (2007), 'Henan yaopin wangshang zhaobiao, 1072 jia yiyuan "tongyao tongjia"' (Henan hospitals purchase medicine through online bidding, 1072 hospitals now charge the same prices for the same medicine), 13 September, available at http://health.sohu.com/20070913/n252127018.shtml.

Yang, Mayfair Mei-Hui (1994), *Gifts, Favors, and Banquets: The Art of Social Relationships in China*, Ithaca, NY: Cornell University Press.

Yang, Mayfair Mei-Hui (1997), Director, *Through Chinese Women's Eyes*, documentary film.

Yang, Mayfair Mei-Hui (1999), *Spaces of Their Own: Women's Public Sphere in Transnational China*, Minneapolis, MN: University of Minnesota Press.

Yang, Mu and Heng Siam-Heng (2011), 'China–ASEAN relations after CAFTA', in

Chong Guan Kwa and Mingjiang Li (eds), *China–ASEAN Sub-Regional Cooperation Progress, Problems, and Prospect*, Singapore: World Scientific.

Yang, T. (ed.) (2003), *Social Policy in China*, Beijing: Chinese Academy of Social Sciences.

Yao, Jianfu (2012), *Chen Xitong qinshu* (Conversations with Chen Xitong), Hong Kong: New Century Press.

Yao, Yang (2009), 'The Political Economy of Government Policies toward Regional Inequality in China', in Yukon Huang and Allesandro M. Bocchi (eds), *Reshaping Economic Geography in East Asia*, Washington, DC: World Bank, pp. 218–240.

Ye, Duchu and Xianfu Lu (2009), *Dictionary of Party Building* (Dang de Jianshe Cidian), Beijing: Central Party School Press (Zhongyangdangxiao chubanshe).

Ye, Xiaonan (2011), 'Zhongguo minying jingji shehui gongxian riyi xianzhu: siqi shuliang chaoguo 840 wan hu' (China's private economy is making increasing social contribution: there are more than 8.4 million private enterprises), *People's Daily* (overseas edition), 22 January, available at http://paper.people.com.cn/rmrbhwb/html/2011-01/22/content_730663.htm.

Yee, Herbert (1983), 'The Three World Theory and Post-Mao China's Global Strategy', *International Affairs*, 59(2): 239–49.

Yeoh, Kok Kheng (2009), *Towards Pax Sinica?: China's Rise and Transformation: Impacts and Implications*, Kuala Lumpur: Universiti Malaya, Institut Pengajian China.

Yeophantong, Pichamon (2013), 'Governing the World: China's Evolving Conceptions of Responsibility', *Chinese Journal of International Politics*, 6(4): 29–36.

Yep, R. (2004), 'Can "Tax-for-Fee" Reform Reduce Rural Tension in China? The Process, Progress and Limitations', *China Quarterly*, 177: 42–70.

Yim, Linda (1990), 'The Foreign Policy of Singapore' in David Wurfel and David Burton (eds), *The Political Economy of Foreign Policy in Southeast Asia*, London: Palgrave MacMillan, pp. 124–145.

Yin, Deyong (2009), 'China's Attitude toward Foreign NGOs', *Washington University Global Studies Law Review*, 8(3): 521–543.

Yoon, Hwy-tak (2004), 'China's Northeast Project: Defensive or Offensive Strategy?', *East Asian Review*, 16(4): 99–121.

Yoshida, Yutaka (2005), *Nipponjin no sensō kan: sengoshi no naka no hen'yō*, Tokyo: Iwanami shoten.

You, Ji (1999), *The Armed Forces of China*, Sydney, Australia; London, UK; New York, USA: Allen & Unwin and I.B. Tauris.

You, Ji (2009), 'The 17th Party Congress and the CCP's Changing Elite Politics', in Dali Yang and Zhao Litao (eds), *China's Reform at 30*, Singapore: World Scientific.

You, Ji (2014a), 'China's New Supreme Command and Xi Jinping's political leadership', in Yongnian Zheng and Lance L.P. Gore (eds), *China Entering Xi Jinping Era*, New York: Routledge.

You, Ji (2014b), 'The PLA and Diplomacy: Unreveiling Myths about the Military Role in Foreign Policy-Making', *Journal of Contemporary China*, 23(86).

Yu, Hong (2010), 'The Rationale, Prospects and Challenges of China's Western Economic Triangle in Light of Global Economic Crisis', *Asian Politics and Policy*, 2(3): 427–461.

Yu, Jianrong (2009), 'Dangqian Woguo Quntixingshijian de Zhuyaoleixing Hiqi Jibentezheng' (Types and basic characteristics of domestic mass incidents), *Zhongguozhengfadaxue Xuebao* (Journal of CUPL), 6: 118–124.

Yu, Verna (2010), 'Has Beijing Got What It Takes To Be a Global Player?', *South China Morning Post*, 2 October.
Yuan, Wen Jin (2012), 'China's Export Lobbying Groups and the Politics of the Renminbi', CSIS Freeman Briefing Report, February.
Zang, Xiaowei (2001), 'Educational Credentials, Elite Dualism, and Elite Stratification in China', *Sociological Perspectives*, 44: 189–205.
Zang, Xiaowei (2004), *Elite Dualism and Leadership Selection in China*, London: Routledge.
Zang, Xiaowei (2008), 'Market Reforms and Han–Hui Variation in Employment in the State Sector in a Chinese City', *World Development*, 36(11): 2341–2352.
Zang, Xiaowei (2010), 'Affirmative Action, Economic Reforms, and Han–Uyghur Variation in Job Attainment in the State Sector in Ürümchi', *China Quarterly*, 202: 344–361.
Zang, Xiaowei (2011), 'Uyghur–Han Earnings Differentials in Ürümchi', *China Journal*, 65: 141–155.
Zang, Xiaowei (2015), *Ethnicity in China: A Critical Introduction*, Cambridge: Polity Press.
Zeng, Douglas Zhihua (2011), 'How do Special Economic Zones and Industrial Clusters Drive China's Rapid Growth?', Policy Research Working Paper, Washington, DC: World Bank.
Zha, Jianying (2006), *Bashi niandai fangtanlu* (Interviews of the 1980s), Beijing: Sanlian Bookstore.
Zhai, Lanyun and Zhao Guoqin (2006), 'Zhengzhou renda foujue zhengfu zhuanxiang baogao zhuizong' (Zhengzhou People's Congress follow-up report on the change of direction), *Procuratorial Daily*, 4 December, available at http://www.jcrb.com/n1/jcrb1135/ca567378.htm.
Zhai, Qiang (1992), 'China and the Geneva Conference of 1954', *China Quarterly*, 129: 103–122.
Zhai, Qiang (2000), *China and the Vietnam Wars 1950–1975*, Chapel Hill, NC: University of North Carolina Press.
Zhang, Bei-Chuan and Chu Quan-Sheng (2005), 'MSM and HIV/AIDS in China', *Cell Research*, 15(11–12): 858–864.
Zhang, Hongli (2001), *Gonggong Yusuan* (Public budget), Beijing: Zhongguo caizheng jingji chubanshe.
Zhang, L. (2001), *Strangers in the City: Reconfigurations of Space, Power, and Social Networks within China's Floating Population*, Stanford, CA: Stanford University Press.
Zhang, L. (2003), 'Zhongguo nongcun shehui baozhang tixi bianqe: huimou yu qianzhan' (Chinese rural social security reform: overview and outlook), *Jiangsu luntan* (Jiangsu Forum), 1: 55–57.
Zhang, L. and S.X.B. Zhao (1998), 'Re-examining China's Urban Concept and the Level of Urbanization', *China Quarterly*, 154: 330–381.
Zhang, L., J. Huang, et al. (2003), 'China's War on Poverty: Assessing Targeting and the Growth Impacts of Poverty Programs', *Journal of Chinese Economic and Business Studies*, 1(3): 301–317.
Zhang, Li (2002), 'Spatiality and Urban Citizenship in Late Socialist China', *Public Culture*, 14(2): 311–334.

Zhang, Liang (2001), *The Tiananmen Papers*, Andrew J. Nathan and Perry Link (eds), New York: Public Affairs.
Zhang, Pingyu (2008), 'Revitalizing Old Industrial Base of Northeast China: Process, Policy and Challenge', *Chinese Georgraphical Science*, 18(2): 109–118.
Zhang, Q.F. and J.A. Donaldson (2008), 'The Rise of Agrarian Capitalism with Chinese Characteristics: Agricultural Modernization, Agribusiness and Collective Land Rights', *China Journal*, 60: 25–47.
Zhang, Shuguang (2012), 'Zhongguo jingji waijiao zhanlue kaocha' (Examining the strategy of China's economic statecraft), 20 August, *Wenhui Bao*, available at http://finance.sina.com.cn/review/hgds/20120820/101512895688.shtml.
Zhang, Weibing (2008), 'On Cultivating Core Values of Contemporary Soldiers', *Political Work in Chinese Military*, No. 8.
Zhang, Weiping (ed.) (1995), *Xinbian dangwu gongzuo quanshu* (A new manual for conducting Party affairs), Beijing: Zhongguo yanshi chubanshe.
Zhang, Weiwei (2011), 'The Analysis of a Miracle: The China Model and its Significance', *Qiushi* (Seeking Truth), 22 March.
Zhang, Weiwei (2012), *The China Wave: Rise of a Civilizational State*, Hackensack, NJ: World Century Books.
Zhang, Xi, Xinghou Yuan and Wei Wang (2001), *Bumen yusuan gaige yanjiu – Zhongguo zhengfu yusuan zhidu gaige poxi* (Study of sector budget reform – analysis of government budget system reform in China), Beijing: Jingji kexue chubanshe (Economic Science Press).
Zhang, Xiaoping, Yuqi Xiong, Jing Ye, Zhaohua Deng, Xinping Zhang (2013), 'Analysis and Government Investment in Primary Healthcare Institutions to Promote Equity during the Three year Health Reform Program in China', *BioMed Central Health Services Research*, 13: 114.
Zhang, Xiaosong (1988), 'Dui "nannü pingdeng kouhao de zhiyi"' (Interrogating the slogan of 'equality between men and women'), *Zhongguo funübao* (China Women's News), 16 May.
Zhang, Xinxin (1981), 'Wo zainaer cuoguole ni?' (Where did I miss you?), *Shouhuo* (Harvest), available at http://www.dushu999.com/xdwx/z/zhangxinxin/000/001.htm (accessed 22 August 2014).
Zhang, Xiulan (2013), 'Evaluating Experimental Policymaking: Lessons from China's Rural Health Reforms', *IDS Policy Briefing*, 46 (October): 4.
Zhang, Yang (2014), 'Gonganbu haiwai jie hu linggeyue 88 ming xianfan luowang' (The Ministry of Public Security apprehends 88 suspects overseas in two months), *Renmin ribao* (People's Daily), 20 September.
Zhang, Yin and Guanghua Wan (2005), *Why Do Poverty Rates Differ From Region to Region?*, United Nations University.
Zhang, Yingli (2014), *China's National Security Strategy in the New Era*, Beijing: PLA National Defense University Press.
Zhang, Yongjin (1998), *China in International Society since 1949: Alienation and Beyond*, Basingstoke: Macmillan.
Zhang, Yunsheng (1988), *Maojiawan jishi: Lin Biao mishu huiyilu* (True account of Maojiawan: reminiscences of Lin Biao's secretary), Beijing: Chunqiu chubanshe.

Zhang, Zhen (2009), 'Review of PLA Building and Reform in the New Era', in Li Jinai (ed.), *The Path of PLA Strengthening, Personal Experiences in the PLA's Major Reform and Development*, Beijing: PLA Publishing House.

Zhao, Guangcheng (2012), 'No-Fly Zones and China's Diplomatic Dilemma', *Contemporary International Relations*, 5: 13–30.

Zhao, Lei (2006), 'Zhong zu bu qian buzhang zhiyan gaoguan guanli' (Former Minister on Management), *Nanfang Zhoumo* (Southern Weekly), 9 November.

Zhao, L. and T.S. Lim (eds) (2010), *China's New Social Policy: Initiatives for a Harmonious Society*, New Jersey: World Scientific Books.

Zhao, Qixuan (2005), 'China's Current Policy on Agricultural Subsidies: Problems and Countermeasures', *Journal of Hainan Normal University*, 115: 98–101.

Zhao, Quansheng (1995a), 'China's Foreign Relations in the Asia-Pacific Region: Modernization, Nationalism and Regionalism', in Lo Chi Kin, Suzanne Pepper and Tsui Kai Yuen (eds), *China Review*, Hong Kong: Chinese University Press.

Zhao, Quansheng (1995b), *Interpreting Chinese Foreign Policy*, Oxford: Oxford University Press.

Zhao, Songqiao (1986), *Physical Geography of China*, Beijing: Science Press.

Zhao, Suisheng (2004), *A Nation-State by Construction: Dynamics of Modern Chinese Nationalism*, Stanford, CA: Stanford University Press.

Zhao, Suisheng (ed.) (2008), *China–US Relations Transformed: Perspectives and Strategic Interactions*, London: Routledge.

Zhao, Suisheng (2010a), 'Chinese Foreign Policy under Hu Jintao: The Struggle between Low-Profile Policy and Diplomatic Activism', *Hague Journal of Diplomacy*, 5(4): 357–378.

Zhao, Suisheng (2010b), 'The China Model: Can It Replace the Western Model of Modernization?', *Journal of Contemporary China*, 19(65): 419–436.

Zhao, Suisheng (2013), *The Rise of China and Transformation of the US–China Relationship: Forging Partnership in the Age of Strategic Mistrust*, London: Routledge.

Zhao, Ziyang (1982), 'Guanyu guowuyuan jigou gaige wenti de baogao' (Report on the institutional reform of the State Council), 8 March, available at http://www.npc.gov.cn/wxzl/gongbao/2000-12/26/content_5328235.htm.

Zhao, Ziyang (1987), 'Advance Along the Road of Socialism with Chinese Characteristics', *Beijing Review*, 30(45): i–xxvii.

Zhao, Ziyang (2009) *Prisoner of the State: The Secret Journal of Premier Zhao Ziyang*, New York: Simon & Shuster.

Zheng, B. (2008), 'Gaige kaifang 30 nian zhongguo liudong renkou shehui baozhangde fazhan yu tiaozhan' (The development and challenges of social security for China's floating population during 30 years of reform and opening up), *Zhongguo renkou kexue* (China Population Sciences), 1: 55–57.

Zheng, B. (2009), 'Zhongguo shebao "suipianhua zhidu" weihai yu "suipianhua chongdong" tanyuan' (Exploration of the sources of China's social insurance 'fragmented system' dangers and 'fragmentation impulse'), *Gansu shehui kexue* (Gansu Social Sciences), 3: 50–58.

Zheng, B. (2012), 'Dui Zhongguo chengzhen zhigong jiben yanglao baoxian xianzhuang de fansi yi yi banshu sheng fenshou bu dizhide benju, cheng yin yu duice' (Reflections on the current situation of China's urban employee basic old-age insurance – the

nature, causes and policies to deal with (the problem of), over half of the province's running deficits), *Shanghai University Journal (Social Sciences)*, 29: 10.
Zheng, B. (2013), 'Zhongguo yanglao gaige zhi wo jian' (China's pension reform in my eyes), *Zhongguo shehui baozhang* (China Social Security), 11: 16–17.
Zheng, Lu and Xiang Deng (2011), 'China's Western Development Strategy: Policies, Effects and Prospects', MPRA Paper No. 35201, available at http://mpra.ub.uni-muenchen.de/id/eprint/35201.
Zheng, S. (1997), *Party vs. State in Post-1949 China: The Institutional Dilemma*, Cambridge, UK and New York, USA: Cambridge University Press.
Zheng, Wei (2009), 'Social Security and Minority Economic Development', *Asian Social Science*, 5(7): 41–43.
Zheng, Y. (2004), *Globalization and State Transformation in China*, New York: Cambridge University Press.
Zheng, Yefu (1994), 'Nannü pingdeng de shehuixue sikao' (Sociological thinking on equality between men and women), *Shehuixue yanjiu* (*Sociological Studies*), 2: 110.
Zheng, Yongnian (1999), *Discovering Chinese Nationalism in China: Modernization, Identity, and International Relations*, Cambridge Asia-Pacific Studies, New York: Cambridge University Press.
Zheng, Yongnian (2007a), *De Facto Federalism in China: Reforms and Dynamics of Central–Local Relations*, Singapore: World Scientific.
Zheng, Yongnian (2007b), *Hu Jintao's Road Map to China's Future*, Singapore: East Asian Institute.
Zheng, Yongnian, Zhengxu Wang and Sow Keat Tok (2006), *Hu Jintao at the Helm: Major Issues in the Aftermath of the 6th Party Plenum*, Singapore: East Asian Institute.
Zhengxie Ningbo Shi Weiyuan Hui (PPCC Ningbo Committee) (2014a), 'Zhengxie ningboshi weiyuan hui ti'an banli gongzuo minzhu pingyi banfa (shixing)' (Measures of PPCC Ningbo Committee on democratic assessment of the handling of proposals (trial)), 28 September, available at http://www.nbzx.gov.cn/art/2014/11/25/art_19281_1137799.html.
Zhengxie Ningbo Shi Weiyuan Hui (PPCC Ningbo Committee) (2014b), 'Shi zhengxie jiang she "quanti huiyi ti'an"' (The City PPCC will establish 'all-members proposals'), 25 September, available at http://zx.ningbo.gov.cn/art/2013/9/25/art_19383_1045571.html.
Zhengxie Ningbo Shi Weiyuan Hui (PPCC Ningbo Committee) (2014c), 'Shi zhengxie shouci kaizhan ti'an gongzuo minzhu pingyi' (The City PPCC had its first democratic assessment of the handling of proposals), 29 October, available at http://www.nbzx.gov.cn/art/2014/10/29/art_19317_1130598.html.
Zhengzhou Shi Renmin Zhengfu (Zhengzhou City People's Government) (2008), 'Zhengzhou Shi chengzhen jumin jiben yiliao baoxian he buchong yiliao baoxian buchongguiding (shixing)' (Zhengzhou City Government's additional regulations on basic medical insurance and supplementary medical insurance for urban residents), 27 May, available at http://www.cnlss.com/LssLaw/CentralSouthRegion/HnLss/200805/LssLaw_20080527211949_5270.html.
Zhengzhou Wanbao (Zhengzhou Evening Daily) (2008), 'Daibiao yi'an huikui: Zhengzhou kanbing nan kanbing gui deidao gaishan' (Feedback on PC deputies' proposals:

improvement in the availability and affordability of medical service in Zhengzhou), 21 April, available at http://health.sohu.com/20080421/n256417293.shtml.
Zhong, Xueping (2000), *Masculinity Besieged? Issues of Modernity and Male Subjectivity in Chinese Literature of the Late Twentieth Century*, Durham, NC: Duke University Press.
Zhong, Y. (2003), *Local Government and Politics in China*, Armonk, NY: M.E. Sharpe.
Zhong, Y. (2010), 'Chinese Township Government: Between a Rock and a Hard Place', in J.H. Chung and T.C. Lam (eds), *China's Local Administration*, London: Routledge, pp. 174–195.
Zhonggong dangshi renwu zhuan (Biographies of Personalities in CCP History), (1980–), Vols 1–60, Xi'an: Shaanxi renmin chubanshe, 1980–96; Vols 61–, Beijing: Zhongyang wenxian chubanshe, 1997–.
Zhongguo Caizheng Xuehui (ed.) (2000), *Goujian yusuan guanli xinmoshi – Bumen yusuan zhidu yu guoku danyi zhanghu zhidu* (Constructing a new model of budget management: departmental budget system and centralized Treasury account), Beijing: Jingji kexue chubanshe.
Zhongguo Renmin Zhengzhi Xieshang Huiyi Chongqing Shi Jiangbei Qu Weiyuanhui (CPPCC Committee of Jiangbei District, Chongqing Municipality) (2013), 'Fahui hao jiceng zhengxie zai defang zhili zhong de zuoyong' (On how PPCCs could play a better role in local governance), 3 May, available at http://www.cqjbzx.gov.cn/newsdisplay.aspx?nid=6692.
Zhou, K.X. (1996), *How the Farmers Changed China: Power of the People*, Boulder, CO: Westview Press.
Zhou, Na (2012), 'Why Competition Cannot Effectively Reduce Corruption: The Case of China's Public Procurement', Doctoral Dissertation, City University of Hong Kong.
Zhou, Ning (2012), 'Zhongguo shangren zaichaoxian touzi sunshi diaocha' (Research into the investment losses of Chinese companies in DPRK), *Caijing blog*, 12 July.
Zhou, Xiaochuan (2009), 'Reform the International Monetary System', *People's Bank of China*, available at http://www.pbc.gov.cn/english/detail.asp?col=6500&id=178 (accessed 4 January 2010).
Zhou, Z.H. (2005), *Zhogguo difang xingzheng zhidu shi* (The history of China's local administrative system), Shanghai: Shanghai People's Publishing House.
Zhou, Z.H. (ed.) (2007–12), *History of the Administrative Divisions of China*, 12 vols, Shanghai: Fudan University Press.
Zhu, Chenghu (2011), 'Guanyu dangqian shijie zhanlue geju de jidian sikao' (Some reflections on the contemporary world strategic structure), *Shijie Jinghji yu Zhengzhi* (World Economics and Politics), 2: 4–12.
Zhu, Jiangnan (2012), 'The Shadow of the Skyscrapers: Real Estate Corruption in China', *Journal of Contemporary China*, 21(74): 243–260. doi:10.1080/10670564.2012.635929.
Zhu, Jiangnan, Jie Lu and Tianjian Shi (2013), 'When Grapevine News Meets Mass Media Different Information Sources and Popular Perceptions of Government Corruption in Mainland China', *Comparative Political Studies*, 46(8): 920–946. doi:10.1177/0010414012463886.
Zhu, Rongji (2002), 'Jinyibu zhuanbian zhengfu zhineng jiaqiang zhengfeng jianshe'

(Further transform government functions and strengthen the political construction), *Zhongguo xingzheng guanli*, 4: 3.

Zhu, Weiqun (2012), 'Duidangqian minzu lingcheng wenti de jidian sikao' (Several thoughts on current nationality problems), *Xuexi shibao* (Study Times), 15 February, available at http://www.cpcnews.cn/BIG5/64093/64102/ 17122242.html.

Zhu, Xuchu (2000), 'Zhengfu zhineng yu gonggong caizheng zhineng' (Government function and public financial function), *Caizheng yanjiu*, 7: 32–35.

Zhu, Zhenming (2010), 'China's Foreign Economic Cooperation for CLMV: Contact Engineering in CLMV', in Mitsuhiro Kagami (ed.), *Japan and Korea with the Mekong River Basin Countries*, Bangkok: Bangkok Research Center.

Zhu, Zhiqun (2006), *US–China Relations in the 21st Century: Power Transition and Peace*, London: Routledge.

Zoellick, Robert (2005), 'Whither China: From Membership to Responsibility. Remarks to National Committee on US–China Relations', available at http://www.cfr.org/publication/8916/whither_china.html (accessed 30 March 2007).

Zou, Lan (1998), 'Central and Western China Attracting More Investments', *Business Reporter*.

Zuo, Xiulan (2007), 'China's Policy Towards Minority Languages in a Globalizing Age', *Transnational Curriculum Inquiry*, 4(1): 80–91.

Index

30 September Movement 431
64Tianwang, Molihua 347
228 Incident 405
1998 reform 90–91

ABC (Agricultural Bank of China) 387
About Face (Mann) 417
accountability 99, 340
activism 338, 339
Adams, James W. 138
Addressing US–China Strategic Distrust (Lieberthal and Wang) 424–5
administrative area economy 158
administrative district economy 158
administrative divisions 150–52
administrative territory 147–64
adult education 227–31
adult education association 227
'Advance Along the Road of Socialism with Chinese Characteristics' (Zhao) 193
affirmative action programmes 210
Africa 383
ageing population 248
Agence France-Presse (AFP) 347
agent and principal dilemma 383, 394
age rule 128
Agnew, John 149
agrarian revolution 276–7
agricultural secondary schools 224
agriculture 295–8, 296, 303, 304, 312, 313, 387
  subsidies 200
Ahn, Byung-joon 60
aid 374–6, 381, 382, 384–5, 388–9, 393
  to North Korea 410
  Taiwanese 405
air pollution 337
Alden, Chris 383
All-China Federation of Trade Unions 340, 343
All-China Women's Federation 296, 343
American Images of China (Turner) 414
America's Challenge (Swaine) 413, 423–4
America's Response to China (Cohen) 413, 415
Anderson, Perry 443
Andersson et al. 196, 199
anger-venting incidents 354–5, 357–8
Angolan Civil War 367
Anhui 153, 355, 357

anti-bureaucratism 254
anti-corruption 84, 93, 253, 258–70
anti-graft 254
Anti-Secession Law, 2005, 407
Anyuan 275
apparat 16
AQSIQ (General Administration of Quality Supervision, Inspection and Quarantine) 91, 92
ARF (ASEAN Regional Forum) 434
Arkush, R. David 414
army 71, 117–33
'Articles of Association of Chinese Trade Unions' 227
ASEAN (Association of Southeast Asian Nations) 48, 372, 388–9, 426, 427–8, 434, 440, 441
  early harvests 393
  trade increase 436–7
ASEAN Plus One mechanism 435
ASEAN Plus Three mechanism 435, 437
Asian Infrastructure Investment Bank 374
Assessment Committee 114
assimilation 207–8, 209
assistant governors 96
Associated Press (AP) 347
audit offices 93, 259–60
authoritarianism
  consultative 342
  fragmented 177
autonomous counties 160
autonomous regions 16, 95–6, 213–14
autonomy, NGOs 335

Ba, Alice 432
Bachman, David 23
Bader, Jeffrey A. 388
Bai, Yang 290
Bai, Zhijian 96
Bandung conference, 1955, 366
Bangladesh 376
Bank of Communications 387
banks 4, 178, 179, 181, 320, 386–7
  see also PBoC
baoli 453
Barabantseva, Elena 205, 207, 208, 210
Barnett, A. Doak 60, 97
basic education 223–4

531

basic living allowance programme 326
Baum, Richard 33
Beautiful Imperialist (Shambaugh) 414
Bebel, August 290
Becker, Jasper 71
Beijing 95, 153, 191, 246, 352, 354, 358
'The Beijing Consensus' (Ramo) 48
Beijing Olympics 372
Beijing Olympic Torch relay, protests 54
Belgium 450
Bergsten, C. Fred 371
Bergsten et al. 419–20
Bernstein, Richard 421
Bevir, M. 104
Beyond Tiananmen (Suettinger) 422
Bian, Yanjie 6
Bianco, Lucien 49
bianzhi 16, 93, 453
Bin, Ke 385
bipolarity 435
'black box' 21, 22, 33, 35, 36, 37, 38
Bo'ao Forum for Asia 372
BOC (Bank of China) 387
Borneo 431
Bourdieu, Pierre 272
bourgeoisie 280, 281, 282, 284
bourgeois revolution 273–4, 278
Bo, Xilai 36, 37–8, 124, 264
Bo, Zhiyue 98, 99, 100–101
Brautigam, Deborah 383
Breznitz, Dan 195
BRICS 372, 374, 375
Brødsgaard, Kjeld Erik 63
Brook, Timothy 334
Brunei 438, 440
budgetary revenues 171, 172, 316
budgeting 143–5
bureaucratism 254
Burma 429
Burns, John P. 62

CAAC (Civil Aviation Administration of China) 92
CADC (2014) database 163
cadre exchange system 62–3
cadres 267, 315, 316, 317–19
  limiting the authority of 214, 327
  recentralization over 322
  selection process 63–4
CAFTA (China–ASEAN Free Trade Agreement) 390, 393, 436–7, 440
Caijing 347
Callahan, William 74
Cambodia 388–9, 395, 430
The Cambridge History of China (Hucker) 153

Cameron, David 450
Canada 389
Canglang 163
'Can the Subaltern Speak?' (Spivak) 297
capital 48, 84, 180, 195, 319, 381, 387, 448
  cultural 284, 306
  human 211, 217, 234
  social 217, 339, 342
capitalism 7, 211, 274, 285, 286, 368, 373
Capitalism from Below (Nee and Opper) 7
capitalist classes 283
Capital Youth May Fourth Memorial debriefing meeting, May 1990, 50
Cartier, C. 155, 156, 162, 163
cash cropping 313
Castellino, Joshua 205, 206, 207
catalysts 332
CBRC (China Banking Regulatory Commission) 91, 387
CCB (China Construction Bank) 387
CCP (Chinese Communist Party) 3, 42–55, 57–75, 77, 106, 365–9
  and civil society 342–3
  and class politics 271–86
  and corruption 253
  nationality policy 207–9, 211, 212
  and NPC 78
  'one China' policy 406
  and 'Patriotic Education Campaign' 400
  and PLA 117–33
  and State Council 85–8
  and 'Three Represents' 109
  and welfare and social security 238
CCP's Survival Strategy (Hishida) 46
CDB (China Development Bank) 387
CDIC (Central Discipline Inspection Commission) 70–71, 87, 253, 258–9, 261, 263, 267, 268–9
Central Anti-Corruption Coordination Group 263
central banks 178, 181, 386–7
  see also PBoC
Central Bureau for the Soviet Areas 59
Central China 161, 162
Central Committee of the CCP 96, 99, 100
'The Central Committee of the Chinese Communist Party's Decision on Reforming the Education System' 225
Central Economic Work Conference 87
Central Financial Work Commission 91
central government 76–95
Central Leading Group for Finance and Economic Affairs 86–7, 88
Central Leading Group for Foreign Affairs 87
central leading small groups (CLSGs) 67

central liaison offices 96
central–local relations 147–8
Central Organization Department 262, 263
Central People's Government Committee 76–7
Central Political and Legal Affairs Commission 86
Central Political and Legal Commission (CPLC) 70
central–provincial relations 97–9
Central Review Committee 260–61
Chahar 153
chairmen 95, 96, 98, 99, 108
Chamberlain, Heath B. 334
Chan, Chris King-chi 335
Chandra, Alexander C. 437
Chang, Chiung-Fang 213
To Change China (Spence) 416
Chang, Kou-t'ao 59
Cha, Victor 408, 409, 411
Cheek, Timothy 48
Chen Bo'er 291
Chen, Duxiu 58, 260
Chen, Gang 213, 214
Chengdu 196
chengfen 16, 279, 453
chengguan 453
Cheng, Joseph Y.S. 435
Chen, Jack 217
Chen, Jerome 44
Chen, Jian 389, 413, 419
Chen, Liangyu 36, 37–8
Chen, Shaofeng 383
Chen, Shui-bian 406, 407
Chen, Xitong 37–8
Chen, Yizi 33
Chen, Yonggui 295, 297
Chen, Yugang 372
Chen, Yun 28, 32, 33, 34, 35, 77, 140
 and CDIC 262
 and economic policy 168, 170–71
Chen, Z. 371
Cheonan 412
Cheung, Peter T.Y. 102
Chiang, Ching-kuo 405
Chiang, Kai-shek 404, 405
Chien, C, 149
China and the EU: A Common Future (Crossick and Reuter) 445–6
China–Arab Nations Cooperation Forum 372
China–Caribbean Economy and Trade Cooperation Forum 372
China CITIC Bank 387
China Coast Guard 92
China Confidential (Tucker) 418–19
China–DAC study group 375

China Daily 388
'China Dream' 72, 74–5, 120
China Everbright Bank 387
The China Fantasy: How Our Leaders Explain Away Chinese Repression (Mann) 417, 421
China Institute for Contemporary International Relations (CICIR) 385
China Labour Bulletin 347
China Leadership Monitor 36
China Model 51
China News Analysis 26
China Overseas Investment Federation 389
China Quarterly 43, 100, 141
China's America (Li) 414
China's Campaign to Open Up the West (Goodman) 155
*China's Decision for Rapprochement with the United State*s (Garver) 418
China's Local Administration: Traditions and Changes in the Sub-National Hierarchy (Chung and Lam) 155
China's New Nationalism: Pride, Politics, and Diplomacy (Gries) 50
China's Provinces in Reform: Class, Community and Political Culture (Goodman) 155
China's Provinces in Reform project 155
China: The Balance Sheet (Bergsten et al.) 419–20
China, the United States, and Global Order (Foot and Walter) 421
China Youth Development Foundation 343
Chinese Academy of Social Sciences (CASS) 51, 84, 139, 284, 450
Chinese Adult Education Association 227
'Chinese Basic Education Reform and Development Compendium' 219
'Chinese Dream' 61
'Chinese Education Reform and Development Compendium' 232
Chinese Films 292
Chinese Nationalism in the Global Era (Hughes) 50
Chinese People's Political Consultative Conference (CPPCC) 76
Chin, Gregory 216, 373
Chizhou 355, 357
Chongqing 113, 150, 168, 196
Chow, Gregory 210
Christensen, Thomas 426
Chuansha 163
Chung, Jae Ho 157, 408, 409
chushen 16, 279, 453
CIC (China Investment Corporation) 387
cities 151–2, 158–9, 160, 161, 162, 163

citizenship education 234–5
city patrol brutality 349, 351–2, 354, 355, 357, 358
Civil Affairs Ministry 150, 157, 245, 246, 335, 336
civilization-state 4–5
civil–military relations 71, 117–33, 122, 128
civil society 333, 334, 340, 342–3
civil war 60
clashes 54
class background 16
class composition 16
class labels 279
class politics 271–86
class struggle 63, 165, 271, 272, 274, 277, 278–9, 281, 284, 285
    and Mao 28
Class Struggle (CCP booklet) 273
Clinton, Hillary 395
Closer Economic Partnership Arrangements 390
Clothey, Rebecca 208, 211
CLSGs (central leading small groups) 67
clubs, workers' 275
CMC 122, 126, 127, 131–2
CMI (Chiang Mai Initiative) 437
CMIM (Chiang Mai Initiative Multilateralization) 437
CNMC (China Nonferrous Metals Co.) 389
coastal provinces 191, 192, 193–4, 196, 197, 202, 203, 339–40
coast guard 92
Cohen, Paul 143
Cohen, Warren 413, 415
'cold politics, hot economics' 398, 399
Cold War 368, 433
collaboration 336
collateral 321
collectively owned enterprises 220, 316, 317, 320, 329
    see also TVEs (township and village enterprises)
collective petitioning 346, 347, 354
The Coming Conflict with China (Bernstein and Munro) 421
Commerce Ministry 364
commercial banks 387
Commission for Economic Restructuring 89
Commission on Foreign Investment 89
Commission on Import and Export Affairs 89
common-fate community 121, 122
Common Programme 76, 106
communes 240–41, 243

Communism, definitions 44
communist parties 431
    see also CCP (Chinese Communist Party)
Communist Youth League of China (CYLC) 46, 343
Comprehensive Reform Leadership Small Group 175
Comprehensive Reform Leading Group 88
compulsory education 219, 220, 223–4, 245
Compulsory Education Law of the People's Republic of China 219
Concept of Scientific Development 72
'Concerning the Situation in the Ideological Sphere' (Document No. 9) 51–2
conditional objective control 125
conditional subjective control 123–6
Confucius Centres 373
Congressional-Executive Commission on China 2005, 210
conscription ratio 122
consultative authoritarianism 342
Contest for Supremacy (Friedberg) 421
Contest of the Century (Dyer) 422
continuing education 227–31
'Continuities and Discontinuities in the Ideology of the Great Proletarian Cultural Revolution' (Israel) 45
control, graduated 342
Cook, Malcolm 405, 406, 407, 408
co-operative medical schemes 241, 243, 246
Cooper, Earle 430
Cooper, Robert 442
corporatism 4, 167, 336
corruption 93, 253–70, 307
Corruption Perceptions Index (CPI) 255, 258, 270
Corruption Prevention Office 267
CoSTIND (Commission of Science, Technology and Industry) 91–2
Council of Europe (CoE) 207
counties 147, 149, 150, 151, 153, 154, 155, 158–62
county-level city 151, 158–9, 159, 160, 161–2, 163
coups 124
the courts 259
Cox, Nigel 426
CPLC (Central Political and Legal Commission) 70
CPPCC (Chinese People's Political Consultative Conference) 76
'crony capitalism' 7
Crossick, Stanley 445–6
Cross Strait Services Trade Agreement (CSSTA) 54

CSC (Central Supervisory Commission) 260, 261–2
cultural activities 215
cultural capital 284, 306
Cultural Revolution 26, 28–31, 44, 60–61, 78
  and assimilation 208
  and education 218
  and New Culture movement 45
  and political extremism 209
currency 183, 374, 381, 382, 386, 453
current account surplus 387
Czech Republic 451

DAC (Development Assistance Committee) 375–6
Dahl, R. 115
Dai, Bingran 446
Dai, Xianglong 181
Dalai Lama 388, 390, 391, 450
dam projects 337
danwei 16, 239, 453
Dato' Ajit Singh 433–4
Davis et al. 334
Dazhai 295, 296–7, 302
Dazhai Conglomerates 306
Debating China (Hachigian) 420
debt 320–21, 323, 383
decentralization 3, 97
'Decision about Deepening the Educational Reform and Comprehensively Promote Quality Education' 229
'Decision by the Central Committee of the Communist Party of China on the Reform of the Education System' 221, 231
'Decision Concerning Health Reform and Development' 243
'Decision Concerning Some Problems in the Construction of the Socialist Market Economy' 243
'Decision on Economic System Reform' 139
'Decision on Reforming and Developing the Adult Education by the National Education Committee' 228
'Decision on Some Issues of Popularizing the Primary Education' 223
'Decision on Strengthening the Construction of the Party's Governance Capability' 230
'Decision on the Reform of the Basic Education by the Chinese Communist Party' 224
Decision on various major issues in 'comprehensively deepening reforms' 267, 268
'Decision on Vigorously Developing Vocational and Technical Education', 1991, 225
'Decision on Vigorously Promoting the Reform and the Development of Vocational Education', 2002, 226
'Decisions on Strengthening Staff Education' 227
Declaration on the Rights of Indigenous Peoples 207
Declaration on the Rights of Persons Belonging to National or Ethnic, Religious and Linguistic Minorities 207
decollectivization of agriculture 312, 317
defence memoranda of understanding (MOUs) 435
de jure federalist state 98, 99
de Mesquita, Bruce Bueno 384
democratization of Taiwan 405–6
demolition 349
Deng, Guosheng 336
Deng, Xiaoping 23, 24, 25, 27, 31, 36, 37, 38, 45, 61, 78–9, 187
  on aid 385
  and the army 124
  biography of 419
  on bourgeoisie 284
  consolidation programme, opposing 30
  on the Cultural Revolution 298
  and economic policy 63, 140, 169, 170, 398
  and education 224, 227
  and foreign policy 431–3
  and 'get rich first' 73
  and Great Leap Forward 28
  and Japanese militarism 401
  and Party-state relations 66
  and photo 32–3
  on price reform 34–5
  and regional development 191–2
  and separating Party and government 168
  and 'Southern Tour' 139
  supporting neoauthoritarians 48
  and 'Theory of the Three Worlds' 367
  on TVEs 318
  and uneven development 203
  and Zhao Ziyang 88
Deng Xiaoping Theory 72
Deng, Yingchao 262
Denmark 450
deputies, quotas 107
developing countries 367
developmental dictatorship 47–9, 55
development finance 374–6
Development Orientated Poverty Alleviation Programme in Rural China 324
DFA (Department of Foreign Aid) 386

dibao 244–6, 247, 248, 453
Dickson, Bruce 7
DICs (Discipline Inspection Committees) 253, 257, 259, 267–8
Dictionary of Party Building 346
diji shi 151
diplomacy, purchasing 388, 389
diplomatic recognition 366
diplomatic relations 434, 439, 440
diqu 149
direct investment 381
disaster relief 342
discipline inspection 263
Discipline Inspection Commission (CDIC) 87
discipline inspection commissions 70–71, 87, 253, 258–9, 261
discipline inspection groups 268
Discovering Chinese Nationalism in China: Modernization, Identity, and International Relations (Zheng) 50
DoC (Declaration on the Conduct of Parties in the South China Sea) 439
Domes, Jürgen 100
Donaldson, John 101, 155, 195
Dong, Biwu 65
Dong, Wang 416
Donnithorne, Audrey 141
Dosch, Jörn 436
DPP (Democratic Progressive Party) 406, 407
DPRK (Democratic People's Republic of Korea) *see* North Korea
Dreyer, June Teufel 207, 210
Drezner, Daniel 383
'dual track' reform strategy 173
Dyer, Geoff 422

Early Harvest Programme (EHP) 436
earthquake, Wenchuan 342
East Asia 397–412
East China 161, 162
ECFA (Economic Cooperation Framework Agreement) 391–2
'Economic Cabinet' 77
economic construction 47, 165, 253
economic development 63, 165–6
economic elite 6, 7
economic leverage 382
economic policy 88, 165–86, 385
Economic Reform Institute 177
economic relations, international 371
economic sanctions 391–3
economic statecraft 381–96
Economic System Reform Commission 182
economy, global 368, 369
education 200, 217–35, 245, 275, 276

Education Law of the People's Republic of China 219, 222, 229
'Education Revitalization Action Plan for the 21st Century' 229
EEZ (Exclusive Economic Zone) 438
Egan, Annabel 447
the Elders 168, 170, 173, 177
Election Study Centre of the National Chengchi University 405–6
elementary education 223
elite men 299, 301, 307
elite politics 21–39
Elmer, Franziska 211
embargo after 1949, 366
Emergency Response Law 128
employment 210–11, 306
Empress of China 413
energy 92, 382, 383
engagement strategies 342
ENGOs (environmental NGOs) 337–8, 343
entrepreneurs 7, 109–10
environmental activism 338
environmental damage 337
environmental NGOs 337–8
Environmental Protection Ministry 92, 93–4
environment-related incidents 349, 350, 354
equality, gender 300, 301–2
equitable development 190, 191, 192
Estonia 450
ethnic autonomous counties 326
ethnic minorities 54, 95–6, 205–16
ethnic minority areas 326–7, 354
ethnic-related conflicts 354, 358
'The EU–China: Closer Partners, Growing Responsibilities' 445
EU (European Union) 205, 207, 216, 372, 393, 441, 442–52
European Court of Human Rights 207
The EU, the US and China: Towards a New International Order? (Jing and Wei) 448–9
evening schools 275
exchange rate policy 364
executive meetings 83
Ex-Im Bank (Export-Import Bank) 387
exit–entry management 91
exporters 184
export-oriented growth strategy 3
exports 322, 369, 387
extremism, political 208–9

factions 24, 100
factories 189
factory workers 349–50
Fairbank, John King 414–15
Falungong 16

Fan, Cindy 196, 199
Fan, Jishe 422
Fan Liqing 54
Farer, Tom J. 207
farmers' vocational and technical education 228
farming 243, 295–8, 312, 313
Fazhi Ribao 347
FDI (foreign direct investment) 193, 198, 387, 398–9
February 28 Incident 405
federalism 97, 98
fees 243, 245, 317, 319, 323, 327
    education 219, 220, 226, 232
female labour 295–8, 303–4
femininity, natural 299, 301, 302, 305, 306
feminism 288, 289–90
Feng, Wei 386
feudalism 294
Fewsmith, Joseph 21, 33
field agencies 149
film industry 290–91
Finamore, Salvatore 448–9
finance 137–46
Finance and Economic Commission 77
Finance and Economics Leadership Small Group (FELSG) 168–9, 175
financial crisis, global 179, 371–2, 379, 383, 389
financial governance, global 374
Fingar, Tom 422
Finland 450
First World 367
fiscal transfers 198, 323–4, 325–7
fiscal transparency 143–4
Fisher et al. 340–41
fishermen 394
Fitzgerald, C.P. 366
Fitzgerald, John 52–3, 150, 155, 156
Five Guarantees *(wubao)* System 200, 240, 243
Five Principles of Peaceful Coexistence 366, 376, 429
Five-Year Plans 77
Fleming, Michael 207
Food and Drug Administration 92
food safety 92
Foot, Rosemary 373, 421, 423
Foreign Affairs Bureau 267
foreign aid *see* aid
foreign exchange reserves 387
Foreign Ministry 87
foreign-owned companies 349, 354, 358
foreign policy 22, 381, 429–35
Former Yugoslavia 442

Forum on China–Africa Cooperation (FOCAC) 372
Four Clean-Ups Movement 254
'Four Trillion RMB Stimulus Programme' 179
Fox, John 449–50, 451
FPDA (Five Power Defence Arrangements) 428
Fragile Relationship (Harding) 417
'fragmented authoritarianism' 177
France 377, 388, 391, 430
free association principle 207
freedom cases 351, 352
free trade agreements (FTAs) 390, 391
free trade area/zone 84, 157, 436–7
Friedberg, Aaron 421
Friedman, Eli 340
Friends of Nature 337
Froissart, Chloe 340
Frolic, B. Michael 334
Fujian 192, 193, 262
Fulda et al. 335–6
full employment 239, 241
functional groups 100
funding of education 220–21, 222–3

G2 371, 372
G20 372, 374
GAC (Government Administrative Council) 76, 77
Gang of Four 24, 25, 30, 31, 32, 262
Gansu 153
Gao, Gang 24, 25, 27, 77
Gaokao 233–4, 453
Garnaut, John 36
Garside, Roger 31
Garver, John 418
gas 393–4
GDP (gross domestic product) 4, 73, 110, 121, 165, 171
    ASEAN-China free trade area 436
    and corruption 257
    cost of pollution 337
    in ethnic regions 211
    a quarter of the world's average 191
    and TVE value added 314
    and welfare 249
    western provinces 198
gender 288–307
General Administration of Quality Supervision, Inspection and Quarantine (AQSIQ) 91, 92
General Agreement on Trade in Services (GATS) 235
General Office 79
general social service delivery NGOs 340–41

generals' tenure 128
Geneva conference, 1954, 366
Germany 388, 450, 451
Ghai, Yash 211, 213, 214
Gibson, John 196, 199
Giddens, Anthony 271
Gilder, George 301
Gilley, Bruce 46–7, 49, 54
Gini coefficient 324, 325
Gladney, Dru C. 207, 211
GlaxoSmithKline 266–7
global economy 368, 369
global financial crisis (GFC) 179, 371–2, 379, 383, 389
global governance 372–6
global politics 363–79
global power 379
GMD (Guomingdang) 76, 253
Godemont, Francois 449–50, 451
Goh, Evelyn 383
Goldstein, Avery 24
Goldstein, Steven M. 45
Goldstone et al. 7
Golley, Jane 197, 199
GONGOs (government-organized NGOs) 342, 343
Goodman, David S.G. 7, 66, 99, 101–2, 155
Good Neighbourliness Policy (GNP) 434
Gordon White et al. 334
governance 104–16
  global 372–6
Governance and Development (World Bank) 104
government
  central 76–95
  finance 137–46
  local 104–16, 167–8, 221, 315, 318–19, 321, 329
  provincial people's 96
  regional 194–5
  representation of minorities 214
Government Work Report 83, 85
governors 95, 96, 100
GPAD (General Political Affairs Department) 131
graduated control 342
graft 254, 256
grain production 202, 313, 328
grain ration 240
grassroots organizations 58, 60
Great Leap Forward 23–4, 27–8, 44, 60, 78, 296
Great Power 370, 371, 373
Greece 389, 450
Gries, Peter Hays 50

grievances 349–50, 351–8
Grossman, Leo 206
group guarantees 206–9
growth 198, 199, 257
Guangdong 24, 84, 95, 168, 192, 193, 262
  and mass incidents 352, 354, 358
  and tax collection 194–5
Guangxi 197
Guangzhou 191
guanxi 16, 453
'Guidelines for Patriotic Education' 50
Guide Weekly 58
Guizhou 101, 191, 195, 316–17
Gu, Jing 339
Guo, Fenglian 295–6, 297, 298, 302, 303, 306
Guoguang, Wu 51–2
Guo, Jingfu 211
Guo, Jinlong 95
Guo, Yong 255–6
Gusu 163
Guy, R.K. 155

Habermas, Jürgen 48, 442–3, 451
Hachigian, Nina 420
Hainan 192
Hale, William 207
Hall, Stuart 271
Han Chinese 205, 208, 210–11
Handbook of the Administrative Divisions of the People's Republic of China (Ministry of Civil Affairs) 157
Hansen, Mette Halskov 210, 213
Hanzhong county 160
Hao, Yufan 419
Harding, Harry 417
'harmonious society' 63, 73, 234, 324
'Harmonious World' 370
Harper, Stephen 389
Harrison, Lawrence E. 58
Hartford, Kathleen 45
Hasmath, Reza 336, 340, 342
Hayhoe, Ruth 217
health care 111, 112, 241, 243, 245, 325
health insurance 200, 247
Health Ministry 92
heavy industry 3–4, 238–41
He, B. 143
He, Baogang 207, 208, 209, 216
Hebei 153, 354
Heberer, Thomas 208
He et al. 274
hegemonic masculinity 307
Heilmann, Sebastian 168, 202–3
Heilongjiang 153, 201

He, Laoliu 291, 292
Henan Province 110
Heng, Siam-Heng 426
Henrard, Kristin 206
heping fazhan 453
heping jueqi 453
Hershatter, Gail 295, 296, 298–9
Hess, Stephen E. 214
hexie shehui 453
He-Ying Zhen 289
He, Zengke 255
higher education 231–2, 234
higher vocational education 225, 226
Hildebrandt, Timothy 335, 336, 339
Hindess, B. 273
Hishida, Masaharu 46
Historical Materialism 273
Historical Resolution 23
'history issue' 399, 400, 401, 402
History of the Administrative Divisions of China (Zhou) 157
HIV/AIDS NGOs 338–9, 343, 344
Ho Chi Minh 430
Holbig, Heike 46–7, 49, 54
Hong Kong 22, 54, 257, 390
Honig, Emily 295, 298–9
Ho, Peter 337
hospitals 111–12
household farming 243, 312, 313
household registration system 4, 17, 313, 339
households 317
housing 114
Howland, Douglas 205
HRC (Human Rights Council) 378
Hsu, Carolyn 336, 341, 343
Hsu, Jennifer 336, 340, 342
Hua, Guofeng 23, 24, 25, 31, 32, 33
Hu, Angang 257
Huang, Philip C. 333
Huangpu 163
Huang, Y. 97, 314, 316
Hubei 352, 354
Hucker, Charles 153
Hughes, Christopher R. 50, 436
Hu, Jintao 36, 38, 61, 66, 71, 93, 199–203
  and the army 124
  and central government, dominance of 88
  and economic policy 171
  and ethnic minorities 216
  and 'harmonious society' 63, 73–4, 324
  and Harmonious World 370
  and international economic relations 371
  and lifelong learning 230
  and the north-east 201
  and rural taxes 245
  on Spratly Islands 438
  and welfare 247–8, 249
hukou 4, 16, 313, 339, 453
  holders 185
human capital 211, 217, 234
human rights 206, 207, 351, 352, 369, 377, 391–2, 446–7
Human Rights in China 2007, 210, 212, 216
Hunan 351
Hundred Flowers 27
Hungary 450
Huntington, Samuel 127, 257
Hunt, Michael 415
HURD (Housing and Urban–Rural Development) 114
Hurst, William 195
Hu, Yaobang 25, 33, 34, 61, 88, 101, 169, 262
Hyer, Eric 207, 208, 209

ICAC (Independent Commission against Corruption) 257
ICBC (Commercial Bank of China) 387
identity 54–5, 271
ideology 42–55, 72–5
Ideology and Organization in Communist China (Schurmann) 42
Ideology and Politics in Contemporary China (Johnson) 44, 45
Ikenberry, G. John 399, 421–2
IMF (International Monetary Fund) 368, 374, 437
'Implementation Rules for the Compulsory Education Law of the People's Republic of China' 219
implementers 332
imports 387
import substitution development strategy 3
incentives 315–18, 329
incidents, mass 345–7, 358
income 312–14, 327
  inequality 258, 324, 325
Indochina 430
Indonesia 428, 429, 431, 440
industrial workers 274
industry 189, 199, 238–9, 314–22, 387
Industry and Commerce Bureau 335, 336
industry associations 90, 183
inequality 235, 249, 322
  ethnic 210–11, 215
  income 258, 324, 325
  regional 188–9, 196, 199, 200, 203
inflation 180–81
infrastructure 202, 388, 390
inland provinces 190, 192, 194, 196, 197
Inner Mongolia 153, 197

inspection teams 268–9
institutional experiences 341
institutionalization 126–9
insurance 111, 112, 247, 248, 325
intellectuals 283, 304–5
interdependence 336
'Interim Management Regulations on School Register Management of Radio and Television University Students' 227
'Interim Measures for County Farmers' Technical Schools' 228
interior regions 190, 191, 202–3
International Commission on Intervention and State Sovereignty 207
International Convention on the Elimination of Forms of Racial Discrimination 206
International Cooperation Bureau 267
International Covenant on Civil and Political Rights 206–7
international relations 363–79
international sanctions 391–3
interregional inequality 196
investments 374–5, 389–91
Iraq 379
Ireland 450
Iron Girls 288, 295–9, 301, 302, 303, 305, 306
Ishihara, Shintaro 403
Israel, John 45
Issacs, Harold R. 414
Iwasaki, Ikuo 48

Jacques, Martin 5
Japan 60, 166, 384, 397, 398–404, 411, 412, 441
   blocking REE shipments 393
   boycott of Japanese products 386, 392
Jerdén, Bjorn 409
Jespersen, T. Christopher 414
Jia, Cunsuo 296
Jiang, Jieshi 59
Jiang, Qing 29, 30
Jiangsu 153, 162–3, 191, 195, 352, 354
Jiang, Zemin 35, 36, 38, 50, 63, 66, 173
   and ASEAN 434
   and class 283
   on foreign policy 435
   and ideology 73, 74
   and lifelong learning 230
   military intervention, coping with 71
   and rural health problems 243
   and rural taxes 245
   and Shanghai Pudong 163
   and 'Three Represents' 45–6, 61, 109, 282
   and unemployment 242
   and Western Regional Development Programme 196, 197
   and Zhu Rongji 88, 171
Jiaozhi 153
Jia, Xinjin 408
Jilin 153, 201, 354
Jin, Baisong 386
Jinchang 163
jingji tequ 157
Jing, Li 414
Jing, Men 448–9
Jiu-San Society 114
Johnson, Chalmers 44–5
Johnson, Emily 210
Johnson Reef 438
joint ventures 193
judiciary 70–71

Kang, Sheng 30
Kanji, Nazneen 332
Kaup, Katherine Palmer 214
Kennedy, Scott 183, 376, 420
Kent, Ann 216
Keohane, Robert O. 382
Kersting et al. 104
kexue fashan 453
Khnaw, Hoon 428
Khrushchev, Nikita 44
Kim Jong Il 411
Kim Jong Un 411
Kim, Samuel S. 408, 409, 410
kindergartens 220–23
'Kindergarten Work Procedure' 222
Kinzelbach, Katrin 446–7
Kissinger, Henry 368, 418
KMT (Kuomintang) 59, 60, 272, 390–91, 404, 405
knowledge 234–5
Koenig, Matthias 207
Kohn, Richard 131
Koizumi, Jun'ichiro 401, 402
Kokaryo controversy 401
Korea
   South 48, 166, 201, 397, 408–9, 410, 411
   see also North Korea
Kostello, Eric 6–7
Koszorus, Frank 206
Kou, Chien-wen 122
Kuhn, Phillip 279
Kunshan 163
Kuomingdang (KMT) 106
Kurlantzick, Joshua 436
Kymlicka, Will 206

labels, class 279
labour disputes 345, 349, 354
labour, female 295–8, 296, 303–4
Labour Insurance Regulations 239
labour market 4, 210–11
Labour Secretariat 58–9
Labour Weekly 58–9
Lai, Hongyi 211, 213, 214
Lampton, David M. 67, 417
Lam, Tao-Chiu 157
Land and Resources Ministry 90–91
land finance 323
land-related grievances 322, 328, 345, 349, 352, 354, 358
languages, minority 212–13
Laos 440
Lardy, Nicholas 141, 368
Large, Daniel 383
Latvia 450
Lau et al. 339
Law of Compulsory Education 223
leader, global 379
leaders, provincial 99–101
leading small groups (LSGs) 67, 171, 175, 176
League of Nations System of Minority Guarantees 206
Lee, Chin-Kwan 340
Lee, O. Lee 414
Lee, Teng-hui 405, 406
legitimacy 52–5
Leibold, James 207, 208, 209, 213, 216
Lenin, Vladimir Ilich 49, 280, 286
leverage
  economic 382
  trading 387
Lewis, David 332
Liaoning 153, 201
liberation of women 300
Libya 377, 378
Li, Chao 196, 199
Li, Da 58
Lieberthal, Kenneth 31, 63, 177, 424–5
lifelong education 229–30
The Life of Wu Xun 291
Li, Gang 96
light industry 3–4
Li, Keqiang 79, 84, 85, 88, 92–3, 170, 264, 383
  and economic policy 171, 175
  and NDRC 183
  and purchasing diplomacy 388
  and social justice 249
Li, L.C. 140
Li, Linda 195
Li, Lisan 59
Li, M. 371

Li, Nanqing 139
Lin, Biao 22, 25, 27, 28, 30, 262
Lindau, Juan 48
Ling, Jihua 264
Li, Peng 35, 88, 169, 171, 173–4, 434
Li, Rongrong 180
Lisbon Treaty 442
'little gang of four' 32
'the little State Council' 84
Liu, Chengjun 121
Liu et al. 299
Liu Guoguang et al. 78, 87
Liu, Jianping 385, 386
Liu, Jiayi 93
Liu, Junde 158
Liu, Muhua 111
Liu, Qingshan 254
Liu, Shaoqi 24, 25, 27, 28, 30, 60, 61, 78, 262
Liu, Tienan 267
Liu, Wei 386
Liu, Weishu 385
Liu, Xiaobo 391
Liu, Xiaoli 295, 296, 297
Liu, Xingwu 212
Liu, Yandong 79
Liu, Zhijun 87, 92, 93, 260
living allowances 326
Li, Xiaojiang 302–3
lobbying 183–4
local and central relations 147–8
local governance 104–16
local governments 104–16, 167–8, 221, 315, 318–19, 321, 329
'Local Leaders' database *(People's Daily)* 106
local liberalism 383
local state corporatism 4, 318–19, 328–9
Loewen, Howard 437
Logan, J.R. 6
Long March 59
Lontoh, Lucky A. 437
Lou, Ji-wei 138, 144
LSGs (leading small groups) 67, 171, 175, 176
Lu et al. 284
Lumbini 390
Lundberg, Maria 210, 213, 214
Lu, Ning 67
Luo, Gan 263
Lu, Xianfu 346
Lu, Xun 289, 290, 291, 293
Lu, Yiyi 335

Macao 390
MacFarquhar, Roderick 25, 217
Mackerras, Colin 205, 207, 208, 209, 210, 212, 213, 216

MacMillan, Margaret 418
macroregions 148, 155, 156, 162, 187, 192
Ma, Jun 142
Ma, Kai 182
Making of a Special Relationship (Hunt) 415
Malaya 431
Malaysia 430–31, 436, 438, 439, 440
male elites 299, 301, 307
Manchuria 153, 189–90
Mandarin Chinese 212
Manion, Melanie 110, 257
Mann, James 417, 421
manufacturing industry 189–90
Mao's China and the Cold War (Chen) 419
Mao, Yuanxin 30
Mao, Zedong 27, 32, 37, 44, 59–60, 76, 77, 88, 106
  on aid 385
  and the army 124
  and class 277–81
  and 'continuous revolution' 65
  and corruption 253, 254
  critique of *The Life of Wu Xun* 291
  and Cultural Revolution 29, 30–31
  and Dazhai 295
  death of 61
  and DPRK 408
  and 'dual enthusiasms' 142
  and foreign policy 22
  and Gao Gang affair 25
  and Great Leap Forward 24
  on imperialism and revisionism 429
  and peasants 276
  and PLA 131
  and regional development 189–91, 203
  and 'second front' 28
  and SPC 77
  speeches and comments 26
  and State Council 78
  and 'Theory of the Three Worlds' 367
  and 'two-line struggle' 23
  and Zhou Enlai 87–8
Mao Zedong Thought 43, 72
Ma, Qiusha 335
marginality complex 299
marketization 47, 241–4
market transition 5, 6, 7
Marriage Law 294
'martyrs' 240–41
Marxism 285
Marxism–Leninism 42, 43–5, 49, 55, 72
Marxism–Leninism Mao Zedong Thought 43–7
Marx, Karl 49, 272–3, 280, 286
masculine potency 307

masculinity, hegemonic 307
masculinization of women 299, 301, 302, 303–4, 306
mass incidents 345–54, 358
mass of people 346
Mastanduno, Michael 382, 399
Matsuzawa, Setsuko 338
Maull, Hans 447–8
Ma Weiguo 54
May Fourth feminism 288
May Fourth New Cultural era 49, 52, 289
Ma, Ying-jeou 390–91
mayors 95
Mearsheimer, John J. 420–21
'mechanisms of power' 67
Medeiros et al. 383
Medeiros, Evan 370, 423
medical insurance 111, 112, 248
medical schemes 241, 243, 246, 248, 325
Meer, Craig 405, 406, 407, 408
Melton, Oliver 202–3
Meng et al. 185
MEP (Ministry of Environmental Protection) 93–4
meritocracy 129
Mexico 48
micro-blog *(weibo)* 16
middle classes 7, 122–3, 283
middle schools 224, 226
migrant NGOs 339–40, 342
migrant workers 349, 358
migration 313–14
MIIT (Ministry of Industry and Information Technology) 92
the military 71, 117–33
Miller, Alice 37
mineral industry 189
Ming dynasty 150, 152–3
Minimum Livelihood Guarantee 112
minorities 201
  rights 205–16
minority areas 199
Minxin, Pei 257
miscarriage of justice 351, 354, 357, 358
Mischief Reef 438
Misra, Kalpana 45
mistresses, multiple 307
mob 346
mobility 100–101, 102
mobilization 273, 275–6, 277, 285
MOFCOM (Ministry of Commerce) 91, 385, 386
MOF (Ministry of Finance) 386, 387
monetary policies 382
money, increased value of 313

Montinola et al. 98
Morgan, W.J. 218, 235
MoR (Ministry of Railways) 92
Moscow 377
MOT (Ministry of Transport) 92
MSM (men who have sex with men) 338
multilateralism 434, 441
multipolarity 435
municipalities 95
municipal party secretaries 95
Munro, Ross 421
Murphree, Michael 195
Mushkat, Roda 216
Muslim population 215
Myanmar 376, 393–4, 395

Nakano, Ryoko 216
Nakasone, Yasuhiro 401
Nanhui district 164
Nanjing 153
Nanjing Massacre 399
Nanshi 163
Nathan, Andrew J. 100, 128
National Audit Office 93, 259–60
national bourgeoisie 282
National Bureau of Corruption Prevention 259
National Bureau of Statistics 249
National College Entrance Examination 233–4
National Compulsory Education Programme for the Poor Regions 219
National Defence Law 71, 121
National Education for Work conference 225
nationalism 49–55
Nationalist Party 290
nationality policy 205–16
'National Plan for Medium and Long-Term Education Reform and Development (2010–2020)' 230–31
National Population and Family Planning Commission 92
National Security Council 131
National Union for the Total Independence of Angola (UNITA) 367
National Work Conference on Education 227
A Nation-State by Construction: Dynamics of Modern Chinese Nationalism (Zhao) 50
natural femininity 299, 301, 302, 305, 306
Navy 130
NDRC (National Development and Reform Commission) 77, 84, 91, 181, 183, 186, 386
  'Four Trillion RMB Stimulus Programme' 179
  and Wen Jiabao 182

NEA (National Energy Administration) 84, 92
Nee, Victor 5, 6, 7
Negotiating with the Enemy (Xia) 419
neibu 16, 33
neighbours, cultivating relationships 390–91
neoauthoritarians 47–8
Nepal 389–90
New Culture movement 45, 289, 290, 291
new democratic revolution 60, 273–4
new poor 283
'new socialist countryside' policy 328
'New Year's Sacrifice' 289, 290
New Year's Sacrifice 291–4
New Youth 58
NGOs (non-governmental organizations) 216, 331–44
nianpu 33
nine-dash line 438
Ningbo City 113–15
Ningxia 153
Nixon and Mao (MacMillan) 418
Nixon, Richard 368, 417
Nobel Peace Prize 391
nomenklatura 16, 62–3, 85, 108
Non-Aligned Movement 366
'Nordpolitik' 408
norms 279–80
Norris, William J. 383, 387
north-eastern provinces 201–2
North Korea 201, 384, 395, 397, 408, 409–11, 412
  investment in 389
  sanctions 392
  seizing Chinese fishing boats 394
North Zhili 153
Norway 391–2
'Notice about Some Issues of Junior Middle School Workers' 227–8
'Notice on Raising Funds for Rural Schools' 223
'Notice on Reforming and Strengthening Farmers' Vocational and Technical Education and Training Work' 228
'Notice on Strengthening the Practical Technical Training for the Rural Youth During the Seven-Five Period' 228
'Notice on Strengthening the Worker's Educational Organizations' 227
NPC (National People's Congress) 76, 77, 83, 85, 88, 106, 214
NRCMS (new rural co-operative medical scheme) 243, 246, 248
NRPS (New Rural Pension Scheme) 200, 247
Number One leader 96
Number Two 96

Nu River dam project 337
Nye, Joseph 257

objective control 123, 124
objective criteria 277
O'Brien, K. 110
occupational strata 284–5
Office for Supervision of Discipline Inspection Cadres 267
officer corps 130–31
O'Hanlon, Michael 424
Oi, Jean 256
oil 369, 393–4
Oksenberg, Michel 141, 177
old-age assistance 240–41, 243–4, 246–7
old democratic revolution 273–4
'Old Rural Pension Scheme' 247
Olympics 372
'One Central Focus, Two Basic Points' 47
'The One-China Principle and the Taiwan Issue' 406
opera 290
Operation Fox Hunt 2014, 269
'Opinions on Accelerating the Reform and Development of Higher Education' 232
'Opinions on Developing the Rural Pre-School Education' 220
Opinions on Further Reform and Development of Adult Higher Education' 228
'Opinions on Reforming the Secondary Education Structure and Developing the Vocational and Technical Education' 224–5
'Opinions on Some Issues about Approval of the Establishment of the Workers' University and Graduate Degrees' 228
'Opinions on Strengthening and Improving the Apprentice Training' 227
'Opinions on the Current Development of Pre-school Education' 222–3
'Opinions on the Enterprises to Open Kindergartens' 221
'Opinions on the Implementation of the Goals of the National Ninth Five-Year Plan Concerning Early Childhood Education' 221–2
'Opinions on Trial Implementation of the New Management Mode and Operation Mechanism of Higher Vocational and Technical Education' 226
'Opinions on Vigorously Developing the Higher Correspondence Education and Evening University' 227
'Opinions on Workers' Education' 227

Opper, Sonja 7
Organic Law of the Central People's Government 76
Organic Law of the State Council 83
Organisation for Economic Co-operation and Development (OECD) 375
Origins of the Chinese Revolution: 1915–1949 (Bianco) 49
'Outline for China's Educational Reform and Development' 229
'Outline for Conducting Patriotic Education' 50
'Outline on the Reform and Development of Chinese Education' 225
outward investment 374–5
overseas development aid (ODA) 384–5
An Overview of Shanghai Husbands 301

Pahl, R.E. 273
Pakistan 376
'pan-blue' camp 406
'pan-green' camp 406, 407
Pan, Suiming 300–301, 378
PAP (People's Armed Police) 128, 131
Paracel Islands 437
'paralyzed villages' 317
participative budgeting 143
partners 332
part-time education 227, 228
Party branches 342, 343
Party committees 69, 86
Party groups 69–70, 86
'Party management of cadres' system 62–3
Party–military relationship 71
party secretaries 95–6, 98–9, 100, 101–2
path-dependence 329
Patriotic Education Campaign 50, 400–401
PBoC 84, 91, 181, 182–3, 184, 364, 386–7
PBSC (Politburo Standing Committee) 85
PC (People's Congress) 106, 107–8, 109, 110–12, 115, 116
'Peaceful Rise of China' *(heping jueqi)* concept 370
peacemaking 377
Peace of Westphalia 206
Pearl River Delta 193, 195, 201
Pearson, Margaret 368
Peasant Nationalism and Communist Power: The Emergence of Revolutionary China, 1937–1945 (Johnson) 44
peasants 274, 276–7, 278, 282, 283, 317, 319, 321
  burdens 323, 324
  incomes 312–14
  protests 322, 350

Pei, Minxin 49
Peng, Dehuai 28
Penghu Islands 403
Peng, Qinghua 96
Peng, Zhen 65
pension fund deficit 249
pension insurance 247
pensions 200, 241, 243, 244, 245, 246–7, 248
Pentassuglia, Gaetono 205, 207
People's Bank of China *see* PBoC
People's Daily 64, 106, 349
People's Government 106
people's livelihood projects 223
People's Supervision Committee 259
Pepper, Suzanne 217
performing arts 212
Perry, Elizabeth 275
personal connections 338
Peters, Anne 207
Peters, B. 104
petit bourgeoisie 282
petitioning, collective 346, 347, 354
the Philippines 332, 430–31, 438, 439, 440
Phillion, JoAnn 207, 212
physical labour 295–8, 303–4, 306
Pierre, J. 104
Pingjiang 163
PKI (Partai Komunis Indonesia) 431
PLA (People's Liberation Army) 71, 117–33
PLCs (Party's Political and Legal Affairs Commissions) 259
plenary meetings 83
pluralization of society 342
pluralization of state–NGO relations 341, 343
Poland 450, 451
police brutality 349, 351, 354, 355, 357, 358
policy banks 387
policy objectives 383
Politburo 95, 96, 99
Political Bureau Standing Committee (PSC) 70, 131
political capital 5, 6, 7, 83, 389
political change 338
The Political Economy of China's Provinces (Hendrischke and Feng) 155
political elite 6, 7
political extremism 208–9
political mobilization 273, 275–6, 277, 285
political transition 337–8
pollution 322, 337
PONGOs (Party-organized NGOs) 342, 343
the poor 283
Popular Movement for the Liberation of Angola (MPLA) 367
popular nationalism 49, 52–4

populist sentiments 52–3
potency, masculine 307
poverty 197, 200, 310, 325
  reduction 101
  relief 326, 327
A Power Audit of EU–China Relations (Fox and Godemont) 449–50
power dynamics 297
'power persistence' theory 6
power relations 300
PPCC (People's Political Consultative Conference) 106–8, 109, 110, 113–15, 116
  representation of minorities 214
pragmatic nationalism 52
Prantl, Jochen 216
PRC–DPRK Economic and Cultural Cooperation Agreement 384
PRC–DPRK Treaty of Friendship, Cooperation, and Mutual Assistance, 1961, 408
Pre-Cultural Revolution Period 25–8
Preece, Jennifer Jackson 206, 207
prefecture-level city 151, 155, 159, 160, 161, 162, 163, 195
prefectures 149, 151, 153, 197
Premiers 79, 80, 83, 85, 87, 168–75, 176–82, 185–6
pre-school education 220–23
prices, state procurement 312
primary education 224
'primary stage of socialism' 72
principal–agent dilemma 383, 394
private companies 316, 317, 329, 349, 352, 354, 358, 394
private sector 7, 109–10, 242, 320, 321
procuratorates 259
pro-democracy movement crackdown 66
production, diversification of 313
professionalism, PLA 129–31
'A Program for China's Education Reform and Development' 50
proletariat 274, 275, 278, 280, 282–3
property rights 316–17
protests 54, 122, 322, 345–59
province-level city 151–2
province-level officials 383
provinces 95–103, 150, 153–4, 156, 190, 191, 192
provincial and central relations 97–9
provincial governors 95, 100
provincial leaders 99–101
provincial party secretaries 95, 98–9, 101–2
Provincial Party Standing Committee 96
Provincial People's Congresses 98
provincial people's government 96

'Provisional Basic Programme for County Level Rural Social Old-Age Insurance' 244
'Provisions on Strengthening the Management of the General Educational Funds' 219
PSC (Political Bureau Standing Committee) 70, 131
public cohesion 234–5
Public Finance in China (Lou and Wang) 138
public order disturbances 348
public sector benefits 242
Public Security Bureau 346
public sphere 333, 334
Pudong 157, 163–4
Pudong New Area 159, 163
purchasing diplomacy 388, 389

Qian, Qichen 433
Qin dynasty 148–9
Qing dynasty 153, 155
Qing Governors and Their Provinces: The Evolution of Territorial Administration in China, 1644–1796 (Guy) 155
Qinghai 153, 354
Qinglin, Jia 95
Qin Shihuang 148–9
qu 157
quntixing shijian 453
quotas 107
Qu, Qiubai 59

Radio Free Asia 347
Ramo, Joshua Cooper 48–9
Rankin, Mary B. 333
raw materials 194
The Reach of the State (Shue) 141
real estate 184, 256
recentralization policies 202
reciprocal accountability 99
recruitment, army 122
Rectification Movement, 1957, 254
Red Army 59
redistribution 6
Redondo, Elvira Dominguez 205, 206, 207
REE (Rare Earth Elements) 393
regional autonomy 213–14
regional development 187–204
regional governments 194–5
registered organizations 335, 336
'Regulation on Charging Tuition and Accommodation Fees at Public Colleges and Universities' 231–2
'Regulations for the National Industrial Enterprises Workers Congress' 227
Rehe 153

relief 240
religion 212–13
relocation 349
Remick, Elizabeth 194
Renwick, Neil 339
Ren, Xuefei 340
Ren, Zhongyi 262
'Report on Rapidly Strengthening Agricultural Technology Training Work' 228
'Report on the Construction of a Prosperous Society in an Inclusive Way; and Creating a New Situation of Socialism with Chinese Characteristics' 230
'Report on the Draft Plan for National Economic of 1979' 227
'Report on the Reform of the Structure of Secondary Education' 224
Republican era 153–5
'The Responsibility to Protect' (International Commission on Intervention and State Sovereignty) 207
reterritorialization 151, 158–9
Rethinking China's Provinces (Fitzgerald) 155
retirement 89
Reuter, Etienne 445–6
revenues 171–5, 317
revenue-sharing system 316
Revive the North-East Programme 201–2
revolution 7, 273–4, 276–7, 278
'Revolutionary Elders' 170
rice-growing south 188
Rigger, Shelly 405, 406
rights 205–16, 340
riots 54
Rise of Central China Programme 201, 202
Rising Star (Gill) 421
Rithmire, Meg 195
river deltas 193
RMB value 179, 183–4
ROC (Republic of China) *see* Taiwan
Roh, Tae Woo 408
ROK (Republic of Korea) *see* South Korea
'Role of Government' 139
Romania 451
ronghe 207–9, 211, 213, 214, 215, 216
Rose, Caroline 400
Ross, Robert S. 422, 447
Rostow, Walter W. 43
Rowe, William T. 333
rural areas 228, 328, 349
rural basic education 223–4
rural compulsory education system 200
Rural Cooperative Medical Scheme 200
rural development 310–29
Rural Development Research Centre 177

rural *dibao* 245–6, 248
rural industry 314–22, 328
Rural Minimum Living Standard Security Scheme 200
rural old-age care 240–41, 243–4
rural pensions 246–7, 248
rural pre-school education 220, 221
rural residents 200, 238–9, 244–5, 340
rural taxes 244, 245
Rural Tax Reform 140, 143
rural vocational middle schools 224
rural welfare 240–41, 243
rural women 295–8, 303–4
Ryukyu Islands 403

SAFE (State Administration of Foreign Exchange) 387
safety net 327
Saich, Tony 335
SAIC (State Administration for Industry and Commerce) 92
Same Bed, Different Dreams (Lampton) 417
sanctions 382, 385, 391–3
San Francisco Treaty, 1951, 403
Sang, Hu 290
Sanlin 163
Sarkozy, President Nicolas 388
SARS (Severe Acute Respiratory Syndrome) 246
SASAC (State-Owned Assets Supervision and Administration Commission) 91, 180, 181, 386
Sata, Michael 395
Sautman, Barry 205, 206, 207, 208, 209, 210, 213, 216
S–C–A chain 272–3, 286
Scarborough Shoal 438
Schell, Orville 420
Schoenhals, Michael 217
schools 224, 225, 226, 275
Schram, Stuart 44, 277
Schurmann, Franz 42, 44
Schwartz, Benjamin 43, 44, 277
Scientific Development Concept 61, 74, 230, 231
SCOPSR (State Commission Office for Public Sector Reform) 90
SCPSR (State Commission for Public Sector Reform) 90
SDPC (State Development and Planning Commission) 91
The Search for Modern China (Spence) 416
SEATO (South East Asia Treaty Organization) 428
Seckington, Ian 50, 54

secondary education 223, 224, 233
secondary vocational and technical education 224–6
Second World 367
secretaries, party 95–6, 98–9, 100, 101–2
Secretary General 79
SEC (State Economic Commission) 181, 182
security 190, 191, 412, 434
Seeberg, Vilma 217
Seeking Truth (Qiushi) 51, 74
self-determination 207
self-governing 16
self-immolation cases 347
sending states 382
Senkaku/Diaoyu Islands 402–4, 411, 412
servicemen 240–41
SETC (State Economic and Trade Commission) 90, 91, 182
'Several Opinions about Deepening the Reform of the Higher Education System' 232
'Several Opinions on Further Strengthening the Vocational Education Work' 226
sex industry 307
SEZs (Special Economic Zones) 24, 34, 157, 192–4, 195, 203, 383
Shambaugh, David 42, 48, 61, 411, 420, 435
on ASEAN 433
Beautiful Imperialist 414
on Korea 409, 410
Shandong 191, 354
Shanghai 157, 159, 163, 168, 189, 191, 195
and mass incidents 353, 354, 358
Shanghai Cooperation Organization 372
Shanghai Disneyland project 164
'Shanghai gang' 36
Shanghai Pilot Free Trade Zone 84
Shanghai Pudong 163–4
Shantou 192
Shan, Wei 213, 214
Shanxi Province 108, 109, 160
Shaoyang 351
Sha, Yexin 301
sheng 453
shengwei 453
Sheng, Yueh 58
Sheng, Yumin 100, 102
Shen, Hongfang 438
Shenzhen 192, 193
Shih, Victor C. 184
Shimonoseki Treaty, 1895, 403
Shirk, Susan L. 99, 127
shuanggui 263, 453
Shue, Vivienne 141
Sichuan 101, 153, 352, 354
Simon, Karla 335

Sina Weibo 16
Singapore 430–31, 440
Sino-Burmese Joint Declaration, 29 June 1954, 429
Sino-Japanese communiqué, 1972, 400
Sino-Japanese relations 398–404
Sino-Japanese Treaty of Peace and Friendship, 1978, 400
Sino-Japanese War 399, 403
Sino-Soviet split 44
skills 234–5
Skinner, William 156, 187
Slovenia 451
Smith, Alastair 384
Smith, Warren 210, 213, 214
social anger-venting incidents 345, 354–5, 357–8
social capital 217, 339, 342
'Socialism is a kind of unrealistic ideal' 46
'socialism with Chinese characteristics' 45
'socialist market economy' 73
socialist revolution 273–4
socialization of pre-school education 222
social justice 249
Social Pension Insurance for Urban Residents 247
social security 238–50, 339
social stability 345
social unrest 345–59
Sociological Studies 300
SOEs (state-owned enterprises) 88, 90, 91, 171, 180, 181, 192–3, 194
 and energy policy 383
 labour disputes 354
 and mass incidents 349, 352
 in north-eastern provinces 202
 reduction 4
 and Western Regional Development Programme 198–9
'soft power' 373
Solinger, Dorothy J. 282
'Some Issues of the Further Requirement by the Central Committee of the Chinese Communist Party for Perfecting the Socialist Market Economy' 230
Song, Lin 267
Song, S. 241, 243, 244
South Africa 367
South China Morning Post 347, 349
South China Sea disputes 437–9, 440
Southeast Asia 426–41
'Southern Tour' 139
Southern Weekend 347
South Korea 48, 166, 201, 397, 408–9, 410, 411
South Vietnam 430
South Zhili 153
sovereign wealth funds 387
Soviet Union 43, 44, 367, 368, 384, 399, 430, 440
spatial administrative hierarchy 157–8
spatial theory 156
SPC (State Planning Commission) 77, 181, 182
special administrative regions 96
special relationship 16
Special Services 130, 131
Special Treatment Work Day Programme 240
Spence, Jonathan 416
Spires, Anthony 341
Spivak, Gayatri Chakravorty 297
sponsors 335
Spratly Islands 437–8
stability 345
stabilization policy 176, 178–81, 185
Stalin, Joseph 276
Standing Committees of Provincial People's Congresses 98–9, 111, 112
'State Budgetary Revenues and Expenditures' 220
state capitalism 7
State Council 76, 77, 78, 79–85, 91–3
State Council Decision on Deepening Budget Management System Reform 144–5
state council leading small groups 67
State Councillors 79
State Council Production Office 182
State Council's Decision on the Reform and Development of the Basic Education 220
State Economic and Trade Commission (SETC) 90, 91, 182
State Education Commission 221
state enterprise reform 242
state nationalism 49, 52–3
State Oceanic Administration 394
state procurement prices 312
state reterritorialization 151
state–society relations 334–6, 341–2
state sovereignty recognition 207
Steinberg, David A. 184
Steinberg, James 424
stimulus programme, November 2008, 179, 180
Stoker, G. 104
Storey, Ian 427, 436, 438
Strand, David 333
Strategic Missile Force 130
'strategic partnership' 445, 446
Strategic Reassurance and Resolve (Steinberg and O'Hanlon) 424

structural groups 100
structural linkage 382
structural policies 176–8, 180, 185
Stuart-Fox, Martin 426
student protests 54, 333
subaltern speech 297
subjective control 123–4, 126
subjectivities 279–80, 281
Sub-Saharan Africa: From Crisis to Sustainable Growth (World Bank) 104
Suettinger, Robert 418, 422
'Suggestions on Accelerating Ningbo's Urban Economic Development' 114
SUIC 347–8, 351
Suiyuan 153
Sukarno, President 428, 429
Su, Lin 419
Sullivan, Roger 368
Sun, Dr Yat-sen, 207, 208
Sun, Liping 295, 296, 297, 345
Sun, Luxi 385
Sun, Sijing 121
Sun, Warren 22, 25, 27, 28, 29, 30, 31, 140
Sun, Yan 257–8
Sun, Yat-sen 74
superpowers 367
Supervision Ministry 259, 263
Supreme People's Procuratorate 259
surcharges 317, 323
surplus, trade 387
Su, Shaozhi 33
Sutter, Robert 415–16, 419
suzhi 340, 453
Suzhou 162–3
Swaine, Michael 413, 423–4
symbolic class 281–5
Syria 376
systems 16, 67–9, 70–71
systems theory 156
Szelényi, Ivan 5, 6–7

Taipei regime 367–8
Taiwan 22, 48, 376, 393, 397, 404–8, 438, 444
  anti-mainland demonstrations 54
  and economic ties 383, 386, 390–91, 395
  recognition by ASEAN 428
Taiwan Relations Act, 1979 (US) 407
Taiyuan City 108, 109
Tanaka, Akihiko 398
Tang, James 369
Tang, Jiaxuan 433–4
Tangled Titans (Shambaugh) 420
Tang, Xiaoyang 383
Tanner, Murray 383

taoguang yanghui 369–70, 453
Tapp, Nicholas 211
taxes 194–5, 245, 316, 354
Tax Sharing Reform, 1994, 142, 144
technical education 224–6, 228
technocrats 130, 131
'technologies of power' 67
Teets, Jessica 340, 342
Teiwes, Frederick C. 22, 25, 27, 28, 29, 30, 31, 140
  on provincial leaders 101
tenure, generals' 128
term limits 89
territorial urbanization 164
'textbook issue' 400
Thailand 430–31, 439
Thakur, Ramesh 216, 373
Thayer, Carlyle 438
Thelle, Hatla 446–7
'The One-China Principle and the Taiwan Issue' 407
'Theory of the Three Worlds' 367
Thiers, Paul 341
Third Front 190, 191
Third Plenum 32, 165, 170, 175, 177
third realm 333
Third World 367
Thornton, Patricia 343
'three agricultural problems' 322
Three-Anti Campaign 254
'Three Fixes' 90
Three Gorges Dam 150, 337
'three nos' 239–40
'Three Represents' 45–6, 61, 72, 73, 109, 282
Tiananmen Incidents 47
Tiananmen Papers (Zhang) 33
Tiananmen protests 333, 352, 368, 400, 433
  attitude of EU 444–5
  attitude of Japan 402
  attitude of US 417
Tiananmen Square 173
Tianjin 194–5
Tibet 246, 354, 444
  refugees 390
Tilak, J.B.G 235
tiliu 317, 453
Tokyo–Beijing Forum 401
tonghua 207
Tong, James 141
Townsend, James R. 44
township-level officials 316–17
town/township 149
trade 369, 381–2, 386, 390–91, 392–3, 398–9, 408
  leverage 387

partner 387
surplus 387
trade unions 227, 275, 340
Tragedy of Great Power Politics (Mearsheimer) 420–21
transfer payments 198, 323–4, 325–7
transnational activism 339
transparency, fiscal 143–4
Transport Ministry 92
Treasury securities 387
Tucker, Nancy Bernkopf 418–19
Tunsjo, Oystein 447
Tuosheng, Zhang 447
Turner, Oliver 414
TVEs (township and village enterprises) 167, 195, 314, 315, 318–19, 320–22
two-class structure 284
'two-line struggle' 23
'two whatevers' 32

Uhalley, Stephen, Jr 58, 59
UK 377, 450, 451
UNCLOS (United Nations Convention on the Law of the Sea) 438, 439
unemployment 241–2
UNITA (National Union for the Total Independence of Angola) 367
United Front Work Department 106
The United States and China (Dong) 416
The United States and China (Fairbank) 414–15
United States (US) 367, 368
  and ASEAN 428–9, 440, 441
  debt 383
  economic statecraft 384
  foreign relations with China 413–25
  and G2 371
  global security policy 412
  Indochina, withdrawal from 432
  and Japan and South Korea 397
  as key ally against Soviets 399–400
  and North Korea 410
  purchasing diplomacy 388
  relations with China 447, 449
  and sanctions 385, 391
  and Taiwan 404, 407
  trying to undermine the dominance of 373
  US Congressional-Executive Commission on China 209, 210, 212, 214
  using UN veto 376
  and Vietnam 430
Universal Declaration of Human Rights 206
universities 225
unlawfulness 346
unregistered organizations 336

unrest 345–59
UNSC 367–8, 376
UN (United Nations) 206–7, 332, 376–8
urban areas 349
urban *dibao* 245, 247
urban districts 159, 160, 161, 162, 163
urban *hukou* holders 185
urbanization 164, 315, 327
urban medical assistance schemes 248
urban residents 244, 340
Urban Residents' Health Insurance 247, 248
Urban Spaces in Contemporary China (Davis et al.) 334
urban welfare 247–8
urban white-collar professionals 184–5
urban workers 238, 239
Ürümchi 210
Urumqi 54
US–China–EU Relations: Managing the New World Order (Ross, Tunsjo and Tuosheng) 447
US–China Relations in the 21st Century: Power Transition and Peace (Zhu) 422
USSR 43, 44, 84, 367, 368, 384, 399, 430, 440
Uyghur workers 210

values 55, 279–80
van Canh, Nguyen 430
van Ness, Peter 367
verdict reversal issue 32
vertical chain of command 97
veterans 240–41
veto, UN 376–7, 378
vice governors 96
Vice Premiers 79, 80, 85, 89
victim mentality 51
Vietnam 430, 431, 432, 437, 438, 439, 440
village debt 320–21
village-level officials 317–18
village-owned enterprise 317
  see also TVEs (township and village enterprises)
violence 354
vocational colleges 225
vocational education 224–6, 227, 228, 229
Vocational Education Law of the People's Republic of China 225–6
vocational middle schools 224
vocational universities 225
Vogel, Ezra 419

wages 312–14
Walker, Richard 43
'walking on two legs' policy 220
Wall, Geoffrey 211

Walter, Andrew 421, 423
Wang, Chenyan 385
Wang, Dong 413
Wang, Dongxing 30, 32
Wang, Jingtao 211
Wang, Jisi 424–5
Wang, Li 386
Wang, Qishan 84, 263–9, 270
Wang, Shulin 138
Wang, Yi 93
Wang, Yizhou 371
Wang, Yuxiang 207, 212
Wang, Zheng 50
Wan, Li 34
war crimes, Japanese 399, 400
Washington Quarterly 422
water pollution 337
Watson, James 279, 280
wealth 283, 387
Wealth and Poverty (Gilder) 301
Weber, Max 42
Wechat 16
Wedeman, Andrew 255, 258
weibo 16, 453
Wei, Jianxing 263
Wei, Shen 448–9
Wei, X. 243
Weixing 16
welfare 238–50, 324
welfare enterprises 239
Wenchuan earthquake 342
Wen, Jiabao 83, 84, 85, 88, 170, 326, 450
 and corruption 93
 and economic policy 171, 174–5, 182–4
 and overseas investments 393
 and purchasing diplomacy 388, 389
 and regional development 199–203
 and rural taxes 245
 and SOEs 91
 and stabilization policy 178–9, 181
 and welfare 247–8, 249
Wenling City 143
Wenran, Jiang 389
Wenzhou 195
West China 161, 162
western provinces 196–9
Western Regional Development Programme 196, 197–8
Western Shaanxi 153
wheat-growing north 188
When China Rules the World (Jacques) 5
'Where Did I Miss You?' (Zhang) 302
white-collar professionals 184–5
White Papers on EU 443–4
'White Terror' 405

Wittfogel, Karl 43–4
women 288–307
Women and Socialism (Bebel) 290
Women of China 296
Wong, Christine P.W. 140–41, 142
Woodman, Sophia 211, 213, 214
Woo, Franklin J. 415
work and Mao 28
work days, extra 240–41
workers 274
 disputes 349–50, 352
workers' clubs 275
working class 282–3
work units 239, 242
World Bank (WB) 104, 138, 141–2, 177, 337, 368, 387
 on NGOs 332
 and quota shares 374
world stage actor 363–79
WTO (World Trade Organization) 88, 174, 369, 378, 390, 391
Wu county 162
Wu, Di 291
Wu, F. 337
Wujiang county-level city 163
Wujiang district 163
Wu, Jiaxiang 48
Wu, Wei 33, 35
Wuxian city 162
Wuzhong 162

Xiamen 192
xian 453
xiang 453
Xiangcheng 162
Xianglin's Wife 288, 289–94, 298
Xianglin's Wife (opera) 290
Xiang, Nan 262
Xiang, Zhongfa 59
xianji shi 151
Xiaobo, Lü 257
xiaokang (shehui) 453
Xiao, Ren 346, 435
Xia, Yafeng 419
Xia, Yan 290, 291, 292–4
Xi, Jinping 36, 37, 38, 48, 50, 61, 88
 and anti-corruption 84, 93, 263–9
 and the army 117, 121, 125
 and 'China Dream' 74–5
 and corruption 270
 'disseminating modern Chinese values' 373
 and economic policy 170, 171, 175
 on the EU 444
 and G2 372
 and NDRC 183

and purchasing diplomacy 388
reducing government powers 185–6
reform agenda 94
and social justice 249
Xikang 153
Xinhua Daily 347
Xinjiang 54, 96, 191, 354
xitong 16, 67–9, 70–71, 453
Xi, Zhongxun 24
Xu, Caihou 264
Xue, Benhui 386
Xueping, Zhong 299
Xu et al. 338

Yang, David 334
Yang, Guobin 338
Yang, Hu 126–32
Yang, Jiang 126–32
Yang, Jiechi 79
Yang, Li 211
Yang, Mu 426
Yangpu 163
Yangshan 164
Yang, Shangkun 120
Yangtze River Delta 193, 195, 201
Yan, Jianying 385
Yan, Xuetong 372
Yao, Yilin 182
Yasukuni Shrine 398, 401, 402
Ye, Duchu 346
Yee, Herbert 367
Yeongpeong island 412
Yew, Roland 49–50
Yim, Linda 430
yinsheng yangshuai 299
Yoshida, Yutaka 402
You, Ji 117
You, Jiangrong 127
yuan 453
Yuan dynasty 150
Yue opera 290
Yugoslavia, Former 442
Yu, Jianrong 354
Yunnan 101, 191, 195, 303–4
Yu, Qiuli 120, 227
Yuzhong District 113

Zambia 389, 395
Zang, Xiaowei 210
Zeng, Peiyan 182
Zeng, Qinghong 64
Zhang, Gaoli 79
Zhang, Guotao 58
Zhang, Jun 446
Zhang, Shuguang 218, 385, 394

Zhang, Tiejun 446
Zhang, Weiping 279, 280
Zhang, Weiwei 5
Zhang, Xiaoming 96
Zhang, Xinxin 302
Zhang, Yongjin 368, 398
Zhang, Zhen 127
Zhang, Zishan 254
Zhanjiang city 84
Zhao, Hongzhu 267
Zhao, Kejin 385
Zhao, Mancang 297
Zhao, Quansheng 368, 433
Zhao, Suisheng 7, 50, 52, 419
Zhao, Ziyang 25, 33, 35, 39, 61, 66, 85
    and corruption 262
    and downsizing 89
    and economic policy 168–9, 170, 171, 173, 182, 385
    and global economy 193
    and Hu Yaobang 88
    and 'primary stage of socialism' 72–3
    and structural policies 177
Zhejiang 143, 352, 354
Zheng, Wei 211
Zheng, Xutao 386
Zheng, Yefu 300, 301
Zheng, Yongnian 50, 97
Zhengzhou City 110
Zhili 153
zhixia shi 151–2
Zhongfa, Xiang 59, 179
Zhong, Y. 149
Zhou, Enlai 27–8, 29–30, 77, 78, 87
    and assimilation 207–8
    at Bandung conference 366
    Dazhai, visit to 302
Zhou, Xiaochuan 181, 182–3
Zhou, Yong 210, 213, 214
Zhou, Yongkang 264
Zhou, Yongsheng 386
Zhou, Z.H. 157
Zhuang, Qubing 408
Zhu, Feng 422
Zhuhai 192
Zhu, Marshall De 261
Zhu, Rongji 90, 139, 171, 182, 434
    and economic policy 88, 169–70, 173, 174, 180–81, 182
    and free trade agreement 436
    and rural taxes 245
    and stabilization policy 178
    and unemployment 242
    on western China 197
Zhu, Weiqun 208, 209

Zhu, Zhiqun 422
Zimbabwe 376
zizhi 16

zizhi (qu) 453
The A to Z of United States–China Relations (Sutter) 419